# REPORT OF THE CONGRESSIONAL COMMITTEES INVESTIGATING THE IRAN-CONTRA AFFAIR

# REPORT OF THE CONGRESSIONAL COMMITTEES INVESTIGATING THE IRAN-CONTRA AFFAIR

## With the Minority Views

Abridged Edition

## Daniel K. Inouye, Chairman
Senate Select Committee

## Lee H. Hamilton, Chairman
House Select Committee

Edited and with an Introduction by
Joel Brinkley and Stephen Engelberg

 **Times** BOOKS

# Contents

Introduction     ix

Editors' Methodology     xiii

Iran-Contra Chronology     xv

Cast of Characters     xxvii

List of Countries     xxxiii


## MEMBERS AND STAFFS OF U.S. SENATE AND HOUSE COMMITTEES     3


## PREFACE: ORIGINS OF THIS REPORT     7


## SECTION I: THE REPORT


### PART I   EXECUTIVE SUMMARY

Executive Summary     11


### PART II   CENTRAL AMERICA

**Chapter 1** Introduction: Background on U.S.-Nicaragua Relations     37

**Chapter 2** The NSC Staff Takes Contra Policy Underground     40

**Chapter 3** The Enterprise Assumes Control of Contra Support     62

**Chapter 4** Private Fundraising: The Channell-Miller Operation     88

**Chapter 5** NSC Staff Involvement in Criminal Investigations and Prosecutions     104

**Chapter 6** Keeping "USG Fingerprints" Off the Contra Operation: 1984–1985     112

**Chapter 7** Keeping "USG Fingerprints" Off the Contra Operation: 1986     125

PART III   THE ARMS SALES TO IRAN
    **Chapter 8** U.S.-Iran Relations and the Hostages in Lebanon    139
    **Chapter 9** The Iran Arms Sales: The Beginning    144
    **Chapter 10** Arms to Iran: A Shipment of HAWKs Ends in Failure    154
    **Chapter 11** Clearing Hurdles: The President Approves a New Plan    169
    **Chapter 12** Arms Sales to Iran: The United States Takes Control    185
    **Chapter 13** Deadlock in Tehran    206
    **Chapter 14** "Taken to the Cleaners": The Iran Initiative Continues    214
    **Chapter 15** The Diversion    233
    **Chapter 16** Summary: The Iran Initiative    239

PART IV   EXPOSURE AND CONCEALMENT
    **Chapter 17** Exposure and Concealment: Introduction    247
    **Chapter 18** October 1986: Exposure Threatened    250
    **Chapter 19** November 1986: Concealment    255
    **Chapter 20** November 1986: The Attorney General's Inquiry    266

PART V   THE ENTERPRISE
    **Chapter 21** Introduction to the Enterprise    289
    **Chapter 22** The Enterprise    292
    **Chapter 23** Other Privately Funded Covert Operations    318

PART VI   CONCLUSIONS AND RECOMMENDATIONS
    **Chapter 24** Covert Action in a Democratic Society    333
    **Chapter 25** Powers of Congress and the President in the Field
       of Foreign Policy    341
    **Chapter 26** The Boland Amendments and the NSC Staff    343
    **Chapter 27** Rule of Law    347
    **Chapter 28** Recommendations    362

SECTION II THE MINORITY REPORT
    The Minority Views of Mr. Cheney, Mr. Broomfield, Mr. Hyde,
       Mr. Courter, Mr. McCollum, Mr. DeWine, Sen. McClure,
       and Sen. Hatch    371

PART I  INTRODUCTION
    **Chapter 1** Introduction         375

PART II  THE FOREIGN AFFAIRS POWERS OF THE CONSTITUTION
        AND THE IRAN-CONTRA AFFAIR
    **Chapter 2** The Foreign Affairs Powers and the Framers' Intentions     397
    **Chapter 3** The President's Foreign Policy Powers in Early
    Constitutional History     399
    **Chapter 4** Constitutional Principles in Court     402

PART III  NICARAGUA
    **Chapter 5** Nicaragua: The Context     409
    **Chapter 6** The Boland Amendments     413
    **Chapter 7** Who Did What to Help the Democratic Resistance?     417

PART IV  IRAN
    **Chapter 8** The Iran Initiative     427
    **Chapter 9** Iran: The Legal Issues     435
    **Chapter 10** The Use or "Diversion" of the Iran Arms Sales Proceeds     437

PART V  DISCLOSURES AND INVESTIGATIONS
    **Chapter 11** From the Disclosure to the Uncovering     443
    **Chapter 12** The NSC's Role in Investigations     447

PART VI  PUTTING CONGRESS' HOUSE IN ORDER
    **Chapter 13** The Need to Patch Leaks     451

PART VII  RECOMMENDATIONS
    **Chapter 14** Recommendations     455

SECTION III SUPPLEMENTAL AND ADDITIONAL VIEWS
    **The Additional Views of Sen. Inouye and Sen. Rudman**     463
    **The Additional Views of Mr. Rodino, Mr. Fascell, Mr. Foley,**
    **Mr. Brooks, Mr. Stokes, Mr. Aspin, and Mr. Boland**     464

**The Additional Views of Mr. Rodino, Mr. Fascell, Mr. Brooks, and Mr. Stokes**                                                                465

**The Additional Views of Sen. Boren and Sen. Cohen**                          466

**The Additional and Separate Views of Sen. Heflin**                              467

**The Additional Views of Sen. Boren**                                                       468

**The Supplemental Views of Sen. McClure**                                             469

**The Additional Views of Mr. Broomfield**                                                 470

**The Supplemental Views of Sen. Hatch**                                                 471

**The Supplemental Views of Mr. Hyde**                                                    472

**The Additional Views of Sen. Cohen**                                                      473

**The Supplemental Views of Mr. McCollum**                                           474

**The Additional Views of Sen. Trible**                                                        475

# Introduction

On a sunny afternoon in September 1985, Robert C. McFarlane, the President's National Security Adviser, took an elevator to the Capitol's fourth floor, where he was escorted past an armed guard into the House Intelligence Committee's small, private hearing room. McFarlane was settling into a green leather chair as the soundproof door closed behind him.

Representative Lee Hamilton had a few pointed questions he wanted to ask.

There had been a troubling story in the press a month before. *The New York Times* had reported that an obscure National Security Council aide named Oliver L. North was raising money for the Contras. He'd been helping them buy weapons, giving them tactical military advice—all that and more at a time when U.S. assistance to the Contras was supposed to be prohibited.

Hamilton was chairman of the Intelligence Committee, the principal Congressional body monitoring the Contra program. He wanted to know what this fellow North was up to.

In his cool, earnest, and unequivocal manner, McFarlane assured the Congressman that the story just wasn't true. Colonel North had not "given military advice of any kind" or "in any way been involved with funds for the Contras."

"We were skeptical, and we asked him the same question in several different ways," the Congressman recalled recently. "But he was he was always positive; he left no doubt."

So Hamilton, a courteous, low-key, southern Indiana lawyer, shook McFarlane's hand and said: "I for one am willing to take you at your word." And with that, the House Intelligence Committee's investigation of the matter was dropped.

Sixteen months passed. But then, in January 1987, Lee Hamilton found himself appointed to a new committee. He was named chairman of the House select committee investigating the Iran-Contra Affair. Hamilton's new committee worked in tandem with its counterpart from the Senate, and the two panels had a combined staff of almost 100 lawyers, investigators, accountants, auditors, and others. They had subpoena power and unusual cooperation from the White House. They studied thousands of pages of records, even read passages from President Reagan's personal diary. They took dozens of private depositions and heard from 28 public witnesses during three months of nationally televised hearings.

Even with all that, it was almost 11 months before the questions Hamilton first posed to McFarlane back in September 1985 were answered. The end result is this extraordinary report.

It's a stunning document, describing in exhaustive detail "confusion, secrecy and deception," "pervasive dishonesty," and "disarray at the highest levels of Government." Some questions about the sale of arms to Iran and the covert program to aid the Contras will never be answered in full. But this study is the closest to a definitive account the nation is ever likely to get. It even comes with Republican dissenting views.

The Committees concluded that "the ultimate responsibility for events in the Iran-Contra Affair must rest with the President." And had this catalog of criticisms landed at another time, under different political circumstances, it might have changed the nation's political landscape for months or years to come. But as it was, at the White House the President and his aides brushed off the Committees' work with a blithe, dismissive wave.

Reagan declined even to discuss the report for the first several days. He finally offered only a brief, disparaging remark, standing in the White House Rose Garden as an aide handed him a large, flapping Thanksgiving turkey—a bit of symbolism that surely was not lost on the President. What did he think of the Committees' report?

"Maybe they labored and brought forth a mouse," he said.

Almost in chorus, others in the White House agreed, saying: "There's nothing new here." And in at least one sense they were correct. By November 1987, the Iran-Contra Affair had already done such grievous damage to the Reagan Presidency that the report, even with its many new revelations, only served to ratify what most people already knew.

To many Americans, the very idea of selling advanced weaponry to the Ayatollah Khomeini was, all by itself, more than enough to send the President's public approval ratings into a steeper, faster free-fall than the polls had ever registered since they were first taken, back when Franklin Roosevelt sat in the White House. In December 1986, just after word of the arms sales came out, the number of Americans who said they approved of the way Reagan was doing his job fell by 30 percent, and the numbers have crept back only a few points since then.

The effect of that drop has been dramatic. During most of 1987 the White House was, in the words of one of the President's senior aides, "catatonic, waiting for it to pass."

Then by fall the Committee hearings had ended and the public seemed to be losing interest in the affair. The background noise had faded, but that only made it easier to gauge the long-range political repercussions the scandal had left behind. All of a sudden, after six years of inarguable political dominance, the White House now seemed unable to do anything right; the problems and embarrassments seemed to follow one after another:

- Two heavily promoted Supreme Court nominations ended in embarrassing failures.
- The President found he had little choice but to accept the idea of raising taxes to reduce the budget deficit, even though for years he had been saying the nation would get tax increases only "over my dead body."
- After six years of making Central America dance to its tune, the White House was forced to watch, grumbling from the sidelines, as Central Americans worked out a peace agreement that Reagan fundamentally deplored.
- And then, just a couple of days before this report was published, the President had to compromise with Congress again, agreeing to limit testing of perhaps his most cherished project, the Strategic Defense Initiative, or Star Wars.

All of that seemed largely a consequence of the President's diminished standing as the nation's leader. Before, he had been able to bend Congressional will by sheer force of determination; senators and representatives knew all too well that the public stood behind him. But Iran-Contra changed all that and emboldened many members of Congress. Reagan couldn't intimidate them so easily anymore.

So for the White House, brushing off this report carried few political risks; the damage was already done. At the same time, there was another benefit. By taking the position that the Iran-Contra Committees' work was not worthy of serious discussion, the President managed to evade answering the major open questions about his own role in the affair. Even this report leaves some of them hanging.

In July, as the Congressional hearings dominated the nation's attention, Reagan said he was eager to tell his story once the hearings ended.

"You won't be able to shut me up," he said. But in speeches, statements, interviews, and public appearances since then, he has carefully skirted the mire of unresolved questions, contradictions, and accusations that the Iran-Contra Committees left behind.

This report shows, for example, that the Committees still wonder what the President really believes about the Iran arms sales. In a nationally televised speech on March 4, the President said: "What began as a strategic opening to Iran deteriorated, in its implementation, into trading arms for hostages." But then in an interview on October 2, as the Committees note in this report, Reagan said flatly: "It was not trading arms for hostages."

And what about William J. Casey, the former CIA director and one of the President's closest aides? Colonel North told the Iran-Contra Committees that Casey was the mastermind behind much of what he did; he knew all about the diversion of Iran arms sales profits to the Contras and thought it was "a neat idea," North said.

Casey was dead by the time North said all that. But last November, before he was hospitalized with a brain tumor, Casey said he hadn't known a thing about the diversion until he happened to stumble onto information about it a few weeks earlier. Which story does the President believe? He has never said.

And then there's the question of how much Reagan really knew about North's covert program to aid the Contras, the one Lee Hamilton first asked about in September 1985.

The Committees' report shows that by the fall of 1986, the Enterprise—the NSC's secret government that North called "Project Democracy"—had accrued $4.5 million in assets, including warehouses, boats, leased houses, communications centers, ordnance, munitions, six airplanes, and a 6,250-foot runway—not to mention secret bank accounts holding about $8 million.

How much did the President know about all that? In October 1986 he said he "did not know the exact particulars" of the Contra supply program. But then in May he said the whole thing "was my idea." That contradiction has never been explained.

Those are just samples from the lingering questions behind the disclosures in this report. But Marlin Fitzwater, the President's spokesman, made it clear that the White House does not intend to answer them. The day this report was released, he said: "It just serves no useful purpose for us to be second-guessing or to be going back and going through what should have happened and shouldn't have happened." The White House wasn't interested in discussing any of it.

As for Lee Hamilton, now that his work is done at last, he says he was wrong to have taken McFarlane's word back in 1985, though he believes that at the time he had little choice. Rhetorically he asks: What can you do when they are so willing to lie?

Serving as chairman of the Iran-Contra Committee after that earlier experience was a little ironic, he acknowledges. But Hamilton also said: "I'm sure it was even more ironic for Bud McFarlane and Ollie North."

Joel Brinkley
White House correspondent, *The New York Times*
Washington editor of the *Times*' Iran-Contra coverage, January through August 1987

# Editors' Methodology

For this book, the report has been abridged to a publishable length. We the editors tried to excise redundancies and keep the basic story line intact. The Committees often repeated anecdotes and findings several times to illustrate different points. We kept the different points but, wherever possible, condensed the anecdotes in the second telling.

Wherever we made substantive deletions that seemed to affect the story line, we added editors' notes summarizing the deleted passages. These notes are shown in **boldface type.** We also used editors' notes to explain ambiguities and to point out occasional relevant facts that the Committees omitted. Unless otherwise indicated, direct quotations in the editors' notes are taken from the report.

In addition, within square brackets throughout the text (also in boldface) we inserted various explanations. For example, when the Committees mention Country 1, we explain that it is **[Israel]**. When the Committees refer to HINDs, we add **[Soviet-made attack helicopters]**.

The introductory summaries as well the conclusions and recommendations of both the majority and the minority reports are presented in full. Some of the other chapters are barely edited at all, while some others are heavily condensed.

Since the minority report does not represent the views of even all the Republicans on the Committees, it is edited more heavily than the rest. We should say that we are offering only samples from the body of the minority report.

For the 13 supplemental and additional views at the end of the report, we have included the introductory passages of each and summarized the rest in editors' notes.

Throughout, the actual text is presented exactly as written, except in a few cases where we have deleted a transition word or phrase—such as "however" or "at the same time"—that was no longer appropriate in the abridged form. Also, we have retained the original numbering of figures and tables in the report; because some were deleted, the numbering is sometimes no longer sequential.

In choosing which passages to keep and which to abridge, we consulted with the Iran-Contra Committees' leadership. But in the end all the editing decisions were our own.

Joel Brinkley
Stephen Engelberg

# Iran-Contra Chronology

**1979**

November 4
Iranian militants take 66 American diplomats hostage in Tehran.

**1980**

September 22
Iraq invades Iran.

**1981**

December
President Ronald Reagan signs a "Finding" authorizing a covert Central Intelligence Agency operation to support the anti-Sandinista rebels, or Contras. The Administration assures Congress the purpose is to limit the spread of communism in the region.

**1982**

December 21, 1982
The first restrictions on Contra aid become law, in the form of an amendment proposed by Representative Edward Boland, Democrat of Massachusetts. It prohibits any use of Federal funds to overthrow the Government of Nicaragua.

**1983**

October 23, 1983
A massive truck bomb kills 241 U.S. Marines in Beirut. Iran is suspected to be behind the bombing.

## December 8–9

New legislation passed by Congress restricts Government expenditures on behalf of the Contras to $24 million.

## December 12

Truck bombs explode at American and French embassies in Kuwait. After an investigation, 17 members of a group named Da'wa, Arabic for The Call, are eventually arrested. They are convicted soon after, and their relatives in Lebanon decide the best way to free the prisoners is to seize American hostages.

## December 14

The State Department instructs embassies abroad to implement Operation Staunch—an effort to prevent foreign countries from arming Iran.

## 1984

## February 21

With money running out for the Contras, Robert C. McFarlane, the National Security Adviser, warns President Reagan that the program will have to be curtailed by May or June unless new money is found.

## March 16

William Buckley, CIA station chief in Beirut, is kidnapped and held in Lebanon by Islamic Holy War, pro-Iranian extremists.

## April

Press accounts report that the CIA has mined Nicaraguan harbors. In the furor that follows, many in Congress push for a complete cutoff of aid to the Contras.

## May

Duane Clarridge, a CIA officer who supervises the Contra program, introduces Lt. Col. Oliver L. North, a National Security Council aide, to Contra leaders in Honduras. Clarridge tells them that if Congress cuts off aid Colonel North will take his place.

McFarlane meets with Saudi Arabia's ambassador to Washington, Prince Bandar Bin Sultan. With the $24 million cap in Contra funding taking effect, Prince Bandar agrees to keep the Contras alive with a contribution of $1 million per month.

## May 8

The Rev. Benjamin Weir is kidnapped.

**August 31**

McFarlane asks for a reassessment of U.S. policy toward Iran.

**October 12**

Reagan signs an appropriations measure containing a new Boland Amendment, Boland II, approved earlier by Congress. It bans any agency or entity involved in intelligence activities from spending money to aid the Contras.

**December 3**

Peter Kilburn of the American University of Beirut is kidnapped.


## 1985

**January 8**

The Rev. Lawrence M. Jenco is seized in Lebanon.

**February**

The Saudis agree to contribute an additional $24 million to the Contra cause after McFarlane tells Prince Bandar the rebels need money.

**March 16**

Another American, Terry A. Anderson of the Associated Press, is kidnapped in Beirut.

**May 3**

Michael A. Ledeen, a consultant to the National Security Council, meets with Prime Minister Shimon Peres of Israel to discuss Iran.

**May 28**

David P. Jacobsen of the American University Hospital in Beirut is kidnapped.

**June 3**

Buckley dies (according to Jacobsen, who tells of this after he is freed in November 1986).

**June 9**

Thomas M. Sutherland of the American University of Beirut is kidnapped.

**June 17**

The NSC staff moves forward with a new policy towards Iran. A draft National Security

Decision Directive circulates to top officials, who are not impressed. Caspar W. Weinberger, the Secretary of Defense, writes: "This is almost too absurd to comment on."

Late June

Reagan meets with hostage families.

July 3

Reagan attends a National Security Planning Group meeting and is frustrated by the apparent lack of options for freeing the hostages.

Early July

David Kimche, Director General of the Israeli Foreign Ministry, tells McFarlane that Iranian officials want to open a "political discourse" with the U.S.

Mid-July

Reagan approves "in principle" the sale of TOW antitank missiles to Iran, subject to further review.

August 2

Kimche meets with McFarlane and asks for specific authorization to ship missiles to Iran.

August 6

McFarlane briefs Reagan on the Israeli proposal to sell American antitank missiles to Iran through Israel. There is dispute on whether the President approved this sale. McFarlane says he did; Reagan at first agrees but later says he cannot recall.

August 10

North flies to Costa Rica and meets with Ambassador Lewis Tambs and CIA station chief Joe Fernandez to discuss construction of a secret airstrip for the Contra operation.

August 20

Israel sends 96 TOW antitank missiles to Iran.

September 5

McFarlane sends a letter to the House Permanent Select Committee on Intelligence that states it his "deep personal conviction" that no one on the NSC staff has violated either the letter or spirit of the Boland Amendment.

In Paris, Ledeen meets with Manucher Ghorbanifar, the Iranian who arranged the first

xviii

TOW shipment, to complain that no hostages have been released. Ghorbanifar asks for more missiles.

September 14

Israel sends 408 more TOW missiles to the Iranian city of Tabriz. Weir is released the same day.

October 3

North is told that Buckley will be released soon, but Islamic Jihad in Lebanon announces that it plans to execute Buckley.

November

Working at the direction of Richard V. Secord, a retired Air Force major general, Richard Gadd, a retired Air Force colonel, searches for airplanes that could be bought by the resupply operation. Secord later testifies that North was to raise the project's money from private donations and friendly foreign governments.

November 24–25

The CIA arranges for a shipment of 18 HAWK antiaircraft missiles from Israel to Iran aboard a CIA front company airplane. Iran rejects the missiles within days after test-firing one of them, finding that they do not meet Iran's requirements. Later, some of the American officials involved in arranging the flight said they were told the plane carried oil-drilling parts, not weapons.

November 25

John N. McMahon, Deputy Director of Central Intelligence, says the CIA cannot provide any more covert assistance without an explicit authorization from the President. On December 5 the President signs a Finding retroactively authorizing the operation. Later, McFarlane's deputy, Vice Adm. John M. Poindexter, testifies that he destroyed this order after word of the Iran arms sales began to become public.

December 4

McFarlane resigns as National Security Adviser. Poindexter is appointed his successor.

December 6

North tells an Israeli official that he plans to use profits from future arms sales to support the Contras.

## December 7

A meeting is held at the White House with Reagan, Secretary of State George P. Shultz, Weinberger, McFarlane, and Poindexter at which the Iran initiative is discussed. Participants at the meeting have different recollections of what took place. Some suggest that a consensus was reached to end the arms shipments to Iran. McMahon has said no such agreement was reached.

## December 8

McFarlane flies to London with North for a meeting with Ghorbanifar, Kimche, and Yaacov Nimrodi, an Israeli arms dealer. McFarlane tells Ghorbanifar that the U.S. does not want to take part in any more arms transfers to Iran, although the U.S. is willing to continue diplomatic contacts.

## 1986

## January 17

Reagan signs an order authorizing arms shipments to Iran in an effort both to improve relations with officials in Iran thought to be moderates and to bring about the release of the hostages. This order authorizes the CIA to assist "third parties" as well as friendly foreign countries in shipping weapons.

## February 17

The U.S. sends 500 TOW missiles to Israel, from American stocks, for shipment to Iran. No hostages are freed.

## February 19

An American delegation arrives in Frankfurt, West Germany, for face-to-face meetings with Iranian officials. The Iranians ask for better weapons, and North presses for hostages. Further high-level meetings are agreed to.

## February 27

Another shipment of 500 TOW missiles is sent to Israel, once again for shipment to Iran. But again no hostages are freed.

## March

The resupply operation, which had gotten off to a slow start, makes some successful airdrops to Contra troops in northern Nicaragua. The planes are flown from the Illopango airbase in El Salvador with the cooperation of the Salvadoran military.

## April 4

In a memorandum, North outlines a plan to have $12 million in profits from the Iran arms sales diverted to the Contras. The memo is prepared for Poindexter to relay to the President. Poindexter later testifies that he never showed the memo to the President. Reagan has denied knowing anything about the diversion to the Contras until November 1986.

## April 17

Kilburn's body is found. His kidnappers say he was killed in retaliation for the American bombing of Libya two days before.

## May 1

Secord sends Robert C. Dutton, a retired Air Force colonel, to Illopango to straighten out the resupply operation. At the same time, Felix Rodriguez, a former CIA operative recruited by North to work at Illopango, meets in Washington with Vice President George Bush. Participants say the air resupply operation is not mentioned.

## May 23–24

508 TOW missiles and 240 spare parts for HAWK missiles are shipped to Israel.

## May 25

McFarlane, North, and other American officials fly to Tehran, carrying with them spare parts for Iran's HAWK antiaircraft missiles. They spend four days meeting with Iranian officials, trying to win the release of all the American hostages. They are not successful.

## June 11

Poindexter tells North that Assistant Secretary of State Elliott Abrams has asked the Sultan of Brunei to donate $10 million for the Contras.

## June 26

Congress approves $100 million in military and non-lethal aid to the Contras beginning October 1.

## July 10

Albert Hakim, an Iranian-American and Secord's business partner, begins looking for a new intermediary in the Iran dealings.

## July 26

Jenco is freed.

August 4

The U.S. sends Iran a shipment of spare parts for HAWK antiaircraft missiles.

August 6

North meets with 11 members of the House Intelligence Committee, and responding to a *New York Times* story, he denies raising any money for Contras or offering them military advice. Later, North testifies that he lied in this session.

August 25

Hakim's efforts succeed; a "Second Channel" to Iran is found. An emissary, identified as an officer in the Revolutionary Guards, meets with Secord and Hakim in Brussels, Belgium.

September 6

North learns that a Costa Rican official was threatening to disclose in a press conference the existence of the secret airstrip in that country that North's enterprise built to serve the Contra resupply program. Ambassador Tambs calls President Oscar Arias Sanchez and urges him to the cancel press conference. Arias does so, but Costa Rican officials still disclose the existence of the airstrip on September 25.

September 9

Frank Herbert Reed is kidnapped.
   New Iranian intermediaries are flown to Washington for meetings with North, Secord, and Hakim. One of them acknowledges the Iranian role in the kidnapping of Reed.

September 12

Another American, Joseph James Cicippio, is taken hostage.

October 5

A cargo plane carrying arms to the Contras, part of the North-Secord resupply operation, is shot down over Nicaragua. Three crewmen are killed and a fourth, Eugene Hasenfus, is taken captive.

October 21

Edward Austin Tracy is kidnapped in Lebanon.

October 28

Another 500 U.S. TOW missiles are sent to Iran.

October 29

Secord, Hakim, and George Cave, a retired CIA officer called in to work on the Iran operation, meet with Iranians in Mainz, West Germany. They disclose that radicals in Iran have published 5 million pamphlets about the McFarlane visit to Iran.

November 2

Jacobsen is released.

November 3

A Lebanese magazine, *Al-Shiraa,* discloses that the U.S. sent arms to Iran and that McFarlane visited Tehran.

November 5–6

Press accounts confirm the story even as the White House issues a denial.

November 10

The President's senior advisers argue over how to respond. Reagan, according to notes taken at the session, agrees there is need for a public statement but tells his aides to "stay away from detail."

November 12–19

North and other White House officials prepare increasingly inaccurate chronologies of events in the Iran affair.

November 19

Reagan holds a press conference and makes major errors of fact. He insists, for example, that no other country was involved, even though Israel was shipping many of the weapons. He says 1,000 TOWs were sent when the number was actually 2,004. Minutes after the press conference ends, advisers correct the misstatement about Israel.

November 21

William J. Casey, the Director of Central Intelligence, appears before House and Senate Intelligence Committees after a major battle within the Administration over what he will say about the CIA's role in the November 1985 arms shipment. Attorney General Edwin Meese III says he is disturbed by confusion over the facts and suggests that the President have him conduct an inquiry. North is told that Justice Department officials will inspect his files the next day, and he begins shredding documents.

**November 22**

A Justice Department official, Bradford Reynolds, finds an April 1986 memo to the President that mentions the diversion of funds to the Contras.

**November 23**

North tells Meese there was a diversion of funds but misstates other crucial aspects of the deal.

**November 24**

Meese goes to the White House and tells the President of the diversion. White House Chief of Staff Donald T. Regan attends, and his reaction to the news is "horror, horror, horror, horror."

**November 25**

Meese announces the diversion of money from the Iran arms sales to the Contras. Reagan announces Poindexter's resignation and North's dismissal.

**December 19**

Lawrence M. Walsh is named special prosecutor in the Iran-Contra Affair.


**1987**

**January 6–7**

The Senate and the House set up committees to investigate the Iran-Contra Affair.

**January 24**

Four teachers—Alann Steen, Jesse J. Turner, and Robert Polhill, Americans, and Mithileshwar Singh, an Indian-born U.S. resident alien—are kidnapped at Beirut University College.

**February 26**

The Tower Commission, set up to study NSC operations and headed by former Texas Senator John Tower, issues its report. It concludes that the President's top advisers were responsible for creating the chaos that led to the Iran-Contra Affair. The report asserts that President Reagan was largely out of touch with the operations undertaken by his National Security Council staff.

**May 5**

Televised public testimony begins before the Senate and House Committees investigating the Iran-Contra Affair. Secord is the first witness.

July 7

North begins six days of testimony before the Congressional Committees. He says he has no idea if the President had any knowledge of the diversion of funds to the Contras. He also says that William Casey was aware of and approved of the diversion and that the arms sales were originally intended as an exchange for the hostages.

July 15

Poindexter begins five days of testimony before the Committees. He says he never told the President of the diversion of funds, to give him "plausible deniability" about the affair.

August 3

The Iran-Contra hearings end after more than 250 hours of testimony from 28 public witnesses.

November 18

The Congressional Iran-Contra Committees issue their report.

# Cast of Characters

**Elliott Abrams:** Assistant Secretary of State for Inter-American Affairs and coordinator of the Administration's Central America policy. He said he was not involved in the covert aid to the Contras despite many meetings with North and his solicitation of $10 million from Brunei for the Contras.

**George Bush:** Vice President of the United States. Attended some but not all of the high-level meetings on the Iran initiative. Appears to have played a minor role. Was not recorded as taking a position at the August 6, 1985, meeting with Reagan when the first Israeli sale of arms to Iran was discussed by top Presidential aides. He met on May 1, 1986, with Felix Rodriguez, a former CIA officer who was working on the Contra airlift in El Salvador. Witnesses, including Rodriguez, insisted that the Contra operation did not come up in the conversation. A memo prepared for the meeting by Bush's staff said its purpose was to provide a briefing on the progress of the war in El Salvador and "resupply of the Contras." A Bush aide said a secretary misunderstood his instructions on what the memo was to say; the secretary said she typed what she was told.

**Adolfo Calero:** A Contra leader who was North's chief contact with the rebels during the two-year ban on U.S. military aid. Had primary responsibility for distributing most private funds received by the Contras. Still a member of the Contra political directorate.

**William J. Casey:** As Director of Central Intelligence, he was instrumental in the creation of the Contra movement and was a central figure in the Iran arms sales. According to North's uncorroborated testimony, Casey wanted to set up a permanent secret fund, not accountable to Congress, that could be used for clandestine activities. Disabled by a brain tumor in November, he died in May without having been questioned in detail about the affair. North said he knew all about the diversion, but some associates find this unlikely.

**Carl R. "Spitz" Channell:** Political fundraiser who pleaded guilty in April to conspiring to defraud the Government by raising tax-exempt funds and funnelling them to the Contras. Named North as a co-conspirator. His highly effective operation raised $10 million, of which only $4.5 million went to or was spent on behalf of the Contras. Another $1 million paid for a range of political advertising.

**Duane Clarridge:** Head of the CIA's Central America task force for several years, he supervised efforts to arm the Contras and mine Nicaraguan harbors. As chief of the CIA's European division, he was a central figure in arranging the arms shipment to Iran in November 1985. Later became head of a special CIA counterterrorism unit.

**Thomas Clines:** Former CIA officer who worked with Secord and Hakim. According to testimony, $1 million in profits from the arms sales was allocated to him.

**Robert C. Dutton:** Retired Air Force colonel and associate of General Secord. Helped supervise the day-to-day running of the Contra network. Credited with making the air operation successful after early failures. Given immunity from prosecution by the independent counsel.

**Robert L. Earl:** A Rhodes scholar, former CIA analyst on Middle Eastern affairs, and North's deputy on the National Security Council. Testified that North had told him that at a White House meeting North was given word he had been "designated the scapegoat" for the Iran-Contra Affair. Also said that North quoted Reagan as saying of the diversion: "It is important that I not know." North denied making that statement.

**Joe Fernandez (alias Tomas Castillo):** Former CIA station chief in Costa Rica. The Agency disciplined him in 1985 for his role in preparation of a manual for training the Contras that advocated assassination. Played a major role in North's resupply network by passing messages to Contras in the field who were waiting for airdrops. Said his supervisors at the Agency were fully aware of his activities.

**Alan Fiers:** Head of the CIA's Central America Task Force, Fiers denies knowing of Fernandez' role helping the Contras. He acknowledges that when other officials made misleading statements to Congress about the Contra operation, he didn't correct them.

**David Fischer:** A former Special Assistant to the President, he arranged for contributors to the Contras to meet Reagan in exchange for a retainer of $20,000 per month, according to Channell. Fischer denies any such deal and said the money was for consulting.

**Clair George:** The CIA's Deputy Director for Operations, George said the U.S. got involved in "harebrained schemes" intended to rescue the hostages. Said Casey knew the agency was reluctant to carry out the Iran operation and so turned to the NSC staff instead.

**Manucher Ghorbanifar:** Iranian arms merchant who arranged the early U.S. arms deals with Iran. CIA officials considered him untrustworthy and in 1984 issued a "burn notice" that advised other intelligence services not to work with him. Flunked every polygraph, or lie detector, test he was ever given by the Agency. Used by the NSC as the principal contact in developing a relationship with Iran in late 1985 and early 1986.

**Francis Gomez:** After leaving his post as Deputy Assistant for Public Affairs at the State Department, Gomez received a State Department contract to do public education on Central America. He and Richard R. Miller had a loose partnership in a company called IBC. It handled a State Department contract and, separately, funnelled money raised from private citizens to the Contras.

**Donald Gregg:** The National Security Adviser to Vice President Bush, Gregg was a CIA veteran and close friend of Felix Rodriguez, who worked on the private resupply operation. When Rodriguez had complaints about the effort, he called Gregg, who set up a meeting in Washington.

**Albert Hakim:** Business partner of Secord who coordinated the financial transactions behind the Iran arms sale and the delivery of supplies to the Contras. Records compiled by the Committees show that large profits were made from the Iran and Contra arms sales. He was instrumental in developing the second set of contacts with Iran after Ghorbanifar was banished and said he felt like he had been Secretary of State for a day.

**Fawn Hall:** Former secretary to North who shredded, altered, and smuggled documents out of the White House in November 1986 in an effort to protect North from the Iran-Contra disclosures. Now a secretary at the Navy Department, where she does not have access to classified material.

**Adnan M. Khashoggi:** Saudi businessman and arms dealer who provided interim financing for the initial arms shipments to Iran. He said he lost money on the deals.

**David Kimche:** Former Director General of the Israeli Foreign Ministry and senior intelligence official, he helped establish contacts between the United States and Iran in 1985 that led to the sale of American arms to Tehran.

**Robert C. McFarlane:** National Security Adviser from October 1983 to December 1985. He testified he had briefed the President "dozens" of times on secret efforts to funnel private aid to the Contras. Said he did not know the full extent of North's activities. In 1985 and 1986 McFarlane assured Congress that North was following the letter and spirit of Boland Amendment restrictions on Contra aid. He personally arranged Saudi Arabia's contribution to the Contras and remained active in the Iran project even after quitting as National Security Adviser in December of 1985.

**Edwin Meese III:** Attorney General. Conducted a much criticized inquiry into the Iran arms sales in fall 1986. Testified he had unearthed the "essential facts," but critics said he should have used experienced criminal investigators. The report notes that before he found the infamous diversion memo, he brought note-takers and witnesses along for all his interviews. But in the days afterward, he met the principals alone and took no notes. Has appeared several times before the grand jury investigating the Iran affair.

**Richard R. Miller:** A former chief of public affairs at the Agency for International Development and Reagan campaign worker, Miller worked with Gomez at IBC. He has admitted helping North solicit tax deductible contributions that were used for a non-deductible purpose: arming the Contras. Miller pleaded guilty to conspiracy charges brought in May by Lawrence Walsh, the special prosecutor.

**Yaacov Nimrodi:** Former Israeli official in Iran, now an arms dealer. Helped organize the first arms shipments to Iran.

**Amiram Nir:** Adviser on terrorism to Shimon Peres when Peres was the Israeli Prime Minister. Seen by many as the "Ollie North of Israel." A former journalist, he took over the handling of Israel's arms deals with Iran from Kimche in early 1986. Was main contact with Ghorbanifar and even flew to Tehran for the May 1986 meeting.

**Oliver L. North:** The Marine lieutenant colonel who, as a staff member at the National Security Council, coordinated the dealings with Iran and the Nicaraguan rebels. Dismissed in November 1986. Testified that all his activities had been approved by superiors to whom he reported regularly. Although no one explicitly told him so, he "assumed" throughout that the President knew what he was doing. He was at the center of every NSC operation uncovered so far and was a charismatic "can-do" officer who worked on terrorism issues and Central America.

**Robert W. Owen:** A North aide under contract with the State Department who served as the colonel's courier to the Contras and described himself as a "private foot soldier" in the Contra supply efforts. Wrote North a series of blistering letters about the Contra movement and its failings.

**John M. Poindexter:** The vice admiral who was National Security Adviser from December 1985 to November 1986. Allowed to resign after investigators learned of the diversion. Took full responsibility for authorizing the diversion of Iran arms sale proceeds to the Contras. Said he had not told the President about the diversion to protect Reagan from political embarrassment. Although praised throughout his Navy career as an officer who had a photographic memory and a penchant for keeping superiors informed, he told the Iran Committees repeatedly that he could not recall key events of his tenure and kept vital information from the President.

**Ronald Wilson Reagan:** President of the United States. The Iran and Contra operations were intended to accomplish two of his most important objectives: keeping the Contras alive and rescuing the American hostages in Lebanon. Uncertainty remains about what he approved. Reagan has insisted he knew nothing of the diversion of Iran arms profits to the Contra cause, and the report found no evidence to the contrary. But the President has acknowledged supporting efforts by the NSC staff to aid the rebels. Since the Iran-Contra Affair became public, Reagan has called North a "national hero" and has faulted himself for becoming too emotionally involved in the fate of the hostages.

**Donald T. Regan:** President Reagan's chief of staff until he resigned in February 1987. Testified he was aware in general of the Iran initiative and said he did not know about the diversion of funds to the Contras until it was publicly revealed last November.

**Glenn A. Robinette:** A private security consultant and former CIA officer. Installed a security system worth $14,000 at North's home, which he said was paid for by Secord.

**Felix I. Rodriguez:** A former CIA agent also known as Max Gomez. Was liaison between the Contra supply operation and authorities in El Salvador. Testified that he discussed the secret Contra program with officials in Vice President Bush's office but never with Mr. Bush.

**Richard V. Secord:** Retired Air Force major general hired by North to direct the arms sales and the covert support of the Nicaraguan rebels. Repeatedly denied he had any interest in profiting from what he called "the Enterprise," but testimony suggested that money was being set aside for him. Had a dim view of the CIA, which he said was filled with "shoe clerks."

**George P. Shultz:** Secretary of State. Testified that Poindexter and Casey had deceived him and the President to keep the Iran arms sales alive. Denounced the efforts of the CIA and the National Security Council to run foreign policy and said he had threatened to resign three times since 1983. Many details of Iran affair were kept from him by White House. Some Republicans say he should have worked harder to stop arms sales.

**John K. Singlaub:** A retired Army major general who was a central figure in the private effort to raise money to buy weapons for the Contras. Testified he did not know that the Secord operation was accumulating millions of dollars from the sale of arms. He arranged one arms shipment of more than $5 million. His main role was to act as a "lightening rod" that could draw public attention from the North/Secord operations.

**Lewis A. Tambs:** As U.S. Ambassador to Costa Rica, North directed him to help open a southern front for the Contras after his appointment in July 1985. He understood North's order actually came from a group managing Central American policy that consisted of North, Abrams, and Alan Fiers, head of the CIA's Central America task force. These three officials denied his assertion.

**Caspar W. Weinberger:** Secretary of Defense. Thought his opposition to the Iran arms sales had killed the Iran dealings in December 1985 but found months later that he was wrong. Testified he had scoffed at the notion of establishing relations with Iranian "moderates" because there are no moderates. Has resigned because of his wife's ill health.

# List of Countries

A number of foreign countries helped the United States with various aspects of the Iran-Contra Affair, in almost all cases with the understanding that their roles would be kept secret. Trying to avoid embarrassing them, the Committees did not name them and instead referred to these countries by pre-assigned numbers—even though in some cases the names of the countries were perfectly obvious.

Not all of the countries discussed during the hearings were mentioned in the final report, so the document uses only a selection of the numbers. These include:

Country 1:  Israel
Country 2:  Saudi Arabia
Country 3:  Taiwan
Country 4:  China
Country 5:  South Korea
Country 6:  South Africa
Country 14: Guatemala
Country 15: Portugal
Country 16: Turkey
Country 17: Cyprus

# REPORT OF THE CONGRESSIONAL COMMITTEES INVESTIGATING THE IRAN-CONTRA AFFAIR

## United States Senate

### Select Committee on Secret Military Assistance To Iran and the Nicaraguan Opposition

Daniel K. Inouye, Hawaii, *Chairman*
Warren Rudman, New Hampshire, *Vice Chairman*

George J. Mitchell, Maine
Sam Nunn, Georgia
Paul S. Sarbanes, Maryland
Howell T. Heflin, Alabama
David L. Boren, Oklahoma

James A. McClure, Idaho
Orrin G. Hatch, Utah
William S. Cohen, Maine
Paul S. Trible, Jr., Virginia

## United States House of Representatives

### Select Committee to Investigate Covert Arms Transactions with Iran

Lee H. Hamilton, Indiana, *Chairman*
Dante B. Fascell, Florida, *Vice Chairman*

Thomas S. Foley, Washington
Peter W. Rodino, Jr., New Jersey
Jack Brooks, Texas
Louis Stokes, Ohio
Les Aspin, Wisconsin
Edward P. Boland, Massachusetts
Ed Jenkins, Georgia

Dick Cheney, Wyoming, *Ranking Republican*
Wm. S. Broomfield, Michigan
Henry J. Hyde, Illinois
Jim Courter, New Jersey
Bill McCollum, Florida
Michael DeWine, Ohio

# United States Senate

## Select Committee on Secret Military Assistance to Iran and the Nicaraguan Opposition

Arthur L. Liman
*Chief Counsel*

| | |
|---|---|
| Mark A. Belnick | Paul Barbadoro |
| *Executive Assistant to the Chief Counsel* | *Deputy Chief Counsel* |

Mary Jane Checchi
*Executive Director*

Lance I. Morgan
*Press Officer*

*Associate Counsels*

| | |
|---|---|
| C. H. Albright, Jr. | W. T. McGough, Jr. |
| Daniel Finn | Richard D. Parry |
| C. H. Holmes | John D. Saxon |
| James E. Kaplan | Terry A. Smiljanich |
| Charles M. Kerr | Timothy C. Woodcock |
| Joel P. Lisker | |

## Committee Staff

| | | | |
|---|---|---|---|
| *Assistant Counsels* | Steven D. Arkin* | *Staff Assistants* | John K. Appleby |
| | Isabel K. McGinty | | Ruth Balin |
| | John R. Monsky | | Robert E. Esler |
| | Victoria F. Nourse | | Ken Foster* |
| *Legal Counsel* | Philip Bobbitt | | Martin H. Garvey |
| *Intelligence/Foreign Policy Analysts* | Rand H. Fishbein | | Rachel D. Kaganoff* |
| | Thomas Polgar | | Craig L. Keller |
| *Investigators* | Lawrence R. Embrey, Sr. | | Hawley K. Manwarring |
| | David E. Faulkner | | Stephen G. Miller |
| | Henry J. Flynn | | Jennie L. Pickford* |
| *Press Assistant* | Samuel Hirsch | | Michael A. Raynor |
| *General Accounting Office Detailees* | John J. Cronin | | Joseph D. Smallwood* |
| | Olga E. Johnson | | Kristin K. Trenholm |
| | John C. Martin | | Thomas E. Tremble |
| | Melinda Suddes* | | Bruce Vaughn |
| | Robert Wagner | *Administrative Staff* | Laura J. Ison |
| | Louis H. Zanardi | | Hilary Phillips |
| *Security Officer* | Benjamin C. Marshall | | Winifred A. Williams* |
| *Security Assistants* | Georgiana Badovinac | *Secretaries* | Nancy S. Durflinger |
| | David Carty | | Shari D. Jenifer |
| | Kim Lasater | | Kathryn A. Momot |
| | Scott R. Thompson | | Cindy Pearson |
| *Chief Clerk* | Judith M. Keating* | | Debra S. Sheffield* |
| *Deputy Chief Clerk* | Scott R. Ferguson | *Receptionist* | Ramona H. Green |
| | | *Computer Center Detailee* | Preston Sweet |

## Committee Members' Designated Liaison

| | |
|---|---|
| Senator Inouye | Peter Simons |
| Senator Rudman | William V. Cowan |
| | Thomas C. Polgar |
| Senator Mitchell | Richard H. Arenberg |

## Part Time*

| | |
|---|---|
| *Assistant Counsel* | Peter V. Letsou |
| *Hearings Coordinator* | Joan M. Ansheles |
| *Staff Assistants* | Edward P. Flaherty, Jr. |
| | Barbara H. Hummell |
| | David G. Wiencek |

*The staff member was not with the Select Committee when the Report was filed but had, during the life of the Committee, provided services.

| | | | |
|---|---|---|---|
| *Senator Nunn* | Eleanore Hill | | |
| | Jeffrey H. Smith | *Interns* | Nona Balaban |
| *Senator Sarbanes* | Frederick Millhiser | | Edward E. Eldridge, III |
| *Senator Heflin* | Thomas J. Young | | Elizabeth J. Glennie |
| *Senator Boren* | Sven Holmes | | Stephen A. Higginson |
| | Blythe Thomas | | Laura T. Kunian |
| *Senator McClure* | Jack Gerard | | Julia F. Kogan |
| *Senator Hatch* | Dee V. Benson | | Catherine L. Udell |
| | James G. Phillips | *Document Analyst* | Lyndal L. Shaneyfelt |
| *Senator Cohen* | James Dykstra | *Historian* | Edward L. Keenan |
| | L. Britt Snider | *Volunteers* | Lewis Liman |
| *Senator Trible* | Richard Cullen | | Catherine Roe |
| | | | Susan Walsh |

# United States House of Representatives

## Select Committee to Investigate Covert Arms Transactions with Iran

### Majority Staff

John W. Nields, Jr.
*Chief Counsel*

W. Neil Eggleston
*Deputy Chief Counsel*

Kevin C. Miller
*Staff Director*

| | | | |
|---|---|---|---|
| *Special Deputy* | Charles Tiefer | *Systems Administrator* | Catherine L. Zimmer |
| *Chief Counsel* | | *Systems* | Charles G. Ratcliff |
| *Staff Counsels* | Kenneth M. Ballen | *Programmer/Analysts* | Stephen M. Rosenthal |
| | Patrick J. Carome | *Executive Assistant* | Elizabeth S. Wright |
| | V. Thomas Fryman, Jr. | *Staff Assistants* | Bonnie J. Brown |
| | Pamela J. Naughton | | Christina Kalbouss |
| | Joseph P. Saba | | Sandra L. Koehler |
| *Press Liasion* | Robert J. Havel | | Jan L. Suter |
| *Chief Clerk* | Ellen P. Rayner | | Katherine E. Urban |
| *Assistant Clerk* | Debra M. Cabral | | Kristine Willie |
| *Research Director* | Louis Fisher | | Mary K. Yount |
| *Research Assistants* | Christine C. Birmann | | |
| | Julius M. Genachowski | | |
| | Ruth D. Harvey | | |
| | James E. Rosenthal | | |

### Minority Staff

Thomas R. Smeeton
*Minority Staff Director*

George W. Van Cleve
*Chief Minority Counsel*

Richard J. Leon
*Deputy Chief Minority Counsel*

5

| | | | |
|---|---|---|---|
| *Associate Minority Counsel* | Robert W. Genzman | *Minority Staff Editor/Writer* | Michael J. Malbin |
| *Assistant Minority Counsel* | Kenneth R. Buck | *Minority Executive Assistant* | Molly W. Tully |
| *Minority Research Director* | Bruce E. Fein | *Minority Staff Assistant* | Margaret A. Dillenburg |

## Committee Staff

| | |
|---|---|
| *Investigators* | Robert A. Bermingham |
| | James J. Black |
| | Thomas N. Ciehanski |
| | William A. Davis, III |
| | Clark B. Hall |
| | Allan E. Hobron |
| | Roger L. Kreuzer |
| | Donald Remstein |
| | Jack W. Taylor |
| | Timothy E. Traylor |
| *Director of Security* | Bobby E. Pope |
| *Security Officers* | Rafael Luna, Jr. |
| | Theresa M. Martin |
| | Milagros Martinez |
| | Clayton C. Miller |
| | Angel R. Torres |
| *Editor* | Joseph Foote |
| *Deputy Editor* | Lisa L. Berger |
| *Associate Editor* | Nina Graybill |
| *Production Editor* | Mary J. Scroggins |
| *Hearings Editors* | David L. White |
| | Stephen G. Regan |
| *Printing Clerk* | G. R. Beckett |

## Associate Staff

| | |
|---|---|
| *Representative Hamilton* | Michael H. Van Dusen |
| | Christopher Kojm |
| *Representative Fascell* | R. Spencer Oliver |
| | Bert D. Hammond |
| | Victor Zangla |
| *Representative Foley* | Heather S. Foley |
| | Werner W. Brandt |
| *Representative Rodino* | M. Elaine Mielke |
| | James J. Schweitzer |
| *Representative Brooks* | William M. Jones |
| *Representative Stokes* | Michael J. O'Neil |
| | Richard M. Giza |
| *Representative Aspin* | Richard E. Clark |
| | Warren L. Nelson |
| *Representative Boland* | Michael W. Sheehy |
| *Representative Jenkins* | Robert H. Brink |
| *Representative Broomfield* | Steven K. Berry |
| | David S. Addington |
| *Representative Hyde* | Diane S. Dornan |
| *Representative Courter* | Dennis E. Teti |
| *Representative McCollum* | Tina L. Westby |
| *Representative DeWine* | Nicholas P. Wise |
| *General Counsel to the Clerk* | Steven R. Ross |

# PREFACE

# Origins of This Report

On November 3, 1986, Al-Shiraa, a Lebanese weekly, reported that the United States had secretly sold arms to Iran. Subsequent reports claimed that the purpose of the sales was to win the release of American hostages in Lebanon. These reports seemed unbelievable: Few principles of U.S. policy were stated more forcefully by the Reagan Administration than refusing to traffic with terrorists or sell arms to the Government of the Ayatollah Khomeini of Iran.

Although the Administration initially denied the reports, by mid-November it was clear that the accounts were true. The United States had sold arms to Iran and had hoped thereby to gain the release of American hostages in Lebanon. However, even though the Iranians received the arms, just as many Americans remained hostage as before. Three had been freed, but three more had been taken during the period of the sales.

There was still another revelation to come: on November 25 the Attorney General announced that proceeds from the Iran arms sales had been "diverted" to the Nicaraguan resistance at a time when U.S. military aid to the Contras was prohibited.

Iran and Nicaragua—twin thorns of U.S.

foreign policy in the 1980s—were thus linked in a credibility crisis that raised serious questions about the adherence of the Administration to the Constitutional processes of Government.

The public and Members of Congress expressed deep concern over the propriety and legality of actions by the staff of the National Security Council (NSC) and other officers of the Government regarding both the arms sales and the secret assistance to the Contras.

The issue of U.S. support for the Contras was not new. The President and Congress had engaged in vigorous debate over the proper course of U.S. policy, and Congress had barred U.S. support of Contra military operations for almost 2 years. Subsequently, senior Administration officials had assured Committees of Congress repeatedly that the Administration was abiding by the law.

The Iran-Contra Affair, as it came to be known, carried such serious implications for U.S. foreign policy, and for the rule of law in a democracy, that the 100th Congress determined to undertake its own investigation of the Affair.

The inquiry formally began on January 6, 1987, when the Senate, by S. Res. 23, established the Select Committee on Secret Military Assistance to Iran and the Nicaraguan Opposition. The next day, the House, by H. Res. 12, established the Select Committee to Investigate Covert Arms Transactions with Iran. The two Chambers charged their respective Committees with investigating four major areas: arms sales to Iran, the possible diversion of funds to aid the Contras, violations of Federal law, and the involvement of the NSC staff in the conduct of foreign policy.

The two Committees took the unprecedented step of merging their investigations and hearings and sharing all the information they obtained. The staffs of the two Committees worked together in reviewing more than 300,000 documents and interviewing or examining more than 500 witnesses. The Committees held 40 days of joint public hearings and several executive sessions. The two Committees then decided to combine their findings in a joint Report.

The conclusions in this Report are based on a record marred by inconsistent testimony and failure on the part of several witnesses to recall key matters and events. Moreover, a key witness—Director of Central Intelligence William J. Casey—died, and members of the NSC staff shredded relevant contemporaneous documents in the fall of 1986. Consequently, objective evidence that could have resolved the inconsistencies and overcome the failures of memory was denied to the Committees—and to history.

Under the American system, Government is accountable to the people. A public bipartisan investigation such as this one helps to ensure that the principle of accountability is enforced for all officials and policies. It strengthens the national commitment to the democratic values that have guided the United States for two centuries.

The President cooperated with the investigation. He did not assert executive privilege; he instructed all relevant agencies to produce their documents and witnesses; and he made extracts available from his personal diaries, although he rejected the Committees' request to refer to those entries in this Report on the ground that he did not wish to establish a precedent for future Presidents.

The Committees also received unprecedented cooperation from a sovereign nation, the State of Israel. Although not willing to allow its officials to be examined, the Government of Israel assembled and furnished the Committees with extensive materials and information, including information affecting its national security.

The Committees' investigation of the Iran-Contra Affair is not the first, following as it does the findings of the Senate Select Committee on Intelligence and the President's Special Review Board (known as the Tower Board); nor will it be the last, for the investigation of the Independent Counsel assigned to this matter continues.

But the Committees hope this Report will make a contribution by helping to explain what happened in the Iran-Contra Affair, and by helping to restore the public's confidence in this Nation's Constitutional system of Government.

# SECTION I

# THE REPORT

# PART I

# EXECUTIVE SUMMARY

The full story of the Iran-Contra Affair is complicated, and, for this Nation, profoundly sad. In the narrative portion of this Report, the Committees present a comprehensive account of the facts, based on 10 months of investigation, including 11 weeks of hearings.

But the facts alone do not explain how or why the events occurred. In this Executive Summary, the Committees focus on the key issues and offer their conclusions. Minority, supplemental, and additional views are printed in Section II and Section III.

## SUMMARY OF THE FACTS

The Iran-Contra Affair had its origin in two unrelated revolutions in Iran and Nicaragua.

In Nicaragua, the long-time President, General Anastasio Somoza Debayle, was overthrown in 1979 and replaced by a Government controlled by Sandinista leftists.

In Iran, the pro-Western Government of the Shah Mohammed Riza Pahlavi was overthrown in 1979 by Islamic fundamentalists led by the Ayatollah Khomeini. The Khomeini Government, stridently anti-American, became a supporter of terrorism against American citizens.

## Nicaragua

United States policy following the revolution in Nicaragua was to encourage the Sandinista Government to keep its pledges of pluralism and democracy. However, the Sandinista regime became increasingly anti-

11

American and autocratic; began to aid a leftist insurgency in El Salvador; and turned toward Cuba and the Soviet Union for political, military, and economic assistance. By December 1981, the United States had begun supporting the Nicaraguan Contras, armed opponents of the Sandinista regime.

The Central Intelligence Agency (CIA) was the U.S. Government agency that assisted the Contras. In accordance with Presidential decisions, known as Findings, and with funds appropriated by Congress, the CIA armed, clothed, fed, and supervised the Contras. Despite this assistance, the Contras failed to win widespread popular support or military victories within Nicaragua.

Although the President continued to favor support of the Contras, opinion polls indicated that a majority of the public was not supportive. Opponents of the Administration's policy feared that U.S. involvement with the Contras would embroil the United States in another Vietnam. Supporters of the policy feared that, without U.S. support for the Contras, the Soviets would gain a dangerous toehold in Central America.

Congress prohibited Contra aid for the purpose of overthrowing the Sandinista Government in fiscal year 1983, and limited all aid to the Contras in fiscal year 1984 to $24 million. Following disclosure in March and April 1984 that the CIA had a role in connection with the mining of the Nicaraguan harbors without adequate notification to Congress, public criticism mounted and the Administration's Contra policy lost much of its support within Congress. After further vigorous debate, Congress exercised its Constitutional power over appropriations and cut off all funds for the Contras' military and paramilitary operations. The statutory provision cutting off funds, known as the Boland

Amendment, was part of a fiscal year 1985 omnibus appropriations bill, and was signed into law by the President on October 12, 1984.

Still, the President felt strongly about the Contras, and he ordered his staff, in the words of his National Security Adviser, to find a way to keep the Contras "body and soul together." Thus began the story of how the staff of a White House advisory body, the NSC, became an operational entity that secretly ran the Contra assistance effort, and later the Iran initiative. The action officer placed in charge of both operations was Lt. Col. Oliver L. North.

Denied funding by Congress, the President turned to third countries and private sources. Between June 1984 and the beginning of 1986, the President, his National Security Adviser, and the NSC staff secretly raised $34 million for the Contras from other countries. An additional $2.7 million was provided for the Contras during 1985 and 1986 from private contributors, who were addressed by North and occasionally granted photo opportunities with the President. In the middle of this period, Assistant Secretary of State A. Langhorne Motley—from whom these contributions were concealed—gave his assurance to Congress that the Administration was not "soliciting and/or encouraging third countries" to give funds to the Contras because, as he conceded, the Boland Amendment prohibited such solicitation.

The first contributions were sent by the donors to bank accounts controlled and used by the Contras. However, in July 1985, North took control of the funds and—with the support of two National Security Advisers (Robert McFarlane and John Poindexter) and, according to North, Director

Casey—used those funds to run the covert operation to support the Contras.

At the suggestion of Director Casey, North recruited Richard V. Secord, a retired Air Force Major General with experience in special operations. Secord set up Swiss bank accounts, and North steered future donations into these accounts. Using these funds, and funds later generated by the Iran arms sales, Secord and his associate, Albert Hakim, created what they called "the Enterprise," a private organization designed to engage in covert activities on behalf of the United States.

The Enterprise, functioning largely at North's direction, had its own airplanes, pilots, airfield, operatives, ship, secure communications devices, and secret Swiss bank accounts. For 16 months, it served as the secret arm of the NSC staff, carrying out with private and non-appropriated money, and without the accountability or restrictions imposed by law on the CIA, a covert Contra aid program that Congress thought it had prohibited.

Although the CIA and other agencies involved in intelligence activities knew that the Boland Amendment barred their involvement in covert support for the Contras, North's Contra support operation received logistical and tactical support from various personnel in the CIA and other agencies. Certain CIA personnel in Central America gave their assistance. The U.S. Ambassador in Costa Rica, Lewis Tambs, provided his active assistance. North also enlisted the aid of Defense Department personnel in Central America, and obtained secure communications equipment from the National Security Agency. The Assistant Secretary of State with responsibility for the region, Elliott Abrams, professed ignorance of this support.

He later stated that he had been "careful not to ask North lots of questions."

By Executive Order and National Security Decision Directive issued by President Reagan, all covert operations must be approved by the President personally and in writing. By statute, Congress must be notified about each covert action. The funds used for such actions, like all government funds, must be strictly accounted for.

The covert action directed by North, however, was not approved by the President in writing. Congress was not notified about it. And the funds to support it were never accounted for. In short, the operation functioned without any of the accountability required of Government activities. It was an evasion of the Constitution's most basic check on Executive action—the power of the Congress to grant or deny funding for Government programs.

Moreover, the covert action to support the Contras was concealed from Congress and the public. When the press reported in the summer of 1985 that the NSC staff was engaged in raising money and furnishing military support to the Contras, the President assured the public that the law was being followed. His National Security Adviser, Robert C. McFarlane, assured Committees of Congress, both in person and in writing, that the NSC staff was obeying both the spirit and the letter of the law, and was neither soliciting money nor coordinating military support for the Contras.

A year later, McFarlane's successor, Vice Admiral John M. Poindexter, repeated these assurances to Congressional Committees. Then, with Poindexter's blessing, North told the House Intelligence Committee he was involved neither in fundraising for, nor in providing military advice to, the Contras.

When one of Secord's planes was shot down over Nicaragua on October 5, 1986, the President and several administration spokesmen assured the public that the U.S. Government had no connection with the flight or the captured American crew member, Eugene Hasenfus. Several senior Government officials, including Elliott Abrams, gave similar assurances to Congress.

Two months later, McFarlane told Congressional Committees that he had no knowledge of contributions made by a foreign country, Country 2 [Saudi Arabia], to the Contras, when in fact McFarlane and the President had discussed and welcomed $32 million in contributions from that country. In addition, Abrams initially concealed from Congress—in testimony given to several Committees—that he had successfully solicited a contribution of $10 million from Brunei.

North conceded at the Committees' public hearings that he had participated in making statements to Congress that were "false," "misleading," "evasive and wrong."

During the period when the Administration was denying to Congress that it was involved in supporting the Contras' war effort, it was engaged in a campaign to alter public opinion and change the vote in Congress on Contra aid. Public funds were used to conduct public relations activities; and certain NSC staff members, using the prestige of the White House and the promise of meetings with the President, helped raise private donations both for media campaigns and for weapons to be used by the Contras.

Pursuant to a Presidential directive in 1983 the Administration adopted a "public diplomacy" program to promote the President's Central American policy. The program was conducted by an office in the State Department known as the Office for Public Diplomacy for Latin America and the Caribbean (S/LPD). S/LPD's activities were coordinated not within the State Department, but by an interagency working group established by the NSC. The principal NSC staff officer was a former senior CIA official, with experience in covert operations, who had been detailed to the NSC staff for a year with Casey's approval, and who upon retirement from the CIA became a Special Assistant to the President with responsibility for public diplomacy matters.

S/LPD produced and widely disseminated a variety of pro-Contra publications and arranged speeches and press conferences. It also disseminated what one official termed "white propaganda": pro-Contra newspaper articles by paid consultants who did not disclose their connection to the Administration. Moreover, under a series of sole source contracts in 1985 and 1986, S/LPD paid more than $400,000 for pro-Contra public relations work to International Business Communications (IBC), a company owned by Richard Miller, whose organization was described by one White House representative as a "White House outside the White House."

The Administration, like Members of Congress, may appeal directly to the people for support of its positions; and government agencies may legitimately disseminate information and educational materials to the public. However, by law appropriated funds may not be used to generate propaganda "designed to influence a Member of Congress;" and by law, as interpreted by the Office of the Comptroller General, appropriated funds may not be used by the State Department for "covert" propaganda activities. A GAO report concluded that S/LPD's white propaganda activities violated the ban on arranging "covert propaganda."

Private funds were also used. North and Miller helped Carl R. "Spitz" Channell raise $10 million, most of which went to Channell's tax-exempt organization, the National Endowment for the Preservation of Liberty ("NEPL"). They arranged numerous "briefings" at the White House complex on Central America by Administration officials for groups of potential contributors. Following these briefings, Channell reconvened the groups at the Hay-Adams Hotel, and made a pitch for tax-deductible contributions to NEPL's Central America "public education" program or, in some individual cases, for weapons. Channell's major contributors were given private briefings by North, and were afforded private visits and photo sessions with the President. On one occasion, President Reagan participated in a briefing.

Using the donated money, Channell ran a series of television advertisements in 1985 and 1986, some of which were directed at television markets covering the home districts of Congressmen considered to be "swing" votes on Contra aid. One series of advertisements was used to attack Congressman Mike Barnes, a principal opponent of Contra aid, and one of the Congressmen to whom Administration officials had denied violating the Boland Amendment in September of 1985. Channell later boasted to North that he had "participated in a campaign to ensure Congressman Barnes' defeat."

Of the $10 million raised by North, Channell and Miller, more than $1 million was used for pro-Contra publicity. Approximately $2.7 million was sent through IBC and off-shore accounts of another Miller-controlled company to Secord's Swiss accounts, or to Calero's account in Miami.

Most of the remainder was spent on salaries and expenses for Channell, Miller and their business associates.

NEPL's charter did not contemplate raising funds for a covert war in Nicaragua, and the Internal Revenue Service never approved such activity when NEPL was granted exempt status. As a consequence, Channell and Miller have each pleaded guilty to the crime of conspiring to defraud the United States Treasury of revenues "by subverting and corrupting the lawful purposes of NEPL." Channell named North as a co-conspirator.

In private fundraising, as in the "white propaganda" campaign, the goal of supporting the Contras was allowed to override sensitivity to law and to accepted norms of behavior.

## Iran

The NSC staff was already engaged in covert operations through Secord when, in the summer of 1985, the Government of Israel proposed that missiles be sold to Iran in return for the release of seven American hostages held in Lebanon and the prospect of improved relations with Iran. The Secretaries of State and Defense repeatedly opposed such sales to a government designated by the United States as a supporter of international terrorism. They called it a straight arms-for-hostages deal that was contrary to U.S. public policy. They also argued that these sales would violate the Arms Export Control Act, as well as the U.S. arms embargo against Iran. The embargo had been imposed after the taking of hostages at the U.S. Embassy in Tehran on November 4, 1979, and was continued because of the Iran-Iraq war.

Nevertheless, in the summer of 1985 the

President authorized Israel to proceed with the sales. The NSC staff conducting the Contra covert action also took operational control of implementing the President's decision on arms sales to Iran. The President did not sign a Finding for this covert operation, nor did he notify the Congress.

Israel shipped 504 TOW anti-tank missiles to Iran in August and September 1985. Although the Iranians had promised to release most of the American hostages in return, only one, Reverend Benjamin Weir, was freed. The President persisted. In November, he authorized Israel to ship 80 HAWK anti-aircraft missiles in return for all the hostages, with a promise of prompt replenishment by the United States, and 40 more HAWKs to be sent directly by the United States to Iran. Eighteen HAWK missiles were actually shipped from Israel in November 1985, but no hostages were released.

In early December 1985, the President signed a retroactive Finding purporting to authorize the November HAWK transaction. That Finding contained no reference to improved relations with Iran. It was a straight arms-for-hostages Finding. National Security Adviser Poindexter destroyed this Finding a year later because, he testified, its disclosure would have been politically embarrassing to the President.

The November HAWK transaction had additional significance. The Enterprise received a $1 million advance from the Israelis. North and Secord testified this was for transportation expenses in connection with the 120 HAWK missiles. Since only 18 missiles were shipped, the Enterprise was left with more than $800,000 in spare cash. North directed the Enterprise to retain the money and spend it for the Contras. The "diversion" had begun.

North realized that the sale of missiles to Iran could be used to support the Contras. He told Israeli Defense Ministry officials on December 6, 1985, one day after the President signed the Finding, that he planned to generate profits on future arms sales for activities in Nicaragua.

On December 7, 1985, the President and his top advisers met again to discuss the arms sales. Secretaries Shultz and Weinberger objected vigorously once more, and Weinberger argued that the sales would be illegal. After a meeting in London with an Iranian interlocutor and the Israelis, McFarlane recommended that the sales be halted. Admiral John Poindexter (the new National Security Adviser), and Director Casey were of the opposite opinion.

The President decided to go forward with the arms sales to get the hostages back. He signed a Finding on January 6, 1986, authorizing more shipments of missiles for the hostages. When the CIA's General Counsel pointed out that authorizing Israel to sell its U.S.-manufactured weapons to Iran might violate the Arms Export Control Act, the President, on the legal advice of the Attorney General, decided to authorize direct shipments of the missiles to Iran by the United States and signed a new Finding on January 17, 1986. To carry out the sales, the NSC staff turned once again to the Enterprise.

Although North had become skeptical that the sales would lead to the release of all the hostages or a new relationship with Iran, he believed that the prospect of generating funds for the Contras was "an attractive incentive" for continuing the arms sales. No matter how many promises the Iranians failed to keep throughout this secret initiative, the arms sales continued to generate funds for the Enterprise, and North and his superior, Poindexter, were consistent advocates for their continuation. What North and Poindexter asserted in their testimony that they did not know, however, was that most of these arms sales profits would remain with the Enterprise and never reach the Contras.

In February 1986, the United States, acting through the Enterprise, sold 1,000 TOWs to the Iranians. The U.S. also provided the Iranians with military intelligence about Iraq. All of the remaining American hostages were supposed to be released upon Iran's receipt of the first 500 TOWs. None was. But the transaction was productive in one respect. The difference between what the Enterprise paid the United States for the missiles and what it received from Iran was more than $6 million. North directed part of this profit for the Contras and for other covert operations. Poindexter testified that he authorized this "diversion."

The diversion, for the Contras and other covert activities, was not an isolated act by the NSC staff. Poindexter saw it as "implementing" the President's secret policy that had been in effect since 1984 of using nonappropriated funds following passage of the Boland Amendment.

According to North, CIA Director Casey saw the "diversion" as part of a more grandiose plan to use the Enterprise as a "stand-alone," "off-the-shelf," covert capacity that would act throughout the world while evading Congressional review. To Casey, Poindexter, and North, the diversion was an integral part of selling arms to Iran and just one of the intended uses of the proceeds.

In May 1986, the President again tried to sell weapons to get the hostages back. This time, the President agreed to ship parts for HAWK missiles but only on condition that all the American hostages in Lebanon be released first. A mission headed by Robert McFarlane, the former National Security Adviser, traveled to Tehran with the first installment of the HAWK parts. When the mission arrived, McFarlane learned that the Iranians claimed they had never promised to do anything more than try to obtain the hostages' release. The trip ended amid misunderstanding and failure, although the first installment of HAWK parts was delivered.

The Enterprise was paid, however, for all of the HAWK parts, and realized more than an $8 million profit, part of which was applied, at North's direction, to the Contras. Another portion of the profit was used by North for other covert operations, including the operation of a ship for a secret mission. The idea of an off-the-shelf, stand-alone covert capacity had become operational.

On July 26, 1986, another American hostage, Father Lawrence Jenco, was released. Despite all the arms sales, he was only the second hostage freed, and the first since September 1985. Even though McFarlane had vowed at the Tehran meeting not to deliver the remainder of the HAWK parts until all the hostages were released, the Administration capitulated again. The balance of the HAWK parts was shipped when Father Jenco was released.

In September and October 1986, the NSC staff began negotiating with a new group of Iranians, the "Second Channel," that Albert Hakim had opened, in part, through promises of bribes. Although these Iranians allegedly had better contacts with Iranian officials, they, in fact, represented the same principals as did the First Channel and had the same arrangement in mind: missiles for hostages. Once again, the Administration insisted on release of all the hostages but settled for less.

In October, after a meeting in London, North left Hakim to negotiate with the Hakim made no secret of his desire to make large profits for himself and General Secord in the $15 billion-a-year Iranian market if relations with the United States could be restored. Thus, he had every incentive to make an agreement, whatever concessions might be required.

As an unofficial "ambassador" selected by North and Secord, Hakim produced a remarkable nine-point plan, subsequently approved by North and Poindexter, under which the United States would receive "one and one half" hostages (later reduced to one). Under the plan, the United States agreed not only to sell the Iranians 500 more TOWs, but Secord and Hakim promised to develop a plan to induce the Kuwaiti Government to release the Da'wa prisoners. (Seventeen Kuwaiti prisoners, connected to "al-Dawa," an Iranian revolutionary group, had been convicted and imprisoned for their part in the December 12, 1983, attacks in Kuwait on the U.S. Embassy, a U.S. civilian compound, the French Embassy, and several Kuwaiti Government facilities.) The plan to obtain the release of the Da'wa prisoners did not succeed, but the TOW missiles were sold for use by the Iranian Revolutionary Guard. Following the transfer of these TOWs, a third hostage, David Jacobsen, was released on November 2, 1986, and more profit was generated for the Enterprise.

Poindexter testified that the President approved the nine-point plan. But other testimony raises questions about this assertion. Regardless of what Poindexter may have told the President, Secretary Shultz testified that when he informed the President on December 14, 1986, that the nine-point plan included a promise about the release of the

Da'wa prisoners in Kuwait, the President reacted with shock, "like he had been kicked in the belly."

During the negotiations with the Second Channel, North and Secord told the Iranians that the President agreed with their position that Iraq's President, Saddam Hussein, had to be removed and further agreed that the United States would defend Iran against Soviet aggression. They did not clear this with the President and their representations were flatly contrary to U.S. policy.

The decision to designate private parties—Secord and Hakim—to carry out the arms transactions had other ramifications. First, there was virtually no accounting for the profits from the arms deals. Even North claimed that he did not know how Secord and Hakim actually spent the money committed to their custody. The Committees' investigation revealed that of the $16.1 million profit from the sales of arms to Iran only about $3.8 million went to support the Contras (the amount representing "the diversion"). All told, the Enterprise received nearly $48 million from the sale of arms to the Contras and Iran, and in contributions directed to it by North. A total of $16.5 million was used to support the Contras or to purchase the arms sold to (and paid for by) the Contras; $15.2 million was spent on Iran; Hakim, Secord, and their associate, Thomas Clines, took $6.6 million in commissions and other profit distributions; almost $1 million went for other covert operations sponsored by North; $4.2 million was held in "reserves" for use in future operations; $1.2 million remained in Swiss bank accounts of the Enterprise; and several thousand dollars were used to pay for a security system at North's residence.

Second, by permitting private parties to

conduct the arms sales, the Administration risked losing control of an important foreign policy initiative. Private citizens—whose motivations of personal gain could conflict with the interests of this country—handled sensitive diplomatic negotiations, and purported to commit the United States to positions that were anathema to the President's public policy and wholly unknown to the Secretary of State.

## The Coverup

The sale of arms to Iran was a "significant anticipated intelligence activity." By law, such an activity must be reported to Congress "in a timely fashion" pursuant to Section 501 of the National Security Act. If the proposal to sell arms to Iran had been reported, the Senate and House Intelligence Committees would likely have joined Secretaries Shultz and Weinberger in objecting to this initiative. But Poindexter recommended—and the President decided—not to report the Iran initiative to Congress.

Indeed, the Administration went to considerable lengths to avoid notifying Congress. The CIA General Counsel wrote on January 15, 1986, "the key issue in this entire matter revolves around whether or not there will be reports made to Congress." Shortly thereafter, the transaction was restructured to avoid the pre-shipment reporting requirements of the Arms Export Control Act, and place it within the more limited reporting requirements of the National Security Act. But even these reporting requirements were ignored. The President failed to notify the group of eight (the leaders of each party in the House and Senate, and the Chairmen and Ranking Minority Members of the Intelli-

gence Committees) specified by law for unusually sensitive operations.

After the disclosure of the Iran arms sales on November 3, 1986, the American public was still not told the facts. The President sought to avoid any comment on the ground that it might jeopardize the chance of securing the remaining hostages' release. But it was impossible to remain silent, and inaccurate statements followed.

In his first public statement on the subject on November 6, the President said that the reports concerning the arms sales had "no foundation." A week later, on November 13, the President conceded that the United States had sold arms, but branded as "utterly false" allegations that the sales were in return for the release of the hostages. The President also maintained that there had been no violations of Federal law.

At his news conference on November 19, 1986, he denied that the United States was involved in the Israeli sales that occurred prior to the January 17, 1986 Finding. The President was asked:

> Mr. President . . . are you telling us tonight that the only shipments with which we were involved were the one or two that followed your January 17 Finding and that . . . there were no other shipments which the U.S. condoned?

The President replied:

> That's right. I'm saying nothing, but the missiles we sold.

And, on November 25, 1986, the Attorney General—with the President at his side—announced at a press conference that the President did not know of the Israeli shipments until after they had occurred. He stated that the President learned of the November 1985 HAWK shipment in February 1986.

In fact, however, the Israeli sales, including the HAWK shipment, were implemented with the knowledge and approval of the President and his top advisers; and the President himself told Shultz on the day of his press conference that he had known of the November 1985 shipment when it occurred. McFarlane, Poindexter, and North were intimately involved in the Israeli shipments; and the CIA had actually transported one delivery from Israel to Iran.

While the President was denying any illegality, his subordinates were engaging in a coverup. Several of his advisers had expressed concern that the 1985 sales violated the Arms Export Control Act, and a "cover story" had been agreed on if these arms sales were ever exposed. After North had three conversations on November 18, 1986, about the legal problems with the 1985 Israeli shipments, he, Poindexter, Casey, and McFarlane all told conforming false stories about U.S. involvement in these shipments.

With McFarlane's help, North rewrote NSC staff chronologies on November 19 and 20, 1986, in such a way that they denied contemporaneous knowledge by the Administration of Israel's shipments to Iran in 1985. They asserted at one point that the U.S. Government believed the November 1985 shipment consisted of oil-drilling equipment, not arms.

Poindexter told Congressional Committees on November 21, 1986, that the United States had disapproved of the Israeli shipments and that, until the day before his briefing, he believed that Administration officials did not know about any of them until

after they had occurred. He then destroyed the only Finding signed by the President that showed the opposite.

Casey told Congressional Committees on November 21, 1986, that although a CIA proprietary airline had actually carried missiles to Iran from Israel in 1985, the proprietary had been told the cargo was "oil-drilling equipment."

McFarlane told the Attorney General on November 21, 1986, that the Israelis said they were shipping oil-drilling equipment in November 1985 and that McFarlane did not learn otherwise until May 1986.

On learning that the President had authorized the Attorney General to gather the relevant facts, North and Poindexter shredded and altered official documents on November 21, 1986, and later that weekend. On November 25, 1986, North's secretary concealed classified documents in her clothing and, with North's knowledge, removed them from the White House.

According to North, a "fall guy" plan was proposed by Casey in which North and, if necessary, Poindexter, would take the responsibility for the covert Contra support operation and the diversion. On Saturday November 22, 1986, in the midst of these efforts to conceal what had happened, Poindexter had a two and one half hour lunch with Casey. Yet Poindexter could not recall anything that was discussed.

North testified that he assured Poindexter that he had destroyed all documents relating to the diversion. The diversion nevertheless was discovered on November 22, 1986, when a Justice Department official, assisting the Attorney General's fact-finding inquiry, found a "diversion memorandum" that had escaped the shredder.

Prior to the discovery of the diversion

memorandum, each interview by the Attorney General's fact finding team had been conducted in the presence of two witnesses, and careful notes were taken in accordance with standard professional practices. After discovery of the diversion memorandum—which itself gave rise to an inference of serious wrongdoing—the Attorney General departed from these standard practices. A series of important interviews—Poindexter, McFarlane, Casey, Regan, and Bush—was conducted by the Attorney General alone, and no notes were made.

The Attorney General then announced at his November 25 press conference that the diversion had occurred and that the President did not know of it. But he made several incorrect statements about his own investigation. He stated that the President had not known of the Israeli pre-Finding shipments, and he stated that the proceeds of the arms sales had been sent directly from the Israelis to the Contras. These statements were both mistaken and inconsistent with information that had been received during the Attorney General's fact-finding inquiry.

Poindexter testified to these Committees that the President did not know of the diversion. North testified that while he assumed the President had authorized each diversion, Poindexter told him on November 21, 1986, that the President had never been told of the diversion.

In light of the destruction of material evidence by Poindexter and North and the death of Casey, all of the facts may never be known. The Committees cannot even be sure whether they heard the whole truth or whether Casey's "fall guy" plan was carried out at the public hearings. But enough is clear to demonstrate beyond doubt that fundamental processes of governance were disregarded and the rule of law was subverted.

## FINDINGS AND CONCLUSIONS

The common ingredients of the Iran and Contra policies were secrecy, deception, and disdain for the law. A small group of senior officials believed that they alone knew what was right. They viewed knowledge of their actions by others in the Government as a threat to their objectives. They told neither the Secretary of State, the Congress nor the American people of their actions. When exposure was threatened, they destroyed official documents and lied to Cabinet officials, to the public, and to elected representatives in Congress. They testified that they even withheld key facts from the President.

The United States Constitution specifies the process by which laws and policy are to be made and executed. Constitutional process is the essence of our democracy and our democratic form of Government is the basis of our strength. Time and again we have learned that a flawed process leads to bad results, and that a lawless process leads to worse.

## Policy Contradictions and Failures

The Administration's departure from democratic processes created the conditions for policy failure, and led to contradictions which undermined the credibility of the United States.

The United States simultaneously pursued two contradictory foreign policies—a public one and a secret one:

— The public policy was not to make any concessions for the release of hostages lest such concessions encourage more hostage-taking. At the same time, the United States was secretly trading weapons to get the hostages back.

— The public policy was to ban arms shipments to Iran and to exhort other Governments to observe this embargo. At the same time, the United States was secretly selling sophisticated missiles to Iran and promising more.

— The public policy was to improve relations with Iraq. At the same time, the United States secretly shared military intelligence on Iraq with Iran and North told the Iranians in contradiction to United States policy that the United States would help promote the overthrow of the Iraqi head of government.

— The public policy was to urge all Governments to punish terrorism and to support, indeed encourage, the refusal of Kuwait to free the Da'wa prisoners who were convicted of terrorist acts. At the same time, senior officials secretly endorsed a Secord-Hakim plan to permit Iran to obtain the release of the Da'wa prisoners.

— The public policy was to observe the "letter and spirit" of the Boland Amendment's proscriptions against military or paramilitary assistance to the Contras. At the same time, the NSC staff was secretly assuming direction and funding of the Contras' military effort.

— The public policy, embodied in agreements signed by Director Casey, was for the Administration to consult with the Congressional oversight committees about covert activities in a "new spirit of frankness and cooperation." At the same time, the CIA and the White House were secretly withholding from those Committees all information concerning the Iran initiative and the Contra support network.

— The public policy, embodied in Executive Order 12333, was to conduct covert operations solely through the CIA or other organs of the intelligence community specifically authorized by the President. At the same time, although the the NSC was not so authorized, the NSC staff secretly became operational and used private, non-accountable agents to engage in covert activities.

These contradictions in policy inevitably resulted in policy failure:

— The United States armed Iran, including its most radical elements, but attained neither a new relationship with that hostile regime nor a reduction in the number of American hostages.

— The arms sales did not lead to a moderation of Iranian policies. Moderates did not come forward, and Iran to this day sponsors actions directed against the United States in the Persian Gulf and elsewhere.

— The United States opened itself to blackmail by adversaries who might reveal the secret arms sales and who, according to North, threatened to kill the hostages if the sales stopped.

— The United States undermined its credibility with friends and allies, including moderate Arab states, by its public stance of opposing arms sales to Iran while undertaking such arms sales in secret.

— The United States lost a $10 million contribution to the Contras from the Sultan of Brunei by directing it to the wrong bank account—the result of an improper effort to channel that humanitarian aid contribution into an account used for lethal assistance.

— The United States sought illicit funding for the Contras through profits from the secret arms sales, but a substantial portion of those profits ended up in the personal bank accounts of the private individuals executing the sales—while the exorbitant amounts charged for the weapons inflamed the Iranians with whom the United States was seeking a new relationship.

## Flawed Policy Process

The record of the Iran-Contra Affair also shows a seriously flawed policymaking process.

## Confusion

There was confusion and disarray at the highest levels of Government.

— McFarlane embarked on a dangerous trip to Tehran under a complete misapprehension. He thought the Iranians had promised to secure the release of all hostages before he delivered arms, when in fact they had promised only to seek the hostages' release, and then only after one planeload of arms had arrived.

— The President first told the Tower Board that he had approved the initial Israeli shipments. Then, he told the Tower Board that he had not. Finally, he told

the Tower Board that he does not know whether he approved the initial Israeli arms shipments, and his top advisers disagree on the question.

— The President claims he does not recall signing a Finding approving the November 1985 HAWK shipment to Iran. But Poindexter testified that the President did sign a Finding on December 5, 1985, approving the shipment retroactively. Poindexter later destroyed the Finding to save the President from embarrassment.

— That Finding was prepared without adequate discussion and stuck in Poindexter's safe for a year; Poindexter claimed he forgot about it; the White House asserts the President never signed it; and when events began to unravel, Poindexter ripped it up.

— The President and the Attorney General told the public that the President did not know about the November 1985 Israeli HAWK shipment until February 1986— an error the White House Chief of Staff explained by saying that the preparation for the press conference "sort of confused the Presidential mind."

— Poindexter says the President would have approved the diversion, if he had been asked; and the President says he would not have.

— One National Security Adviser understood that the Boland Amendment applied to the NSC; another thought it did not. Neither sought a legal opinion on the question.

— The President incorrectly assured the American people that the NSC staff was adhering to the law and that the Government was not connected to the Hasenfus airplane. His staff was in fact conducting a "full service" covert operation to support the Presidents which they believed he had authorized.

— North says he sent five or six completed memorandums to Poindexter seeking the President's approval for the diversion. Poindexter does not remember receiving any. Only one has been found.

## Dishonesty and Secrecy

The Iran-Contra Affair was characterized by pervasive dishonesty and inordinate secrecy.

North admitted that he and other officials lied repeatedly to Congress and to the American people about the Contra covert action and Iran arms sales, and that he altered and destroyed official documents. North's testimony demonstrates that he also lied to members of the Executive branch, including the Attorney General, and officials of the State Department, CIA and NSC.

Secrecy became an obsession. Congress was never informed of the Iran or the Contra covert actions, notwithstanding the requirement in the law that Congress be notified of all covert actions in a "timely fashion."

Poindexter said that Donald Regan, the President's Chief of Staff, was not told of the NSC staff's fundraising activities because he might reveal it to the press. Secretary Shultz objected to third-country solicitation in 1984 shortly before the Boland Amendment was adopted; accordingly, he was not told that, in the same time period, the National Security Adviser had accepted an $8 million contribution from Country 2 even though the State Department had prime responsibility for dealings with that country. Nor was the Secretary of State told by the President in February 1985 that the same country had pledged another $24 million—even though

the President briefed the Secretary of State on his meeting with the head of state at which the pledge was made. Poindexter asked North to keep secrets from Casey; Casey, North, and Poindexter agreed to keep secrets from Shultz.

Poindexter and North cited fear of leaks as a justification for these practices. But the need to prevent public disclosure cannot justify the deception practiced upon Members of Congress and Executive branch officials by those who knew of the arms sales to Iran and of the Contra support network. The State and Defense Departments deal each day with the most sensitive matters affecting millions of lives here and abroad. The Congressional Intelligence Committees receive the most highly classified information, including information on covert activities. Yet, according to North and Poindexter, even the senior officials of these bodies could not be entrusted with the NSC staff's secrets because they might leak.

While Congress's record in maintaining the confidentiality of classified information is not unblemished, it is not nearly as poor or perforated as some members of the NSC staff maintained. If the Executive branch has any basis to suspect that any member of the Intelligence Committees breached security, it has the obligation to bring that breach to the attention of the House and Senate Leaders—not to make blanket accusations. Congress has the capability and responsibility of protecting secrets entrusted to it. Congress cannot fulfill its legislative responsibilities if it is denied information because members of the Executive branch, who place their faith in a band of international arms merchants and financiers, unilaterally declare Congress unworthy of trust.

In the case of the "secret" Iran arms-for-hostages deal, although the NSC staff did not inform the Secretary of State, the Chairman of the Joint Chiefs of Staff, or the leadership of the United States Congress, it was content to let the following persons know:

— Manucher Ghorbanifar, who flunked every polygraph test administered by the U.S. Government;
— Iranian officials, who daily denounced the United States but received an inscribed Bible from the President;
— Officials of Iran's Revolutionary Guard, who received the U.S. weapons;
— Secord and Hakim, whose personal interests could conflict with the interests of the United States;
— Israeli officials, international arms merchants, pilots and air crews, whose interests did not always coincide with ours; and
— An unknown number of shadowy intermediaries and financiers who assisted with both the First and Second Iranian Channels.

While sharing the secret with this disparate group, North ordered the intelligence agencies not to disseminate intelligence on the Iran initiative to the Secretaries of State and Defense. Poindexter told the Secretary of State in May 1986 that the Iran initiative was over, at the very time the McFarlane mission to Tehran was being launched. Poindexter also concealed from Cabinet officials the remarkable nine-point agreement negotiated by Hakim with the Second Channel. North assured the FBI liaison to the NSC as late as November 1986 that the United States was not bargaining for the release of hostages but seizing terrorists to exchange for hostages—a complete fabrication. The lies,

omissions, shredding, attempts to rewrite history—all continued, even after the President authorized the Attorney General to find out the facts.

It was not operational security that motivated such conduct—not when our own Government was the victim. Rather, the NSC staff feared, correctly, that any disclosure to Congress or the Cabinet of the arms-for-hostages and arms-for-profit activities would produce a storm of outrage.

As with Iran, Congress was misled about the NSC staff's support for the Contras during the period of the Boland Amendment, although the role of the NSC staff was no secret to others. North testified that his operation was well-known to the press in the Soviet Union, Cuba, and Nicaragua. It was not a secret from Nicaragua's neighbors, with whom the NSC staff communicated throughout the period. It was not a secret from the third countries—including a totalitarian state—from whom the NSC staff sought arms or funds. It was not a secret from the private resupply network which North recruited and supervised. According to North, even Ghorbanifar knew.

The Administration never sought to hide its desire to assist the Contras so long as such aid was authorized by statute. On the contrary, it wanted the Sandinistas to know that the United States supported the Contras. After enactment of the Boland Amendment, the Administration repeatedly and publicly called upon Congress to resume U.S. assistance. Only the NSC staff's Contra support activities were kept under wraps. The Committees believe these actions were concealed in order to prevent Congress from learning that the Boland Amendment was being circumvented.

It was stated on several occasions that the

confusion, secrecy and deception surrounding the aid program for the Nicaraguan freedom fighters was produced in part by Congress' shifting positions on Contra aid.

But Congress' inconsistency mirrored the chameleon-like nature of the rationale offered for granting assistance in the first instance. Initially, Congress was told that our purpose was simply to interdict the flow of weapons from Nicaragua into El Salvador. Then Congress was told that our purpose was to harass the Sandinistas to prevent them from consolidating their power and exporting their revolution. Eventually, Congress was told that our purpose was to eliminate all foreign forces from Nicaragua, to reduce the size of the Sandinista armed forces, and to restore the democratic reforms pledged by the Sandinistas during the overthrow of the Somoza regime.

Congress had cast a skeptical eye upon each rationale proffered by the Administration. It suspected that the Administration's true purpose was identical to that of the Contras—the overthrow of the Sandinista regime itself. Ultimately Congress yielded to domestic political pressure to discontinue assistance to the Contras, but Congress was unwilling to bear responsibility for the loss of Central America to communist military and political forces. So Congress compromised, providing in 1985 humanitarian aid to the Contras; and the NSC staff provided what Congress prohibited: lethal support for the Contras.

Compromise is no excuse for violation of law and deceiving Congress. A law is no less a law because it is passed by a slender majority, or because Congress is open-minded about its reconsideration in the future.

## Privatization

The NSC staff turned to private parties and third countries to do the Government's business. Funds denied by Congress were obtained by the Administration from third countries and private citizens. Activities normally conducted by the professional intelligence services—which are accountable to Congress—were turned over to Secord and Hakim.

The solicitation of foreign funds by an Administration to pursue foreign policy goals rejected by Congress is dangerous and improper. Such solicitations, when done secretly and without Congressional authorization, create a risk that the foreign country will expect and demand something in return. McFarlane testified that "any responsible official has an obligation to acknowledge that every country in the world will see benefit to itself by ingratiating itself to the United States." North, in fact, proposed rewarding a Central American country with foreign assistance funds for facilitating arms shipments to the Contras. And Secord, who had once been in charge of the U.S. Air Force's foreign military sales, said "where there is a quid, there is a quo."

Moreover, under the Constitution only Congress can provide funds for the Executive branch. The Framers intended Congress's "power of the purse" to be one of the principal checks on Executive action. It was designed, among other things, to prevent the Executive from involving this country unilaterally in a foreign conflict. The Constitutional plan does not prohibit a President from asking a foreign state, or anyone else, to contribute funds to a third party. But it does prohibit such solicitation where the United States exercises control over their receipt and expenditure. By circumventing Congress' power of the purse through third-country and private contributions to the Contras, the Administration undermined a cardinal principle of the Constitution.

Further, by turning to private citizens, the NSC staff jeopardized its own objectives. Sensitive negotiations were conducted by parties with little experience in diplomacy, and financial interests of their own. The diplomatic aspect of the mission failed—the United States today has no long-term relationship with Iran and no fewer hostages in captivity. But the private financial aspect succeeded—Secord and Hakim took $4.4 million in commissions and used $2.2 million more for their personal benefit; in addition, they set aside reserves of over $4 million in Swiss bank accounts of the Enterprise.

Covert operations of this Government should only be directed and conducted by the trained professional services that are accountable to the President and Congress. Such operations should never be delegated, as they were here, to private citizens in order to evade Governmental restrictions.

## Lack of Accountability

The confusion, deception, and privatization which marked the Iran-Contra Affair were the inevitable products of an attempt to avoid accountability. Congress, the Cabinet, and the Joint Chiefs of Staff were denied information and excluded from the decision-making process. Democratic procedures were disregarded.

Officials who make public policy must be accountable to the public. But the public cannot hold officials accountable for policies of which the public is unaware. Policies that

are known can be subjected to the test of reason, and mistakes can be corrected after consultation with the Congress and deliberation within the Executive branch itself. Policies that are secret become the private preserve of the few, mistakes are inevitably perpetuated, and the public loses control over Government. That is what happened in the Iran-Contra Affair:

— The President's NSC staff carried out a covert action in furtherance of his policy to sustain the Contras, but the President said he did not know about it.

— The President's NSC staff secretly diverted millions of dollars in profits from the Iran arms sales to the Contras, but the President said he did not know about it and Poindexter claimed he did not tell him.

— The Chairman of the Joint Chiefs of Staff was not informed of the Iran arms sales, nor was he ever consulted regarding the impact of such sales on the Iran-Iraq war or on U.S. military readiness.

— The Secretary of State was not informed of the millions of dollars in Contra contributions solicited by the NSC staff from foreign governments with which the State Department deals each day.

— Congress was told almost nothing—and what it was told was false.

Deniability replaced accountability. Thus, Poindexter justified his decision not to inform the President of the diversion on the ground that he wanted to give the President "deniability." Poindexter said he wanted to shield the President from political embarrassment if the diversion became public.

This kind of thinking is inconsistent with democratic governance. "Plausible denial," an accepted concept in intelligence activities, means structuring an authorized covert operation so that, if discovered by the party against whom it is directed, United States involvement may plausibly be denied. That is a legitimate feature of authorized covert operations. In no circumstance, however, does "plausible denial" mean structuring an operation so that it may be concealed from—or denied to—the highest elected officials of the United States Government itself.

The very premise of democracy is that "we the people" are entitled to make our own choices on fundamental policies. But freedom of choice is illusory if policies are kept, not only from the public, but from its elected representatives.

## Intelligence Abuses

### Covert Operations

As former National Security Adviser Robert McFarlane testified, "it is clearly unwise to rely on covert action as the core of our policy." The Government cannot keep a policy secret and still secure the public support necessary to sustain it. Yet it was precisely because the public would not support the Contra policy, and was unlikely to favor arms deals with Iran, that the NSC staff went underground. This was a perversion of the proper concept of covert operations:

— Covert operations should be conducted in accordance with strict rules of accountability and oversight. In the mid-1970s, in response to disclosures of abuses within the intelligence community, the Government enacted a series of safeguards. Each covert action was to be approved personally by the President, funded by Congressional appropriations, and Congress was to be informed.

In the Iran-Contra Affair, these rules were violated. The President, according to Poindexter, was never informed of the diversion. The President says he knew nothing of the covert action to support the Contras, or the companies funded by non-appropriated monies set up by North to carry out that support. Congress was not notified of either the Iran or the Contra operations.

— Covert actions should be consistent with publicly defined U.S. foreign policy goals. Because covert operations are secret by definition, they are of course not openly debated or publicly approved. So long as the policies which they further are known, and so long as they are conducted in accordance with law, covert operations are acceptable. Here, however, the Contra covert operation was carried out in violation of the country's public policy as expressed in the Boland Amendment; and the Iran covert operation was carried out in violation of the country's stated policy against selling arms to Iran or making concessions to terrorists. These were not covert actions, they were covert policies; and covert policies are incompatible with democracy.

— Finally, covert operations are intended to be kept from foreign powers, not from the Congress and responsible Executive agencies within the United States Government itself. As Clair George, CIA Director of Operations, testified: "to think that because we deal in lies, and overseas we may lie and we may do other such things, that therefore that gives you some permission, some right or some particular reason to operate that way with your fellow employees, I would not only disagree with that I would say it would be the destruction of a secret service in a democracy." In the Iran-Contra Affair, secrecy was used to justify lies to Congress, the Attorney General, other Cabinet officers, and the CIA. It was used not as a shield against our adversaries, but as a weapon against our own democratic institutions.

**The NSC Staff**

The NSC staff was created to give the President policy advice on major national security and foreign policy issues. Here, however, it was used to gather intelligence and conduct covert operations. This departure from its proper functions contributed to policy failure.

During the Iran initiative, the NSC staff became the principal body both for gathering and coordinating intelligence on Iran and for recommending policy to the President. The staff relied on Iranians who were interested only in buying arms, including Ghorbanifar, whom CIA officials regarded as a fabricator. Poindexter, in recommending to the President the sale of weapons to Iran, gave as one of his reasons that Iraq was winning the Gulf war. That assessment was contrary to the views of intelligence professionals at the State Department, the Department of Defense, and the CIA, who had concluded as early as 1983 that Iran was winning the war. Casey, who collaborated with North and Poindexter on the Iran and Contra programs, also tailored intelligence reports to the positions he advocated. The record shows that the President believed and acted on these erroneous reports.

Secretary Shultz pointed out that the intelligence and policy functions do not mix, because "it is too tempting to have your analysis on the selection of information that is presented favor the policy that you are advocating." The Committees agree on the need to separate the intelligence and policy functions. Otherwise, there is too great a risk that the interpretation of intelligence will be skewed to fit predetermined policy choices.

In the Iran-Contra Affair, the NSC staff not only combined intelligence and policy functions, but it became operational and conducted covert operations. As the CIA was subjected to greater Congressional scrutiny and regulation, a few Administration officials—including even Director Casey—came to believe that the CIA could no longer be utilized for daring covert operations. So the NSC staff was enlisted to provide assistance in covert operations that the CIA could not or would not furnish.

This was a dangerous misuse of the NSC staff. When covert operations are conducted by those on whom the President relies to present policy options, there is no agency in government to objectively scrutinize, challenge and evaluate plans and activities. Checks and balances are lost. The high policy decisions confronting a President can rarely be resolved by the methods and techniques used by experts in the conduct of covert operations. Problems of public policy must be dealt with through consultation, not Poindexter's "compartmentation"; with honesty and confidentiality, not deceit.

The NSC was created to provide candid and comprehensive advice to the President. It is the judgment of these Committees that the NSC staff should never again engage in covert operations.

## Disdain for Law

In the Iran-Contra Affair, officials viewed the law not as setting boundaries for their actions, but raising impediments to their goals. When the goals and the law collided, the law gave way:

— The covert program of support for the Contras evaded the Constitution's most significant check on Executive power: the President can spend funds on a program only if he can convince Congress to appropriate the money.

When Congress enacted the Boland Amendment, cutting off funds for the war in Nicaragua, Administration officials raised funds for the Contras from other sources—foreign Governments, the Iran arms sales, and private individuals; and the NSC staff controlled the expenditures of these funds through power over the Enterprise. Conducting the covert program in Nicaragua with funding from the sale of U.S. Government property and contributions raised by Government officials was a flagrant violation of the Appropriations Clause of the Constitution.

— In addition, the covert program of support for the Contras was an evasion of the letter and spirit of the Boland Amendment. The President made it clear that while he opposed restrictions on military or paramilitary assistance to the Contras, he recognized that compliance with the law was not optional. "[W]hat I might personally wish or what our Government might wish still would not justify us violating the law of the land," he said in 1983.

A year later, members of the NSC staff were devising ways to continue support and direction of Contra activities during the period of the Boland Amendment. What was previously done by the CIA—and now prohibited by the Boland Amendment—would be done instead by the NSC staff.

The President set the stage by welcoming a huge donation for the Contras from a foreign Government—a contribution clearly intended to keep the Contras in the field while U.S. aid was barred. The NSC staff thereafter solicited other foreign Governments for military aid, facilitated the efforts of U.S. fundraisers to provide lethal assistance to the Contras, and ultimately developed and directed a private network that conducted, in North's words, a "full service covert operation" in support of the Contras.

This could not have been more contrary to the intent of the Boland legislation.

Numerous other laws were disregarded:

— North's full-service covert operation was a "significant anticipated intelligence activity" required to be disclosed to the Intelligence Committees of Congress under Section 501 of the National Security Act. No such disclosure was made.
— By Executive order, a covert operation requires a personal determination by the President before it can be conducted by an agency other than the CIA. It requires a written Finding before any agency can carry it out. In the case of North's full-service covert operation in support of the Contras, there was no such personal determination and no such Finding. In fact, the President disclaims any knowledge of this covert action.
— False statements to Congress are felonies if made with knowledge and intent. Sev-

eral Administration officials gave statements denying NSC staff activities in support of the Contras which North later described in his testimony as "false," and "misleading, evasive, and wrong."

— The application of proceeds from U.S. arms sales for the benefit of the Contra war effort violated the Boland Amendment's ban on U.S. military aid to the Contras, and constituted a misappropriation of Government funds derived from the transfer of U.S. property.

— The U.S. Government's approval of the pre-Finding 1985 sales by Israel of arms to the Government of Iran was inconsistent with the Government's obligations under the Arms Export Control Act.

— The testimony to Congress in November 1986 that the U.S. Government had no contemporaneous knowledge of the Israeli shipments, and the shredding of documents relating to the shipments while a Congressional inquiry into those shipments was pending, obstructed Congressional investigations.

— The Administration did not make, and clearly intended never to make, disclosure to the Intelligence Committees of the Finding—later destroyed—approving the November 1985 HAWK shipment, nor did it disclose the covert action to which the Finding related.

The Committees make no determination as to whether any particular individual involved in the Iran-Contra Affair acted with criminal intent or was guilty of any crime. That is a matter for the Independent Counsel and the courts. But the Committees reject any notion that worthy ends justify violations of law by Government officials; and the Committees condemn without reservation the making of false statements to Congress and the withholding, shredding, and alteration of documents relevant to a pending inquiry.

Administration officials have, if anything, an even greater responsibility than private citizens to comply with the law. There is no place in Government for law breakers.

## Congress and the President

The Constitution of the United States gives important powers to both the President and the Congress in the making of foreign policy. The President is the principal architect of foreign policy in consultation with the Congress. The policies of the United States cannot succeed unless the President and the Congress work together.

Yet, in the Iran-Contra Affair, Administration officials holding no elected office repeatedly evidenced disrespect for Congress' efforts to perform its Constitutional oversight role in foreign policy:

— Poindexter testified, referring to his efforts to keep the covert action in support of the Contras from Congress: "I simply did not want any outside interference."

— North testified: "I didn't want to tell Congress anything" about this covert action.

— Abrams acknowledged in his testimony that, unless Members of Congressional Committees asked "exactly the right question, using exactly the right words, they weren't going to get the right answers," regarding solicitation of third-countries for Contra support.

— And numerous other officials made false statements to, and misled, the Congress.

Several witnesses at the hearings stated or implied that foreign policy should be left solely to the President to do as he chooses, arguing that shared powers have no place in a dangerous world. But the theory of our Constitution is the opposite: policies formed through consultation and the democratic process are better and wiser than those formed without it. Circumvention of Congress is self-defeating, for no foreign policy can succeed without the bipartisan support of Congress.

In a system of shared powers, decision-making requires mutual respect between the branches of government.

The Committees were reminded by Secretary Shultz during the hearings that "trust is the coin of the realm." Democratic government is not possible without trust between the branches of government and between the government and the people. Sometimes that trust is misplaced and the system falters. But for officials to work outside the system because it does not produce the results they seek is a prescription for failure.

## WHO WAS RESPONSIBLE

Who was responsible for the Iran-Contra Affair? Part of our mandate was to answer that question, not in a legal sense (which is the responsibility of the Independent Counsel), but in order to reaffirm that those who serve the Government are accountable for their actions. Based on our investigation, we reach the following conclusions.

At the operational level, the central figure in the Iran-Contra Affair was Lt. Col. North, who coordinated all of the activities and was involved in all aspects of the secret operations. North, however, did not act alone.

North's conduct had the express approval of Admiral John Poindexter, first as Deputy National Security Adviser, and then as National Security Adviser. North also had at least the tacit support of Robert McFarlane, who served as National Security Adviser until December 1985.

In addition, for reasons cited earlier, we believe that the late Director of Central Intelligence, William Casey, encouraged North, gave him direction, and promoted the concept of an extra-legal covert organization. Casey, for the most part, insulated CIA career employees from knowledge of what he and the NSC staff were doing. Casey's passion for covert operations—dating back to his World War II intelligence days—was well known. His close relationship with North was attested to by several witnesses. Further, it was Casey who brought Richard Secord into the secret operation, and it was Secord who, with Albert Hakim, organized the Enterprise. These facts provide strong reasons to believe that Casey was involved both with the diversion and with the plans for an "off-the-shelf" covert capacity.

The Committees are mindful, however, of the fact that the evidence concerning Casey's role comes almost solely from North; that this evidence, albeit under oath, was used by North to exculpate himself; and that Casey could not respond. Although North told the Committees that Casey knew of the diversion from the start, he told a different story to the Attorney General in November 1986, as did Casey himself. Only one other witness, Lt. Col. Robert Earl, testified that he had been told by North during Casey's lifetime that Casey knew of the diversion.

The Attorney General recognized on November 21, 1986 the need for an inquiry. His staff was responsible for finding the diversion memorandum, which the Attorney General promptly made public. But as described earlier, his fact-finding inquiry departed from standard investigative techniques. The Attorney General saw Director Casey hours after the Attorney General learned of the diversion memorandum, yet he testified that he never asked Casey about the diversion. He waited two days to speak to Poindexter, North's superior, and then did not ask him what the President knew. He waited too long to seal North's offices. These lapses placed a cloud over the Attorney General's investigation.

There is no evidence that the Vice President was aware of the diversion. The Vice President attended several meetings on the Iran initiative, but none of the participants could recall his views.

The Vice President said he did not know of the Contra resupply operation. His National Security Adviser, Donald Gregg, was told in early August 1986 by a former colleague that North was running the Contra resupply operation, and that ex-associates of Edwin Wilson—a well known ex-CIA official convicted of selling arms to Libya and plotting the murder of his prosecutors—were involved in the operation. Gregg testified that he did not consider these facts worthy of the Vice President's attention and did not report them to him, even after the Hasenfus airplane was shot down and the Administration had denied any connection with it.

The central remaining question is the role of the President in the Iran-Contra Affair. On this critical point, the shredding of documents by Poindexter, North, and others, and the death of Casey, leave the record incomplete.

As it stands, the President has publicly stated that he did not know of the diversion. Poindexter testified that he shielded the President from knowledge of the diversion. North said that he never told the President, but assumed that the President knew. Poindexter told North on November 21, 1986 that he had not informed the President of the diversion. Secord testified that North told him he had talked with the President about the diversion, but North testified that he had fabricated this story to bolster Secord's morale.

Nevertheless, the ultimate responsibility for the events in the Iran-Contra Affair must rest with the President. If the President did not know what his National Security Advisers were doing, he should have. It is his responsibility to communicate unambiguously to his subordinates that they must keep him advised of important actions they take for the Administration. The Constitution requires the President to "take care that the laws be faithfully executed." This charge encompasses a responsibility to leave the members of his Administration in no doubt that the rule of law governs.

Members of the NSC staff appeared to believe that their actions were consistent with the President's desires. It was the President's policy—not an isolated decision by North or Poindexter—to sell arms secretly to Iran and to maintain the Contras "body and soul," the Boland Amendment notwithstanding. To the NSC staff, implementation of these policies became the overriding concern.

Several of the President's advisers pursued a covert action to support the Contras in disregard of the Boland Amendment and of several statutes and Executive orders requiring Congressional notification. Several of these same advisers lied, shredded documents, and covered up their actions. These facts have been on the public record for months. The actions of those individuals do not comport with the notion of a country guided by the rule of law. But the President has yet to condemn their conduct.

The President himself told the public that the U.S. Government had no connection to the Hasenfus airplane. He told the public that early reports of arms sales for hostages had "no foundation." He told the public that the United States had not traded arms for hostages. He told the public that the United States had not condoned the arms sales by Israel to Iran, when in fact he had approved them and signed a Finding, later destroyed by Poindexter, recording his approval. All of these statements by the President were wrong.

Thus, the question whether the President knew of the diversion is not conclusive on the issue of his responsibility. The President created or at least tolerated an environment where those who did know of the diversion believed with certainty that they were carrying out the President's policies.

This same environment enabled a secretary who shredded, smuggled, and altered documents to tell the Committees that "sometimes you have to go above the written law;" and it enabled Admiral Poindexter to testify that "frankly, we were willing to take some risks with the law." It was in such an environment that former officials of the NSC staff and their private agents could lecture the Committees that a "rightful cause" justifies any means, that lying to Congress and other officials in the executive branch itself is acceptable when the ends are just, and that Congress is to blame for passing laws that run counter to Administration policy. What may aptly be called the "cabal of the zealots" was in charge.

In a Constitutional democracy, it is not true, as one official maintained, that "when you take the King's shilling, you do the King's bidding." The idea of monarchy was rejected here 200 years ago and since then, the law—not any official or ideology—has been paramount. For not instilling this precept in his staff, for failing to take care that the law reigned supreme, the President bears the responsibility.

Fifty years ago Supreme Court Justice Louis Brandeis observed: "Our Government is the potent, the omnipresent teacher. For good or for ill, it teaches the whole people by its example. Crime is contagious. If the Government becomes a law-breaker, it breeds contempt for law, it invites every man to become a law unto himself, it invites anarchy."

The Iran-Contra Affair resulted from a failure to heed this message.

PART II

# CENTRAL AMERICA

**Figure 1-1. Map of Central America.**

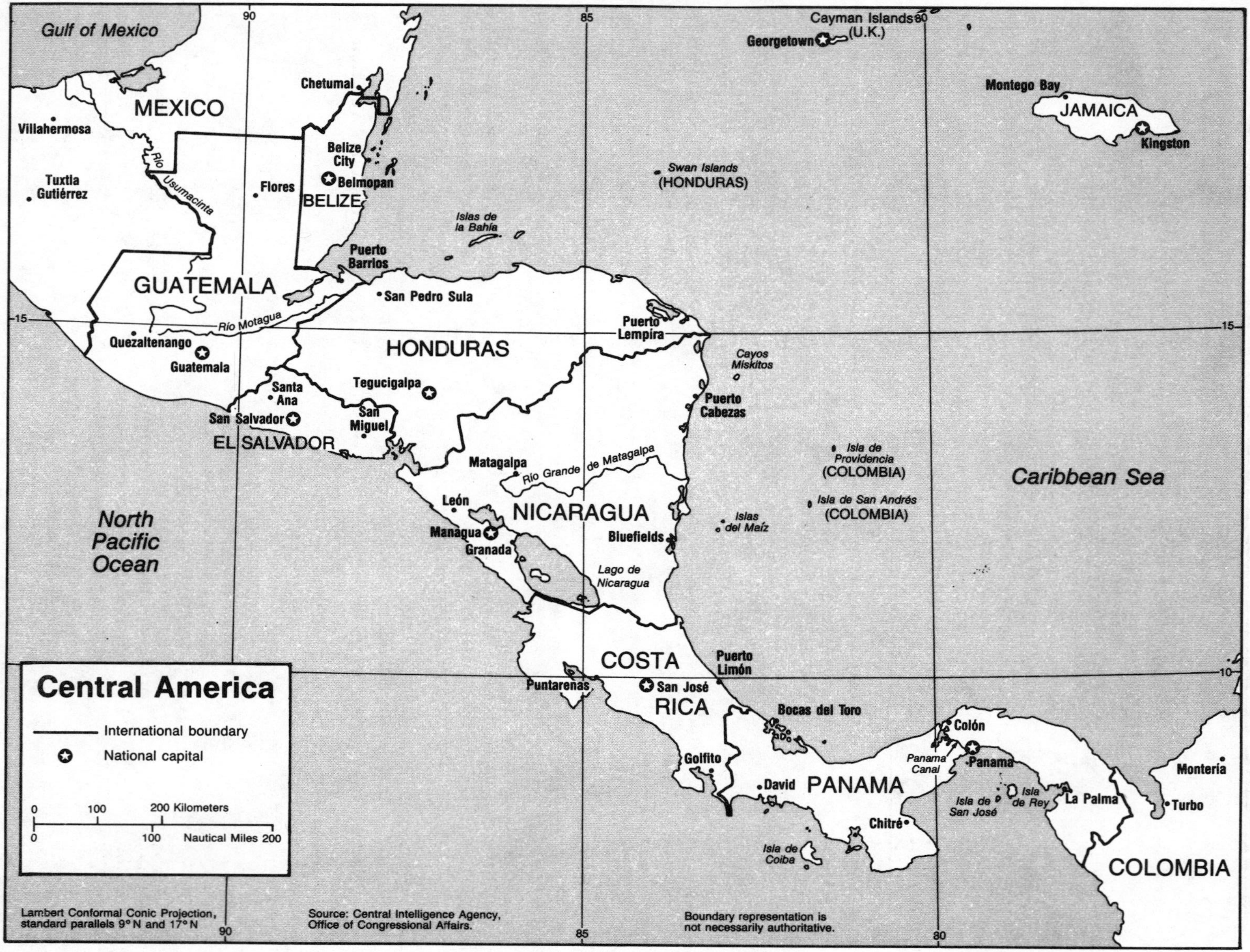

# CHAPTER 1

# Introduction: Background on U.S.-Nicaragua Relations

On July 17, 1979, President Anastasio Somoza Debayle and his family fled Nicaragua. A civil war that had devastated the nation's economy and caused more than 130,000 casualties was at an end, as was the autocratic and corrupt 43-year rule of the Somoza family. But the battle for Nicaragua's future was just beginning.

The Sandinistas were enormously popular when they began their rule. A Provisional Government of National Reconstruction was formed to lead the country. At its head was a five-person directorate composed of Violetta Chamorro (widow of the murdered La Prensa editor), Alfonso Robelo, Sergio Ramirez, Moises Hassan, and Daniel Ortega. Hassan and Ortega came from the militant wing of the Sandinista Party. Members of the 18-member cabinet and the 33-member council were drawn from a broad spectrum of Nicaraguan public life. Though Nicaraguans were generally satisfied that the new Government represented the Somoza opposition, the United States was not, pointing to Ortega and Hassan as left-wing radicals.

## The Sandinistas Take Over

The Sandinistas set out to court public favor and international support. They promised free elections, a free press, free enterprise, an independent judiciary, and an end to political oppression.

Yet, the Sandinistas took over television and radio stations and censored the newspaper La Prensa, which opposed repression whether by the Sandinistas or by Somoza. The Sandinistas forced the two moderate members of Nicaragua's governing council, Chamorro and Robelo, to resign, pressured opposition parties, continued political detentions, and expropriated land. The revolutionary party organization assumed the functions of state. On September 19, 1980, the Government announced that it would not hold national elections until 1985.

The United States was ambivalent about the Sandinistas at first. The Carter Administration gave the new Government $39 million in emergency food aid, but even as it accepted that money,

37

Nicaragua's ties to Cuba and the Soviet Union grew stronger. U.S. intelligence also found that the Sandinistas were helping the Marxist rebels in El Salvador. President Carter suspended the aid, and as he took office, President Reagan vowed that Nicaragua would get no more United States assistance until it was fully democratic.

Concerns about Nicaragua's internal repression, its growing military force, its ties to the Soviet bloc and its support for the Salvadoran insurgency led the Administration to consider ways to assist the regime's opponents, who came to be known as the Contras.

## The Contras

As the Sandinistas consolidated their hold on Nicaragua in 1979 to 1981, the concerns of the United States were matched within Nicaragua itself. In response, a new Nicaraguan rebel movement—anti-Sandinista "Contras"—emerged.

The Contras were not a monolithic group, but a combination of three distinct elements of Nicaraguan society: former National Guardsmen and right-wing figures who had fought for Somoza and against the revolution; anti-Somocistas who had supported the revolution but felt betrayed by the Sandinista Government; and Nicaraguans who had avoided direct involvement in the revolution but opposed the Sandinistas' increasingly anti-democratic regime.

The largest and most active of these groups, which later came to be known as the Nicaraguan Democratic Force (FDN), was led by Adolfo Calero Portocarrero. Calero had been an accountant and businessman, and had been active in the movement to oust Somoza. Following the liberation, he served as the political coordinator of the Conservative Democratic Party and became an outspoken critic of the Sandinista Government. Calero joined the resistance movement after his office and home were attacked and he was forced into exile.

Although Calero had opposed Somoza, the FDN had its roots in two insurgent groups made up of former National Guardsmen who fled Nicaragua after the fall of Somoza. In 1981, this branch of the resistance consisted of only a few hundred men.

In addition to the main force of FDN fighters centered primarily in the northern portion of the country, other resistance forces became active in other parts of Nicaragua. These include several Indian groups operating along the Atlantic coast and, after 1981, a group formed by the charismatic figure and former Sandinista guerrilla leader and hero, Eden Pastora. Forces under Pastora were based along the southern border with Costa Rica.

Initial support for the Nicaraguan resistance came from another country [**Argentina**], which organized and supplied paramilitary forces in early 1981. By the end of 1981, however, the Contras were looking to the United States for their support. They were to find a receptive audience—President Reagan.

## Figure 1-2. Map of Nicaragua

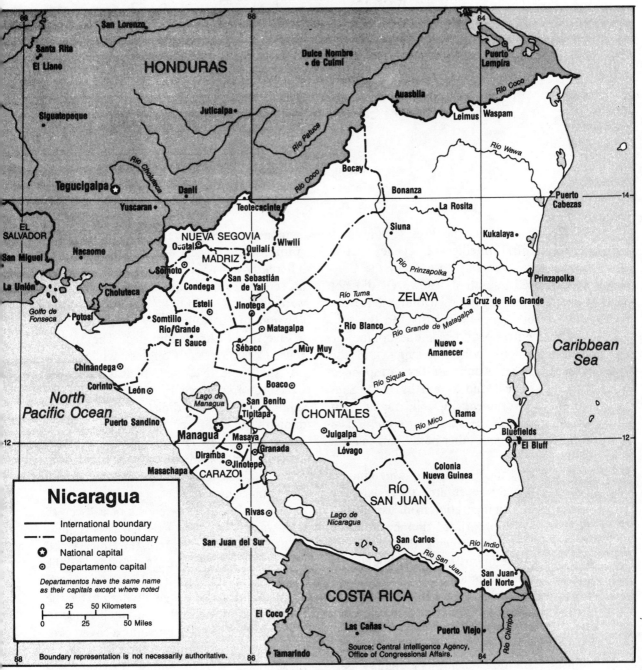

Nicaragua

— International boundary
—·— Departamento boundary
National capital
Departamento capital

*Departamentos have the same name as their capitals except where noted*

0  25  50 Kilometers
0  25  50 Miles

Boundary representation is not necessarily authoritative.

Source: Central Intelligence Agency, Office of Congressional Affairs.

39

# CHAPTER 2

# The NSC Staff Takes Contra Policy Underground

In December 1981, the President authorized a Central Intelligence Agency (CIA) covert action program to support the Contras. The CIA's activity, however, did not remain covert for long: within months, it was the topic of news reports and the subject of Congressional debate questioning the Administration's policy in support of the Contras. The Administration responded that it did not intend to overthrow the Sandinista Government in Nicaragua, but sought to check the spread of communism to El Salvador and other nations in Central America.

In 1982, in the first Boland Amendment, Congress sought to enforce that claim by barring the Administration from using Congressionally appropriated money for the "purpose" of overthrowing the Sandinista regime. The Administration, although not pleased with the amendment, nevertheless accepted it, because the amendment allowed the Administration to maintain support for the Contras so long as that support had as its "purpose" stopping the spread of the Sandinista revolution outside Nicaragua's borders.

With the first Boland Amendment, then, came a temporary compromise between the Administration and Congress. But it was an inherently uneasy compromise, based more on semantics than substance: The Contras were not in the field to stop Sandinista arms flowing to El Salvador; they were in the field to overthrow the Sandinistas. The Intelligence Committees of Congress, while rejecting that objective, nevertheless approved CIA use of contingency reserve funding to support the anti-Sandinistas. And the Administration embraced the contradiction inherent in the new law, by emphasizing that U.S. support was aimed only at interdicting arms destined for other Central American Communist insurgencies.

During 1983, press reports of a "secret" CIA war in Nicaragua led to increased questioning in Congress. In July, the House voted to end all Contra aid. Meanwhile, in the hopes of forestalling an aid cutoff, the Administration accepted an invitation by the Senate Select Committee on Intelligence to clarify its intentions in pursuing a covert program. Despite Administration efforts to meet those concerns, by the winter, the House and Senate had agreed to cap Contra funding at $24 million, a sum that both the Administration and the Congress knew would not last through fiscal 1984.

Nonetheless, the Administration decided to escalate the operations in Nicaragua. When the Nicaraguan harbor mining was disclosed in April, it created a storm of protest in Congress and around the country and, chiefly as a result, Congress declined to appropriate more money for the Contras. With the CIA out of funds for the Contras, the NSC staff took over the program of supporting the Contras. But this time, the operation was covert in a new sense—it was concealed from Congress.

Beginning in May 1984, when the CIA-appropriated funds for the Contras ran out, the National Security Council (NSC) staff raised money for Contra military operations from third countries with the knowledge of the President, supervised the Contras' purchase of weapons, and provided guidance for the Contras' military operations. The operational responsibilities fell largely to Lt. Col. Oliver L. North, a member of the NSC staff who reported to the National Security Adviser, Robert C. McFarlane, and his deputy, Vice Admiral John M. Poindexter.

In October 1984, the Congress passed and the President signed the second Boland Amendment prohibiting the expenditure of any available funds in support of Contra military operations by any agency or entity involved in intelligence activities. Rather than halting U.S. support for the Contras, the CIA's withdrawal was treated as a call for the NSC staff to take over the entire covert operation, raising more money from a third country, arranging for arms purchases, and providing military intelligence and advice. The NSC staff went operational—and underground.

## THE DECEMBER 1981 FINDING

In December 1981, President Reagan signed his first Finding specifically authorizing covert paramilitary actions against the Sandinista Government in Nicaragua. Under the law, covert actions may be initiated only by a personal decision of the President. A Finding is an official document embodying that decision. By signing a Finding, a President not only authorizes action, but accepts responsibility for its consequences.

Sponsoring the CIA's new covert program in Central America was the Director of Central Intelligence, William J. Casey. Casey was a veteran of covert operations, having served with the Office of Strategic Services (OSS), the predecessor to the CIA, during the Second World War.

Casey was a firm believer in the value of covert operations, and took an activist, aggressive approach to his craft. In the words of the CIA's Deputy Director of Operations, Clair George, "Bill Casey was the last great buccaneer from OSS."

### Pastora Defects

Casey saw the opportunity to make military headway against the Sandinistas in early 1982, when rebel leader Eden Pastora defected from the ruling Sandinista junta. Pastora appeared to be an ideal candidate for Contra military leadership. Known to his followers by the *nom de guerre*, "Comandante Zero," he had been one of the heroes of the fight against Somoza. From 1977 to 1978, he served in the Sandinista National Liberation Front and later held several high posts in the new Government until his abrupt resignation in 1981. In April 1982,

41

Pastora organized the Sandinista Revolutionary Front (FRS) and declared war on the Sandinista Government.

Although Pastora was a popular, charismatic leader with the potential to challenge the Sandinistas, his geographic base presented a problem for the Administration. He insisted on operating in the southern part of Nicaragua. The Administration, however, claimed that its only purpose in aiding the Contras was to interdict arms flows to El Salvador, which lies to the north of Nicaragua. Support for Pastora in the South contradicted that claim.

Casey's deputy, Admiral Bobby R. Inman, an intelligence professional who had headed the National Security Agency, objected to this broadening of the covert program. He believed that it was unsound, and unauthorized by the existing Presidential Finding. Yet Casey was determined to proceed. Inman retired at the end of June 1982 and the CIA supported Pastora without any change in the Presidential Finding.

## A Proposal for a New Finding

Pastora's rebel group "develop[ed] quickly." By July 12, 1982, Donald Gregg, then head of the NSC's Intelligence Directorate and responsible for all covert action projects, proposed a new draft Finding to keep pace with Pastora's developing operations. Gregg, like Inman, believed that broad support for Pastora was outside the scope of the December 1981 Finding.

Vice Admiral Poindexter, then military adviser to the National Security Adviser, disagreed. In a hand-written note, Poindexter stated: "I don't see this really needs to be approved since the earlier Finding covers it, but maybe it would be good to get a confirmation since we now have a better idea as to where we are going."

## BOLAND I

By the fall of 1982, press reports told of a growing U.S. involvement in Nicaragua. Administration spokesmen responded by stating that the U.S. Government was seeking not to overthrow the Nicaraguan Government, but merely to prevent it from exporting revolution to El Salvador. Aid to the Contras was presented as an act in defense of El Salvador, not a hostile act against Nicaragua.

Congress soon began to question this explanation. Some Members believed that the Sandinistas were trying to spread a Marxist revolution to neighboring states. They argued that no Communist regime had ever stepped down or consented to free elections and that support for the Contras was necessary to bring about democracy in Nicaragua.

Out of this debate emerged an amendment to the Defense Appropriations bill for fiscal year 1983, later known as Boland I. Introduced by Representative Edward P. Boland, the amendment passed the House by a vote of 411–0, and was adopted, in December 1982, by a Conference Committee of the House and Senate. This first Boland Amendment prohibited CIA use of funds "for the purpose of overthrowing the Government of Nicaragua."

In December 1982, The New York Times reported intelligence officials as saying that Washington's "covert activities have . . . become the most ambitious paramilitary and political action operation mounted by the

C.I.A. in nearly a decade. . . ." One month later, in January 1983, Senator Patrick J. Leahy, accompanied by staff of the Senate Intelligence Committee, visited Central America to review U.S. intelligence activities related to Nicaragua. His findings, supplemented by followup Committee briefings and inquiries, revealed that the covert action program was "preceding policy," that it was "growing beyond that which the Committee had initially understood to be its parameters," and that "there was uncertainty in the executive branch about U.S. objectives in Nicaragua."

Questions about compliance with the Boland Amendment increased throughout 1983. In March, 37 House Members sent a letter to the President warning that CIA activities in Central America could be violating the law. In April, news reporters visiting Contra base camps wrote that "[t]he U.S.-backed secret war against Nicaragua's leftist Sandinista regime has spilled out of the shadows."

Challenged to defend the Administration's compliance with the law, the President asserted in April that there had been no violation of the Boland Amendment. There would be none, said the President, because even a law he disagreed with had to be observed: "We are complying with the law, the Boland Amendment, which is the law." "[W]hat I might personally wish or what our government might wish still would not justify us violating the law of the land." When asked if his Administration was doing anything to overthrow the Government of Nicaragua, he replied, "No, because that would be violating the law."

It soon became clear that the President had not made the case for the Administration's Contra support policy with either the Congress or the American people. He was not helped by the Contras' performance on the ground. The Contras had failed to win either popular support or military victories in Nicaragua and could not, without both, sustain public support in the United States.

## THE ADMINISTRATION RESPONDS TO CONGRESSIONAL UNREST: MAY–SEPTEMBER 1983

### White Propaganda

In June of 1983, the Administration decided upon a new method of trying to win public support for the President's policy in Central America. On July 1, 1983, then National Security Adviser Clark announced that "the President had decided that the Administration must increase our efforts in the public diplomacy field to deepen the understanding of the support for our policies in Central America."

As a result, an office of Public Diplomacy for Latin American and the Caribbean (S/LPD) was established in the State Department, headed by Otto Reich, who eventually was given the rank of Ambassador. The mission of the office—public diplomacy—was a "new, non-traditional activity for the United States government," according to the State Department. In fact, "public diplomacy" turned out to mean public relations-lobbying, all at taxpayers' expense. The office arranged speaking engagements, published pamphlets, and sent materials to editorial writers. In its campaign to persuade the public and Congress to support appropriations for the Contras, the office used Government employees and outside contractors—including Richard Miller and Francis Gomez who would later work with North to provide Contra assistance.

A Deputy Director of S/LPD, Jonathan Miller, reported the office's success in what he labeled a "White Propaganda Operation," which sought to place op-ed pieces in major papers by secret consultants to the office. By Reich's own description, the office adopted "a very aggressive posture vis-a-vis a sometimes hostile press." It claimed that "[a]ttacking the President was no longer cost free."

Later, the Comptroller General would find that some of the office's efforts, in particular Jonathan Miller's "White Propaganda," were "prohibited, covert propaganda activities," "beyond the range of acceptable agency public information activities. . . ."

## The CIA Tries to Stockpile

In the summer of 1983, while efforts were underway at the State Department to change public opinion, the CIA began secret preparations in the event Congress decided to cut off aid to the Contras. In that event, the Agency planned to obtain equipment free of charge from the DOD.

On July 12, the President directed that the DOD provide enhanced support for the CIA in its efforts to assist the Contras. One day later, the CIA sent a "wish list" to the DOD, requesting that $28 million in equipment be transferred to it, "free-of-charge." The list covered everything from medical supplies to aircraft, and included a request for personnel. The Joint Chiefs of Staff proposed that each of the four services carry a quarter of the cost of these transfers. The equipment then could be stockpiled by the CIA and

provided to the Contras if the need arose. The CIA would not run afoul of any aid ceiling since it had not paid for the equipment.

By late summer, the DOD's General Counsel concluded that a nonreimbursable transfer would violate the Economy Act, a law requiring that the DOD be reimbursed for the cost of interagency transfers. The CIA would have to pay for all items except surplus equipment. The project was finally terminated on February 12, 1985, after the CIA had obtained, without cost, 3 surplus Cessna aircraft and, at cost, 10 night vision goggles, 1 night vision sight, and a Bushmaster cannon.

## The September 1983 Finding: A New Rationale for Covert Aid

Trying to forestall a complete cutoff of Congressional aid, the Administration accepted the Senate Intelligence Committee's proposal that it draft a new Finding defining and delimiting the purposes of the covert program. By August, Director Casey had presented the Committee with a first draft and later, in September, proceeded to "informally discuss the finding with Senator Goldwater and other key Senators of the SSCI." Within the Administration, the Finding was, as North put it, "thoroughly scrubbed" by the State Department and NSC staff as well by as the Justice Department and lawyers from DOD and CIA.

The new Finding also reflected a change of tactics. Congress would not accept a Finding broad enough to permit paramilitary operations conducted by U. S. citizens. The Administration gave its assurances that aid for paramilitary operations would be limited to third-country nationals. Casey told the President that the "new Finding no longer lets us engage in PM [paramilitary operations]."

The new Finding, however, was not without problems. The Administration's stated objective in supporting the Contras was now to pressure the Sandinistas into accepting a treaty that had to include free elections. If, as the President believed, the Sandinistas could not win such an election, they would never agree to such a treaty. Only the prospect of a military defeat would push them toward a negotiating posture. Yet, the renunciation of a military victory was the price set by Congress for a bipartisan compromise. The Finding thus contained within it a paradox that would haunt the Administration's Nicaragua policy.

## FORCING THE ISSUE: THE DECEMBER FUNDING CAP AND INTENSIFYING COVERT OPERATIONS

One day after the September Finding was briefed to the Intelligence Committees, an unnamed Administration official was quoted in The New York Times explaining the rationale of the new Finding: "Yes, we are supporting the rebels until the Nicaraguans stop their subversion," an "approach," the official urged, that "should end the argument over whether the Administration was violating its pledge by doing more than just stopping the arms flow."

But Administration hopes that the September Finding, and its new rationale for covert action, would end the debate on Contra aid were quickly dashed. Discussions were held on the House floor over the advisability of continuing covert aid, and the President took his cause to the public in his radio addresses. In October, the House voted to halt all aid to paramilitary groups fighting the Nicaraguan Government. The Senate, however, wanted to continue aid. In early December, the House and Senate agreed to a compromise: A "cap" of $24 million would be placed on Contra funding, and the CIA would be barred from using its contingency reserves to make up any shortfall.

## The Decision to Bring the Situation to a Head

Having survived the threat of a total cutoff of funds for the Contras, the Administration decided to intensify the CIA's covert activities while funding still remained. Charged by the new National Security Adviser, Robert McFarlane, to prepare an "in-depth review" of the Administration's Central America policy, a Special Interagency Working Group (SIG) concluded: "Given the distinct possibility that we may be unable to obtain additional funding in FY-84 or FY-85, our objective should be to bring the Nicaragua situation to a head in 1984."

Even before the decision had been officially acknowledged, plans had been implemented to step-up paramilitary operations in Central America. In the fall, speedboats carried out attacks against Sandinista patrol craft and fuel tanks. By November, a more heavily armed speedboat had been developed for follow-on operations.

At the end of December, and thereafter, the mining and other operations increased. In early January, the CIA proposed attacks against fuel supply depots and transmission lines along the "entire Pacific coast of Nicaragua." On January 7, three magnetic mines were placed in Sandino harbor; on February 3, an air attack destroyed a Sandinista "communications and naval arms depot"; and on February 29, more mines were placed at Corinto. By March 29, plans had been made to support an attack by Eden Pastora on San Juan del Norte; it was hoped that the attack would result in the installation of a provisional government.

## The Role of Lt. Col. Oliver North

At the NSC, Lt. Col. Oliver North became the liaison with the CIA in its intensified covert effort. A graduate of the U. S. Naval Academy, he had distinguished himself on the battlefield in Vietnam, winning a Silver Star, a Bronze Star, and two Purple Hearts. He was assigned to the NSC in October 1981, where he quickly established a reputation with his superiors as a staffer who could get a job done.

North was energetic, articulate, action-oriented, and had a reputation for bypassing red tape. His superiors could depend on him not only to carry out orders, but to keep them informed. North was a prodigious writer, often staying in his office until late at night to complete lengthy papers or other work.

As described by a number of his colleagues, North's relationship to McFarlane was very close. With McFarlane's rise to the position of National Security Adviser, North came to play an increasingly large role not only in the operational aspects of Contra policy, but also in forging that policy. North already had contacts in Central America who were pleased with his success. On November 7, 1983, John Hull, Indiana native, ranch owner in Costa Rica, and Contra sup-

porter, wrote that "B.G.," or "blood and guts," as North was known, was to have a new boss, Robert McFarlane. Hull hoped this would make North "more powerful as we need more like him."

North became a strong advocate within the NSC staff of intensified covert support for the Contras. He was the point of contact, transferring information from the CIA to the National Security Adviser for the President's approval. For every significant, and sometimes insignificant, operation, he provided a memorandum to the National Security Adviser destined for the President. His reports were detailed and enthusiastic, his recommendations supportive of further operations.

In his new assignment, North looked to Casey for guidance. In his words, Director Casey was a "teacher or philosophical mentor" of sorts, to whom he looked for help and advice on a regular basis.

## Tension Between the 1983 Finding and Intensified Operations

In a series of memorandums written between October 1983 and March 1984, North recorded the CIA's increasing covert presence in the region. Relatively minor operational details were given to the President, as on November 4, when North advised McFarlane to suggest an increase in the number of weapons supplied to the Contras by 3,000. The President approved the recommendation. North not only sought approval for, but also reported the results of, various actions proposed to him by Agency personnel. On February 3, he reported a successful attack on a Sandinista communications and naval arms depot. Admiral Poindexter penned, "Well done," and checked North's recommendation that the President would be briefed.

In memoranda to McFarlane, [**North**] proposed significant military actions against the Sandinistas, the details of which cannot be disclosed for national security reasons, but which give substance to the testimony of Clair George, CIA Deputy Director for Operations, that North's ideas were often extreme, "crazy," or "hairbrained." The memos reveal the same enthusiasm for covert paramilitary operations that North would later bring to his work as the "switching point" for Contra support during the next 2 years.

## The Money Begins to Run Out

By February 1984, the $24 million earmarked by Congress for the Contras was being quickly depleted. On February 13, North wrote to McFarlane, emphasizing the importance of obtaining "relief from the $24M ceiling," but recognizing that "[c]ongressional resistance on this issue is formidable."

## The Harbor Mining Disclosures

In early April, the country learned that the U.S. Government was involved in the mining of Nicaraguan harbors. U.S. Government presence in Nicaragua had become "embarrassingly overt." As McFarlane testified: "The disclosure that harbors had been mined in Nicaragua was received very badly. . . ."

On April 26, Director Casey "apologize[d] profoundly," conceding inadequate disclosure. But the "apology" could not heal the "fracture" between Congress and the Ad-

ministration that the mining had created. The Administration's policy to bring the situation "to a head" had backfired: the plan, rather than attracting support, lost it.

## KEEPING THE CONTRAS TOGETHER: SPRING–SUMMER 1984

The Administration's proposal for $21 million in supplemental assistance for the Contras now lay in doubt as Congress debated the course of U. S. policy in Central America. The uproar over the mining incident made any further appropriation unlikely. Indeed, House Speaker Thomas P. (Tip) O'Neill, Jr. declared that, in his view, the President's funding request was "dead."

With or without appropriated funds, the Administration planned to continue supporting the Contras. In McFarlane's words, the President directed the NSC staff to keep the Contras together "body and soul." In Poindexter's words, the President "wanted to be sure that the contras were supported."

McFarlane assigned this responsibility to North, who testified:

I was given the job of holding them together in body and in soul.

\* \* \*

To keep them together as a viable political opposition, to keep them alive in the field, to bridge the time between the time when we would have no money and the time when the Congress would vote again, to keep the effort alive, because the President committed publicly to go back, in his words, again and again and again to support the Nicaraguan resistance.

47

## Tapping Foreign Sources—The First Efforts

With the appropriated funds projected to run out in May or June, the Contras could be kept together only if an alternative source of funding could be found. The Administration began to look beyond the U.S. Treasury to foreign countries for monetary support.

### Looking to Country 1 for Contra Support

McFarlane testified that perhaps as early as February 1984, he considered "the possibility of in effect farming out the whole contra support operation to another country, which would not only provide the funding, but give it some direction." In February or March, McFarlane pursued the idea with an official from Country 1 [**Israel**]. He inquired whether Country 1 would have any interest in instructing "the contras in basic tactics, maneuver[s], and so forth." Country 1 officials eventually declined the invitation.

But McFarlane was not dissuaded from attempting a less ambitious plan for third-country support. On March 27, McFarlane met with Director Casey and proposed a plan to approach third countries, including Country 1, for Contra assistance. Secretary of State George P. Shultz testified that during other discussions within the Administration about third-country funding, he questioned the legality and wisdom of any third-country approach. Shultz testified that by April 18, McFarlane knew he (Shultz) felt it was a mistake to approach Country 1 for Contra support.

Nevertheless, McFarlane followed through with the plan recounted in Director Casey's March 27 memo. He directed Howard J. Teicher, the Director of Near East Affairs at the NSC, to speak to an official in Country 1's Ministry of Foreign Affairs about obtaining monetary support. Teicher made the approach, but Country 1 declined to be a part of the plan.

In May, Secretary Shultz learned of Teicher's approach from the U. S. Ambassador to Country 1, and he confronted McFarlane at the White House. According to Shultz, McFarlane told him that Teicher's approach to Country 1 was without authorization and that Teicher was operating "on his own hook." But Shultz later learned, to the contrary, from his Ambassador, that Teicher had made a point of telling the Ambassador he was in Country 1 at McFarlane's instructions. Later, McFarlane told the Committees that he had directed Teicher to seek a contribution from Country 1.

### Looking to Country 6 for Contra Support

**In 1984 the CIA considered asking South Africa (Country 6) to aid the Contras. When South African officials were approached, "the initial reaction had been favorable." But in the end the idea was dropped because some officials realized it would be embarrassing if exposed.**

### Country 2 Contributes Funds

By May 1984, the Contras had exhausted the last portion of the $24 million Congressional appropriation for fiscal 1984. McFarlane testified that possibly as early as May, he met with the Ambassador from Country 2 [**Saudi Arabia**] and explained that it was almost "inevitable that the Administration would fail" to win Congressional support for the Contras. According to McFarlane, the Ambassador offered to "provide a contribution of $1 million per month, ostensibly from private funds that would be devoted to—as a humanitarian gesture—to sustenance of the Contras through the end of the year." In his testimony, McFarlane denied that any solicitation of Country 2 had occurred, and insisted the Country 2 contribution was merely a gift.

After receiving the contribution and informing his deputy, Admiral Poindexter, McFarlane charged North with the responsibility for arranging the transfer of funds: "[I] asked him to be in touch with the contra leaders and to find out where the bank account was kept. . . . Lieutenant Colonel North came back and provided the name of the bank, its address and the contras' account number for the bank in Miami. . . ."

According to McFarlane, the President was informed of the Country 2 contribution shortly after it took place. McFarlane placed a note card into the President's morning briefing book. He chose this method of informing the President of the contribution to reduce any chance that others at the President's daily briefing might become aware of the funding scheme. After the meeting, McFarlane was called in to "pick up the note card which," he recalled, "expressed the President's satisfaction and pleasure that this had occurred."

**McFarlane told some Cabinet officers of the donation but not others, starting a pattern that would persist to the end of the Iran-Contra Affair.**

## The June National Security Planning Group Meeting

On June 25, the National Security Planning Group met to consider options for funding the Contras. In attendance were the President, Vice President Bush, Secretary Shultz, Secretary Weinberger, Director Casey, Meese, and McFarlane. Director Casey urged the President to seek third-country aid. Secretary Shultz responded that Chief of Staff James Baker had told him that if the U.S. Government acted as a conduit for third-country funding to the Contras, that would be an "impeachable offense." Casey responded that it was permissible if the plan called for direct contributions from third countries to the Contras. Meese recalled that there was an opinion by Attorney General William French Smith that provided authority for such a plan, but also noted that if an opinion were sought, Justice Department lawyers should be given guidance on what the opinion should say. The meeting ended without any firm conclusion. McFarlane advised that no one was to do anything without the necessary Justice Department opinion. Although McFarlane had already secured the contribution from Country 2, neither he nor anyone else mentioned it.

And although McFarlane had urged those at the National Security Planning Group meeting not to do anything, that very day North arranged for the transfer of Country 2 funds to Contra leader Adolfo Calero.

North made these plans to send the Country 2 funds to Calero despite his apparent knowledge of the legal difficulties expressed earlier that day at the National Security Planning Group meeting. His notes reflect that he was advised of those discussions by Clarridge of the CIA. North recorded phrases such as "impeachable offense" (presumably referring to Secretary Shultz's remark), and "going to French Smith—reading on US seeking alternative funding." The note continues: "Seek 3d party funding."

The next day, June 26, Director Casey met with Attorney General Smith. A CIA note on the meeting quoted Smith as saying that asking other countries to fund the Contras was legal, as long as the other countries used their own money, not funds given to them by the U.S.

The Intelligence Committees were not advised of the Country 2 contribution until 1987.

## Providing Support—The Private Network

With funds available from Country 2, North turned to creating a mechanism for providing materiel support for the Contras.

North testified that, at Casey's suggestion, he turned to Retired U.S. Air Force Maj. General Richard V. Secord:

> I approached General Secord in 1984 and asked that he become engaged in these activities. . . .
>
> I went back to him again and at some point in '84, he agreed to become actively engaged. He agreed to establish, and did, private commercial entities outside the United States that could help carry out these activities. It was always viewed by myself, by Mr. McFarlane, by Director Casey, that these were private commercial ventures, private commercial activities. . . .
>
> [I]t was always the intention to make this a self-sustaining operation and that there always be something there which you could reach out and grab when you needed it. Director Casey said he wanted something you could pull off the shelf and use at a moment's notice.

The network, albeit privately run, was created for the purpose of pursuing "foreign-policy goals." According to North: "It was never envisioned in my mind that this would be hidden from the President."

The President has publicly stated that he was kept informed of some of the efforts by private citizens to aid the Contras. Poindexter testified the President "knew the contras were being supported . . . by third-country funds and by private support activity. . . ." There is no evidence, however, to suggest that the President was ever informed about an "off-the-shelf" covert operation.

### Secord's Initial Role

In summer 1984, Secord's first assignment from North was to assist the Contras in buying weapons with the funds sent to Calero by Country 2. In July, Secord, accompanied by his associate and former CIA operative, Rafael Quintero, met with Calero to discuss the Contras' need for low-priced weapons. He left the meeting with a weapons list. Although Secord was not an arms dealer, he agreed to act as a broker to procure the weapons with his business partner, Albert A. Hakim, a naturalized American of Iranian descent. In his testimony, Secord referred to the operation that he and Hakim used for Contra support as "the Enterprise."

### Owen's Role

North also obtained the assistance of Robert W. Owen to act on his behalf with Contra leaders. Owen was a private citizen who was a teacher before he joined the staff of Senator Dan Quayle in 1982. After leaving Senator Quayle's staff in 1983, Owen joined Gray & Co., a public relations firm in Washington, D.C.

Taking a leave of absence from his firm,

Owen traveled to Central America in late May or early June 1984 and met with Contra leaders. He was told, and subsequently repeated to North, that the Contras "would need $1 million a month, and if they wanted to increase in size they would need about a million and a half dollars a month." Between October 1984 and March 1986, Owen made more than seven trips to Central America collecting information and delivering intelligence and money to the Contras on North's behalf. He was given the code name "T.C." (The Courier), and in his own words, he served as North's "eyes and ears" in Central America.

## BOLAND II

In the summer of 1984, CIA covert assistance to the Contras began to wane as funds were depleted. Meanwhile, legislation—the second Boland Amendment—that would bar the Agency from future support for the Contras had been passed by the House in early August. According to McFarlane, as the CIA stepped out of the picture, the task of supporting the Contras fell to the NSC: "[t]he President had made clear that he wanted a job done. The net result was that the job fell to the National Security Council staff."

In late August, North traveled to Central America to meet with Calero to resolve "immediate operational/logistic problems." McFarlane advised North: "Exercise absolute 'stealth.' No visible meeting. No press awareness of your presence in the area."

By early October, Congress had adopted the Boland Amendment to an omnibus appropriations bill. Signed into law by the Pres-

ident on October 12, 1984, the bill would later be referred to as Boland II. It provided in relevant part:

> During fiscal year 1985, no funds available to the Central Intelligence Agency, the Department of Defense, or any other agency or entity involved in intelligence activities may be obligated or expended for the purpose or which would have the effect of supporting, directly or indirectly, military or paramilitary operations in Nicaragua by any nation, group, organization, movement or individual.

While Boland II cut off all funding for the Contras, it held out some hope for renewing Contra aid in the future by providing that the Administration could seek a $14 million appropriation on an expedited basis after February 28, 1985. But, even as the bill held out a future hope, its sponsors made clear that the law was intended to achieve an immediate cutoff of aid.

Poindexter and North, who admitted assisting the Contras in their military activities, had a different view. Both testified that they did not believe that Boland II was applicable to the NSC staff and that while the CIA could no longer provide any assistance to the Contras, the NSC staff was free to do so. Poindexter put it succinctly: "I never believed, and I don't believe today, that the Boland Amendment ever applied to the National Security Council staff. .. .."

Their former superior, Robert McFarlane, was surprised by that view. In "cutting off money for the Contras," he understood Congress to say "we don't want any money raised for the Contras." McFarlane testified that he repeatedly addressed the NSC staff with "a kind of litany of mine, . . . [not to] 'solicit, encourage, coerce, or broker'" financial contributions for the Contras. According to McFarlane, he specifically told North to "stay within the law and to be particularly careful not to be associated with or take part in any fundraising activities."

North and Poindexter both denied hearing McFarlane's warnings against solicitation and entreaties to observe the law. Both claimed that they were acting within their legal rights in aiding the Contras. North stated that all of his acts were authorized by his superiors, and Poindexter, speaking as one of those superiors, confirmed that he had given North a "broad charter" to support the Contras and had "authorized in general" North's actions in carrying out that charter. McFarlane testified he was unaware of the breadth of North's activities.

In any case, Poindexter and North were not deterred by Boland II in assisting the Contras. Indeed, Boland II was a spur to action. The CIA had to withdraw from supporting the Contras and, according to North, this meant he "was the only person left talking to them."

As Poindexter summed up North's role, "[O]nce the CIA was restricted," North was the "switching point that made the whole system work . . . the kingpin to the Central American opposition . . . ."

Boland II did not deter North—it simply reinforced the need to keep what he was doing secret from Congress, the public, and others in the Government.

## CONTRA AID—FALL 1984 TO WINTER 1985

Boland II did not cause any immediate crisis for the Contras. Steps taken months before

ensured their survival. As McFarlane testified, "[T]here wasn't any need" for funds at the time. The $1 million-a-month pledged by Country 2 in June 1984 would "bridge the gap" at least until December.

## Arms Shipments Begin and Blowpipes Are Sought

While Second undertook to procure weapons, North remained heavily involved. Calero testified that he consulted with North regarding weapons needs and purchases and North's notebooks confirm this.

In the fall, the Contras' most pressing need was ground-to-air missiles. The Sandinistas had just obtained Soviet-designed HIND-D helicopters, sophisticated assault helicopters. North devoted his efforts to finding a missile capable of shooting them down.

**North tried to help the Contras buy British Blowpipe shoulder-fired antiaircraft missiles from Chile but failed. At about the same time he helped Secord convince the Chinese Government to sell the Contras some of their surface-to-air missiles.**

Meanwhile, the Contras were also running out of basic weapons. According to Secord, in November, Secord, using money provided by Calero, made a downpayment on a shipment of arms which was to come by sea from the Far East. But the shipment was delayed and, in fact, it would not arrive until the spring of 1985.

To make the first arms shipment, the Enterprise needed an end-user certificate (EUC)—a document certifying that the arms were for the exclusive use of the country to which the arms were being sent. By February 14, 1985, North had the end-user certificates, and Secord was able to ship more than 90,000 pounds of East European munitions by chartered aircraft from Defex, a European arms dealer, to a Central American country for the Contras.

## Providing Intelligence and Military Advice

North's role was not limited to assisting arms purchases. On direction from McFarlane, he gave political advice to the Contras on unifying the different factions and adopting a platform recognizing human rights and pledging a pluralistic society. Even more critical for the Contras, North provided military intelligence and advice.

The CIA and the DOD could not provide military intelligence directly to the Contras, so North provided it himself. North would obtain maps and other intelligence on the Sandinista positions from the CIA and DOD, ostensibly for his own use. North would then pass the intelligence to the Contras using Owen as a courier.

Director Casey was eager to keep the CIA bureaucracy insulated from North's activities in supporting the Contras. Indeed, in November, Casey complained to Poindexter that North was conducting his support activities "indiscreetly," and had disclosed to CIA officials that he was raising funds for, and providing intelligence to, the Contras.

Learning of the complaint, North wrote McFarlane on November 7, 1984, to defend his behavior. North insisted he had not implicated the Chief of the CIA's Central American Task Force in his Contra support activities. "Clarifying who said what to whom," North acknowledged that he had passed intelligence to Calero to assist him in

destroying the Sandinistas' newly acquired HIND-D helicopters. North stated that he had gone to both the CIA and to the DOD for information on the helicopters' location and passed this on to Calero.

In early February 1985, North became concerned about a shipment of weapons bound for the Sandinistas aboard the ship, the *Monimbo*. In a memorandum to McFarlane and Poindexter, North recommended the vessel be seized or sunk:

If asked, Calero would be willing to finance the operation. He does not, however, have sufficient numbers of trained maritime special operations personnel or a method of delivery for seizing the ship on the high seas. . . . If time does not permit a special operation [on the high seas] . . . Calero can quickly be provided with the maritime assets required to sink the vessel before it can reach port at Corinto. He is in contact with maritime operations experts and purveyors of materiel necessary to conduct such an operation.

North asked McFarlane for authorization to provide Calero "with the information on Monimbo" and for permission to approach him "on the matter of seizing or sinking the ship."

This time, Admiral Poindexter raised a legal question, but only to advise McFarlane about how North's recommendation should be handled. On the bottom of the memorandum, Poindexter agreed with North that, "We need to take action to make sure ship does not arrive in Nicaragua. JP." But in a cover note to McFarlane, Admiral Poindexter wrote:

Except for the prohibition of the intelligence community doing anything to assist the Freedom Fighters I would readily recommend I bring this up to CPPG [Crisis Pre-Planning Group] at 2:00 today. Of course we could discuss it from the standpoint of keeping the arms away from Nicaragua without any involvement of Calero and Freedom Fighters. What do you think?

No action was taken on North's recommendation to seize the *Monimbo*.

**North also managed to secure the help of David Walker, a British paramilitary expert who helped the Contras carry out a special military operation inside Nicaragua. The operation is not described, though one plan had been to blow up one or more of the Sandinistas' powerful Soviet-made MI-24 HIND attack helicopters. The White House liked to call the HINDs flying tanks; they had come to be symbols of Nicaragua's oversized military.**

## Singlaub Efforts with Countries 3 and 5

Country 2 had pledged funds only through the end of 1984. Therefore, by the end of the year, an urgent need existed to find money for the Contras to continue into 1985.

In late November 1984, North approved the efforts of Retired U.S. Army Maj. Gen. John K. Singlaub to obtain funds from third countries to support the Contras. Singlaub met in Washington with officials of Country 3 [**Taiwan**] and Country 5 [**South Korea**] to request aid. Singlaub was blunt about the Contras' needs: bullets, guns, and anti-aircraft missiles. The foreign country officials, however, expressed concern about running afoul of "Congress by openly defying the Boland Amendment." At the same time they were willing to help "if this could be done in a way that did not attract attention." They

agreed to send Singlaub's request to their respective governments.

Singlaub followed up on his request, travelling to Countries 3 and 5 in January. He met with highly placed officials and reiterated his earlier request for military donations to the Contras. Singlaub provided the officials with an index card bearing the name of the bank and account number, under Calero's control, where the funds could be deposited directly. Singlaub told the officials he was a private citizen, but wanted to make it clear he was not an "unguided missile ricocheting around to that part of the world." He expressed the belief that "it would be possible . . . to have someone in the Administration send a signal to them . . . to indicate that [he] . . . was not operating entirely on [his] . . . own, without the knowledge of the Administration."

On February 1, 1985, North's notes reflect that Singlaub called North and told him that Country 3 needed a signal that the Administration would be "greatly pleased" by a donation before Country 3 would be willing to contribute.

Countries 3 and 5 did not contribute any money as a result of Singlaub's efforts. Not until late 1985, after a signal was in fact given by an NSC official, did Country 3 make a contribution.

## Country 2 Makes an Additional Contribution

With the Contras running out of funds, McFarlane turned once more to Country 2. McFarlane made the initial approach to its Ambassador for more funds. He testified that he did not "solicit" funds because the Boland Amendment prohibited such solicitation. He merely told the Ambassador of the plight of the Contras and hoped for a contribution. According to Secord, North asked him to follow up on McFarlane's initial meeting.

In early February 1985, Country 2 agreed to contribute an additional $24 million. McFarlane informed the President of the contribution by placing a note card in the President's daily briefing book. The President again reacted with "gratitude and satisfaction," expressing no surprise. Unknown to McFarlane, the Country 2 head of state had already informed the President directly of the new contribution. But the President did not mention this when he briefed the Secretary of State and McFarlane on his meeting with the government leader.

Nor did McFarlane tell the Secretary of Defense. Both Secretary Weinberger and General John W. Vessey, Jr., the Chairman of the Joint Chiefs of Staff, learned of the contribution from other sources.

The new donation from Country 2, like its predecessor, was sent to Calero's accounts. Between June 1984 and March 1985, Country 2's contributions, totaling $32 million, were virtually the only funds the Contras had.

## CONTRA AID: WINTER–SPRING 1985

### The Administration Returns to Congress

In the winter of 1985, the Administration pinned its hopes on obtaining the $14 million in aid held out by the Boland legislation.

The chances for success were dim from the start. The new Chairman of the Senate Intelligence Committee, David Durenberger, had warned publicly that he would oppose both the release of the $14 million and any future Contra aid. But the President had not given up. He told a group of reporters, "We're going to do our best."

North was optimistic that "[w]ith adequate support the resistance could be in Managua by the end of 1985."

Any legislative proposal for increased aid depended upon the Contras' survival in the field. McFarlane testified he told North that "unless the Contras become a credible military force, they would never gain political support in Congress and among the American people." North was counting on the Enterprise to provide the support necessary to maintain the Contras as a viable force.

### The Weapons Shipments from the Enterprise Continue

In the spring of 1985, two weapons shipments arranged by Secord in consultation with North and Calero would finally reach the Contras: first, in February, a planeload of 90,000 pounds of munitions from Europe and, second, in the spring, a sealift. Both shipments were arranged through Transworld Armament, and both apparently required end-user certificates.

North needed the cooperation of Central American countries to provide documentation and to receive the shipments for the Contras. On March 5, 1985, he proposed that one country be rewarded for its assistance. In a memorandum to McFarlane, North suggested that the Secretaries of State and Defense and Chairman Vessey of the Joint Chiefs of Staff be asked to grant the Central American country additional security assistance.

The "real purpose" of this memo, North explained, was to:

find a way by which we can compensate [Country 14] for the extraordinary assistance they are providing to the Nicaraguan freedom fighters. At Tab II are end-user certificates which [Country 14] provided for the purchase of nearly $8M worth of munitions to be delivered to the FDN.

In the attached memorandum to Weinberger, Shultz, and Vessey, drafted by North, the real purpose behind the request was not stated. The memorandum contained no reference to the end-user certificates, "to the arrangements which have been made for supporting the resistance through [Country 14]," or to the Country 14 **[Guatemala]** munitions "wish list" North attached for McFarlane's information. Instead, the request for aid was predicated on its merits.

McFarlane testified that he recommended that the Cabinet approve increased assistance based solely on his assessment of Country 14's need, without taking into account its support of the Contras. North testified that he had not promised a "quid pro quo." There was no "need" to make such a promise to a country threatened by the Sandinista presence, he said.

## Disbursements to Other Contra Leaders

During the winter and spring of 1985, North decided to use the money sent directly to Calero from Country 2 to support other Contra leaders. To do this, funds were withdrawn from Calero's account using traveler's checks, and hand-carried to North. North stored the checks in his safe. Additional cash was secured from Secord.

North testified that the idea for maintaining this fund came from Director Casey:

My recollection is that the very first traveler's checks came either very late '84 or certainly early 1985 and that the sum total of traveler's checks was probably in excess of $100,000 or thereabouts.

I also had cash which I estimated to be somewhere in the neighborhood of 50 to 75 thousand dollars in cash, so we are talking about an operational account that went from somewhere around 150 to 175 thousand dollars. At various points in time there would be considerable sums in it and at various points in time there would be none in it.

\* \* \*

What is important that you realize is that meticulous records were kept on all of this. I kept a detailed account of every single penny that came into that account and that left that account. All of the transactions were recorded on a ledger that Director Casey gave me for that purpose. Every time I got a group of traveler's checks in, I would report them, and I would report them when they went out, even going so far as to record the traveler's check numbers themselves.

The ledger for this operational account was given to me by Director Casey, and when he told me to do so, I destroyed it because it had within it the details of every single person who had been supported by this fund, the addresses, their names, and placed them at extraordinary risk.

One of the principal beneficiaries of North's fund was a Resistance leader. With McFarlane's approval, North decided to assume support for the Resistance leader, using funds drawn from the Calero account.

By February 27, 1985, "Adolfo [Calero] ha[d] agreed to provide [the] requisite funds in the blind without [the] [Resistance leader] becoming aware of the source." Eventually, Calero was to "deposit $6,250 per month in [Resistance leader's] checking account without [his] knowledge [of the source]." But before the direct deposit mechanism could be put into operation, North enlisted Robert Owen and Jonathan Miller, then-Deputy Coordinator for Public Diplomacy at the State Department, to pass the money to the Resistance leader. Sometime in early March, North handed Owen and Miller traveler's checks from his office safe, and requested that the checks be cashed. Miller and Owen did so, and returned to North's office. Later that day, at his apartment, Owen passed $6,000 to $7,000 in cash to the Resistance leader.

Owen handled a number of transfers to Contra leaders. He testified that he paid "[s]omewhere between six and ten" Contra leaders, and the total amount paid was "[s]omewhere around $30,000." On March 22, 1985, for example, Owen traveled to Central America carrying several thousand dollars in cash or traveler's checks for delivery to a Contra leader. In some cases, Owen's efforts did not take him far from the White House itself. In April, for example, he waited outside the Old Executive Office Building in the rain. A car drove up, and Owen passed cash to a Nicaraguan Indian leader sitting inside.

## KEEPING THE OPERATION SECRET

North provided the logistical and funding assistance the Contras needed to keep going in Central America at the same time that he worked to keep their cause alive in Washington. To persuade Congress to vote for renewed aid, it was critical that the NSC staff's Contra assistance remain secret. As North warned Calero: "Too much is becoming known by too many people. We need to make sure that this new financing does *not* become known. The Congress must believe that there continues to be an urgent need for funding."

North actively cultivated an image of Contra self-sufficiency within the Administration. For example, he urged the CIA's Chief of the Central American Task Force to reject the State Department's opinion that the Resistance had become largely ineffective since U.S. funding ran out in May 1984. "I told [the Chief of the Central American Task Force]," wrote North, "that it was important that the SNIE [Special National Intelligence Estimate] reflect the fact that there was substantial outside support which had continued for some months and showed no signs of abating."

But even without such active encouragement, the secrecy shrouding North's efforts contributed to the appearance of Contra self-sufficiency. As funds arrived and weapons were shipped, CIA intelligence reports confirmed that the Contras remained not only a viable force, but were surviving on their own, without apparent U.S. Government assistance.

The secret of North's involvement, however, was not to last. North's name had begun to appear periodically in the press along with that of Singlaub. By March, Singlaub already had become something of a "lightning rod" in the press, attracting attention as a private fundraiser for the Contras. According to Singlaub, North told him that his frequent visits to the NSC were a source of concern. But North "understood and agreed" that Singlaub had to keep a "high profile" in order to raise funds, and he supported the effort. If Singlaub "had high visibility, [he] might be the lightning rod and take the attention away from [North] and others who were involved in the covert side of support."

## COVERT OPERATION AND LEGISLATIVE STRATEGY INTERTWINE

While maintaining the secrecy of his Contra support activities, North worked to promote a legislative strategy that would change both the Congressional and the public perception of the Nicaraguan threat. In March, he and Donald Fortier sponsored an elaborate plan calling for lobbying, a media blitz, and culminating in almost daily Presidential speeches and phone calls in support of the initiative. At its most ambitious stage, the plan included a 10-page, day-by-day chronology to describe each of the players' appointed tasks.

**North proposed what he called a "fallback plan" in case Congress did not renew aid. Under it, the Saudis would be asked to contribute an additional $25 to $30 million, and a tax-exempt foundation would be set up to receive it. But McFarlane ruled that out.**

During March 1985, North focused his attention on the elaborate legislative strategy plan he had been working on since late February. The plan was developed in conjunction with a peace initiative drafted by North in a Miami hotel room with FDN head Adolfo Calero and other Contra leaders, which became known as the San Jose Declaration. North arranged the deadline for a Sandinista response to the peace plan to coincide with the vote by Congress. If the Sandinistas rejected the overture, as North anticipated, then "special operations against highly visible military targets in Nicaragua," were timed to follow in the hopes that successful and "visible" Contra military activities might favorably influence Congress's decision on Contra aid.

## THE ADMINISTRATION RESPONDS TO CONGRESSIONAL DEFEAT

In early April, the Administration submitted a Contra aid proposal to the Congress, along with its own peace plan modeled on the San Jose Declaration. The President pledged that lethal aid would only be provided if the Sandinistas rejected the proposal. The plan provoked controversy, and on April 23, the House rejected the Administration's proposal.

Publicly, the President expressed his determination "to return to the Congress again and again." Soon after the House defeat, the Administration was back on Capitol Hill hoping to mold a compromise in support of nonlethal aid.

Meanwhile, Nicaraguan President Daniel Ortega traveled to the Soviet Union and throughout Europe, seeking renewed assistance for the Sandinista forces. President Ortega's visit to Moscow prompted the President to issue a warning to Congress:

And whatever way they may want to frame it, the opponents in the Congress of ours, who have opposed our trying to continue helping those people, they really are voting to have a totalitarian Marxist-Leninist government here in the Americas, and there's no way for them to disguise it. So, we're not going to give up.

President Ortega's Moscow trip also prompted a renewed sense in Congress that something had to be done to support the Contras. With strong support from Congressional leaders, President Reagan announced the imposition of economic sanctions against Nicaragua on May 1, 1985.

## MAINTAINING THE COVERT OPERATION

Before the Congress rejected the Administration's aid proposal, North was optimistic about the Contras' prospects. The image of Contra military capability cultivated by North was arguably at odds with reality. U.S. Army General Paul F. Gorman, Commander of the Southern Command from May 1983 through February 1985, told the Committees that "the prospects of the Nicaraguan resistance succeeding [were] dim at best." Specifically referring to Congressional testimony he gave in June and December 1985, Gorman testified:

what I was saying in those days was that I did not see in the Nicaraguan resistance a combination of forces that could lead to the overthrow of the government or the unseating of the Sandinistas.... The training of the Contras was, when I last saw them in 1985, abysmal. . . . I didn't regard them as a very effective

military organization, based on what I could see in reflections of battles, in communications on both sides. The Sandinistas could wipe them out.

Regarding North's reaction to his views, Gorman added:

Oliver was terribly concerned about my attitude, and he knew that I was travelling up here on the Hill and in other circles where I was being asked to comment on the prospects of these people.

Gorman concluded by telling the Committees, "it was also very clear to me, he [North] saw me as a problem in terms of what I was saying, and I think he was just doing his damndest to get me to shut up—old General, put a cork in it."

**In the spring, North made ambitious new plans for the Contras, but everything was stalled when Congress rejected the Administration's new funding request, sending Contra morale into a tailspin.**

Meanwhile, in Congress, a consensus was building in favor of humanitarian aid. By May 15, 1985, Congressional leaders were seeking counsel from the NSC on the Administration's position about a Contra support bill that was limited to nonlethal aid.

By the end of May, North was optimistic that the Boland Amendment restrictions would be lifted, at least with respect to the CIA's provision of intelligence and political support. But even if they were lifted, and Congress appropriated humanitarian aid, North did not contemplate that his covert operation would end. He told McFarlane in a May 31 memo:

Plans are underway to transition from current arrangements to a consultative capacity by the CIA for all political matters and intelligence, once Congressional approval is granted on lifting Section 8066 [Boland Amendment] restrictions. The only portion of current activity which will be sustained as it has since last June, will be the delivery of lethal supplies.

## THE SECORD GROUP AND ITS COMPETITION

As humanitarian aid measures were debated in Congress, Secord's Enterprise was continuing to procure weapons for the Contras. By May, Secord was using Thomas G. Clines, rather than the original broker. Clines' source was a European arms dealer. Secord was also using Rafael Quintero to handle the logistics of the arms deliveries in Central America. As North put it, Quintero was the "Second man on [the] scene." He coordinated the arms reception in Central America, and "all of the liaison with the Contras and with the local authorities." From Quintero, Secord would obtain the information necessary to provide North with what North termed "views from on [the] scene" in Central America. Clines, Quintero, and Secord were to play an increasingly large role in the Contra support structure as the summer progressed.

During May, Secord arranged through Clines for the third in a series of arms transfers to the Contras. This time, the shipment was to arrive by sea. Periodically, Secord would call North with the latest update, as on May 8: "Came out of in . . . now in Paris; -Tested every item; -ship arrived 4–5 hours

ago; -40,000 M-79 . . . ." Later, on May 24, North recorded: "Call from Dick; -Vessel needs shipping agent for receiving; -Need to do long lead plan for Aug–Sep delivery; -need to make deposit for M-79 buy." As Secord testified, North "was in the information collection business" and "[h]e wanted to know if I would provide him with details of any deliveries or deals that were made, and I did so gladly."

General Secord was not the only weapons dealer seeking the Contra account during the summer of 1985. For example, Ronald Martin, a Miami arms dealer, was by May "setting up [a] munitions 'supermarket' " in Central America. As North testified: "You had a very competitive environment down there. Once the U.S. Government withdrew in '84 from directly supporting the resistance, you ended up with a lot of folks out there running a very cutthroat business."

North discouraged Calero from dealing with some of Secord's competitors. He testified that CIA Director Casey had suspicions that the arms warehouse operation run by Martin was supported by U.S. funding that had been diverted to Martin by a Central American country. According to North, Casey told him "that there shouldn't be any further transactions with that broker until such time as he resolved or they were able to resolve where" the money to stockpile "several millions of dollars worth of ordnance" had come from.

Secord's other competitor for procuring arms for the Contras during the spring of 1985 was General Singlaub. As early as April, Singlaub had begun to arrange for a major weapons purchase, after meeting at FDN base camps in March with the FDN military commander, Enrique Bermudez. The list of weapons Singlaub drew up with Bermudez included AK-47 rifles, RPG-7 rocket launchers, light machine guns, and SA-7 surface-to-air missiles. Singlaub took the weapons list to North, who made "some additions and subtractions." North and Singlaub "reach[ed] a clear-cut statement of what we were going to buy."

Sometime later that month, Singlaub introduced Calero to a European arms dealer. Calero was astonished at the low prices he had been quoted; "at least in the case of the AK-47s that price was about half of what we had previously had to pay." (In part, this can be attributed to the fact that Singlaub did not take a commission.)

Part of the explanation for the difference between Secord's prices and those of Singlaub's dealer was Secord's profit margin—a margin of which Calero was unaware. Secord testified that his markup on all Contra shipments "averaged out almost exactly 20 percent." In fact, the actual commission charged on the cost of arms averaged 38 percent.

Secord candidly admitted that he was to make a profit:

Q: I take it from what you are saying that you were to make a profit on these arms transactions?

A: Yes . . . . It was intended that the profits generated would be shared by Hakim, myself, and, of course, the arms dealer.

Calero testified he was unaware that Secord was earning money off the arms sales. He believed that Secord was supplying the weapons at cost. North, on the other hand, testified that it was his understanding from his conversations with Casey in 1984 that those running the off-the-shelf covert entities were entitled to fair compensation.

**In early May, both General Singlaub and General Secord tried to sell antiaircraft missiles to the Contras. Singlaub's prices were far lower, and he did manage to sell the Contras one shipment. But thereafter, North gave any money he raised directly to Secord, who made Contra arms purchases himself.**

# CHAPTER 3

# The Enterprise Assumes Control of Contra Support

In the summer of 1985, Congress voted to appropriate $27 million for the Contras' humanitarian needs, including food, medicine and clothing. At the same time, the covert program, run by the National Security Council (NSC) staff, entered a new and bolder phase. With the Contras' daily living needs taken care of by Congress, and their requirements for arms having been met through Country 2's prior donations, the NSC staff was able to focus on attempting to improve the Contras' military effectiveness. This involved establishing an air resupply program for the main Contra fighting force operating in the North of Nicaragua, the Nicaraguan Democratic Force (FDN), and promoting the opening of a second Contra front in the South of Nicaragua by supporting other Contra fighters, independent of the FDN, who were operating there. This support for the southern forces included the procurement of arms as well as the establishment of an air resupply program.

Disappointed at the failure of Adolfo Calero to develop a logistics infrastructure, Lt. Col. Oliver North asked Gen. Richard Secord and his associates to assume new responsibilities that under the Boland Amendment the U.S. Government could not undertake. Secord agreed to continue to handle all future weapons procurement for the Contras and to acquire and operate a small fleet of planes to make air drops of weapons, ammunition, and other supplies to the Contras in both northern and southern Nicaragua. North arranged the funding for Secord to carry out these activities, directing third-country and private contributions to Secord that previously went to Calero. These funds were later augmented by the diversion from the Iranian arms sales that North, with Admiral John Poindexter's approval, initiated.

Financed by contributions and the diversion, the Secord group purchased and operated five airplanes, built an emergency airstrip in Costa Rica, maintained an air maintenance facility and a warehouse in another Central American country, and hired pilots and crew to fly the air drop missions. They also purchased weapons and ammunition in Europe and delivered them to Central America for use by the Contras in the south and north. North called the organization "Project Democracy." Secord and his partner, Albert Hakim, referred to it as the Enterprise.

The Enterprise, though nominally private, functioned as a secret arm of the NSC staff in conducting the covert program in Nicaragua. While Secord controlled the operational decisions of the Enterprise, North remained in overall charge of the Contra support program. He set the priorities and enlisted the support of an Ambassador, Central Intelligence Agency (CIA) officials, and military personnel to carry out the air resupply operation. He dealt with crises as they arose, sometimes on a daily basis. In carrying on these tasks, North had the unqualified support of Admiral Poindexter, who had replaced Robert McFarlane as National Security Adviser in December 1985.

The efforts of the NSC staff and the Enterprise to carry out a government function with a makeshift covert organization were, however, dogged by problems from the beginning. The Enterprise's aircraft were in poor condition and the group had to overcome numerous tactical problems in carrying out its mission. While the Enterprise conducted routine air drops in northern Nicaragua, it was not able to begin a regular air drop operation in the south until late summer of 1986—at a time when both Houses of Congress had voted to authorize the CIA to resume its support for the Contras with appropriated funds and when the Enterprise was trying to sell its assets to the CIA. The operation ended abruptly in October 1986 when the plane that Eugene Hasenfus was on was shot down while on a mission to drop supplies to the Contras in Nicaragua.

Before that and for more than 2 years, the NSC staff had secretly achieved what Congress had openly disapproved in the Boland Amendment—an extensive program of military support for the Contras. The Boland Amendment operated as a restraint on dis-

closure, not on action, as the NSC staff placed policy ends above the law.

## THE ENTERPRISE'S MISSION IS EXPANDED

On June 12, 1985, the House passed a bill approving $27 million in humanitarian assistance to the Contras, paving the way for final approval and signature by the President in August 1985. While that vote virtually ensured that the Contras would have adequate food, medical supplies, and other provisions, it also strictly limited the money to nonmilitary uses.

The provision of covert military assistance remained the secret business of the NSC staff. In the summer of 1985, articles appeared in the press speculating about the role of the NSC staff in assisting the Contras and Congress began inquiring of the National Security Adviser whether this was true. Yet, at this very time, the NSC staff decided to extend its covert program to include a system for resupplying Contras in the field. Some of the Contras fighting within Nicaragua were as many as 30 days away by land from border areas. To keep them supplied and to encourage other fighters to move from border sanctuaries to Nicaragua, a capacity to make aerial drops of ammunition and other supplies was essential.

In early July, North held a meeting in Miami of Contra leaders and members of Secord's group to arrange for what Congress had refused to fund—the air resupply of lethal material for the Contra forces inside Nicaragua. Present were North, FDN leader Adolfo Calero, Enrique Bermudez, the FDN military commander, Secord, and his associates, Thomas Clines and Rafael Quintero.

North began the meeting with an expression of a loss of confidence in the way the FDN was handling the donated funds he had directed to the FDN. North's solution, though not unveiled at the meeting, was to have Secord and his group take over the procurement function for the Contras. As Robert Owen, North's courier, testified, "I think he and General Secord felt they probably could do a better job" of handling the funds than the Contras.

North had decided to furnish the FDN directly with arms, air support, and other supplies. He would no longer leave to the Contras the task of spending their own money on these goods and services. Almost immediately after the Miami meeting, Secord's partner, Albert Hakim, established the Lake Resources account in Geneva, Switzerland, and thereafter virtually all donated funds were directed by North to the Lake Resources account in Switzerland, not Calero's accounts. The Secord group—the Enterprise—would no longer function simply as an arms broker from which Calero would purchase the arms. With the contributions, it would make all the decisions on arms purchases and supply the Contras with the weapons and the other support they needed, without receiving from the Contras payment for the arms.

The participants in the Miami meeting also agreed on the need to open a Southern front. With the FDN, the principal Contra force, operating in the North, the Sandinistas could concentrate their military forces on the Northern front. Forcing the Nicaraguans to fight a two-front war by building up a Contra force in the South was elemental military strategy. Calero, however, continued to concentrate his resources on his own organization in the North, the FDN.

## THE NEW HUMANITARIAN AID

As the Enterprise began implementing the plans laid in Miami, the Contras received a boost from Washington. On August 8, 1985, President Reagan signed legislation authorizing $27 million in humanitarian aid to the Contras. For the first time since May 1984, the Contras would receive U.S. Government funding as well as intelligence support from the CIA. Although the Boland Amendment remained in effect, new legislation specified that the Amendment did not prohibit exchanging information with the Contras.

The legislation prohibited the CIA or the Department of Defense (DOD) from administering the new humanitarian funds and required that the President ensure that any assistance "is used only for the intended purpose and is not diverted" for the acquisition of military hardware. The State Department was chosen to administer the aid. By executive order signed on August 29, 1985, the President created the Nicaraguan Humanitarian Assistance Office (NHAO) in the State Department.

The State Department was reluctant to accept this responsibility. The Department had no experience and lacked the organization to feed and provide for the daily needs of troops. To run NHAO, Secretary George P. Shultz tapped Ambassador Robert Duemling, a seasoned diplomat, but with no prior experience in administering an aid program. Secretary Shultz cautioned Duemling to administer the aid not only with "enthusiasm" but also with "care." Ambassador Duemling found the program difficult to administer from the start.

## Preparations for the Resupply Operation

In the beginning of August, Secord met with North and others to discuss the steps necessary to establish the resupply program. First, a logistics organization consisting of aircraft, spare parts, maintenance, communications, and trained personnel had to be set up. For that, Secord turned to former Air Force Lt. Col. Richard Gadd, who since his retirement from the military in 1982 had been providing, through a private business, air support to the Pentagon.

The second task was to obtain a secure operating base from which the aircraft could launch their missions. For this, Quintero, on Secord's instructions, consulted with the Contra leaders and chose a military airbase in a Central American country [El Salvador] ("The Airbase"). Secord and North concurred in this choice.

Finally, Secord concluded that to establish a sustained air resupply operation on the Southern front, an emergency airstrip was necessary in the South. North suggested to Secord Santa Elena in the northwest corner of Costa Rica, which North believed could also be used as a covert secondary operating base for resupply to the Southern front.

## U.S. SUPPORT FOR THE COVERT OPERATION

The plans made in Miami for a resupply operation and a Southern front could not have been implemented without the active support of U.S. Government officials.

In July 1985, almost immediately after the Miami meeting, North asked Lewis Tambs, the newly appointed Ambassador to Costa Rica, to help open a Southern front for the Contras, a request that Poindexter approved. Tambs agreed without consulting Secretary Shultz. Later that summer, North specifically asked for Tambs' help, as well as that of CIA Chief Tomas Castillo, to facilitate the construction and use of the airfield.

North testified that he had received authorization from Director of Central Intelligence William J. Casey to bring Castillo into the resupply operation. Moreover, according to North, the airstrip was discussed in the Restricted Interagency Group on Central American Affairs, which consisted of, among others, North, the Chief of the Central American Task Force (CATF) at the CIA and the group's chairman, Elliott Abrams, Assistant Secretary of State for Inter-American Affairs. Abrams acknowledged the discussions, but testified that he believed "private benefactors, as we used to call them, were building the airstrip."

## The Airfield Is Planned

On August 10, 1985, North flew to Costa Rica where he met with Castillo and Tambs. North and Castillo discussed the establishment of a secret airbase that would permit moving all Contra military operations inside Nicaragua for resupply by air. Castillo and Tambs then worked to achieve the establishment of the airfield and air resupply depot for the Contra forces. Castillo reported these developments to the Chief of the CATF at CIA headquarters. The Chief replied that he was pleased with these developments but he "emphasize[d]" to Castillo that neither the CIA nor DOD could "become involved directly or indirectly" in the project.

### The Airbase Is Secured

Once the Airbase in the other Central American country was selected as the most desirable main base for the air resupply operation, North also took the necessary steps to obtain host-government approval, which required the assistance of other U.S. Government officials. North's notebooks reflect that on September 10, 1985, he met with Col. James Steele, a U.S. Military Group Commander stationed in Central America, and Donald Gregg, Vice President Bush's National Security Adviser. Among the discussion topics North listed was a "Calero/Bermudez visit to [the Airbase] to estab[lish] log[istical] support/maint[enance]," as well as other possible locations for the resupply base. Gregg, however, testified that he did not know of the resupply operation prior to the summer of 1986.

Securing suitable aircraft that the Enterprise could afford proved difficult. In the summer of 1985, North met with both Secord and Calero on the most immediate aircraft needs of the FDN and the resupply operation. They decided that their first need was a C-7 Caribou, a twin-engine propeller aircraft capable of carrying a 5,000-pound cargo over a 900-mile range. By November 1985, Gadd, whose task it was to locate and purchase the airplanes, had found three surplus C-123 airplanes belonging to a Latin American Air Force. Gadd had earlier formed Amalgamated Commercial Enterprises (ACE), a shelf company registered in Panama, to hold title to the aircraft. ACE

was owned equally by Gadd and Southern Air Transport of Miami, which was to provide maintenance and other logistical support.

The logistics director of the Latin American Air Force was unwilling to sell the airplanes—whose use was for military transport—to Gadd without a sign of official U.S. Government approval. So, Gadd turned to North for assistance, who decided to intercede in an effort to obtain the airplanes. North told Gadd and Secord that he requested both Robert McFarlane and the State Department's assistance. On November 15, North indicated in his notebook that he called "Elliott" "re call to [the Latin American country]" for the purpose of telling [that country] that "ACE is OK." Abrams, however, denied any knowledge of the planes belonging to the Latin American country's Air Force. In addition, North asked Vince Cannistraro, a colleague at the NSC, to intercede with the Latin American country. Nonetheless, the Government of the Latin American country did not approve, and the Enterprise had to look elsewhere.

## Country 3 Comes Through

More third-country money was needed to support the Contras. McFarlane had barred a return to Country 2, and John K. Singlaub had since the end of 1984 been trying unsuccessfully to obtain money from Country 3 [Taiwan].

In the summer of 1985, North turned to Gaston Sigur, a Senior Director for Far Eastern and Asian Affairs on the NSC staff, to seek his assistance with Country 3. According to Sigur, North told him that it was an "emergency situation," and that he and

McFarlane were aware that Country 3 "might have an interest in giving some assistance, financial assistance in the humanitarian area to the Contras." North, too, testified that he had gone to Sigur with the knowledge, and approval, of McFarlane. McFarlane testified to the contrary, claiming that he was "firm" with North "in saying to him absolutely no participation by you or any other staff member in any kind of approach to this country."

Sigur recalled that when North asked him to set up the meeting, he inquired, "[N]ow everything here is quite legal?" to which North replied, "[O]h yes, we have checked all that out and there is no question about that."

Sigur met with a Country 3 official and, without mentioning any specific amount of money, learned that the representative needed "to go back to his home government on it." The same day, Sigur went to McFarlane and told him that any contribution from Country 3 would have to be made directly through U.S. Government channels. According to Sigur, "Mr. McFarlane's response to that was that this is not possible, that cannot be done, and so I saw that as the end of that, and I told Colonel North about it."

North was not deterred. He asked Sigur to arrange a face-to-face meeting with the Country 3 representative. At the ensuing meeting at the Hay-Adams Hotel in the fall of 1985, North told the Country 3 representative that "this country [U.S.] would be very grateful if they were to make the contribution." North's plea was successful. Sometime later, the Country 3 official responded with a $1 million contribution in "humanitarian" assistance. North then sent Owen to give the official an envelope containing the

Swiss bank number of the Enterprise's Lake Resources account. The $1 million was transferred to Lake Resources and another $1 million followed in the early months of 1986.

## The Link With NHAO

Without the knowledge of its supervisors, the Nicaraguan Humanitarian Assistance Office (NHAO) program was used to further the Enterprise's activities. Robert Owen became the first link between NHAO and the covert operation. In mid-September 1985, Owen applied to Ambassador Duemling for a position in the humanitarian aid office. North recommended Owen as a "can do" person "who knows the scene," but Duemling declined to hire him.

Duemling still refused to hire Owen even after the three directors of the United Nicaraguan Opposition (UNO)—Calero, Arturo Cruz, and Alfonso Robelo—wrote Duemling requesting Owens help. North, however, continued to press for Owen's employment. At a Restricted Interagency Group meeting on October 11, North complained about the October 10 NHAO resupply flight impounded by Central American authorities, claiming that it would never have happened if Owen had been working for NHAO. Only then did Duemling relent and agree to fund a UNO contract with Owen's company, the Institute for Democracy, Education and Assistance, Inc. (IDEA), to assist in disbursing the humanitarian aid.

North exploited Owen's new position by using his trips, funded by humanitarian aid dollars, to transfer and receive information about the Contra war and the fledgling resupply operation. Following his trips to Central America, Owen would submit two reports—one to NHAO describing humanitarian services performed and another to North describing his activities in coordinating lethal aid. The grant agreement with the State Department barred Owen from performing "any service" related to lethal supply "during the term of this grant."

## NEW LEGISLATION— CONGRESSIONAL SUPPORT INCREASES

On November 21, 1985, the Senate agreed to a conference report on the Intelligence Authorization Bill providing two significant Contra support measures: the CIA was granted additional money to provide communications equipment to the Contras and the bill specifically provided that the State Department was not precluded from soliciting third countries for humanitarian assistance. The U.S. Government was still barred from expending funds to provide lethal assistance to the Contras but, according to North, "the instructions were to bite off a little at a time and start moving back toward full support."

**In December 1985, Poindexter, just appointed as National Security Adviser, took a quick trip through Central America, ostensibly to meet regional leaders but actually to assure them that the U.S. intended to "pursue a victory" against the Sandinistas, according to a memo by North. Poindexter was also briefed on the secret Santa Elena airstrip being built in Costa Rica. Poindexter said he told the President about the airstrip when he got back.**

## Legislative Plans and a New Finding

At a January 10, 1986, NSC meeting, the first in 15 months on Nicaragua, the President heard the views of his advisers. CIA Director Casey described a buildup of Soviet weaponry and increasing Sandinista repression in Nicaragua; Admiral William J. Crowe, Jr., discussed the inability of the Department of Defense to provide logistical assistance that the Contras badly needed; and Secretary Shultz voiced his approval for resumption of Congressional funding for a covert program. The President ended the meeting by instructing his advisers to prepare to go back to Congress with a request for full funding ($100 million) of a covert action program.

A week after the meeting, the President signed a new Finding on Nicaragua, consolidating what had been separate Findings governing various aspects of the program. The Finding authorized the CIA to implement the newly granted aid and to establish the communications network for which Congress had just provided funding.

## The Resupply Operation Begins

In January 1986, the plans set in motion by North in the fall of 1985 were beginning to give shape to the resupply operation. Gadd recruited flight crews, agreed with Southern Air Transport that it would handle all aircraft maintenance, and purchased the first aircraft, a C-7 Caribou. A team was also sent to Santa Elena and construction of the airstrip began in earnest. Moreover, the problem of secure communications was solved with the help of the National Security Agency.

According to North, both Casey and Poindexter had told him to seek some type of secure communications support. North turned to the National Security Agency for secure communications equipment.

The National Security Agency provided KL-43 encryption devices to North. On January 15, North gave KL-43s to the principal members of the covert operation: Secord, Gadd, Steele, Castillo, Quintero, and William Langton, president of Southern Air Transport. North also put a device in his office at the Old Executive Office Building. Each month newly keyed material was distributed to the group to enable them to communicate with each other in a secure manner.

Throughout January 1986, North also pursued discussions with Steele and CIA representatives about arrangements for using the Airbase and for establishing the airstrip at Santa Elena. North's notebooks indicate a series of telephone conversations with Steele relating to obtaining the permission of Central American officials for the resupply aircraft to operate from the Airbase.

During that same period, North wrote to Poindexter that General John Galvin, Commander of U.S. Southern Command, was "cognizant of the activities under way in both Costa Rica and at [the Airbase] in support of the DRF [Democratic Resistance Force]." North added, "Gen. Galvin is enthusiastic about both endeavors."

In February, after consultation with Enrique Bermudez and various commanders connected with the Southern front, North and Secord decided to deliver approximately 90,000 pounds of small arms and ammunition geared for airdrop to the FDN, which also could be delivered to the Southern front. This was the first delivery of arms that North and Secord provided to the Contras without payment from them and out of funds that had been contributed directly to the Enterprise.

Yet by February, supply problems still plagued the operation. There was only one plane at the Airbase, and it was damaged. On its arrival flight, the C-7 plane had developed mechanical problems. The crew jettisoned spare parts, and even training manuals, but the plane crash-landed nonetheless.

Faced with the Contras' requests for resupply and lacking aircraft to perform the job, North sought to deliver arms to the Contra soldiers using aircraft that had been chartered by NHAO to take humanitarian supplies from the United States to Central America.

In February 1986, North called Gadd at home and told him to charter an NHAO flight from New Orleans to the Airbase in Central America. Once the plane arrived at the Airbase, it was directed to an FDN base where ammunition and lethal supplies were loaded and airdropped to the FDN. NHAO later refused to pay for the portion of the charter that covered the delivery of lethal supplies.

In the South, however, the Contra forces remained without necessary supplies.

## Lethal Deliveries Begin

By the end of March 1986, the C-7 Caribou aircraft was operating and flights finally began to ferry lethal and nonlethal supplies for the FDN in the North. But the problem of resupplying the Southern front remained.

On March 28, Owen wrote to North that he, Steele, Rodriguez, and Quintero reached a consensus on what steps had to be taken to successfully resupply the South: lethal and nonlethal supplies should be stockpiled at the Airbase; the Caribou or better yet a C-123 should load at the Airbase, deliver to the South, and refuel at Santa Elena on the return to the Airbase; and the Southern Air Transport L-100 should be used until Santa Elena was prepared to refuel the C-7 and C-123.

While Gadd completed the purchase of a second C-7 Caribou and the first C-123 in early April, North responded to the growing needs of the southern forces. Between early April and April 11, North coordinated virtually every aspect of the first drop of lethal supplies into Nicaragua by way of the Southern front. He was in regular communication with Secord and others to ensure that the drop was successful. KL-43 messages among the planners involved in this drop show both the level of detail in which North was concerned and the coordination among various U.S. Government agencies to ensure that the drop succeeded. The first message, from North to Secord, established the essential elements of the drop:

The unit to which we wanted to drop in the southern quadrant of Nicaragua is in desperate need of ordnance resupply. . . . Have therefore developed an alternative plan which [Chief of the CIA's CATF] has been briefed on and in which he concurs. The L-100 which flies from MSY [New Orleans] to [an FDN base] on Wednesday should terminate it's NHAO mission on arrival at [the FDN base]. At that point it should load the supplies at [the Airbase] which—theoretically [the CIA's Chief of

Station in the Central American country] is assembling today at [the FDN base]—and take them to [the Airbase]. These items should then be transloaded to the C-123. . . . On any night between Wednesday, Apr 9, and Friday, Apr 11 these supplies should be dropped by the C-123 in the vicinity of [drop zone inside Nicaragua]. The A/C shd penetrate Nicaragua across the Atlantic Coast. . . . If we are ever going to take the pressure off the northern front we have got to get this drop in—quickly. Please make sure that this is retransmitted via this channel to [Castillo], Ralph, Sat and Steele. Owen already briefed and prepared to go w/ the L-100 out of MSY if this will help. Please advise soonest.

Secord and Gadd arranged to lease the L-100 plane from Southern Air Transport. Secord transmitted the following instructions to Quintero on April 8:

CIA and Goode [North's code name] report Blackys [a Southern front military commandante] troops in south in desperate fix. Therefore, [CIA's Chief of Station in a Central American country] is supposed to arrange for a load to come from [the FDN base] to [the Airbase] via L100 tomorrow afternoon. . . . Notify Steele we intend to drop tomorrow nite or more like Thurs nite. . . . Meanwhile, contact [Castillo] via this machine and get latest on DZ [drop zone] coordinates and the other data I gave you the format for. . . . CIA wants the aircraft to enter the DZ area from the Atlantic. . . .

On April 9, Secord relayed to North that "all coordination now complete at [the Airbase] for drop—[Castillo] has provided the necessary inputs." After the Southern military commanders relayed the drop zone information to Castillo's communications center, Castillo sent a cable to the Chief of the CATF at CIA headquarters, requesting flight path information, vectors based on the coordinates of the drop zone, and hostile risk evaluation to be passed to the crew. CIA headquarters provided the information, as it did on three other occasions that spring.

After Secord's April 9 message, the L-100 arrived and was loaded with a considerable store of munitions for airdrop to the South on April 10. Castillo had provided the location of the drop zone to Quintero, and Steele told the Southern Air Transport crew how to avoid Sandinista radar. Despite North's intricate planning, the L-100 was unable to locate the Contra forces. The maiden flight to the Southern front had failed.

On April 11, the L-100 tried again, airdropping more than 20,000 pounds of lethal supplies inside Nicaragua. This was the first successful drop to the southern forces. Before the plane left, Steele checked the loading of the cargo, including whether the assault rifles were properly padded.

## THE RESUPPLY OPERATION STEPS UP ITS ACTIVITIES

While the April 11 mission to the South was the only successful airdrop in that region, the air resupply operation was, by April, operating regular, almost daily, supply missions for the FDN in the North. Most missions delivered supplies from the main FDN base to the FDN's forward-operating positions. Other flights dropped lethal cargo to units operating inside Nicaragua. Many of these flights were helped informally by CIA field officers on the ground, who prepared flight plans for aerial resupply missions, brief the air crews on Nicaraguan antiaircraft installations, and

provided minor shop supplies to the mechanics. On one occasion, the CIA operations officer at an FDN base flew Ian Crawford, a loadmaster for the resupply operation, in a CIA helicopter with lethal supplies on board over the border area so Crawford could see where he and his crew were airdropping cargo three to four times daily. However, the resupply operation was not without problems. Poor maintenance hampered the performance of the aircraft and a lack of a closely knit organization contributed to the Enterprise's troubles.

Secord took another step to overcome the resupply problems. He recruited Col. Robert Dutton to manage the resupply operation on a daily basis. Secord knew Dutton from their active duty together in the U.S. Air Force, where Dutton had considerable experience in managing covert air resupply operations. Gadd's role was phased out and on May 1, Dutton, retiring from the Air Force, was placed in operational command of the resupply operation, reporting to Secord, and increasingly over time, directly to North on all operational decisions of consequence.

At the outset, Secord emphasized to Dutton that the air program would receive very little in the way of additional funding. Dutton was instructed to manage the operation with existing equipment and conserve resources carefully as the money provided was all "donated."

When Dutton took over, he traveled to Central America to assess the operation. There were approximately 19 pilots, loadmasters and maintenance operators at the Airbase. In addition, Felix Rodriguez and his associate Ramon Medina coordinated with the Commander and oversaw the local fuel account. Dutton also examined the aircraft—two C-7s, one C-123, and the

Maule—and found that, indeed, they were in "very poor operating condition."

The resupply operation at the Airbase maintained a warehouse stocked with an assortment of munitions—light machine guns, assault rifles, ammunition, mortars, grenades, C-4 explosive, parachute rigging, uniforms, and other military paraphernalia. The crews lived in three safe houses and used a separate office with maps and communications equipment. By May, the Santa Elena airstrip, along with emergency fuel storage space and temporary housing, was finished.

Because Secord (and later North) had impressed on Dutton the need for strict accountability given the limited nature of the donated funds, Dutton enforced a stringent set of accounting requirements: Expenditures had to be carefully documented and all missions fully reported. Moreover, Dutton devised an organization, based on a military hierarchy, that delineated each person's role and responsibility. Dutton also defined the legal constraints on the organization as he had understood from Secord: no Contra combatants could be airdropped into battle. These new requirements of accountability, reporting, and organization were followed for the remaining life of the operation.

Despite these impending changes, North wrote to Poindexter expressing his weariness and warning that without Congressional authorization for CIA involvement, "we will run increasing risks of trying to manage this program from here with the attendant physical and political liabilities. I am not complaining, and you know that I love the work, but we have to lift some of this onto the CIA so that I can get more than 2–3 hrs. of sleep at night."

## The Southern Front Resupply

On May 24, 1986, the day after Dutton left Central America, another planeload of munitions, paid for by the Enterprise arrived at the Airbase for the Southern front. Because the FDN was reluctant to make arms available to the independent southern Contra forces, North and Secord decided in April 1986 that arms and other supplies would now be stored under the control of the Enterprise at the Airbase. This second direct shipment of arms to the Airbase to be delivered to the Southern front was part of the new plan. Together with the late April shipment, there were now more than $1 million in arms at the Airbase available for airdrop to the Southern front forces.

The warehouse, however, was not large enough to accommodate the new munitions. Dutton had to ask the Commander for permission to expand the warehouse, while seeking North's approval for the additional cost of construction. After the Commander authorized the expansion, North relayed to Secord his approval for construction to proceed.

With new arms and an expanded warehouse, Dutton had the material to deliver to the Southern front. However, while regular deliveries with the C-7 continued to the FDN in the North, no flights were being made to the South. North told Dutton that the Southern forces were adding 150 new recruits a day, but that they had neither enough weapons for the fighters nor enough medicine to treat the growing problem of mountain leprosy.

On June 2, Castillo called North and told him that drops to the southern units were needed as soon as possible. Castillo advised North that Quintero had all the necessary vector information to make the drops. Following Castillo's request, two deliveries were prepared for the South totalling about 39,000 pounds, and on June 9, after coordinating with Castillo the location and needs of the Southern troops, the C-123 airplane tried to make an air drop. However, the plane could not locate the troops inside Nicaragua, and when it landed at the Santa Elena airstrip, it got stuck in the mud.

The stuck plane caused consternation at the U.S. Embassy in Costa Rica. The month before, Oscar Arias had been inaugurated as the new President of Costa Rica. The new Costa Rican Government had told Ambassador Tambs that it had instructed that the airstrip not be utilized. Tambs, in turn, told Castillo to notify North and Udall Corporation that the airstrip had to be closed. Now Tambs was faced with explaining to President Arias why a munitions-laden airplane was stuck in the mud at Santa Elena. A plan was devised by Tambs, Castillo, and others at the U.S. Embassy to borrow trucks from a nearby facility to free the aircraft, but the plane was able to take off before the plan could be carried out.

The needs of the FDN still had to be met. On June 10, North met with Calero who requested that the Caribou planes fly more missions inside Nicaragua. The Enterprise was just about to purchase additional arms for the FDN. However, the most pressing need, North wrote to Poindexter, was neither money nor arms, but rather: "to get the CIA re-engaged in this effort so that it can be better managed than it now is by one slightly confused Marine Lt. Col." North further reported to Poindexter that "several million rounds of ammo are now on hand . . . Critically needed items are being flown in from Europe to the expanded warehouse facility at

[the Airbase]. At this point, the only liability we still have is one of Democracy, Inc.'s airplanes is mired in the mud (it is the rainy season down there) on the secret field in Costa Rica."

Despite the difficulties, North wanted to continue to airdrop supplies, especially to the South. As soon as the C-123 was freed from the mud, it embarked on another mission with a full lethal load for the southern troops. But this time, fog covered a mountain, and William Cooper, the chief pilot for the resupply operation, hit the top of a tree, knocking out an engine. After the plane reached the drop zone, Cooper could not locate the troops.

Communicating by KL-43, North told Castillo that to facilitate further airdrops to the southern forces, he had "asked Ralph [Quintero] to proceed immediately to your location. I do not think we ought to contemplate these operations without him being on scene. Too many things go wrong that then directly involve you and me in what should be deniable for both of us."

## ALTERNATIVE FUNDING SOURCES: NORTH'S RESPONSE TO CONGRESSIONAL ACTION

The Administration continued to seek an appropriation for the CIA to resume its program of covert assistance to the Contras. In early May, according to Poindexter, the President told him, "If we can't move the Contra package before June 9, I want to figure out a way to take action unilaterally to provide assistance." Poindexter wrote his deputy, Donald Fortier, "The President is ready to confront the Congress on the Constitutional question of who controls foreign policy. . . . George [Shultz] agrees with the President that we have to find some way and we will not pull out."

North, who received a copy of Poindexter's PROF note, responded immediately with a suggestion: The Contras should capture some territory inside Nicaragua and set up a provisional government. The President would respond by recognizing the Contras as the true government and provide support. Asked by Poindexter whether he had talked to Casey about his plan, North replied, "Yes, in general terms. He is supportive, as is Elliott [Abrams]. It is, to say the least, a high risk option—but it may be the only way we can ever get this thing to work."

## The Money: Third Country Assistance

By the end of April 1986, the Contras' funding needs were critical. North told Fortier: "We need to explore this problem urgently or there won't be a force to help when the Congress finally acts." The same day, North wrote to McFarlane that "the resistance support acct. is darned near broke," and asked for assistance in filling the gap:

> Any thoughts where we can put our hands on a quick $3–5M? Gaston [Sigur] is going back to his friends who have given $2M so far in hopes that we can bridge things again, but time is running out along w/ the money.

### An Aborted Solicitation

Despite North's reference to "Gaston," it was not Gaston Sigur, but Singlaub who went to the Far East in May 1986 in search of Contra aid. This time, Singlaub wanted to be sure that he would receive the official U.S. "signal" these countries had previously told him was a condition to their aid. Before he traveled to Countries 3 and 5, Singlaub spoke to Elliott Abrams at the State Department and, according to Singlaub, explained that he wanted to know "how the U.S. would send a signal." Singlaub testified that Abrams told him that he (Abrams) would send the signal.

Singlaub arrived in Country 3, but before he could meet with his contact, Abrams told him to stop the plan. When Singlaub and Abrams later met, Singlaub testified that Abrams told him that the solicitation was "going to be handled by someone at the highest level." Singlaub assumed that it would be someone from the White House, although Abrams never gave him a specific name. However, Abrams disputed Singlaub's testimony. While acknowledging that he spoke to Singlaub about Singlaub's proposed solicitation, Abrams testified that he never agreed to provide to Singlaub a U.S. Government signal for the solicitation. Abrams' account is supported by the testimony of Richard Melton, at the time Director of the Office of Central American Affairs at the State Department, who was present during Abrams' conversations with Singlaub.

## The May 16, 1986, NSPG Meeting

On May 16, 1986, the President and his advisers discussed the issue of obtaining funds from third countries. In a memorandum to the President for the National Security Planning Group (NSPG) meeting, North suggested three ways to "bridge the gap" in funding: (1) a reprogramming of funds from DOD to the CIA ($15 million in humanitarian aid); (2) a Presidential appeal for private donations by U.S. citizens; and (3) a "direct and very private Presidential overture to certain Heads of State." The last source of funds would, as North put it, eliminate the need "to endure further domestic partisan political debate."

Director Casey opened the meeting and explained the Contras' needs. The good news, he told the President, was that the Contras had infiltrated more troops into Nicaragua than ever before, and the troops were now being resupplied by air. The "bad news" was that the Resistance was operating under the assumption that it would receive new funding at the end of May. Only $2 million remained from the humanitarian assistance appropriation.

Later in the discussion, Secretary Shultz returned to the Contras' need for funds. Noting the unlikelihood of an immediate Congressional appropriation and the improbability that the intelligence committees could be persuaded to reprogram funds, Secretary Shultz suggested that third countries be approached for humanitarian aid. North added that the Intelligence Authorization Act of 1986 permitted the State Department to approach other governments for non-military aid.

No one at the meeting discussed the fact that Country 2 had already given $32 million to the Contras, including a $24 million donation committed to the President personally. Nor was it mentioned that several Far Eastern countries had been approached for donations or that Country 3 had given $2 million only 6 months earlier. Instead, Shultz was instructed to prepare for review by the President a list of countries that could be solicited.

Later that day, North told Poindexter that the urgency of the need had lessened: The Enterprise had that day received the last $5 million of the $15 million arms sales to Iran. North wrote Poindexter: "You should be aware that the resistance support organization now has more than $6 million available for immediate disbursement. This reduces the need to go to third countries for help." North later testified that he wrote the message because "it was important he [Poindexter] understand that Secretary Shultz didn't need to go out that afternoon and go ask for additional help." Poindexter testified that he understood the $6 million to which North referred was coming from the Iranian arms sales, but he did not tell the President the $6 million was available. North testified that as he was leaving the NSPG meeting, he mentioned to Poindexter that Iran was supplying $6 million for the Contras, but that he did not know whether he was overheard.

North wrote Poindexter that he did not know whether all those present at the NSPG meeting, such as Chief of Staff Donald Regan, knew of "my private U.S. operation." On the other hand, North noted to Poindexter, "the President obviously knows why he has been meeting with several select people to thank them for their 'support for Democracy' in CentAm."

North also realized that disclosure of a significant sum of money earmarked for Contra support, but only made possible by arms sales to Iran, could prove politically embarrassing.

Poindexter approved North's recommendation to seek the $15 million reprogramming and responded to his concerns: "Go ahead and work up the paper needed for the $15M reprogramming. . . . I understand your concerns and agree. I just didn't want you to bring it up at NSPG. I guessed at what you were going to say. Don Regan knows very little of your operation and that is just as well."

Meanwhile, the concerns that prompted North's silence at the May 16 NSPG meeting persisted: Who knew about the secret aid third countries had given earlier? In the prior 2 years, members of the NSC staff had approached several countries for financial assistance to the Contras. Of these, two had provided funds or other forms of assistance. Those solicitations were made without the knowledge of the Secretary of State and other senior diplomatic officials.

The December amendment expressly provided that solicitations for humanitarian aid were not precluded. Now, Secretary Shultz and others were discussing making approaches to countries that had already contributed. Poindexter and North became concerned that their prior actions would be uncovered.

North recommended that Poindexter and McFarlane meet to discuss "how much Sec Shultz does or does not know abt [Country 2 and 3] so that we don't make any mistakes." Poindexter declined to follow North's advice: "To my knowledge Shultz knows nothing about the prior financing. I think it should stay that way."

Nonetheless, McFarlane informed Secretary Shultz. As the Secretary described the event, on June 16, 1986, he received a telephone call on a secure phone from McFarlane, who had by then been out of the Government for approximately 6 months. In a conversation that occurred completely out of context and long after the donation had been made, McFarlane told Secretary Shultz about the Country 2 donation to the Contras.

Soon thereafter, Abrams recommended Brunei as a likely country from which to seek humanitarian assistance for the Contras. As

Poindexter put it, "[t]hey have lots of money." Brunei also qualified for another reason. The Secretary of State did not want to be beholden to any country that was a recipient of U.S. aid. Brunei was not. Originally, the Secretary of State was to make the approach during a meeting with the Sultan of Brunei in June. Before Secretary Shultz left, Abrams asked North for a Contra account to which the money could be sent. North directed his secretary to prepare an index card with the account number on it. North told Abrams that the account was controlled by the Contras and Abrams so informed Secretary Shultz. Following Poindexter's instructions, North did not reveal that the NSC staff "had access to the accounts." North gave the index card to Abrams, who gave it to the Secretary of State. The Secretary decided, however, that he would discuss the general issue of Central America with the Sultan but that he would not make an actual solicitation. The card was not used on that trip.

On August 8, 1986, Abrams met in London with a representative of the Government of Brunei. In an unusual occurrence for Abrams, he traveled under an alias. The two men first met at a London hotel, then walked in a nearby park where Abrams requested $10 million in bridge financing for the Contras. Asked by the official what Brunei would receive in return, Abrams responded, "Well, . . . the President will know of this, and you will have the gratitude of the Secretary and of the President for helping us out in this jam." The official persisted, asking, "What concrete do we get out of this?" Abrams responded, "You don't get anything concrete out of it." Abrams then gave the account number that he had received from North to the Brunei official.

Although the Sultan of Brunei eventually

transferred the $10 million, the funds never reached the account for which they were intended. North testified that he had intended to give Abrams the number of the Lake Resources account controlled by Secord and Hakim, but the account numbers had been inadvertently transposed by North or by his secretary, Fawn Hall.

## Felix Rodriguez Becomes Disaffected

Shortly after North traveled to Central America in late April 1986, Rodriguez decided to leave Central America. Rodriguez testified: "I don't know if I got a sixth feeling or something, but after I saw the people in there, I didn't feel comfortable with it and I thought we had better leave." Rodriguez informed Steele, citing fatigue as the reason for his departure.

Rodriguez met with Vice President Bush in Washington on May 1. He had arranged the meeting through the Vice President's National Security Adviser, Donald Gregg. The appointment scheduling memo for the meeting states: "To brief the Vice President on the status of the war in [El Salvador] and resupply of the Contras." Members of the Vice President's staff gave conflicting testimony over how this description was printed on his schedule. Sam Watson, the Vice President's Deputy National Security Adviser, testified that the memo was inaccurate, and that he did not provide the description. Phyllis Byrne, the secretary who typed the memo, testified that Watson had given her the description.

In the Old Executive Office Building on his way to the Vice President's office, Rodriguez stopped by to tell North he was leaving the operation. Rodriguez said North asked him to remain in Central America, but he ignored the request. Escorted by Gregg and Watson, Rodriguez then met with the Vice President.

Before Rodriguez could tell the Vice President that he was leaving Central America, North arrived and told the Vice President about the good job Rodriguez was doing. Embarrassed to tell the Vice President he was going to leave, Rodriguez left the meeting without discussing his resignation, and eventually returned to Central America. Rodriguez testified that "at no point in any of this conversation did I ever mention doing anything that was remotely connected to Nicaragua and the contras." Moreover, former Senator Nicholas Brady, who was also present at the meeting, testified that the resupply operation was not discussed.

Rodriguez stayed in Central America, but his relationship with Dutton became increasingly strained. According to Dutton, they disagreed on how the operation should be run. At the same time, North had his own reservations that Rodriguez was "something of a loose cannon" who might reveal the operation.

Rodriguez was summoned to meet with North and Dutton in Washington on June 25. Rodriguez testified that at the end of the meeting, he asked to see North alone. Rodriguez told North that he had learned "that people are stealing here," in particular Thomas Clines, a former associate of Edwin Wilson. Rodriguez expressed his concerns that arms were being sold at inflated prices. North disputed Rodriguez's conclusions and told Rodriguez that Clines was a patriot, and that he was not buying equipment, only helping to transport the goods. In fact, none of the arms furnished to the FDN and the

Southern front since Rodriguez became involved in the operation were sold to the Contras. Instead, the Enterprise purchased arms with money obtained from the arms sales to Iran and private U.S. donors.

At the close of the meeting, according to Rodriguez, North made one last comment. Congress was voting that day on the $100-million Contra aid legislation, and the television in North's office carried the floor debate. According to Rodriguez, North looked at the television and said: "Those people want me but they cannot touch me because the old man loves my ass." North did not recall that part of his conversation with Rodriguez. That meeting was the last between the two.

## New Legislation

On June 25, 1986 the House approved the Administration's request for $100 million in Contra aid. The $100 million aid package marked the first time in more than 2 years that the House had voted to provide lethal assistance to the Contras. By June 1986, North had established air resupply to both the Northern and Southern fronts. The Enterprise had succeeded in flying lethal material to the Contra fighters inside Nicaragua; even Americans in the employ of North's organization were flying into that country, all financed by donated funds and proceeds from the Iranian arms sales overseen by North. None of North's activities were disclosed to Congress in advance of the House vote. Only 1 month later, before the aid bill had been signed, Poindexter would write to Congress that the NSC was complying with the letter and spirit of the Boland Amendment.

## Selling the Assets to the CIA

With the House vote in June, North's hopes to reengage the CIA in Nicaragua were on the verge of being realized. North was increasingly occupied with the Iran arms initiative, and he was anxious to give the Contra resupply operation back to the CIA. But North wanted the Enterprise to recoup its investment, and urged the CIA to buy the assets of the resupply operation in Central America.

Secord had Dutton prepare a plan to present to the CIA. North wrote to Poindexter:

We are rapidly approaching the point where the PROJECT DEMOCRACY [PRODEM] assets in CentAm need to be turned over to CIA for use in the new program. The total value of the assets (six aircraft, warehouses, supplies, maintenance facilities, ships, boats, leased houses, vehicles, ordnance, munitions, communications equipment, and a 6520' runway on property owned by a PRODEM proprietary) is over $4.5M.

All of the assets—and the personnel—are owned/paid by overseas companies with no U.S. connection. All of the equipment is in first rate condition and is already in place. It wd be ludicrous for this to simply disappear just because CIA does not want to be "tainted" with picking up the assets and then have them spend $8–10M of the $100M to replace it—weeks or months later. Yet, that seems to be the direction they are heading, apparently based on NSC guidance.

If you have already given Casey instructions to this effect, I wd vy much like to talk to you about it in hopes that we can reclaim the issue. All seriously believe that immediately after the Senate vote the DRF [Nicaraguan Democratic Resistance] will be subjected to a major Sandinista effort to break them before the U.S. aid can become effective. PRODEM currently has the only assets available to support the DRF and the CIA's most ambitious estimate is 30 days after a bill is signed before their own assets will be available. This will be a disaster for the DRF if they have to wait that long. North predicted "disaster" if his plan was not followed.

The plan drafted by Dutton at Secord's request offered two options. The first was to sell the assets of the organization to the CIA at cost; the second would continue the operation on behalf of the CIA for a monthly fee. The plan indicated a preference for a sale because the funds generated would permit the Enterprise to engage in other covert action projects: "[W]e prefer option I with the proceeds from the sale going back into a fund for continued similar requirements."

North testified that the idea to sell the Enterprise's assets to the CIA was Director Casey's.

Concluding his efforts to "sell" the project, North offered to send Poindexter a copy of Dutton's "prospectus," or, as he wrote, "the PROJECT DEMOCRACY status report. It is useful, nonattributable reading."

Poindexter responded that he had not given Casey any "guidance" against the sale and, indeed, that he approved of North's plan. Poindexter explained that he had told CIA Deputy Director Robert Gates "the private effort should be phased out," but he agreed with North and asked him to talk to Casey about the plan to sell Project Democracy to the CIA.

Clair George, the CIA Deputy Director for Operations, testified that North asked him to buy the aircraft, but that he declined because their use in private resupply could result in criticism of the CIA. "I wouldn't

buy those planes if they were the last three planes in Central America," he said.

**Through the summer, the people running the resupply operation continued to bicker, and an argument developed over who really owned the airplanes. In August, Felix Rodriguez even "made off with an airplane," North complained in one memo. The arguments back and forth brought the operation to a halt for a short time, until the warring parties reached an uneasy truce, mediated by Colonel Steele.**

During the fall of 1986, problems continued in the resupply operation, but some success on both the Northern and Southern fronts was finally achieved. The resupply operation delivered more than 180,000 pounds of lethal supplies to the Southern front in September alone.

In late August, North attended a Restricted Interagency Group meeting at which the Chief of the CATF and others were asked what steps the airlift—i.e., according to North, the "covert operation being conducted by this government to support the Nicaraguan Resistance"—should take now that the CIA was due to assume control. According to North, he described at that meeting the activities in which the Enterprise was engaged and sought approval from the Restricted Interagency Group to continue until the CIA could take over. While the Chief of CATF acknowledged that North discussed airdrops to the Contras, he testified that he did not recall North discussing "his full service covert action program."

On August 22, Dutton met with Quintero and devised a new plan for Southern front resupply that he presented to North: The initial arrival over the drop zone should be at dusk; once the zone has been identified by the pilots, repeated sequential drops would be made in the evening without communication to the troops. Castillo agreed with the plan, as did Steele. North also approved it.

On September 4, North met with Poindexter. North asked Poindexter for the "go/no go" on sequential air deliveries to the Southern forces. Shortly afterwards, North told Secord to implement the new drop plan and conduct a "force feed" operation to the South where all supplies would be delivered sequentially in accordance with Dutton's plan.

On September 9, Dutton flew with the crew in the second C-123 (now operational) inside southern Nicaragua to attempt a lethal drop to the troops Castillo had identified. But this mission was unable to locate the troops, prompting Dutton to propose to North using two aircraft on each mission to increase delivery potential once troops were located and to protect against increased Sandinista antiaircraft fire. Dutton also asked North for help on weather information and troop location. North approved the use of two aircraft and told Dutton to obtain weather information from Steele, and that he would speak to Castillo about troop locations. North cautioned Dutton not to personally fly inside Nicaragua again: The operation could not afford the exposure if the plane were shot down inside Nicaragua with Col. Robert Dutton at the controls.

The pace of delivery stepped up. The resupply operation was finally becoming effective only weeks before the CIA would be back in the business. On September 11, a lethal drop was successfully made to the South using the C-123 while the C-7 delivered more arms for the FDN in the northern regions. Dutton reported the success of the southern delivery to North. On the 12th, three aircraft made more deliveries: a C-123

delivered 10,000 pounds to the South and a C-7 and a Maule delivered to the FDN. September 13 was "a red letter day," Dutton wrote to North. All five aircraft flew at the same time, with lethal loads dropped in both the North and South. "The surge is now in full force," Dutton relayed to North. The plan at last was working.

Things were going so well that Dutton advised North that an additional $20,000 in cash was needed for the fuel fund and that the "C-123 is now armed with HK-21/7.62 machine gun on the aft ramp, bring on the MI-24 [attack helicopter]." In fact, before Dutton returned to Washington, he could report to North that "all troops should now have equipment. Will stand by for direction from [Castillo]. He already told us not to send any more to [a Southern commandante] for a while. Never thought we would hear that."

The "hand-to-mouth" operation that had limped along on limited resources for so long had, with the support of certain individuals, finally delivered the goods. Under North's direction, Dutton's operational control, Castillo's critical assistance in locating, dispatching, and scheduling the needs of the Southern troops, and Steele's coordination with the Commander, the South received arms, while deliveries continued apace to the FDN in the North. Indeed, for the rest of September, lethal drops were successfully made to both the FDN and the Southern forces. North duly reported the operation's success to Poindexter.

When Dutton returned from Central America later that month, he met with North. North asked him to arrange a 1-day trip to the region so that he could personally thank the pilots and crew. North told him, "Bob, you will never get a medal for this, but some day the President will shake your hand and thank you for it."

Dutton had also prepared a photograph album depicting the operation: the operational bases, drop zones, aircraft, munitions, and the crew replete with assault machine guns and other assorted weapons. Dutton showed the album to North, who liked it and said he wanted to show it to "the top boss." North testified that he sent the album to Poindexter to show to the President, but never heard further about the album. Poindexter testified that he did not show the album to the President.

## North Expands His Special Operations

Even with the $100 million in appropriated funds becoming available in the near future, North tried to get other aid for the Contras. In May, Israeli Defense Minister Yitzhak Rabin had offered to provide Israeli military advisers for the Southern front. Although nothing came of this offer, North and Rabin met again in September and discussed an Israeli transfer of Soviet bloc weapons to the Contras. Rabin wanted "to know if we had any need for SovBloc weaps and ammo he could make avail." Rabin asked whether North's ship, the *Erria*, had left the Mediterranean. When North responded that it was in Lisbon, Rabin suggested that it dock at Haifa and "have it filled w/whatever they cd assemble" of a "recently seized PLO shipment captured at sea."

Poindexter sanctioned the Israeli arms offer: "I think you should go ahead and make it happen. It can be a private deal between Dick [Secord] and Rabin that we bless. . . . Keep the pressure on Bill [Casey] to make

things right for Secord." Later, Poindexter cautioned "[a]bsolutely nobody else should know about this. Rabin should not say anything to anybody else except you or me." On September 15, North told Poindexter that "orders were passed to the ship this morning to proceed to Haifa to pick up the arms. Loading will be accomplished by Israeli military personnel."

Despite Poindexter's caution, North later recounted the offer in a memorandum briefing the President for a visit from Israeli Prime Minister Shimon Peres. North wrote that Prime Minister Peres was likely to raise certain sensitive issues, such as the transfer of Soviet bloc arms by the Israelis "for use by the Nicaraguan democratic resistance." North recommended: "If Peres raises this issue, it would be helpful if the President thanked him since the Israelis hold considerable stores of bloc ordinance compatible with what the Nicaraguan resistance now uses." Next to this sentence, Poindexter penciled: "Rabin. Very tightly held."

As another expansion of his special operations, North received an offer from a third party to engage in sabotage and other activities inside Nicaragua, to be financed with Enterprise funds [the Panamanian Government]. Poindexter approved the sabotoge plan, but instructed North not to become involved in conspiracy or assassinations. According to North, the plan was never implemented because North was dismissed.

## THE OPERATION BEGINS TO UNRAVEL: DISCLOSURE OF THE AIRSTRIP

Along with others in the Administration,

North had helped to prevent the disclosure of his operation to Congress. The extent of his involvement in Central America, however, made him open to exposure. Although the U.S. Congress was not told of North's role in supporting the Contras, Central American governments—including that in Managua—were aware of it. Eventually, one of those governments chose not to remain silent.

Early in the morning on September 6, North learned that a Costa Rican official was threatening to hold a press conference announcing the existence of the Santa Elena airfield and alleging violations of Costa Rican law by North, Secord, and Udall Resources. North immediately called Assistant Secretary Abrams and told him that the press conference had to be stopped. half an hour later, North had reached Ambassador Tambs and placed a conference call to Abrams.

President Arias was scheduled to visit the United States, and Abrams "instructed Tambs to advert to the visit in a way which made it clear to President Arias that his visit was at risk." Abrams testified, "It was supposed to be diplomatic, but the message was supposed to be clear." North's notes reflect the idea of a greater threat than the cancellation of a White House visit: "Conf. call to Elliott Abrams and Amb. Lew Tambs;—Tell Arias; —Never set foot in W.H.;—Never get 5 [cents] of $80M promised by McPherson." An hour or two later, Tambs had made the call (but did not threaten the cutoff of aid), and the press conference was cancelled.

In his report to Poindexter, North exaggerated his own role in the crisis. In a PROF note, North told Poindexter he had personally forestalled the crisis by calling the President of Costa Rica and threatening to cut off aid. North conceded to Poindexter that he may have overstepped the bounds of his authority: "I recognize that I was well beyond my charter in dealing with a head of state this way and in making threats/offers that may be impossible to deliver." Poindexter responded: "Thanks, Ollie, you did the right thing, but let's try to keep it quiet." North admitted in his testimony that he had not called President Arias. He claimed, instead, that the PROF message "was specifically cast the way it was to protect the other two parties engaged."

The Costa Rican officials were delayed but not deterred by the call. On September 25, Costa Rican authorities held a press conference announcing the discovery of a "secret airstrip in Costa Rica that was over a mile long and which had been built and used by a Co. called Udall Services for supporting the Contras." Olmstead was named as the man who set up the airfield as a "training base for U.S. military advisors."

The New York Times picked up the story. North, with assistance from Abrams and others, drafted press guidance for the Administration's response. The "guidance," approved by Poindexter, stated that the airstrip had been offered to the Costa Rican Government "by the owners of the property who had apparently decided to abandon plans for a tourism project." It concluded: "No U.S. Government funds were allocated or used in connection with this site nor were any U.S. Government personnel involved in its construction. Any further inquiries should be referred to the Government of Costa Rica." The U.S. Government's role in facilitating the construction of the airfield was concealed.

At the same time North was promoting this cover story, he suggested to Poindexter that steps be taken to "punish" the Costa Rican Government for the disclosure.

On September 30, North again argued that any attempt to benefit President Arias should be quashed: "Those who counsel such a course of action are unaware of the strategic importance of the air facility at Santa Elena and the damage caused by the Arias' government revelations."

## THE COVERT OPERATION ENDS

The triumph of the airlift was short-lived. When Bill Cooper wrote to Dutton in late September after another successful drop, "Ho-Hum, just another day at the office," Dutton warned him to be careful.

On October 5, a C-123 left the Airbase at 9:50 A.M. local time with 10,000 pounds of ammunition for a drop to the FDN inside Nicaragua. Cooper was in command, Buzz Sawyer the co-pilot, and Eugene Hasenfus the loadmaster who would actually drop the supplies. An FDN fighter was also on board for radio communications to the troops on the ground. Although the mission was to support the northern FDN forces, the plane flew a southern route to avoid Sandinista guns.

First reports had the plane missing. Castillo sent Southern front troops to look for the plane and Dutton notified North's office in an attempt to mount a search operation. Earl attempted to arrange for a U.S. military search and rescue mission, while friendly governments in the region also organized a discreet search effort. Felix Rodriguez called the Vice President's Deputy National Security Adviser at his home, telling him the plane could not be found. It was all to no

avail: the plane had been hit by a Sandinista SAM-7 over Nicaraguan territory. Three crew members were killed. Only Hasenfus survived, captured by the Sandinistas.

Abrams called North and asked him to arrange to retrieve the bodies. The State Department issued press statements claiming no U.S. involvement in the mission.

But the Enterprise had begun to unravel. The bodies of the crew were found bearing Southern Air Transport identification cards. The Federal Aviation Administration and the U.S. Customs Service began to investigate. With secrecy no longer possible, the resupply operation was shut down.

## PRESIDENTIAL AUTHORIZATION AND KNOWLEDGE

The President told the Tower Review Board that he did not know that the NSC staff was assisting the Contras. After the Tower Report was issued, the President stated that private support for the Contras was "my idea." In fact, the President knew of the contributions from Country 2. According to Poindexter, the President's policy was "to get what support we could from third countries."

In general, Poindexter understood that the President wanted the NSC staff to support the Contras, including encouraging private contributions. The President also knew, according to Poindexter, that North was the chief staff officer on Central America who was responsible for carrying out the President's general charter to keep the Contras alive. Poindexter regularly reported to the President on the status of the Contras, the fact that they were surviving, and "in general terms" North's role in facilitating their survival. As a result of these briefings, Poindexter thought that the President understood that both he and North were coordinating the effort to support the Contras. Poindexter also believed the President understood that "Col. North was instrumental in keeping the Contras supported without maybe understanding the details of exactly was he was doing."

As to the level of detail provided to the President on the Contra support operation, Poindexter testified that he:

> would not get into details with the President as to who was doing what. The President knew that there was a Boland Amendment, he knew there were restrictions on the government. As he has said, I think, since November of 1986, that he did not feel that the Boland Amendment applied to his personal staff and that that was his feeling all along. I knew that.

> He knew the Contras were being supported, and we simply didn't get into the details of exactly who was doing what.

Poindexter testified that on one occasion, he briefed the President with some specificity about the Contra support program, but understood that the President did not recall the briefing:

> Now, you know, the President doesn't recall apparently a specific briefing in which I laid out in great detail all of the ways that we were going about implementing the President's policy, and I frankly don't find that surprising. It would not, frankly, at the time have been a matter of great interest as to exactly how we were implementing the President's policy.

Without getting to the "extraneous detail[s]" of how the President's policy was being implemented, however, Poindexter briefed the President on the Santa Elena airstrip in Costa Rica. Poindexter testified that in December 1985, after he returned from Central America, he specifically briefed the President about the local assistance provided in establishing the airstrip. In addition, Poindexter informed the President that the "private individuals" were also involved in establishing the airstrip. At the same time, Poindexter excluded the "extraneous detail" that North, through Tambs and Castillo, had facilitated the construction of the airstrip. Similarly, while Poindexter thought that the President was aware of North's role in supporting the Contras, "it did not include something as specific as directing Col. North to conduct air supply operations." North testified that he believed that the President approved his efforts to resupply the war. In fact, his actions support that belief. While Poindexter testified that he did not show the photograph album detailing the operation to the President, North testified that he sent the album to the President through Poindexter and told Dutton that the President would thank Dutton for his efforts.

## CONCLUSION

Although the North-Secord resupply operation ended on a disastrous note, with the shooting down of the Hasenfus plane, North had successfully managed, with the approval of his superiors, the covert program to assist the Contras for almost 2 years. The covert program that North had developed inevitably created conflicts of loyalties and shadings of duties among the persons whom he coopted to assist him. Felix Rodriguez was a close associate of Donald Gregg, the National Security Adviser to the Vice President. Yet North instructed Rodriguez not to tell Gregg that he was secretly working for North, and Rodriguez testified that he complied until the summer of 1986. According to North, Director Casey wanted to insulate the CIA's career employees from North's operation so that the CIA could not be charged with a violation of the Boland Amendment. CIA officials admitted that, far from their traditional role, they "actively shunned information. We did not want to know how the Contras were being funded . . . we actively discouraged people from telling us things."

The CIA's attempt to remain uninformed failed as North sought out the assistance of CIA personnel in Central America. Particularly after Congress amended the law to allow the CIA to exchange intelligence with the Contras, many flights undertaken by the Enterprise were reported by CIA field offices to CIA headquarters; and at least one CIA Chief of Station provided information necessary for the Enterprise to make accurate airdrops and avoid Sandinista fire.

A CIA Chief of Station, the U.S. Ambassador to Costa Rica, and other operatives—both Government employees and private citizens—that North recruited with the approval of his superiors provided necessary support to his covert program of military support for the Contras. Yet throughout this time, the NSC staff repeatedly assured Congress that it was complying with the letter and spirit of the Boland Amendment.

The NSC staff's resupply operation provided essential support to the Contras' during 1986. Not only did North coordinate that effort, but he decided with Secord, after consulting the Contras' military commanders, what supplies were needed in order to conduct the entire Contra operation, both on the ground and in the air.

North directed the Enterprise's efforts on behalf of the Contras with Poindexter's approval and in the belief that the President likewise concurred. The result was that, with the help of other U.S. Government officials, North managed to provide to the Contras what Congress had not: a full-scale program of military assistance.

## Table 3-1.—Resupply Flights Made by the North/Secord Resupply Operation During 1986

These excerpts from the Committees' table—the first two months of airdrops compared with the final month—show how much more effective the resupply flights were at the end.

| DATE | AIRCRAFT | FDN/SOUTHERN | NOTES |
|------|----------|--------------|-------|
| 23 March 86 | C-7 Caribou | N/A | Local Flight-No Cargo |
| 24 March 86 | C-7 Caribou | N/A | Local Flight-No Cargo |
| 25 March 86 | C-7 Caribou | N/A | Local Flights-No Cargo |
| 26 March 86 | C-7 Caribou | N/A | 3 Local Flights-No Cargo |
| 28 March 86 | C-7 Caribou | N/A | 2 Local Flights |
| 28 March 86 | C-7 Caribou | N/A | 2 Local Flights |
| 28 March 86 | C-7 Caribou | N/A | 2 Local Flights-No Cargo |
| 31 March 86 | C-7 Caribou | N/A | Local Flight-No Cargo |
| 31 March 86 | C-7 Caribou | N/A | Local Flight-No Cargo |
| 31 March 86 | C-7 Caribou | N/A | Training-No Cargo |
| 1 April 86 | C-7 Caribou | FDN | Lethal Cargo 3,440 lbs. |
| 1 April 86 | C-7 Caribou | N/A | Local Flight-No Cargo |
| 4 April 86 | C-7 Caribou | FDN | Lethal Cargo (2 flights) 9,200 lbs. |
| 6 April 86 | C-7 Caribou | N/A | Training |
| 7 April 86 | C-7 Caribou | FDN | Lethal Cargo (2 flights) 8,600 lbs. |
| 8 April 86 | C-7 Caribou | FDN | Lethal Cargo (2 flights) 11,500 lbs. |
| 9 April 86 | C-7 Caribou | FDN | Lethal Cargo (3 flights) 18,000 lbs. |
| 10 April 86 | C-7 Caribou | FDN | Lethal Cargo (2 flights) 7,900 lbs. |
| 10 April 86 | L-100 | Southern | Arrived DZ on time but never saw inverted or strobe light. Aborted after staying in area 25 minutes. Lethal Cargo: 18 bundles |
| 11 April 86 | C-7 Caribou | FDN | Lethal Cargo (3 flights) 16,250 lbs. |
| 11 April 86 | L-100 | Southern | Lethal drop UNO/ South received 20,000 lbs. ammo, grenades, rockets, launchers, rifles, magazines, etc. |
| 7 Sept 86 | C-123 | Southern | Lethal HK-21 machine guns, cartridges, C-4 explosive, hand grenades, shells |
| 9 Sept 86 | C-123 | Southern | Lethal No drop No contact in DZ Troops on ground unable to identify coordinates of DZ. Bad weather. Arrived at coordinates early |
| 10 Sept 86 | C-7 Caribou | FDN | Weapons & supplies. |
| 11 Sept 86 | C-7 Caribou | FDN | Lethal 384 81mm shells |
| 11 Sept 86 | C-123 | Southern | Lethal load 10,000 lbs. No drop made Bad weather. Called North's office to get assistance w/ weather reports. |
| 12 Sept 86 | C-123 | Southern | Drop 10,000 lbs. Rifles, grenades mortar shells, cartridges and non-lethal |
| 12 Sept 86 | C-7 Caribou | FDN | 3800 lbs. of ammo grenades and non-lethal |
| 13 Sept 86 | C-123 | Southern | 10,000 lbs. dropped cartridges, hand grenades and non-lethal |
| 13 Sept 86 | C-123 | FDN | 5,000 lbs food 4,630 grenades |
| 13 Sept 86 | C-7 Caribou | FDN | 1500 lbs of chutes & straps |
| 13 Sept 86 | C-7 Caribou | FDN | Additional delivery |
| 14 Sept 86 | C-123 | Southern | 10,000 lbs cartridges, shells, machine guns, and grenades |
| 14 Sept 86 | C-7 Caribou | FDN | mortar shells |
| 17 Sept 86 | C-123 | Southern | 9850 lbs. cartridges, C-4 explosive, fuses, detonators, and grenades. |

| DATE | AIRCRAFT | FDN/SOUTHERN | NOTES |
|---|---|---|---|
| 19 Sept 86 | C-123 | Southern | 10,500 lbs. lethal |
| 20 Sept 86 | C-123 | FDN in the Southern Provinces | 10,500 lbs. lethal 3 machine guns, ammo, grenades, all received in good shape. |
| 23 Sept 86 | C-123 | Southern | 10,100 lbs 15 pallets Lethal: grenades, AK's 702 ammo |
| 29 Sept 86 | C-123 | Southern | Lethal Drop Cartridges, shells, and grenades |
| 29 Sept 86 | C-7 Caribou | FDN | 2,400 hand grenades |
| 30 Sept 86 | C-7 Caribou | FDN | Lethal Drop |
| 30 Sept 86 | C-7 Caribou | FDN | Lethal |
| 5 Oct 86 | C-123 | FDN in the Southern Provinces | Lethal; Plane shot down. Carrying guns & other ammo. Left Airbase at 0950. Full fuel and 10,000 lbs. route same as usual. Planned to return to Airbase 1530. Never reached DZ. |

Source: Flight logs and mission reports compiled by air resupply operation pilots and flight crew.

# CHAPTER 4

# Private Fundraising: The Channell-Miller Operation

While donations from other countries and profits from the Iran arms sales provided most of the money for lethal assistance to the Contras after the Boland Amendment, the network of private foundations and organizations formed by Carl R. "Spitz" Channell and Richard R. Miller also played a role. Channell's principal organization, the tax-exempt National Endowment for the Preservation of Liberty (NEPL), used White House briefings and private meetings with the President to raise more than $10 million from private contributors, almost all for the Contra cause. Over half of this total came from two elderly widows—Barbara Newington and Ellen Garwood—who made the bulk of their contributions after receiving private and emotional presentations by Lt. Col. Oliver North on the Contras' cause and military needs. One dozen contributors accounted for 90 percent of NEPL's funds in 1985 and 1986.

Of the $10 million that was raised, only approximately $4.5 million was funnelled to, or spent on behalf of, the Contras, including more than $1 million for political advertising and lobbying. The rest was retained by Miller and Channell for salaries, fees, and expenses incurred by their organizations, including compensation to their associates, David Fischer and Martin Artiano.

The NEPL money spent for direct and indirect assistance to the Contras was disbursed primarily by Miller at the direction of North. Approximately $1.7 million was "washed" by Channell through Miller's domestic and Cayman Island entities—International Business Communications (IBC) and I.C., Inc.—to the Enterprise, where it was commingled with funds from third-country contributions and the Iranian arms sale. Another $1 million was passed at the direction of North through Miller's entities to accounts controlled by Adolfo Calero, and approximately $500,000 was distributed at North's request to other persons and entities engaged in activities relating to the Contras.

Channell and Miller made elaborate efforts to conceal the nature of their fundraising activities and North's role. Certain funds received by NEPL for Contra assistance were allocated on Channell's books to a project denominated "Toys," a euphemism for weapons. The NEPL and IBC employees were instructed to refer to North by a code name, "Green." Funds were transferred to the Contras, not directly—which would be traceable—but through Miller's anonymous offshore entity, I.C., Inc. North misrepresented to several White House officials the nature of the network's fundraising activities. For instance, the President apparently was led to believe that the funds were being raised for political advertising; the President's Chief of Staff, Donald Regan, was deliberately kept in the dark by North and Admiral John Poindexter; and North misrepresented to Congress and White House personnel the nature of his involvement in the activities of NEPL and IBC. As a result, the network was able to operate successfully until the latter part of 1986, when increased Government aid to the Contras and public disclosure of both the Iranian arms sales and the Contra resupply network made further assistance efforts unnecessary and unwise.

By using a tax-exempt organization to funnel money to the Contras—for arms and other purposes—Channell and Miller provided tax deductions to donors. As a result, the U.S. Government effectively subsidized a portion of contributions intended for lethal aid to the Contras. In the spring of 1986, Channell and Miller pled guilty to criminal tax charges of conspiring to defraud "the United States Treasury of revenues to which it was entitled by subverting and corrupting the lawful purposes . . . of NEPL by using NEPL . . . to solicit contributions to purchase military and other non-humanitarian aid for the Contras." At his plea hearing, Channell identified Miller and North as his co-conspirators.

## THE BACKGROUND

## Carl R. "Spitz" Channell

**Channell was a successful political fundraiser who started his own consulting firm in 1982 and then formed a network of political action committees and tax-exempt foundations, including the NEPL.**

According to Channell, when he formed NEPL in late 1984, most "Washington insiders" doubted that anyone could raise money to advance foreign policy. Channell, however, believed that he could succeed because his major donors were committed to President Reagan and his philosophy toward foreign affairs.

At first, NEPL concentrated on raising funds to publicize "European issues," e.g., SALT, summits, and nuclear freeze proposals. In January 1985, after NEPL ran a large newspaper advertisement congratulating President Reagan on his inauguration, Channell received a call from Edie Fraser of the public relations firm, Miner & Fraser. According to Channell, Fraser indicated that she admired the ad and asked for NEPL's assistance in organizing and promoting a fundraising dinner for the Nicaraguan Refugee Fund (NRF). This was Channell's introduction to the Contras' cause.

To assist him, Channell recruited Daniel Conrad, a fundraising consultant from San Francisco, with whom Channell had dealt on earlier occasions. Conrad came to Washington, and together he and Channell initiated NEPL's involvement in the Nicaraguan issue.

Lines of authority in Channell's organization were informal. Fundraisers reported either to Conrad or Channell, who shared responsibility for training them. Channell, however, was generally in charge of preparing the script to be used for soliciting prospective donors.

## Richard R. Miller and IBC

Miller, 35, received a bachelors degree in 1976 from the University of Maryland. During parts of 1979 and 1980, he served as director of broadcast services for the Reagan campaign.

After the 1980 election, Miller served on the transition team and then briefly as special assistant to the director of public affairs in the Department of Transportation. From February 1981 to February 1983, he was chief of news and public affairs for the Agency for International Development (AID). He was then promoted to public affairs director at AID, where he remained until 1984.

Upon leaving AID, Miller established IBC as a sole proprietorship to engage in media relations, strategic planning for public affairs, political analysis, and executive branch liaison. In 1984, he began to work with Francis Gomez who recently had left his position as Deputy Assistant Secretary for Public Affairs in the State Department. Miller had first met Gomez in February 1982.

Immediately upon leaving the State Department in February 1984, Gomez received a contract from the State Department to assist its newly formed Office of Public Diplomacy for Latin America and the Caribbean (S/LPD) with public relations advice and support. The original purchase order for the contract specified that Gomez was to write talking point papers on Central America, prepare speaker kits, identify and refute distortions and false allegations regarding U.S. policy, draft sample speeches, prepare op-ed pieces and feature articles, assist Central American refugees and exiles visiting Washington, arrange media events for them, and make them available for Congressional interviews.

This contract was renewed with Gomez in May 1984 and then assumed by IBC in August or September 1984. Before it terminated in September 1986 after several renewals, Gomez and IBC received a total of $441,084 from the State Department.

In September 1984, IBC also began to represent one of Adolfo Calero's organizations, the Nicaraguan Development Council (NDC). Initially, IBC charged NDC $3,000 a month for public relations services, a fee that was later raised to $5,000 a month when IBC hired a full-time employee to do work for NDC. This relationship gave Miller and Gomez significant opportunities to work closely with Calero, Alfonso Robelo, and Arturo Cruz.

In the course of assisting the Contras with their public relations, Miller was introduced to North, apparently by either Otto Reich or Jonathan Miller (no relation)—Director and Deputy Director of S/LPD—who were IBC's principal contacts at the State Department. In early 1985, Richard Miller became involved with the NRF dinner, with which Channell and Conrad were also engaged. This was the beginning of their relationship, although the dinner demanded little of their respective energies and was organized and run principally by others.

90

## The NRF Dinner

According to Channell, the NRF dinner had to be postponed several times and was an organizational disaster. When it finally took place on April 15, 1985, President Reagan attended and delivered the keynote address. The NRF dinner proved to Channell that large and expensive functions were not an efficient method of raising money for the Contras, but the President's commitment to the Contra cause convinced Channell that the Nicaraguan issue was fertile ground for fundraising and public education.

Thereafter, Channell and Conrad, with the assistance of Miller, concentrated on private meetings with potential large donors, who would be given an audience with North and, in some cases, a photo opportunity with the President.

## CHANNELL-MILLER NETWORK—THE BEGINNINGS

In late March or early April 1985, Channell, Conrad, Miller, and to a significantly lesser degree, Gomez, embarked on an effort to assist the cause of the Contras. Their joint efforts would extend into the latter portion of 1986. According to Miller, Channell initially offered to IBC a retainer of $15,000 per month, which IBC accepted.

At first, IBC lent support to the American Conservative Trust and NEPL in their efforts to educate the public on the Nicaraguan issue. Very quickly, however, Channell expressed to Miller an interest in raising money for the Contras. Because of their prior contact with the Contras' organization and leaders, Miller and Gomez believed that they could be of assistance. One of Channell's first steps, with IBC help, was to secure a letter from Adolfo Calero authorizing NEPL to solicit contributions on behalf of his organizations. This letter, dated April 10, 1985, opened "Dear Spitz," and read in part:

> Please help us to achieve our dream, a free and democratic Nicaragua, not tied to a hostile Soviet threat but to a peaceful democratic American tradition.
>
> All resources you can raise will be appreciated. We can put all of them to good purposes.
>
> Richard Miller and Frank Gomez can keep you informed of our progress and serve as our contact point in the United States.

## The Initial Solicitations

In early April 1985, Channell spoke with one of his prior contributors, John Ramsey of Wichita Falls, Texas, who Channell felt might be interested in contributing to support the Contras. Ramsey seemed receptive to the idea, but wanted to meet Calero in person to ensure that any money he contributed would, in fact, be used to support the Contras.

Channell scheduled a dinner for himself, Conrad, Miller, Gomez, Ramsey, and Calero in Washington, D.C., on April 10, 1985. At the last minute, however, Calero was unable to attend and the dinner went forward without him. Going into the dinner, Channell had told Miller and Gomez that Ramsey was a "tough cookie" who probably would be most interested in the Contras' need for arms and other lethal supplies.

91

At the dinner, in a private room at the Hay-Adams Hotel, Miller and Gomez spoke at length about the Contras' need for supplies, both lethal and non-lethal. Gomez showed Ramsey a book of photographs taken during a recent trip Gomez had made to various Contra bases in Central America. This collection included pictures of Contra fighters, mortars, and machine guns.

Conrad openly tape-recorded the conversation during dinner, supposedly because he was learning new information about the Contras and wanted to preserve it. The transcript of the tape, as further interpreted by Channell, Conrad, and Miller during depositions, confirms that Channell, Miller, and Gomez discussed the Contras' military and non-military needs at length, often in response to questions from Ramsey. At one point, Miller deflected a suggestion by Ramsey that people be solicited to send used shotguns to the Contras:

RAMSEY: "The best I can tell, a shotgun is the best thing to use in jungle warfare."

GOMEZ(?): "Or a very rapid fire machine gun. That's why the AK-47s [**Soviet infantry rifles**] and the M16s are the best weapons."

MILLER: "The M16 fires a 22.5 caliber bullet."

RAMSEY: "I bet I could get 10,000 people to give their old shotguns to this."

MILLER: "Only one problem. You can't export guns without a license."

Later, Channell itemized some of Calero's needs:

CHANNELL: "Calero wants those red eye [U.S.-made shoulder-fired antiaircraft missiles] missiles. He wants boots. He wants

back packs. He wants AK-47 rounds which you can get on the international market. He wants communications equipment."

Ramsey, however, returned again to his suggestion to provide the Contras with donated arms, which is not what Channell and Miller had in mind:

RAMSEY: "We're going to call it the Shotgun Drive. And we're going to get Remington to put up the amo [sic]. Dupont owns Remington.

"We're going to start on CBs. We're not even going to invoke the electronic media until we get support or we have about three semis going north on Tobacco Road out of North Carolina full.

"And they keep calling on another semi.

"We got an empty semi out there? Somebody got an 18-wheeler empty can come down and help liberate Central America?"

Near the end of the transcript, the Channell-Miller group succeeded in turning the discussion back to missiles and money:

UNKNOWN: "Between now and May 1 the red eye missiles could be the entire key.

"Because if they succeed at this point in launching an offensive including tanks and MI24 helicopters into that region and go for the cans. . . .

"There's two different kinds of red eye missiles. There's one that's very unsophisticated which is just a direct shot missile. And then there's one that's able to take on the Hind [sic] because the Hind has major decoy devices, has heavy armament, and it has these flares on the back of the exhaust from the jets—the expulsion from the engine—that mask the heat.

"So you have to have the $8,000 red eye to make it work."

The transcript concludes with an observation, attributed to Miller, summing up well the philosophy with which Channell, Conrad, and Miller approached their solicitations:

MILLER: "If you provide money for ammunition, the money they've set aside for ammunition can go to boots.

"On the other hand, if you provide money for boots, what they've set aside for boots can go to ammunition."

The solicitation was a success. The next morning Ramsey had breakfast with Calero and, at that time or shortly thereafter, donated $20,000 directly to the Nicaraguan Development Council. As noted earlier, the NDC had previously retained IBC as a public relations consultant.

The Ramsey solicitation was not, however, to become the model. It did not produce enough money for the effort and the donation was sent directly to Robelo so that the Channell-Miller group was not compensated. A new approach was undertaken.

## North's Maiden Presentation

After the Ramsey solicitation, Channell drew on his experience with NCPAC briefings, and worked with Miller to sponsor a White House "event" for prior and potential NEPL contributors. This event was intended to educate contributors about the situation in Nicaragua and to solicit funds for the Contras. Through North, Miller and other IBC associates were successful in arranging a White House briefing for a group invited by NEPL.

The briefing was held on June 27, 1985, in the Old Executive Office Building next to the White House with North as the principal speaker. According to Channell, North delivered what became his standard speech about Nicaragua and the Contras. North showed slides during his presentation, some of which had been provided by IBC.

North's speech was an impassioned plea. He discussed the Communist threat posed to Nicaragua's neighbors by the Soviet and Libyan military buildup in Nicaragua, the political and religious repression in Nicaragua, the humanitarian and military needs of the Contras, and the importance of United States support for the Contras. North also emphasized that the United States would be flooded with millions of refugees if Nicaragua continued under its existing regime and policies. This briefing was the initial substantive encounter between Channell and North.

After the briefing, the potential donor group was taken across the street for a reception and dinner at the Hay-Adams Hotel. As was to become customary, NEPL arranged and paid for food and lodging at the Hay-Adams for persons attending this special White House briefing. At the dinner, Channell presented Calero with a check for $50,-000, which represented all Contra-related contributions received to date by NEPL. At Miller's instruction, the check was made payable to a Calero account.

Channell testified that his understanding was that the contributed funds would be used for humanitarian supplies. This understanding was based on Calero's specific appeal that night for medicine and food.

## The Establishment of I.C., Inc.

**Miller set up a Cayman Islands corporation known as I.C., Inc. Later the name was changed to Intel Co-Operation, Inc. Miller also arranged a meeting between Channell and North at a restaurant near the White House, and there it was agreed that any money Channell raised for the Contras would be given to Miller, who would deposit it in his International Business Communications or I.C. accounts.**

## CHANNELL-MILLER NETWORK— THE OPERATION

### White House Briefings and Hay-Adams Gatherings

The North briefing in June 1985 served as the blueprint for other similar briefings during the next year for NEPL contributors or potential contributors. These group briefings occurred on October 17, 1985, November 21, 1985, January 30, 1986, and March 27, 1986.

The White House briefings were meticulously planned by NEPL, IBC, North, and White House personnel. Internal White House memorandums obtained by the Committees show that North was the switching point for arranging and coordinating the briefings with White House liaison, White House Counsel, and White House security.

NEPL prepared and sent invitations to persons selected by Channell and his associates. A typical invitation to a briefing stated in pertinent part:

You are one of a small group of dedicated Americans who has stood by President Reagan . . . in support of his agenda. . . . It will be a pleasure to meet you in Washington on [date] when you attend our special security briefing followed by a working dinner. . . . Please be reminded that your accommodations at the Hay-Adams Hotel are taken care of and there is no expense to you.

For those who attended, NEPL met them at the airport with a limousine and escorted them to the Hay-Adams Hotel, where all expenses were paid by NEPL.

The group typically was taken from the Hay-Adams to a reception room in the Old Executive Office Building, where they were introduced to North and other White House personnel. Other than North, among those who participated in these briefings were Patrick Buchanan, White House Communications Director; Mitch Daniels, Political Assistant to the President; Linas Kojelis, Special Assistant to the President for Public Liaison; Linda Chavez, Deputy Assistant to the President and Director of the Office of Public Liaison; and Elliott Abrams, Assistant Secretary of State for Inter-American Affairs. For the January 30 briefing, David Fischer—a former Special Assistant to the President who became a highly paid consultant to NEPL and IBC—even arranged for a Presidential "drop-by."

North always delivered the principal speech and slide presentation along the lines of the June 1985 briefing. While he was an effective speaker, North generally was careful not to ask for money, often telling the audience that he could not solicit funds because he was a Federal employee. He did, however, suggest that persons interested in contributing funds for the Contras should speak with Channell. At least one attendee at these briefings recalled North's stating that there were certain matters he could not discuss with them "on this side of Pennsylvania Avenue" but that Channell would raise later "on the other side of the street," a reference to the Hay-Adams Hotel.

An account of North's presentation was provided at the public hearings by an eventual contributor in attendance at the March 1986 briefing, William O'Boyle:

[North] described the military and political situation in Nicaragua. He had photographs of an airport in Nicaragua that had been recently built; the purpose of the airport was ostensibly commercial, but it was in fact a disguised military airport. One of the uses for which the airport was intended was to recover the Russian Backfire bombers after they made a nuclear attack on the United States.

Another possible use of this airport was to fly a certain kind of mission that was currently being flown out of Cuba, up and down the east coast of the United States. Apparently every day a Russian plane leaves Cuba, as I recall, and goes right up the 12-mile limit, has some kind of large device on the outside of the plane. . . . This Nicaraguan air base would allow the Russians to fly the same kind of mission up the west coast to the United States. . . .

He described the refugee problem . . . and we could look forward in the next few years to millions of refugees flooding across our borders as this happened. . . .

He showed photographs which indicated that the Nicaraguan government officials were indicated in smuggling dope. . . . He also told an anecdote about some Nicaraguan agents that were recently caught with dope and money and so forth and disguised as American agents.

O'Boyle indicated also that North furnished him with classified information designed to show that the Soviets were managing the diplomacy of the Nicaraguans before the United Nations.

After the briefings, Channell, Miller, and their associates hosted a cocktail party and dinner at the Hay-Adams, often attended by Contra leaders and some U.S. Government officials. During the reception and dinner, NEPL and IBC employees attempted to determine which attendees were the most likely contributors. The enticement of purchasing lethal supplies for the Contras was often used with potential contributors. Those persons who expressed a serious interest in contributing money for the Contras were offered the opportunity to meet one-on-one with North, and, if they gave enough, a meeting with the President. Large contributors to NEPL uniformly received thank you letters from North (and often from the President) for their support of the President's policies in Central America, although without specific reference to any contribution.

## North's Involvement in Solicitations Intended for the Purchase of Lethal Supplies

In his public testimony, North testified that "I do not recall ever asking a single, solitary American citizen for money." He readily admitted, however, that "I showed a lot of munitions lists" to Contra contributors or potential contributors "in response to questions about the cost of lethal items." The Committees received evidence on North's activities that shed light on these statements.

*1. "Big Ticket Items" and "Ollie's New Purchase" Lists.* In the late fall or early winter of 1985, Channell asked Miller to have North prepare and provide a list of "big ticket items" to be used in soliciting contributions for the Contras. At Miller's request, North recited a list that included heavy lifting of cargo by aircraft (approximately $675,000 worth); training and outfitting of an "urban tactics unit"; the resupply of a Contra fighting unit known as the "Larry McDonald Brigade" (a Contra unit); and probably missiles of some kind.

Miller typed the list onto his computer, printed a single copy, gave that copy to Channell, and deleted the computer entry. Channell used this list, which totalled approximately $1.2 million, to solicit contributions. An apparently different "big ticket items" list was prepared by North and used by him and Channell in a solicitation of Nelson Bunker Hunt. Handwritten notes produced by Miller indicate other conversations with North about fundraising for lethal supplies. A note dated September 18, 1985, contains entries reading "$415,000-Weapons, C4, M79" and "520,000 MAUL." "C4" refers to an explosive, "M79" likely refers to a grenade launcher, and "$520,000 MAUL" refers to the cost of eight Maule airplanes. Miller testified that North provided this information to him with the understanding that it would be used for fundraising.

*2. North's Special Appeals.* As North testified publicly, he met with scores of potential contributors to convey the plight and needs of the Contras. Insofar as North's actual role, the more revealing of these meetings are those that were conducted in private.

*a. Nelson Bunker Hunt*—In September 1985, Channell arranged a meeting in Dallas between North and Nelson Bunker Hunt, a wealthy Texas businessman who had contributed $10,000 to NEPL the previous July.

Channell rented a private airplane for $8,000 to $9,000 to transport North to and from Dallas.* The trip was worth the cost.

In Dallas, there was a private dinner at the Petroleum Club attended by Hunt, Conrad, Channell, and North. North gave his standard briefing, without slides, and showed Hunt a list of various Contra needs. The list was divided about evenly between lethal and non-lethal items, and included Maule aircraft and a grenade launcher possibly described as an "M-79." The total price was about $5 million. According to Channell, after discussing the items on the list and their prices, North "made the statement that he could not ask for funds himself, but contributions could be made to NEPL, or words . . . to that effect." North then left the room, a maneuver that had been "pre-arranged."

Channell explained that the list was his idea because he wanted a "fundraising objective" to take to Hunt. He therefore had asked North to prepare a list totalling about $5 million for use in the solicitation of Hunt.

Despite this evidence, Hunt has told the Committees that Channell never spoke to him about the Contras' need for weapons. According to Hunt, Channell told him that the Contras had "unpaid bills" for "[f]ood and shelter, medicine, [and] general expenses. . . ." Hunt testified that he does not recall any conversation he had with North at the dinner.

Nonetheless, as a result of this dinner, Hunt made two payments to NEPL of $237,500 each. One of them was a contribution and one was a loan. The loan was evi-

---

*This was the first time North used an airplane supplied by NEPL; on one other occasion, NEPL chartered a plane to fly North and his family for a weekend visit to Barbara Newington's house in Connecticut.

denced by an unsigned promissory note because Channell would not agree to the loan (especially after he was unable to find a contributor to guarantee the loan on NEPL's behalf). Nevertheless, he held the $237,500 principal for 4 months, repaying it to Hunt in January 1986 without interest. Hunt subsequently paid $237,000 to NEPL in March 1986 as a contribution, making his total contributions to NEPL $484,500.

*b. Barbara Newington*—Barbara Newington, a wealthy widow from Greenwich, Connecticut, had been a large contributor to Channell organizations (and at least one predecessor organization) for a few years. In 1985 and 1986, Newington contributed a total of $2,866,025 to NEPL. On June 25 or 26, 1985, she met privately with North because she was unable to attend the Channell group meeting arranged for the next day. She also met privately with President Reagan on two occasions.

In early November 1985, North, Miller, and Channell participated in a solicitation of significant contributions from Newington. Miller's handwritten notes leading up to the meeting indicate that Channell prepared a proposed "pitch" for "Green"—the code name for North used by NEPL and IBC—to use with Newington. This "pitch" included statements such as "[you are] the most secure person we know in the U.S." and "[w]e are asking you to take on a project that requires your kind of person." Although Miller does not specifically recall, he might have relayed a somewhat softened version of this solicitation to North.

In further preparation for the solicitation, Miller created a file folder that contained an unclassified photograph of a Soviet HIND helicopter on one side of the folder and a picture of a shoulder-held surface-to-air missile on the other side. He also included an article from The New York Times on the capabilities of the HIND helicopter.

The critical meeting took place in Newington's suite at the Hay-Adams Hotel where Channell, Miller, and Newington were joined by North. At the meeting, North referred to the file folder prepared by Miller, placed The New York Times article in front of Newington, and described the capability of the pictured surface-to-air missile to counteract HIND helicopters. In response to a question from Newington, North indicated that he knew where to obtain such missiles, although Miller cannot recall whether North quoted any prices. North left the room shortly thereafter. According to Miller, North's absence was not specifically prearranged, "but it was his practice not to be in the presence of the donor when they were asked for money."

Channell then solicited Newington for a substantial amount of money. Over the course of the next 4 to 6 weeks, Newington made stock contributions to NEPL worth approximately $1.1 million. Like Hunt, Newington has denied that she ever made a contribution intended for the purchase of lethal supplies.

At some point in the spring of 1986, Channell and Newington decided to invite North and his family to Newington's house for a weekend of recreation and relaxation. Miller, North, and North's family travelled to Connecticut in a private plane chartered by Channell. It is unclear whether there was any discussion of Contra assistance that weekend.

**Both William O'Boyle and Ellen Clayton Garwood testified that they too were solicited in a similar manner. O'Boyle made two donations to-**

talling $160,000, and Mrs. Garwood gave more than $2.5 million for the purchase of weapons and ammunition from a list North and Channell had shown her.

The Committees interviewed or deposed 13 of NEPL's significant contributors during the relevant time period, nearly all of whom reported personal contact with North. The Committees have received evidence that several of these contributors—including John Ramsey of Wichita Falls, Texas, and C. Thomas Claggett, Jr., of Washington, D.C.—made donations intended for the purchase of lethal supplies. Channell's records reveal that 12 contributors, including Newington and Garwood, accounted for slightly more than 90 percent of NEPL's contributions in 1985 and 1986.

By giving to the tax-exempt NEPL, the contributors were able to claim tax deductions even though their contributions were intended for the purchase of lethal supplies. The Committees have received evidence that several of these contributors claimed tax deductions for their NEPL contributions. For taxpayers in the 50 percent tax bracket, this meant that the public in effect paid for half their gifts.

## The Role of the President

In a May 19, 1986, PROF note to Poindexter, North wrote "the President obviously knows why he has been meeting with several select people to thank them for their 'support for Democracy' in Cent[ral] Am[erica]." In fact, what the President knew is a matter of some doubt.

The President, in his March 19, 1987, press conference said that he believed that contributors he met had donated money for political advertising for the Contras. The minutes of the May 16, 1986, National Security Planning Group (NSPG) meeting reveal the same understanding on the part of the President. He stated, "What about the private groups who pay for ads for the Contras? Have they been contacted? Could they do more than ads?" Similarly, in preparation for the January 30 briefing, Linda Chavez wrote a memorandum to the President, stating that "ACT and NEPL spent in excess of $3 million supporting the President's programs through public awareness using television and newspaper messages." In fact, much of the $3 million was directed toward Contra support activities, including arms.

Poindexter, however, testified at his deposition that "[t]here wasn't any question in my mind" that the President was aware that the contributors he was thanking were giving to the Contras. He added that "in the White House during this period of time that we were encouraging private support, we really didn't distinguish between how the money was going to be spent." North testified that in writing his May 19 PROF note, he assumed that the President was aware that the contributions were for munitions, as well as other things, although he denied ever discussing this with the President.

The President met with and thanked several large contributors for their support of his policies. David Fischer, former Special Assistant to the President, arranged Presidential photo opportunities or meetings with at least seven major Channell-Miller contributors in 1986. Fischer and Martin Artiano, a Washington lawyer, were paid steep fees by IBC (which charged these fees to NEPL) for arranging these meetings (among other services).

98

All told, between December 1985 and February 1987, IBC paid Fischer $397,400 and Artiano $265,000. Artiano transferred $60,000 of his payments to Fischer. All of the payments were reimbursed to IBC by NEPL.

When asked about allegations that Fischer was paid $50,000 for each meeting arranged with the President, Donald Regan, the President's Chief of Staff, testified that he had no independent knowledge of such an arrangement, but, if true, the allegations would be a "real embarrassment." According to Regan, "we thought he was doing it out of his concerns for the contras and the goodness of his heart, a public pro bono type of thing." He continued: "To find out he was being paid for it was a real shock. . . . [A]nyone getting paid to get a group into the White House, we tried to block that."

Fischer, however, contends that Regan knew by the first meeting between the President and Channell supporters—in January 1986—that Fischer was acting as a paid consultant to the Channell organization. When he raised the subject with Regan, according to Fischer, Regan responded, "I hope you're being compensated for this."

## What Happened to the Money

Just as only a small fraction of the Iranian arms profits was used for the Contras, so only a small part of the money Channell raised for the Contras reached them. Fischer and Artiano received more than $650,000 or more than five percent of the total money raised, and Miller, Gomez, and their companies retained a large percentage of the $5 million that IBC received from NEPL. A total of $2,740,000 was transferred by IBC to

I.C., Inc., and $430,000 directly to Lake Resources. After deducting the payments to Fischer and Artiano—which eventually were reimbursed by NEPL—the balance, approximately $1.2 million, was retained by IBC for fees-for-services and expenses on NEPL's behalf. This amount, however, is not all that Miller and Gomez received from the venture. Miller testified that North agreed in late 1985 that he and Gomez could begin to collect a 10 percent commission on the payments funnelled to the Contras through IBC and I.C., Inc. Miller stated that North said that the 10 percent was reasonable since "most of the other people in the business of providing assistance to the Contras were taking 20% to 30%." North, in his testimony, denied that he had agreed to any specific percentage, but rather stated that he had approved "fair, just, and reasonable" compensation to Miller and Gomez. Nonetheless, North's notebooks contain an entry for November 19, 1985, which states "IBC—10%."

Including these commissions, IBC, Miller, and Gomez received more than $1.7 million from the money raised by NEPL for the Contras. Channell's take was also substantial, though apparently not of the magnitude of Miller's and Gomez's total compensation. He furnished his offices extravagantly and was lavish in his expenditures. He drew compensation for 1985 and 1986 totalling $345,-000, while Conrad and his organization received more than $270,000, extraordinary earnings for nonprofit fundraisers.

Out of the money raised by NEPL, the Contras and their affiliated entities received only $2.7 million, with approximately $500,-000 going to other persons and entities engaged in activities relating to the Contras. The money was routed through IBC and I.C., Inc. and disbursed at the direction of

North to Lake Resources, Calero, and the other persons and entities. In virtually every case, Miller would tell North when money was available and North would then instruct him on what to do with it. Figure 4-1 depicts the flow of money. In addition, as described in the next section, more than $1.2 million was spent on political advertising and lobbying for the Contras.

## Political Advertising for the Contras

Apart from financial assistance to the Contras, the major project of the Channell and Miller organizations in 1985 and 1986 was a "public education" and lobbying program in support of U.S. Government aid for the Contras.

The major vehicle in the "public education" campaign was a series of television advertisements prepared by the Robert Goodman Agency in Baltimore that cost NEPL $1 million. Adam Goodman of that agency, following the Senate's approval of the Contra funding bill in 1986, wrote a letter to Channell describing their achievement:

By design, we launched the four-week national television and campaign in Washington, DC, in late February. This reflected the economy of reaching all 435 Members of the House (and 100 United States Senators) in one sitting. Beginning with Week 2, and running through the first decisive House vote in late March, we also aired spot commercials in 23 additional television markets across the country. These targeted markets, covering the home Districts of nearly thirty Congressmen experts considered to be at the core of the key 'swing vote' on Contra funding, added scope and credibility to the ad campaign. In fact, N.E.P.L.'s national

television spot series was ultimately seen by more than 33 million people, or one out of every seven Americans.

Supplementing the television programs were press conferences and speaking tours by persons supporting the Contras. These were arranged by IBC and another public relations firm, Edelman, Inc., retained by Channell, which was paid $92,000 by NEPL.

NEPL paid $115,000 for extensive polling by the Finkelstein Company as an aid to selecting areas where television advertisements and speaking tours would most likely have a favorable effect on a Congressional vote. He also retained two companies, Miner & Fraser and the Lichtenstein Company, to generate letters to Congressmen supporting Contra aid, and he paid two lobbyists for their services in support of this effort: Dan Kuykendall, who concentrated on undecided Republicans and conservative Democrats, and Bruce Cameron, who focused on liberal Democrats.

Another organization, Prodemca, which had concentrated on Central American issues, also received payments from Channell. Its representatives apparently participated in strategy sessions about enlisting Congressional support.

Finally, it appears that Channell engaged in advertising targeted to defeat Representative Michael Barnes's bid for a Senate seat in Maryland. Representative Barnes had been a vocal opponent of military assistance to the Contras. Channell's Anti-Terrorism American Committee ran a series of television advertisements opposing Representative Barnes during the primary campaign. When Representative Barnes was defeated in the primary, Channel and his associates (Cliff Smith and Krishna Littledale) sent a telegram to North exulting in this result:

> We have the honor to inform you that Congressman Michael Barnes, foe of the freedom fighter movement, adversary of President Reagan's foreign policy goals and opponent of the President's vision for American security in the future has been soundly defeated in his bid to become the Democratic candidate for the U.S. Senate from Maryland.
>
> His defeat signals an end to much of the disinformation and unwise effort directed at crippling your foreign policy goals.
>
> We, at the Anti-Terrorism American Committee (ATAC), feel proud to have participated in a campaign to ensure Congressman Barnes' defeat.

## CHANNELL-MILLER NETWORK: THE END

### The Beginning of the End

On October 18, 1986, the President signed legislation appropriating $100 million for the Contras ($30 million for humanitarian assistance and $70 million in unrestricted aid). The anticipation of this legislation led to a downturn in the activities of the Channell-Miller fundraising and Contra assistance network (see Figure 4-1) after the summer of 1986.

With the disclosure in early November of the sale of arms to Iran, however, persons involved in the network became concerned that the story of the network would unravel and become public. This prescient concern led to meetings between Miller and North on November 20 and 21.

The initial meeting was requested by Miller. They met in the hallway outside of North's office in the Old Executive Office Building. Miller told North that he was worried about the possible legal ramifications and the costs associated with a legal defense. North told Miller that he should use the money left in the Intel Co-Operation (or I.C., Inc.) account (approximately $200,000) for any legal fees that might arise.

North called Miller the next day, November 21, to arrange a meeting later that afternoon. Miller met North in the Old Executive Office Building, and North asked him for a ride to Dupont Circle. Miller told North that money was needed from a foreign source to fund public relations and congressional activities on behalf of the United Nicaraguan Opposition (UNO). Miller suggested contacting the Sultan of Brunei or an Arab country. North's response was "I gave one to Shultz already and he [screwed it up]." North also stated that "if Shultz knew that the Ayatollah was bankrolling this whole thing he'd have a heart attack." Miller did not understand either reference.

Either that day or the day before, North told Miller that the Attorney General had advised North to obtain legal counsel.

### NEPL Activities in December 1986

In December 1986, NEPL's staff received an unusually lengthy holiday vacation from December 15 to January 5, 1987. The reason given for this lengthy break was that the media were making it too difficult for the organizations to conduct their work and that the most sensible response was to close operations for a couple of weeks.

Immediately prior to the extended holiday, two NEPL accounting employees were instructed by their supervisors to delete from the accounting records any and all references to the "Toys" project. As mentioned above, contributions intended for the purchase of lethal supplies generally were designated on NEPL's books for the "Toys" project. Alterations in the accounting records and related floppy discs were made to modify prior references to "Toys" to a neutral project named "CAFP TV" (presumably Central American Freedom Project—Television Advertising).

In addition, NEPL's principal accountant took all NEPL accounting materials home with him during the vacation, including financial records, bank statements, check books, deposit slips, and the like. The evidence obtained by the Committees suggests that all such records were taken to perform year-end accounting tasks and were returned by the accountant without further alteration.

## February 1987 Report from IBC to NEPL

On February 16, 1987, IBC issued a report to NEPL that reconstructed the disposition of the Contra assistance payments made by NEPL to IBC and I.C., Inc. during the period from July 1985 through the end of 1986. The report contained supporting documentation for many of the relevant transactions.

In a summary at the beginning of the report, IBC acknowledged that most of the disbursements of these funds were made "at the request of Lt. Col. Oliver L. North." Moreover, the summary states that "we were assured by [North] at the time that the funds were to be applied solely for humanitarian assistance." Miller has told the Committees that he would write these statements differently if he were writing them today.*

## Guilty Pleas of Channell and Miller

On April 29, 1987, Channell pled guilty to a one-count criminal information filed the same day by the Independent Counsel. As noted above, the information charged that Channell, Miller, "and others known and unknown to the Independent Counsel" conspired "to defraud the IRS and deprive the Treasury of the United States of revenue to which it was entitled by subverting and corrupting the lawful purposes . . . of NEPL by using NEPL . . . to solicit contributions to purchase military and other types of non-humanitarian aid for the Contras," in violation of 18 U.S.C. Section 371. The acts identified by the information as part of the conspiracy include the Ramsey, Hunt, Newington, O'Boyle, Garwood, and Claggett solicitations. At the hearing in which Channell's guilty plea was accepted by the Federal district court, Channell named Miller and North as his co-conspirators.

Miller pled guilty to a substantively identical criminal information on May 6, 1987. Both Channell and Miller are awaiting sentencing.

---

*According to Miller, he told North in late 1986 that he "hoped to hell the account had been used for humanitarian assistance." North responded "Oh hell, yes."

# Figure 4-1. The Channell-Miller Contra Assistance Network

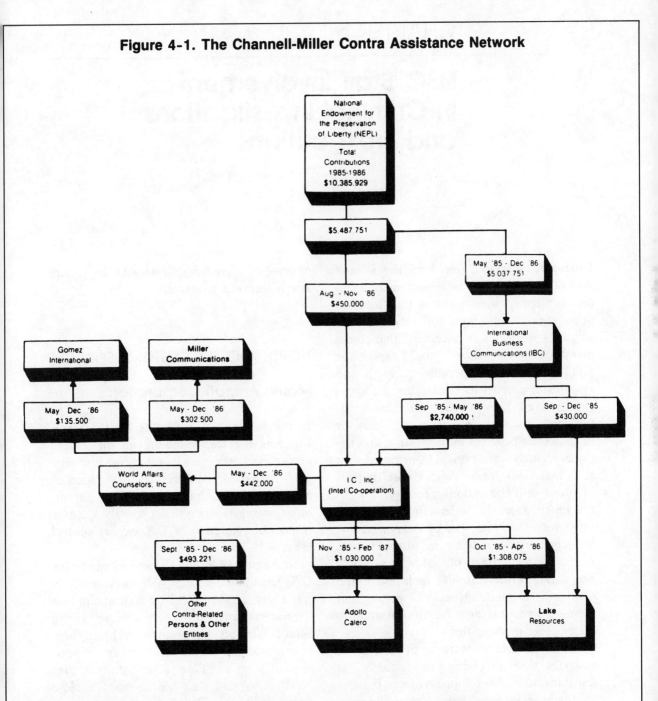

This chart represents the money flow of the Channell-Miller Contra Assistance Network.

Source: Senate Select Committee on Secret Military Assistance to Iran and the Nicaraguan Opposition and House Select Committee to Investigation Covert Arms Transactions with Iran.

# CHAPTER 5

# NSC Staff Involvement in Criminal Investigations and Prosecutions

During the period covered by the Boland Amendment, federal law enforcement agencies conducted investigations that touched upon various aspects of the secret Contra support operation. Concerned that these investigations, if pursued, would expose the NSC staff's covert operations, North and Poindexter reacted by contacting the agencies involved. They sought to monitor investigations and, in some cases, to delay or impede their progress by suggesting that national security was at stake. Confronted with such assertions from White House officials involved with the nation's security, law enforcement agencies understandably cooperated with the NSC staff by delaying some investigations, arranging to move a convicted former foreign official whom North was afraid would disclose facts about the Contras to a minimum security prison, and giving Poindexter and North information about other investigations.

The Committees are aware of seven such episodes, three involving the United States Customs Service and four involving the Department of Justice. They represent an integral part of the NSC staff's efforts to keep its operations even from those with legitimate law enforcement interests.

## NORTH AND THE CUSTOMS SERVICE

### Maule Aircraft Corporation

In the summer of 1986, the United States Customs Service, following up on a CBS news report, began an investigation into allegations that Maule Aircraft Corporation of Macon, Georgia, had shipped four aircraft into Central America to support the Contras in possible violation of U.S. export control laws.

In August 1986, the Commissioner of the U.S. Customs Service, William von Raab, was approached by North, who told him that Customs agents in Georgia were giving Maule Aircraft Corporation a hard time. North said the Maule Corporation shipped aircraft such as "Piper Cubs" down south. North also said that Maule was "a close friend of the President." Commissioner von Raab told North he would look into the Customs Service investigation and assigned the matter to William Rosenblatt, Assistant Commissioner for Enforcement.

Rosenblatt contacted North, who told Rosenblatt that the people involved in the sale and export of the four Maule aircraft were "good guys" and had done nothing illegal. North insisted that the aircraft were simply "super Piper Cubs" and were exported only to a Central American country, where they were used to supply the Contras with medical and humanitarian supplies. Rosenblatt explained that in order to verify the legality of the transactions, Customs needed certain documents and photographs of the aircraft, which North promised to produce. In exchange, Rosenblatt agreed to postpone issuance of subpoenas.

Over the course of the next several weeks, Rosenblatt continued to contact North periodically to request the promised documentation, which North led him to believe would be forthcoming "momentarily." Because of North's promises, Rosenblatt told the agent in charge to suspend issuing a grand jury subpoena for Maule, although the agent asserted that the Maule officials were "stonewalling" him.

On November 10, Rosenblatt met with Commissioner von Raab to discuss North's assertions that the Customs investigation could compromise national security, including an effort to obtain the release of the hostages. At that meeting, von Raab advised Rosenblatt to speak with Robert Kimmitt, General Counsel to the Treasury Department, about his inability to obtain the Maule and SAT records. Rosenblatt scheduled that meeting for the afternoon of November 17.

On the morning of November 17, Rosenblatt called North to attempt again to get the promised documents on Maule Aircraft. To Rosenblatt's surprise, North indicated that he had the documents and would send them right over. When they arrived, however, Rosenblatt was quite disappointed. They did not include purchase orders, photographs, or other documents sufficient to dispose of the Customs inquiry. That afternoon, Rosenblatt met with Kimmitt and related the entire episode involving Maule and SAT. At that point, the investigation resumed, 6 weeks after it had been halted at North's request.

## MIAMI NEUTRALITY INVESTIGATION

In connection with another investigation, this one conducted by the Office of the United States Attorney for the Southern District of Florida, North and Poindexter were able to obtain information concerning the vulnerability of the Enterprise.

### The Roots of the Investigation

On July 21, 1985, the Miami Herald published an article by reporters Martha Honey and Tony Avirgan. In that article, a mercenary for Civilian Military Assistance (CMA) named Steven Carr, who was then imprisoned in Costa Rica, spoke of an arms shipment from Fort Lauderdale to a Central American location. The article caught the attention of the FBI in the Southern District of Florida, which opened an investigation into Carr's allegations and alerted FBI headquarters in Washington, D.C., as required in any matter involving the Neutrality Act.

## Garcia Allegations

In December 1985, an individual named Jesus Garcia was convicted in the Southern District of Florida on charges of possessing an unlicensed machine gun.

While Garcia was awaiting sentence, he offered through his attorney to provide federal authorities with information relating to paramilitary plots in Central America. As a result of that offer, he was interviewed on January 7, 1986 by two FBI agents. He claimed that he had been set up on the machine gun charge by a person who supposedly worked for Tom Posey and the CMA, a pro-Contra paramilitary group. According to Garcia, Posey was attempting to neutralize him because of his knowledge of a CMA plot to assassinate Ambassador Lewis Tambs to collect a reward offered by a notorious drug kingpin in Central America. The assassination, Garcia told the FBI, would, as an added benefit, be blamed on the Sandinistas, thereby assisting the Contras' cause. Garcia also gave the FBI further details on the gun shipment reported earlier in the Miami Herald.

The FBI agents and Jeffrey Feldman, the Assistant United States Attorney conducting the investigation, were all skeptical. Nevertheless, given the gravity of Garcia's allegations, the investigation continued. At the request of the FBI, embassy officials in Costa Rica interviewed Carr and other American mercenaries imprisoned in that country. Hotel records at the alleged site of a critical meeting seemed to confirm its occurrence. Flight plans and records suggested that the alleged arms shipment also could have occurred.

During this phase of the investigation, the FBI received allegations that North, Owen, and John Hull were involved in, or at least aware of, the gun running plots. This information was not supplied by Garcia, but came through other sources.

On March 14, 1986, an FBI agent and Feldman met with Anna Barnett, the Executive Assistant United States Attorney. While the FBI agent and Feldman were in Barnett's office discussing the investigation, United States Attorney Leon Kellner came in to inquire whether anyone was aware of an alleged plot to assassinate Ambassador Tambs. According to Kellner, he had just received a call from someone at the Department of Justice in Washington who wanted information about the investigation. At or shortly after that meeting, it was decided that the FBI agents and Feldman would travel to New Orleans to interview Jack Terrell, a/k/a "Colonel Flaco," a former CMA mercenary who, they had been told, knew more details of the conspiracy.

## Terrell and Costa Rica

In New Orleans, Terrell provided the FBI agents and Feldman with additional information on the alleged assassination plot and arms shipment. When pressed, however, Terrell admitted that most, and perhaps all, of his information was based on hearsay rather than on his direct participation or observation.

Feldman and the FBI agents traveled to Costa Rica on March 31, 1986, and reported to the U.S. Embassy. There they met with Tambs, who wanted to know the purpose of their visit. Feldman briefed Tambs thoroughly on their investigation and intentions. During that briefing, Feldman showed Tambs a chart he had drawn to illustrate the supposed conspiracy that had been described to him. The chart showed a pyramid of participants, with lines of involvement running up through John Hull and Robert Owen to Oliver North at the top.

When he saw the chart, Tambs summoned "Thomas Castillo," who introduced himself to the investigators as a CIA station chief. Castillo provided them background information on Hull. According to Feldman, Castillo also spoke of North warmly as "the person who introduced me to the President of the United States last week."

Over the course of the next two days, Feldman, the FBI agents, and various embassy personnel interviewed Steven Carr and several other imprisoned mercenaries. They attempted to set up an interview with Hull, who initially agreed and then declined to speak to them. Feldman was also told by an employee at the U.S. Embassy that Hull had been contacted by the NSC about the investigation.

## April 4 Meeting

Feldman met late on the afternoon of April 4, 1986, with Kellner and Barnett to discuss the results of his trip to Costa Rica. Also present were Larry Scharf (Special Counsel to the United States Attorney) and Richard Gregorie (Chief Assistant United States Attorney).

Feldman explained to them that, while the assassination plot seemed to be fading as a cause for concern or a vehicle for prosecution, the gun-running charges seemed to have some basis in fact. Others at the meeting believed, however, that Feldman was having a difficult time fitting a complex combination of facts, witnesses, and actors into a coherent theory of prosecution.

At one point, the topic of the Boland Amendment was raised. Because no one in the room was familiar with the details of that legislation Barnett asked Assistant United States Attorney David Liewant to locate it with the research computer.

According to Liewant, when he arrived at Kellner's office with the printout, only Kellner, Barnett, and Feldman were present and Keller was on the telephone talking to someone at the Department of Justice. According to Liewant, when Kellner hung up, he turned to Barnett, Feldman, and Liewant and said that the Department wanted them to "go slow" on the investigation. Liewant could tell from Kellner's expression and tone of voice that Kellner was disdainful of that suggestion and had no intention of actually slowing the investigation.

If Liewant's account of this meeting is correct, the Department of Justice would appear to have been exerting improper influence to delay an investigation, albeit influence brushed aside by Kellner. But each of the other participants in the April 4 meeting deny that any such telephone conversation took place. Richard, Trott, Jensen, and Meese also deny that any telephone call like that described by Liewant occurred or that anyone, to their knowledge, attempted to slow the investigation at any time.

At the end of the meeting on April 4, Kellner asked Feldman to draft a memorandum pulling together the results of the investigation to date as well as Feldman's approach to any possible prosecution.

## The Meese Aside

On April 12, Meese, along with Jensen and Revell, arrived in Miami to visit a number of FBI agents wounded in a shoot-out the day before. Kellner accompanied Meese on his visits.

During the day, Meese pulled him aside and asked him about the Garcia investigation. Kellner believes that he told Meese that there did not appear to be much substance to the assassination allegations, but that the gun-running investigation was continuing. Kellner testified that Meese neither stated nor implied that the investigation should be slowed or conducted in any other particular manner.

**Feldman first concluded it was time to issue grand jury subpoenas for various documents and witnesses but then decided further investigation was needed first. At one point Feldman said Kellner told him to suspend the investigation until Kellner returned from Washington because "politics" was involved. In Washington, meanwhile, FBI and Justice Department officials were showing unusual interest in the investigation. Deputy Attorney General D. Lowell Jensen discussed the case directly with Meese, and it was decided that Poindexter should be advised. But when Kellner returned to Miami, he told Feldman to proceed.**

Upon receiving approval from Kellner, Feldman proceeded with the investigation. The Independent Counsel subsequently declined to take over the case and Feldman was continuing to investigate the matter at the time he was deposed by the Committees.

## REWARD FOR A FRIEND

In one episode, the NSC staff undertook to persuade the Department of Justice to "reward" someone characterized by North as a "friend" who had been convicted of plotting to assassinate a Central American leader. In that episode, the NSC staff's motive appears to have been a desire to prevent disclosure of certain questionable activities.

According to a North PROF to Poindexter, the "friend" was an official in a Central American country with whom North, the U.S. Ambassador, General Gorman, and Dewey Clarridge arranged for bases for the Contras as well as overall logistics, training and support.

This official and other plotters were indicted prior to 1986 for conspiracy to assassinate a Central American leader. Pursuant to a plea agreement, the official pleaded guilty to two felony counts which carried a significant maximum sentence; and he was later sentenced to two shorter, though still significant, prison terms to run concurrently.

At the sentencing hearing, U.S. military officials assigned to the State Department testified on behalf of the official. The court provided that the official could be immediately eligible for parole if so determined by the Parole Commission and recommended he serve his sentence at a minimum security institution. Meanwhile, Assistant Secretary of State Elliott Abrams promised the official's government that he would look into the case.

In a September 17, 1986 PROF message to Poindexter, North noted that the official was under the impression he would serve only a matter of days or weeks at the minimum security institution and then be released. North was concerned that once the official realized he was really going to serve a long sentence, "he will break his longstanding silence about the Nic[araguan] Resistance and other sensitive operations." North noted the next morning he would meet with Oliver Revell, Steven Trott, and Elliott Abrams to explore the possibility of a pardon, clemency, deportation, or sentence reduction. The objective of this exercise, as North put it, was "to keep [the official] from feeling like he was lied to in legal process and start spilling the beans." Admiral Poindexter responded: "You may advise all concerned that the President will want to be as helpful as possible to settle this matter."

Representatives of different agencies of the Administration met to discuss the request for leniency. Deputy Assistant Attorney General Mark Richard attended a meeting where Defense Department representatives argued on the official's behalf. Richard concluded their reasons were not sufficiently specific. No one ever gave a detailed account of what the official had actually done for the United States to deserve leniency. He was always simply described as a "friend of the United States." The State Department agreed with the Department of Justice that the official was a terrorist and should be punished. The CIA did not express an opinion.

In early October, North tried again with the Department of Justice, this time with help from General Gorman and Dewey Clarridge. Also at this meeting were Mark Richard (filling in for Trott), Revell, and Elliott Abrams. North, Gorman and Clarridge all argued for leniency for the official, explaining only that the official was a "friend of the government" who was "always ready to assist us" and "was helpful in accommodating our military." Abrams agreed that the U.S. should do what it could for the official, thereby reversing the State Department's earlier position.

North said Trott and Revell believed this should result in the release and deportation of the official. North suggested that the official's attorney should be discreetly briefed to mollify the concerns of those involved that the official "will start singing songs nobody wants to hear."

Richard soon determined that neither Trott nor Kellner had any objection to redesignating the official to the minimum security institution, as contemplated in the original court's recommendation and made the appropriate arrangements with the Bureau of Prisons.

## THE FAKE PRINCE

In April 1985, a man who said he was a Saudi "prince" offered to donate $14 million to the Contras but ended up swindling North and Miller, to the tune of $370,000, according to Miller. North tried to obstruct the FBI's investigation of bank fraud charges against the "prince." In the end North told Miller he could reimburse himself for the $370,000 by taking the money from Contra assistance funds. The Saudi "prince" turned out to be an Iranian con man who was later incarcerated in a Federal penitentiary in Texas.

## INSTIGATION OF INVESTIGATIONS

North attempted to exploit his contacts with the FBI to attempt to instigate or intensify investigations of people and organizations perceived as threats to the Enterprise. He was ultimately assisted in this effort by Richard Secord and Glenn Robinette.

In early 1986, Secord had been the target of allegations that he was running guns and drugs between Central America and the United States. In May 1986, these allegations blossomed into a lawsuit filed in United States District Court for the Southern District of Florida. The lead plaintiffs in the action were reporters Martha Honey and Tony Avirgan, who were represented by the Christic Institute. The defendants included Secord, Thomas Clines, Theodore Shackley, and John Hull.

At some point after the lawsuit was filed, North again contacted Oliver Revell, this time to suggest that the federal government ought to investigate the plaintiffs because he thought they were probably being funded or supported by the Sandinistas. Revell told him that the FBI did not engage in that type of investigation.

On May 9, the FBI interviewed North about alleged measures taken against him. North claimed that his car had been vandalized, he had been followed, and his dog had been poisoned. North also claimed a fake bomb device had been left in his mailbox. He had not kept the device, however, for the FBI to analyze. North told the FBI that he had written down the license number of the car that was used to follow him, but, after several requests from the FBI, he failed to provide it, claiming he lost the number.

The FBI checked with the local police regarding the fake bomb device placed in North's mailbox. North had told them he discarded it before it could be examined. The FBI concluded it was probably a prank rather than a threat.

On June 3, 1986, North met with FBI agents to discuss an investigation they had been conducting into allegations by North that he was the target of politically motivated vandalism and harassment, perhaps by foreign intelligence sources. At this meeting, North expressed his displeasure about the FBI's alleged lack of effort in the investigation. In particular, he complained that the FBI had never contacted an NSC staffer who supposedly was the source of allegations linking North to drug traffic, had not investigated Daniel Sheehan of the Christic Institute, had not interviewed a reporter who claimed North had threatened him, had not examined allegations made by Senator Kerry against North, and had not attempted to interview Senator Durenberger and Representative Hamilton to determine the sources for allegations made against North about which they had raised questions. Despite these complaints, the FBI ultimately closed its investigation after concluding that none of North's complaints could be traced to foreign intelligence sources.

North ultimately hit on a better formula, however, with Secord's assistance. In March 1986, Secord had retained Glenn Robinette, a security consultant and former CIA officer, to conduct a private investigation of some of the individuals ultimately involved in the Honey and Avirgan lawsuit. One of the people Secord singled out for such treatment was Jack Terrell, also known as "Colonel Flaco." Terrell had at one time been a pro-Contra mercenary associated with Tom Posey and CMA. He ultimately became disillusioned with the Contras, however, and began to cooperate with the plaintiffs in the lawsuit. He threatened to testify that North had helped provide secret funding to the Contras and that he, Terrell, had used CMA as a cover from which to carry out CIA-sponsored assassinations.

In mid-1986, the FBI received information from a classified source that pro-Sandinista individuals might have been contemplating an assassination of President Reagan. The FBI suspected that Terrell might be involved and disseminated this information to the CIA, Secret Service, State Department, Department of Justice, and NSC.

110

Shortly thereafter, on July 15, 1986, Revell received a call from North, who indicated that he knew a person familiar with Terrell's activities and would make his contact available for debriefing. The FBI met that evening with Robinette, North's contact, who told them he had met Terrell on July 11 while posing as an attorney exploring the possibility of collaborating with Terrell on a book, movie, and television program. Robinette, who was in daily contact with Terrell, offered to assist the FBI in gaining information about him.

On July 22, 1986, FBI agents interviewed North. He told them he had heard of Terrell eighteen months earlier when a Contra intelligence officer complained of Terrell's brutality. North claimed he suggested at the time of that incident that local officials should expel Terrell. North stated that he had heard that Terrell had tried to import guns into a Central American country and had claimed to be formerly with U.S. Army Special Forces and the CIA.

The FBI agents asked North about Secord and Robinette. North said Secord ran an import-export business and was a consultant to the Defense Department and emphasized Secord did not work for him. He said Robinette was a security consultant hired by Secord to investigate Terrell. North acknowledged he met with Robinette prior to sending him to the FBI and that Robinette gave him copies of the Terrell manuscript and the other materials Robinette shared with the FBI. North stated that neither he nor his staff was responsible for arming, funding, or administering Contra programs and denied he was involved with covert operations being run from the U.S.

The FBI decided to watch Terrell with Robinette's help. Although Robinette refused to wear a recording device, he reported back to the FBI after he met with Terrell. Shortly thereafter, Terrell went to Miami at the same time President Reagan visited Miami. Agents observed him there and concluded he was not a threat to the President. The FBI then terminated this investigation.

## SUMMARY

We do not mean to impugn the integrity of the law enforcement officials involved. Suggestions that national security could be compromised, coming from NSC aides, inevitably were given weight by law enforcement officials and led them on occasion to provide information to the NSC staff and to delay investigations. The fault lies with the members of the NSC staff who tried to compromise the independence of law enforcement agencies by misusing claims of national security.

# CHAPTER 6

# Keeping "USG Fingerprints"* Off the Contra Operation: 1984–1985

In October 1984, the President signed into law a version of the Boland Amendment barring the Central Intelligence Agency, the Department of Defense, and "any other agency or entity of the United States involved in intelligence activities" from providing support to Contra military activities. Explaining the statute on the floor of the House of Representatives immediately before its passage, Representative Edward P. Boland, then Chairman of the House Permanent Select Committee on Intelligence, was clear about the legislation's intent: the provision "ends U.S. support for the war in Nicaragua." National Security Adviser Robert C. McFarlane acknowledged that intent: "the Boland Amendment governed our actions," he told these Committees. Although Congress eventually approved humanitarian aid for the Contras and authorized intelligence sharing, the full prohibition on lethal support remained in effect until October 1986.

Despite the Boland Amendment's prohibition, U.S. support for the Nicaraguan Resistance continued. As set forth fully in Chapters 2 and 3, members of the National Security Council staff—with help from officials of other Government agencies—supervised a covert operation supporting the Contras. They provided weapons and military intelligence to the Resistance and resupplied troops inside Nicaragua, using funds raised from foreign countries, private citizens, and ultimately the Iranian arms sales. They did so despite the unambiguous intent of Congress that the U.S. Government, including the NSC staff, could not aid the Contras' military effort.

Secrecy, therefore, was vital to the success of the Contra operation. Disclosure of U.S. support, Oliver North wrote to John Poindexter in May 1986, "could well become a political embarrassment for the President and you." Moreover, disclosure would surely doom the project. Poindexter told these Committees: "It was very likely if it became obvious what we were doing that Members of Congress would have maybe tightened it [the law] up. I didn't want that to happen."

But just as secrecy was vital to the operation's success, even limited success jeopardized that secrecy. As the Contras continued

---

*North's term used in two PROF notes to Poindexter dealing with the possible disclosure of the U.S. Government link to the Contra operation.

to purchase supplies and equipment despite the cut-off of aid, Congress and the media inquired, inevitably, about the sources of Resistance support and funding.

Officials involved in the Contra support operation took every precaution to ensure that the project remained secret. They withheld the facts from some Administration officials who spoke out frequently on U.S. policy in Central America, forcing them to mislead Congress and the American people. They discouraged reporters from pursuing the link between the NSC staff and the Contras. And they responded to direct inquiries with half truths and false statements.

## 1983–1984: SUSPICIONS, AND THE "CASEY ACCORDS"

Even before the full-prohibition Boland Amendment was enacted in October 1984, Members of Congress were concerned that the Administration was not providing sufficient information about the covert program in support of the Nicaraguan Resistance.

In April 1983, Senator Daniel Moynihan, Vice Chairman of the Senate Select Committee on Intelligence, spoke of a "crisis of confidence" between Congress and the intelligence agencies running the operation. A year later, Committee Chairman Barry Goldwater rebuked the CIA in the wake of the revelations related to Nicaragua harbor mining.

After the mining incident became public in April 1984, Director Casey was called before an extraordinary secret session of the Senate—60 Members were present—to explain the failure to consult adequately ahead of time. The Director apologized at the ses-

sion, and promised a new spirit of cooperation. The promise would soon be formalized in what became known as the "Casey Accords," an agreement between the CIA and the Senate Intelligence Committee on consultation guidelines for covert operations.

The accords reflected the recognition that cooperation and forthrightness on covert activities were essential in the relationship between the Executive and Congress. But the subsequent actions of Casey and members of the NSC staff did not reflect that recognition.

## 1984: TESTIMONY BEFORE CONGRESS ON THIRD-COUNTRY ASSISTANCE

In December 1983, the President signed into law legislation limiting funding for the Contras in fiscal year 1984 to $24 million.

The Administration, however, sought funding for the Contras beyond the $24 million appropriation. On several occasions in 1984, officials tried to obtain aid for the Contras from third-country sources. Those attempts occurred as early as February, when the Administration began to suspect that Congress was not likely to approve supplemental funding for the Contras when the $24 million ran out. Shortly thereafter, McFarlane sought to obtain equipment, materiel and training for the Contras from Country 1.

Stories about the third-country contacts soon began appearing in the media. Prompted by the reports, the House Permanent Select Committee on Intelligence requested an appearance on May 2 by CIA Director Casey and Kenneth W. Dam, then Deputy Secretary of State. The testimony occurred about 5 weeks after Casey had sent the memorandum to McFarlane outlining the CIA's efforts to obtain lethal assistance for the Contras from Country 1 and Country 6 and indicating Casey's awareness of McFarlane's attempt to obtain assistance from Country 1. Coming only days after he had pledged to be fully candid with Congress, Casey's testimony was inconsistent with his memorandums:

STOKES: . . . There has been some talk in the media with reference to [Country 1] or [Country 2] being alternative funding sources. What can you tell us about that?

CASEY: Well, there has been a lot of discussion. We have not been involved in that at all.

FOWLER: Who has?

CASEY: I do not know.

\* \* \*

FOWLER: . . . Is any element of our Government approaching any element of another Government to obtain aid for the Contras?

CASEY: No, not to my knowledge.

Kenneth Dam acknowledged to the Committees that "there have been conversations with [Country 1]" about aid to the Contras and explained that those talks had led nowhere. He also said that there had been no "high level" approach to Country 2. Asked about Administration activities, Dam denied that the U.S. Government was approaching other countries for assistance. Dam's denials accurately reflected State Department policy but not Administration activities. There is no evidence that Dam was aware of the Casey and McFarlane third-country efforts or that he did not make his statements in good faith. However, Casey, who knew at least about the

approaches to Countries 1 and 6, did not correct Dam's statements.

On September 9, two major newspapers, The New York Times and the Miami Herald, published reports suggesting that third countries and private U.S. citizens had replaced the CIA in providing aid to the Contras. The reports prompted another Congressional inquiry. Three days after the stories appeared, the House Intelligence Committee called officials from the CIA and the State Department to appear before it. Members assumed that these officials —Dewey Clarridge, the CIA's Latin American Division Chief, and Ambassador Anthony Langhorne Motley, Assistant Secretary of State for Inter-American Affairs—would know whether the reports were true or false.

Clarridge told the Members that the CIA believed the Contras had been receiving about $1 million per month—precisely what Country 2 had provided. He added, however, "We know of no place or no country that has supplied any funds in any real amount."

**Asked several times, several ways, if the U.S. was soliciting foreign help for the Contras, Motley repeatedly said no.**

## EARLY 1985: THE SECOND COUNTRY 2 CONTRIBUTION

In February 1985, the Administration obtained an additional donation from Country 2. A $5 million deposit was made on February 27, 1985; by the end of March 1985, the amount totaled $24 million, bringing the total donation from that country to about

114

$32 million. Again, officials took steps to ensure that the funding remained secret.

Within weeks of the new donation, Assistant Secretary Motley was called to testify before the Senate Committee on Foreign Relations. On March 26, 1985, Senator Christopher Dodd asked about "a number of rumors or news reports around this town about how the Administration might go about its funding of the Contras in Nicaragua. There have been suggestions that it would be done through private groups or through funneling funds through friendly third nations, or possibly through a new category of assistance and asking the Congress to fund the program openly." Motley replied that the Boland Amendment prohibited "any U.S. assistance whether direct or indirect, which to us would infer also soliciting and/or encouraging third countries; and we have refrained from doing that because of the prohibition."

**Even as the CIA was directly or indirectly helping the Contras in several ways, Casey told the Senate Intelligence Committee that his Agency had "carefully kept away from anything which would suggest involvement in their activities."**

## DEFLECTING MEDIA INQUIRIES

By June 1985, reporters were close to establishing a link between the NSC staff and Contra support. A June 3 memo from North to Poindexter illustrates North's efforts to discourage reporters from pursuing the story. North boasted in the memo that at his request, Adolfo Calero told Alfonso Chardy of the Miami Herald "that if he (Chardi) [sic] printed any derogatory comments about the FDN or its funding sources that Chardi [sic]

would never again be allowed to visit FDN bases or travel with their units." North added: "At no time did my name or an NSC connection arise during their discussion."

North and retired Major General John K. Singlaub had already devised a plan to divert press attention away from the NSC staff's Contra operation, which by then was being coordinated under North by Richard Secord, Richard Gadd, and their employees. North encouraged Singlaub to court the media, realizing that, as Singlaub put it, "If I [Singlaub] had high visibility, I might be the lightening rod and take the attention away from himself [North] and others who were involved in the covert side of support."

The plan seems to have had some success. Shortly after his discussion with North, Singlaub was the subject of a long article in The Washington Post connecting him to support for the Contras, and in the coming months, he would be featured in virtually all the major newspapers. Although North himself soon would be the subject of press reports, Secord was not mentioned in the media until mid-1986, and details of North's resupply operation were not revealed until the plane carrying Eugene Hasenfus was shot down in October 1986.

## June–August 1985: Press Reports on NSC Staff and Contra Support

By April, third-country funding had not only sustained the Contras but had "allowed the growth of the Resistance from 9,500 personnel in June 1984 to over 16,000 today—all with arms," according to an April 11, 1985, memo from North to McFarlane. During May, according to a May 31 memo, "the Nicaraguan Resistance recorded significant advances in their struggle against the Sandinistas."

In June, reporters first linked the Contras' success with North. By mid-August, most major news organizations had published or broadcast reports on this "influential and occasionally controversial character in the implementation of the Reagan Administration's foreign policy."

News stories in June 1985 explored the sources of Contra funding. On June 10, the Associated Press distributed an article by Robert Parry suggesting that the White House had lent support to private fundraising efforts. The article named North as the White House contact for such efforts, which according to the report, revolved around John Singlaub.

Two weeks later, the Miami Herald reported that the Administration "helped organize" and continued to support "supposedly spontaneous" private fundraising efforts. The article quoted extensively from ousted Nicaraguan Democratic Force (FDN) leader Edgar Chamorro, who described a trip by North and a CIA officer to a Contra base in the spring of 1984. North and the CIA officer assured the rebels, according to the article, that the White House would "find a way" to keep the movement alive. Neither North nor the CIA officer specifically promised private aid, although "it was clear that was their intent," Chamorro was quoted as saying.

In August, reports in The New York Times, The Washington Post, and other major newspapers asserted that White House support for the Contras involved more than fundraising. Oliver North had given the Contras "direct military advice" on rebel attacks, exercising "tactical influence" on military operations, The New York Times

reported. The newspaper reported that North had also "facilitated the supplying of logistical help" to the Contras, filling in where the CIA could no longer help. The information was attributed to anonymous "administration officials."

## Denials

The day after this story appeared, President Reagan responded to the allegations. "[W]e're not violating any laws," the President said as he signed legislation providing $27 million in humanitarian aid for the Contras and authorizing the exchange of intelligence. In a statement released later that day, the President added that he would "continue to work with Congress to carry out the program as effectively as possible and take care that the law be faithfully executed."

The National Security Adviser made his first comments on the allegations about North in an interview with The Washington Post. In an August 11 article, McFarlane said he had told his staff to comply with the Boland Amendment. "We could not provide any support," he said, but he also stated that the NSC staff could and did maintain contact with the Contras.

## SUMMER AND FALL AUGUST 1985: CONGRESSIONAL INQUIRIES

In the third week of August, Representative Michael Barnes, Chairman of the Subcommittee on Western Hemisphere Affairs of the House Committee on Foreign Affairs, and Representative Lee H. Hamilton, Chairman of the House Permanent Select Committee on Intelligence, separately wrote the President's National Security Adviser, inquiring into NSC support for the Contras. Representative Barnes' letter, dated August 16, cited press accounts as the cause of concern about NSC staff support for the Contras. The reports, Barnes wrote, "raise serious questions regarding the violation of the letter and spirit of U.S. law."

## RESPONSES TO CONGRESS: THE MCFARLANE LETTERS

On September 5, McFarlane sent the first of his responses to Congress. He wrote to Representative Hamilton: "I can state with deep personal conviction that at no time did I or any member of the National Security Council staff violate the letter or spirit" of Congressional restrictions on aid to the Contras. In denying allegations about NSC staff activities, the letter echoed the language of the Boland Amendment:

> I am most concerned . . . there be no misgivings as to the existence of any parallel efforts to provide, directly or indirectly, support for military or paramilitary activities in Nicaragua. There has not been, nor will there be, any such activities by the NSC staff.

This letter, drafted by McFarlane himself, served as the model for five additional letters prepared by North, signed by McFarlane, and sent in September and October in response to Congressional inquiries. In testimony before these Committees, McFarlane called these responses "too categorical." He said: "I did not give as full an answer as I should have." North went further, acknowl-

edging that statements in the letters were "false," and summarizing the responses as "erroneous, misleading, evasive, and wrong."

## First Reaction: Conceal the Facts

**Citing the *New York Times* story telling of North's involvement with the Contras, Representative Barnes' letter also made a broad request for NSC documents on the subject. But an NSC information policy officer decided to conduct only a narrow search of NSC office files.**

Within a few days, some 50 relevant documents were identified, and 10 to 20 were deemed worthy of review. They were given to Commander Paul Thompson, the NSC's General Counsel. On or about August 26, Thompson gave the documents to McFarlane, warning him that some warranted concern and raising the possibility of asserting executive privilege in response to the Barnes inquiry.

## The Six "Troubling" Memos

McFarlane reviewed the documents and selected six memorandums which, despite the narrow focus of the search, "seemed to me to raise legitimate questions about compliance with the law." He added: "[A]n objective reading would have taken passages in each of these memorandums to be either reflective of a past act that was not within the law or a recommendation that a future act be carried out that wouldn't be."

**One of the memos told of North's meeting with the Chinese Government to discuss the sale of**

antiaircraft missiles to the Contras. In another North proposed helping the Contras attack and sink a Nicaraguan merchant ship that was delivering weapons to the Sandinistas. In a third memo, North proposed increasing foreign aid to Guatemala as compensation for "extraordinary assistance" given to the Contras. The fourth memo described North's "fallback plan" for aiding the Contras if Congress did not renew aid. In the fifth, North described the current status of Contra forces and said efforts should be made to raise $15 to $20 million so the Contra force could grow to between 30,000 and 35,000 men, compared to about 12,000 then. And in the final memo North provided an update of Contra military and political activities.

## Undiscovered Documents

The memos Thompson presented to McFarlane in late August 1985 did not represent all the memos written by North to McFarlane demonstrating North's involvement in supporting the Contras. Because it was limited by the information policy officer to official NSC and Presidential Advisory files, the search would not uncover "nonlog" memorandums. In one such memo, dated November 7, 1984, North made clear that he was attempting to pass intelligence information about Sandinista HIND helicopters to Calero.

Nor did the search turn up relevant logged memorandums in which North indicated that he and Contra leaders had planned the timing of rebel military operations. For example, a March 20, 1985, memo stated:

> In addition to the events depicted on the internal chronology at Tab A, other activities in the region continue as planned—including military operations and political action. Like the

chronology, these events are also timed to influence the vote:

— planned travel by Calero, Cruz and Robelo;
— various military resupply efforts timed to support significantly increased military operations immediately after the vote (we expect major Sandinista crossborder attacks in this time frame—today's resupply . . . went well); and
— special operations attacks against highly visible military targets in Nicaragua.

## MCFARLANE-NORTH ALTERATION DISCUSSIONS

On August 28, McFarlane and North began a series of lengthy meetings to fashion a response to the Congressional inquiries. According to a chronology prepared by McFarlane, they met six times and spoke by phone four times between August 28 and September 12, the date of the response to Representative Barnes. Although both McFarlane and North acknowledged to the Committees that they discussed altering the documents, the two dispute the purpose of the meetings.

The two reviewed the documents and, according to McFarlane, North explained that his memos were being misinterpreted. For example, in one memo North wrote that the FDN "has responded well to guidance on how to build a staff," and that "all FDN commanders have been schooled" in guerrilla warfare tactics. McFarlane said North told him, contrary to any implication in the document, that the guidance came not from him but from retired military officers hired by the Contras. As McFarlane related the events, North offered to alter the documents and McFarlane gave him a tentative go-ahead. McFarlane testified:

> Well, as we went through them, he pointed out where my own interpretation was just not accurate . . . and he just said, you are misreading my intent, and I can make it reflect what I have said if this is ambiguous to you, and I said all right, do that.

North shortly returned with a sample alteration. McFarlane's testimony indicates that the document North had altered was "FDN Military Operations," dated April 11, 1985. The recommendation in the document, "that the current donors be approached to provide $15–20M additional between now and June 1, 1985" was replaced with a recommendation that "an effort must be made to persuade the Congress to support the Contras." North had asserted, according to McFarlane, that the problem with the documents was one of interpretation and that the changes would be slight. McFarlane acknowledged that this alteration left the document "grossly at variance with the original text."

McFarlane testified that he did not replace any original NSC documents with altered documents and did not instruct North to do so. He said he took with him when he resigned the pages North had altered and eventually destroyed them.

North's version of events is substantially different. McFarlane, North testified, brought the selected documents to his attention, "indicated that there were problems with them, and told me to fix them." This meant, he testified, that he was to "remove references to certain activities, certain undertakings on my behalf or his, and basically clean up the record."

## RESPONSES TO CONGRESS: THE DENIALS

Within days of his document review and discussions with North, McFarlane sent the first of his responses to Congress. In addition to the broad assurance that the NSC staff was complying with the "letter and the spirit" of the Boland Amendment, the responses contain specific denials of allegations that the NSC staff had provided fundraising or military support to the Nicaraguan resistance.

### Fundraising

McFarlane's September 12 response to Representative Barnes stated: "None of us has solicited funds, [or] facilitated contacts for prospective potential donors. . . ."

In his October 7 letter, McFarlane replied as follows to a written question from Representative Hamilton:

MR. HAMILTON: The Nicaraguan freedom fighters, in the last two months, are reported by the U.S. Embassy, Tegucigalpa, to have received a large influx of funds and equipment with some estimates of their value reaching as high as $10 million or more. Do you know where they have obtained this assistance?

MR. MCFARLANE: No.

In fact, according to his own testimony, McFarlane not only knew how the Contras obtained financial assistance, he personally facilitated the main donation to the Contras:

Q: . . . I was referring to Country Two and the fact that the actual donors had, as I understand it, Country Two was the actual donors—

A: Yes.

Q: And that you had not only facilitated contacts, but you had facilitated the actual contribution.

A: I will accept that, yes.

## Military Assistance

In his September 5 letter, McFarlane stated:

> At no time did we encourage military activities. Our emphasis on a political rather than a military solution to the situation was as close as we ever came to influencing the military aspect of their struggle.

North was heavily involved in the military aspect of the Contra struggle. He testified that this statement was false. In addition to helping arm the Contras, and to providing intelligence and cash to Contra leaders, North also, beginning in the summer of 1985, coordinated the efforts to set up a resupply operation to provide lethal and nonlethal supplies to troops inside Nicaragua. Several weeks before the letters were drafted, North asked Secord to set up the operation, and he called on Ambassador Lewis Tambs to facilitate the construction of an airfield for refueling resupply aircraft. Yet, McFarlane wrote to Representative Hamilton on October 7:

> Lieutenant Colonel North did not use his influence to facilitate the movement of supplies to the resistance.

North acknowledged that this statement was false.

It is unclear whether McFarlane was fully aware of North's activities. McFarlane testified he was not. But the documents McFarlane reviewed and about which he was concerned shortly before drafting the first response to Congress showed that North repeatedly attempted to influence the military aspect of the Contras' struggle.

Furthermore, McFarlane specifically denied in his October 7 letter to Representative Hamilton that North had provided the Contras "tactical advice":

> The allegation that Lieutenant Colonel North offered the resistance tactical advice and direction is, as I indicated in my briefing, patently untrue.

North acknowledged to the Committees that although he never "sat down in the battlefield and offered direct tactical advice . . . I certainly did have a number of discussions with the Resistance about military activities, yes, to include the broader strategy for the Southern front and an Atlantic front and an internal front." And McFarlane testified: "I felt it was likely that an officer of the qualifications and excellence of Col. North, when he was down visiting in Central America, probably did extend advice." Indeed, McFarlane admitted in his testimony that he felt in 1985 that "it was likely" that North had gone "beyond the law" on giving military advice to the Contras.

**McFarlane's written denials were repeated in face-to-face meetings with Members of Congress. Representative Lee Hamilton, Chairman of the House Intelligence Committee, told McFarlane, "I for one am willing to take you at your word," and he dropped his investigation.**

120

## MCFARLANE-BARNES DOCUMENT DISPUTE

In his first response to Representative Barnes on September 12, McFarlane ignored the Congressman's request for documents. A PROF note to Paul Thompson on September 20 indicated that McFarlane believed he had successfully sidestepped the document issue: "Now that we have the Barnes letter behind us you can return the Contra papers to Ollie please."

Ten days later, however, Representative Barnes renewed his document request. In a letter to McFarlane dated September 30, 1985, the Congressman wrote:

> I am sure you understand that the pertinent documents must be provided if the Committee is to be able to fulfill its obligation to adopt legislation governing the conduct of United States foreign policy and to oversee the implementation of that policy under the law.

Representative Barnes and McFarlane met at the White House on October 17. The day before the meeting, NSC General Counsel Paul Thompson prepared a memo for McFarlane suggesting that Representative Barnes should be told that the National Security Adviser had no legal authority to turn over the documents.

At the meeting with Congressman Barnes, McFarlane, referring to a stack of documents on his desk, explained that a document search had been made and that McFarlane had selected documents relevant to Congressional inquiries. He told Congressman Barnes he would not permit the documents to leave his office but would allow the Congressman to read them there.

McFarlane acknowledged that he made the offer knowing Representative Barnes would likely refuse it:

Q: And I take it—it was part of your thinking that if a busy Congressman came down to your office and saw a substantial stack of documents, and you were having a short meeting [McFarlane had budgeted one hour for the session], it was very unlikely that he would ask to read through the documents from one end to the other?

A: I think that is true, yes.

Indeed, Representative Barnes deemed the offer not to be serious. He understood McFarlane to imply that the documents on the desk were not all the documents but only the ones McFarlane had concluded were "relevant." This, Barnes felt, "was not an adequate way to ascertain the truth of the allegations."

On October 29, Representative Barnes wrote McFarlane again expressing his view that the procedures mandated by McFarlane were "inadequate." He requested that McFarlane turn the documents over to the House Intelligence Committee, thereby assuring that the classified materials would be appropriately handled. Representative Barnes wrote: "I believe that this proposal would surely resolve any concerns that the Administration might have about the security of the information, while at the same time fulfilling the responsibilities of the House." This was the last correspondence between McFarlane and Representative Barnes on this issue.

## MCFARLANE'S 1986 TESTIMONY

In the wake of the November 1986 revelations and a full year after he left office, McFarlane testified before several panels investigating the Iran-Contra Affair: the Senate and House Intelligence Committees, the Senate and House Foreign Affairs Committees, and the President's Special Review Board (The Tower Board). Again, Members of Congress—and this time officials on the Tower Board staff as well—were unable to learn the crucial facts about the Government's actions in support of the Nicaraguan Resistance.

The former National Security Adviser acknowledged to the panels that North had told him in May 1986 about the diversion of Iranian arms sales funds to the Contras. That aspect of Administration support for the Resistance, by the time of McFarlane's December 1986 testimony, had been revealed by the Attorney General. Beyond that, McFarlane withheld virtually all other relevant information in his possession about U.S. support for the Contras during the period of Congressional restrictions. He concealed new information he learned of North's activities in 1986, and he repeated many of the inaccurate statements that he had made orally and in writing to Members of Congress while he was National Security Adviser.

In his testimony before the Select Committees, McFarlane acknowledged that his remarks to investigating panels between December 1986 and February 1987, like his statements about U.S. support of the Resistance in 1984 and 1985, had been "clearly too categorical."

**Even after the Iran-Contra scandal broke open, in December 1986, McFarlane steadfastly continued to deny any knowledge of most of North's activities. Asked again if other countries, including Saudi Arabia, had donated money to the Contras, he said: "I have no idea of the extent of that or anything else."**

## SUMMER 1985: INQUIRY OF THE INTELLIGENCE OVERSIGHT BOARD

The flood of press allegations about possible NSC violations of the Boland Amendment prompted no investigations by executive branch law enforcement agencies. Only one small executive oversight organization, the Intelligence Oversight Board, responded to the widespread charges. In late August 1985, the Board conducted an inquiry into NSC staff activities. After a brief investigation by its counsel, Bretton G. Sciaroni, the Board concluded that Oliver North had not provided military or fundraising assistance to the Nicaraguan Resistance.

Sciaroni began his inquiry with a 30 to 40 minute interview of Paul Thompson. Shortly before that interview, Thompson turned over to McFarlane the NSC file documents on North's activities. Those documents included the six "troubling" memorandums that indicated, as Thompson later put it, that "if he [North] was in effect doing what was reflected in the documents, he was perhaps not aware of the constraints of the . . . Boland Amendment." In his interview with Sciaroni, Thompson made no mention of North's activities as depicted in the memorandums. Indeed, he denied that North had provided "military support" to the Contras and asserted that North had limited himself to providing political encouragement and "moral support" while funds were unavailable. Although the Committees cannot be certain what Thompson knew directly of North's activities, it is clear that his denials cannot be squared with the memorandums he had given McFarlane.

Furthermore, Thompson withheld from Sciaroni the six "troubling" memorandums included in the batch he gave McFarlane. During their meeting, Thompson provided Sciaroni an inch-thick pile of documents and told him he was producing "the relevant documents for my review," according to Sciaroni. The only documents to which Sciaroni would not be permitted access, Thompson told him, were North's personal working files. Thompson also told Sciaroni that the pile of documents he was turning over were the same as those that had been "shown to the Hill." Missing from the pile were many of the documents Thompson himself acknowledged raised questions about North's activities.

Sciaroni's next investigative step was to talk with North. During a 5-minute discussion, North gave Sciaroni a "blanket denial" of charges that he was actively involved in aiding the Contras. Although North did not recall the conversation with Sciaroni, he was clear in his testimony that he had no intention of being candid with the Intelligence Oversight Board Counsel: "I am sure if he asked me" about supporting the Contras, "I denied it, because after all we viewed this to be a covert operation and he had absolutely no need to know the details of what I was doing."

Still, Sciaroni stressed in his testimony that he was justified in expecting cooperation from NSC staff officers. Both Thompson and North, he said, "understood who I represented, the mandate of the Board to look into matters of legality, and the seriousness of the allegations that had been raised." His investigation was "an anomaly" in that he had no legal authority over the NSC staff, and therefore, Sciaroni said, he "was relying upon the good will of other officers at the White House." Once again, however, North chose to conceal. This time, the object of his deception was a board established by and operating within the executive branch, an entity privy to intelligence information and programs of the highest sensitivity.

## SUMMARY

While exercising its responsibility to oversee the implementation of the law cutting off aid to the Nicaraguan Resistance, Congress tried repeatedly through 1984 and 1985 to learn how the Resistance was staying alive and whether the U.S. Government was involved with the Contras' survival. The President, the Vice President, the National Security Adviser, and officials on the NSC staff were aware that a multimillion dollar donation from Country 2, facilitated by McFarlane, was largely responsible for the Contras' survival. North, Poindexter, and perhaps other high Administration officials, were aware that the NSC staff was directly providing lethal support to the Nicaraguan Resistance. McFarlane denied knowledge of North's activities, but documents he reviewed following Congressional inquiries show that North actively assisted the Contras' military effort.

Yet Congressional inquiries on U.S. support for the Contras were invariably met with categorical denials. So too were inquiries made by the media. In both cases, the information sought related not to sensitive operational details, but to a controversial foreign policy issue. The question repeatedly asked was whether it was the policy and practice of the U.S. Government during this period to provide lethal support to the rebels fighting in Nicaragua. It was to that question that Administration officials repeatedly responded with denials.

The record leaves no doubt that some of the officials making these denials did so as part of a deliberate attempt to deceive Congress and the public. North, who testified, "I didn't want to show Congress a single word on this whole thing," admitted that the letters sent to Congress over McFarlane's signature were "false." In meetings with Members of Congress, McFarlane repeated the statements in the letters. He acknowledged in testimony before these Committees that he had been "too categorical." Poindexter testified that his intent during this period was to "withhold information." And it is difficult to reconcile CIA Director Casey's testimony in this period with his knowledge of the facts as demonstrated by the documentary evidence, and with his pledge to the Senate Intelligence Committee that he would abide by a new spirit of cooperation.

Other officials who denied the existence of U.S. support, including the State Department officials who testified before Congress in 1984 and 1985, and the press liaison of the NSC staff, were unaware of the truth, themselves victims of concealed information.

As 1986 began, a new National Security Adviser was supervising the NSC staff, promoted from within. But the covert Contra operation continued, as did the overriding concern to keep the fact that the United States was providing lethal aid to the Contras secret from Congress and the American people.

# CHAPTER 7

# Keeping "USG Fingerprints" Off the Contra Operation: 1986

In 1986, the Contra support project finally achieved a degree of operational success. By mid-year, weapons and other material were being dropped to Resistance troops inside northern Nicaragua; by fall, similar airdrops were being made in the South. Congress had appropriated funds for the humanitarian needs of the Contras, it had authorized third-country solicitation for humanitarian aid, and it had allowed the CIA to provide intelligence to the Resistance. But Congress had maintained the prohibition on lethal support. Following the pattern of 1984–1985, allegations in the media and independently obtained information prompted Congressional inquiries, which in turn were met with categorical denials by Administration officials, some of whom knew the statements to be misleading and false.

The expansion of the covert operation's activities in 1986 also created new problems for officials still seeking to maintain secrecy. In September, a new Costa Rican Government threatened to reveal the existence of the Santa Elena airfield, exposing the involvement of U.S. citizens and Government officials in providing support to the Con-tras. Administration officials mobilized quickly to squelch the threatened press conference. Successful at first, the officials were unable to prevent disclosure by the Costa Rican Government three weeks later. Concerned that reporters might discover the link between the airfield and U.S. officials, North immediately took steps to ensure that no "USG fingerprints" would be found on Santa Elena.

In October, the Sandinistas shot down an Enterprise plane on a resupply mission (the Hasenfus flight). Administration officials, not all of whom knew the true facts, denied before Congress and to the media that the U.S. Government was involved in the Hasenfus flight. Even the President spoke out. With no protest from his National Security Adviser or others aware of the facts, the President told the American people: "[T]here is no government connection with that at all."

For most of 1986, efforts to determine whether the U.S. Government was providing lethal support to the Contras despite the legal restrictions were thwarted by the same techniques used in 1985.

## JANUARY TO JUNE 1986: PRESS REPORTS

Through the first quarter of 1986, Congressional and media attention on the NSC staff's involvement with the Contras abated. In Washington, Congressional Committees had accepted the categorical denials the previous fall by the National Security Adviser. In Central America, the resupply project was not fully operational and Resistance activities slowed. A New York Times reporter in the region in January found the "Nicaraguan guerrillas . . . back in their camps;" in early March, the correspondent described the Resistance as being "in its worst military condition since its formation in 1982."

By the end of March, the Contras' fortunes began to shift, and articles again appeared discussing the sources of Resistance funds and supplies. Some focused on charges that the Contras had received lethal support from American mercenaries and funds from drug trafficking; others explored how the Contras were spending the $27 million appropriated by Congress in August, 1985, for humanitarian aid. By the end of April, North had reemerged as the focus of attention. The allegations in the new series of articles were almost always attributed to anonymous officials, and some of the details were incorrect. But the main charge—that U.S. Government officials had continued to provide lethal aid to the Contras despite the Boland Amendment—was accurate. The renewed reporting provided the context for a new round of Congressional inquiries that would begin at the end of June.

**Through the spring, *The Miami Herald* published several articles about North's activities in support of the Contras.**

126

## Concern for Secrecy

As the Contra support operation expanded during 1986, the task of maintaining secrecy became more challenging. National Security Adviser John Poindexter, who admitted to the Committees, "I wanted to withhold information on the NSC operational activities in support of the Contras from most everybody," did what he could to conceal the NSC connection.

North oversaw two of the most important NSC "accounts," but Poindexter kept North's title artificially low because "we wanted to provide a significant amount of cover for Colonel North and his activities." According to Poindexter, North's responsibilities warranted the title Special Assistant to the President, the third-level rank in the White House. Instead, he kept North as Deputy Director of Political Military Affairs. "We didn't want to call public attention to Colonel North," Poindexter testified.

In July, shortly after the renewal of Congressional inquiries, Poindexter tried further to downplay North's responsibilities. He apparently leaked to the Washington Times the story that North's position at the NSC staff was "precarious" and that "NSC soft liners" were maneuvering "to edge him out." In a PROF Note sent the day the article appeared, Poindexter reassured North about his intentions: "I do not want you to leave and to be honest cannot afford to let you go." He told North to call two reporters at the Washington Times and "tell them to call off the dogs." Poindexter wrote: "Tell them on deep background, off the record, not be published, that I just wanted to lower your visibility so you wouldn't be such a good target for the Libs [Liberals]."

For purposes of secrecy North stopped writing "logged memos" that went into NSC files. Instead he began communicating using the NSC computer system, figuring (incorrectly) that it was more secure. These computer messages were called PROF notes, named for the IBM professional office computer system. Poindexter arranged it so North could communicate directly with his computer terminal, bypassing the normal NSC channels by using a special file called "Private Blank Check."

Poindexter also stressed to North the need to avoid speaking of his secret operational activities with anyone, including other Administration officials. In May 1986, Poindexter learned that North had discussed his plan to offer the *Erria* to the CIA for use in a covert activity with Ken deGraffenreid, Senior Director of Intelligence Programs at the NSC, the officer who maintained NSC documents of the highest sensitivity. The *Erria* was a ship under North's control, purchased by the Enterprise for use in various covert operations. In a PROF he titled "Be Cautious," Poindexter directed North to maintain absolute silence about his activities:

I am afraid you are letting your operational role become too public. From now on I don't want you to talk to anybody else, including [CIA Director] Casey, except me about any of your operational roles. In fact you need to quietly generate a cover story that I have insisted that you stop.

Poindexter testified that he was particularly concerned about keeping Casey ignorant of the operation because the CIA Director could be called to testify before Congressional Committees.

Poindexter also kept the existence of the covert operation hidden from officials who did not ordinarily testify before Congress, such as former Chief of Staff Donald Regan. Poindexter explained: "Based on my feeling that if we were going to keep this up and avoid more restrictive legislation, that we simply had to limit the knowledge of the details to those that had absolutely the need to know. I simply didn't think that he [Regan] had an absolute need to know." In addition, Poindexter testified that he felt Regan "talked to the press too much. I was afraid he'd make a slip." Despite Poindexter's directive, North kept the CIA Director apprised of everything, according to his testimony. But North shared Poindexter's desire to conceal U.S. Government coordination of Contra support activities from Congress and the American public. He told these Committees: "I didn't want to show Congress a single word on this whole thing."

The next month, as airdrops became more frequent, North tried to ensure that resupply activities in Central America could not be traced back to him or other U.S. officials. On June 16, he informed Tomas Castillo, a CIA Station Chief in Central America, that he had sent Rafael Quintero to Central America to facilitate a supply drop to the FDN. "I do not think we ought to contemplate these operations without him being on the scene," North wrote via KL-43. "Too many things go wrong that then directly involve you and me in what should be deniable for both of us."

Shortly after this message to Castillo, Karna Small, the press liaison for the NSC staff, asked North to comment on allegations that would be broadcast in a CBS News program, "West 57th Street." Small sent a note to North saying she had declined the show's request to speak with North, but that since it would include interviews with people making charges about North, she should call back with a comment. She remarked, "I can't just give them the 'bullshit' response."

The segment aired on June 25. It charged that "the White House secretly directed a private aid network to arm the Contras when it was illegal for the White House to do that." The show focused on John Hull, suggesting that he played an important role in helping the Contras from his ranch in Costa Rica. It also alleged that Robert Owen acted as "the NSC representative" to the Contras and their supporters in Costa Rica. Describing Owen as "the bag man for Ollie North," the report charged that he carried $10,000 a month from the NSC to John Hull for use in purchasing lethal and nonlethal supplies for the Nicaraguan Resistance. The segment also reported: "The White House today quoted Colonel Oliver North as calling the private aid network 'nonsense.' The White House also said, quote, 'The President never approved any such plan' [to aid the Contras]".

Two days after the show aired, North sent a PROF to Karna Small:

I have just had a chance to watch the W57th piece. As far as I am concerned, it is the single most distorted piece of 'reporting' I have ever seen. . . . The only charges made about the NSC are made by people who are in jail, on their way to jail or just out of jail. If this is supposed to be credible, then I'll eat my shirt.

**In June 1986, Representative Ron Coleman of Texas called for an investigation of NSC aid to the Contras " 'to get at the truth' behind the widely publicized allegations." Poindexter wrote to Congress, saying all these charges had been answered before. Once again the investigation was dropped.**

## AUGUST 1986: NORTH'S MEETING WITH MEMBERS OF CONGRESS

In response to the Resolution of Inquiry, the House Intelligence Committee sought to meet with North. On August 6, North met with 11 members of the House Intelligence Committee in the White House Situation Room. North began the session with a presentation about his activities. The description echoed closely McFarlane's letters the year before to Representatives Hamilton and Barnes: North's principal mission was to coordinate contacts with the Contras; a main purpose of his job was to assess the viability of the Nicaraguan Resistance as a democratic organization; and he explained to Contra leaders the limitations on U.S. support as imposed by the Boland Amendment. According to a memorandum based on notes taken at the meeting, North said "that he did not in any way, nor at any time violate the spirit, principles or legal requirements of the Boland Amendment."

In response to specific questions, North denied that he had raised funds for the Contras or offered them military advice. North told the Members that his relationship with Robert Owen was "casual," that Owen never took guidance from him. He stated that he had not been in contact with John Singlaub at all in 1985 or 1986.

By his own testimony, North lied to the Members of the Intelligence Committee at this meeting:

A: . . . I will tell you right now, counsel, and all the Members here gathered, that I misled the Congress. I misled—

Q: At that meeting?

A: At that meeting.

Q: Face to face?

A: Face to face.

Q: You made false statements to them about your activities in support of the Contras?

A: I did.

At the conclusion of the meeting, according to an observer, Representative Hamilton "expressed his appreciation for the good-faith effort that Admiral Poindexter had shown in arranging a meeting and indicated his satisfaction in the responses received."

## Authority to Lie

North conceded in his testimony that Poindexter did not give him specific prior authority to make false statements. Before meeting with the Members of the House Intelligence Committee, North expressed to his aide Robert Earl "concern . . . [about] what he was authorized to say" at the session. According to Earl, North tried to obtain guidance from Poindexter but could not reach him. Poindexter "was on leave, yes, out of the office" during this period, according to Earl, who testified: "My impression was that the leave was not accidental. The timing of the leave was just not a coincidence." In his testimony, Earl characterized his observation as follows:

Q: So that your impression of it, your observation of it, was that Colonel North had some information to protect and that he was being left to figure out how to protect it on his own?

A: I think that's a fair statement.

North and Poindexter differ on whether North had general authority from the National Security Adviser to lie at the session. North testified that he was acting under such authority: "I went down to that oral meeting with the same kind of understanding that I had prepared those memos in 1985 and other communications." North added: "[Poindexter] did not specifically go down and say, 'Ollie, lie to the Committee.' I told him what I had said afterwards, and he sent me a note saying, "Well done.""

While Poindexter did send such a note, he claimed it did not indicate approval of North's lies. Poindexter acknowledged that North and he had a "general understanding that he [North] was to withhold information about our involvement." But Poindexter told these Committees that he did not know North had lied at his meeting with the Intelligence Committee, and that he had not expected North would do so.

The evidence is clear, however, that Poindexter knew North had misled the Members of Congress. Poindexter attached his "well done" message to a PROF Note summarizing the meeting.

In his testimony, Poindexter acknowledged that he did not expect North to disclose the truth:

I did think that he would withhold information and be evasive, frankly, in answering questions. My objective all along was to withhold from the Congress exactly what the NSC staff was doing in carrying out the President's policy. . . . I thought that Colonel North would withhold information. There was no doubt about that in my mind.

## SEPTEMBER 1986: THE SANTA ELENA AIRFIELD

Soon after North had turned aside the Congressional inquiry, he learned of a new threat of exposure, this one involving the Santa Elena airfield in Costa Rica. It came just as Congress was taking steps to fund the Contras again.

North told a good deal of the story in a PROF sent the next day to Poindexter: "Last night at 2330 our Project Democracy rep. in Costa Rica called to advise" that the Arias Government would hold a press conference the next morning "announcing that an illegal support operation for the Contras had been taking place from an airfield in Costa Rica for over a year." North wrote that Secord and CIA Station Chief Tomas Castillo would be "predominantly mentioned." From North's notebook it appears that he too was in danger of being mentioned at the press conference. The first entry relating to the incident reads: "0005—call from [Castillo]— Security Minister plans to make public Udall role w/ Base West [Santa Elena airfield] and allege violation of C[osta] R[ican] law by Udall, Bacon, North, Secord, et al."

North immediately arranged a conference call with Elliott Abrams and Louis Tambs. North claimed in his PROF note to Poindexter that the three officials agreed that North would call President Arias and make two threats: if the press conference proceeded as scheduled Arias would not be permitted to meet with President Reagan and he "w[ould] never see a nickel of the $80M that [Agency for International Development Director M. Peter] McPherson had promised him" the day before. North's notebook also reflected his intention to threaten a foreign govern-ment if necessary to maintain secrecy. The entry reads:

> 0008—Conf. . . . Call to Elliott Abrams and Amb Lew Tambs
>
> —Tell Arias:
>
> —Never set foot in W.H.
>
> —Never get 5 [cents] of $80M promised by McPherson.

Ambassador Tambs did call President Arias. The purpose, he testified, was to "dissuade him from this press conference." Abrams recalled instructing Tambs before the call to President Arias that revelation of the airfield would put at risk Arias' upcoming meeting with President Reagan. Tambs testified that he merely told President Arias that it would not be prudent to hold the planned press conference in light of the pending case before the International Court of Justice.

In his PROF note, North assured Poindexter that steps had been taken to ensure that the NSC-coordinated Contra operation would not be linked to the airfield: "As a precaution the Project a/c [aircraft] were flown to [another base] last night and no project personnel remain on site at the field." The next day, Poindexter indicated his approval of North's actions. He wrote in a PROF: "Thanks, Ollie. You did the right thing, but let's try to keep it quiet."

## Airfield Revealed: Damage Control

Although the initial news conference was cancelled, the Costa Rican Government announced the existence of the airfield three weeks later. On September 26, the Costa Rican Interior Minister told reporters that his government had discovered and shut down an airfield that had been used for resupplying the Contras, for trafficking drugs, or both. Secord and North were not mentioned, although the name of the Enterprise Panamanian company that built the airfield, Udall Resources, Inc., was revealed, as was the pseudonym (Robert Olmstead) of William Haskell, the man who purchased the land.

The airfield had not been used in the resupply operation for several months, and the press conference had compromised its location and purpose. Nonetheless, action was taken to ensure that the roles of U.S. officials and the Enterprise remained concealed. In a PROF note, North told Poindexter: "There are no USG fingerprints on any of the operation." Udall Resources, which North described as "a proprietary of Project Democracy," will "cease to exist by noon today." The company's resources—$48,000 —were moved to another Panamanian account. And Udall's office in Panama "is now gone as are all files and paperwork." Olmstead, North added, "is not the name of the agent—Olmstead does not exist."

**In a second PROF note to Poindexter, North wrote: "Believe we have taken all appropriate damage control measures to keep any USG [U.S. Government] fingerprints off this."**

## THE HASENFUS DOWNING

On the morning of October 5, 1986, one of the aircraft belonging to the Enterprise left its operational base with 10,000 pounds of ammunition and gear for FDN forces inside northern Nicaragua. William Cooper was in command, Wallace "Buzz" Sawyer was the co-pilot, and a 17-year-old FDN fighter was handling radio communication with the troops on the ground. Also on board, as the "kicker" who would actually drop the supplies to forces waiting below, was Eugene Hasenfus.

Within a few hours, the aircraft was reported missing. Officials later learned that the plane had been hit by a Sandinista SAM-7 missile over Nicaraguan territory. Three crew members were killed. Hasenfus survived and was captured by the Sandinistas.

The Sandinistas found in the wreckage, and showed reporters, an identification card issued to Hasenfus by the air force in the operational base's host country identifying him as an "adviser" in the "Grupo U.S.A." group at the base, and a business card belonging to an official at the NHAO office in Washington. They also found and displayed an ID card issued to Cooper by Southern Air Transport.

## The U.S. Government Connection

The Hasenfus flight was part of the resupply operation coordinated by North with the support and approval of the President's National Security Adviser. North acknowledged in testimony about the flight: "I was the U.S. Government connection." James Steele, a U.S. Military Group Commander in Central America; Lewis Tambs, the U.S. Ambassador to Costa Rica; and Tomas Castillo, a CIA Station Chief in Central America, all provided assistance to the secret operation to support the Contras. Yet, virtually every newspaper article on the incident in the days after the downing would quote senior Government officials, including the President himself, denying any U.S. Government connection with the flight. And within a week, high Government officials would offer the same categorical denials before Congressional Committees.

## The Initial Response

When the Sandinistas shot down the Hasenfus plane, North was in West Germany negotiating with the Second Channel. He returned to Washington within 48 hours of the downing to help deflect inquiries about the flight, leaving Albert Hakim behind to complete his negotiations.

Two days later, plans were made at a Restricted Interagency Group (RIG) meeting in which Abrams and CIA Central American Task Force Chief (C/CATF) participated to ensure that the U.S. Government would not be implicated by the flight. A PROF from NSC staff member Vincent Cannistraro to Adm. Poindexter described decisions made at the meeting. Among them, Cannistraro wrote, "UNO to be asked to assume responsibility for flights and to assist families of Americans involved." Also, the group decided that press guidance would be prepared "which states no U.S.G. involvement or connection, but that we are generally aware of such support contracted by the Contras."

A few days later The New York Times reported: "Nicaraguan rebels took full responsibility today for the flight of a military cargo plane that was downed over Nicaragua last week." A "senior Administration official" was quoted in the story as saying that the U.S. Government had asked the rebels to take responsibility. While denying that any such request was made, Bosco Matamoros, UNO's Washington-based spokesman, told the reporter, "There was no United States government connection." Similar denials by Administration officials would soon follow. North was not at the RIG meeting, but he testified that the guidance stating no U.S. Government connection was "not inconsistent with what we had prepared as the press line if such, if such an eventuality occurred."

## The Denials

The President: There is no evidence the President knew of U.S. involvement in the Hasenfus flight. But the National Security Adviser and officials on the NSC staff did know. Also, the day of the downing, Felix Rodriguez called Col. Sam Watson in Vice President Bush's office, suggesting to him that North was involved with the flight. Donald Gregg, Assistant to Vice President Bush, earlier had been alerted to the possibility that North was linked to the resupply operation.

Nevertheless, the President was permitted to deny any U.S. Government connection with the flight. In an exchange with reporters on October 8, the President praised the efforts to keep the Contras armed, comparing resupply efforts to those of the "Abraham Lincoln Brigade in the Spanish Civil War." But when asked whether the Hasenfus plane had any connection with the American Government, the President replied, "Absolutely none." He told reporters:

There is no government connection with that at all . . . We've been aware that there are private groups and private citizens that have been trying to help the Contras—to that extent—but we did not know the exact particulars of what they're doing.

**Assistant Secretary of State Elliott Abrams, a member of the Contra RIG, offered perhaps the most vehement denials. Asked if he could categorically affirm that Hasenfus was not in any way controlled, guided, or directed by anyone connected with the U.S. Government, he said: "Absolutely. That would be illegal. We are barred from doing that, and we are not doing it. This was not in any sense a U.S. Government operation. None."**

North claimed, however, that his Contra-related activities were discussed at some RIG meetings. In his testimony, North specifically mentioned only one RIG meeting, initially asserting that Abrams attended. North's notebook entry of that meeting, however, indicates Abrams was not present. Nonetheless, North maintained that Abrams knew details of his Contra-support activities. An entry in North's notebook for April 25, 1986, suggests that North and Abrams discussed "support for S. front," the fact that the "air base [was] open in C[osta] R[ica]," and "100 BP's [Blowpipe missiles]." North testified that he did not specifically recall that conversation, "but do not deny that I discussed those [items listed in North's notebook] at various points in time with Mr. Abrams and others." (Abrams was not asked about this notebook entry.)

Moreover, the third key member of the RIG, the CIA Chief of the Central American Task Force (C/CATF), testified that he was "taken aback" by Abrams' categorical denials of North's involvement. While he insisted that he did not want "to impeach" Abrams' testimony, C/CATF told these Committees: "I thought he [Abrams] would have a broad brush understanding, as did a lot of other people, Ollie was in and around those things."

Abrams argued in defense of his statements that he or someone on his staff had checked with other key agencies—the Central Intelligence Agency (CIA) and the Department of Defense (DOD)—and verified that no U.S. officials were involved with the Hasenfus flight. In their testimonies, two key CIA officials—the C/CATF and the Deputy Director for Operations—mentioned no call from Abrams' office, and testified they were surprised by Abrams' categorical denials.

Similarly, Abrams noted that soon after the crash, while North was out of the country, he called an NSC staff officer and received assurances that the NSC staff was not involved in the Hasenfus flight. Abrams said the official "may have been Mr. Earl." Earl, however, was aware that the flight was part of "Democracy, Inc." and that North played an important role in that organization. (Earl was not asked about a call from Abrams.)

During the period he was making his denials, Abrams spoke with North. But Abrams did not ask whether North was involved with the Hasenfus flight, despite the fact that Abrams, in his words, "knew that he [North] was monitoring" the private Contra support network. Abrams said he did not ask North because "it was very clear that [confirming his involvement in the flight] would have been completely contradictory to what he had previously told me." North had a different explanation: "He didn't have to ask me . . . He knew."

## ABRAMS' BRUNEI TESTIMONY

In addition to denying any U.S. role in the Hasenfus flight, Elliott Abrams denied on several occasions that the U.S. Government actions had sought third-country funding for the Contras. His statements were made despite his previous involvement in soliciting funds from the Government of Brunei. In testimony before Congressional Committees in late 1986, Abrams repeatedly deflected questions about the Contras' funding, giving responses which were, in his word, "misleading."

Appearing before the House Intelligence Committee on October 14, 1986, together with Clair George, Abrams again denied that third countries had aided the Contras:

ABRAMS: "I can only speak on that question for the last fifteen months when I have been in this job, and that story about [Country 2], to my knowledge is false. I personally cannot tell you about pre-1985, but in 1985–1986, when I have been around, no."

CHAIRMAN: "Is it also false with respect to other governments as well?"

ABRAMS: "Yes, it is also false."

## CONCLUSION

Throughout the period of Congressional restrictions on lethal aid to the Contras, Administration officials were asked repeatedly whether the U.S. Government was in any way providing such support. In every instance, officials responded to the inquiries with evasive answers or categorical denials. Some of these officials made their statements as part of a deliberate attempt to conceal what they knew about U.S. Government support for the Nicaraguan Resistance.

These Committees found no direct evidence suggesting that the President was a knowing participant in the effort to deceive Congress and the American public. But the President's actions and statements contributed to the deception.

Congressional Committees overseeing the implementation of the Boland Amendment repeatedly sought to determine how the Contras were being funded. The President knew that Country 2 had provided substantial sums of money to the Resistance; he had personally discussed such a contribution with the leader of that country. But knowledge of this contribution was not widely shared within the Administration. Indeed, high-ranking State Department officials were permitted on several occasions to testify to Congress that it was not the policy of the United States to facilitate or encourage third-country donations, and that the Administration had not in fact done so. In one instance, following the enactment of the full prohibition Boland Amendment in October 1984, Ambassador Motley testified that "soliciting" or "encouraging" third country donations would violate the law.

In October 1986, the President denied that the U.S. Government had any connection with the Hasenfus flight, depicting it as part of a "private" operation. According to Poindexter the President "understood that the Contras were being supported and that we were involved in—generally involved in coordinating the effort." These Committees found no evidence suggesting that the President knew his statements about the flight were false. He merely echoed the denials made the day before by State Department officials. The National Security Adviser and others who knew the President's remarks were false appear to have made no effort to ensure that the President's statements were accurate and his knowledge complete. Poindexter testified he was too busy with the Reykjavik summit to correct the public record.

## REASONS FOR THE DECEPTION

North endeavored to explain the need for the deception by arguing that he was forced to weigh "the differences between lives and lies." He told the Committees:

> [t]he revelations of the actual details of this activity . . . would have cost the lives of those with whom I was working, would have jeopardized the governments which had assisted us, would have jeopardized the lives of the Americans who in some cases were flying flights over Nicaragua, would have put at great risk those inside Nicaragua and in Eastern Europe and other places where people were working hard to keep them alive. . . .

North's justification for his decision to deceive does not withstand analysis. Congress is routinely briefed on covert operations where lives are at risk. Beyond that, Congress publicly debated and then approved the support of the Contras prior to enactment of the Boland prohibition. Operational details that would have put at risk the personnel conducting those operations were not publicly revealed. The same is true for the Congressionally approved operation in support of the Contras currently underway.

Even in 1985 and 1986, Congress was not asking about operational details such as drop-zone coordinates or flight paths. Members of Congress simply wanted to know whether it was true that the U.S. Government was providing lethal support to the Nicaraguan Resistance.

Indeed, North testified that his efforts were known widely outside the United States, even by this Country's enemies: "Izvestia knew it . . . . My name had been in the newspapers in Moscow, all over Daniel Ortega's newscasts. Radio Havana was broadcasting it." Moreover, it was important to the success of the resupply operation that friendly countries in Central America knew that the U.S. Government support for the Contras was continuing so that they would not drive the Contras out of their countries.

Only the American people and the Congress were kept in the dark. Had they known, it would not have been lives at risk but the NSC staff's secret operation itself. Poindexter told these Committees he believed during his tenure in the White House that disclosure of the NSC staff operation would have almost surely triggered tighter restrictions on aid to the Contras. McFarlane testified that disclosure of the "troubling" documents on North's activities which he had gathered in response to a Congressional inquiry "would be an extremely torturous, conflicting, disagreeable outcome and that I hoped we didn't come to that."

North's contemporaneous actions and words provide clear evidence that the reasons for the deception had more to do with the political risk to the operation than to the physical risk to operation personnel. The record is clear that North's actions after the revelation of the Santa Elena airfield were motivated by a desire to prevent the discov-

135

ery of "USG fingerprints," in his words, on the airfield.

In addition, in a May 1986, PROF note to Poindexter, North warned that Members of Congress were bound to become "more inquisitive" as the Contra operation's level of activity increased. He wrote: "While I care not a whit what they say about me, it could well become a political embarassment for the President and you."

PART

# THE ARMS SALES
# TO IRAN

# CHAPTER 8

# U.S.-Iran Relations and the Hostages in Lebanon

For many Americans, the most surprising and alarming aspect of the Iran-Contra Affair was President Reagan's decision to sell arms to Iran. Only a few years before, that nation had humiliated the United States. From November 1979 to January 1981, Iran held American diplomats hostage, while Iranian mobs in the streets of Tehran chanted slogans calling for the death of President Carter and the destruction of U.S. interests throughout the Middle East.

## No Regional Guarantees

Partly in reaction to the war in Vietnam, the United States in 1969 began to shift to a worldwide policy of no longer directly guaranteeing the security of its regional allies. Instead, the United States would work with its friends to ensure that they had the military capability to defend themselves against internal subversion or external threat. Under the Nixon Doctrine, the United States looked to regional powers, such as Iran, to serve as guardians of American interests in distant corners of the world.

Iran's armed forces, under Shah Mo-

hammed Reza Pahlavi, served as a deterrent to regional aggression in this conception of American policy. "Iran," President Carter declared during a 1977 trip to Tehran, "because of the great leadership of the Shah, is an island of stability in one of the more troubled areas of the world."

The Shah's power proved illusory. Growing protests by students, leftists, and, most importantly, Muslim religious opponents led in February 1979 to the Shah's overthrow and his replacement by a Shiite Muslim religious leader, Ayatollah Khomeini, who had been forced into exile in 1964, first to Iraq and then to France. The new regime was contemptuous of both the United States—the "Great Satan"—and the West. Fiery Shiite clerics accused the United States of imperialism and the murder of thousands during the Shah's rule. America's fortunes in Iran had crumbled.

If any doubt remained about the nature of the new regime, it was removed on November 4, 1979, when youthful Iranian militants—the Revolutionary Guards—stormed the U.S. Embassy in Tehran and took 66 American diplomats hostage. The hostage crisis lasted 444 days. It helped to drive one

President from office and to elect another who pledged that America would not be so humiliated again.

## ARMS SALES TO IRAN

In response to the Embassy seizure, the United States on November 14, 1979, embargoed all arms shipments to Iran as part of a general embargo on trade and financial transactions. Ten months later, however, the invasion of Iran by Iraq, on September 22, 1980, raised the question of who might ultimately be punished by this punitive measure. The prospect of an Iranian defeat and an increase in Soviet influence in the region was of concern.

Iran's armed forces were in disarray; the officer corps and enlisted ranks had been decimated by government purges and desertions. Iran's military arsenal was also in poor shape. Modern aircraft, armor, and naval vessels purchased by the Shah had been left unattended during the 24-month revolution and were badly in need of spare parts and maintenance.

Against this background, the Reagan Administration's Senior Interdepartmental Group (SIG) convened on July 21, 1981, to discuss U.S. policy toward Iran. SIG members concluded "that U.S. efforts to discourage third country transfers of non-U.S. origin arms would have only a marginal effect on the conduct and outcome of the war, but could increase opportunities for the Soviets to take advantage of Iran's security concerns and to persuade Iran to accept Soviet military assistance."

Despite the U.S. embargo, Iran obtained weapons and military support services on the thriving world arms market. Oil was often the medium of exchange in elaborate barter deals, and Persian Gulf trade became an irresistible lure for international arms merchants. The Reagan Administration listed no fewer than 41 countries that had provided Iran with weapons since the start of the war.

As a result, by the spring of 1983, the tide in the Gulf war had turned in favor of Iran.

## Operation Staunch

At this point the Administration decided to initiate Operation Staunch, a plan seeking the cooperation of other governments in an arms sales embargo against Iran. On December 14, 1983, the State Department instructed its Embassies in countries believed to be involved in arms trade with Tehran to urge their host governments to "stop transferring arms to Iran because of the broader interests of the international community in achieving a negotiated end to the Iran-Iraq war."

## IRAN'S SUPPORT OF TERRORISM

The long-suppressed Shiite community in Lebanon, with close religious and familial ties to Iran, had found inspiration in the rule of the Ayatollah Khomeini. In the aftermath of the Israeli invasion of Lebanon in June 1982, some Shiite groups in Lebanon used political kidnappings and terrorism against Americans and American institutions as retaliation against perceived U.S. support for the Israeli invasion and occupation of their country. The United States became aware in July 1982 that Iran was supporting groups in

140

# Figure 8–1. Map of Iran

141

Lebanon, such as Islamic Jihad and the Hizballah (Party of God), that were suspected of terrorism.

United States Marines had been sent to Lebanon briefly in August and September 1982 to supervise the withdrawal of forces of the Palestine Liberation Organization (PLO) from Beirut and returned to Lebanon soon thereafter in the aftermath of the Sabra and Shatila massacres.

A series of bold attacks followed against Americans and American interests throughout Lebanon. The U.S. Embassy in Beirut was destroyed in April 1983, killing 63, including 17 Americans. A suicide bombing on October 23, 1983, killed 241 Marines in their barracks in Beirut. This incident was followed in December by a series of bombing attacks against the U.S. and French Embassies in Kuwait. The 17 men who were apprehended in the Kuwait attack were tried and sentenced to prison. The release of these "Da'wa prisoners" (as they came to be known after a pro-Khomeini party with supporters in several countries) became a key demand of the Hizballah as attacks against U.S. targets and the taking of American hostages continued in Lebanon.

**Although American intelligence recognized that the Hizballah was not completely controlled by Iran, the broad connection between Tehran and terrorism was clear. On January 20, 1984, the State Department formally designated Iran a supporter of international terrorism.**

## Hostage-Taking Begins

Three Americans were seized in Beirut in 1984: Jeremy Levin, Beirut Bureau Chief for the Cable News Network, on March 7; William Buckley, CIA's Chief of Station, on March 14; and the Reverend Benjamin Weir, a Presbyterian minister who had lived in the Lebanese capital for 30 years, on May 8, 1984. Buckley's capture was of special concern for CIA Director Casey. It was suspected at the time—and later confirmed —that Buckley was being tortured, and Casey wanted to spare no effort to get him back.

Four Americans were seized in 1985: Father Lawrence Martin Jenco, Director of Catholic Relief Services in Beirut, on January 8; Terry Anderson, chief Middle East correspondent for the Associated Press, on March 16; David Jacobsen, Director of the American University Hospital, on May 28; and Thomas P. Sutherland, Dean of the American University's School of Agriculture, on June 9.

On June 14, 1985, Shiite terrorists struck again, hijacking TWA flight 847 and murdering one of its passengers, Navy diver Robert Stetham. National Security Adviser Robert McFarlane publicly stated: "It is my purpose to remind terrorists and to keep them on notice that no act of violence against Americans will go without a response."

The President spoke on the same subject on June 30, 1985, "The United States gives terrorists no rewards and no guarantees. We make no concessions. We make no deals."

These were strong and unambiguous words from the President and a senior American official. Yet a few weeks later, President Reagan authorized Israel to sell TOW antitank missiles to the government of the Ayatollah Khomeini, the Hizballah's spiritual leader. Seven months later he authorized the direct sale of arms to Iran.

**A chapter footnote says the Committees investigated allegations that Iranian intermediaries had**

reached an agreement with Reagan campaign committee officials in 1980 that arms would be shipped to Iran if the hostages were released after the election. The Committees said they found no credible evidence to support this assertion and were told the offer had been rejected.

# CHAPTER 9

# The Iran Arms Sales: The Beginning

In August 1985, the President decided that the United States would allow arms sales to Iran. The decision represented a reversal of U.S. policy against selling arms to Iran and, as it later turned out, against making concessions for the return of hostages. Yet it was made so casually that it was not written down, the President did not recall it 15 months later, and the Secretaries of State and Defense were not even told of it at the time.

The President's decision triggered a series of arms transactions with Iran that continued for 15 months. At the initial transaction, the Iranians established a pattern of dealing that never changed: Iran would agree to get the hostages freed in return for arms; once the arms arrived, the Iranians would demand still more weapons; only after another arms shipment would a single hostage—not a group, as promised—be freed. But, instead of breaking off the transactions, the Americans continued to accede to the Iranian demands. What follows is the story of how the arms sales began.

## THE ACTORS TAKE THEIR PLACES

Long before the President made his decision, the individuals and circumstances that propelled the sales were at work in Washington, Jerusalem, and Tehran.

Since the fall of 1984, the National Security Council (NSC) staff had been pressing other Government agencies to develop a plan for opening a relationship with Iran and moderating that government's anti-American stance. The State Department and the Defense Department opposed the notion, and while the Central Intelligence Agency (CIA) was favorably inclined, officials there said renewed relations hinged on the release of seven U.S. hostages held by the pro-Iranian Hizballah in Lebanon and on a pledge by Iran to stop terrorist activities.

In Jerusalem, officials were eager for better relations with Iran, for two very pragmatic reasons: commercial and diplomatic. Israel had friendly relations with Iran under the Shah. Despite revolutionary Iran's vow to destroy Israel, the Israelis regarded Iraq as a greater threat to their security than Iran. Israel's goal was to create conditions for the resumption of commercial and diplomatic relations with a post-Khomeini regime.

Tehran had its own agenda. Rhetoric notwithstanding—the United States was considered "The Great Satan" and Israel a blasphemy—Tehran wanted modern tanks and high-technology antitank and antiaircraft missiles to counter Iraq's Soviet-made fighter planes and modern tanks. It needed spare parts to maintain the arsenal of weapons that the Shah had purchased from the United States.

The unlikely catalyst for bringing these disparate parties together was Manucher Ghorbanifar—a resourceful Iranian merchant living in Paris who understood the intersection of interests and saw how the American hostages could be used as an incentive for the sale of missiles to Iran.

## Ghorbanifar

Since fleeing Iran in 1979, Ghorbanifar had sought to make a career as a broker through whom Western governments could develop contact with Iran. By 1984, Ghorbanifar was well known to U.S. intelligence services, and details of his activities filled a thick file in the CIA's Operations Directorate. The CIA viewed Ghorbanifar with particular disfavor, but that did little to discourage the Iranian from trying to interest U.S. intelligence agencies in various schemes, all of which would financially benefit him.

His CIA file describes Ghorbanifar as an Iranian businessman and self-proclaimed "wheeler dealer" who, prior to the 1979 revolution, had been the managing director of an Israeli-connected Iranian shipping company. According to rumors, Ghorbanifar also was an informant for SAVAK, the Shah's intelligence service, and had a relationship with Israeli intelligence; but those relationships have never been confirmed.

In January 1984, Ghorbanifar contacted U.S. Army Intelligence in West Germany with tales of "Iranian terrorist organizations, plans, and activities." In mid-March, a CIA officer met with Ghorbanifar in Frankfurt to explore the data Ghorbanifar was offering. At that meeting, Ghorbanifar indicated he had information on the kidnapping, in Beirut, of CIA Chief of Station William Buckley. He identified an Iranian official (the Second Iranian), who would play a key role in the arms-for-hostages transactions a year later, as the "individual responsible" for the kidnapping. He also described an Iranian plot to assassinate U.S. Presidential candidates.

A CIA-administered polygraph examination of Ghorbanifar on this information indicated he was lying. Ghorbanifar gave no satisfactory explanation for the results. Undeterred, he again approached the CIA in June 1984, this time trying to broker a meeting between the U.S. Government and another Iranian official (the First Iranian). The First Iranian was also to be a key player in the arms-for-hostages transactions of 1985 and 1986. According to Ghorbanifar, the First Iranian was favorably disposed towards the United States.

Again, Ghorbanifar was polygraphed, and again, the examination indicated he was lying. This time, the CIA responded by publishing, on July 25, 1984, a rarely issued "Fabricator Notice," warning Agency personnel and other U.S. intelligence and law enforcement agencies that Ghorbanifar "should be regarded as an intelligence fabricator and a nuisance."

145

## Ghorbanifar Proposes to Ransom the Hostages

Ghorbanifar continued to seek a relationship with the U.S. Government. His first chance came in November 1984 when he met Theodore Shackley, a former Associate Deputy Director for Operations of the CIA who had retired from the Agency in 1978. On behalf of his "risk management" firm, Research Associates, Inc., Shackley maintained contact with the former head of the Shah's SAVAK Counterespionage Department VIII, General Manucher Hashemi. At the suggestion of Hashemi, Shackley traveled to Hamburg, West Germany, where he met with a group of Iranians, including Ghorbanifar, the First Iranian and a Dr. Shahabadi, chief of the Iranian purchasing office in Hamburg and purportedly a friend of Saudi entrepreneur and arms dealer Adnan Khashoggi. At one meeting, on November 20, Ghorbanifar told Shackley that for a price he could arrange for the release of U.S. hostages in Lebanon through his Iranian contacts. Ghorbanifar said he required a response on the "ransom deal" by December 7. Ghorbanifar added that he would not work with the CIA because the Agency was "unreasonable and unprofessional." Upon his return to the United States, Shackley sent a memorandum about his meetings with Ghorbanifar to Lt. Gen. Vernon Walters, Ambassador-at-Large in the State Department and a former Deputy Director of the CIA. Walters referred the memorandum to Hugh Montgomery, Director of Intelligence and Research in the State Department. Montgomery, in turn, passed the Shackley memorandum to Ambassador Robert B. Oakley, head of the State Department's counterterrorism efforts, and Assistant Secretary of State for Near Eastern Affairs Richard W. Murphy. Oakley and Murphy regarded the hostage ransom proposal as a "scam," and on December 11, 1984, Montgomery told Shackley that the State Department was not interested in pursuing the Ghorbanifar ransom proposal.

## Ghorbanifar Tries Again

Ghorbanifar still did not give up. Having failed with the CIA, the Army, and the State Department, he found another and ultimately more fruitful channel into the U.S. Government through Israel. A New York businessman, Roy Furmark, served as the contact point. Furmark had previously worked for Adnan Khashoggi, and was a friend of CIA Director William Casey. Furmark also knew Cyrus Hashemi, a naturalized U.S. citizen of Iranian extraction whom Furmark tried to interest in a number of business ventures. In January 1985, Furmark and Ghorbanifar met while Furmark was in Europe to discuss business opportunities in Iran.

Furmark later introduced Ghorbanifar to Hashemi and Khashoggi. Ghorbanifar, at this time, was looking for sophisticated weapons for Iran, and Khashoggi suggested that Ghorbanifar try to develop access to the United States and its weapons through Israel. Sometime later, Khashoggi put Ghorbanifar and Hashemi in touch with an Israeli group: Al Schwimmer, an adviser to then Israeli Prime Minister Shimon Peres, and Ya'accov Nimrodi, an Israeli businessman with government service background. Both Khashoggi and Hashemi saw the potential for huge profits if Ghorbanifar were to become the conduit for U.S. arms to Iran and gain control of trade between the United States and Iran.

At Khashoggi's initiative members of the Israeli team met with Hashemi and Ghorbanifar in London, Geneva, and Israel in early spring. Weapons sales to Iran were discussed but the meetings produced nothing concrete. In late April, Ghorbanifar proposed to one of the Israelis that he be permitted to purchase U.S.-manufactured TOW antitank missiles from Israel, and, in return, he would obtain the release of CIA Beirut Chief of Station Buckley, then a hostage in Lebanon.

## Ledeen Gets Involved

At about that same time, NSC consultant Michael Ledeen was trying to persuade National Security Adviser Robert McFarlane to use him as an informal channel to get intelligence on Iran from Israel, using his close personal relationships with several high-ranking Israeli officials. In March 1985, Ledeen met in Europe with a senior official from a western European nation who told Ledeen that the United States could play a significant role in Iran. The foreign official recommended that the United States contact Israel because the Israelis had the best intelligence resources on Iran. Upon his return to the United States in early April, Ledeen proposed to McFarlane that he be authorized to meet with Israeli Prime Minister Peres and other Israeli officials to explore potential Israeli-U.S. cooperation on Iran. Although the NSC staff told McFarlane that "none of us feel Mike should be our primary channel for working the Iran issue with foreign governments," they were impressed with Ledeen's access to Prime Minister Peres, and therefore recommended that Ledeen informally meet with the Israelis to express interest in developing "a more serious and coordinated strategy for dealing with the Iranian succession crisis." McFarlane agreed.

Ledeen traveled to Israel in early May. On May 3 he met with Prime Minister Peres and then with a former senior official of the Israel Defense Forces. During the meetings, Ledeen said he was acting on McFarlane's behalf, although in a private rather than official capacity, and expressed interest in sharing intelligence on Iran. According to Ledeen, the Americans held hostage in Lebanon were not discussed at these meetings in early May. An Israeli official, however, recalls Ledeen's telling him about offers by various Iranians to help get the hostages released. According to Ledeen, the Prime Minister asked him to advise McFarlane that Israel wanted to sell artillery shells or pieces to Iran but would do so only if it received U.S. approval.

## THE NSC RECONSIDERS IRAN POLICY

On June 3, 1985, McFarlane approved a second Ledeen trip to Israel, but Ledeen's return to Israel was delayed when Secretary of State George P. Shultz protested Ledeen's earlier trip. Shultz had heard from the U.S. Ambassador to Israel that Ledeen had been in Israel talking to Israeli officials about obtaining intelligence on Iran, without notice to the U.S. Embassy. Shultz complained to McFarlane that neither he nor the U.S. Ambassador to Israel had been informed of the trip, and pointed out that Israel and the United States had differing interests in Iran. He also questioned the wisdom of relying upon Israeli intelligence about Iran. McFarlane told Shultz that Ledeen had taken the

May trip "on his own hook." He also said he was "turning [the Iran initiative] off entirely." In fact, McFarlane told Ledeen to postpone, not cancel, the trip.

Major policy changes call for consultation with the Secretaries of State and Defense and an opportunity for the President to consider their views. McFarlane thus began the established process of interdepartmental policy formulation. He had earlier requested the CIA to prepare the updated SNIE on Iran, and in June he asked members of his staff to prepare a draft National Security Decision Directive (NSDD). An NSDD is a Presidential directive establishing policy in a particular area. It is the result of an analytical process, including discussions among the interested parties.

Fortier and Howard Teicher of the NSC staff submitted the draft NSDD to McFarlane on June 11, and on June 17, McFarlane circulated this draft to Secretary Shultz, Secretary of Defense Caspar W. Weinberger, and CIA Director Casey. The draft NSDD recommended, among other things, that anti-Khomeini factions in Iran should be supported, and that U.S. allies and friendly states should be encouraged to "help Iran meet its import requirements . . . includ[ing] provision of selected military equipment." To bolster the NSC's analysis, McFarlane cited the CIA's earlier intelligence estimate that had recommended such arms sales, and warned of the Soviet threat to Iran.

Only Casey endorsed the draft NSDD. Secretary Weinberger wrote on the transmittal note accompanying the draft, "This is almost too absurd to comment on. . . . It's like asking Quadaffi to Washington for a cozy chat." Weinberger's response to the National Security Adviser was less sarcastic but

unambiguously negative. Secretary Shultz's response was also negative. He criticized the idea of relaxing the arms embargo against Iran, warned against the danger of strengthening Iran, and disagreed with the notion that Iran was in danger of falling into Soviet hands.

During the same period, the President was sharply critical of Iran. In a speech to the American Bar Association on July 8, 1985, the President declared Iran to be part of a "confederation of terrorist states . . . a new international version of Murder Incorporated." He added, "Let me make it plain to the assassins in Beirut and their accomplices that America will never make concessions to terrorists."

## The Discussions Continue

In late June, according to McFarlane's testimony, David Kimche, the Director General of the Israeli Foreign Ministry, became involved in the project. Kimche had an established relationship with McFarlane and Ledeen. While in Washington for another purpose in early July, he briefed McFarlane on the ongoing contacts of Israeli and Iranian officials, and the Iranians' interest in establishing contact with the United States. Kimche recommended that the discussions with the Iranians continue. McFarlane told Secretary Weinberger about the meeting, and Weinberger's military assistant, Lt. Gen. Colin Powell, recalled that McFarlane discussed both the sale of arms to Iran and the hostages.

On July 8, 1985, members of the Israeli team met in Hamburg with Ghorbanifar, Khashoggi, Khashoggi's son-in-law, and the

First Iranian. Before the meeting, Ghorbanifar told the Israelis that the sale of 100 TOWs was essential to enhance his credibility with Iran, and claimed that the sale would be followed by the release of the American hostages.

Ghorbanifar described the First Iranian as a politically powerful individual in his own right, with close personal connections to Khomeini, and a leader of one of Iran's revolutionary organizations.

At the meetings, the First Iranian spoke of the need for a party who could act as a bridge between Iran and the United States, of the threat of Soviet influence in Iran, and of the risks he had taken in meeting with Israel in order to promote an opening with the United States. The participants also discussed missiles and hostages. The First Iranian promised to present a comprehensive written proposal within a week.

Shortly after that meeting, according to Ledeen's testimony, Schwimmer flew to Washington and met with Ledeen on July 11, 1985. He briefed Ledeen on Ghorbanifar's proposal to obtain the release of the American hostages in exchange for TOW missiles. Ledeen then wrote McFarlane, "The situation [concerning Iran] has fundamentally changed for the better." On July 13, he briefed McFarlane orally on the Israeli talks with the Iranians.

## The President Is Informed

McFarlane decided to take the matter to President Reagan, even though the President was in the hospital recuperating from surgery. By this time, the release of the hostages had become an immediate concern to the President. He had met with the hostage families for the first time in late June, and had been moved by the experience. On July 3, he had attended a National Security Planning Group meeting to discuss the hostages, and had come away frustrated at the lack of alternatives.

McFarlane met with the President at the hospital on July 18. Donald Regan, the White House Chief of Staff, was present. What was discussed at this meeting is not clear: Apparently no one took notes. Regan did not recall any mention of arms at the meeting, and McFarlane's accounts have varied: More than a year later, on November 21, 1986, McFarlane wrote in a PROF note to Poindexter that the President "was all for letting the Israelis do anything they wanted at the very first briefing in the hospital." But during the public hearings McFarlane stated that the President's position was that no U.S. owned items from the United [S]tates [could be] proper[ly] shipped at that time. This left open the possibility that the Israelis were free to ship from Israel Israeli-owned TOWs that had been acquired from the United States.

McFarlane testified that the Israelis were informed that the President was unwilling to allow the United States to supply arms directly to Iran. Ledeen testified, however, that, in accordance with McFarlane's instructions, he informed the Israelis that the President approved "in principle" the sale of TOWs by Israel subject to further review of the details.

But Israeli Defense Minister Yitzhak Rabin would not proceed unless he received assurances that the Secretary of State knew of the plan and that the President unequivocally approved.

149

## The Israeli Arms Sales Are Authorized

On August 2, according to McFarlane's testimony, Kimche flew to Washington to meet with McFarlane and to obtain the specific U.S. position on Israel's sale of the TOWs. The meetings occurred on August 2 and 3. McFarlane made no memorandum of the meetings, and recollections differ. All agree, however, that the Israelis asked for permission to sell 100 TOWs, and that McFarlane agreed to present the issue to the President.

The White House log records an August 6 meeting between McFarlane and the President, the Vice President, Secretaries Shultz and Weinberger, and Regan. McFarlane reported that the Iranians wanted a dialogue with the United States and 100 TOWs from Israel in return for which four hostages would be released. McFarlane also said that the United States would be able to deny any connection to or knowledge of the sale, a suggestion the Secretary of State regarded as untenable. Secretary Shultz told the President that it "was a very bad idea," and that despite the talk of better relations, "we were just falling into the arms-for-hostages business and we shouldn't do it."

Secretary Weinberger also opposed the sale. He and Secretary Shultz argued that the initiative would not work, and that the sale would contradict the U.S. efforts to persuade other countries to observe the embargo. None of the witnesses recalls the Vice President's position, and there is no evidence that Casey was consulted by the NSC staff at this stage. McFarlane, according to Ledeen, directed that Casey and the CIA not be informed for fear that the CIA might leak.

Chief of Staff Regan testified that the President told McFarlane to "go slow" at the August meeting and to "make sure we know who we are dealing with before we get too far into this." According to all the participants, the President announced no decision at the meeting.

Several days later, the President telephoned McFarlane and, according to McFarlane, authorized the Israelis to proceed with the sale in modest quantities of "TOW missiles or other military spares" that would be replenished by the United States. The President stipulated that the sales not affect the balance of the Iran-Iraq war, not be used for terrorist purposes, and not include such major items as aircraft. McFarlane told Poindexter about the conversation, but Poindexter did not recall its contents. Regan recalled that the President appeared upset when he learned in September that TOWs had been shipped.

The President, in his Tower Board interview, originally confirmed that he had authorized the sale, but later stated that he had no actual recollection one way or another. No documents record the decision.

The Tower Board concluded that the President most likely approved the Israeli sales before they occurred. The evidence supports that conclusion. The Israelis expressly sought the President's approval of the Israeli sales and confirmation that the Secretary of State had been consulted. By McFarlane's own admission, he told the Israelis that they were authorized to sell the TOWs. McFarlane had no motive to approve a sale of missiles to Iran if the President had not authorized it. Moreover, Ledeen testified that McFarlane told him of the President's decision. McFarlane also contemporaneously reported the President's approval to Kimche.

The President's decision on the arms sale

conveyed by McFarlane to the Israelis committed the United States to the policy unsuccessfully advocated in the draft NSDD—the sale of weapons by an American ally to Iran.

## Israel Ships 96 TOWs—But No Hostage Is Released

On August 19, Ghorbanifar returned to Israel where he met with the Israeli team. Ghorbanifar advised that he had made payments in Iran but he was not certain how many hostages would be released. As for CIA Station Chief Buckley, Ghorbanifar said that the Iranians recognized his "special value" and, therefore, would return him last. That same day, the DC-8 transport aircraft arrived in Israel, and was loaded with 96 (rather than 100) TOW missiles. In the early morning hours of August 20, the plane left Israel bound for Iran, with Ghorbanifar on board. The TOWs were then delivered and the aircraft returned to Israel late that same day.

But no hostages were released. Ghorbanifar had an explanation: contrary to his plan, delivery of the missiles was taken by the Commander of the Iranian Revolutionary Guards rather than by the Iranian faction for whom they were intended. Still, Ghorbanifar remained hopeful that he could produce the hostages. With McFarlane's assent, Ledeen met with Kimche in London on August 20 to discuss ways to bring the hostages out of Lebanon.

## 400 More TOWs for 1 Hostage

On September 4 and 5, Ledeen met in Paris with Ghorbanifar and members of the Israeli team. Since no hostages had been released despite the delivery of the 96 TOWs on August 20, severe arguments occurred at the meeting. Ghorbanifar indicated that one hostage would be released provided the Israelis sold Iran an additional 400 TOW missiles. We are satisfied from our review of all the evidence that the President was informed and approved of the transaction in the hope that the hostages would be released. The second shipment was approved by Prime Minister Peres and Defense Minister Rabin on September 9. On September 10, Khashoggi ordered the transfer of $4 million into an Israeli intermediary's account to finance Ghorbanifar's purchase of the 400 TOWs. The money reached the Israeli account on September 13 and Ghorbanifar repaid Khashoggi that $4 million the following day.

The aircraft used to transport the second shipment of TOWs to Iran arrived in Israel on September 14. The DC-8 was loaded with 408 missiles (bringing the total of TOWs shipped to 504), and, early the next morning, it flew to Tabriz to make delivery. On board was Ghorbanifar's Iranian assistant, Mahadi Shahista. Tabriz, rather than Tehran, was used as the Iranian delivery point to prevent this shipment from falling into the hands of the Revolutionary Guards.

The Iranians made it clear that this was an arms-for-one-hostage bargain. They gave McFarlane the choice of any hostage other than Buckley. Ghorbanifar told the Israelis that Buckley was too ill to be released. In fact, Buckley had died in June of a pulmonary condition brought on by prolonged interrogation, torture, and mistreatment.

On September 15, American hostage Reverend Benjamin Weir was released near the U.S. Embassy in Beirut.

On September 17, the Israeli intermediary's account received an additional $290,000 from Ghorbanifar for the expense of transporting the 504 TOWs to Iran, and on September 18, Iran transferred $5 million to Ghorbanifar's Swiss account for the additional TOWs.

Despite the fact that all the TOWs were delivered, only one hostage had been produced, not the group that Ghorbanifar originally had promised. Still, the President continued to receive optimistic reports on the initiative. However, no other hostages were released for the 504 TOWs.

**In September North asked the CIA to gather intelligence on Ghorbanifar. It was given to McFarlane but was not shared with Secretaries Shultz or Weinberger. When Weinberger found out, he demanded and received the information.**

## The Initiative Continues: The Ante Is Upped

Despite Ghorbanifar's failure to secure the release of the four or five hostages originally promised, discussions of further arms deals continued. In late September, Ghorbanifar met with members of the Israeli team and Ledeen in Paris. This time, Ghorbanifar asked for antiaircraft missiles, including a new HAWK missile to attack high-flying aircraft. (The HAWKs do not have that capability, but apparently none of the participants was aware of this.) Ledeen reportedly consented to a HAWK transaction with Iran, but demanded that the hostages be released. Ledeen recalls that McFarlane approved the sale of HAWKs before November, but Ledeen could not recall when. Nor could he recall this Paris meeting.

In the meantime, North had received information that another U.S. hostage, allegedly Buckley, would be released between October 3 and 5. However, the Islamic Jihad in Lebanon announced, on October 3, that it planned to execute Buckley. North asked Ledeen to arrange for Ghorbanifar to come immediately to the United States to discuss the hostages. On October 8, Ghorbanifar arrived in Washington, accompanied by Schwimmer and Nimrodi, and met with Ledeen at the Old Executive Office Building.

## Meeting in Europe, October 1985

According to Ledeen, the purpose of the late October meeting was not to strike an arms-for-hostages deal with the Iranians, but rather to approach the U.S.-Iranian initiative from the strategic, geopolitical perspective. Ledeen testified that he and the First Iranian discussed ways to improve U.S./Iranian relations without trading arms for hostages. In fact, Ledeen maintained that like himself, this Iranian was "vociferously opposed to what had been done in providing weapons to the Iranian regime over the course of the past couple of months, said that all we could achieve by sending arms to Iran was to strengthen the Khomeini regime, which was the opposite of what he thought we were about." It was Ledeen's belief that "so long as the Iranians are able to obtain weapons from the United States as a result of [a] dialogue with us, they will say anything and they will do anything in order to continue to get these weapons, and so long as that pipeline of weapons functions, we will never be able to evaluate their real intentions."

Ledeen stated that upon his return from Europe, he reported to McFarlane that the First Iranian thought he could have his people occupy "key positions in the [Iranian] government" if the United States would help by providing a quantity of "small arms and training."

By other accounts, however, such political discussions are not all that transpired at the late October meeting. According to one of the Israeli intermediaries, the Iranian official emphasized that efforts must be continued for the release of the four remaining hostages in exchange for arms, particularly HAWK missiles. Also according to the Israeli intermediary, Ledeen was pressing, on behalf of the U.S. President, for all four hostages to be released as soon as possible and all at once, and he promised that following their release the U.S. would assist Iran as far as it could.

This appears to have been the last meeting among Iranian, Israeli, and American representatives before the shipment of HAWK missiles to Iran in late November 1985.

## THE LESSONS OF THE FIRST ARMS SHIPMENT

The August-September 1985 TOW transaction set the pattern for the entire Iran initiative:

— A promise by the Iranians to release the hostages in exchange for an agreed quantity of weapons.
— The breach of that promise after delivery of the weapons.
— The delivery of more weapons in response to new demands by the Iranians.
— The release of a single hostage as an enticement to further arms transfers.

The lesson to Iran was unmistakable: All U.S. positions and principles were negotiable, and breaches by Iran went unpunished. Whatever Iran did, the U.S. could be brought back to the arms bargaining table by the promise of another hostage.

# CHAPTER 10

# Arms to Iran: A Shipment of HAWKs Ends in Failure

An Israeli-American plan to sell HAWK missiles to Iran in exchange for American hostages crystallized in November 1985. The plan—which grew out of the late October meeting in Geneva among Michael Ledeen and Iranian and Israeli officials and intermediaries—ultimately led to a shipment of 18 HAWK antiaircraft missiles by a CIA airplane from Israel to Tehran on November 24 and 25. As the plan evolved, National Security Adviser Robert McFarlane had contacts with senior Israeli officials, brought aspects of the plan to the attention of the President, Chief of Staff Donald Regan, and the Secretary of State, and gave Oliver North increasing responsibility for overseeing the plan's implementation. The planning and execution of the operation did not proceed smoothly, and in the end, no hostages were released.

## LEDEEN BRINGS HOME A PLAN

NSC consultant Michael Ledeen returned to Washington from the Geneva meeting at the end of October 1985. He told North and McFarlane of the National Security Council Staff of the proposal by Manucher Ghorbanifar and the other Iranians that the United States provide specified missiles in return for the release of U.S. hostages in Lebanon. On October 30, 1985, Ledeen first met alone with North and then with both North and McFarlane. In the first meeting, Ledeen said that the "First Iranian," a highly placed Iranian official who acted as a go-between in the arms sales negotiations, "wants to be U.S. ally—has support in Tehran." Ledeen spelled out the Iranians' demands for securing the American hostages' freedom. He told North that, "to get hostages out," the Iranians wanted a "blanket order" of 150 HAWK missiles, 200 Sidewinder missiles, and 30 to 50 Phoenix missiles. The proposal contemplated that the hostages would be released in three groups, with separate arms deliveries to Iran to occur before the second and third releases. Ledeen raised the unresolved problem of U.S. replenishment of the 500 TOWs withdrawn from Israeli reserves and shipped to Iran in August and September 1985 prior to the release of hostage Benjamin Weir. Ledeen said Israeli Defense Minister Yitzhak Rabin was "complaining about" the United

States' failure to make good on its promise to replace those items.

North and Ledeen met with McFarlane later that day to continue the discussion. Ledeen, claiming that improved U.S.-Iranian relations could follow an agreement, advocated cooperation with the Israelis "to bring out credible military and political leaders" in Iran. McFarlane expressed skepticism even about the existence of moderate elements in Iran, let alone their ability to come to power. Nevertheless, he did not oppose renewing arms shipments to Iran. McFarlane instructed North and Ledeen that "not one single item" of armaments should be shipped to Iran without the release of "live Americans." McFarlane, Deputy National Security Adviser John Poindexter, and other senior American officials often repeated this instruction over the next several months, but it was consistently disregarded.

Ledeen's meeting with the First Iranian in Geneva led to meetings between the Americans and Israelis in early November 1985. The Iranians had significantly increased their demands for weapons. Moreover, the Israelis still sought replenishment of the TOWs they had sold to Iran.

## North-Nir Dialogue Begins

North and Amiram Nir, the Israeli Prime Minister's Adviser on Combatting Terrorism, met in Washington on November 14. Although they apparently did not discuss arms sales to Iran, they did set the foundation for a variety of future Israeli-U.S. covert operations. North jotted notes indicating that this operation could require at least a million dollars a month "for near term and probably mid-term rqmts [requirements]."

North's notes list several unanswered questions:

- How to pay for
- How to raise $ . . .
- Use Israelis as conduit?
- Go direct?
- Have Israelis do all work w/U.S. pay?
- Set up joint/Israeli cover op

On November 19, North and Nir discussed two code-named covert operations, "T.H. 1," the one they had discussed on November 14, and "T.H. 2." North's notes reflect that the second operation would also require a source of "op[erational] funds." In mid-November, North did not have answers to the funding question. But, according to North, within a few months, he and Nir had solved the problem: they would use the Iran arms sales profits. Planning for the privately funded joint covert activities began.

## McFarlane Briefs CIA

On November 14, McFarlane told the CIA of an Israeli plan to deliver arms to "certain elements of the Iranian military who are prepared to overthrow the Government." The next day, Israeli Defense Minister Rabin asked for reassurances that the arms shipments were approved by the President. McFarlane said the previous authorization for arms sales and replenishments from American stocks still held.

## McFarlane Briefs the President

McFarlane told the President about the developing plans for the HAWK transaction shortly before they left on November 17 for a summit meeting with Soviet leaders in Geneva. Regan, who was present, said it was:

> [J]ust a momentary conversation, which was not a detailed briefing to the President, that there [is] something up between Israel and Iran. [McFarlane said] [i]t might lead to our getting some of our hostages out, and we were hopeful. . . .

## THE NOVEMBER HAWK SHIPMENT

By the third week of November, the Israeli intermediaries and the Americans believed they had reached an agreement with Ghorbanifar on a plan that would gain release of all the hostages by Thanksgiving. The plan was, in essence, a straight swap: U.S.-made missiles in Israeli stocks would be sold to Iran in exchange for American hostages. As the exchange date approached, many details remained unresolved. They were only hammered out in separate and frantic long-distance negotiations among the Israeli intermediaries and Ghorbanifar, Ghorbanifar and his contacts in the Iranian Government, and Israeli Government officials and NSC officials.

### How Many Missiles?

One critical component of the plan was unsettled until the eleventh hour—the number and type of missiles that the Israelis would ship to Iran. As evidenced by their late October proposal, the Iranians wanted to purchase immediately hundreds of millions of dollars worth of sophisticated U.S.-made missile systems for use in their war with Iraq.

The Israelis were concerned about depleting their stocks. The Americans, who had not found a solution to the replenishment requirements arising out of the August and September missile shipments, sought an agreement involving smaller quantities of missiles shipped over time. The middlemen in the transaction—Ghorbanifar and Al Schwimmer and Yaacov Nimrodi, Israeli arms dealers also involved in the negotiations—had substantial monetary incentives to negotiate a deal in which large quantities of weapons and money would change hands.

By Sunday, November 17, the planners had decided on an initial shipment of 80 HAWK missiles. This shipment was to be just the start of a much larger, phased transaction.

On November 18, North called Schwimmer, who was in direct contact with Ghorbanifar. They discussed a sale of 600 HAWKs to Iran in groups of 100 spread out over the next 3 or 4 days. Schwimmer told North that the first shipment of 100 missiles had been "approved" in Tel Aviv and that it was to be followed by the release of five "boxes," the code name for the American hostages. After the call, North wrote in his Notebook: "Schwimmer to P/U [pick up] HAWKs in U.S." That day, an Israeli official told Prime Minister Shimon Peres that the Americans were willing for 500 HAWK missiles to be supplied, but it was proposed that Israel supply 80 HAWKs.

By November 20, the plan—as reported by North to Poindexter—had moved away from one involving 500 to 600 HAWKs toward one that included these components: First, 80 HAWKs from Israeli stocks were to be moved to Iran on Friday, November 22, on three planes spaced apart by 2 hour intervals. After the planes were launched, but before they landed in Iran, five American and possibly one French hostage would be released. After the hostages were freed, 40 more HAWKs would be moved to Iran. The United States would replenish Israel's stocks promptly by sale at a mutually agreed price.

North's notes from the same day confirm that the initial delivery was to be 80 items, but indicate a key difference from what he had reported to Poindexter: the American hostages would not be freed all at once in advance of the arrival of any HAWKs, but rather would be released sequentially after each shipment. After referring to the total of 80 HAWKs, North wrote:

—One 27-2
  27-3
  26-1
  6+1 French

This notation appears to mean that 2 hostages were to be released after a first shipment of 27 missiles, 3 hostages were to be released after a second shipment of the same amount, and 1 hostage would be released after a third shipment of the remaining 26 items. In fact, within a few days, an initial load of HAWKs arrived in Tehran without any prior hostage release.

McFarlane's instruction not to ship weapons without the prior release of the hostages thus was not followed.

## McFarlane Puts North in Charge

While McFarlane was at the Geneva summit with the President, North became immersed in the details of the HAWK transaction. North testified that he was "thrown into this on the night of November 17," in almost simultaneous telephone calls from Rabin and McFarlane. Rabin told North that the plan called for Israel to move 80 HAWK missiles by November 20. He said that Israel was unwilling to commence the shipment without satisfactory arrangements for replenishment by the United States. According to North's notes, McFarlane told North to solve Rabin's replenishment problem, and "to keep orders under $14M" each—the threshold figure for reporting foreign military sales to Congress.

The next day, North or Poindexter asked Lt. Gen. Colin Powell, then military assistant to Secretary of Defense Casper Weinberger, about the availability and price of HAWKs and TOWs, and the legality and method of transferring such missiles. The requester initially sought information on a proposed transfer of 500 HAWKs, but, in accordance with the evolving plan, soon cut the number to 120. Powell understood that the ultimate destination of the weapons would be Iran and that Israel was acting as an intermediary.

After receiving this request, Powell contacted Noel Koch, Principal Deputy Assistant Secretary of Defense for International Security Affairs, who in turn asked Henry Gaffney, Director of Plans, Defense Security Assistance Agency (DSAA), to find out how many HAWKs were available for immediate transfer. DSAA is the entity within the Department of Defense that is primarily responsible for arms sales to other governments. Koch asked Gaffney to prepare a Point Paper examining the requirements for notification of Congress and whether the ultimate destination of the weapons might be concealed.

Gaffney testified that he understood from his superiors that the Point Paper should

157

cast a negative view of the transaction to reflect Secretary Weinberger's presumed opposition to arms transfers to Iran. He completed his paper, entitled "HAWK Missiles for Iran," on November 22 or 23 and submitted it to Powell. Powell testified that he gave the paper to Secretary Weinberger, who did not, however, recall receiving it.

Gaffney testified that under the Arms Export Control Act, Iran was not an eligible country for direct sales from the United States, and that, in his view, even if Iran were to become eligible, the contemplated sales of HAWKs could not be made directly or indirectly (through Israel or otherwise) unless the President notified Congress.

## McFarlane Informs the President and the Secretary of State

While they were still in Geneva, McFarlane updated the President and Chief of Staff Donald Regan on the status of the HAWK shipment and the anticipated hostage release. McFarlane informed them that the Israelis were about to ship the weapons, and expressed hope that the hostages would come out by the end of the week. McFarlane specifically told the President that Israel was about to deliver 80 HAWK missiles to Iran via a warehouse in Country 15, and that Israel wanted the United States to replace those missiles.

McFarlane testified that he simply told the President that the Israelis were about to act, but did not ask for specific approval:

> [T]he President provided the authority in early August for Israel to undertake, to sell arms to Iran, and to then come to the United States for replenishment, to buy new ones. That didn't

require then the Israelis to come back to us on each occasion and get new approval.

The President asked McFarlane to arrange a meeting at which the President and his top advisers would review the initiative after the summit.

At about the same time, McFarlane also told Secretary of State George Shultz of the impending arms-for-hostages swap. McFarlane called Secretary Shultz by secure phone "out of the blue, about a hostages release and arms sales to Iran." McFarlane explained that Israel was about to ship 100 HAWKs to Iran through Country 15 **[Portugal],** that the shipment would occur only if the hostages were released, and that the United States would sell replacements to Israel. Secretary Shultz understood it as "a straight-out arms-for-hostages deal." He expressed his opposition, and rebuked McFarlane for not informing him about it earlier: "I told him I hoped that the hostages would get out, but I was against it, and I was upset that he was telling me about it as it was just about to start so there was no way I could do anything about it." When asked about Secretary Shultz' account, McFarlane testified: "I don't recall it that way."

## North Recruits Secord

As McFarlane had explained to the President and Secretary Shultz, the plan was to move 80 HAWKs from Tel Aviv to the capital of Country 15, transfer them to other planes, and then ship them on to Iran. The planners chose this circuitous routing because direct flights from Israel to Iran would draw attention given the poor relations between Israel and Iran. Because the cargo was arms, special clearances had to be obtained from the government of Country 15. As the pilot who ultimately flew the HAWKs to Iran stated:

> Everybody can fly [in Europe] without clearances unless you have . . . sensitive stuff like arms aboard, and then you have to have diplomatic clearance.

A problem developed on November 18: The government of Country 15 was unwilling to grant the special clearances. On that day, North asked Richard Secord—his confederate in the covert operation supporting the Contras—to fly to Country 15 to "see what he could do to straighten out the mess."

McFarlane testified he was not aware that North was providing this letter to Secord, and that his permission was not sought to send it out.

Secord arrived in Country 15 on November 20. He and his associate Thomas Clines, who Secord said "had really been handling all of the matters for the Enterprise" in Europe, together started "to work the problem . . . through our colleagues in the armament industry . . ."

## Million-Dollar Deposit to Lake Resources

On November 18—the same day that he brought Secord into the deal—North began to arrange for a $1-million transfer from Israeli intermediaries to the account of Lake Resources, a Panamanian company controlled by Secord and referred to by North as "our Swiss Co[mpany]." Lake Resources and its account at Credit Suisse in Geneva had been established by North and Secord in May 1985 "to receive monies in support of the covert operations." Prior to this deposit, which was made on November 20, Secord and North had used the company exclusively for supporting the Contras.

The purpose for this $1-million deposit is unclear. North and Secord testified that the payment was for chartering planes to move the 80 HAWKS to Iran. The Israeli Historical Chronology affirms this explanation.

Some evidence suggests that Secord made, or contemplated making, expenditures in Country 15. One of the persons with whom Secord was working, an officer of a European arms company, reportedly attempted to bribe an official of the government of Country 15 to obtain the necessary clearances, and there are references to Secord having spent substantial sums in Country 15. However, bank records do not show any such payments out of the Lake Resources account.

Whatever the initial purpose of the deposit, the Committees have ascertained its use. Secord used approximately $150,000 to pay for air charters relating to the HAWK shipment, and the remaining $850,000 was spent to support the Contras and to make profit distributions to Secord and his business associates, Albert Hakim and Thomas Clines. North testified that in early 1986 he told the Israelis that the money had been used "for the purpose of the Contras" and that they acquiesced. The first "diversion" to the Contras of money received in connection with the Iranian arms sales had occurred.

## Confusion in Country 15

The plan to ship the HAWKs through Country 15 faced collapse because the government there refused to grant the necessary clearances. Upon arriving in Country 15, Secord and his associates—the European business-man and Clines—tried to overcome this problem. All three were fully aware that the cargo to be moved was HAWK missiles. Be-cause their efforts were outside normal diplo-matic channels and in contradiction to stated U.S. policy, they were not well-received by the government of Country 15.

## North Updates Poindexter

As the operation faltered on November 20, North reported to Poindexter and portrayed a mission well under control. He made no mention of the obstacles faced in Country 15:

> The Israelis will deliver 80 Mod HAWKS to [the capital of Country 15] at noon on Friday 22 Nov. These 80 will be loaded aboard three chartered aircraft, owned by a proprietary which will take off at two hour intervals for Tabriz, [Iran]. The aircraft will file for overf-light through the [capital of Country 16] FIR enroute to Tabriz [from Country 15]. Appro-priate arrangements have been made with the proper . . . [Country 16] air control personnel. Once the aircraft have been launched, their departure will be confirmed by Ashghari [a pseudonym for Ghorbanifar] who will call [the Second Iranian official] who will call [an Iranian in Damascus] who will direct [another Iranian in Beirut] to collect the five rpt five Amcits [American citizen hostages] from Hiz-ballah and deliver them to the U.S. Embassy. There is also the possibility that they will hand over the French hostage who is very ill.

This PROF message is clear evidence that North informed Poindexter in detail of the HAWK transaction—including the involve-ment of Secord and the replenishment ar-rangements—well in advance of the shipment.

## North Asks the CIA for Assistance

Secord and the European businessman were unable to budge the government of Country 15. With only hours left before an Israeli plane carrying 80 HAWKs was to depart for the capital of Country 15, North urgently sought assistance from McFarlane, the CIA, and the State Department. North called McFarlane on the evening of November 21; they discussed whether McFarlane should call Country 15's Prime Minister or Foreign Minister in the morning.

Informed by Secord of the difficulties in Country 15, North immediately asked CIA official Duane Clarridge to assist in obtaining clearances for the plane going there. Clar-ridge said Secord should contact the CIA Chief in Country 15, whose name North then relayed to Secord. At the same time, Clar-ridge sent "flash" cables instructing the CIA Chief in Country 15 and his deputy to report immediately to the office for a "special as-signment."

The next morning, November 22, Secord, using his Copp pseudonym, called the CIA Chief and said that he urgently needed clear-ance for an El Al charter flight scheduled to leave Tel Aviv in 20 minutes and fly to the capital of Country 15. Secord urged the CIA Chief to call an official of Country 15 and emphasize the urgency of obtaining the clearance. At this point, the CIA Chief sug-gested enlisting the help of the Deputy Chief of Mission at the U.S. Embassy in Country 15.

**North secured the help of the U.S. Embassy in Portugal by telling a false story to Robert B.**

Oakley, then the Director of the Office of Counterterrorism and Emergency Planning at the State Department. He said he had learned by accident that Israel was having trouble getting clearance; "one of his people" buying arms for the Contras discovered that Israel was moving a shipment of arms obtained from the same source.

## Jumbo Jet Departs for Country 15 Transit Point

Although the clearance for landing in Country 15 had not been authorized on the morning of November 22, the El Al 747 carrying the 80 HAWK missiles was ordered to take off for that country's capital. As the plane neared its "go—no go point," frantic efforts were underway to change the country's government's position. Clarridge cabled the CIA Chief in Country 15 and ordered him to "pull out all the stops" to solve the problem. Secord called an official in Country 15's foreign ministry, who said that the government had decided to withhold permission based upon the U.S. Embassy's previous statement that the United States did not concur in the shipment. Hoping to reverse this position, the Deputy Chief of Mission made hurried phone calls attempting to summon the Country 15 Foreign Minister out of a cabinet meeting; and Secord told the CIA Chief that "McFarlane was being pulled out of [a] meeting with [the] Pope" to call the Foreign Minister.

All these efforts were in vain. By early afternoon, Secord, who was in radio contact with the El Al plane, telephoned North and informed him that the government of Country 15 had refused permission. He said the aircraft had been ordered back to Tel Aviv.

## North and Clarridge Bring in a CIA Airline

Due to the delays, the El Al plane, which the Israelis had reserved for this operation for only a limited time, was no longer available. Clarridge, North, and Secord scrambled to find other ways to transport the HAWK missiles to Iran. Within hours, Clarridge met with the Chief of the CIA's air branch and told him "we [have] a very sensitive mission in the Middle East and we need a 747 aircraft right away." The branch chief could not locate such a large aircraft on short notice, but suggested that a CIA airline proprietary might be able to move the cargo. At 4 P.M. on November 22, an air branch official called the CIA project officer for the proprietary, and asked whether its Boeing 707 cargo planes were available to move 80 pieces of "sensitive hi priority cargo" from Tel Aviv to the capital of Country 15. The project officer reported that at least one of the airline proprietary's planes was available.

Clarridge's actions resulting in the involvement of the air proprietary were at North's request and with the authority of CIA Associate Deputy Director of Operations, Edward Juchniewicz. Juchniewicz spoke with both Clarridge and North on November 22, and told them he had no objection to giving Secord the commercial name of the airline proprietary to charter the necessary flights. Over the next 48 hours, Clarridge and CIA air branch personnel closely managed the proprietary's flight activities in support of this covert operation. Before the operation was over, the proprietary's project officer also became directly involved in coordinating matters.

161

## Schwimmer's DC-8 Charter Falls Through

On the evening of November 22, Schwimmer called North to say the charter of the DC-8s for the Country 15-to-Iran leg of the mission had fallen through. In a PROF note to Poindexter, North updated the situation as of 7:00 P.M.:

> Unbelievable as it may seem, I have just talked to Schwimmer, in TA [Tel Aviv,] who advises that they have released their DC-8s in spite of my call to DK [David Kimche] instructing that they be put on hold until we could iron out the clearance problem in [the capital of Country 15]. Schwimmer released them to save $ and now does not think that they can be re-chartered before Monday.

Within minutes of Schwimmer's call, North and Secord discussed a substitute method of transporting the missiles from Country 15 to Iran. Secord suggested that the European businessman's company try to find some planes. North wrote to Poindexter that Secord would solve the problem by diverting a plane from the Contra operation to the Iran operation:

> Advised Copp of lack of p/u [pick up] A/C [aircraft]. He has advised that we can use one of our LAKE Resources A/C which was at [the capital of Country 15] to p/u a load of ammo for UNO [United Nicaraguan Opposition]. He will have the a/c repainted tonight and put into service nlt [no later than] noon Sat so that we can at least get this thing moving. So help me I have never seen anything so screwed up in my life. Will meet with Calero tonite to advise that the ammo will be several days late in arriving. Too bad, this was to be our first direct flight to the resistance field

> . . . inside Nicaragua. The ammo was already palletized w/ parachutes attached. Maybe we can do it on Weds. or Thurs.

> More as it becomes available. One hell of an operation.

In fact, it appears that Lake Resources had no planes at this time. Nevertheless, this PROF note reveals that North was beginning to meld the two operations he was overseeing and to recognize that the Lake Resources enterprise could operate in a variety of settings.

## The Oil-Drilling Equipment Cover Story

During the planning of the HAWK missile shipment, the Israeli and American participants agreed to keep the true nature of the operation secret. They would use a false "story line" that the cargo to Iran was oil-drilling equipment. Several American officials who knew of the operation were advised of this cover story but understood that it was false and knew that the cargo was missiles.

At the time, the President and Regan knew that the cargo comprised HAWK missiles and were specifically told of the false story before the shipment was made, presumably by McFarlane. Regan testified: "I recall that that was to have been a cover story if discovered, it was to have been said that these were oil-drilling parts."

North claims he used the cover story when he brought Clarridge and Allen into the operation. As he later testified, "I lied to the CIA because that was the convention that we had worked out with the Israelis, that no one else was to know." Allen testified that North "stated emphatically" that the cargo was oil-drilling equipment, but that he (Allen) had "serious doubts" about whether this was true.

If Clarridge did not know the contents of the cargo at the start, he soon learned it. In Country 15, late in the morning of November 23, Secord gave the CIA Chief a full accounting of the mission. Their meeting occurred in a car in a hotel parking lot. Secord revealed his identity, explained he was formally associated with the NSC, and specifically told the officer that the planned flight would contain HAWK missiles being sent to Iran in exchange for hostages.

The CIA Chief testified that he returned to his office and sent two cables to Clarridge through the "Eyes Only" privacy channel he was using on the HAWK project. The first cable contained a general report, mentioning the discussion with Secord but not setting forth the substance of the conversation. The second cable reported that the flights would contain HAWK missiles sent to secure the release of the hostages. The Committees' investigation did not locate this cable. But the CIA Chief's subsequent testimony about its existence was corroborated in testimony by the CIA Deputy Chief and by the Deputy Chief of Mission—who at the time either read the cable or was told about it by the CIA Chief. In addition, the CIA communicator, who transmitted the cable from Country 15, vividly recalls being shocked when he read the message and learned that the United States was sending arms to Iran.

Clarridge received additional information that revealed that the cargo was HAWKs: North testified that shortly after the shipment occurred, if not before, he had told Clarridge the true nature of the cargo. Moreover, on November 23, Allen showed Clarridge a report that, according to Allen,

would cause "one [to] think that this initiative had involved arms in the past." Allen suspected that the November shipment also involved arms and "couldn't help but believe that [Clarridge] suspected that. Particularly he could see the [report] as clearly as I, and he leafed through [its contents] . . . I left the folder with him and then picked it up later." After the shipment, Clarridge received additional information that made clear that the cargo was missiles.

Clarridge insisted in testimony before these Committees that he had no recollection of having learned that the cargo was missiles prior to early 1986. This testimony conformed to the false story certain Administration officials put out in November 1986 when they were trying to conceal the advance knowledge in the U.S. Government of the shipment of HAWK missiles.

The Committees are troubled by the fact that the cable informing Clarridge of Secord's detailed account of the operation, and an earlier cable Clarridge sent to the CIA Chief at the outset of the operation, are inexplicably missing from an otherwise complete set of 78 cables sent by CIA officials during the operation.

## Country 15 Routing Is Abandoned

By the afternoon of November 23, the plan to transship the missiles through Country 15 was abandoned. The previous evening, McFarlane had called the country's Foreign Minister and believed he had received a "green light" for the flights. However, the foreign government still insisted that the United States provide a diplomatic note setting forth the nature of the cargo and the shipping route, and stating that the release of

163

American hostages was the purpose of the shipment. The foreign government wanted this documentation because it saw the operation as "so directly in conflict with known U.S. policy and [its own] policy." Clarridge cabled the CIA Chief in the capital of Country 15 that in light of the diplomatic message, "it is obvious . . . that we are closing down [the Country 15] aspect of this operation."

Meanwhile, still on November 23, Israeli military personnel began to load the HAWKs into the CIA proprietary airplane at the Tel Aviv airport. If they had not already been told, the proprietary's crew surmised from the appearance of the crates that their cargo was missiles and reported this to the airline manager.

Later that day, the participants decided to move the shipment directly from Tel Aviv to Iran, without transiting a third country. Under the new plan, one of the proprietary's planes would make a series of flights to move the 80 HAWKs. After dismissing one route, the planners selected a shorter—but more dangerous—route across Country 16. But obtaining overflight clearances from Country 16 remained a problem, so Clarridge once again cabled the CIA Chief there. Several hours later, the CIA Chief replied that the Government of Country 16 was supportive, but needed "some idea of what the aircraft would carry as presumably they would not be empty." Late that night, Clarridge sent two more increasingly urgent cables to the CIA Chief in Country 16. In conformity with the cover story, these cables told the CIA Chief to advise the government of Country 16 that "the aircraft are carrying sophisticated spare parts for the oil industry" and that the five flights would be spread over a number of days.

North and Clarridge, working with Schwimmer, continued to coordinate the flight activity on Sunday, November 24. At the last minute, they decided that, at least on the first sortie, the plane should land at a transit point in another country, Country 17, to disguise the fact that the shipment was moving from Israel to Iran. While this decision was being made, the CIA Chief in Country 16 informed Clarridge that the government there had approved the five overflights, but that "incoming flight cannot come directly from [Country 17]."

## CIA Airline Proprietary Moves the Missiles

On November 24, the CIA proprietary aircraft [St. Lucia Airways] carrying 18 HAWK missiles flew from Tel Aviv to the transit point in Country 17 [Cyprus]. Because Schwimmer had sent the plane without a cargo manifest, the pilot lacked the documentation required by customs officials at the transit point, who wanted to inspect the cargo. Simultaneously, Schwimmer and the proprietary manager, along with North and Clarridge, frantically discussed how to solve this. While there is evidence to the contrary, it seems the pilot simply talked his way out of the problem.

After getting out of the transit point in Country 17, the pilot ran into trouble while flying over Country 16 [Turkey]. According to the airline manager's report,

nothing was prepared for overflight in [Country 16] and [the pilot] had again to talk his way through. Since they [the Country 16 ground controllers] repeatedly insisted on a diplomatic clearance number, he made one up which was not accepted after long negotiations and then he filibustered one hour and 30 min his way through [Country 16], using different altitudes, positions and estimates that he told [Country 16's] Military with whom he was obviously in radio contact . . .

However, radar realized his off-positions which gave additional reason for arguments and time delays.

Cables the next day from the CIA Chief in Country 16 to Clarridge suggested several reasons why the pilot encountered these difficulties. For example, the destination of the plane was changed at the last minute from Tabriz to Tehran, which "provoked query" from Country 16 because it did not square with the clearance request. Other discrepancies caused outright anger:

[An official of Country 16 was] quite upset over multiple flight plans received, fact first flight came directly from [the transit point in Country 17] and did not request clearance beforehand and conflicting stories about plane's cargo. [The CIA Chief] told [the official] it was oil industry spare parts, telex from carrier stated medical supplies and the pilot told ground controllers he was carrying military equipment. . . .

Bottom line is that [the government of Country 16] still wants to assist but has developed a little cynicism about our interaction with them on the matter.

Ironically, the pilot reportedly told the flight controllers the true nature of the cargo even while Clarridge was spreading the cover story to high level officials of Country 16.

The only part of the operation that went smoothly was the flight into Tehran. The Second Iranian Official and Ghorbanifar, who were in Geneva, passed word to officials in Tehran to prepare to receive the plane. The plane landed in Tehran early in the morning.

## AFTERMATH OF THE HAWK FLIGHT

### The Failure Sinks In

On November 25, with the Americans still entertaining the hope that one or more hostages might be released, senior White House and CIA officials were informed about the weekend's activities. Poindexter told the President at his regular 9:30 A.M. briefing that a shipment of arms to Iran had just taken place.

At 7 A.M. that morning at CIA headquarters, Edward Juchniewicz told McMahon that Secord and "those guys" at the NSC had "used our proprietary to send over some oil supplies" to Iran. McMahon's reaction was anger:

I said goddam it, I told you not to get involved. And he [Juchniewicz] said, we're not involved. They came to us and we said no. And they asked if we knew the name of a secure airline and we gave them the name of our proprietary. I said, for Christ's sake, we can't do that without a Finding.

McMahon said that at the time he accepted Juchniewicz's report that the cargo had been oil-drilling equipment: "[M]y focus was that we had done something wrong . . . and I didn't care what was on that airplane." McMahon's view was that any use of the CIA airline proprietary at the direction of CIA but without a Presidential Finding was illegal.

165

Shortly after talking to Juchniewicz, McMahon went to Deputy Director for Operations Clair George's office where several staffers were discussing the weekend's activities. McMahon told them "that they weren't going to do anything more until we got a Finding."

McMahon also moved quickly to contact CIA General Counsel Stanley Sporkin on the matter of the airline proprietary's activity. McMahon testified that "during the day I called Sporkin several times and I told him that I wanted a Finding and I wanted it retroactive to cover that flight." Sporkin recalled that McMahon simply asked him to look into the legal aspects of the activity, but did not declare that a Finding was necessary.

Late in the day, two officers from the Operations Directorate, an air branch officer and his group chief, were directed to brief Sporkin on the proprietary's flight.

The participants' accounts of the briefing of Sporkin differed significantly. The air branch subordinate officer said that the meeting lasted about 45 minutes and that he and his superior explained to the lawyers that the airline proprietary—acting at the direction of the NSC staff and with the approval of Juchniewicz—had moved some cargo from Israel to Iran. He testified that as of November 25, he knew nothing about the cargo other than its weight and dimensions and that that was the only information about the cargo that was discussed at the briefing. He recalled that the lawyers exhibited no curiosity about the nature of the cargo and that there was no mention that the cargo was either oil-drilling equipment or military equipment. He also testified that nothing was said to indicate that the proprietary's flight was related to an effort to free hostages.

The CIA group chief said he did not even

know of the activity being scrutinized until that morning. He stated in an interview that he and the subordinate explained that a CIA proprietary plane, acting in a strictly commercial capacity, had carried "commercial cargo" into Iran.

Notwithstanding these divergent accounts from officials of the Operations Directorate, it is clear that the briefers told Sporkin that missiles had been transported, and the shipment was part of an effort to free the hostages. Sporkin testified: "What they told me indicated an involvement in a shipment of arms to Iran." Sporkin's deputy, Deitel, specifically recalled that the briefers said the cargo was missiles. Sporkin testified that the briefers probably specified the exact type of missiles being shipped.

During the briefing, Sporkin tentatively concluded that a covert action Finding was necessary to authorize the previous activity. He stated that there should be no more flights to move the rest of the cargo in Israel until the matter could be looked into further.

Sporkin then dictated a draft Finding that authorized the CIA to assist in "efforts being made by private parties" to obtain the release of hostages through the provision of "certain foreign materiel and munitions" to the Government of Iran. In its entirety, the Finding stated:

*Finding Pursuant to Section 662 of The Foreign Assistance Act of 1961, As Amended, Concerning Operations Undertaken by the Central Intelligence Agency in Foreign Countries, Other Than Those Intended Solely for the Purpose of Intelligence Collection.*

I have been briefed on the efforts being made by private parties to obtain the release of Americans held hostage in the Middle East, and hereby find that the following operations in foreign countries (including all support necessary to such operations) are important to the national security of the United States. Because of the extreme sensitivity of these operations, in the exercise of the President's constitutional authorities, I direct the Director of Central Intelligence not to brief the Congress of the United States, as provided for in Section 501 of the National Security Act of 1947, as amended, until such time as I may direct otherwise.

SCOPE: Hostage Rescue—Middle East
DESCRIPTION

The provision of assistance by the Central Intelligence Agency to private parties in their attempt to obtain the release of Americans held hostage in the Middle East. Such assistance is to include the provision of transportation, communications, and other necessary support. As part of these efforts certain foreign materiel and munitions may be provided to the Government of Iran which is taking steps to facilitate the release of the American hostages.

All prior actions taken by U.S. Government officials in furtherance of this effort are hereby ratified.

The draft Finding referred to no objective of opening a diplomatic channel with Iran. Yet, this was the justification for the arms deals that the Administration offered after they were exposed in November 1986. Rather, the Finding depicted a straight swap of arms for hostages.

Sporkin sent the proposed Finding to Casey on November 26. That morning, Clair George phoned North to tell him that Sporkin had determined a Finding was necessary. Later that day, after Casey called McFarlane and Regan "to ascertain that indeed this had Presidential approval and to get assurances that a Finding would be so signed," Casey,

who agreed a Finding was needed, delivered the text to Poindexter. Poindexter did not immediately present it to the President. Over the next several days, Casey, McMahon, and George made repeated inquiries to Poindexter and other "NSC personnel" and "continuously receive[d] reassurances of the President's intent to sign the Finding."

## The President Renews His Approval

On the day the CIA sent the proposed Finding to the White House, November 26, the President authorized continuing the arms-for-hostages transaction.

## The Iranians Feel Cheated

After midnight on November 26, Allen learned that officials in Iran were upset that the wrong model of HAWKs had been delivered. The Iranians also complained through Ghorbanifar that the missiles had Israeli markings, which "the Iranians took to be a prov[o]cation."

On November 25 or 26, Ghorbanifar, "on the very edge of hysteria," called NSC consultant Michael Ledeen, and said "the most horrible thing had happened. . . . [T]hese missiles had arrived and they were the wrong missile." Ghorbanifar gave Ledeen an urgent message from the Prime Minister of Iran for President Reagan: "We have done everything we said we were going to do, and you are now cheating us, and you must act quickly to remedy this situation." Ledeen conveyed this to Poindexter.

At this point, North dispatched Secord to Israel. During meetings with Kimche and Schwimmer, Secord quickly deduced the source of Iran's displeasure: according to him, Schwimmer and Nimrodi had promised Ghorbanifar that the missiles being provided could shoot down high-flying Soviet reconnaissance planes and Iraqi bombers. The I-HAWK missiles that were provided, like all HAWKs, had no such capability. The Iranians were insisting that "these embarrassing missiles" be removed from Tehran.

## CONCLUSION

The shipment of HAWKs to Iran was bad policy, badly planned and badly executed. In contradiction to its frequently emphasized public policy concerning the Iran-Iraq war and nations that support terrorism, the United States had approved the sale of arms to Iran. The United States had agreed to a sequential release of hostages following successive deliveries of weapons; thereafter, this departure from policy became the norm. This precedent, established in November 1985, gave the Iranians reason to believe that the United States would retreat in the future

from its demand for the release of hostages prior to any weapons shipments.

The planning and execution of the operation were also flawed. By the time the U.S. Government became directly involved, official disclaimers by unwitting State Department officials had already complicated the foreign relations aspect of the project. And the mission itself jeopardized the security of the CIA airline proprietary's operation.

Finally, the cover story that was used by certain NSC and CIA officials in November 1986 was first employed in November 1985 for purposes of operational security. The President, Secretary Shultz, McFarlane, Poindexter, North, and various CIA officials, however, were fully aware in November 1985 that Israel was shipping HAWKs to Iran—not oil-drilling equipment—with U.S. approval and assistance to obtain the release of the American hostages.

**A chapter footnote says that crew members aboard the CIA proprietary company, St. Lucia Airways, were not supposed to know they were shipping weapons. But they did and joked that "we should be firing them at Iran rather than flying them into Iran."**

# CHAPTER 11

# Clearing Hurdles:
# The President Approves
# a New Plan

The difficulties with the November 1985 HAWK shipment and the failure to secure the release of more hostages did not end the arms-to-Iran initiative. Having already traveled down the path of bargaining for the hostages' lives, the President and his NSC staff were reluctant to turn back. North quickly began to plan another arms deal, and the President signed the Finding that Stanley Sporkin prepared immediately after the HAWK shipment. North claimed repeatedly in December that reversing course would cause the radical captors to kill the hostages.

North had another motivation for continuing the arms deals. As he explained to Israeli officials in early December, he wanted to divert profits to benefit the Contras he was supporting in Nicaragua.

In December 1985 and January 1986, the Secretaries of State and Defense argued aggressively to the President against trying to trade arms for hostages. Among other things, they asserted that this initiative was illegal and contrary to longstanding U.S. public policy against providing arms to terrorist states and bargaining with terrorists.

Secretary Weinberger and Secretary Shultz' arguments, together with a first-hand assessment by McFarlane that the Iranian intermediary was the "most despicable man" he had ever encountered, caused the initiative to lose momentum in December. However, in early January the Israelis approached Poindexter—who had replaced McFarlane as National Security Adviser—with a new plan that Poindexter and North quickly embraced. The President decided to go forward. He signed an expanded Finding and directed that the covert activity not be reported to Congress.

Unlike the 1985 transactions, the President decided that the weapons for Iran would now come directly from U.S. stocks. The NSC staff took charge of the initiative, relegating the Israelis to a secondary role. Secord was designated as the agent of the U.S. Government in the future transactions. This created the opportunity to generate profits on the arms sales that the Enterprise could use for its other covert projects—including support of the Contras.

## THE PLAYERS CHANGE

John Poindexter—soon to be elevated to National Security Adviser—and Oliver North met on November 27, 1985, to devise a new plan. Poindexter directed North to have Richard Secord or Israeli official David Kimche deliver a message to soothe the Iranians' feeling of having been cheated because the HAWKs delivered three days earlier did not meet their expectation. North and Poindexter also discussed a "change of team" on the operation. North's notes of the meeting indicate that the United States was prepared to deliver 120 items (probably a new version of HAWKs) in exchange for all the hostages after the first delivery and a commitment by Iran of no future terrorism.

The change in team included removing Michael Ledeen, the NSC terrorism consultant, as an intermediary. When Ledeen gave Poindexter the message that the Iranians felt cheated, Poindexter told him, "We're going to take you off this thing for awhile because we need somebody with more technical expertise." This was the last time Ledeen spoke to Poindexter on the Iran initiative, "since from the time [Poindexter] became National Security Adviser, [Ledeen] was unable to get an appointment with him."

In late November, Secord, Iranian go-between Ghorbanifar, Kimche, and Israeli arms dealers Al Schwimmer and Yaacov Nimrodi met in Paris. According to notes North took when Secord briefed him on the meeting, Ghorbanifar was "angry," apparently because the Iranians wanted "something to deal w[ith] Soviet Recon[naissance]"—such as Phoenix or Harpoon missiles—rather than the HAWKs that were delivered. Ghorbanifar advanced a set of proposals that "blatantly" called for the swapping of arms for hostages. The first proposal, as later related to North by Secord, provided for a phased exchange of 3200 TOW missiles for hostages:

600 TOWs = 1 release
H + 6 hrs later = 2000 TOWs = 3 release
H + 23 hrs = 600 TOWs = 1 release

The other options were variations in which other armaments—such as Maverick air-to-surface missiles, Dragon surface-to-surface missiles, Improved-HAWK missiles, spares for F-4 air planes, ground artillery, and bombs—would be substituted for some or all of the TOWs. Ghorbanifar's proposal also contemplated arms deliveries beyond the initial swap. The Paris group agreed to meet with U.S. representatives in London on December 6 to pursue these proposals.

**North began looking for new ways to move weapons and met with Assistant Secretary of Defense Richard L. Armitage, who asked another Pentagon official to research the matter. The resulting memo said there was no way to transfer American weapons to Iran, either through Israel or directly, without informing Congress under the Arms Export Control Act. Armitage briefed Weinberger on this before the December 7, 1985, showdown among senior officials on the Iran issue.**

## North Lays Out a Plan

On December 4, North wrote a PROF message to Poindexter setting out the current situation and proposing a new arms-for-hostages transaction. He described the "extraordinary distrust" the Iranians developed because Schwimmer and Ledeen had promised that the missiles shipped in November could fly high enough to stop Soviet reconnaissance flights. He said, "None of us [Kimche, Meron, Secord] have any illusions about the cast of characters we are dealing with on the other side. They are a primitive, unsophisticated group who are extraordinarily distrustful of the West in general and the Israelis/U.S. in particular."

While acknowledging "a high degree of risk" in continuing the operation, North emphasized, "we are now so far down the road that stopping what has been started could have even more serious repercussions." He exhorted Poindexter to press on in a way that suggested the United States was already subject to Iranian extortion:

> If we do not at least make one more try at this point, we stand a good chance of condemning some or all [of the hostages] to death and a renewed wave of Islamic Jihad terrorism. While the risks of proceeding are significant, the risks of not trying one last time are even greater.

North outlined the proposal slated for the upcoming meeting in London. He said the "package" would comprise deliveries from Israel of "50 I HAWKs w/PIP (product improvement package) and 3300 basic TOWs" and reported that the Iranians had already deposited $41 million to pay for these items and that this sum was "now under our control." The schedule that North laid out made plain that this would be an unadulterated swap of arms for hostages:

H-hr: 1 707 w/300 TOWs = 1 AMCIT
H + 10hrs: 1 707 (same A/C) w/300 TOWs = 1 AMCIT
H + 16hrs: 1 747 w/50 HAWKs & 400 TOWS = 2 AMCITs

H + 20hrs: 1 707 w/300 TOWs = 1 AMCIT
H + 24hrs: 1 747 w/2000 TOWs = French Hostage

As it had been previously, the schedule was set up so that the Americans had to deliver weapons before the Iranians would produce any hostages.

The following day, North put the proposal into an unsigned, unaddressed memorandum. This memorandum made clear that all 3,300 TOWs and all 50 Improved HAWK missiles would come from Israel's "prepositioned war reserve." North's memorandum proposed not only that Congress not be notified about the operation and replenishment, but also that there be a cover story to explain why Israel needed to buy weapons:

> The Israelis have identified a means of transferring the Iranian provided funds to an Israeli Defense Force (IDF) account, which will be used for purchasing items not necessarily covered by FMS. They will have to purchase the replenishment items from the U.S. in FMS transaction from U.S. stocks. Both the number of weapons and the size of the cash transfer could draw attention. If a single transaction is more than $14.9 M, we would normally have to notify Congress. *The Israelis are prepared to justify the large quantity and urgency based on damage caused to the equipment in storage.*

Although the Finding CIA Counsel Stanley Sporkin drafted in November contemplated *delayed* Congressional notification, North's proposal represented an entirely different approach: structuring the transaction so as to evade Congressional reporting altogether.

As North was putting together his plan for a new arms-for-hostages deal, the CIA stood by to provide support for more flights into Iran. In the days after the HAWK shipment,

Clarridge and CIA stations in Countries 16 and 18 exchanged numerous cables relating to clearances for anticipated flights from Israel to Iran transiting at Country 18 and overflying Country 16. On November 27, Clarridge told the stations that the "operation is still on but we have encountered delays" and that "whatever was supposed to happen after the first sortie did not happen and we are regrouping." On December 3, he reported to them: "We are still regrouping. Key meetings of principals will take place this weekend with earliest possible aircraft deployments sometime mid to late week of December 8." Clarridge left the United States on other business in early December. However, before leaving he told his deputy to expect another flight to Iran on a project being run by the NSC for which the CIA would be asked to obtain clearances. (For an organizational chart of the CIA in 1985, see Figure 11-1.)

## THE PRESIDENT SIGNS A FINDING

McFarlane returned to his office on December 3 for the first time after the Geneva summit. He had already told the President of his decision to resign, and he tendered his resignation the following day. On December 3 and 4, McFarlane had several lengthy meetings with Poindexter. However, he does not recall any discussion of the status of the covert action Finding—which CIA Director William Casey had delivered to Poindexter with a recommendation that the President sign it and about which McMahon had been anxiously pestering Poindexter for days.

On December 5, in one of his first acts as National Security Adviser, Poindexter pre-

sented the Finding to the President at his daily national security briefing. The President signed it. Poindexter's notes of his daily briefing of the President refer to the Finding. Chief of Staff Donald Regan was present at this briefing, but testified that he has no recollection of the Finding or the President's signing it:

> I have racked my brains since I've read about it in the press, that you have had testimony to that effect. I've checked with my members of the staff, the White House staff who were working with me at the time, as to whether they remember it. No one can remember seeing that document.

Poindexter testified that he was never happy with the Finding because it failed to mention any objectives other than trading arms for hostages. He said he submitted it to the President without the staffing and review that normally accompanies a Finding. In fact, other than Casey and McMahon—who both urged that the Finding be signed—Poindexter did not recall discussing it with anyone else.

The original of the signed Finding was kept in Paul Thompson's safe at the NSC. Contrary to normal practice, the CIA and other agencies were not given a copy. Indeed, no copies were made. McMahon said that he knew of no other occasion when this occurred.

When the Iran initiative was unraveling almost a year later, Poindexter destroyed this Finding. He believed that if the Finding came to light it would cause "significant political embarrassment" to the President because it would reinforce the emerging picture that the United States had traded arms for hostages. In addition, the Finding was evi-

# Figure 11-1. Organization Chart of the Central Intelligence Agency.

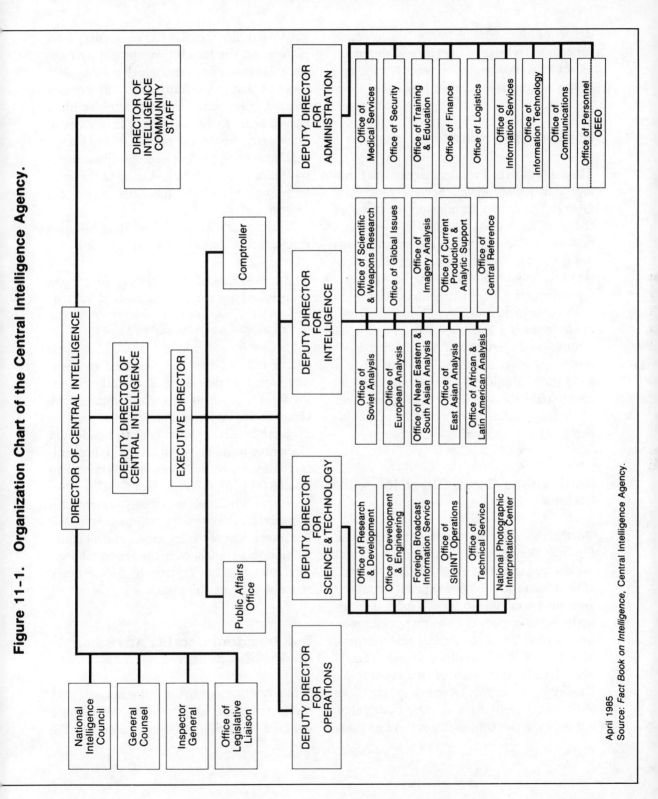

April 1985
Source: *Fact Book on Intelligence*, Central Intelligence Agency.

173

dence of the Administration's contemporaneous knowledge of the HAWK shipment, a fact that Poindexter, Casey, North, and others sought to conceal in November 1986.

## Poindexter Briefs Shultz

The same day the President signed the Finding, Poindexter briefed Secretary of State George Shultz by telephone on the status of the Iran initiative. The briefing—Shultz's first from Poindexter on the subject—was not complete: Poindexter did not even mention the Finding. Not knowing he was hearing only part of the story, Shultz commented at the time to an aide, "he [Poindexter] told me more than I had known before of what went on in the latter half of 1985 and I felt this was a good thing and we were off to a good start." Shultz told Poindexter that the Iran initiative was a "very bad idea" and that "[w]e are signaling to Iran that they can kidnap people for profit."

## North Raises Contra Diversion with Israelis

On the day after the President signed the Finding, December 6, North remarked during a meeting with Israeli officials that the United States wanted to use profits from the upcoming arms sale to Iran to fund U.S. activity in Nicaragua. The meeting, which was held in New York, concerned replenishment of Israeli TOWs. One of the Israeli officials made handwritten notes of this meeting on December 12, 1985. According to these notes, the Israelis were told by North that not only did the United States have no bud-

get to pay for the 504 TOW missiles (and planned on the Israeli Government's receiving this money from the Israeli intermediaries), but that in the future the United States wanted to generate profits from this transaction in order to finance part of its activity in Nicaragua. According to the Israeli Historical Chronology, North had a position paper with him at the meeting that he said was to be presented to the President at a meeting the following day.

North testified that he recalled no such conversation, though he could not rule it out:

> My recollection was that the first time it [the diversion] was specifically addressed was during a [later] meeting with Ghorbanifar. It may well have come up before, but I don't recall it.

North testified that his "clearest recollection" was that the notion of using the residuals for the Contras was first suggested by Ghorbanifar in January 1986.

North flew from New York to London on December 6 and met with Secord, Ghorbanifar, Kimche, Schwimmer, and Nimrodi to discuss the 50-HAWK, 3,300-TOW proposal that North had previously presented to Poindexter. Ghorbanifar acknowledged that the Iranians were having increasing difficulty maintaining control over the Hizballah captors and pressed vigorously for a quick renewal of arms shipments.

## The President and His Advisers Review the Initiative

While North was moving full-steam ahead in the negotiations, the President and his top national security advisers debated the

Iranian initiative at an informal meeting on the morning of Saturday, December 7, in the White House residence. Present were the President, Secretaries Shultz and Weinberger, McMahon (sitting in for Casey, who was out of town), McFarlane, Poindexter, and Regan.

Secretary Shultz, Secretary Weinberger, and Regan all voiced strong opposition to the initiative. Secretary Shultz advanced multiple policy reasons for not pursuing it. His "talking points" for the session stated that the initiative would "negate the whole policy" of not making "deals with terrorists"; that he doubted it would buy the United States influence with moderates in Iran; that it would undoubtedly become public and "badly shake[]" moderate Arabs when they learned that the United States was "breaking our commitment to them and helping the radicals in Tehran fight their fellow Arab Iraq"; and that U.S. allies would be "shocked if they knew we were helping Iran in spite of our protestations to the contrary."

Secretary Weinberger also forcefully voiced opposition, including on legal grounds. He said the proposed arms deal would violate both the U.S. embargo against the shipment of arms to Iran and the restrictions on third-country transfers of U.S.-provided arms in the Arms Export Control Act. He later testified: "[T]here was no way in which this kind of a transfer could be made if that particular Act governed."

The President, along with McFarlane and Poindexter, spoke in favor of continuing the initiative. According to Secretary Shultz:

The President, I felt, was somewhat on the fence but rather annoyed at me and Secretary Weinberger because I felt that he sort of—he was very concerned about the hostages, as well as very much interested in the Iran Initiative.

Secretary Shultz testified that the President was "fully engaged" in the conversation and frustrated with the situation.

In response to Weinberger's legal objections, Shultz recalls that the President responded: " 'Well, the American people will never forgive me if I fail to get these hostages out over this legal question,' or something like that." Weinberger replied: " '[B]ut visiting hours are Thursday', or some such statement."

The participants left the meeting with different views about whether the initiative would proceed. According to Poindexter, the President wanted to pursue every means of trying to get the hostages back. But McFarlane recalled that the President, with disappointment and frustration, approved the position of no more arms sales to Iran, at least pending the London meeting.

Despite varying impressions of the meeting, the President directed McFarlane to go to London to meet with Ghorbanifar and others. Poindexter testified that the purpose was to "check out" the Israeli channel to Iran so that the President could have firsthand information on which to base a decision. McFarlane testified that his purpose was to stress to Ghorbanifar that the United States was open to political discourse with Iran but no arms sales. But there is evidence of a more specific purpose: McFarlane was to try to talk Ghorbanifar into arranging a release of the hostages outside the framework of an arms deal, or at least before any more arms deliveries.

## MCFARLANE MEETS GHORBANIFAR IN LONDON

On December 8, McFarlane joined Kimche, Secord, North, Nimrodi, and Ghorbanifar in London. McFarlane presented an agenda that focused on a political opening with Iran and on areas of possible common interests between the United States and Iran. In contrast, Ghorbanifar wanted to talk only about specified numbers of TOW missiles for each hostage. Ghorbanifar explained that the Iranians were very angry over receiving the wrong kind of HAWK missiles. McFarlane responded: "[G]o pound sand, that is too bad." McFarlane was "revolted" by the bargaining and found Ghorbanifar to be a "borderline moron."

North was unhappy with McFarlane's negative reaction and that day wrote an "eyes only" memorandum to McFarlane and Poindexter entitled "Next Steps." In it, North reviewed options that he saw as necessary "[i]f we are to prevent the death or more of the hostages in the near future." After reviewing the problems of Ghorbanifar's untrustworthiness, Schwimmer's arrangement of previous deals that angered the Iranians and left Israel with inadequate funds for replenishment, and the United States' "lack of operational control over transactions with Ghorbanifar," North initially set out four options: the arms-for-hostage swap discussed in London, an Israeli delivery of 400 to 500 TOWs to Iran to restore "good faith," a military raid, and "do nothing." North summarily rejected the "do nothing" approach.

North testified that Casey shared his view that terminating the negotiations would lead to the death of the hostages.

At the end of the memo, North described a "fifth option": the United States would directly sell arms to Iran, acting pursuant to a Presidential Finding and using Secord as an operational "conduit." The Iran initiative was restructured over the next few weeks to closely resemble this "fifth option." Moreover, using the Enterprise as a conduit for the arms sales proceeds facilitated the diversion of funds to the Contras that North had mentioned to the Israelis only a few days earlier.

## McFarlane Briefs the President on the London Meeting

On December 10, McFarlane briefed the President on the London meeting. Also present were Casey, Poindexter, North, and Regan. McFarlane emphasized that Ghorbanifar lacked integrity and that the initiative was unlikely to bear fruit if he remained the channel to the Iranians. At the same time, McFarlane or North said that abandoning the initiative would risk the lives of the hostages. The President seemed influenced by this concern.

No decision was reached about the future of the initiative, and again there were differing perceptions about what would happen. The President continued to hope that its continuation might lead to freedom for the hostages. McFarlane recalled that the President asked,

> [W]hy couldn't we continue to let Israel manage this program, and was expressing and searching for, I think understandably, ways to keep alive the hope for getting the hostages back, and it is quite true that the President was profoundly concerned for the hostages.

Casey left the meeting with "the idea that the President had not entirely given up on encouraging the Israelis to carry on with the Iranians."

> I suspect he would be willing to run the risk and take the heat in the future if this will lead to springing the hostages. It appears that Bud [McFarlane] has the action.

## The CIA Evaluates Ghorbanifar

Ledeen, with North's approval, aggressively urged the CIA to establish an intelligence relationship with Ghorbanifar. In early December, Ledeen met with the CIA's Duane Clarridge and Charles Allen. He told Allen the history of the Iran initiative, including the HAWK missile debacle. He then explained why he believed Ghorbanifar had contacts that could help the CIA gain insights into the Iranian regime and assist its counterterrorism efforts. Ledeen said Ghorbanifar was "a good fellow who is a lot of fun" and "praised [him] to the hilt."* Allen passed the information to the CIA's Near East Division for evaluation.

After meeting with Ghorbanifar in mid-December in Switzerland, Ledeen met with Casey on December 19 and repeated his arguments for dealing with the Iranian. Casey reacted favorably but indicated a need to clear up the controversy over Ghorbanifar's poor record with the CIA.

Casey called Deputy Director for Operations Clair George and instructed him to arrange a new evaluation of Ghorbanifar. On December 22, the Chief of the Iran branch at

the CIA interviewed Ghorbanifar at Ledeen's home. The Chief of the Iran branch reported to his CIA superiors that he was "only further convinced of the untruthfulness or lack of trust that we could put in Mr. Ghorbanifar." They decided that Ghorbanifar should be given a polygraph test, and Ghorbanifar agreed. After hearing the briefing on Ghorbanifar, Casey sent the President an "eyes only" letter stating that one of the ongoing initiatives to free the hostages was a plan involving Ghorbanifar. Casey wrote of Ghorbanifar: "He has 3 or 4 scenarios he would like to play out."

The decision to consider continued reliance on Ghorbanifar was remarkable. Previously, Agency officials had found his information so marked by deceit, lies, and self-serving proclamations that it had issued a "burn notice" warning the U.S. intelligence community that he could not be trusted and should not be dealt with. Moreover, the information Ghorbanifar was providing was almost impossible to corroborate. He alone was explaining the Iranian position on the hostage issue. The last deal he had helped arrange, the November HAWK shipment, had been a complete disaster.

## ACCELERATION OF THE INITIATIVE: JANUARY 1986

In mid-December, 1985, Amiram Nir, adviser to the Prime Minister of Israel, became involved in the Iran operation; he later became the liaison to the Americans and Ghorbanifar.

---

*At this time, Ledeen also outlined Ghorbanifar's proposal for an anti-Libyan "sting" operation in which the assassination of a leading opponent of Qadhafi would be staged and later revealed to be faked.

## Nir Comes to Washington

On January 2, 1986, Nir flew to Washington to meet with Poindexter and North at the request of Prime Minister Peres. In an opening meeting with North in a hotel, Nir said that he had an idea about how to improve the progress of the Iranian operation. Nir met later that morning with Poindexter, North, and Don Fortier, Poindexter's deputy, and laid out his plan. The central features of the proposal were recorded by Poindexter in his notes: the Israelis would ship to Iran 4,000 "unimproved TOWs"; after the delivery of the first 500, all five American hostages would be released; simultaneously the Southern Lebanon Army would release "20–30 Hizballah prisoners who don't have blood on their hands." If the American hostages were released, Israel would ship to Iran the other 3,500 TOWs and Iran would "confirm" its agreement for "no more hostages [and] terror." Under the plan, the United States would replace the TOWs only if the hostages were released. If the hostages were not released, replenishment was not required and Israel would have lost 500 TOWs. If they were freed, then the United States would replace the 4,000 TOWs, plus the 500 TOWs the Israelis had shipped in 1985.

## Nir and North Discuss Use of Residuals

Nir's proposal included another feature: generating profits that could be diverted to other covert projects. This was not a new concept: Nir and North had talked generally about joint covert operations in November, and North had told other Israelis in December that the United States wanted to use profits

from the arms sale under discussion at that time to finance U.S. activities in Nicaragua.

## A New Finding Is Prepared

Poindexter realized from the start that if the United States embraced the Nir proposal for revitalizing the Iranian initiative, a new covert action Finding would be essential. In notes that he wrote on a flight to join the President in California immediately after the January 2 meeting he jotted: "Covert Finding—already pregnant for 500." Poindexter testified that the "500" was a reference to the TOWs that Israel had already shipped to Iran with U.S. approval but without a Finding.

A first draft of the new Finding, prepared by a CIA staff lawyer who was told nothing of the November Finding, did not mention the objective of gaining the release of American hostages. It did authorize shipment of arms to Iran. This draft included the standard provision calling for the Director of Central Intelligence to report the activity to the Intelligence Committees of Congress.

On January 3, Sporkin edited the draft Finding, making several significant changes. First, he put the provision calling for Congressional notification in brackets, and above it inserted new language directing that the Director instead "refrain from reporting . . . until I [the President] otherwise direct." Sporkin made this change to present squarely to the President the alternatives on notification. Sporkin also changed the description section of the Finding. He apparently sent this draft to North during the day on January 3. The draft contained no references to hostages.

The next day, North drafted a cover memorandum for Poindexter to send to the President with the Finding. North wrote that Nir had proposed a plan "by which the U.S. and Israel can act in concert to bring about a more moderate government in Iran." He said that under the plan, this goal was to be achieved by providing "military materiel, expertise and intelligence" to "Western-oriented Iranian factions." Providing such items to moderates would enable them to come to power by "demonstrat[ing] their credibility in defending Iran against Iraq and in deterring Soviet intervention," North said.

North's draft cover memorandum described the role to be played by the United States under the plan:

> As described by the Prime Minister's emissary [Nir], the only requirement the Israelis have is an assurance that they will be allowed to purchase U.S. replenishments for the stocks that they sell to Iran. Since the Israeli sales are technically a violation of our Arms Export Control Act embargo for Iran, a Presidential Covert Action Finding is required in order for us to allow the Israeli sales to proceed and for our subsequent replenishment sales.

North's memorandum thus makes plain that he understood that, without a Finding, the sale of U.S.-made weapons by Israel to Iran would violate the Arms Export Control Act.

On Monday, January 6, North hand-carried the draft Finding and cover memorandum to Attorney General Meese for his review. Jensen testified that North presented the papers for "informational" purposes only, and that the Attorney General was not asked for, and did not offer, any opinion.

## The President and Advisers Consider the New Proposal

At the morning national security briefing on January 6, Poindexter told the President of the Nir proposal. The Vice President, Regan, and Don Fortier were also present. The President "indicat[ed] he was in general agreement" with the proposal and decided there would be a full NSC meeting the following day on the proposal and the Finding. Poindexter presented the President with the January 6 draft of the Finding at this briefing. Poindexter did not intend that it be signed at this point because it had not yet been "fully staffed" and discussed among the President's national security advisers. But the President, not realizing that the Finding was only a proposal for discussion, read it and signed it, reflecting his agreement.

At the full NSC meeting on January 7 were the President, the Vice President, Secretaries Shultz and Weinberger, Attorney General Meese, Casey, Poindexter, and Regan. While Secretaries Weinberger and Shultz continued to object strenuously, all others favored the plan or were neutral. Secretary Weinberger, who said he had no advance knowledge about the subject, found it to be "very much a re-run" of the December meeting, except that now the President decided to go forward with the plan. There is no record that the Vice President expressed any views.

At the meeting, Attorney General Meese provided a legal opinion that the arms sales could be done legally with Israel making the sales and the United States replenishing Israel's stocks. Secretary Weinberger again objected that the proposed transaction would violate the Arms Export Control Act; the Attorney General responded that there were mechanisms outside the AECA through which the operation could proceed legally, including "the President's inherent powers as Commander in Chief, the President's ability to conduct foreign policy. . . ." Meese referred to a 1981 written legal opinion by Attorney General William French Smith stating that the CIA could legally sell to third countries weapons obtained from the Defense Department under the Economy Act. On this authority, he "concurred with the view of Director Casey that it would be legal for the President to authorize arms transfers pursuant to the National Security Act."

## North Proceeds with Plans for Replenishment

That day, North called Nir in Israel and said that the United States was prepared to proceed with Nir's plan, subject to certain conditions. North said that both the President and Secretary Weinberger had agreed to the plan. North gave Nir this encoded message:

1. Joshua [President Reagan] has approved proceeding as we had hoped.

2. Joshua and Samuel [Secretary Weinberger] have also agreed on method one [replenishment by sale, as opposed to "method two," replenishment by prepositioning].

3. Following additional conditions apply to Albert [Code name for operation?].

A. Resupply should be as routine as possible to prevent disclosure on our side. May take longer than two months. However, Albert says if crisis arises Joshua promises that we will deliver all required by Galaxie [apparently C 5A cargo plane] in less than eighteen hours.

B. Joshua also wants both your govt and ours to stay with no comment if operation is disclosed.

4. If these conditions are acceptable to the Banana [Israel] th[e]n Oranges [U.S.] are ready to proceed.

Neither of the "additional conditions" proposed by the U.S. side dealt with the substance of the operation. North's notes reflect that the purpose for "routine" resupply spread over a period of months was to enable the purchases by Israel to be broken "into lots of less than Cong[ressional] limit" and to avoid "raising eyebrows." The "no comment" proposal would enable the United States—even after the operation was publicly exposed—to avoid acknowledging its central role.

Nir and North also discussed terms for replenishment sales. By this time, the Chief of the Israeli Procurement Mission in New York and Noel Koch, Principal Deputy Assistant Secretary of Defense for International Security Affairs, had been designated as the Israeli and American contacts for hammering out the details.

**Israeli officials continued to negotiate with American officials over how much they would pay to buy replacements for the missiles shipped in 1985. Meanwhile, a Pentagon official suggested that one way to avoid problems with the Arms Export Control Act was to "go black" and use the CIA. Under this plan, the Pentagon would sell arms to the Agency, which would transfer them to Iran.**

## Ghorbanifar Fails Polygraph

Ghorbanifar returned to Washington in January for his new polygraph. The examination was conducted at the CIA on January 11 and lasted five hours. The CIA polygraph operator concluded that Ghorbanifar lied on 13 of 15 items on which he was questioned. According to George, "The only questions he passed were his name and his nationality."

After the test, a CIA officer reported in a memorandum to Casey, McMahon, and Clair George: "Ghorbanifar is a fabricator who has deliberately deceived the U.S. Government concerning his information and activities. It is recommended that the Agency have no dealing whatsoever with Ghorbanifar." Afterwards, Ghorbanifar showed up at Ledeen's house "furious" and "hurting" because the questioning was more expansive than he had expected and because he claimed to be physically injured by the examination techniques.

The following day, the Chief of the CIA's Iran branch briefed George and the Chief of the Near East Division (C/NE) on the negative results. They instructed him to have no further contact with Ghorbanifar or Ledeen. George viewed the polygraph results as confirming his view of Ghorbanifar and declared to Casey that the Operations Directorate would have nothing more to do with the Iranian. He told North of this decision on January 13. A few days later, the Operations Directorate disseminated a notice saying the CIA would do no more business with Ghorbanifar.

Ghorbanifar's polygraph failure, however, did nothing to squelch his relationship with Casey and the NSC staff. Indeed, North—who "wanted" Ghorbanifar to pass—had braced himself for a negative result. He told Ledeen beforehand that the CIA would make sure Ghorbanifar flunked because they did not want to work with him. Casey, notwithstanding Clair George's advice to termi-

nate the Ghorbanifar relationship, found a way to deal with Ghorbanifar outside the normal Operations Directorate headed by George. Casey ordered Charles Allen, who was the CIA's senior antiterrorism analyst, to meet with Ghorbanifar "to determine and make a record of all the information that he possessed on terrorism, especially that relating to Iranian terrorism—just take another look at this individual." In George's view, Allen virtually became the case officer for Ghorbanifar. To George, there could not have been a "better mismatch" between Allen—who had no experience managing an agent—and Ghorbanifar—who was especially "complex" and difficult to control.

Allen spent five hours with Ghorbanifar at Ledeen's home on January 13 "to assess Subject's access to Iranian Government leaders" and to obtain information from him on terrorists. During this session, Ghorbanifar told Allen that funds generated through the projects he was discussing could be used for "Ollie's boys in Central America." Allen recorded this remark in his handwritten notes of the meeting as "can fund Contras." He did not, however, refer to it in his memorandum to Casey and others on the session. He later explained that at the time he did not "consider it important or even relevant to my particular mission," that he did not discuss it with anyone else, and that he "promptly forgot it."

On January 14, Allen briefed Casey on his session with Ghorbanifar. He told Casey that Ghorbanifar was "very hard to pin down," "very flamboyant," "very clever, cunning." Indeed, Allen called him a "con man," to which Casey jokingly responded: "Maybe this is a con man's con man then." For the moment, Allen said, he was given no further assignment concerning Ghorbanifar.

## Restructuring the Deal

In mid-January, the plan for the operation was restructured in two significant respects. First, weapons to be shipped to Iran would come from U.S.—not Israeli—stocks. Second, at the direction of Poindexter, Casey, and North, Richard Secord was brought into the operation as a "commercial cut-out": a conduit for the money to be paid by Iran to the United States for the missiles. This latter change enabled the "diversion" of funds to support the Contras, which had already begun in November with the use of a part of the Israelis' $1 million deposit to Lake Resources, to continue in a more direct manner.

**After some discussion, Administration officials decided to use Secord for the operation.**

On January 14, Casey told North, according to North's notes, that "Secord Op [is] O.K."

North met with Poindexter that evening. They discussed inserting Secord into the transaction as an "agent for the CIA. . . ." Under this arrangement, the Iranians would receive missiles from Israeli stocks; and Secord, acting as an agent for the CIA, would simultaneously buy basic TOW missiles from DOD and sell and ship them to Israel as replacements. The CIA would not actively participate in the operation. Poindexter directed North to discuss this approach with Casey. This plan called for the private North/Secord enterprise in lieu of the CIA. The CIA would have a role in name only. The Economy Act authorized *intergovernmental* transfers of weapons, but would not permit DOD to sell directly to Secord unless he were designated an "agent" of the CIA.

The barrier to the plan was Secretary Weinberger. Although Casey was on board, Secretary Weinberger continued to raise objections both to the plan and to Secord's involvement.

North met with Sporkin to discuss Secord's role. Sporkin interrupted this meeting to telephone one of his staff lawyers, George Clarke, to discuss whether there would be any "problems or reporting requirements" with the North/Poindexter proposal to use Secord as an "agent" of the CIA but to otherwise leave the CIA out of the operation. Sporkin recalled an "argument with one of my people" about whether there was a way to structure the transaction without the CIA's getting involved. "The answer was no way."

After this meeting, Sporkin prepared a paper for Casey. He advised that the "preferred way to handle the proposal" was for the CIA to take control of the materiel through an Economy Act transfer from DOD before it was moved to the Middle East. Sporkin wrote that he could find no precedent for the purchase of materiel from DOD by someone acting as a CIA "agent," where the CIA had no other role in the transaction.

One of Sporkin's main concerns was the question of notifying Congress:

The key issue in this entire matter revolves around whether or not there will be reports made to Congress. Each of the Acts involved—the Foreign Assistance Act, the Arms Export Control Act, and indeed the National Security Act as amended—have certain reporting provisions in them. While the National Security Act provides for a certain limited reporting procedure, it is my view that there may be other ways of making a suitable report by exercise of the President's constitutional prerogatives.

One such possibility would be not to report the activity until after it has been successfully concluded and to brief only the chairman and ranking minority members of the two Oversight Committees. This would maximize the security of the mission and reduce the possibility of its premature disclosure.

Later that afternoon, North spoke again with Sporkin, who urged that the "final proposal" be "run by" the Attorney General.

That same afternoon, Poindexter convened in his office a meeting of senior administration officials to discuss the structuring of the transaction, the continuing objections of Secretary Weinberger, and the proposed Finding. Present were Secretary Weinberger, Casey, Attorney General Meese, Sporkin, and possibly North. The Attorney General said Israel should not ship weapons out of its stocks and recommended that the United States instead sell directly to the Iranians. Restructuring the operation in this way, he explained, would avoid the restrictions of the Arms Export Control Act, including Congressional reporting requirements.

Sporkin recalled that no decision was made at the meeting and that Secretary Weinberger wanted additional time to examine the revised structure of the plan:

[A]s we were breaking up, the Secretary of Defense said that I want to review all this. I want to have my lawyers look at it and to see if that analysis is correct. And so the meeting broke up without there being any decision made.

The next day, I received a call from the Director—I think it was the next day—in which he said that he received a call from the—from the Secretary of Defense, who said that his people

have looked it over and they agree with the analysis and they have signed off on the project.

Secretary Weinberger was unable to recall, or find anyone at the Defense Department who had performed, any such legal review.

## President Signs a New Finding

Poindexter now arranged to get the President to sign the Finding. At the January 17, 1986 national security briefing attended by the President, the Vice President, Regan, Poindexter, and Fortier, Poindexter discussed the plans and referred to a new cover memorandum. The President did not read the memorandum, but he signed the Finding. To indicate the President's decision, Poindexter wrote "RR per JMP" on the approval line of the memorandum. At the bottom of the memorandum, he also wrote: "President was briefed verbally from this paper. VP, Don Regan and Don Fortier were present."

The January 17 Finding was almost identical to the draft Finding presented to the President on January 6. The only change was the insertion of the words "third parties" in the list of entities to be assisted by the CIA. The Committees have received from NSC files a copy of the January 6 version of the Finding that bears Sporkin's handwritten insertion of this phrase. Sporkin testified that this change was made merely to make the first paragraph of the Finding symmetrical with the second, which already contained a reference to "third parties." He said that the term did not refer to Secord but to Ghorbanifar and other Iranian intermediaries.

The cover memorandum, which North prepared and Poindexter signed, contained the same summary of the Nir proposal that North had included in his January 4 draft cover memorandum. However, the new memorandum stated that for legal reasons the operation should not be conducted as Nir proposed and should instead proceed with sales of arms from the CIA through an agent directly to Iran. Following the advice Attorney General Meese had provided the previous day, the memorandum stated:

> We have researched the legal problems of Israel's selling U.S. manufactured arms to Iran. Because of the requirement in U.S. law for recipients of U.S. arms to notify the U.S. government of transfers to third countries, I do not recommend that you agree with the specific details of the Israeli plan.

The memorandum outlined the new plan to make direct sales from the CIA to Iran through Secord, who was identified only as "an authorized agent."

As was the case with North's earlier draft, the cover memorandum to the President from Poindexter stated that "[t]he Israelis are very concerned [about] Iran's deteriorating position in the war with Iraq" and "believe it is essential that [Israel] act to at least preserve a balance of power in the region." In fact, Secretaries Weinberger and Shultz and Deputy Director McMahon all subsequently testified that this assessment of the state of the Iran-Iraq conflict was contrary to U.S. intelligence estimates.

Defense Secretary Weinberger testified to the Committees that he was unaware that a Finding had been signed. However, he recalled that around January 18, Poindexter told him the President had decided to sell 4,000 TOW missiles to Iran and instructed him to make the missiles available.

Secretary of State Shultz testified he was unaware even of the Presidential decision to sell the weapons. He recalled a luncheon with the President's other top advisers on January 17, during which he expressed opposition to what he thought was still an unapproved plan to sell weapons to Iran.

According to the Tower Board, in his diary entry for January 17, 1986, the President wrote: "I agreed to sell TOWs to Iran."

## CONCLUSION

With the signing of the Finding, the Administration was embarked on an arms-for-hostages initiative with Iran in which the United States—not Israel—would play the lead role. The President set this course over the continued objections of his Secretaries of Defense and State, and notwithstanding the CIA's renewed determination that the Iranian intermediary, Ghorbanifar, could not be trusted.

In a change from the 1985 arms deals, Poindexter, Casey, and North had structured the transactions planned for 1986 in a manner that would leave the United States in possession and control of the large "residuals" that would flow from the sales. Secord and the Lake Resources Enterprise were established as a conduit for the money paid for the missiles by Iran. North and Nir had several ideas about how these profits would be used. Foremost in North's mind was the potential for diversions to the Contra effort.

# CHAPTER 12

# Arms Sales to Iran: The United States Takes Control

The President's decision to sign the Finding on Friday, January 17, 1986, marked the beginning of U.S. control over the Iran arms sales initiative. In November 1985, the United States had acted as a necessary and supporting player to the Israeli plan to ship weapons; the January 17 Finding established that weapons from U.S. stocks would be transported and sold under U.S. control.

The Finding also brought the Central Intelligence Agency (CIA) into the initiative in a more substantial way than it had been in the prior shipment. Yet despite the Finding, the CIA would continue to play only a supporting role to the National Security Council (NSC)-sponsored initiative. While providing logistic and technical support—and a mechanism for getting the weapons from the Department of Defense (DOD) under the Economy Act—the CIA deferred to the NSC staff in evaluating the reliability of the intermediaries and the likelihood of success of the initiative.

Over the next few months, negotiations among the Iranian representatives, the intermediary, and the American officials continued. The pattern established in the 1985 sales would continue. In February, the United States sold 1,000 TOW missiles to Iran and no hostages were released. Instead, the Iranians insisted on the sale of HAWK spare parts and the United States agreed.

Although the arms sales were a failure in achieving the goals set forth in the Finding, they were successful in another way. The Iranians were willing to pay substantially more for the military goods than they cost, and part of the excess filled the bank account of the Enterprise. As North testified, the possibility of using these profits to aid the Contras provided additional incentive to pursue the Iranian initiative.

## THE FINDING IS IMPLEMENTED

On January 18, CIA General Counsel Stanley Sporkin, CIA Deputy Director for Operations Clair George, and the CIA Deputy Chief of the Near East Division (DC/NE) met in the White House Situation Room with National Security Adviser John Poindexter, Oliver North, and Richard Secord to define the Agency's responsibilities. Poindexter and North told the CIA representatives that the Finding had been signed and discussed with them the CIA's role in the arms sales initiative. The CIA's "point man," DC/NE, was to arrange for the Agency to acquire 4,000 TOW missiles from the DOD for sale to Iran. He was also instructed to establish a CIA account through which funds could be delivered to the Department of Defense for purchase of the missiles. Although the Finding was directed to the CIA, the Agency's responsibilities as outlined at the meeting put it in a role of lending logistic support for the NSC staff, which would be principally conducting the negotiations.

At the January 18 meeting, George met Secord for the first time when Secord was introduced as a consultant to the NSC. George knew of Secord's past association with Edwin Wilson, the former CIA officer who was then serving time in a Federal prison for a variety of offenses. George was concerned about Secord's involvement and following the January 18 meeting advised Director Casey of his opinion. George cautioned Casey: "If they are going to ship arms to Iran for hostages . . . don't use Secord."

George expressed even greater disapproval when he discovered that Iranian intermediary Manucher Ghorbanifar was to be involved. The exact point at which George became aware of Ghorbanifar's role in the Iran initiative is unknown, although he implied in testimony that he knew either as a result of, or shortly following, the January 18 meeting. Shortly after Ghorbanifar failed a CIA polygraph test on January 11, 1986, George issued a "field notice"* to senior

---

*A "field notice" is a fabricator warning issued to specific CIA stations, as opposed to a "burn notice," which receives world-wide CIA distribution.

CIA officials in Europe instructing them to avoid dealing with Ghorbanifar. Only a few days later while in the White House, George was "given the Finding to which, surprise, the guy I am going to be dealing with or supporting the National Security Council to deal with, is Ghorbanifar."

Prior to the signing of the January 17 Finding, George advised North of Ghorbanifar's polygraph test results. He also recalled warning Casey against dealing with Ghorbanifar, but "before I could go through one more fight about Mr. Ghorbanifar, [the CIA] received a Presidential order which . . . ended up meaning we were dealing with Mr. Ghorbanifar." Eventually, Casey designated Charles Allen to oversee Ghorbanifar's activities.

DC/NE asked North for a contact at DOD with whom he could arrange to obtain the TOWs. North told DC/NE to contact Secretary Weinberger's military aide, then-Maj. Gen. Colin Powell. When DC/NE telephoned Powell several days later, the general explained that he was aware of the sensitivity of the operation, knew where the weapons were to be delivered, and knew the covert activity was supported by a Finding. Powell named Lt. Gen. Vincent M. Russo as the CIA's contact at DOD.

Russo told DC/NE originally that the price would be around $6,000 per TOW, a price with which North had problems. DC/NE recalled North's reaction to that figure:

The initial price was precisely—it was Russo telling me it was going to be something around 6,000 per. And I recall telling North that and he recalled—it doesn't make any difference to me [DC/NE] whether they charge three or six or nine—I recall North saying, 'well, that is too high, they must be giving you a brand new missile replacement cost figure, and they should be charging for the oldest model TOW in stock. We don't care if these things in fact work real well. Tell the Army that we want the oldest thing they can find in the warehouse.' So I went back to Russo and said, let me make clear that we don't need the very best, latest thing right off the factory line.

The eventual price was approximately $3,400 per TOW, including freight costs.

North's attitude that he did not "care if these things in fact work real well" is inconsistent with the goals of opening a broader initiative with Iran and freeing the hostages. Demonstrably antiquated or unworkable merchandise most likely would promote distrust; indeed, the controversy over the November 1985 HAWK shipment had been caused in part by the Iranians' claim that the 18 HAWKs did not meet their expectations.

On January 20, North noted: "Price must be firm for Defense [Department]—Must be less than 6K." Under the figure showing 4,504 TOWs, North jotted, "Nir knows 10K upper limit—Dick [Secord] arrange w/Nir". The notes suggest that Nir and North had agreed that the TOWs sold to Iran must not exceed $10,000 per unit but that the CIA would not pay more than the original DOD price of $6,000 per TOW. In the plan to sell 1,000 of the missiles to Iran in February, North and Nir were expecting to obtain $4 million above the cost of the missiles. When North learned he could obtain the basic TOW for substantially less, the anticipated profit for the Enterprise increased.

## The Army Executes the Tasking

On January 18, Powell telephoned Gen. Maxwell R. Thurman, Vice Chief of Staff of the Army, with a secret, "close hold" assignment for the Army: to prepare 4,000 basic TOW missiles to be shipped to the CIA. Within a week, the number was increased to 4,508 to cover the 508 missiles Israel had shipped in September that McFarlane had agreed to replenish. Thurman, who was not told the ultimate destination of the missiles or the purpose of the shipment, delegated the responsibility down the chain of command and ultimately to Maj. Christopher Simpson.

The instructions were to maintain a degree of secrecy unusual even for weapon transfers to the CIA: no notes; communications only by secure telephone or face to face; and the number of people privy to the operation kept to a minimum. The imposition of such extraordinary secrecy led the Army to bypass its normal system for interagency transfers, with that system's safeguards against underpricing, depleting stockpiles, and affecting defense readiness. Even though the secrecy guidelines were strictly observed, an apparently accidental error in the price became crucial. By inadvertently using the wrong stock number for the TOW, the Army underpriced the missile and created a price differential broad enough to generate a significant surplus of funds for the Enterprise.

## Pricing the TOW Missiles

Simpson went directly to the TOW Project Manager at the Army Missile Command at Redstone Arsenal in Huntsville, Alabama. Powell had been asked to provide a "basic," or "vanilla," TOW—one that had not been manufactured since 1975. The basic TOW, however, had experienced mechanical problems that required the Army to make design modifications. The TOW Deputy Project

Manager informed Simpson he had sufficient basic TOWs to meet the order but that the TOWs needed the safety modification, which would add to the expense.

Simpson set about pricing the TOWs in what seemed to be a logical manner—he checked the Army's catalogue of inventoried items, complete with national stock numbers and prices. Simpson found the price to be $3,169 for a basic TOW, to which he estimated an additional $300 for the safety modification—a total of $3,469 per missile. Simpson quoted that price to the CIA.

There were, however, eight different models of TOWs listed in the catalogue. Unknown to Simpson, when safety modifications became a required feature, the Army created a new stock number for the basic TOW with the modification and a corresponding new, and much higher, price. Using the correct stock number, the Army should have provided the CIA a cost of $8,435 per missile.

Although Simpson's testimony is inconsistent on the question of whether he was aware that the Army catalogue price for the basic TOW with modifications was $8,435, there are indications that some officials in the Army became aware of the erroneous price. The transfer documents accompanying the first and third shipments from the Army and the CIA carried the Simpson price, the receipts for the second shipment did not reflect any price. Testimony from Army officials about the changing prices in these documents has been inconsistent and inconclusive.

Army officials included in these pricing decisions have denied any intent to lower the price of the TOWs, and the Committees have found no evidence to the contrary. What is apparent, however, is that in fulfilling the CIA request for TOWs in early 1986, the Army bypassed its usual method of obtaining, pricing, and transferring weapons. The emphasis on keeping the transaction secret, even from those involved in the process, led to a significant pricing error, one that North exploited to the advantage of the Enterprise. Without this pricing error, there would have been a much smaller difference between the $10,000 per TOW Ghorbanifar was willing to pay and the actual cost of the TOWs—and the diverted profits to the Enterprise would have been minimal.

## The London Meeting

Armed with a low, firm price for the TOWs, North, Secord, and Amiram Nir, an adviser to Israeli Prime Minister Shimon Peres, met with Ghorbanifar in London on January 22, their first meeting following the President's approval of the Finding. North testified that he was dissatisfied with the notion of selling weapons to Iran until this meeting with Ghorbanifar. North's stated reluctance is inconsistent with the testimony of Sporkin and others, who described North as a strong advocate for the plan and a leader in getting it adopted by the President. Nevertheless, according to North, the inducement that caused him to embrace the plan was a suggestion by Ghorbanifar to divert profits from the arms sales to the Contra forces.

North described his conversation with Ghorbanifar during a lull in the London meetings:

Mr. Ghorbanifar took me into the bathroom and Mr. Ghorbanifar suggested several incentives to make that February [TOW] transaction work, and the attractive incentive for me was the one he made that residuals could flow to support the Nicaraguan resistance. He made it point blank and he made it by my understanding with the full knowledge and acquiescence and support, if not the original idea of the Israeli intelligence services, the Israeli Government.

The tape recording of that meeting does not reflect the private conversation which North described. Instead, it reveals that Ghorbanifar discussed assisting the Contras openly, in the presence of North, Nir, and Secord:

GHORBANIFAR: "I think this is now, Ollie, the best chance because we never would have found such a good time, we never get such a good money out of this. [Laughingly] We do everything. We do hostages free of charge; we do all terrorists free of charge; Central America for you free of charge; American business free of charge; [First Iranian Official] visit. Everything free."

NORTH: "I would like to see, . . . some point this, uh, idea, and maybe, y'know, if there is some future opportunity for Central America. You know that there is a lot of Libyan, a lot of Libyan and Iranian activity with the Nicaraguans."

Poindexter declared that he first learned of the possibility of diverting arms sales proceeds from North in early February 1986. He said that following North's meetings in London, North briefed him on progress being made domestically by CIA and DOD in procuring TOW missiles. Poindexter recalled North casually mentioning, "Admiral, I think I have found a way that we can provide some funds to the democratic resistance [Contras] through funds that will accrue from the sale of arms to the Iranians." Poin-

dexter claimed that he considered the diversion to be "a very good idea" that he approved orally after only a few minutes conversation.

Poindexter stated that the diversion was merely an implementation of the President's policy and a decision Poindexter had authority to make without consulting the President. Nevertheless, Poindexter admitted knowing that public revelation of the diversion's approval by him would result in his leaving the Administration, although he said that he "probably underestimated" the effect public knowledge of the operation would eventually have on the Administration. Poindexter stated that he made the diversion decision without consulting the President in order to give the President "deniability." He acknowledged, however, that he had never acted that way before and that he had a reputation for keeping his superiors informed.

What had begun as an initiative to obtain the release of the American hostages had now assumed a second, inherently conflicting goal. The Finding set forth a policy of selling weapons in order to obtain the release of hostages and to secure an opening to Iran. Use of the arms sales to aid the Contras created an incentive to charge the highest price the Iranians would pay while selling the least expensive equipment, a policy unlikely to win Iranian confidence or the hostages' freedom.

On January 24, North prepared a sophisiticated "notional timeline" for Poindexter under the name "Operation Recovery," which proposed the transfer of TOW missiles and intelligence information to Iran in exchange for the release of the American hostages. "Operation Recovery" reflected the ambitions of the planners who recently met in London. An agreement was reached that the TOWs were to be shipped to Iran in four increments of 1,000 missiles, with an additional 508 TOWs delivered to Israel as replenishment for that country's stocks. On February 8, the Southern Lebanon Army was to release 25 Hizballah prisoners after Iran received the first 1,000 TOWs. On February 9, "all U.S. Hostages [were to be] released to the U.S./British or Swiss Embassy" and "a second group of Hizballah [was to be] released by [the Southern Lebanon Army]." The following day, as preparations were underway to deliver the second increment of TOWs to Iran, Hizballah was to release certain other hostages. The notional timeline also made reference to another ambition of the planners: "February 11, Khomeini steps down." Following this sequential release of prisoners for arms, the United States would deliver the final two increments of missiles. The last deliveries were to be in exchange for hostages of other nationalities and the recovery of hostage William Buckley's remains.

## THE FEBRUARY SHIPMENT

In the delivery schedule agreed upon in the London meeting, North noted, "10 days from money—move TOWs." The same schedule indicated that a deposit of $10 million would occur on January 29. The deposit was not made, and on January 31, DC/NE and Secord met with North to develop another schedule based on an anticipated bank transfer to the CIA account on February 4. However, on that day, North jotted in his notes, "Gorba going to bank to make transaction tomorrow," indicating another delay in the transaction.

On February 10, $1,850,000 was wire-transferred to the CIA Swiss account from the Enterprise's Credit Suisse account, Lake Resources. The following day, another $1,850,000 was wire-transferred to the CIA account "by the order of one of our clients" without further explanation or identification. CIA headquarters then arranged through the Treasury Department to pay $3,700,000 to DOD for 1,000 TOW missiles.

Possession of the 1,000 TOWs was transferred from DOD to CIA once DOD received notice that CIA had the money to cover the cost of the TOWs. Thereafter, on February 15 and 16, separate flights of Southern Air Transport aircraft departed Kelly Air Force Base, each carrying 500 TOWs to Tel Aviv. Upon arriving in Israel, the cargo was unloaded from the planes and stored by Israeli military officials for transshipping to Iran. On February 17, the first Israeli charter plane delivered 500 TOWs to Bandar Abbas. Before departing Iran, the aircraft was loaded with 17 I-HAWK missiles which had been rejected by Iranian Defense officials following the November 1985 shipment. The Israeli aircraft returned on the next day to Tel Aviv.

Based on his meetings with Ghorbanifar, DC/NE understood that upon the delivery of 1,000 TOWs to Iran, all American hostages would be released. Sessions with Iranian delegates would follow, and these could lead to a strategic U.S.-Iran meeting in a neutral location. After the strategic meeting, the remaining 3,000 TOWs would be delivered. All of these arrangements had been made using Ghorbanifar as the interlocutor. Despite having shipped 18 HAWK missiles and 1,004 TOWs, North and Secord had yet to meet an Iranian official. Rather, they had relied solely on Ghorbanifar to present the Iranian demands and to convey the U.S. response. The American understanding—that delivery of 1,000 TOWs would cause the release of all the hostages—was contrary to the advice of the CIA professionals. As Clair George later told these Committees: "Under no conditions would the Government of Iran ever allow all the hostages to be released . . . because the only leverage that those who held the hostages have is the hostages, so why would they give them up."

## The First Frankfurt Meeting

On February 19, 1986, the U.S. delegation arrived in Frankfurt, West Germany, for what was to be its first opportunity to meet with a representative of the Iranian Government. When the Second Iranian Official failed to appear, Ghorbanifar began to offer excuses for his absence. Nevertheless, North decided to return to the United States until the Second Iranian Official arrived in Frankfurt.

Albert Hakim, Secord's associate, had joined the U.S. delegation from Geneva. Earlier in February, Secord had told Hakim that his translating skills would be required at a meeting with Ghorbanifar and an Iranian Government official. Hakim said that Ghorbanifar, when he learned of Hakim's participation, objected violently and branded Hakim "an enemy of the State." Hakim said he eventually joined the meeting in disguise and under the name "Ibrahim Ibrahim" without Ghorbanifar knowing his true identity.

On the return trip to the United States from the aborted Frankfurt meeting, North announced that Hakim would be the translator because he distrusted Ghorbanifar. When

DC/NE objected to the use of so many "outsiders" for a covert activity, North professed his trust in both Secord and Hakim and attested to their expertise. DC/NE later ordered a name trace on Hakim, which revealed allegations of illegal foreign sales of U.S. equipment.

## The Meeting with an Iranian Official

On February 25, the Second Iranian Official arrived in Frankfurt at the airport Sheraton Hotel and the U.S. delegation promptly returned for the meeting. The first session with him "was a disaster." Hakim said the discussion began to deteriorate when Ghorbanifar misled both the Iranian and the Americans in his translation of conversation. After several minutes of discussion, Hakim knew that the two sides were on "different frequencies," with little hope of successfully communicating. Ghorbanifar tried to placate both sides, even though their objectives were entirely different.

The delegations met again the following day in the Second Iranian Official's hotel suite at the Sheraton. The Iranian continued to argue for the purchase of Phoenix missiles, advising the Americans that if Phoenix missiles were made available, "then we will start on the hostages . . . you might not get them all immediately, but we will at least start on it." The parties eventually agreed that the delivery of 1,000 TOWs would be immediately followed by the release of "a couple of hostages." The remaining hostages would be released after a meeting among high-level officials at Kish Island off the coast of Iran. When the hostage "problem" was resolved, the United States would deliver the remaining 3,000 TOWs.

With their first meeting with the Second

191

Iranian Official behind them, certain members of the NSC staff felt they had established formal communications with Iran. This line of communication consisted of the Second Iranian Official as the representative of Iran's government and Ghorbanifar as the intermediary for the two governments. Nir remained an active participant in the first channel proceedings, particularly in monitoring Ghorbanifar's activities.

## THE SECOND INSTALLMENT OF TOWS IS DELIVERED

On February 27, North and DC/NE met with Casey, Poindexter, and George at the Old Executive Office Building to report on the meeting with the Second Iranian Official. They anticipated the imminent release of as many as two hostages and arrangement for a strategic Iran-U.S. conference. Ghorbanifar's unreliability, which had been noted by the Second Iranian Official as well as the Americans in Frankfurt, was discussed. DC/NE noted that Hakim telephoned the Iranian following the Frankfurt meeting in an attempt to exclude Ghorbanifar from future negotiations.

DC/NE later complained to George about using Secord and Hakim as U.S. negotiators. DC/NE recommended replacing Hakim as a translator with George Cave, a former CIA officer still on contract with the Agency and whose knowledge of Iran and command of the Farsi language were well-known. In a second effort to remove "outsiders" from political negotiations, DC/NE urged George to propose that Secord be eliminated from any future meetings with Iranian officials.

Also on February 27, Israeli charter aircraft delivered the second load of 500 TOW missiles from Tel Aviv to Bandar Abbas. Again, Secord coordinated the flight using a Southern Air Transport crew. In a KL-43 message, Secord discussed a meeting he attended with Hakim, Ghorbanifar, and the Second Iranian Official after all other Frankfurt participants had departed. Secord revealed that, once again, a shipment of weapons would not gain the release of any hostages. Instead, a new condition—the meeting at Kish Island—would first have to be met:

> Met with Nir and Gorba this A.M. . . . Subsequently I met with the [Second Iranian Official] for about one hour. . . . the [Second Iranian Official] emphasized need for quick meeting at Kish and said he would possibly, repeat, possibly surprise us by getting some hostages released before meeting. . . . [S]uggest you make contingency plan to accommodate early release (i.e., as early as Sunday). So, bottom line is on to Kish ASAP to seize the potential opening now created. Regards, Richard.

North reported on his Frankfurt meeting with the Second Iranian Official to McFarlane, who had remained interested in the arms sales initiative following his departure from the National Security Council in December 1985. McFarlane had agreed earlier to meet with Iranian Government officials at a designated location, possibly Kish Island. First, North assessed the meeting:

> Just returned last night from mtg w/[Second Iranian Official] in Frankfurt. If nothing else the meeting serves to emphasize the need for direct contact with these people rather than continue the process by which we deal through intermediaries like Ghorbanifahr. . . .

Throughout the session, Gorbanifahr intentionally distorted much of the translation and had to be corrected by our man on occasions so numerous that [Second Iranian Official] finally had Albert translate both ways. Assessment of mtg & agreement we reached as follows:—[Second Iranian Official] has authority to make his own decisions on matters of great import.—He does not have to check back w/Tehran on decisions take.—The govt. of Iran is terrified of a new Soviet threat.—They are seeking a rapprochment but are filled w/ fear & mistrust.—All hostages will be released during rpt during the next meeting.—They want next mtg urgently and have suggested Qeshm Is. off Bandar Abbas.—They are less interested in Iran/Iraq war than we originally believed.—They want technical advice more than arms or intelligence.—Tech advice shd be on commercial & military maintenance—not mil tactics—They committed to end anti-U.S. terrorism.—They noted the problems of working thru intermediaries & prefer dir. contact-[the Second Iranian Official] noted that this was USG/GOI contact in more than 5yrs. Vy important—[the Second Iranian Official] recognizes risks to both sides—noted need for secrecy.—[the Second Iranian Official] stressed that there were new Sov. moves/ threats that we were unaware of. While all of this could be so much smoke, I believe that we may well be on the verge of a major breakthrough—not only on the hostages/terrorism but on the relationship as a whole. We need only to go to this meeting which has no agenda other than to listen to each other to release the hostages and start the process.

McFarlane replied:

Roger Ollie. Well done—if the world only knew how many times you have kept a semblance of integrity and gumption to US policy, they would make you Secretary of State. But they can't know and would complain if they did—such is the state of democracy in the late 20th century. But the mission was terribly promising. As you know I do not hold Ghorbanifar in high regard and so am particularly glad to hear of [the Second Iranian Official's] apparent authority . . .

In February, it was apparent that the hostage problem would not be resolved quickly. In mid-February, the United States had shipped 500 TOWs to Iran. The Second Iranian Official, however, did not attend the first scheduled meeting. Several days later, when he did meet with the Americans, he promised to release hostages only after a meeting among high-level officials at some unspecified time in the future. On that promise alone, the United States immediately sent an additional 500 TOWs to Iran.

The American participants could attribute the failure to obtain the release of any hostages after the November 1985 HAWK transaction to the Iranians' apparent anger over the outdated missiles they received. No similar justification could explain the lack of action by the Iranians after they received 1,000 TOWs. The Americans kept their part of the bargain and shipped the weapons; the Iranians broke their promise and delivered no hostages. Instead, the United States received only another promise, not of hostages, but of another meeting.

## The Diversion Continues

The sale of the 1,000 TOWs was successful in one respect. The "attractive incentive" that North had seen in the arms sales materialized—profits to be used for the Contras.

The February TOW shipment had generated a $10 million payment to Secord. After Secord paid $3.7 million to the CIA's Swiss account, North discussed the use of residuals with Secord: "I described for General Secord the purposes to which I thought that money ought to be applied. . . . There were points in time when we discussed these activities. I had to tell him what the government was going to charge for various commodities, but ultimately the decision (pricing) was his." North said that the purpose of the residuals was "to sustain the Iranian operation, to support the Nicaraguan resistance, to continue other activities which the Israelis very clearly wanted, and so did we, and to pay for a replacement for the original Israeli TOWs shipped in 1985." The January 17 Finding, however, made no mention of support to the Contras or of other intelligence activities as goals of the covert action.

North said that residuals intended for the Contras were a small segment of a larger, comprehensive covert activity support plan. The decision on how to apply the residuals was stated by North: ". . . residuals from those transactions would be applied to support the Nicaraguan Resistance with the authority that I got from my superiors, Admiral Poindexter, with the concurrence of William J. Casey and, I thought at the time, the President of the United States." Those superiors, according to North, also approved the use of Iranian arms sales proceeds to compensate Secord:

> The arrangement that I made with General Secord starting in 1984 recognized that those who were supporting our effort were certainly deserving of just and fair and reasonable compensation. . . . It was clearly indicated [by] Mr. McFarlane and Admiral Poindexter and in fact almost drawn up by Director Casey, how these would be outside the U.S. Government, and that I told them right from the very begin-

ning that those things that he (Secord) did deserved fair and just compensation.

Poindexter recalled no such authorization. Although he felt that Secord was deserving of "reasonable compensation," Poindexter testified that the subject "never came up." Poindexter was unaware of any particular profits Secord and others realized from the arms sales.

North left further definition of "fair and just compensation" up to Secord. He claimed that he did not review the records of the Enterprise, rarely knew how much money had actually been transferred for the Contras, and never knew how much of the profits had gone to Secord and Hakim. Secord and Poindexter also testified that they were unaware of Hakim's method of controlling the accounts.

## THE INITIATIVE CONTINUES

Even though the sale of 1,000 TOWs had not produced a single hostage, the initiative went forward. But Nir became concerned that he would be excluded from further meetings and that Israeli interests would be ignored. Within days after the meeting with the Second Iranian Official in Frankfurt, Israeli Prime Minister Peres wrote to President Reagan summarizing the results of the Frankfurt meeting and discussing the next steps.

The February decision to supply U.S. intelligence information to the Iranian delegation concerned CIA officials. The NSC staff forwarded to the CIA the Iranians' request for a map depicting Iraqi battle positions at its border with Iran. When CIA Deputy Director John McMahon learned of this request, he cabled Casey who was traveling overseas:

1. A new dimension has been added to this program as a result of meeting held in London between North and Ghorbanifar. We have been asked to provide a map depicting the order of battle on the Iran/Iraq border showing units. Troops, tanks, and what have you . . .

\* \* \*

3. Everyone here at Headquarters advises against this operation not only because we feel the principal involved is a liar and has a record of deceit, but, secondly, we would be aiding and abetting the wrong people. I met with Poindexter this afternoon to appeal his direction that we provide this intelligence, pointing out not only the fragility in the ability of the principal to deliver, but also the fact that we were tilting in a direction which could cause the Iranians to have a successful offense against the Iraqis with cataclysmic results. I noted that providing defensive missiles was one thing but when we provide intelligence in the order of battle, we are giving the Iranians the wherewithal for offensive action.

4. Poindexter did not dispute our rationale or our analysis, but insisted that it was an opportunity that should be explored. He felt that by doing it in steps the most we could lose if it did not reach fulfillment would be 1,000 TOWs and a map of order of battle which is perishable anyway.

\* \* \*

6. I have read the signed Finding dated 17 January 1986 which gives us the authority to do what the NSC is now asking. Hence, in spite of our counsel to the contrary, we are proceeding to follow out orders as so authorized in the finding.

Casey did not order McMahon to do otherwise. Once again, concerns voiced by career officials at the CIA were brushed aside and the intelligence was provided.

By early March, career officials at the CIA were pressing their doubts that Ghorbanifar and his principals could deliver on their promises to free the hostages. Iran had not demonstrated any ability to gain release of hostages since early September 1985, nearly six months earlier. On March 7, DC/NE expressed his doubts in a memorandum to his supervisor, the Chief of the Near East Division in the Operation Directorate:

Ghorbanifar insisted on another meeting after which the Keesh Island matter will be set. North is prepared to stonewall in Paris. There will be no more "slices of salami" handed out. However, our other friend, NEER [sic], will also be present. We sense strongly . . . that he is unilaterally providing additional arms as an incentive to the Keesh Island. I have briefed Ed Juchniewicz on the above. I tried to get into McMahon, but he did not have time. I will be back Saturday PM and will give you a ring. *What we may be facing is evidence that [the Secord Iranian Official] does not have the authority in Tehran to make it work.* [Emphasis added.]

## Cave Joins the Team

By March 5, the CIA prevailed in its bid to have intelligence professional George Cave replace Hakim as the interpreter. At CIA Headquarters that day, Cave was briefed by DC/NE, George, and Allen. DC/NE asked Cave if he would travel to Tehran to translate during a meeting with the Iranian Speaker of Parliament, Rafsanjani. Cave had prior experience with Ghorbanifar and had been involved in the 1984 decision to issue a worldwide "burn notice" on him. Cave was appalled that a sensitive operation would depend so heavily on a man with a long record of self-serving lies and distortions. Cave was equally concerned that the Israelis had such a prominent role in the affair, because Israeli and American goals in the region were not always compatible.

North, DC/NE, and Cave flew to Paris on March 7 to meet with Ghorbanifar and Nir. Ghorbanifar told the Americans that the Second Iranian Official's internal political position had not been improved by the Frankfurt meeting. Upon examining their military stockpiles, Iranian military representatives felt that they needed no additional TOWs; instead, they wanted the Americans to sell them 240 types of spare parts to repair the HAWK missiles in Iran's stocks. Nir encouraged the U.S. delegation to pursue this avenue, contending that such a sale would result in the release of all American hostages. Before concluding the Paris meeting, Ghorbanifar told the Americans that the Kish Island site was unacceptable to the Iranians, who would agree only to meet in Tehran. The altered meeting site created further delays.

North's notes of the Paris meeting reflect fear that his channel to Iran might be seriously flawed. He commented that all prior effort focused on the purchase of arms rather than political change and that "we cannot verify that there is anyone else in G.O.Ir [Iran] aware or even interested in talking to USG." In spite of these concerns, North continued to pursue the plan.

In a report for Casey after the Paris meeting, Cave addressed several points raised by Ghorbanifar during the meeting. The last paragraph set forth Ghorbanifar's suggestion to divert profits from the sale of arms to Iran to aid the Contras: "He also proposed that we use profits from these deals and others to fund [other operations]. We could do the same with Nicaragua." Charles Allen read Cave's memorandum, but dismissed the statement as a typically expansive remark by Ghorbanifar. Yet, this was not the first time that Allen had learned that Ghorbanifar was attempting to use North's interest in the Contras to "sweeten the pot" for the Americans. During a meeting between Allen and Ghorbanifar in January 1986, Ghorbanifar had mentioned the possibility of using monies generated from various projects to aid "Ollie's boys in Central America."

## New Doubts About Ghorbanifar

**After the Paris meeting, North became increasingly frustrated with Ghorbanifar. In memos, he wondered whether the Iranians Ghorbanifar had contacted were interested only in personal gain and arms sales. Allen and others, however, remained convinced that Ghorbanifar was the sole channel, and Cave quoted the Israelis as saying he would "blow the whole thing" if he were pushed out.**

Ghorbanifar realized that the meeting between the Americans and the Second Iranian Official had rendered him superfluous. After the Frankfurt meeting in late February, Hakim had called the Iranian official to recommend that Ghorbanifar be bypassed in further negotiations. As a result, at the early March meeting in Paris, Ghorbanifar had continually emphasized to the Americans that he was essential, a position he would continually restate.

To placate Ghorbanifar, North invited him to Washington in late March. In a telephone call several days prior to Ghorbanifar's arrival, Nir told Allen of Ghorbanifar's concerns and advised that any attempt to eliminate Ghorbanifar from the negotiations was "unwise . . . because of the hold that [Ghorbanifar] has over the [Second Iranian Official]."

While Nir was promoting Ghorbanifar to the CIA, Nir and North were discussing how to divide up the profits from the sale of HAWK spare parts. An entry in North's notebooks related a conversation with Nir: "price data on 240 . . . timing per acquisition . . . need to know residuals on—price per unit ($6068), price in Aaron's place, how much is left for use by Israelis." "Aaron" was the code name for DOD official Noel Koch; "Aaron's place" was, presumably, the Pentagon. The conversation reflects the Israelis' desire to know how much of the residuals would be available to finance the Israelis' purchase of the 504 replacement TOWs.

### Ghorbanifar Visits Washington

On April 2, 1986, Ghorbanifar and an Israeli official met in London to discuss financial arrangements for shipping the HAWK spare parts. Ghorbanifar flew to Washington the next day and met with the CIA Chief of the Near East Division (C/NE) Cave, and North at a hotel in Herndon, Virginia. They discussed the availability of the HAWK spare parts on the list that Ghorbanifar had earlier supplied. CIA logistics personnel then attempted to locate the items, many of which were not in production or not available.

C/NE remembered Ghorbanifar saying that the Iranians had agreed to release all American hostages as soon as the U.S. delegation arrived in Tehran. Based on Ghorbanifar's prior performance, the CIA officers were skeptical. Two days later, Cave drove Ghorbanifar to Dulles International Airport outside Washington. During the drive, Cave reminded Ghorbanifar that all hostages had to be released before any of the HAWK spare parts would be delivered. Cave said that Ghorbanifar "took the statement under advisement."

Following the April meeting with Ghorbanifar, North and Nir continued to discuss the arms sales and the use of the residuals. On April 7, North received an update on Nir's most recent contact with the Second Iranian Official and Ghorbanifar. Without further explanation, North jotted in his notebook on that date, "Merchant [Ghorbanifar] needs $1.5M from HAWKs." Nir commented that the Second Iranian Official did not trust Ghorbanifar and trusted the United States even less.

### Planning the Tehran Mission

During March and April, U.S. planners considered dispatching an advance U.S. party to meet with Iranian officials equivalent to NSC staff representatives. Specifically, Casey, Poindexter, and others contemplated Cave and North traveling with Ghorbanifar to Iran in advance of the McFarlane visit. Even before the meeting had been moved from Kish Island to Tehran, Cave believed that an advance trip was a practical step. He pointed out, "With all my Iranian experience and my distrust for Ghorbanifar, I thought there was an awful lot of personal risk in us going in [to Tehran without an advance trip]."

Secord later reflected that a trip without advance work was a mistake:

It was strongly recommended by three of us—Nir, myself, and North—were all recommending that a preparatory meeting take place. There was, after all, as far as I knew, no agenda agreed to for this meeting (McFarlane's), and so it seemed to me at least—and I think to the others—to be not well organized. In fact, I have been to many, many international meetings, and I don't think I have ever been to one where there wasn't some preparatory work done in advance.

Poindexter ruled out the possibility of an advance trip by North and others, claiming "that was more dangerous and that if we had a more senior person there with the group that there was less risk to the whole group." According to North, Poindexter's view was echoed by Director Casey, who argued:

This advance trip is so hidden, we are going to use non-U.S. Government assets throughout, European or Middle Eastern airlines, no U.S. Air registration, air flights. You might never be heard from again. The Government might disavow the whole thing.

## North's Diversion Memorandum

Around April 4, 1986, North prepared an extensive report for Poindexter entitled "Release of American Hostages in Beirut." In the memorandum, North summarized the Iran initiative, beginning with a June 1985 meeting between certain "private American and Israeli citizens." Under the report's subheading, "Current Situation," North detailed the agreement reached at the most recent meeting between Ghorbanifar and U.S. officials:

Subject to Presidential approval, it was agreed to proceed as follows:

— By Monday, April 7, the Iranian Government will transfer $17 million to an Israeli account in Switzerland. The Israelis will, in turn, transfer to a private U.S. corporation account in Switzerland the sum of $15 million.
— On Tuesday, April 8 (or as soon as the transactions are verified), the private U.S. corporation will transfer $3.651 million to a CIA account in Switzerland. CIA will then transfer this sum to a covert Department of the Army account in the U.S.
— On Wednesday, April 9, the CIA will commence procuring $3.651 million worth of HAWK missile parts (240 separate line items) and transferring these parts to [a CIA storage facility]. This process is estimated to take seven working days.

The "Current Situation" section included a timetable that placed McFarlane and his team of negotiators in Tehran on April 19 to meet with Rafsanjani. It also forecast that all of the American hostages would be released sometime following sequential arms deliveries to Iran.

Under a second subheading, "Discussion," North listed nine points to be discussed with the Iranian Government through Ghorbanifar. The nineth topic follows:

— The residual funds from this transaction are allocated as follows:
— $2 million will be used to purchase replacement TOWs for the original 508 sold by Israel to Iran for the release of Benjamin Weir. This is the only way that we have found to meet our commitment to replenish these stocks.

— $12 million will be used to purchase critically needed supplies for the Nicaraguan Democratic Resistance Forces. This materiel is essential to cover shortages in resistance inventories resulting from their current offensives and Sandinista counter-attacks and to 'bridge' the period between now and when Congressionally-approved lethal assistance (beyond the $25 million in 'defensive' arms) can be delivered.

The last page of the report contained a recommendation that the President approve the plan:

> That the President approve the structure depicted above under "Current Situation" and the Terms of Reference at Tab A.
>
> Approve_____ Disapprove_____

North transmitted a PROF message on April 7 to McFarlane stating that North had prepared the memorandum at Poindexter's request for "our boss":

> Met last week w/ Gorba to finalize arrangements for a mtg in Iran and release of hostages on or about 19 Apr. This was based on word that he had to deposit not less than $15M in appropriate acct. by close of banking tomorrow . . . Per request of JMP have prepared a paper for our boss which lays out arrangements. Gorba indicated that yr counterpart in the T. mtg wd be Rafsanjani. If all this comes to pass it shd be one hell of a show.

During her testimony, Fawn Hall, North's secretary, expressed familiarity with the early April memorandum. She recalled typing it as North stood behind her and dictated. She also believed that one of the drafts of this memorandum was edited by Poindexter and returned to her for typing correction. She testified that Poindexter never suggested that the memorandum was improper in any fashion nor did he ever suggest the outlined policy not be pursued. Further, Hall stated that her understanding of the phrase "our boss" in the April 7 PROF referred to President Reagan. Poindexter testified that he did not recall seeing any memorandums discussing the diversion of funds to the Contras until the day before he resigned in late November 1986.

In testifying about the diversion of funds, North stated that he believed his superiors had approved all his actions during the Iran initiative. He said that he may have written as many as five or six memorandums in which he asked for the President's approval for the diversion of profits from the sale of weapons to Iran. North explained that each of the memorandums was prepared for Presidential approval when a proposed sale of weapons to Iran neared its final stage.

Even though North said he prepared "diversion" memorandums for five or six transactions, there were only three successful shipments of arms during the initiative: "It is my recollection I sent each one up the line, and that on the three where I had approval to proceed, I thought that I had received authority from the President." North stressed that, unlike other memorandums he had submitted for Presidential approval, he never saw a memorandum about diversion reflecting the President's initials in the "Approval" space. He denied receiving instructions from Poindexter to discontinue the drafting of such memorandums.

Poindexter's recollection differed sharply. He said that North first discussed with him the idea of using the proceeds of the arms sales to support the Contras in late January or early February 1986. He could not remember ever receiving a written memorandum calling for the President's approval and never directed North to prepare such a memorandum. According to Poindexter, he directed North to put nothing in writing about the diversion, a direction North denied receiving. Poindexter admitted leading North to believe that the President had approved the plan, but he denied ever discussing it with the President.

Poindexter testified that his decision not to tell North that he had hidden the diversion from the President was risky in light of his "plausible deniability" plan. Without Poindexter's knowledge, North told both McFarlane and Casey about the diversion. North's associate, Robert Earl, also knew. Not knowing of Poindexter's supposed plan to give the President "plausible deniability," any of them may have spoken to the President about the diverted funding for the Contras.

The diversion to the Contras was not the only use of funds that North had in mind in April. On April 15, he received a call from Nir about joint covert operations to be conducted by the Americans and the Israelis. According to North, the operations—named TH-1 and TH-2—were to be financed out of the proceeds of the arms sales. None of them progressed beyond the planning stages, but North was prepared to dedicate funds from the Enterprise to those covert operations.

## Complications

Around April 22, 1986, CIA officers reviewed information noting that Ghorbanifar complained bitterly of his arrest by Swiss police. Ghorbanifar had allegedly funded a transaction that violated certain U.S. Federal laws and was coordinated by Cyrus Hashemi, an Iranian arms dealer. This incident was the first these CIA officers knew of a U.S. Customs "sting" operation targeting a group of individuals who had allegedly attempted to sell U.S. arms to Iran. Allen avoided discussing the subject with Ghorbanifar. However, Allen believed that the arrest would have little effect on the NSC operation.

## NEW DEMANDS

In late April and early May, Allen continued to communicate with Ghorbanifar to gauge any changes in Iran's position on the long-promised meeting in Tehran. Following the February delivery of 1,000 TOWs, the Second Iranian Official had promised that the hostages would be released if the Americans agreed to a meeting with top-level Iranian officials. By mid-April, the requirement of a sale of HAWK spare parts was added. On April 14, Ghorbanifar called Allen with new demands. In that conversation, Ghorbanifar relayed an Iranian proposal for the sequential release of hostages following the arrival of the Americans in Tehran and the delivery of the spare parts. The Iranians were withdrawing their original promise to release the American hostages upon the arrival of the American delegation and instead demanded additional arms sales. During his conversation with Allen, Ghorbanifar recommended that North reject the Iranian proposal.

The following day, Allen prepared a memorandum outlining what he perceived to be obstacles in the initiative and his own recommendations. Allen recognized that unless the

United States was willing to provide additional weapons, it had no alternative but to wait, a decision that would lead to "additional hostages and threat of exposure." He cautioned, "Every day that passes, raises the risk of embarrassing disclosures." Allen also suggested "sweetening the pot" by an act of U.S. omission, that is, permitting the Israelis to become an arms supplier to Iran, a position the Israelis were "anxious" to take because "they would like to see Iran prevail." Allen recognized that without a sweetener, the Iranians had little motivation to fulfill their bargain to release the hostages.

Poindexter responded sharply to the new Iranian proposal, purporting to communicate the President's own frustrations with the operation. In a PROF message to North written shortly before a meeting in Frankfurt among North, Cave, Nir, Ghorbanifar, and the Second Iranian Official, Poindexter issued North specific instructions:

> You may go ahead and go [to the meeting in Frankfurt], but I want several points made clear to them. There are not to be any parts delivered until all the hostages are free in accordance with the plan that you layed (sic) out for me before. None of this half shipment before any are released crap. It is either all or nothing. Also you may tell them that the President is getting very annoyed at their continual stalling. He will not agree to any more changes in the plan. Either they agree finally on the arrangements that have been discussed or we are going to permanently cut off all contact. If they really want to save their asses from the Soviets, they should get on board. I am beginning to suspect that [the Second Iranian Official] doesn't have such authority.

The Israelis also came to believe that the Ghorbanifar channel might be doomed. Se-

cord conveyed this message to North: "I talked to Adam [Nir] this A.M. He [is] quite pessimistic re Gorba/[Second Iranian Official] cabal. He know[s] time is nearly over."

In mid-April, North wrote in his notebooks that he had received "1st acknowledgement that Iranians are committed." While this encouraged North, it suggested that the American demands would not be met. In light of Poindexter's concern that the Second Iranian Official might lack sufficient authority, the Americans could not be certain that the Iranian delegation would be able to secure the release of the hostages.

Allen's April 15 memorandum noted that one of Ghorbanifar's efforts to have the Americans "sweeten the pot" for Iran included the sale to Iran of two U.S.-made radar systems. Even though the radars were a subject of prior negotiations, North had treated them as separate from the spare parts sale. In a PROF note on April 29, North sought Poindexter's approval to sell the radars during the upcoming Frankfurt meeting. In the process, North pressured Poindexter for an immediate decision on this additional concession to the Iranian demands.

In contrast to North, Allen was pessimistic about progress made by the Second Iranian Official and Ghorbanifar toward the release of American hostages. In a formal memorandum to Casey on May 5, Allen detailed his interpretation of events in Iran:

> 1. [Most recent information] suggests that the White House initiative to secure release of American hostages in Lebanon remains dead in the water. We surmise . . . that [the Second Iranian Official] is unable to provide the assurances and to make the arrangements demanded by our side. Ghorbanifar has not

deposited the funds necessary to move the spare parts.

2. We believe that the Iranian government has not been able to convince the holders of the hostages to release them to Iranian custody. This belief is fortified by the experience of [another government]. Ghorbanifar's failure to deposit the necessary funds indicates that he has doubts about [the Second Iranian Official's] ability to obtain the release of the hostages. Ghorbanifar is in a bind and he knows that once he deposits the money he cannot get it back. He also is aware that we have insisted that the spare parts will [be] delivered eight hours after the release of the hostages and only after the release of the hostages.

**In February, Poindexter told Secretary Shultz of plans for a high-level meeting in Iran. He did not mention that arms deliveries were on the agenda. In March, Poindexter said the meeting was off. But two months later the State Department heard rumors about the ongoing Iran weapons deal from an unlikely source: the American Embassy in Britain. In May, Nir, Ghorbanifar, and the Saudi businessman Adnan Khashoggi invited a British entrepreneur, Tiny Rowlands, to participate in a U.S.-endorsed plan to sell arms to Iran. Rowlands queried an Embassy official, who immediately cabled Shultz at the Tokyo summit. Shultz first found Regan, who was surprised. Shortly afterward, Poindexter told the Secretary, "This is not our deal." Poindexter then wrote North about the incident, saying of Nir: "We really can't trust those SOB's."**

## Another Meeting in London

On May 6, North, Nir, Cave, and Ghorbanifar met at the Churchill Hotel, London. The meeting focused on pricing of the spare parts shipment. Cave denied discussing the issue, noting that North, Nir, and Ghorbanifar were always careful to exclude him from such conversations.

In discussing the upcoming meetings in Tehran, Ghorbanifar named Iranian Government representatives whom the Second Iranian Official said would meet the American delegation: Prime Minister Musavi, Speaker Rafsanjani, and President Khameni, with a possible visit by the Imam's son, Ahmed Khomeini.

Cave had his first telephone conversation with the Second Iranian Official while he was in London. He described a "major snag" that arose regarding the sequence of the spare parts delivery. The Second Iranian Official was allegedly adamant that all the parts be delivered simultaneously with the arrival of McFarlane in Tehran. The Second Iranian Official finally agreed that when the American delegation arrived in Tehran with as many spare parts as the aircraft could hold, an Iranian delegation would be dispatched to Lebanon to barter for the release of the hostages. When the hostages were released, the remaining spare parts were to be delivered. An Israeli present during the meeting later confirmed this agreement.

Once again, the American position had slipped. Poindexter's firm resolve only weeks earlier to refuse to deliver any parts until the hostages were released had eroded. The Iranians were insisting on complete delivery and the American negotiators began to relent.

## Cave Becomes Concerned About Pricing

Several days following the London meeting, Cave received information that he claimed was the first time he had heard of price manipulation by Ghorbanifar. Cave recalled his shock when he learned of Ghorbanifar's exorbitant price. Concerned that such pricing could jeopardize the operation, Cave approached North. Cave said that North expressed alarm at the price and may have indicated that he would speak to Nir about it.

According to Cave, Ghorbanifar's pricing of the May shipment was confusing. During the May meeting in London, Ghorbanifar complained about having spent $1 million of his own money to support the NSC operation. This complaint, coupled with CIA's knowledge of Ghorbanifar's legal concerns following his arrest and probable loss of funds through the U.S. Customs "sting" operation, caused some CIA participants to conclude that Ghorbanifar was simply trying to raise as much money as possible from the transaction. C/NE rationalized that the price of the radars, an additional $6.2 million, could have accounted for the inflated figure. According to their testimony, neither C/NE, Cave, nor Allen associated the inflated price with an effort by North and others to obtain profits in support of Contra activities.

During March and April the intelligence information gathered on the initiative was available to a restricted group at the CIA. Cave routinely examined the information, which was controlled by National Intelligence Officer Charles Allen. Casey, Gates, Clair George, C/NE, and the Chief/Iran Branch were among others to whom the intelligence reports were disseminated. At least three reports showed that the Iranians were paying an exorbitant price for the spare parts. Information showed an attempt by the Second Iranian Official and Ghorbanifar to raise $21 million to purchase the two radars and over $20 million for the spare parts. Seven highly placed CIA officials thus had access to information that showed a huge mark up in the price of the spare parts and radar shipments. Yet all of them denied suspecting a diversion of funds until much later.

## THE MEETING IS SET

By May 6, North told Poindexter that he had achieved what Poindexter demanded—all hostages would be released before the parts were delivered. He reported this to Poindexter in a hopeful PROF note:

I believe we have succeeded. Deposit being made tomorrow (today is a bank holiday in Switzerland). Release of hostages set for 19 May in sequence you have specified. Specific date to be determined by how quickly we can assemble requisite parts. Thank God—he answers prayers. V/R, North.

On May 12, C/NE had advised the CIA Office of Finance that they should expect a deposit of $13 million to the CIA account in Switzerland. The deposit would allow the CIA to purchase the 240 HAWK spare parts and two radars from DOD. Two days later, C/NE changed the amount the Office of Finance should expect to $10 million. Finally, on May 16, 1986, the CIA Swiss account received a deposit of $6.5 million from "Hyde Park Square." C/NE advised North of the deposit and recalled North's comments: "Yes, 6.5. is in and the remaining 6.5 is going to come later [for the radars]." Iranian funds were never sent for the radars. Additionally, C/NE was not certain of arrangements to pay for the 508 TOWs and had assumed that the Israeli Government handled that expense in a separate transaction.

## The National Security Planning Group Meeting

Also on May 16, Poindexter and North attended a National Security Planning Group meeting chaired by the President. They discussed soliciting financial support from third countries to support the Nicaraguan Resistance. Poindexter recalled that Secretary of State Shultz said that Congress would probably not renew funding for the Contras as early as Administration officials had hoped. To develop "bridge funding" for the Contras, Poindexter asked Secretary Shultz to prepare a list of countries for the President to consider for solicitation.

Following the meeting, Poindexter received a PROF message from North declaring, "There is now $6M available to the resistance forces." This message was sent the same day one of the Enterprise's Swiss accounts received a deposit toward the purchase of spare parts. Poindexter testified that he understood the $6 million had come from the diversion; however, the National Security Adviser claimed he did not tell the President of the sudden availability of "bridge funds." Generally, according to Poindexter, when opportunities arose for him to discuss the diversion with President Reagan, he avoided doing so in order to permit the President to be able to deny knowledge of the issue. Poindexter claimed that he never volunteered to the President that diverted funds were available to "bridge" the Contra financial requirements.

## Final Planning for Tehran

With the 1-week delay in receiving the deposit from Ghorbanifar, participants in the initiative adjusted their schedules. North notified Poindexter on May 17 of travel plans for the Americans going to Tel Aviv and Tehran.

On May 22, a Southern Air Transport 707 airplane delivered 13 pallets of HAWK missile spare parts to Israel. The following day, Southern Air Transport flight crews arrived in Israel for the trips to Tehran.

On May 24, a second 707 arrived in Israel with 508 TOW missiles to replace the Israeli arms issued to Iran in 1985. After an examination by Israeli Defense Force personnel, the weapons were judged to be in "poor condition" and were rejected. One pallet of HAWK parts and the Tehran delegation departed on May 25 aboard a disguised Israeli Government aircraft. Another Israeli plane loaded with the remaining 12 pallets of HAWK spare parts was ready for immediate departure to Tehran.

## U.S. War Readiness Suffers

The CIA obtained the 13 pallets of HAWK missile spare parts using much the same procedures employed to obtain the TOWs a few months earlier. Once again, the usual method of dealing with CIA requests for weapons from DOD was ignored. Bypassing the system in February created a large enough pricing error to make the diversion of excess profits feasible. Bypassing the system in obtaining the HAWK spare parts was equally serious, this time affecting U.S. war readiness.

When the Army received from the CIA the list of HAWK spare parts the Iranians were demanding, Major Simpson began to fill the order. But the Iranians had prepared the list using outdated documents and obsolete stock numbers, making it difficult for the Army to identify the parts; indeed, HAWK Project officials could not identify 11 of the items on the list.

Out of 148 items, only 99 existed in the Army's stocks in sufficient quantities such that the transfer to Iran would have no readiness impact. In the case of 15 items, Army stocks would be completely depleted if the Army provided all quantities requested. Supplying 11 items would have depleted more than half the available stocks.

Simpson was able to adjust the quantities on many of the items requested. On April 23, however, he instructed his subordinates to ship all of the items on the revised list. Readiness impact remained critical for 10 to 12 of the parts. The parts were ordered to be shipped even though U.S. HAWK missile batteries would be deficient if they were needed.

The availability of one part was particularly acute. The Iranians had requested a quantity of one particular part used in the HAWK radar. If the part fails, the system does not work; if there are no replacements, the system remains useless. The Army had only a limited supply of this part. Shipping the parts would put the readiness impact in the "high risk" category. Simpson protested to his superiors that the Army's stock of this part could not be depleted. The CIA insisted on delivery, and all of the parts were shipped. U.S. readiness was thus adversely affected.

## CONCLUSION

The President's decision to sign the Finding in mid-January 1986 carried with it a deci-

sion not to notify Congress of the covert operation. As the participants recalled, the scheme contemplated a quick sale of weapons and an immediate release of all the hostages. Indeed, the memorandum accompanying the Presidential Finding provided that the initiative would be closed down if the hostages were not released after the first 1,000 TOWs were sold.

By the end of May, the Americans had seen one pledge after another evaporate. When the first sales took place in mid-February they were not followed by a hostage release. Iran was subsequently rewarded with the promise of the sale of HAWK parts, but the Americans insisted that all the hostages first had to be released. That American demand was abandoned as well, however, as the McFarlane delegation prepared for their trip to Tehran in an airplane containing a quantity of HAWK spare parts.

While freedom for American hostages had not materialized, a funding mechanism to support various clandestine programs was flourishing. By the time McFarlane and North were preparing for their journey to Tehran, part of the profits obtained from the sale to Iran of both the TOW missiles and the HAWK spare parts had been diverted to support the Nicaraguan Resistance movement. The remainder of the profits were stored in secret Swiss bank accounts to support "off-the-shelf" clandestine operations.

**A chapter footnote says the Committees learned that the NSC was preparing to sell Iran two radars the Shah of Iran had already paid for years earlier. The radars, valued at $6.3 million, had been kept in a warehouse because of the arms embargo against Iran. When Iran failed to come up with the money for this purchase, the idea was dropped.**

# CHAPTER 13

# Deadlock in Tehran

The Presidentially approved McFarlane mission to Tehran in the spring of 1986, was intended to crown a 9-month effort to free the hostages and establish a dialogue with Iran. McFarlane likened the mission to Henry Kissinger's historic secret meeting with Premier Chou En-lai that paved the way to U.S.-China reconciliation. Eight years after an Iranian Prime Minister, Mehdi Bazargan, was dismissed for meeting with President Carter's National Security Adviser, McFarlane was to meet with Speaker Rafsanjani, Prime Minister Musavi, and President Khamenei, the three most powerful leaders in Iran under Ayatollah Khomeini. What is more, McFarlane believed that the hostages were to be released upon his arrival and that the HAWK parts were not to be delivered until the hostages were safe. Hopeful of success, North arranged logistical support for the return of the hostages and prepared a press kit for the White House. North added his own flourish: He ordered a chocolate cake from an Israeli baker as a gift for the Iranians.

The Iranians had very different ideas—centering on arms and Da'wa prisoners. As a result, the Tehran mission ended in acrimo-nious confrontation with the hostages still in captivity.

## PREPARING FOR THE MISSION

The American delegation consisted of McFarlane, North, former CIA official George Cave, then-NSC staff member Howard Teicher, Amiram Nir, adviser to the Israeli Prime Minister on combatting terrorism, and a CIA communicator who was to remain on the plane and forward messages via secure means to Poindexter in Washington and Secord in Tel Aviv. McFarlane included Nir at the request of the Israelis who viewed this as a joint U.S.-Israeli operation. All members of the delegation used aliases and Nir passed himself off as an American.

The delegation took one pallet of HAWK parts with them in the aircraft. The remaining 11 pallets of parts were left in Israel with Secord, who was poised to deliver them upon the release of the hostages.

The Tehran trip was both an extraordinarily heroic and a very foolish mission for McFarlane and his companions. As the immediate predecessor of the National Security Adviser, McFarlane knew many of the Nation's most sensitive secrets. North was privy to some of them as well, as was Teicher. Yet, the plan called for them to go to Tehran under false passports and pseudonyms without even safe conduct documents from the Iranian Government. Ghorbanifar and the Second Iranian arranged the visit. Ghorbanifar was a private citizen and the Second Iranian, was, according to Ghorbanifar, the person responsible for the kidnapping of CIA agent William Buckley. The Iranian government had demonstrated during the U.S. Embassy seizure that it could not prevent the holding of diplomats as hostages by its Revolutionary Guards. The State Department was unaware of the mission because Poindexter had told Shultz back in March that a proposed high-level meeting between McFarlane and the Iranians had been cancelled, never informing Shultz that it had been rescheduled. Further, Poindexter had rejected North's suggestion . that Shultz, Poindexter, and McFarlane meet before the trip. And friendly governments with embassies in Iran were not alerted. McFarlane and his party were, in effect, on their own in Tehran—even subject to legitimate arrest for entering under false passports and with missile parts.

Moreover, the plan contemplated that after the hostages were freed, McFarlane and the delegation would remain in Tehran until the promised HAWK parts were delivered. The former National Security Adviser and ranking members of the NSC staff were, in effect, to substitute themselves for the hostages. In fact, the delegation had cause for concern during the negotiations when the Iranians repeatedly delayed refueling the aircraft. The original plan for the mission entailed less risk. It called for the meeting to be on Kish Island within reach of U.S. naval forces.

Even the timing of the trip was wrong. As North and McFarlane soon discovered, the trip took place during a holy period in the Islamic calendar, and Muslim officials were not fully available. The Iranian officials had to fast throughout the negotiations.

## ARRIVAL IN TEHRAN

The mission arrived in Tehran on the morning of May 25 and the first signs of failure were evident almost immediately. McFarlane expected to be greeted at the airport by Speaker Rafsanjani or some other high official. The Americans waited more than an hour, but no one showed up to greet them. Then, only Ghorbanifar and the Second Iranian arrived. McFarlane described his reactions in a cable he sent soon after arrival:

It may be best for us to try to picture what it would be like if after nuclear attack, a surviving tailor became Vice President; a recent grad student became Secretary of State; and a bookie became the interlocutor for all discourse with foreign countries. While the principals are a cut above this level of qualification, the incompetence of the Iranian government to do business requires a rethinking on our part of why there have been so many frustrating failure[s] to deliver on their part.

As events proved, however, the Iranians were tough, competent negotiators.

Under the pre-Tehran timetable, no HAWK parts—including the pallet on the plane—were to be delivered until the hostages were freed. But even before the American delegation left the airport, the Iranians had removed the pallet. The Iranians were nevertheless disappointed, for the Second Iranian had told his superiors that at least 50 percent—not merely 1 out of 12 pallets—of the parts would be delivered.

## The Misunderstanding

The McFarlane delegation went from the airport to the Independence Hotel (the Hilton in pre-Revolution days), where the entire top floor was assigned to them. In 4 days of talks, virtually the only points on which the Americans and the Iranians could agree were generalities such as the United States' acceptance of the Iranian Revolution and Iran's sovereignty, and common fear of the Soviet Union, including their intervention in Afghanistan. On concrete issues such as the hostages and arms sales, the parties were poles apart.

In accordance with his instructions and the agreement that he believed had been made with the Iranians in Frankfurt, McFarlane insisted that the hostages be released before the HAWK parts were delivered. The Iranians took the opposite position: The HAWK parts had to be delivered first and then the release of the hostages would be negotiated. The Iranians maintained that they had not agreed in Frankfurt to a release of the hostages upon the arrival of the McFarlane delegation. Yet Poindexter had rejected the Iranian position before the President authorized the mission and had so instructed McFarlane:

> [The Iranian official] wants all the HAWK parts delivered before the hostages are released. I have told Ollie that we cannot do that. The sequence has to be (1) meeting; (2) release of hostages; (3) delivery of HAWK parts. The President is getting quite discouraged by this effort. This will be our last attempt to make a deal with the Iranians.

The Americans made contemporaneous notes and reports of the discussions that provide a full account of what happened at Tehran. The key points are summarized here.

## Days 1 and 2—Marking Time

For the first 2 days, May 25 and 26, no high-level Iranian official appeared. The Second Iranian and other "third and fourth level officials" in the Prime Minister's office represented Iran. With no Iranian decisionmaker present, the discussions consisted mainly of exchanges of platitudes, a "diatribe" by the Iranians against the Americans for not bringing "enough" HAWK parts, and protests by McFarlane about the Iranians' failure to produce the hostages. Ghorbanifar tried to reassure the U.S. delegation that the hostages would be released, but the Americans had lost confidence in his promises. McFarlane's anger flared. McFarlane regarded the meeting with low-level Iranians as a waste of time and a degrading breach of protocol. He stated that he had come to "meet with Ministers." The Second Iranian promised to produce an official at the sub-Minister level but McFarlane was still dissatisfied, saying:

> As I am a Minister, I expect to meet with decision-makers. Otherwise, you can work with my staff.

True to his word, McFarlane withdrew from the discussion and left the staff to meet with the Iranians, including the Prime Minister's designee, a member of the Majlis and foreign affairs adviser to Rafsanjani (the "Adviser") who arrived at 9:30 P.M. on the second day and became the leader of the Iranian delegation. Because the Adviser had not attended any prior meetings, North reiterated the U.S. position:

If your government can cause the release of the Americans held in Beirut 10 hours after they are released, aircraft will arrive with the HAWK missile parts. Within 10 days of deposit [of money], two radars will be delivered. After that delivery, we would like to have our logistics and technical experts sit down with your experts to make a good determination of what is needed.

If the initial discussions hinted at the misunderstanding about the terms of the meeting, the Second Iranian made it unambiguous. He rebuffed North's request for a meeting between McFarlane and ministers, saying "We did not agree to such meetings for McFarlane."

North reported to McFarlane that evening. In a message sent to Poindexter that night describing the day's events, McFarlane, relying on North's assessment, stated that the Adviser was "a considerable cut above the Bush Leaguers we had been dealing with."

## The Final Days—McFarlane Remains Firm

For the American delegation and the Iranian representatives, May 27 was a long day. The discussions, termed "marathon" by Cave, lasted from 10 A.M. until 2:10 A.M. on May 28. They began with North, Cave, and Teicher holding a preliminary meeting with the Adviser and the other Iranians. The Adviser delivered bad news about the hostages:

Our messenger in Beirut is in touch with those holding the hostages by special means. They made heavy conditions. They asked for Israel to withdraw from—the Golan Heights and South Lebanon. Lahad must return to East Beirut, the prisoners in Kuwait must be freed, and all the expeses paid for hostage taking. They do not want money from the U.S. Iran must pay this money.

The Adviser, held out hope, however, particularly if the HAWK parts were delivered. He told North that the Iranians were negotiating to scale down the captors' demands. However, "only a portion of the 240 spare parts had been delivered. The rest should come. This is an important misunderstanding."

McFarlane then met with the Adviser, one on one, for 3 hours. He sent a message to Poindexter immediately afterward that included the following:

He [the Adviser] reported that Hizballah had made several preconditions to the release: (1) Israeli withdrawal from the Golan: (2) Israeli withdrawal from Southern Lebanon; (3) Lahad movement into East Beirut; and (4) someone (undefined) to pay the bills the hostages have accumulated. How's that for Chutzpa. . . . He hurriedly added [before I unloaded on him] that these demands are not acceptable and we are negotiating with them and believe that the only real problem is when you deliver the items [the HAWK parts and the radar] we have requested.

I then carefully recounted . . . that he [the President] had only reluctantly agreed to this meeting under a very clear and precise understanding of the arrangements. I then went over in detail what those arrangements were: 1. the U.S. would send a high-level delegation to Tehran. They would bring with them a portion of the items they had requested and paid for (which we had done); 2. upon our arrival, they had agreed to secure the release of the hostages promptly, upon release of the hostages to our custody, we would call forward the balance of items that had been paid for and those that had not been paid for would be dispatched as soon as payment had been received.

* * *

At this point he became somewhat agitated wanting to know just who had agreed to these terms. (I fingered Gorba and the Second Iranian). He stated that these were not the terms as he understood them. The basic difference was that they expected all deliveries to occur before any release took place.

* * *

He was obviously concerned over the very real possibility that his people (Gorba and the Second Iranian) had misled him and asked for a break to confer with his colleagues. I agreed noting that I had to leave tonight. (Actually I don't have to leave tonight but recognizing that we have been here for three working days and they have not produced I wanted to try to build a little fire under them. . . . )

* * *

I tend to think we should hold firm on our intention to leave and in fact do so unless we have word of release in the next six or seven hours. I can imagine circumstances in which if they said tonight that they guarantee the release at a precise hour tomorrow. We would stand by but not agree to any change in the terms or call the aircraft forward.

* * *

My judgment is that they are in a state of great upset, schizophrenic over their wish to get more from the deal but sobered to the fact that their interlocutors may have misled them. We are staying entirely at arms length while this plays out. We should hear something from them before long.

McFarlane's threat to leave had its intended effect. Several hours later, the Adviser reported that the Hizballah had dropped all their demands except for the release of the Da'wa terrorists held prisoner in Kuwait:

The only remaining problem is Kuwait. We agreed to try to get a promise from you that they would be released in the future.

The request for U.S. intervention with Kuwait flew in the face of U.S. policy. The Da'wa had been convicted in Kuwait for a number of terrorist acts, including the bombing of the U.S. Embassy. Kuwait had stood up to threats of reprisal from Da'was for imprisoning the terrorists, and the U.S. had supported Kuwait. The United States wanted other countries to follow Kuwait's example. American policy was clear: Terrorists should be punished—not freed, as the Iranians were now asking.

Accordingly, McFarlane offered no hope of U.S. intervention with Kuwait on behalf of the convicted Da'wa prisoners, saying that U.S. policy was to respect the judicial policies of other nations.

McFarlane adhered to his instructions. The Adviser then tried to cajole McFarlane to send the other HAWK parts prior to any hostage release:

> Since the plane is loaded why not let it come. You would leave happy. The President would be happy. We have no guilt based on our understanding of the agreement. We are surprised now that it has been changed. Let the agreement be carried out. The hostages will be freed very quickly. Your President's word will be honored. If the plane arrives before tomorrow morning, the hostages will be freed by noon. We do not wish to see our agreement fail at this final stage.

McFarlane responded, "We delivered hundreds of weapons. You can release the hostages, advise us, and we will deliver the weapons." Given McFarlane's firmness, the Adviser suggested another way of breaking the impasse: the U.S. and Iranian representatives should meet without McFarlane to try to formulate an agreement on the hostages and HAWK parts, which could be presented to both sides. McFarlane consented with the caveat that "staff agreements must be approved by our leaders."

The NSC staff and the Iranians met for several hours until near midnight. The group hammered out a proposal that provided that Secord's aircraft with the remaining HAWK parts would take off for Tehran but turn around in midflight if the hostages were not released by morning.

**The draft agreement said that while the U.S. launched a plane carrying the remaining spare parts Iran would release all hostages by 0400 Tehran time. If this did not occur, the plane would be turned around. But if all went well, the U.S. would also deliver two radar sets for HAWK missiles and set up a team of Americans in Iran who would handle secret satellite communications between the two governments.**

The Adviser pressed North for concessions on the Da'wa. North, more flexible than McFarlane, proposed a statement such as:

> The U.S. will make every effort through and with international organizations, private individuals, religious organizations and other third parties in a humanitarian effort to achieve the release of and just and fair treatment for Shi'ites held in confinement as soon as possible.

The Iranians had another problem. The Adviser said that Iran could not arrange the release of the hostages by 4 A.M. He pleaded with McFarlane for more time. McFarlane was in no mood to compromise. However, he gave the Adviser until 6:30 A.M. to arrange for the release of the hostages. If the Iranians did not guarantee their freedom by then, the U.S. delegation would leave Tehran.

## Departure

Prior to the 6:30 A.M. deadline, the Second Iranian returned to the hotel with an eleventh-hour compromise. He offered to release two hostages immediately and two more after the HAWK parts were delivered. McFarlane refused, strictly observing his instructions that all the hostages had to be released before any parts could be delivered.

211

Eager to keep the Iran initiative alive, North recommended that McFarlane accept the two-hostage compromise. He testified that McFarlane overruled him, and that he "saluted smartly and carried it out." McFarlane testified that North was so determined to accept a compromise that, while McFarlane was asleep, North violated McFarlane's orders and directed Secord to send the plane from Israel with the remaining HAWK parts. Upon awakening, McFarlane ordered the plane, midway in its voyage, to return to Israel. North denied this allegation, and contended that McFarlane had approved sending the plane subject to its recall. Secord testified that it was always part of the plan to send the plane. Cave testified that he was unaware that the plane had taken off. In any event, the 6:30 A.M. deadline passed without any indication that any hostages had been released.

The Iranians made last-minute efforts to sell the compromise and obtain the HAWK parts. At 8 A.M., just before the delegation left the hotel, the Adviser arrived and repeated the two-hostage proposal. McFarlane rejected it out of hand: "You are not keeping the agreement. We are leaving."

Even at the Tehran airport, the Second Iranian tried to persuade McFarlane to change his mind. But there was no reprieve. McFarlane had come to Tehran with instructions and on the understanding that no more HAWK parts would be delivered unless all of the hostages were freed. He had expected the hostages' release upon his arrival. He had allowed the Iranians to temporize for 3 days. He once again rejected the last-minute compromise and ordered the plane airborne. As McFarlane left, he asked the Second Iranian to tell his "superiors that this was the fourth time that they had failed to honor an agreement. The lack of trust will endure for a long time."

The plane left Tehran at 8:55 A.M. and landed in Tel Aviv several hours later. During the layover there, North consoled McFarlane with the news that the efforts with Iran had produced one benefit: some of the proceeds of the arms sales were being used for the Contras. McFarlane assumed that Poindexter had approved this use of the money, and that, because of the magnitude of the decision, it was not something that Poindexter would have undertaken on his own authority. McFarlane testified that he, therefore, never raised the "diversion" with Poindexter or the President when he reported on the trip.

## WHY THE TEHRAN MISSION FAILED

The participants had different explanations for why the Tehran mission failed. Secord testified that McFarlane, who had demonstrated firmness, was responsible for the failure by insisting on release of all the hostages:

> But as far as I know and this will surprise some people I guess, but as far as I know, there was no Iranian agreement to produce all the hostages at the time of the meeting in Tehran . . . I don't know how exactly that expectation got into McFarlane's head.

Hakim, who had been the interpreter at Frankfurt, agreed:

> I cannot recall any time that was spoken that all hostages would be released. That must have been [a] misconception by someone at sometime somewhere.

McFarlane testified that he was "surprised" at Secord's statement: "[I]n talking to my own staff at the time, Colonel North and others, all of them reconfirmed, yes, we do expect and have all along the complete release of the hostages." And North's messages and reports to Poindexter before the Tehran mission confirm that the President and Poindexter shared that understanding. Indeed, in conveying the President's approval for the mission, Poindexter made clear to North that he would tolerate no more backing down on the conditions. He wrote North more than a month before the trip:

> You may go ahead and go, but I want several points made clear to them [the Iranians]. There are not to be any parts delivered until all the hostages are free in accordance with the plan that you layed out for me before. None of this half shipment before any are released crap. It is either all or nothing. Also you may tell them that the President is getting very annoyed at their continued stalling.

North and Cave blamed the misunderstanding, and the consequent failure of the mission, on Ghorbanifar. North testified that "it turns out that the Iranians did not" agree to the release of all the hostages, even though Ghorbanifar said they had. In his report on the trip, Cave stated that Ghorbanifar was a "dishonest interlocutor," who "gave each side a different picture of the structure of the deal." But Cave was confident that greed would overcome the problems, and he favored continuing the initiative: "Since both Gorba and the Second Iranian stood to make a lot of money out of the deal, they presumably will work hard to bring it off."

Based on long experience with Iranians, Cave was not wholly optimistic. He detected in the Tehran discussions a new dimension to the problem. He concluded that the Kuwaitis held the key to the impasse, and that the American hostages would not be released until Kuwait released the Da'wa prisoners. He grounded his conclusion on the independence of the hostage-holders in Lebanon. Until then, he believed that the Hizballah would not release all the hostages. The Iran initiative now threatened to move from an arms-for-hostage exchange to an arms-and-prisoners-for-hostages trade.

**A chapter footnote says North testified that Casey told him to be prepared to take his own life with a suicide pill if he went to Tehran. But Cave, the retired CIA officer brought into the initiative, said he did not have a poison pill himself and knew of no one in the delegation who did.**

# CHAPTER 14

# "Taken to the Cleaners":* The Iran Initiative Continues

The United States had taken a firm position in Tehran. Although offered two hostages, McFarlane had refused to deliver the remaining HAWK parts unless all the hostages were released first. But this was to be the last show of toughness by the United States: just 2 months later, the United States delivered the same HAWK parts after obtaining the release of only one hostage.

The Iran initiative continued until public reaction following its exposure in November 1986 forced its cancellation. Before then, some of the players had changed: a new channel to Iran (the "Second Channel") with a new Iranian emissary was found; Nir was cut out of the negotiations; and Secord and Hakim took his place. More missiles were sent to Iran, where they went to the radical Revolutionary Guard. But fundamental problems remained, and the Second Channel turned out to represent the same Iranian leaders as did the First Channel. In the end, the United States secured the release of another hostage but three more were seized, at least one allegedly at the instigation of one of

the Iranians with whom the U.S. negotiators had dealt earlier. Despite this, however, the U.S. negotiators agreed not only to sequential release of the hostages but also to seeking the freedom of the convicted Da'wa terrorists from prison in Kuwait.

## THE BARTERING CONTINUES

The deadlock in Tehran did not end Manucher Ghorbanifar's role as an intermediary. A strange interdependence had developed among the parties: Iran still wanted the remaining HAWK parts and other high technology weapons from the United States; the United States wanted the hostages; Israel wanted direct or indirect relations with Iran; and Ghorbanifar wanted to be paid.

Ghorbanifar had borrowed $15 million from Saudi entrepreneur Adnan Khashoggi to finance the HAWK parts shipment and Khashoggi, in turn, had borrowed the money from his financiers. But only one pallet of HAWK parts had been delivered in Tehran and Iran refused to pay. Ghorbanifar could

---

*"Our guys . . . they got taken to the cleaners." Secretary of State, George P. Shultz, testifying at the public hearings.

214

repay his debt to Khashoggi only by inducing the United States to ship the rest of the parts.

## IRAN DISCOVERS THE OVERCHARGE

By the end of June, Iran had raised another reason for refusing to pay Ghorbanifar and release the hostages: The Iranians had obtained a "[m]icrofiche of factory prices" that "does not compare w/ prices charged."

On June 30, Cave spoke by telephone to the Second Iranian who complained that the Iranians had a microfiche price list showing the true price of the HAWK parts and that they had been overcharged by 600 percent. The same day, Ghorbanifar called CIA official Charles Allen and told him that while he was being blamed for the overcharge, his markup was only 41 percent.

## TRYING FOR AN INDEPENDENCE DAY PRESENT

Since the Iranians' complaints rested on the microfiche list, Cave asked for proof of the overcharge. In the meantime, Ghorbanifar and an Israeli official attempted to keep the initiative alive. The Israeli hoped to gain the release of at least one hostage in time for the July 4 Independence Day celebration of the Statute of Liberty's 100th anniversary. Ghorbanifar told the Israeli that he could deliver and, on July 2, Amiram Nir, adviser to Israeli Prime Minister Shimon Peres on combatting terrorism, called North and predicted the release of an American hostage in time for the celebration. North immediately dispatched an interagency team to Wiesbaden. But when the release did not occur, Poindexter criticized North for falsely raising expectations and North, in frustration, let it be known to Nir that he would not take any more calls from him until further notice.

On July 26, Ghorbanifar and the Israelis registered a success: Reverend Lawrence Jenco was released. The Israeli intermediary had forced the issue, telling Ghorbanifar after the July 4 disappointment that the initiative was over unless a hostage was released. Shortly thereafter, Ghorbanifar announced that Jenco would be freed. Although welcome, the release of Father Jenco generated confusion and concern; it was unclear what Ghorbanifar had promised to gain his release.

The next day North and Cave met in Frankfurt with Ghorbanifar and an Israeli official to clarify matters. Ghorbanifar described the arrangements he had made with the Iranians to obtain the release of Rev. Jenco. These included the sequential release of the hostages and the delivery of arms to Iran. Ghorbanifar also told the group that, on his own accord, he had promised the Iranians that if they could prove the claim that they had been overcharged by $10 million for the HAWK spare parts, the United States would make up for it by giving Iran 1,000 free TOWs.

In a July 29 memorandum to Poindexter, North set forth Ghorbanifar's 6-step plan for the sequential release of the hostages in exchange for the remaining HAWK parts, 2 HAWK radars and 1,000 TOWs.

Step 1: One hostage released and $4M to Ghorbanifar for items removed from the aircraft in Tehran during the May visit (Ghorbanifar received the $4M on July 28)

215

Step 2: Remainder of 240 parts plus full quota of electron tubes (item 24 on Iranian parts list) and 500 TOWs delivered to Iran.

Step 3: Second hostage released and Ghorbanifar paid for remainder of 240 parts.

Step 4: 500 TOWs and 1 HIPAR [HAWK] radar delivered.

Step 5: Third hostage released and Ghorbanifar paid for one radar.

Step 6: Meeting in Tehran to discuss future followed by release of the last hostage and delivery of second HIPAR radar.

We believe that the mixture of HAWK parts and TOWs was designed to satisfy both the military and the Revolutionary Guards in Iran.

The proposed terms left the United States in an awkward position. McFarlane had withdrawn his delegation from Tehran when the Iranians had failed to produce all four remaining hostages in exchange for the 12 pallets of HAWK spares sitting on the ground in Israel. They had also discussed the HIPAR radars in Tehran but they, too, were to be delivered only after the radars were paid for and all of the hostages were released.

North repeatedly warned that one of the hostages might be killed if the HAWK parts were not delivered. In his July 29 memorandum to Poindexter, North predicted that "[i]t is entirely possible that if nothing is received, [the Second Iranian] will be killed by his opponents in Tehran, Ghorbanifar will be killed by his creditors . . . and one American hostage will probably be killed in order to demonstrate displeasure."

North recommended that Poindexter brief the President and "obtain his approval for having the 240 HAWK missile parts shipped

from Israel to Iran as soon as possible, followed by a meeting with the Iranians in Europe." Poindexter noted on the memorandum: "7/30/86 President approved."

The decision in Tehran not to ship the parts unless *all* the hostages were released first had been reversed. On August 4, 1986, the HAWK parts were flown into Iran. Secord provided the crew and Israel provided the airplane.

## THE DA'WA PRISONERS

The Adviser, the member of the Iranian Parliament who met with the McFarlane delegation, had told McFarlane and North in Tehran that the freeing of the Da'wa prisoners in Kuwait was essential to the release of all the United States hostages. The demand was taken seriously and North closely monitored the status of the Da'wa prisoners. North saw signs of hope, both that the captors of the Americans would relent on this condition and that Kuwait might, on its own, release the Da'wa prisoners.

## CROWE IS APPRISED

At a meeting of the Terrorist Incident Working Group (TIWG) chaired by North in late June or early July, an allusion was made to the Iranian arms sales. One of the members of the TIWG was Lt. General John Moellering, then-Special Assistant to Admiral William J. Crowe, Jr., Chairman of the Joint Chiefs of Staff. The Joint Chiefs had not been informed of the sales and Moellering was perplexed by the reference to arms sales.

Later, Assistant Secretary of Defense Richard L. Armitage, who had been at the TIWG meeting, briefly explained the Iranian arms sales to Moellering.

Moellering relayed what he had learned from Armitage to Admiral Crowe, a 40-year veteran who served in World War II, Korea and Vietnam. Crowe, though Chairman of the Joint Chiefs, had not been consulted or informed about the decision to ship weapons to Iran, or the McFarlane mission to Tehran. Crowe was "startled" by the "nature of the transaction" because it was "contrary to our policy."

Crowe confronted Defense Secretary Weinberger and asked him to explain why the Joint Chiefs of Staff had been excluded from the decisionmaking process. Weinberger offered no defense of the initiative. Instead, he merely told Crowe that the decision had been made by the Commander in Chief; that "he (the President) can do what he wants to do;" and that "consultation with others below the Commander in Chief level would not have perhaps been very fruitful."

For the first time, at Crowe's direction, the military focused on the effect that the previous sales to Iran had had on the strategic balance in the Middle East and the defense capability of the United States. Given Iran's avowed hostility to the United States, and to U.S. allies in the region, such a study by military experts should have been completed before any sales were authorized. The obsession with secrecy and the desire to avoid possible criticism led to the concealment of the sales not only from Congress but from the President's principal military advisers. Only after determining how the TOWs were actually being deployed was Crowe able to conclude that the arms sales did not significantly affect United States military interests.

## THE VICE PRESIDENT IS BRIEFED

At North's request, Nir briefed Vice President George Bush during his visit to Jerusalem on July 29, shortly before the HAWK parts shipment. Nir described the initiative as "having two layers—tactical and strategic." The tactical layer was an effort "to get the hostages out." The strategic layer was designed "to build better contact with Iran and to insure we are better prepared when a change (in leadership) occurs." Nir told the Vice President that Iran was using the retention of the hostages as leverage: "the reason for the [Iranians'] delay [in releasing the hostages] is to squeeze as much as possible as long as they have assets." But the Iranians were, Nir stated, arranging to release one hostage with another to follow. In return, the Iranians wanted HAWK spare parts and TOWs.

Nir then framed the issues awaiting decision:

Should we accept sequencing? What are alternatives to sequencing? They fear if they give us all hostages they won't get anything from us. If we do want to move along these lines we'd have to move quickly. It would be a matter still of several weeks not several days, in part because they have to move the hostages every time one is released. . . . It is important that we have assets there 2 to 3 years out when the change occurs. We have no choice other than to proceed.

Nir also told the Vice President that "we are dealing with the most radical elements."

The Vice President did not comment except to thank Nir "for having pursued this effort despite doubts and reservations throughout the process."

## THE MICROFICHE ARRIVES

The dispute about overcharging remained unresolved. By August 6, the Israelis had received the microfiche list from Iran. It consisted of pages showing prices as of November 1, 1985, and was authentic. The Iranians had clear evidence that they had been grossly overcharged. But North never considered a refund, even though the Enterprise had more than enough money to mollify the Iranians. North had no intention of eliminating the markup on future shipments. At North's instruction, Robert Earl, North's National Security Council colleague, was calculating prices on possible future shipments using a 3.7 multiplier against cost.

North's solution to Iran's complaint was to ask the CIA to prepare a phony price list to justify the prices charged Iran. According to Allen, this effort failed because the CIA's Office of Technical Services proved incapable of preparing a credible forged list.

As a further complicating factor, when the Iranians inspected the HAWK parts shipped in August, they rejected many of the parts and found the shipment incomplete. By August 20, Iran had identified 177 items that it had originally ordered and had not been included in the shipment. Iran had also determined that 63 of the items that had been sent were defective and asked that they be returned.

Ghorbanifar was thus left in difficult straits; pursued on the one hand by his creditors and criticized, on the other, by Iran for participating in a scam. Ghorbanifar complained hysterically to Allen. Even after Iran paid Ghorbanifar $5 million for the HAWK parts it received on August 4, Ghorbanifar claimed he was still $10 million short of meeting his obligations to his creditors.

From North's point of view, an alternative to Ghorbanifar, with all his financial problems, was needed.

## THE SEARCH FOR A NEW CHANNEL

Ghorbanifar had never been a popular emissary with the Americans. McFarlane in December 1985 had, according to Secord, found him "one of the most despicable characters [he] had ever met. . . ."

On February 27, North wrote of the need to "get Gorba out of the long range picture ASAP." By the time of the Tehran meeting in May therefore, Ghorbanifar was in jeopardy. When the Americans attributed the failure of the McFarlane mission to Ghorbanifar's misrepresentations to both sides, his replacement was certain.

Shortly after the Tehran breakdown, Poindexter authorized North to seek a new opening to Iran for continued negotiations—a "Second Channel." Hakim testified that he believed that the idea for a second channel originated with his associate, Richard Secord. Hakim took the lead in finding the appropriate contacts while keeping North and Secord informed.

Hakim thus had the opportunity to promote his business interests and to serve both his newly adopted country, the United States, and his native country, Iran. Hakim contacted an Iranian expatriate (the "First Contact") whom he had employed in the past. The First Contact made it clear that he expected to be paid for his work. In Cave's presence, Hakim assured him that "if anything goes through" he would realize a "good commission." The demand for remuneration was no surprise to Hakim. Transactions in the Middle East frequently call for "baksheesh"—a payoff to intermediaries. He had made such payoffs in the past. Hakim would draw the money for baksheesh from the profits of the arms deals with Iran.

With the promise of a payoff, the First Contact turned to a fellow Iranian businessman (the "Second Contact") with direct connections to the Iranian Government. How many others helped open the new channel is unclear. But, by the time it was in use, Hakim had obligated for payoffs an indefinite portion of $2 million set aside for such expenses from the Iran profits.

## THE SECOND CHANNEL'S DEBUT

The First and Second Contacts quickly found another avenue into Iran. North first got reports that an emissary from the "Second Channel" had been identified in late July. By July 31, the emissary's relationship to a leading Iranian official had been verified. On August 19, North learned that the emissary would meet with Secord and Hakim in Brussels, Belgium.

The meeting occurred on August 25. The emissary ("the Relative") was an Iranian, who had distinguished himself in the ranks of the Iranian Revolutionary Guard Corps in the war with Iraq. [He has never been publicly identified but is related to Rafsanjani, speaker of the Iranian parliament.]

The Relative impressed Secord. In a message to North after the Brussels meeting, Secord described the discussions as a "comprehensive tour de force" covering matters ranging from Soviet activities to the conduct of the Iran-Iraq war. Arms, however, remained the currency for dealing with Iran.

The Relative knew of the efforts of Ghorbanifar and his contacts. He described Ghorbanifar as a "crook," but promised not to interfere in that channel. He offered to help Ghorbanifar win the release of more hostages. Secord reported to North on August 26, "[m]y judgment is that we have opened up a new and probably much better channel into Iran."

Nonetheless, North also continued working with Ghorbanifar. They met in London on August 8 and worked out one last deal that combined a sequence of arms shipments and hostage releases. Simultaneously, plans moved ahead for an arms shipment involving the Second Channel. Poindexter met the President on September 9 and afterward told North to eliminate Ghorbanifar from future shipments. Allen saw trouble in this and wrote that North would have to raise at least $4 million to keep Ghorbanifar quiet. The banishment of Ghorbanifar reversed the roles of Israel and the Secord/Hakim operation. The Israelis, through Nir, had been the principal contact with Ghorbanifar. With the Second Channel, Secord and Hakim began attending the key meetings. Ghorbanifar kept trying to swing an arms deal, and when North heard of this he had Allen tell the U.S. Customs Service. As of September, plans for the Second Channel were well under way.

Secord arranged for the Relative to be flown to Washington for a 2-day visit on September 19. The first day the Relative met with North, Secord, and Cave in North's office in the Old Executive Office Building. Hakim attended part of the meeting. On the second day, the group met at the headquarters of Stanford Technology Trading Group International in Vienna, Virginia.

Each side assured the other that its objective was a long-term relationship and a common defense against Soviet aggression. But arms, hostages, the Da'wa—and a new subject, the status of Iraq's President, Saddam Hussein—dominated the discussion. The key points of those meetings follow.

*Arms:* The Relative brought an extensive arms "wish list." It included previously requested items, such as HAWK spare parts and radars, and many other items, including offensive weapons, critical to their war effort. To operate the equipment, Iran also could use "minimum levels of technological assistance" from the United States.

*Hostages:* North pressed for the release of all the hostages, not only as a condition of arms sales but as the first step toward a normal relationship with Iran. According to Secord's notes, North said:

> With respect to the document we prepared in Teheran, you will note a considerable emphasis on hostages. We consider them to be an obstacle. An obstacle to the understanding of the American people. The widespread perception here in America is that Iran is basically responsible for these hostages. The issue of hostages and terrorism must be dealt with since it is a political obstacle. On the other hand, you should realize that 52,000 people in the United States died last year in automobile accidents and 130,000 died from lung cancer. Five United States hostages rarely make the newspapers or the television, but because this is a democracy, if the President is found to be helping Iran with this obstacle still in the way, it would be very difficult to explain to our people.

*The Da'wa Prisoners:* Less that two weeks before the meeting with the Relative, Allen had observed that "[m]ore and more, we suspect that some Hizballah leaders would be willing to settle for the release of the [hos-

tages] for Shia prisoners held by [the] the Southern Lebanese Army."

Cave agreed with this analysis. He believed that the families of the Southern Lebanese Army prisoners might place enough pressure on the Hizballah to force an exchange of the American hostages for the Lahad prisoners.

Despite these assessments, the Da'wa prisoners were discussed at the meeting with the Relative. North said the United States could not intervene in Kuwait. He predicted, however, that Kuwait would free the prisoners in phases "if the Government of Iran goes privately to Kuwait and promises them no terrorism." North said that the Kuwaiti position "seem[ed] reasonable" and advised the Iranians to approach Kuwait. Later, when the parties prepared a summary of the two days of meetings, North himself added "the point about the Da'wa hostages and Kuwait and Kuwait's desire for a guarantee against terrorism" to the list.

*Saddam Hussein:* The Relative also sought to enlist the support of the United States in the removal of Iraq's president, Saddam Hussein. The Relative said the Gulf countries, friendly to the United States, should end their support for Hussein. North responded that the United States could "make no commitment about getting rid of Hussein," even though "[w]e agree that there is a need for a non-hostile regime in Baghdad." The Relative was not satisfied with this response. He returned to the issue the next day. He said that "he knows we can bring our influence to bear with certain friendly Arab nations and it is 'within the power of the Arab nations to get rid of Sadam (sic) Hussein.' "

*Other Issues:* The Relative asked that the United States join Iran in trying to raise the price of oil. North did not address this proposal at the time but later he observed that the oil market was "naturally depressed." He also stated that the United States and Iran had "similar interests with respect to oil."

The Relative said that the Second Iranian had "played a role" in the kidnapping of Frank Reed to put "additional pressure on the United States to send the next shipment [of weapons]."

The Relative also stated that William Buckley "was not killed; . . . he died of natural causes; . . . he had three heart attacks." According to Cave, the Americans challenged the Relative's assertion that Buckley had died a natural death. They also questioned the Relative on the complicity of the Revolutionary Guards in Buckley's interrogation and torture, but the Relative denied it. Cave nevertheless concluded that the Revolutionary Guards had interrogated Buckley.

*Joint Commission:* The Relative proposed a joint commission of Iranians and Americans to develop the relationship between the countries, and North appointed Secord, Cave, and himself as the American representatives.

North also promised the Relative that President Reagan would signal his appreciation for Iran's withholding of landing rights for a hijacked Pan American flight.

*The Intermediaries:* The Second Contact accompanied the Relative to the United States. In the midst of the negotiations, he raised with Hakim the question of his compensation for participating in the opening of the Second Channel. Hakim returned to the room and, with North, Secord, Cave, and the Relative present "made sure" that the subject of "financial remuneration" for himself and the other Iranians "would not be forgotten."

When the first day of talks had concluded, North and Hakim led the Relative from the Old Executive Office Building to the White House and conducted a guided tour. Hakim said the tour covered "every corner of the White House," including the Oval Office.

During the tour, North paused before the portrait of President Theodore Roosevelt and told the Relative of Roosevelt's arbitrating an end to the Russo-Japanese War of 1904–05, for which Roosevelt won the Nobel Peace Prize. He said that the United States would be willing to arbitrate an end to the Iran-Iraq conflict.

## PREPARATIONS FOR FRANKFURT

At the Washington talks, the Relative had suggested another meeting. In the meantime, the Relative kept in touch with North through Secord and Hakim.

North advised Poindexter in an October 2 memorandum that the Relative reported that there was now an "internal consensus on how to proceed with regard to the hostages 'obstacle,'" and that, at the next meeting, he would bring one of the officials who had been involved in the discussions with McFarlane in Tehran. The Relative also asked for a "definitive sampling of intelligence." North said the Relative gave the intelligence a "higher priority . . . than any other assistance we could provide." He also reported that the Relative was bringing a Koran for the President.

The memorandum recommended that:

— North be authorized to meet again with the Relative.

— The President inscribe a Bible with an appropriate inscription from Galatians, 3:8 to be given to the Relative.
— Poindexter prohibit anyone other than North, Cave, and Secord from having contacts with Iranian intermediaries.
— The United States provide intelligence to Iran.

North explained how intelligence could be provided without giving Iran an advantage in the war. He suggested that a "mix of factual and bogus information could be provided at this meeting which will satisfy their concerns about 'good faith' . . ."

In conclusion, North observed that:

A memo from you to the President has not been prepared for obvious reasons. It is hoped that between now and 3:00 P.M. Friday you will have an opportunity to privately discuss this with the President and obtain his approvals/signatures on the steps indicated above.

North did not explain the "obvious reasons" for not preparing a memorandum for the President. By giving the Iranians a Bible signed by the President, North provided Iran with proof that was used as evidence of the President's involvement.

More Americans were kidnapped in Lebanon shortly before the meeting with the Relative in Washington. Reed was seized on September 9, and Joseph Ciccipio was taken hostage three days later. In an attachment to his October 2 memo, North attributed the Ciccipio kidnapping to the Second Iranian but blamed Reed's abduction, which the Relative had fixed on the Second Iranian, on another group. And on October 21, just before the second set of October meetings in Germany, Edward Tracy was kidnapped.

## CHASING THE HORIZON— FRANKFURT, OCTOBER 6–8

The U.S. negotiating position suffered dramatic erosion in Frankfurt. The concessions made included mainstay principles of American policy on the Middle East and terrorism. In his testimony, when questioned about these concessions, North asserted that he had "lied every time [he] met the Iranians."

The meetings began on October 6. North, Secord, Hakim, and Cave represented the United States. The Relative appeared for the Iranians, along with a Revolutionary Guard intelligence official. The intelligence officer was not a new face for North, Secord, and Hakim. He had attended the first meeting with Ghorbanifar and the Second Iranian in Frankfurt on February 25–26, and was given a briefing there on U.S. intelligence by Secord. He had also participated in the negotiations with the McFarlane party in Teheran in May.

Because of his persistently negative positions and his insistence on concessions to Iran, the Americans called him "the monster." Hakim, for his part, saw the man as "the engine" because he was the "heart" behind the Iran initiative. To Hakim, this man was the key to an agreement.

In the negotiations, the Engine described himself as the "extraordinary representative of the cooperative that has been assigned to deal with the relationship with the United States." He made clear, however, that there was no unanimity within the Government of Iran on establishing a relationship with the United States.

The agenda at Frankfurt was the familiar one:

*Arms and Intelligence:* Speaking for the Americans, Secord told the Iranians that the

President had approved the transfer of HAWK parts, high-powered radars, 500 TOWs, and three pallets of free medical supplies.

North went further by dropping the restriction against offensive weapons. The "only" limitation was that the sales not include items that would "allow or encourage" the Army or the Revolutionary Guards to seize Baghdad. The Relative had candidly admitted in Washington that he wanted artillery to make Iranian infantry attacks more successful.

*Hostages:* North and Secord said that only the hostages stood in the way of a great era of Iranian-American relations, a period that would include arms transfers involving the Foreign Military Sales Program from the United States to Iran and great financial support for rebuilding the war-torn economy. The hostages were the "obstacles," the term used to describe them throughout the meetings.

The Engine insisted that the Iranians did not hold the hostages and that, if they did, they would have resolved the problem as they had the Embassy hostages. Iran could not guarantee that the Lebanese would listen "100 percent" to Iranians on hostage matters, he said.

*Saddam Hussein:* In Frankfurt, the Americans accepted the Iranians' position on Hussein. Poindexter testified that the matter was not discussed with the President. The President told the Tower Board that the statements made by the American negotiators were "absolute fiction."

North said that the United States sought peace in a way that "it becomes very evident to everybody that the guy who is causing the problem is Saddam Hussein." North said that Iran was no threat to the other countries in the region, and he repeated that Hussein prevented peace. The Engine asked North, "[D]o you really believe this?" North replied that he did and that the "inner circle of our Government knows that."

North purported to convey the President's view of President Hussein: "Sadam Hussein is a [expletive]." Hakim, acting as interpreter, demurred at the harshness of the expletive, but North urged a faithful translation saying, "Go ahead. That's his [the President's] word, not mine."

As the negotiations continued, North returned to the fate of President Hussein. He declared that "[w]e also recognize that Saddam Hussein must go," and North described how this could be accomplished.

*The Da'wa Prisoners:* When the Engine asked North to "show me the way" to gain the confidence of the Lebanese captors and his fellow Iranian officials, North provided two quick answers: First, he said, "[l]et me give you some ammunition for your guns." Then he brought up the Da'wa prisoners.

North said he recognized the desire of the Shi'ite captors to obtain the release of their "brethren who are held in Kuwait as convicted terrorists." He assured the Iranians, that, although the United States had told Kuwait that the Da'wa prisoners were "their business," the United States would not criticize Kuwait should Kuwait release them. The United States had recently conveyed this position to Kuwait, North added. Although a North notebook entry indicates that he and Poindexter had met with the Kuwaiti Foreign Minister on October 3, the Committees have been unable to determine what was discussed. What is indisputable is that at various meetings with the Second Channel, representatives of Iran—a nation classified

223

by the United States as a supporter of terrorism—North offered assistance in gaining the release of Da'wa terrorists. Whether that assistance consisted of not protesting the release, or more, it was contrary to U.S. policy against terrorism.

Thus, North claimed to the Iranians that the Kuwaiti position was "simple": Kuwait would release the prisoners over time in exchange for a promise from "somebody in authority" that there would be no more attacks on the Amir of Kuwait.

*Peace Broker:* From time to time North discussed President Reagan's interest in resolving the Iran-Iraq war on "honorable" terms. North even created a fanciful meeting between himself and the President at Camp David in which he showed the President the Relative's arms list. According to North, President Reagan then ordered North to "[s]top coming in and looking like a gun merchant." At this point, he said, President Reagan struck the table and declared, "I want to end the war."

As North presented the Bible inscribed by the President, he created another apocryphal session with the President. President Reagan was depicted as having returned from a weekend of prayer for guidance on whether to authorize North to tell the Iranians that "[w]e accept the Islamic Revolution." North said that the President gave him the passage that he later inscribed in the Bible with the observation: "This is a promise that God gave to Abraham. Who am I to say that we should not do this?"

*Starting Points:* North presented a handwritten list of seven points that he said the President had authorized.

1. Iran provides funds for 500 TOWs and remainder of HAWK parts.

2. Within 9 days we deliver [HAWK] parts and TOWs (500) plus medical supplies.

3. All American hostages released.

4. Iran provides funds for 1500 TOWs.

5. Within 9 days we will deliver:
*1500 TOWs
*Technical support for HAWKs
*Updated intelligence on Iraq
*Communications team

6. Iran will then:
*Release [John] Pattis
*Provide body of [William] Buckley
*Provide copy of Buckley debrief

7. United States will then:
*Identify sources for other items on [the Relative's arms] list. . . .
*Iran will then work to release other hostages.

*Counterpoints:* The next day, the Engine responded with his own list:

1. The United States would establish a timetable for the delivery of the arms on the Relative's list, thus committing itself to providing offensive and defensive arms.

2. One hostage would then be released.

3. A timetable and a location would be established for the exchange of intelligence; and the United States and Iran would evaluate the Russian, Afghanistan, and Iraq situation.

4. Iran would "only promise" to gain the release of the remaining two American hostages but this was to be linked to American progress on the Da'wa prisoners. The Engine made clear that the release of the Americans and the Da'was would have to "wash." "They would have to coincide or have some other logical correlation."

5. Shipment of the eight items on the Relative's

list would proceed based upon mutually agreed-upon priorities and quantities. Iran would try—but not promise—to locate and arrange the release of the other two hostages.

6. The United States would contact Kuwait to make sure that there are no problems with the release of the Da'wa prisoners.

7. The United States and Iran would agree to work within the framework of the Hague settlement process to provide Iran with military items, such as F-14 spare parts, that Iran had paid for under the Shah's rule but that had been embargoed after the Embassy seizure.

By way of "clarification," the Engine added two other points to his list: John Pattis, a United States citizen, who had been arrested in Tehran as an alleged spy, would not be considered in this round of discussions, and the status of the Shi'ite prisoners held by the Southern Lebanese Army in Lebanon would be left to the Lebanese themselves to resolve.

## AMBASSADOR EXTRAORDINAIRE

The Engine presented his counterproposals to an anxious group. North had to return to Washington, and all parties were worried that their prolonged discussions might attract the attention of local authorities. As North prepared to leave, he told the Iranians that their differences were so great that Iran and the United States would "pass each other like ships in the night." The Relative, in turn, accused the Americans of maintaining that they were pursuing long-term relations with Iran while focusing on the hostages as "the only thing that is being discussed."

North was not prepared to give up and suggested to the group, "[W]hy don't you guys hold this discussion after I'm gone, OK?" He left his seven-point proposal behind, saying "[t]his list was given to me by the President of the United States of America. And there's no way on God's green earth that I'm going to violate my instructions. . . . That's the President's authorized list. That's all he authorized. . . . In fact, he told me 'don't give away more than you have to'—that is everything he authorized me to talk about."

Hakim testified that North left him to negotiate with the Iranians.

Q: Did you feel like you had been the Secretary of State for a day?

A: I would not accept that position for any money in the world, sir.

Q: Well, you had it better than the Secretary of State in some sense. You didn't have to get confirmed; correct?

A: I still believe that I have it better than the Secretary. . . . I can achieve more, too.

Hakim completed the negotiations by the time North arrived in Washington. In his public testimony, Hakim stated that he would be "honored" if the agreement was known as the "Hakim Accords."

The agreement's nine-point plan differed sharply from North's seven-points. Under his grant of immunity, Hakim produced the original version in Farsi.

The Hakim Accords contain a number of concessions. These include the release of only 1½ hostage; the delivery of 500 TOWs before any release and a promise to supply 1,000 more TOWs; technical support for the HAWKs; updated intelligence; and prices for the other weapons Iran had listed. In negotiating the nine-point agreement, Hakim felt under intense pressure from North. In addition to the short deadline to complete the agreement, Hakim testified North also told him that the President wanted a hostage back by Election Day.

The plan represented a retreat for the United States. The Iranians' position on sequential deliveries had been accepted, and the plan did not expressly provide a mechanism for the release of all three of the remaining American hostages kidnapped before 1986. Iran had agreed to release only one hostage.

Moreover, the U.S. position on the Da'wa prisoners was bargained away by promising to develop a plan for the release of some of the 17 prisoners. The United States had criticized allies who, fearing reprisals, had freed terrorists. It had cited Kuwait as an example of a nation with courage: a nation that, although small and vulnerable to terrorism, was nonetheless willing to imprison terrorists. As the Secretary of State testified: "And here was little Kuwait, very vulnerable, standing up to it [terrorism]. So we have to support them. They are much more vulnerable than we. If they can stand up for it, doggone it, so should we."

There were other concessions: a $2,400 reduction in price for each of the 500 TOW missiles; an agreement to prepare a list showing the price and delivery schedule of the items on the Relative's long weapons list; and an abandonment of the demand for the return of William Buckley's remains and the transcript of his interrogation. The fate of Pattis was left for another day. The Americans seized in September 1986 were not mentioned.

Secretary Shultz said of the plan at the public hearings: "Our guys . . . they got taken to the cleaners."

In recommending that Poindexter approve the plan, North minimized his concessions. He asserted that the "[o]nly changes from my proposal is sequential nature of their plan and lack of mention of Buckley body & transcript of interrogation." The release of the Da'wa and the contemplated supply of artillery, he said, could be managed "w/o any great complications." He stated that Cave, Director Casey, and the Chief of the Near East Division all believed that the plan was the "best and fastest way to get two more out—probably within the next 14 days." He added, as the Division Chief had reported, "the situation in Lebanon is getting much worse and we may be getting close to the end of the line for any further movement."

North concluded that the agreement was a bargain: the United States would get two more hostages out for "nothing more than the two sets of 500 TOWs." As for the future, North recommended to Poindexter that "we shd push them to include the Buckley remains and transcript and then get on with it." Poindexter testified, "I discussed those with the President, and he approved the ones that applied to the U.S. Government.

Poindexter and North had different rationales for approving the concessions on the Da'was. North testified that, sooner or later, Kuwait would release the prisoners "as sure as I'm sitting here" and so "the United States might as well get something for them."

Poindexter maintained that since Secord, a private citizen, was to develop the plan to facilitate the release of the Da'wa prisoners, his actions would not compromise U.S. policy against concessions to terrorists. Poindexter held to this position even though

Secord represented the United States in the negotiations and North had appointed him, with Poindexter's approval, to the joint U.S.-Iran commission suggested by the Relative. Cave stated that he understood that the United States approach to the Kuwaitis would be official but that the United States would not seek relief for the three Da'wa prisoners who had been sentenced to death.

Whatever the rationale, any intervention to free the Da'wa prisoners conflicted with official U.S. policy, which was being publicly proclaimed at the very time the secret negotiations with the Second Channel were under way.

## ARMS TRANSFER PREPARATIONS

North, Secord, and an Israeli official met in Geneva on October 22 to iron out the details of the next arms shipment to Iran. They agreed that the 500 TOWs sent to Iran would be taken from the 508 sent to Israel in May and rejected as inadequate by the Israeli Defense Forces, and that the United States would supply Israel with another 500 replacement missiles.

The switch of TOWs, which North approved, was not without risk. The Relative had already complained to North that the TOWs the United States had sent earlier had misfired in battle. Secord said in his testimony that he had heard the Iranians complain that the TOWs had gone "ballistic."

## ARMING THE GUARDS

As the Americans knew, both the Relative and the Engine were members of the Iranian Revolutionary Guards Corps. The Revolutionary Guard is the military arm of the most radical elements in Iran. As Cave explained, "they were the executive arm of the revolution." The Revolutionary Guard was competing with and trying to replace the regular Iranian Army.

Early in the Iran initiative, the Americans were on notice that the weapons sent to Iran might go to the Revolutionary Guards. Ghorbanifar had, in fact, contended that the first shipment of TOWs in August of 1985 had been seized by the Guards when it arrived at Tehran.

According to Cave, the Relative told the Americans that the February shipment of TOWs had gone to the Revolutionary Guards. In November, the Engine shared with North his hope to build an air wing for the Guard.

To the best of the Committees' information, the President was never told that the United States was arming the Revolutionary Guard. Cave stated that he recalled no discussion of whether arming the Guard was consistent with the Finding. In his last interview with the Committees, Cave still characterized the Second Channel as "middle roaders."

## MAINZ MEETING

North, Secord, Hakim, Cave, the Relative, and the Engine met in Mainz, Germany, south of Frankfurt, on October 29, 1986, to discuss the promised release of one or two hostages and the implementation of the rest of the nine points.

The Mainz discussions began with ominous news. The Relative reported that dissension in Iran over the initiative had prompted students associated with a political faction to publish "five million copies" of pamphlets describing the McFarlane visit to Iran. Moreover, although the Hizballah was "basically under the control of the Iranian Government," a faction of Hizballah radicals had published an account of the negotiations between the United States and Iran for distribution in Lebanon. These events almost prevented the Engine and Relative from coming to the meeting.

The Relative then insisted that North tell him who in the U.S. Government supported the Iran initiative. North said the President, the Vice President, Poindexter, Casey, and Regan were in favor, and Secretaries Shultz and Weinberger opposed. "No one else counts," and Congress would not be told "until we get the hostages out."

North told the Iranians that the United States had persuaded another Western government to terminate arms shipments to Iraq. The United States also allegedly had private discussions with certain Arab governments. When the Engine stated that an Arab government had agreed to put pressure on Iraq, North said "That's us doing that." The Committees have no evidence that North's statement of U.S. pressure was true. North testified, though not with reference to this, that "I lied every time I met the Iranians."

*Hostages:* North expressed bewilderment that the Iranians did not simply "exercis[e] every possible amount of leverage they've got to get those people out." He found this particularly confounding because ". . . we agree that as soon as they're out, we can do all kinds of good things." North included on the list of "good things," foreign military sales contracts and the "formal relationship that

McFarlane had held out in Teheran." "The big problem I've got," North said, "is the whole damn appearance of bartering over . . . bodies."

In discussing the plan for the release of the hostages, North divulged to the Iranians classified material of particular sensitivity.

*Arms, Intelligence, Assistance:* The prospect of American military assistance to Iran if more hostages were released dominated the Mainz meetings. The Relative informed the Americans that Rafsanjani had taken a personal interest in restoring inoperable Phoenix missiles. The Relative held out the hostages as bait: "I'll tell you what I'll do. You send that technician to help us with the Phoenixes, I will personally get the third guy out, and I could tell you where the rest of the guys are. I will learn where they are."

The Phoenix was a complicated missile that required several technicians to repair. The Americans expressed concern that if the United States sent technicians, their presence might be discovered by America's allies. North explained, "If there is a visible effort made by the United States Government when there's a long list of hostages being held in Lebanon, this President is going to get stoned by" U.S. allies. To this, Secord added: "[A]nd by his own people."

*The Da'wa:* North emphasized to the Iranians that he had "already started" on the Da'wa plan. He claimed that he had "already met with the Kuwaiti Foreign Minister, secretly. In my spare time between blowing up Nicaragua." (North, in an aside to the American participants, stated that he had spent 7 days putting together a plan on the Da'wa.) However, when asked about the particulars of North's seven days of effort, Cave said he never heard about it.

*The Interlocutors:* Ghorbanifar was not

228

the only Iranian intermediary demanding money. The Relative told Secord and Cave that he had received "ten calls from [the Second contact] asking where his money was." Secord responded that the financial straits of the Second Contact were "our responsibility; we'll take care of it." The discussion then turned to Albert Hakim. The Relative complained that Hakim was "trying to push this [the whole relationship] too fast." Secord explained that "we have placed Albert [Hakim] under pressure on the hostages."

*Joint Commission:* As the United States shifted from the First Channel to the Second, there were strong indications that, notwithstanding the change, the United States was dealing with the same political consortium in Iran.

The Relative then announced the Iranian membership on the "joint commission." The appointees were the Engine, a participant in meetings held under the auspices of both channels; the Adviser, who negotiated with McFarlane in Tehran; a member of the Iranian Parliament, the Majlis; and the Second Iranian, the primary Iranian official in the First Channel and the man who the Relative had said was responsible for Reed's kidnapping. The Americans did not object even though the composition of the Commission, including the Second Iranian, "really blew our minds." The Commission membership demonstrated to the Americans the true breadth of the political union with which they had been dealing all along.

*Saddam Hussein:* The removal of Iraqi President Hussein from power remained on the Iranian list. Secord said that "we" would talk to another country in the region. He added, "It's going to take a lot of talk, a lot of talk."

## THE RELEASE OF JACOBSEN

When the negotiators in Mainz disbanded, North reported to Poindexter through Lt. Col. Robert Earl. Earl advised Poindexter that the Relative "assures us we will get 2 of 3 US hostages held by Hizballah in next few days—probably Fri or Sat but NLT [not later than] Sunday." North proposed that he and Secord go to Lebanon to coordinate the release of the hostages and to brief the American Ambassador on both the third hostage and the "remaining three . . . when we get info from Rafsanjani on locations. . . ." North also wanted to arrange to pick up a Soviet tank that Iran had promised.

So that the President would get credit for the release, North urged that the President announce the hostages' release "after the AMCITS are in USG hands" but "before CNN knows it has happened." North hoped that under this arrangement, President Reagan would be "seen to have influenced the action. . . ."

On Sunday, November 2, two days before the mid-term elections, David Jacobsen was released.

## EXPOSURE

The next day, the initiative was exposed. The source was neither Ghorbanifar nor his financiers, who had made earlier threats to do so, but the Lebanese magazine, *Al-Shiraa.* It had picked up the story that had been circulating in the Hizballah broadsides. On November 4, Rafsanjani addressed the Iranian Parliament and acknowledged that an American delegation had visited Tehran. After the speech, the Relative conveyed to

North that the Iranians still wished to continue the initiative.

North continued to seek the release of another hostage in return for concessions on the Da'wa. North's notebooks show entries about his desire to resolve quickly the "Kuwaiti United States Da'wa problems and the hostages."

North's notebooks reflect his belief that the goal of securing the release of the hostages justified the initiative, and that the public would approve once the facts were out. Noting this, he wrote his conclusion and included a notable misstep: "Ultimately on side of angles [sic]."

## TAKING STOCK IN GENEVA

On November 8, 1986, Cave, North, Secord, and Hakim met with the Engine in Geneva.

By now, each side had its own acute problems. The Engine worried that Ghorbanifar, whom the Iranians now suspected of being an Israeli agent, might cause trouble. He asked Cave's advice on how to "appease" him. North, on the other hand, stated that the burgeoning publicity surrounding the initiative made it all the more imperative that the hostages be released. North assured the Iranians he was "here at the order of the President and we still have the same objectives as explained in Washington and Frankfurt." The Engine made it clear that the freeing of the Da'wa prisoners was a prerequisite to the release of the "other two hostages." Once the Da'wa prisoners were released, there would be "no problem" with the two hostages.

The Americans responded that "we had done all that was humanly possible by talk-

ing dsirectly (sic) to the Kuwaitis . . ." The Americans concluded by strongly recommending that the Iranians send a delegation to Kuwait with the assurance that it would be "warmly received."

When North returned from Geneva, he briefly acted, at Hakim's suggestion, as a ghostwriter for Rafsanjani. The Iranians were contemplating making a public statement in the light of the exposure of the initiative in Iran. On November 11, Hakim asked North to "create something for Rafsanjani to say." North drafted a statement that he sent Hakim by KL-43 computer to be transmitted to the Engine. North added instructions that the statement be issued "from Iran." He said that it would "help with the Kuwaiti situation on which we are now working."

In North's proposed statement, Iran proclaimed "the enduring reality of its Islamic Revolution," its interest in peace, and "His Holiness the Imam['s] . . . gracious[ ] command[ ] that acts of terrorism are not acceptable to advance the aims of the Islamic Revolution." North asked that the Engine "carry this message for me as a personal favor for the cause we both believe in. . . ."

## THE CIRCLE OPENS

The Secretary of State testified that he did not receive confirmation of the arms sales that had been reported in *Al-Shiraa* until November 10, when he attended a meeting in the Oval Office with the President and principals of the NSC. He feared the arms sales would continue. He saw the Administration's statement—that the arms embargo would remain in effect "as long as Iran advocates the use of terrorism"—as a license to ship arms to Iran by pretending that it was no longer supporting terrorism.

On November 14, a day after the President's televised speech on the issue, Secretary Shultz, at his regular weekly meeting with the President, urged him not to sell any more arms to Iran. The President did not commit himself. Shultz then tried another approach. The next day, he submitted a proposal to Chief of Staff Regan permitting the State Department to take control of U.S./Iran policy. This would have given State the authority to block further sales. Regan said he favored this step, but the President was unwilling to adopt it.

North called Nir on November 23 and informed him that he had been interviewed by Attorney General Meese. North said that Meese had asked him about the diversion of some of the Iran arms money to Nicaragua. North then asked Nir to have Israel accept responsibility for the plan but Nir rejected the request. North's notes quote Nir as saying: "I cannot back this story."

## THE FINALE

In early December, Cave asked Hakim to set up another meeting with a representative of the Second Channel. Hakim did so and, on December 12, Under Secretary of State Michael Armacost and Director Casey met to discuss ground rules for the meeting. They agreed that the Iranians would be informed that the channel would, henceforth, be used only for intelligence purposes between the two countries.

The following day, Casey met alone with Regan and succeeded in reversing the

ground rules. Under the new decision, the Second Channel could be used for policy purposes as well as intelligence exchanges. Secretary Shultz learned of this change only after the fact. He observed: "Nothing ever gets settled in this town."

The meeting with the Engine took place in Frankfurt on December 13. Once the meeting was underway, the Engine told Cave and Dunbar that, despite the press revelations, Iran was ready to proceed within the "already established framework." He noted that "[m]uch had been accomplished by North, Secord, and Cave."

The Engine brought up the nine-point plan, saying that five or six of the points had been executed. This was the first that Dunbar or the State Department had heard of the nine points, and Cave had to confirm to Dunbar that there was such a plan. Cave told the Committees that the State Department did not act on his invitation to brief Dunbar, and as a result, Dunbar was not well prepared for the meeting.

When he spoke, Dunbar conveyed the new ground-rules for the Iranian-American dialogue. He told the Engine that arms from the United States would no longer be a part of the initiative, and the Engine, in a quiet and unemotional voice, responded that that "would bring us back to zero." He suggested that Dunbar must be mistaken and that he should return to Washington for a full briefing.

When Dunbar told Secretary Shultz of the nine-point plan, the Secretary was shocked. He insisted on immediately telling the President about it in person.

Poindexter testified that the President had approved the nine-point plan as it applied to the U.S. Government. Poindexter contends that the deal with Secord and Kuwait was private. North told Cave of the President's approval. Secretary Shultz testified, however, that when he told the President of the plan, the President gave no indication that he was familiar with it, but "reacted like he had been kicked in the belly." Shultz continued:

And I told the President the items on this agenda, including such things as doing something about the Dawa prisoners, which made me sick to my stomach that anybody would talk about that as something we could consider doing. And the President was astonished, and I have never seen him so mad. He is a very genial, pleasant man and doesn't—very easy going. But his jaws set and his eyes flashed, and both of us, I think felt the same way about it, and I think in that meeting I finally felt that the President understands that something is radically wrong here.

The President's meeting with Secretary Shultz laid the Iran initiative to rest. The President authorized Shultz to tell Iran that the United States repudiated the nine-point plan and unequivocally rejected further arms sales. Further, Secretary Shultz sent a cable to Kuwait affirming strong U.S. support for Kuwait's refusal to yield on the Da'wa prisoners. The Iran initiative was over.

**A chapter footnote says the Relative told American officials that the Iranians had a 400-page transcript from a debriefing of Buckley, the CIA officer taken hostage and killed. He said the transcript contained 200 to 300 sensitive names. The CIA did a damage assessment but never systematically tried to find out whether there was such a document. Neither the Committees nor the Agency found any direct evidence that the transcript exists.**

# CHAPTER 15

# The Diversion

The term "diversion" entered the vocabulary of American history on November 25, 1986, when the media, covering Attorney General Edwin Meese's press conference, reported a "diversion of funds" for the Contras from the Iran arms sales. The diversion immediately became the focus of the public's attention: Whose idea was it? Who approved it? When? Who knew of it? How much was diverted?

The Committees were able to answer these questions, but only partly, because of contradictions in the record, the destruction of evidence, and apparent forgetfulness by officials.

Lt. Col. Oliver North, Vice Admiral John Poindexter, and Richard Secord all vigorously rejected the term diversion, because it implies that the arms sales proceeds were earmarked for the U.S. Government, and were misappropriated. To North, Poindexter, and Secord, providing assistance to the Contras was only one of a number of intended uses of those proceeds. North named several projects that he was planning to finance from the proceeds. Indeed, Poindexter saw the generation of money for the Contras from the arms sales as no more exceptional than raising money from foreign countries, which the NSC staff had been doing with the President's approval for 18 months. Thus, for North, Poindexter, and Secord, the "diversion" was no diversion. But that was one of the few things upon which they agreed.

## WHOSE IDEA?

The generation of profits for covert uses from the sale of arms was not a novel idea when North first seized upon it. Sophisticated weapons bring premium prices in the international grey market for arms, and can thereby create slush funds for improper covert activities that could not be financed through appropriated money.

General John Singlaub had presented such a proposal in a memorandum to North and Director of Central Intelligence William J. Casey during 1985. The memorandum, prepared by Singlaub's associate, Barbara Studley, defined the "problem":

> With each passing year, Congress has become increasingly unpredictable and uncooperative

233

regarding the President's desire to support the cause of the Freedom Fighters despite growing Soviet oppression. The funds have not been forthcoming to supply sufficient arms necessary for the Freedom Fighters to win.

The "objective" was "to create a conduit for maintaining a continuous flow of Soviet weapons and technology, to be used by the United States in support of Freedom Fighters in Nicaragua, Angola, Cambodia, Ethiopia, etc."

The memorandum proposed a three-way trade in which the United States would provide high technology equipment to another country, that country would deliver from its stockpiles military equipment of equal value to a third country, and the third country would export Soviet-compatible arms to a trading company at the direction of the United States. "The United States," the memorandum observed, would then be able to dispense the arms to "Freedom Fighters worldwide, mandating neither the consent or awareness of the Department of State or Congress."

By the end of November 1985, the Enterprise received a portion of the arms sales proceeds. At North's request, the Israeli intermediaries paid the Lake Resources account $1 million from the proceeds of its August-September TOW shipments. According to North and Secord, the money was to cover the Enterprise's expenses in arranging five shipments of HAWKs to Iran. But when the deliveries were halted after one shipment, the Enterprise held $800,000 in unexpended funds. North received the Israelis' permission to use the $800,000 for "whatever purpose we wanted," and he directed Secord to spend the money for the Contras.

Thus, by early December, the notion that the Iran sales could be used as a vehicle for financing the Contras was firmly planted in North's mind. On December 6, 1985, North remarked to Israeli Ministry of Defense officials that he needed money and that he intended to divert profits from future Iranian transactions to Nicaragua. On December 9, North recommended to Poindexter that the United States take control of the arms sales from Israel, and use "Secord as our conduit to control [Iranian intermediary] Ghorbanifar and the delivery operation." This mechanism was adopted in the President's January 17, 1986, Finding, thereby avoiding the Arms Export Control Act requirement of Congressional notification for Israel to continue sales to Iran of the U.S. weapons. The mechanism allowed the CIA to sell arms to Iran directly *or through a "third party,"* although it did not authorize or even mention the generation of profits. Nevertheless, by permitting the CIA to sell through a third party, the Finding created an opportunity for profits to be generated and placed in the hands of the third party—an opportunity that would not have existed if the CIA sold the arms directly. So far as the record shows, this possibility was never suggested to the CIA attorneys who drafted the Finding, nor did Poindexter discuss it with the President in connection with the President's execution of the January 17 Finding.

North testified that the proposal to support the Contras from arms sales proceeds was first suggested by Ghorbanifar in late January 1986. He did not recall discussing the idea in December 1985 with Israeli Ministry of Defense officials, although he said the "subject may well have come up before [late January], but I don't recall it." According to North, during a meeting abroad with Nir and Ghorbanifar relating to the February

234

1986 TOW shipment to Iran, "Ghorbanifar took me into the bathroom and . . . suggested several incentives to make that February transaction work, and the attractive incentive for me was . . . that residuals could flow to support the Nicaraguan resistance."

The tape of the meeting shows that the idea of assisting the Contras was, in fact, discussed, not alone with North in the bathroom, but with the whole group present. This fact does not negate earlier consideration by North. Indeed, Ghorbanifar does not seem to have been referring to using the sales proceeds, but rather to Iran's assisting U.S. interests in Central America in return for receiving U.S. military assistance.

Regardless of its origin, North believed that using the funds from the arms sales for the Contras was a "neat idea," and he advocated it to Poindexter. He testified that he sought Poindexter's approval upon returning from the meeting with Ghorbanifar and Nir, and that Poindexter pondered the decision for at least several weeks. Poindexter testified, however, that he approved the diversion idea after thinking about it for only a few minutes.

## WHO ELSE KNEW—A STUDY IN CONTRADICTIONS

### Presidential Knowledge

Although both Poindexter and North testified that they never told the President about the diversion, the substance of their testimony diverges from there.

Poindexter testified that he made "a very deliberate decision not to ask the President" about the diversion in order to "insulate [the President] from the decision and provide some future deniability for the President if it ever leaked out." Although Poindexter asserted that the President would have approved of the diversion as an "implementation" of his policies, he nevertheless chose to protect the President from knowledge of the diversion because it was a "politically volatile issue." Poindexter testified as to the success of his efforts to provide the President with "future deniability" of the diversion. When Poindexter was questioned about the White House statement (issued the day after his initial hearing testimony) that the President would not have authorized the diversion, Poindexter responded: "I understand that he [the President] said that, and I would have expected him to say that. That is the whole idea of deniability."

Poindexter testified that he considered the diversion so controversial that he understood he would have to resign if it ever were exposed. Nevertheless, he also testified that, in approving the diversion, he did not consult Casey, a political expert who had managed the 1980 Reagan campaign, and that, only 2 months after taking office as National Security Adviser, he made this decision on his own. Poindexter had been commended in the Navy for keeping his superiors informed. He testified that he had never before withheld information from any of his commanders in order to give them deniability. Moreover, McFarlane, for whom Poindexter had worked for 2 years, assumed that Poindexter would have informed the President. Preempting a decision by the President to provide political deniability—which Poindexter testified that he did—was totally uncharacteristic for a naval officer schooled in the chain of command.

Poindexter's story on Presidential knowledge of the diversion was that he had constructed a situation whereby only he and the President would know whether the President had been advised of the diversion. In this regard, Poindexter testified that he never told North that the President was not privy to the diversion decision.

In contrast, North testified that he always "assumed that the President was aware of [the diversion] and had, through my superiors, approved it." North estimated that he prepared as many as five or six memorandums in final form referring to the use of the arms sales proceeds for the Contras. These memorandums went "up the line" to Poindexter and covered each actual or proposed arms transaction for which payment would be received. The use of proceeds was described in only one paragraph in each memorandum. North's memorandums concluded with the recommendation that Poindexter brief the President to secure approval for the transfer and provided lines on which someone could indicate whether the transfer had been "approved" or "disapproved." North further testified that he did not recall any instruction from Poindexter or anybody else not to write and send such memorandums, adding that "had I been given [such an instruction], I would have followed it." Instead, North created records such as the surviving copies of the April diversion memorandum that called for Presidential briefings and approval.

North assumed without asking Poindexter explicitly that the President knew and approved of the diversion. North had worked under three National Security Advisers. Based on that experience, he concluded that a decision of this magnitude would be taken only with Presidential approval—a view that McFarlane shared.

North said that he continued until November 21, 1986, to assume that the President had approved the diversion. He testified that, on or about that day, he asked Poindexter directly, "does the President know?" He told me [the President] did not." North testified that the President confirmed this lack of knowledge on November 25 when the President told him by telephone that, "I just didn't know." Robert Earl, North's aide, testified that North had told him that the President had said "it is important that I not know." Lt. Cmdr. Coy, the third officemate, who was also present, did not recall any conversation about the President's knowledge. Fawn Hall testified that North told her that the President had "called him an American hero" and said that "he [the President] just didn't know."

## Casey's Knowledge

Discrepancies about Casey's knowledge of the diversion also abound. Poindexter testified that he "purposely" did not discuss the subject with Casey. Poindexter's reasoning was that Casey frequently had to testify before Congress and he did not want to place Casey in a position of having to lie. Poindexter further testified that he had no indication that Casey was aware of the diversion aspect of the arms sales operation.

North, on the other hand, testified that he "had consulted very carefully with Director Casey [about the diversion], and he . . . was very enthusiastic about the whole program." He stated that he had told Casey of the plan to use the proceeds for the Contras before the fact, and that he had reviewed with Casey (probably in February 1986) at least one memo referring to the diversion before sending it "up the line" for Presidential approval.

While still at the NSC, North made inconsistent statements about Casey's knowledge. He told Earl in the spring of 1986 that Casey knew. But on November 23, when questioned by the Attorney General, North omitted Casey from the list of persons privy to the diversion. According to North, this omission occurred after Casey had suggested a "fall guy plan" in which North and, if necessary, Poindexter would take the blame.

Another CIA official, Charles Allen, became aware as early as January or February 1986 of the possibility of a diversion. Allen effectively acted as Ghorbanifar's CIA case officer from their first meeting in January 1986. Allen's notes record that, early in their relationship, Ghorbanifar told him that money could be generated from the arms sales to support the Contras and other activities. Allen found Ghorbanifar's statements so "far-fetched" and "trivial" that, although he recorded them in his notes, he did not report them to his superiors.

Allen remained "very troubled in September that the operation was to spin out of control." On September 9, he met with North following a meeting between North and Poindexter on the Iran initiative. North told Allen that the First Channel into Iran was to be shut down, and that the Second Channel had "flourish[ed] into full bloom."

Allen was surprised by this information. He returned to the CIA "very nonplussed because I couldn't figure out why we would so abruptly shut down the first channel unless we had a very good plan for shutting it down in a way that Ghorbanifar and other creditors of Ghorbanifar would feel assuaged. . . ." Nevertheless, the next day Allen reported this conversation to Casey matter-of-factly and without comment, including a flat, unexplained observation that "[t]o cut Ghorbanifar out, Ollie will have to raise a minimum of $4 million."

On October 1, Allen took his worries to Gates. He told Gates that the Ghorbanifar channel was a "running sore," and that he was concerned that the Iran initiative was "going to be exposed if something isn't done." He also told Gates that "perhaps the money has been diverted to the contras." According to Allen, Gates was "deeply disturbed by that and asked me to brief the Director." When Allen briefed Casey a week later, he found that Roy Furmark—a business associate of Saudi entrepreneur Adnan Khashoggi's and former client of Casey's—had been there before him.

As discussed more fully in Chapter 18, Furmark and Casey met on October 7. Although Furmark knew of Ghorbanifar's speculation about the diversion, it is not clear that he shared this speculation with Casey. Furmark's testimony before the Senate Select Committee on Intelligence is somewhat inconsistent on this point. North testified that Furmark had told Casey in early October about the speculation surrounding the diversion to the Contras.

In any event, according to North, the meeting with Furmark triggered Casey to instruct North "that this whole thing was coming unravelled and that things ought to be 'cleaned up' . . ." In response, North testified that he "started cleaning things up"; he "started shredding documents in earnest after [this] discussion with Director Casey in early October. . . ."

Before Casey suffered a stroke on December 15, 1986, he maintained that he had not known of the diversion prior to the Attorney General's press conference. He died on May 6, 1987.

## HOW MUCH WAS DIVERTED?

Even the amount of arms sales profits that were used, and that were intended to be used, for the Contras is the subject of contradictory testimony. The Committees have concluded that at least $3.8 million of the $16.1 million in arms sales profits were used for Contra assistance. Poindexter testified that he believed the entire surplus was used for that purpose. In contrast, North testified that the surpluses were to be used for a number of other covert projects, and that Secord and his partner, Albert Hakim were entitled to a fair profit.

Secord and Hakim testified that no agreement existed on how much of the money would be used for the Contras: it was within their discretion whether to accept or reject any request for expenditure by North. North and Poindexter were both surprised that the Enterprise still has more than $8 million. Poindexter was repeatedly told by North that Secord was losing money, and he assumed that all of the Enterprise's funds had been spent.

Whatever the amount or expectations, the diversion did occur. Money generated by arms sales authorized by a Presidential Finding for only one covert purpose—the Iranian initiative—was used for a wholly different covert purpose—Contra support. Arms-for-hostages also became arms-for-Contras, a purpose that was not authorized by any Finding and that was proscribed by the Boland Amendment for appropriated funds.

# CHAPTER 16

# Summary:
# The Iran Initiative

It was not a mistake for the President to seek an opening to Iran. Nor was it an error for the President to seek the release of kidnapped American citizens. What was wrong with the Iran initiative was the way in which the Administration tried to achieve these objectives.

The Administration had pledged that the United States would not bargain with terrorists. This Nation would not make concessions in exchange for American hostages, because such concessions could only encourage more kidnapping. Painful as the consequences might be, the Administration had recognized that the United States could not undermine its foreign policy to win the freedom of its captive citizens—for otherwise, the entire Nation would be held hostage.

Similarly, the Administration had recognized that it was not in the Nation's interest to prolong the Persian Gulf War and strengthen the hand of the Ayatollah against Iraq. The Administration had therefore pledged that the United States would not arm either side, but would maintain a policy of strict neutrality, and would urge U.S. allies and friends to do the same.

The Iran initiative broke both of these pledges and violated both of these policies.

It is true, of course, that policies are subject to change. Foreign policy is not immutable. But when policies are thought ripe for change, established processes exist in the U.S. Government for making informed judgments. These processes are not mere formalities. They are intended to draw on the knowledge and expertise of accountable officials, and to produce reasoned determinations. In the Iran initiative, those processes were deliberately bypassed, and deception replaced consultation.

The President undertook the arms initiative in 1985 against the advice of his own Secretaries of State and Defense, without obtaining the views of intelligence community professionals, and without adequate analysis. Secretary of State Shultz warned that the proposed initiative amounted to trading arms for hostages. Secretary of Defense Weinberger warned in 1985 that it violated the law. Both Cabinet officers rejected the notion that the United States could use the leverage of arms sales to open a new relationship with Iran. A draft National Security Decision Directive proposing the new arms policy was dropped. And the Central Intelligence Agency warned that the proposed interlocutor of the new relationship, Manucher Ghorbanifar, was a talented fabricator. There was, in short, no adequate basis for reversing U.S. policy against arms sales to Iran or concessions to terrorists. Yet the plan proceeded.

The manner in which the President made his decision epitomized the larger problem. His decision was at once too casual and too influenced by emotional concern for the hostages. It constituted a major shift in U.S. policy, yet it was not recorded in any writing. Public knowledge of the original decision comes almost entirely from Robert McFarlane, whose recollection has fluctuated. Reasoned analysis was sacrificed for the sake of secrecy and deniability. The President's decision was therefore never fully exposed to the members of the National Security Council itself. Secretary Shultz, for example, argued against the proposed policy in December 1985 and January 1986 at three White House meetings, unaware that the President had signed Findings authorizing the arms sales prior to each of those meetings. Secretary Weinberger believed during 1986 that the United States would ship no more than 500 TOWs unless and until all the hostages were released, unaware that the United States had in fact shipped 1,500 TOWs plus HAWK spare parts to obtain the release of just two hostages.

The results in these circumstances were predictable. Indeed, given the manner in which the Iran initiative was conceived and conducted, there is no mystery in why it failed, only in why it continued, particularly when promise after promise was broken by the Iranian side:

- At least four hostages were to be released in September 1985 after Israel shipped the 504 TOWs. But only one was.
- All of the hostages were to be released in November after Israel shipped the HAWK missiles. But none was.
- The Speaker of the Iranian Parliament, Hofshan Rafsanjani, was to meet McFarlane during his Tehran trip. But Rafsanjani never appeared.
- All of the hostages were to be released when the United States completed the delivery of the HAWK parts in 1986. But only one was.
- The Iranians were to release one hostage and to exert best efforts to release another after the United States shipped 500 more TOWs in October 1986. But only one was released, while the Iranians demanded additional weapons before they made any effort to release a second.

As Secretary Shultz testified, "[o]ur guys, . . . they got taken to the cleaners." Indeed, by the end of the initiative, the Administration had yielded to virtually every demand the Iranians had ever put on the table. Concessions that the Administration was unwilling even to consider in 1985, it made in 1986. No price seemed too high to North and Poindexter, not even promises to help overthrow the Government of Iraq or to pressure Kuwait into releasing the murderous Da'wa terrorists. And in the meantime, three more Americans were kidnapped in Lebanon.

The record affords some explanation of why the Administration persisted—and capitulated—when the Iranians repeatedly reneged: the decisionmakers were moved by different objectives in hopeless conflict with one another. The goals of freedom for the

American hostages and better relations with Iran required that the United States create trust in Tehran. But generating surpluses for the Contras and other secret operations required that the United States overcharge the Iranians. Stinging the Ayatollah may have provided some ironic laughter in the Old Executive Office Building, as North testified, but it was no basis for building an improved relationship with Iran or for gaining release of the hostages. North boasted that, "I lied every time I met the Iranians." But the Iranians North was so willing to deceive were the same people the Administration was depending on to foster a new relationship with Tehran.

With these thoughts in mind, the Committees now examine the record in greater detail for the reasons that the President and his advisers continued the Iran initiative long after the handwriting was on the wall.

## THE ATTORNEY GENERAL'S ADVICE

Attorney General Edwin Meese advised the President that he did not have to notify Congress before selling arms to Iran. The Attorney General based this advice on an opinion of his predecessor, William French Smith, who concluded that the President could export arms pursuant to a Finding, without complying with the Arms Export Control Act. But Attorney General Smith's opinion explicitly stated that the President should notify the Intelligence Committees before the arms were actually exported. Meese took this advice one step further and approved the sales without advance notification.

In taking this aggressive position, the At-torney General, out of concern for secrecy, did not consult with the Office of Legal Counsel in the Justice Department or with any of his aides. He did no research on legislative history, and his advice was not reduced to writing. The Attorney General appears to have done little more than to express his "concurrence with the CIA view."

The sale of arms pursuant to a Presidential Finding without prior notification to the Intelligence Committees or Congress itself was, so far as the Committees can determine, unprecedented. The President was entitled to more careful legal advice from the Attorney General before the President approved the sales. The Committees believe that sound analysis and judgment would have led Attorney General Meese, like his predecessor, to advise the President that the Intelligence Committees had to be notified. Had the President been required to take this step, he may well not have proceeded with the sales, and the President and the country would have been spared serious embarrassment.

The Attorney General served as a member of the NSC by appointment of the President. There is only one reason to have an Attorney General on the NSC: to give the President independent and sound advice. That did not happen in the Iran Affair, and the President was poorly served.

## THE HOSTAGE OBJECTIVE

In his address to the Nation on August 12, 1987, the President stated:

[O]ur original initiative got all tangled up in the sale of arms, and the sale of arms got tangled up with the hostages. . . . I let my preoccupation with the hostages intrude into areas where it didn't belong.

The record supports this candid self-criticism.

Freeing the hostages was a primary objective for the President in the Iran initiative. It was foremost in his mind. Yet the President failed to see that, by pursuing this objective through the sale of arms, the Administration was violating its own basic principles, and putting all the cards in the terrorists' hands. The Administration, in effect, was creating an incentive for the Iranians to continue escalating their demands, and worse, to continue kidnapping Americans.

The President seems to have been vulnerable to the pleas of the hostage families. His aides sought to keep those families from meeting with him. But this quarantine ended in June 1985, when the President held the first of several meetings with the hostage families.

Although the President was also undoubtedly interested in promoting moderation of Iranian policies and opening a new relationship with that regime, his primary focus throughout the venture was on the hostages. Indeed, North told the Attorney General in November 1986 that, with the President, "it always came back to the hostages." And to be sure, from the very outset in the summer of 1985, the NSC staff stressed that the initiative could lead to the release of the hostages.

Perhaps the best expression of the President's concern was his statement at the December 7, 1985, meeting with members of the NSC. There, as recalled by Secretary Shultz, the President brushed aside arguments that the arms sales might violate the Arms Export Control Act with the statement that "the

American people will never forgive me if I fail to get these hostages out over this legal question."

**The Iranians preyed on the President's vulnerability with threats to kill the hostages. In August 1986, the President approved a shipment of HAWK parts after being told the hostages might be killed. There were also domestic political considerations. North wrote in his notebook that the hostages should be released in time for the President's 1986 State of the Union address. Later, he hoped for release by July 4.**

The Committees do not fault the President for his concern about the hostages. It is a testament to the values of this Nation that the leader of the greatest power on Earth would devote so much energy and thought to the fate of six citizens. But when fundamental foreign policy decisions are sacrificed in the hope of freeing six hostages, then the Nation itself becomes the victim. Every American who travels abroad becomes a potential hostage, and U.S. policy can be dictated by hostage-takers.

As the President himself now recognizes, emotion must never be allowed to substitute for judgment in the conduct of U.S. foreign policy. The stakes are simply too great.

## THE POSITION OF ISRAEL

Israel's sponsorship of the Iran initiative, and of Ghorbanifar as an intermediary, carried great weight with the President and his advisers. Israel has taken a strong stand against international terrorism; and Israeli intelligence services are among the most respected in the world. McFarlane turned to

Israel in the spring of 1985 for intelligence on Iran because of dissatisfaction with CIA capabilities.

The Israelis strongly advocated the initiative, viewing it as a joint U.S.-Israel operation, and were willing to give the United States deniability—so long as it did not subject them to criticism by Congress and the Secretary of State was fully informed. McFarlane and Poindexter discussed with the Israelis at various times in 1985 the Administration's view that, since Israel—and not the United States—was selling to Iran, U.S. policy was not being violated.

Moreover, the Israelis made a particularly attractive proposal in January 1986 when Nir told Poindexter that if the hostages were not released after the delivery of another 500 TOWs, Israel would bear that loss and the United States would not have to replenish the Israeli inventory. Even after this "no lose" proposition was rejected in favor of the United States selling to Iran through Secord, Amiram Nir continued to urge the initiative.

Yet, the President was under no illusion that the interests of the United States and Israel were synonymous. As early as June 1985, Secretary Shultz had pointed out to McFarlane that Israel had little to lose by promoting the initiative: it had no policy against arms sales to Iran, and, given the hostility of most of its neighbors, Israel was more willing to gamble on the prospect of changes in the Iranian Government.

No foreign state can dictate the conduct of U.S. foreign policy. Superpowers make their own decisions. And the United States did so in this instance. Nevertheless, Israel's endorsement of the Iran initiative cannot be ignored as a factor in its origin or in its continuation.

## THE CONTRA OBJECTIVE

If Israel had its own interests in promoting the initiative, and if the President was preoccupied with the hostages in pursuing the initiative, North was obsessed with the Contras. From North's first substantive involvement with the arms sales in the fall of 1985, the initiative produced money for the Contras.

After the Enterprise became the selling agent for the CIA in January 1986, North set prices to create a surplus for the Contras. He and Secord used a markup of more than 200 percent. And when the Tehran mission failed, North sought to cheer up McFarlane with the news that the arms sales had at least achieved some benefit—they were subsidizing the Contras.

It is not necessary, however, to rely on inference for the effect of profits on North's recommendations to continue the weapons sales. North testified that when he was beginning to doubt the wisdom of the initiative in January 1986, he found the opportunity to support the Contras from the proceeds of future sales an "attractive incentive" to continue.

North's promotion of the initiative continued to the end, as he drafted memorandums to Poindexter for the President, always recommending that the initiative proceed, warning that the hostages might be killed if it ended, and predicting ultimate success in retrieving the hostages if the United States stayed the course. There is no evidence that North ever saw or understood that gouging the Iranians on behalf of the Contras was at cross purposes with gaining freedom for the hostages. Arms-for-hostages and profits-for-Contra-support were conflicting goals that could not be reconciled.

## THE PROFIT OBJECTIVE

While North sought profits for the Contras (and other covert operations), Albert Hakim sought profits for himself. He made no secret of his personal motive to North or to George Cave of the CIA in promoting the Second Channel as a means of continuing the collapsing initiative.

Above all, Hakim was a businessman. He candidly testified that he saw an opportunity to make a 3 percent piece of the annual $15 billion Iranian market if the Second Channel initiative succeeded. While Hakim saw no conflict between his personal interests and those of the United States, he negotiated the nine-point agreement as if basic principles were commodities open for trade. This unappointed diplomat was willing to bargain away the most fundamental precepts of U.S. foreign policy to open the doors for business with Iran.

The fault, however, does not lie with Hakim. He was left by North to negotiate the agreement; his plan was approved by North and Poindexter, and according to Poindexter, by the President (who was not told that Hakim had negotiated it); and his ulterior purposes were well known.

Arms-for-profit thus entered the list of colliding objectives in the Iran initiative. Privatization of foreign policy had its costs.

* * *

Too many drivers—and never the right ones—steering in too many different directions took the Iran initiative down the road to failure. In the end, there was no improved relationship with Iran, no lessening of its commitment to terrorism, and no fewer American hostages.

The Iran initiative succeeded only in replacing three American hostages with another three, arming Iran with 2,004 TOWs and more than 200 vital spare parts for HAWK missile batteries, improperly generating funds for the Contras and other covert activities (although far less than North believed), producing profits for the Hakim-Secord Enterprise that in fact belonged to the U.S. taxpayers, leading certain NSC and CIA personnel to deceive representatives of their own Government, undermining U.S. credibility in the eyes of the world, damaging relations between the Executive and the Congress, and engulfing the President in one of the worst credibility crises of any Administration in U.S. history.

PART IV

# EXPOSURE
# AND CONCEALMENT

# CHAPTER 17

# Exposure and Concealment: Introduction

The covert operation to support the Contras had been functioning for over a year when, on October 5, 1986, one of the resupply planes was shot down in Nicaragua with Eugene Hasenfus on board—and the secret program began to unravel.

Administration officials denied both publicly and in testimony to Congress that the U.S. Government had any connection to the Hasenfus flight. Nonetheless, investigations were commenced by the FBI and the Customs Service, which, if continued uninterrupted, might have uncovered both the Contra and Iran covert actions and Secord's Swiss bank accounts. North and Poindexter moved promptly to delay and narrow those investigations.

At about the same time, a threat of exposure came from a different quarter. Roy Furmark, a business associate of Saudi financier Adnan Khashoggi and a former client of CIA Director Casey, told Casey that Khashoggi and two Canadian investors had lost $10 million on the Iran arms sales. He warned Casey that the Canadians might sue for return of the $10 million, claiming that the money had been used by the U.S. Government for activity in Central America. Ac-

cording to North, Casey advised him at about this time to destroy documents relating to the covert Contra support operation.

Then, on November 2, 1986, David Jacobsen was released from captivity in Lebanon—the last of the three Americans to be released as part of the Iran initiative. His release was announced and applauded by the White House on November 3, 1986.

On the same day, a Lebanese magazine, Al-Shiraa, reported that the United States had sold arms to Iran, and that Robert McFarlane had visited Tehran. This report soon surfaced in the American press, evoking strong criticism from all quarters. The President was accused of making concessions to terrorists and of violating the law in selling arms to Iran.

The Administration's first response to the disclosures was silence. Encouraged by Poindexter and others on the NSC staff, the President told his advisers that comment should be withheld so as not to jeopardize release of the hostages.

Silence proved infeasible, however, and the President was forced to comment. The President's first public statement was to assert that the press reports of arms sales to

247

Iran had "no foundation." Shortly thereafter, on November 13, 1986, the President conceded publicly that arms had been sold to Iran, but branded as "wildly false" the charge that he had traded arms for hostages.* The President also denied on November 13, 1986 that the sales violated any laws.

A preliminary Justice Department analysis written on or about November 13, 1986 concluded the sales were lawful because they were done pursuant to an Intelligence Finding signed by the President on January 17, 1986. But the writer of the analysis was unaware that the United States had been involved in shipments of U.S. arms by Israel in 1985 *prior* to any Finding.

The President's advisers discussed the legal problems raised by the pre-Finding Israeli shipments on November 18 and 19, 1986, while preparing for the President's press conference scheduled for the evening of November 19. When the President was asked about the pre-Finding shipments at his press conference, he denied that the United States was in any way involved.

In fact, however, the United States had approved the 1985 Israeli shipments, and a CIA proprietary airline had actually carried a November 1985 shipment of HAWK missiles to Iran.

Nonetheless, in the two days following the press conference, North and McFarlane prepared a false chronology, Poindexter and Casey gave misleading statements and testimony, respectively, to Congressional committees, and McFarlane gave a false statement to the Attorney General, denying in each case that the United States knowingly participated in the pre-Finding Israeli shipments. In the afternoon on November 21, 1986, Poindexter destroyed a key document—a Presidential Finding—which would have exposed these statements as false.

Not all Administration officials participated in this effort to rewrite history. Secretary Shultz argued repeatedly for prompt and full disclosure of the facts. He warned the President directly on November 19 and 20 that certain of his subordinates were giving out inaccurate information. Abraham Sofaer, Legal Adviser to the State Department, warned the White House and the Justice Department that a false story was being put forward regarding the November 1985 HAWKs shipment. Provided with this information, the Attorney General sought and received authority from the President to commence an inquiry on November 21.

Shortly after learning of the Attorney General's inquiry, both North and Poindexter destroyed documents. North also altered documents relating to the NSC staff's Contra support operation, and he assured Poindexter that all documents relating to the use of proceeds from the Iran arms sales to support the Contras had been destroyed.

Notwithstanding North's efforts, Justice Department investigators found a memorandum on November 22 that referred to the diversion; and on November 25, the Attorney General and the President made public the fact that arms sales proceeds had been used for the Contras.

The existence of the Enterprise, however, remained a secret until the public hearings of these Committees. North concealed the Enterprise—Secord's companies and Swiss

---

*The President maintains this position today. He stated in a recent interview that the Iran arms initiative "was not trading arms for hostages" (*The New Republic*, 10/26/87, at 10) despite his concession on March 4, 1987 (in response to the Tower Board findings) that "what began as a strategic opening to Iran deteriorated in its implementation into trading arms for hostages."

bank accounts—even while admitting to the diversion. He falsely told the Attorney General on November 23, 1986 that the Iran arms sales proceeds had gone directly from the Israelis into accounts set up by Contra leader Adolfo Calero, and omitted any reference to Secord's accounts in which the funds had actually been placed. The Attorney General repeated this incorrect account of the diversion to the public on November 25.

The disclosures made by the Attorney General on November 25 precipitated the President's request for appointment of an Independent Counsel, the establishment of the Tower Board, an investigation by the Senate Select Committee on Intelligence, and the creation of these Committees; and the secret "off-the-shelf" companies used in both the Iran and Contra covert operations were eventually exposed.

# CHAPTER 18

# October 1986:
# Exposure Threatened

## THE HASENFUS PLANE IS SHOT DOWN

On October 5, 1986, a C-123 aircraft carrying ammunition, uniforms, and medicine for the Contras was shot down over Nicaragua. One crew member, Eugene Hasenfus, survived and was captured by the Sandinistas. Documents on board the airplane connected it to Southern Air Transport (SAT), a former CIA proprietary charter airline based in Miami, Florida.

The U.S. Government denied involvement, but several investigations by Government agencies, as well as the press, commenced shortly thereafter. A CIA Station Chief in Central America, Tomas Castillo, sent a secret message to Robert Dutton, Secord's top aide in the Contra resupply operation, alerting him that the "situation requires we do necessary damage control."

## North Tries to Slow the FBI Investigation of SAT

Within days of the Hasenfus crash, FBI agents began interviewing SAT employees.

They sought to determine whether arms or combatants had been sent from the United States to support insurrection in Nicaragua, in violation of the Neutrality Act. Before the FBI agents could obtain any subpoenas, North called FBI Executive Assistant Director Oliver Revell on October 8 and told him he was concerned about the SAT investigation. North assured Revell that SAT was not involved in illegal activities. North also indicated to Revell that SAT was involved in the arms sales to Iran. North had earlier told Revell about the Iran arms sales in late July 1986 during an Operations Sub Group meeting. North told Revell that he did not know anything about the C-123 that was shot down. North said that SAT was still flying arms shipments to Iran, and those missions would inevitably be disclosed if SAT was investigated.

Revell contacted the Miami FBI office and asked for a written briefing on the investigation, but he did not slow it down. Instead, he obtained authority from Deputy Assistant Attorney General Mark Richard to begin an official investigation on October 10, 1986.

## North Tries to Slow the Customs Investigation of SAT

The U.S. Customs Service also began an investigation after the crash. Upon tracing the purchase of the C-123 to SAT, Customs agents served a broad administrative subpoena on SAT. A full-scale investigation would have revealed payments for both the Iran flights and for arms shipments to the Contras from the Enterprise's Lake Resources and Hyde Park Square accounts in Switzerland. In fact, during the May 1986 Tehran mission, the SAT crew stopped in a European country on their return flight, loaded arms, and flew them to a base in Central America for the Contra resupply operation. One wire transfer from Hyde Park Square paid for both missions.

On October 9, 1986, North called U.S. Customs Assistant Commissioner for Enforcement William Rosenblatt and said he was concerned about the SAT subpoena. North told Rosenblatt that the SAT people were "good guys" who had done nothing illegal. North denied that the SAT airplane contained arms when it left the United States. Relying on North's assurances, Rosenblatt took steps to narrow the focus of the investigation to the airplane itself, and whether arms or ammunition were being exported without a license.

In late October, Poindexter called the Attorney General and asked for delays in Customs and FBI investigations of Southern Air Transport. The Justice Department asked William Webster, FBI Director, to delay the inquiry 10 days. Meanwhile, Democratic House Judiciary Committee members asked the Attorney General to appoint an independent counsel to investigate North, Poindexter, Casey, and others. The matter was referred to the Justice Department's Criminal Division.

## FURMARK VISITS THE CIA: TALK OF "DIVERSION"

While the investigations precipitated by the Hasenfus downing threatened to expose the covert Contra support operation, another event in October 1986 threatened to expose the diversion: Roy Furmark, a business associate of Adnan Khashoggi warned the CIA that, unless certain investors in the Iran arms sales were repaid, they would publicly disclose what they knew of the arms sales and the use of arms sales proceeds for the Contras.

Furmark—who was also a former law client of Director Casey—met with Casey, at Khashoggi's request, on October 7 in Casey's office. Furmark said that Khashoggi and two Canadian investors had supplied financing for the Iran arms sales. They claimed to have lost their $10 million advance when the United States overcharged and then abandoned the First Iranian Channel in favor of dealing with the so-called Second Channel. Khashoggi wanted Furmark to see if Casey could get the U.S. Government to make good on this loan.

At their October 7 meeting, Furmark informed Casey of Khashoggi's role, discussed the financial problems that had arisen, and said that Khashoggi was under pressure from the two Canadians who had participated in the $10 million financing. Furmark warned Casey that Manucher Ghorbanifar—the initial go-between for the

251

United States with the Iranians—was also upset and was threatening to tell members of the Senate Select Committee on Intelligence (SSCI) about the arms sales. When Casey suggested that the transaction sounded like an Israeli arrangement, Furmark told Casey that North was directing the deal.

Charles Allen of the CIA had heard from North in early September that the First Channel was being shut down and that the Second Channel had "flourished into full bloom." Allen was disturbed by this news, "because I couldn't figure out why we would so abruptly shut down the first channel unless we had a very good plan for shutting it down in a way that Ghorbanifar and these creditors of Ghorbanifar would feel assuaged." Allen shared his concerns with Robert Gates of the CIA on October 1. Gates, too, was disturbed and asked Allen to brief the CIA Director.

Allen and Gates arrived in Casey's office together on October 7, after Furmark had departed. Allen told Casey of his misgivings. Casey rejoined that he had just met with Furmark, who had described Khashoggi's financial problems with other investors whom Allen understood to be Canadian. Casey did not mention that funds might have been diverted to the Contras. gone to the Contras; rather, it recorded Ghorbanifar as stating that, "some of . . . [the] profit was redistributed to other projects of the US and of Israel."

Gates and Casey met with Poindexter the following day, October 15. Poindexter read Allen's memorandum. Although Poindexter acknowledged in his testimony that the memorandum contained the news that Ghorbanifar or his financiers were saying that their money went to Central America, and although Poindexter and Casey met alone, Poindexter testified that he and Casey did not discuss the diversion. Casey simply recommended, according to Poindexter, that Poindexter seek the advice of White House Counsel with respect to disclosure of the initiative. Poindexter, however, did nothing because he did not trust the White House Counsel.

After meeting with Poindexter, Gates and Casey directed Allen to meet with Furmark the next day, October 16. Allen met Furmark, and sent a memorandum of the meeting to Casey. Allen's memorandum recited Furmark's account of the origins of the Iran arms transactions and Ghorbanifar's current financial condition. Furmark recommended that the United States consider yet another arms transaction to maintain credibility with the Iranians and to provide Ghorbanifar with enough capital to make a partial repayment to Khashoggi's creditors. As with Allen's October 14 memorandum, this memorandum contained no specific reference to a diversion of funds to the Contras. According to Allen, he wished to protect himself from any indiscriminate use of the memorandum.

North's notebooks show that Furmark's recommendation to generate funds to pay Khashoggi's creditors received serious consideration. North wrote of a conversation with Israeli official Amiram Nir on October 22: "Best way to recoup funds to pay off Furmark, et al is to overcharge on subsequent deliveries."

On October 22, Charles Allen, George Cave, and Roy Furmark met in New York. In the course of that meeting, Furmark raised, for the first time with Allen, the possibility that funds used to finance the arms sales might have been diverted to the Contras.

Allen and Furmark met once more on November 6. By this time the feared publicity of the Iran initiative had occurred. Allen prepared a memorandum for Casey the following day, which reported that the Canadian investors—having been deprived of the threat of exposing the initiative—were now threatening a lawsuit over their failure to be paid. The memorandum also showed that Furmark again alerted Allen to the remaining trump card in the investors' deck: linking the overcharges on the HAWK spare parts to the diversion. Furmark also told Allen of his discovery that Secord was involved in both the arms sales and the Contra resupply operation.

Allen reported to Casey that Furmark was most interested in prompting another arms deal so that Ghorbanifar could recoup his money, and that unhappy investors could make some "nasty allegations against the US Government and key officials" if the matter went unresolved. On the latter point, however, Allen added reassuringly that "much of what they know is speculation and cannot be proven."

At Furmark's request, Casey met with him again on November 24 at CIA headquarters. Furmark and Casey reviewed the finances of the Iran arms transactions beginning in February 1986. This review established that the transactions had resulted in excess funds; Casey told Furmark that he did not know where that money had gone.

In Furmark's presence, Casey unsuccessfully tried to reach the President's Chief of Staff, Donald Regan. He then called North and said "there's a guy here says you owe him $10 million. . . ." North reportedly responded: "[T]ell the man that the Iranians or the Israelis owe them the money."

## THE TRAVELERS CHECK LEDGER

As set out in Chapter 2, North received from Contra leader Adolpho Calero a large number of travelers checks for distribution to Contra leaders and for a variety of other programs. North asserted that he maintained "meticulous records" of the receipt and disbursement of these checks in a ledger provided by Casey. Fawn Hall and Robert Owen testified to seeing North make entries in such a ledger.

North destroyed this ledger, according to his testimony, at the direction of Casey to protect sensitive names and information. North told the Committees that Casey had instructed him sometime between October 13 and November 4 to " 'get rid of that book because the book has in it the names of everybody, the addresses of everybody. Just get rid of it and clean things up.' "

As a result of this destruction, no written record exists to verify North's testimony that checks he cashed for his personal use actually were reimbursements for his out-of-pocket expenses on behalf of the Contras.

## THE FALL GUY PLAN

Throughout the events of the Iran-Contra Affair, deception was viewed as a necessary component. At the same time, according to North's testimony, Casey recognized the need for an ultimate coverup in the event of public disclosure.*

---

*As noted earlier, North's testimony attributing knowledge and statements to Casey after Casey's death should be viewed with caution, particularly insofar as such testimony, albeit under oath, tends to exculpate North.

As far back as the early spring of 1984, North said he and Director Casey had discussed a "fall guy plan." Their discussion took place in the context of Congress' impending cutoff of U.S. aid for the Contras (the Boland Amendment). According to North, when "we eventually decided to pursue availing ourselves of offers from foreign governments [to fund the Contras], it was seen that there would need to be someone who could . . . take the fall" in the event of public disclosure. The idea was to provide North's superiors with "plausible deniability"—although in this instance, that term meant avoiding accountability to the U.S. Government rather than avoiding disclosure to U.S. adversaries.

As North's operational role expanded to the Iran arms sales and the diversion of proceeds derived therefrom, he testified, he volunteered to be the "fall guy" for both the Contra support and the arms sales operations. In his words, "I'm not sure Director Casey ever said, 'It has to be you, Ollie.' It was probably Ollie saying, 'Well, when that [disclosure] happens, it will be me.'"

North made no secret among his colleagues that he was to be a "scapegoat" or "fall guy" if the Iran or Contra support activities became public. He made this comment to at least Poindexter, Robert Earl (one of North's aides), and Owen.

Disclosure of the arms sales in early November 1986 triggered discussions about implementing the fall guy plan. According to North, shortly after the initial November disclosures, Casey told him that he [North] might not be "big enough" to be the "fall guy." Casey indicated that "it's probably going to go higher," and he suggested that "Poindexter might have to be a fall guy." Although North did not recall a conversation with Poindexter about this specific aspect of the plan for "plausible deniability," he did recall that he and Poindexter discussed in early November the likelihood that both of them would have to bear the blame.

North testified that he previously had discussed both the fact and necessity of the "fall guy plan" with Poindexter and McFarlane (as well as with Casey), and that he did not recall any discussion with anybody about the legal propriety of this plan. Poindexter testified, however, that he "was not a party to any plan to make Colonel North or to make me, for that matter, a scapegoat." He nevertheless admitted that "[periodically] Ollie would indicate that he was 'willing to take the rap.'" McFarlane flatly denied that any "fall guy plan" ever existed.

North testified that, but for the criminal investigation of the Iran-Contra Affair, he was prepared to go through with the "plan, resign in disgrace, and take the heat for the President." (There is no evidence that the President was aware of or condoned the "fall guy" plan.) Nevertheless, when an Independent Counsel was appointed and North was the only person specifically named in the order of investigation, North, who by then had retained counsel, changed his mind and decided to protect himself.* North testified that he did not tell Casey or Poindexter of this change in attitude.

*North testified that, "I never in my wildest dreams or nightmares envisioned that we would end up with criminal charges."

# CHAPTER 19

# November 1986: Concealment

## THE ADMINISTRATION'S INITIAL RESPONSE TO THE ARMS SALES DISCLOSURES

The reports of U.S. arms sales to Iran in early November 1986 generated conflict within the Government. Some officials, including Members of Congress and the Secretary of State, demanded prompt and full disclosure. Several individuals on the inside of the Administration, however, insisted on maintaining tight control of the information. The President, denying any arms-for-hostages trade, wanted to say no more than that. Members of the National Security Council (NSC) staff and the Director of Central Intelligence knew that the report from Beirut was only the tip of the iceberg. Accordingly, their first move was to exploit the President's desire to protect the hostages through silence as a way of concealing the truth.

The conflict manifested itself almost at once in an exchange between Secretary of State George Shultz and National Security Adviser John Poindexter shortly after the news broke.

## THE SHULTZ/POINDEXTER CABLES

The Secretary of State was largely without knowledge concerning the Iran initiative. Among other things, Secretary Shultz testified that he did not know prior to November 1986 that the United States had made direct sales of arms to Iran during 1986 or that the President had signed a Finding authorizing such sales. He did know, after the fact, that McFarlane had travelled to Tehran in May, but not that the McFarlane mission had carried weapons with it, or that additional weapons had been delivered thereafter. Moreover, so far as the Secretary of State was advised, the failed McFarlane mission had signaled an end to the Administration's effort to find an opening to Iran.

Thus, the report in Al-Shiraa was news to the Secretary of State. He was then in Europe and found himself peppered with questions from the press about the revelations in Beirut. The Secretary reported these questions in a cable to Poindexter, informing Poindexter that "[t]he big story the press is after is to establish that the U.S. violated its own policy by cutting a big secret arms deal with

255

Iran in order to get our hostages released." Secretary Shultz further informed Poindexter that, "[i]n accordance with the agreed guidance," he had refused to answer any related questions, stating that all such inquiries should be directed to the White House.

The Secretary went on to say that he had been "racking my brains all day to figure out a way to help turn this situation in the best possible direction." To this end, Secretary Shultz recommended that "the best way to proceed is to give the key facts to the public." In addition, apparently based on the arms shipment reported by Al-Shiraa, the Secretary suggested that "[w]e could make clear that this was a special, one-time operation based on humanitarian grounds and decided by the President within his Constitutional responsibility to act for the service of the national interest—and that our policies toward terrorism and toward the Iran/Iraq war stand."

Poindexter, who knew the true facts, rejected Secretary Shultz's proposal. In a return cable Poindexter stated, "I do not believe that now is the time to give the facts to the public," although he asserted that "when we do lay out the facts that it will be well received since it is a good story." Poindexter advised Secretary Shultz that he had spoken that day with the Vice President, the Secretary of Defense, and the Director Casey, and that they all agreed that no statement should be made.

## THE PUBLIC DENIALS CONTINUE

The issue of public comment on the arms sales was discussed during Poindexter's morning meetings with the President on No-

vember 6 and 7. The President agreed that "no comment" was the best policy given his hope, bolstered by Poindexter, that additional hostages would yet be freed. According to notes of the briefings taken by Rodney McDaniel of the NSC staff, the President said that "[n]o way can comment without further damage to chances of getting hostages out."

## THE NOVEMBER 10 MEETING AT THE WHITE HOUSE

On November 10, the President convened a meeting at the White House to establish guidelines for that statement. The Vice President, Secretary Shultz, Secretary Weinberger, Attorney General Meese, Casey, Regan, Poindexter and Alton Keel, then Deputy National Security Adviser attended. The President said there was a need for a public statement, but he instructed his advisers to "stay away from detail."

Keel and Regan made notes during the November 10 meeting; Secretary Weinberger wrote a subsequent memorandum; and Secretary Shultz dictated his recollections of the meeting to his Executive Assistant, Charles Hill. These records contain no material differences. They all show that the meeting was marked by a number of misleading statements and significant omissions by Poindexter as he purported to lay out the facts of the Iran initiative.

For example:

- Poindexter discussed only the January 17, 1986, Finding, omitting any mention of the earlier Finding signed by the President on December 5, 1985, or of the January 6, 1986, superseded Finding.

256

- Poindexter claimed, falsely, that the Iran initiative had begun when the United States stumbled upon an Israeli arms warehouse in Europe while attempting to learn whether the Israelis were shipping arms to Iran.
- Poindexter asserted that the first 500 TOW missiles were shipped from Israel to Iran in August and September 1985, without U.S. permission, even though the Administration had approved this shipment.
- Poindexter stated that the total number of TOW missiles sold to Iran during the initiative was 1,000, when the actual number was 2,004.
- Poindexter indicated that the last 500 TOWs sent in October 1986, had been shipped by Israel rather than the United States. But in fact, Israel had acted as the NSC staff's request because the U.S. shipment was delayed, and the United States had replenished the Israeli TOWs within days after the shipment.

In other words, as late as November 10, and in the presence of the President and senior Cabinet officers, Poindexter either was confused or purposely dissembled. Despite the fact that the President had opened the meeting by declaring the need for a public statement, Poindexter continued to argue that "no statement [is] needed, news has peaked, no hearings until Jan[uary], so [we] should not say anything."

The meeting concluded as it began, when, according to Regan's notes, the President had outlined the type of statement he wanted:

We have not dealt directly w[ith] terrorists, no bargaining, no ransom. Some things we can't discuss because of long-term consideration of

people w[ith] whom we have been talking about the future of Iran.

## PHASE 2 OF THE ADMINISTRATION RESPONSE: LIMITED DISCLOSURE

### Preparing for the President's Address to the Nation

After November 10, the White House began preparing a formal statement for the President to deliver personally to the Nation. This statement was discussed at the daily national security briefing between Poindexter and the President, both of whom expressed continued hope that more hostages would be released that coming weekend. They agreed that the President's upcoming statement would focus on the legality of the arms initiative and emphasize that the arms sales did not constitute ransom.

On the same day, McFarlane sent a PROF message to Poindexter in which he stated that "the only way—the only way—the Administration can expect to come out of this with any element of credibility is for there to be some evidence that it was worth it to try to engage moderates in Iran." This required, according to McFarlane, a statement from Iran. He recommended that the United States concentrate all efforts on convincing the Iranians to change their rhetoric immediately. McFarlane told Poindexter that he had "drafted up some words and left them with Ollie to be sent to Iran."

McFarlane also produced and sent to Poindexter a draft statement for the President, focusing on the effort to open a political dialogue with Iranian moderates. Poindexter wrote back that he had reviewed the draft with North and that they had agreed there was a need to show the final product to George Cave of the CIA in order to "get an 'Iranian reaction' on it."

On November 12, the day before the President was to address the Nation, he presided over a national security briefing of Congressional leaders on the arms sales. The executive branch attendees included the Vice President, Secretary Shultz, Secretary Weinberger, Attorney General Meese, Casey, Regan, Poindexter, and appropriate staff. Senate Leaders Robert Dole and Robert Byrd and House Majority Leader Jim Wright and Representative Dick Cheney represented Congress. The President opened the meeting by stating that no laws were broken, no ransom paid for hostages, and no officials or agencies within the U.S. Government bypassed.

At the morning security briefing the next day, November 13, there was discussion of the elements of the President's upcoming statement, including that the arms shipments had not altered the balance in the Iran-Iraq war; that the arms sold were defensive in nature; and that there would be no additional shipments. There was discussion, too, of whether the total arms shipped to Iran would have fit in one 747 or C-5 cargo plane. The President also stated, according to notes of the meeting, that the Administration "should have gone public sooner."

## The President Addresses the Nation

The President addressed the Nation on November 13. He disclosed that the diplomatic initiative with Iran had been underway for some 18 months. The purposes of this initiative, he said, were (1) to forge a new relationship with Iran, (2) to bring an honorable end to the Iran-Iraq war, (3) to eliminate state-sponsored terrorism, and (4) as part of the new relationship, to attain the safe return of the American hostages held in Lebanon.

The President stated that he had authorized "the transfer of small amounts of defensive weapons and spare parts. . . . These modest deliveries, taken together, could easily fit into a single cargo plane." He elaborated that the weapons shipped "could not, taken together, affect the outcome of the 6-year war between Iran and Iraq nor could they affect in any way the military balance between the two countries." He asserted that since the initiative had commenced, there had been no evidence of Iranian complicity in acts of terrorism against the United States. The President also emphasized that the arms initiative was conducted in full compliance with the law, and that all appropriate Cabinet officers "were fully consulted." He attacked "the wildly speculative false stories about arms for hostages and alleged ransom payments." The President concluded by stating that "[w]e did not—repeat—did not trade weapons or anything else for hostages nor will we."

The President thus committed himself categorically to the proposition that there had been no trade of arms for the hostages and no violations of law. Certain members of the NSC staff and of the CIA, in turn, committed themselves to creating a version of the facts for internal and public consumption that would sustain this proposition.

## EVENTS BETWEEN NOVEMBER 13 AND THE NOVEMBER 19 NEWS CONFERENCE

The Secretary of State testified that, throughout the first weeks of November after the Beirut report, he believed that the President was being misled and misinformed by his staff, particularly Poindexter. Secretary Shultz said he repeatedly argued to the President and Poindexter that nobody looking at the record would credit the assertion that the initiative did not involve arms-for-hostages, and that it was critical there be no tinkering with the facts. It was, the Secretary said, a "battle royal" to get out the truth.

Secretary Shultz also pressed for a definitive statement that the United States would not under any circumstances sell any more arms to Iran. He met with the President on November 14 to urge that he make precisely that statement, and he repeated this recommendation in a draft paper delivered to Regan on November 15. But the statement was not made, nor was Secretary Shultz assured that the arms shipments would be halted. Consequently, when Secretary Shultz appeared on *Face The Nation* on November 16 and expressed the view that the United States should not sell additional weapons to Iran, he felt constrained to answer in response to a question that he, the Secretary of State, did not have authority to speak for the Administration on this point.

The next day the White House stated definitively that there would be no further arms sales to Iran. The White House also reaffirmed that the Secretary of State spoke for the Administration on matters of foreign policy.

Meanwhile, at the Attorney General's request, Charles J. Cooper, Assistant Attorney General for the Office of Legal Counsel, had been looking into the legal issues surrounding the Iranian arms sales. On November 12, 1986, Cooper sent a legal memorandum to the Attorney General that concluded, among other things, that so long as there was a Finding pursuant to the Hughes-Ryan Amendment, the arms sales did not violate the law. In a meeting with Poindexter and Thompson that same day, Cooper had been shown only the January 17 Finding and had been left with the impression that this Finding predated any arms shipments to Iran.

On November 17, Cooper received a draft chronology of events in the Iran initiative prepared by the NSC staff. In reviewing this chronology, Cooper learned for the first time that arms had been transferred by Israel to Iran prior to the January 17, 1986, Finding. Cooper informed the Attorney General, who said that he, too, had been unaware of any arms shipped to Iran prior to the January Finding.

[On] November 18, Poindexter and Casey spoke by secure telephone. A transcript of their conversation indicates that they discussed meeting to prepare for their Congressional briefings and for Casey's scheduled November 21 testimony on Capitol Hill. Poindexter told Casey that the NSC staff had been "putting together all the chronologies and all the facts that we can lay our hands on. . . ." With respect to the proposed preparation meeting, Casey asked whether Poindexter intended to have many people present, specifically mentioning "State" and "Defense." Poindexter responded, "I'd like to spend some time just the two of us. . . . Ed Meese indicated . . . he should want to be helpful and so he would like to be in at least one of the meetings."

## THE PRESIDENT'S NOVEMBER 19 NEWS CONFERENCE

On November 19, the President vouched for facts that were wrong. In his nationally televised news conference, the President made the following assertions—all of which were incorrect:

- The President denied any involvement by a third country in the arms sales. When asked if he could explain the Israeli role, he replied, "No, because we, as I say, have had nothing to do with other countries or their shipment of arms or doing what they're doing."
- When asked whether he was saying that "the only shipments with which we were involved were the one or two that followed your January 17 Finding and that . . . there were no other shipments which the United States condoned," the President responded, "That's right. I'm saying nothing, but the missiles we sold. . . ."
- The President asserted that 1,000 TOW missiles were transferred (in fact, 2,004 were transferred), and that the 1,000 transferred TOWs "didn't add to any offensive power on the part of Iran."
- The President stated that "everything that we sold [Iran] could be put in one cargo plane, and there would be plenty of room left over."

In addition, the President repeated his assertion that the United States had not traded arms for hostages, relying on the distinction that the Iranian Government itself did not hold the hostages.

Commenting on the numerous errors at the press conference, Regan testified that Poindexter and his staff had spun so many stories in preparing the President that "this sort of confused the Presidential mind as to what he could say and couldn't say and what he should say and shouldn't say."

The Secretary of State, who had watched the press conference, sought an immediate meeting with the President.

## THE PRESIDENT AND SECRETARY OF STATE MEET ON NOVEMBER 20

When he asked the President for a meeting, Secretary Shultz said that he could demonstrate that a number of facts had been misstated at the press conference. In Secretary Shultz's view, the President's skillfulness as a communicator was being exploited by the NSC staff for its own purposes—to spread inaccurate information.

The Secretary and the President met on November 20. Donald Regan was also there. It was, Secretary Shultz testified, a "long, tough discussion. Not the kind of discussion I ever thought I would have with the President of the United States."

According to Secretary Shultz, he reviewed with the President the factual errors at the press conference. The President "corroborated" the facts concerning his approval of various arms shipments—including the November 1985 HAWK shipment. The President said, however, that "what he expected to have carried out was an effort to get an opening of a different kind to Iran and the arms and the hostages were ancillary to that,

that was not his objective." Shultz replied, "Well I recognize that, Mr. President, and that is a good objective, but that isn't the way it worked."

The Secretary also asserted that the President was being given wrong information, including "information that suggested that Iran was no longer practicing terrorism." He testified that his message overall to the President was: "You have got to look at these facts."

## THE NSC STAFF'S CHRONOLOGIES

Information was in fact being prepared by the NSC staff in the form of "chronologies," documents setting forth key events relating to the Iran initiative in chronological order. The NSC staff had begun preparing a chronology shortly after the disclosure of the Iran arms sales. The chronology started out as a one- or two-page outline. As time passed, however, the chronology was transformed into a 17-page single-spaced document containing background information and rationales for the various events and decisions.

Although a number of persons worked on the NSC staff chronologies, not all participated in falsifying the facts. That was the province of North, McFarlane, and Poindexter. North testified that the three had purposefully misrepresented significant events in the chronologies.

The most glaring misrepresentations concerned the Israeli shipments made before the President's January 1986, Finding—the August–September 1985 shipments of 504 TOW missiles and the November 1985, shipment of 18 HAWK missiles from Israel to Iran. The initial versions of the chronology,

prepared by North on November 7 included fairly accurate references to those shipments. McFarlane then sent a PROF message to Poindexter on November 7 suggesting that "[i]t might be useful to review what the truth is." But McFarlane's version was not the "truth":

- He asserted that the August–September TOW shipments occurred when the Israelis "went ahead on their own" after McFarlane had disapproved; and
- He made no mention at all of the November 1985 HAWK shipment.

On November 20, North and others turned to the proposed testimony that Casey was to give Congressional Intelligence Committees the next day. They faced the problem that a CIA proprietary airline had actually carried the HAWK missiles to Iran in November 1985, but the President had denied U.S. involvement in that weapons shipment at his press conference the day before. Certain members of the NSC staff developed what Regan later termed a "cover story": that the U.S. Government had been told by the Israelis that the November 1985 shipment carried by the proprietary was "oil drilling equipment," not arms.

Following the November 20 meeting to prepare Casey's testimony, and the subsequent objections to the proposed Casey testimony raised by the State Department, the cover story was amended—in what is believed to be the last version of the chronology—to delete all references to oil drilling equipment. The U.S. authorization of the November 1985 shipment, however, was still denied.

The fictional accounts in the chronologies were not limited to the 1985 shipments. For example, the chronologies omitted the President's December 1985 Finding (which retroactively "authorized" the November shipment that the United States had supposedly objected to); affirmatively misrepresented that there had been consultation with "all appropriate" or "relevant" Cabinet officers during the initiative; and baldly asserted that all arms sales were "within the limits of established policy and in compliance with all U.S. law."

All of this was not the result of any memory lapse. The consequences of this exercise in falsifying the facts were severe. As North testified, by creating an erroneous version of the facts in the chronologies, those responsible were "committing the President of the United States to a false story."

On November 20 and 21, Poindexter and Casey would take further steps in the same direction.

## CASEY AND POINDEXTER PREPARE FOR CONGRESS

On November 21, Casey was scheduled to testify before the House and Senate Intelligence Committees, and Poindexter was to brief delegations of the same Committees. On November 20, a meeting was held in Poindexter's office to review a CIA draft of Casey's proposed testimony and coordinate it with Poindexter's upcoming briefing. In attendance were Casey, Attorney General Meese, Poindexter, North, Cooper, Thompson, and Robert Gates of the CIA. The CIA brought a proposed insert dealing with the November 1985 HAWK shipment. It said that the CIA had been told the shipment was oil drilling equipment. During discussion of the insert, North suggested changing it to say that "no one in the U.S. Government" knew at the time that the November 1985 shipment contained arms. According to Cooper, North also stated at the meeting that the United States had to force Iran to return the 18 HAWKs that Israel had delivered in November, after learning a few months after-the-fact that arms had been shipped. Both Meese and North made handwritten notes of North's points on the draft insert. North's version was accepted.

The meeting lasted approximately 2 hours. Attorney General Meese had to leave early to make a speech that evening at West Point. After the meeting ended, Cooper was asked to come to White House Counsel Wallison's office. He went there with NSC general counsel Thompson. Wallison, Counsel to the President, strenuously objected to not having been included in the just-concluded meeting.

During this session in Wallison's office, State Department Legal Adviser Abraham Sofaer telephoned Wallison, and indicated that there was a problem with Casey's proposed testimony. At Cooper's suggestion, Wallison returned Sofaer's call on a secure line. Sofaer advised Wallison that Secretary Shultz recalled a conversation with McFarlane in November 1985, in which McFarlane made specific reference to the shipment of HAWK missiles from Israel to Iran. Sofaer testified that he had also spoken with Deputy Attorney General Arnold Burns earlier in the day to apprise him of the discrepancy between Casey's draft testimony and Secretary Shultz's recollection. Burns told Sofaer that Attorney General Meese had been advised of this problem, and was aware of facts that would explain everything.

Wallison advised Cooper and Thompson of Sofaer's report. Cooper then asked

Thompson to contact North and McFarlane to get the facts straight. Cooper reminded Thompson of North's statement at the meeting earlier in the day that no one in the U.S. Government knew that the November 1985 shipment contained arms. Thompson agreed to contact North and McFarlane.

Cooper then returned to his office, spoke by telephone to Sofaer, and asked if Secretary Shultz was certain of his November 1985 conversation with McFarlane. Sofaer replied that the State Department had a contemporaneous note written by Secretary Shultz's Executive Assistant, Charles Hill, of a conversation between McFarlane and Shultz on November 18, 1985, which contained the word "HAWKS." Sofaer told Cooper that if Casey's testimony were given in its current form, "he [Sofaer] would leave the Government," to which Cooper replied, "We may all have to."

Cooper then telephoned Thompson, who said that North and McFarlane each stuck by his earlier story, that they had no contemporaneous knowledge that arms were shipped to Iran in November 1985. Cooper did not know who was right or wrong. Moreover, Sofaer told Cooper that if Casey testified that no one in the U.S. Government knew of the weapons shipment, Undersecretary Armacost would have to testify otherwise.

Cooper then placed a secure call to Attorney General Meese at West Point, and the two agreed that the problem language should be deleted from Casey's proposed testimony. Attorney General Meese agreed also with Cooper's suggestion that he return immediately to Washington and take responsibility for "getting his arms around this. . . ."

Cooper next spoke directly to Poindexter (who already had heard from Thompson), and Poindexter agreed that they would have to refrain from making the incorrect statement. Poindexter said he had attempted to discuss the issue with Casey, but that Casey was half-asleep when Poindexter called. Accordingly, Cooper called CIA General Counsel David Doherty to advise him that the problem statement should be deleted. Doherty told Cooper that he already had changed Casey's testimony in that regard.

In his public testimony, North conceded that the oil drilling equipment cover story agreed to at the meeting on November 20, 1986, was false. He played down his role in preparing Casey's testimony, however, and claimed that he acted promptly in a later private meeting with Casey to correct it. He testified that he corrected the proposed testimony even though "there are a lot of heroes walking around that have claimed credit" for causing the correction.

## POINDEXTER, CASEY, AND THE INTELLIGENCE COMMITTEES: NOVEMBER 21

November 21 was the day that Casey and Poindexter appeared before the Intelligence Committees of Congress—the event for which they had attempted to coordinate their statements on November 20. Their efforts continued on Friday morning, November 21, beset by the fact that their plan to present a well-orchestrated "cover story" about the November 1985 HAWK shipment had broken down.

At approximately 8:00 A.M., Cooper arrived at the CIA to ensure that the disputed language regarding the November HAWK shipment had been deleted from Casey's

Congressional testimony. Cooper met with Casey. Casey accepted the revisions without comment. After the meeting, CIA Associate General Counsel Jameson whispered to Cooper that during the November 1985 shipment, one of the pilots had radioed to the ground that the cargo was weapons.

Poindexter was the first to brief members of the House and Senate Intelligence Committees. He related the cover story, not the actual facts. According to the memorandums of that meeting, Poindexter maintained that:

- The United States only learned of the August-September 1985 TOW shipments after the fact, whereupon the President expressed both his displeasure at the arms transfer and his appreciation for the subsequent release of hostage Benjamin Weir.
- The United States did not learn until January 1986 that Israel had transferred 18 HAWK missiles to Iran in November 1985, and the United States persuaded the Iranians to return the missiles to Israel in February 1986.
- He (Poindexter) had learned only the day before that there may have been prior U.S. knowledge concerning the November 1985 shipment.
- Finally, Poindexter promised the Senate Intelligence Committee that he would check into the facts and report back.

Casey testified next as part of a panel including Undersecretary of State Armacost and Assistant Secretary of Defense Armitage. In his opening statement, Casey testified that the CIA was asked in November 1985 to recommend a proprietary to transport "bulky cargo." The crew was told, he said, that the cargo consisted of spare parts for the

oil drilling fields in Tehran. The phrase "no one in the U.S. Government found out that our airline had landed HAWK missiles into Iran until mid-January" had been deleted from his opening statement. But Casey gave no indication that the CIA and NSC staff knew that the shipment was arms, not oil drilling equipment.

Under questioning by Senate Committee Members, Casey, like Poindexter, reverted to the cover story:

SENATOR LEAHY: . . . On November 25th a plane owned by a CIA proprietary . . . delivered 18 HAWK missiles from Israel to Iran. I discussed this at some length with Admiral Poindexter this morning. You referred to it here. The Admiral did not have many details on it. I think he said that he learned of this only yesterday, this shipment by a CIA proprietary of these HAWK missiles. Now, did the CIA know what was on that aircraft, the November 25th '85 aircraft?

MR. CASEY: There is some question about that. I was told yesterday the CIA didn't know it until later on.

SENATOR LEAHY: Did not know until later on?

MR. CASEY: Did not know until later on. Did not know until the Iranians told them some time in January by way of complaining about the inadequacy of whatever was delivered.

SENATOR LEAHY: But my concern is that the NSC says now that they didn't know what was going on and that it just found out that the CIA sent that flight over, and they are trying to figure out why nobody knew what was on it, and now the CIA says well, we did this because the NSC requested it, and we didn't know exactly what they wanted. Do you understand why somebody raised the questions wondering whether there was just plausible deniability being set up here.

MR. CASEY: Hadn't thought about it. I hadn't thought about it.

SENATOR LEAHY: The question I ask, and I would hope that the Agency will give me a very full, clear, specific answer, is did they know at the time, and if they didn't know at the time, why not?

MR. CASEY: Well, I have inquired into that myself, and have been told, and as far as I can find out, the Agency did not know what it was handling at the time. Now, I am still going to inquire further into that."

# CHAPTER 20

# November 1986: The Attorney General's Inquiry

## THE ATTORNEY GENERAL'S INQUIRY IS LAUNCHED

When Attorney General Edwin Meese returned to Washington on the morning of November 21, he immediately convened his top advisers to discuss the Administration's conflicting versions of what had actually happened in November 1985. Present were Deputy Attorney General Arnold Burns, John Richardson (the Attorney General's Chief of Staff), William Bradford Reynolds (Assistant Attorney General for the Civil Rights Division), and Charles Cooper (Assistant Attorney General for the Office of Legal Counsel). Cooper briefed the group on the discrepancies between the proposed Casey testimony and the facts as recalled by others in the Administration. The Attorney General decided to propose to the President that he be commissioned to gather the facts so that the Administration would be speaking with one voice.

At 9:22 A.M., the Attorney General called Poindexter on a secure telephone and told him to arrange a meeting among themselves, the President, and Donald Regan. According to Regan, Attorney General Meese met

with him before they went to see the President on the morning of November 21. Attorney General Meese told Regan he was having trouble getting the facts in one place, and that a full investigation should be made.

At approximately 11:30 A.M., Attorney General Meese, Regan, and Poindexter met with the President. According to Attorney General Meese, he told the President that the Administration did not have a coherent picture of the Iran initiative because the operation was so heavily compartmentalized. Attorney General Meese suggested that he be authorized to gather the facts to present an accurate overview for the President and the public. The President acceded. It was agreed that over the weekend the Attorney General would try to gather the facts in time for the previously scheduled National Security Planning Group (NSPG) meeting on Monday, November 24. Attorney General Meese testified that when he embarked on this effort he was acting as "legal adviser to the President."

Meanwhile, at 11:00 A.M., Ledeen and McFarlane met at Ledeen's home to discuss the extent of the arms sales transactions. McFarlane said he was clear on everything except the November 1985 shipment. North appeared at Ledeen's home about 12:30 P.M., "in some distress" according to McFarlane. Ledeen testified that both North and McFarlane referred to meetings with the Attorney General. McFarlane agreed to drive North back downtown. During the drive, North told McFarlane that he was concerned Ledeen may have made money on the arms transactions, a concern that North denied in his public testimony. North also told McFarlane that he was going to have a "shredding party that weekend." McFarlane testified that he responded, "Ollie, look, you have acted under instruction at all times and I'm confident that you have nothing to worry about. Let it all happen and I'll back you up." North denied using the term "shredding party," but recalled telling McFarlane that all key documents already had been destroyed.

Meese arrived back at the Justice Department at 12:45 P.M. and advised Reynolds, Cooper, and Richardson that the President had authorized him to "get his arms around the Iranian initiative." Meese then met with FBI Director William Webster on an unrelated matter. When Webster brought up the confusion surrounding the Iran arms sales, Attorney General Meese advised that the President had asked him to conduct a factual inquiry because different participants had different pieces of knowledge to be reconciled. Attorney General Meese declined an offer of FBI assistance from Webster, stating that he saw nothing criminal in the arms sales. Webster agreed that absent evidence of a crime, the FBI should not be involved. Attorney General Meese did not relate the details surrounding Casey's testimony or the possible violations of the Arms Export Control Act arising from the 1985

shipments. The Attorney General also testified that he did not bring in the FBI because he and Webster concluded that it would not be "appropriate."

According to North's deputy, Robert Earl, North came to his office during the afternoon of November 21 and told Earl that he had just attended a meeting at the White House, and that the Attorney General was sending a Justice Department team to the National Security Council because the Congressional briefings had raised questions. According to Earl, North said he had asked Attorney General Meese, "Can I have or will I have 24 or 48 hours" and Meese responded that he did not know whether North would have that much time. The Attorney General recalled no such conversation with North; North denied it; and there is no other evidence that North met with the Attorney General that day. Earl testified further that North asked for Earl's Iran file, remarking that "It's time for North to be a scapegoat." Earl stated that, when he gave his file to North, he could tell that he would never see it again. Earl was right.

That afternoon, Attorney General Meese selected his factfinding team. He chose two political appointees and one person from his personal staff. He selected Cooper because he was already looking into the matter as head of the Office of Legal Counsel, which provides advice to the executive branch on various legal matters, including national security. Richardson was the Attorney General's Chief of Staff. Reynolds was assigned because, in addition to his responsibilities as Assistant Attorney General for Civil Rights, he coordinated certain national security matters and was Counselor to the Attorney General.

Meese testified that he never considered

assigning attorneys from the Office of Intelligence Policy and Review, whose job it is to review covert action findings and applications for intelligence surveillance activities. Nor, according to the Attorney General, did he consider assigning additional attorneys to assist with the formidable tasks of document review and witness interviews. No members of the Criminal Division were included, even though William Weld (Assistant Attorney General in charge of the Criminal Division) told Cooper and Reynolds at a staff meeting that morning that he thought the Criminal Division should be involved. Meese testified that it was his view at the time that there was no reason to believe any crime had been committed or that any criminal investigation was required.

At their meeting on Friday afternoon, the factfinding team formulated a list of witnesses to be interviewed. It included McFarlane, North, Secretary Shultz, Secretary Weinberger, the Vice President, Paul Thompson, Stanley Sporkin, John McMahon, Charles Allen, the CIA's Deputy Director for Operations, the CIA Deputy Chief Counsel, and CIA operations officers. Meese listed items that needed action, including contacting Poindexter to gather documents and Casey to arrange interviews of Sporkin and McMahon. The focus of the inquiry was to be the November 1985 HAWKs shipment.

## The NSC Staff Responds by Altering and Destroying Evidence

Once those at the center of the Iran arms sales were alerted to the Attorney General's inquiry, they took steps, in Colonel Earl's words, to "close down the compartment"—destroy all the documentary evidence.

North met with Poindexter at 1:30 P.M. and then again at 2:25 P.M. on November 21. Sometime that same afternoon, North instructed his secretary, Fawn Hall, to alter a series of official action memorandums that he had written during the previous year to then-National Security Adviser McFarlane. These memorandums related to North's activities in raising funds and arranging military assistance for the Contras during the period of the Boland Amendment. McFarlane had told North a year earlier, during the 1985 Congressional inquiry, that these memorandums raised significant problems under the Boland Amendment. McFarlane had given North a handwritten list containing the NSC's "System IV" identification numbers of the problem documents. North kept McFarlane's list taped to his desk near the computer terminal during the ensuing year.

Sometime on November 21, 1986, North requested the originals of the documents on McFarlane's list from the System IV security officer, who found and provided North with all but one. There is no evidence that the System IV security officer knew of North's purpose in requesting these documents.

North then proceeded to alter the original System IV documents by hand. The gist of his alterations was to eliminate references to the funds raised for the Contras from third countries during the Boland cutoff, and also to eliminate or obscure passages in the documents that showed the NSC staff's active role in facilitating the provision of military intelligence and other lethal assistance for the Contras during the same period.

North gave the doctored documents to

Hall and instructed her to prepare new originals containing North's changes. Hall testified that she followed North's instructions without paying attention to the nature of the alterations or asking their purpose. She admitted, however, that she did not feel comfortable, but assumed North had a valid reason. She stated also that she did not then know that the Attorney General had commenced an investigation or that his representatives would shortly be reviewing NSC documents.

After making the alterations, Hall destroyed the original documents and was preparing to replace her file copies of the original versions of the documents with copies of the altered originals when she was distracted by North's shredding of documents and volunteered to help.

The document shredding involved North, Hall, and Earl. North pulled documents from his safe; Hall shredded them. Earl brought documents down from his office, and these, too, were shredded. Hall asked North if she should shred his telephone logs, and he agreed. Hall also shredded PROF notes and KL43 messages. She could not recall what other types of documents went into the shredder. But the quantity was large—approximately one and one half feet of documents. Indeed, so many documents were destroyed that the shredding machine actually jammed and Hall needed assistance from the Crisis Management Center to reactivate it. Hall testified that, although documents were normally shredded in North's office, never before had there been such an organized program of document destruction or such a large volume of documents destroyed.

Although Hall stated that, when she participated in the shredding—as in the alteration of documents—she did not know of the Attorney General's inquiry, North and Earl certainly knew. Yet they both maintained in their testimony that the document destruction was justified to protect the security of the covert action or, as Earl put it, "the compartment." But in fact, the investigators from whom North and Earl were suppressing this evidence were officials of their own Government who had been directed to investigate by the President.

Poindexter, too, destroyed evidence. At approximately 3:00 P.M. on November 21, the Attorney General telephoned Poindexter and requested that he make available for review all documents relating to the Iran initiative. Poindexter then ripped up the only signed copy of the President's December 1985 Finding, which retroactively authorized U.S. participation in the November 1985 arms shipment. Poindexter admitted at the public hearings that he destroyed this Finding because it described the Iran initiative as unambiguously arms-for-hostages, and therefore would have been politically embarrassing to the President. It also would have stripped away the cover story concocted by the NSC staff. It would never reach the investigators.

Since the President had obviously been aware of the December 1985 Finding when he signed it, Poindexter could not explain why he thought that destroying of this Presidential record would nullify its existence—unless he somehow felt confident that the President would either fail to recall the Finding or deny that he had ever signed it. As recently as a week before Poindexter's public testimony, the White House announced that "[o]ur position is that [the Finding] never went to the President, period."

Poindexter's participation in destroying evidence did not stop with the Finding. He also tore up certain PROF notes possibly used to brief the President, which had been stored with the Finding. Although Poindexter said he could not recall their content, these documents were of sufficient importance to be locked with the original Finding in Poindexter's secure safe.

In addition, during the afternoon of November 21, North came to Poindexter with his 1985 spiral notebook which contained North's contemporaneous notes regarding the November 1985 HAWK shipment. Those notes showed that North and others in the U.S. government were involved with that shipment. Like the Finding, the notes belied Poindexter's statement to Congress earlier that day that the United States did not learn of the true contents of the shipment until after it was made. Moreover, although Poindexter testified at the public hearings that North's notes did not reflect that the President had approved the HAWK shipment, in fact, North's notes of November 26, 1985 actually read: "R.R. directed operation to proceed. If Israelis want to provide different model, then we will replenish." Poindexter did not object to North's announced intention to destroy the notebook.

North, Poindexter, and their aides were not the only persons involved in the Iran-Contra Affair to destroy evidence in November 1986. Documents were also shredded at the offices of Secord's company, Stanford Technology Trading Group International (STTGI). According to the testimony of Secord's Administrative Assistant, Shirley Napier, the documents destroyed at STTGI included steno books, telephone logs, and telexes. The destruction continued over a period of days. The participants were Secord,

Robert Dutton, Napier, and an STTGI secretary.

Napier originally testified that the shredding activity occurred early in December 1986. Several weeks after her deposition, Napier submitted an affidavit changing her testimony, based on refreshed recollection, to place the shredding during the week of November 17, 1986, "probably the 19th through the 21st"—the same week as the shredding in the White House.

North and McFarlane took other actions on November 21 in response to the Attorney General's investigation. At 3:15 P.M., North met again with Ledeen, this time in North's office, and discussed the November 1985 HAWK shipment. North knew that Ledeen could testify to U.S. involvement. He asked how Ledeen would respond to questions regarding the shipment. Ledeen replied that he would say he was aware of the shipment but did not know who authorized it or how or when the authorization took place. North said that was fine. North stated also that he had been saving things for "his grandchildren" which he would now have to shred.

The Attorney General's investigation went forward later that afternoon with an interview of McFarlane by Meese and Cooper. Attorney General Meese urged McFarlane to tell the whole truth, assuring him this was in the President's interest. McFarlane said he believed that the November 1985 shipment contained oil drilling equipment until he was told otherwise in May of 1986. When asked if he had told Secretary Shultz in 1985 about the HAWK shipment, McFarlane said he could not recall, but did not dispute it. Cooper testified that neither he nor the Attorney General told McFarlane that Secretary Shultz had a contemporaneous note indicating that

McFarlane had told him about the HAWK shipment before it occurred. But McFarlane testified that he learned of the note from the Attorney General at that same interview. McFarlane's version is corroborated by the fact that he called the State Department right after the interview asking for a copy of the note. The note, of course, was highly significant, because it was the only existing document known to McFarlane that indicated that U.S. officials did indeed know of, approve, and had participated in, the HAWK shipment. North and Poindexter apparently believed they had destroyed or otherwise removed all other such documentary evidence.

At the conclusion of the interview, after Cooper had left, McFarlane stayed behind to speak privately to Meese. He told Attorney General Meese that although he had taken full responsibility in a speech delivered the night before to "protect the President," he wanted Meese to know that the President was "four square" behind the Iran initiative. According to McFarlane, the Attorney General said it was preferable legally if the President had authorized the early shipments.

Immediately after leaving the Attorney General's office, McFarlane used a pay telephone outside of the Justice Department to call North. North's notes of that call indicate that McFarlane said he was told that the Arms Export Control Act was not a problem and that "RR" [Reagan] would be supportive of a "mental finding." McFarlane sent Poindexter a PROF note later that evening similarly describing his meeting with the Attorney General. In that note he stated:

[I]t appears that the matter of not notifying [Congress] about the Israeli transfers can be covered if the President made a 'mental finding' before the transfers took place. Well in that sense we ought to be OK because he was all for letting the Israelis do anything they wanted at the very first briefing in the hospital. Ed [Meese] seemed relieved at that.

On November 21, Attorney General Meese called Casey to let him know about the inquiry and what he would be doing at the CIA. Meese also mentioned he wanted to meet with Casey over the weekend.

As the day drew to a close, North remained late in his office to meet with Richard Miller, a private fundraiser for the Contra cause, who arrived at North's office as North was packing his briefcase. North asked Miller to drive him to Dupont Circle. Either during that drive, or the day before, North told Miller that the Attorney General had advised him to get an attorney. The Attorney General denied telling North to get an attorney; and North testified that it was Casey who so advised him. Miller dropped North at the office building of North's attorney.

## NOVEMBER 22: DIVERSION IS DISCOVERED

With the first McFarlane interview behind them, Attorney General Meese and Cooper began their interview schedule in earnest early Saturday morning. At 8:00 A.M. they interviewed Secretary Shultz and his assistant Charles Hill at the State Department. Regarding the November 1985 shipment, Secretary Shultz said that on November 18, 1985, McFarlane told him that Israel was going to send HAWK missiles to Iran in a trade for the release of U.S. hostages. Secretary Shultz also informed Meese and Cooper that the President had told him earlier that week that he [the President] had contemporaneous knowledge of the November 1985 HAWK shipment. Meese and Cooper asked Hill for the notes of the Shultz/McFarlane conversation, which Hill provided on Monday morning, November 24.

Secretary Shultz testified that, during his interview, he expressed concern that the Iran arms sales might be connected to the Contras. Secretary Shultz said in his testimony he based this concern on the fact that Southern Air Transport's name had come up in the Contra resupply operation and also in the Iran arms transactions. Secretary Shultz's version of this event is corroborated by Hill's contemporaneous notes of Meese's interview of Shultz. Those notes reflect that Secretary Shultz told Meese: "Another angle worries me. Could get mixed up with help for freedom fighters in Nicaragua. One thing may be overlapping with another. May be a connection."

After Secretary Shultz's interview, the factfinding team decided that Reynolds and Richardson should go to the NSC to review documents. They were to look in particular for documents that would indicate whether the 1985 shipments were authorized by the U.S. Government.

After Reynolds and Richardson left for the NSC, Attorney General Meese and Cooper interviewed Stanley Sporkin, former General Counsel to the CIA. Sporkin told them that he drafted a Finding in November 1985 after he learned that the CIA had assisted in arranging transportation of the HAWK missiles to Iran.

Reynolds and Richardson arrived at the West Wing of the White House sometime after 11:00 A.M. NSC General Counsel Paul Thompson escorted them to North's office in the Old Executive Office Building, where they met Earl. The Justice Department officials told Earl they only wanted to see documents relating to the Iran initiative. Earl pulled out accordion-style brown folders from the shelves behind North's desk and placed them on the table.

Richardson also asked for documents from Poindexter's and Thompson's files. Thompson replied that they did not have any because as soon as they had read the documents, they sent them back to the originating office.

Reynolds and Richardson began to review the documents on the table at approximately noon. According to Reynolds, sometime during the first hour of their review, Reynolds came across an undated, unsigned memorandum describing the particulars of a proposed Iran arms transaction to take place in early April 1986. He read the memorandum and put it back. He saw another version of the memorandum with additional information describing an upcoming shipment of arms to Iran including a financial breakdown of the transaction. Reynolds did not set aside either of these memorandums for copying. He recalled that neither version included any section setting forth the diversion of arms sales funds to the Contras. To the best of the Committees' knowledge, these versions have never been recovered.

Reynolds continued his document review of a folder containing intelligence reports. In the back of this folder was a white folder stamped with a red White House label which contained what appeared to be a third version of the memorandum he had seen earlier. He quickly flipped through it. He noted that page 5 included a paragraph stating that $12 million worth of residual funds from the arms sales would be used to purchase supplies for "the Nicaraguan Democratic Resistance Forces." This materiel was needed to "bridge" the gap between current shortages and "when Congressionally approved lethal assistance . . . can be delivered."

Reynolds was shocked. He passed the memorandum to Richardson. Richardson read it and was also surprised. Reynolds intentionally did not clip the document so as not to draw attention to it, but returned it to the file where he could later find it. He continued reviewing other documents.

At approximately 1:45 P.M. Reynolds and Richardson broke for lunch with Cooper and Attorney General Meese. On the way out, they met North. Reynolds told North they had not seen any 1985 files, and North promised to produce them.

During lunch at the Old Ebbitt Grill, Reynolds told Attorney General Meese and Cooper he had found a memorandum which indicated that $12 million generated from the Iran arms sales may have gone to the Contras. Attorney General Meese and Cooper expressed great surprise. There was discussion of whether North wrote the memorandum. The remainder of the lunch was devoted to a discussion of the 1985 shipments and the data collected by McGinnis. There was no discussion of securing documents.

The Attorney General's methodology for conducting the inquiry changed at this point. Before discovery of the diversion memorandum, all interviews were conducted by the Attorney General with another Justice Department official and notes were taken. Thereafter, with the exception of the North interview, all interviews conducted by Meese were one-on-one, with no notes taken—including interviews of Casey, McFarlane, Poindexter, Regan and the Vice President.

After Reynolds and Richardson had left the NSC for lunch on November 22, North reviewed more documents and selected some for shredding. North's office shredder was jammed, however, and other likely locations in the Old Executive Office Building were not open. Later, Earl saw North with a file full of documents standing beside Paul Thompson. North indicated he was going to the White House Situation Room to use the shredder there.

North testified that he was actually shredding documents in his office while Reynolds and Richardson were present. However, Reynolds and Richardson denied this, and Earl, as noted, testified that North's office shredder was jammed.

While the Attorney General's team was meeting at the Old Ebbitt Grill, Casey and Poindexter were also having lunch together. They were joined by North. In his testimony, Poindexter recalled very little about that 2-hour lunch other than that it was initiated by Casey and that Casey discussed his testimony before the House and Senate Intelligence Committees the day before.

Reynolds and Richardson returned to the NSC at approximately 3:30 P.M. where they found North and Earl. Richardson testified that everything appeared to be as they had left it.

While Reynolds and Richardson reviewed documents, North worked at this desk and spoke on the telephone. Richardson took notes of some of these calls. He overheard North speak to an Israeli using various code words, including "Beethoven" in reference to Poindexter. North told the Israeli that a lot had come out about the Iran initiative already, but the most sensitive informaton had not been exposed.

During that afternoon, North sat down

273

with Reynolds and Richardson and told them he was ready to answer their questions. They responded that they were there only to review documents and the Attorney General would interview North later. According to Richardson, North said "he knew he would not be long for this job."

Reynolds and Richardson reviewed documents until approximately 7:15 P.M., at which time they and North left North's office. Reynolds and Richardson made plans to complete their review Sunday morning.

North called Attorney General Meese at 3:40 P.M. that afternoon to arrange the interview. Meese asked to interview North on Sunday morning, but North said he wanted to attend church and take his family to lunch first. Meese agreed to set the interview for 2:00 P.M.

Six minutes after North spoke to Meese on November 22, Casey called Meese and said there were matters he wanted to discuss with him. The two met at Casey's home at 6:00 P.M. By the time of this meeting, Attorney General Meese had reason to believe that the CIA's version of Casey's proposed testimony was almost certainly false. Indeed, by then Attorney General Meese had interviewed Secretary Shultz, who had contemporaneous documentation for his recollection of the November 1985 HAWKs shipment, and former CIA General Counsel Sporkin, who had been told by Casey's subordinates in November 1985 that missiles were shipped. On another issue, the Attorney General had strong reason to believe there was a connection between the arms sales (in which the CIA had been involved) and the Contras: the diversion memorandum.

Despite Casey's obviously central position in any investigation of these matters, Attorney General Meese chose to meet Casey alone. He took no notes of the meeting, nor was the meeting otherwise recorded. The Committees' information about the meeting is thus derived solely from Attorney General Meese's testimony.

According to Meese, Casey said that he had been contacted in October 1986 by a former business associate named Roy Furmark. Furmark told Casey that certain Canadians who had financed the Iran arms sales had not been repaid and were therefore threatening to expose the arms sales. Furmark had represented that the Canadians would claim that the proceeds had been used for "Israeli or United States Government projects." The Attorney General explained that Casey said he had not told him about the Furmark visit earlier because, before the factfinding inquiry began, there was no reason to tell the him.

In testimony before the Senate and House Intelligence Committees in December 1986, Attorney General Meese was not specifically asked about, and he did not volunteer any reference to, proceeds being diverted to Israeli or U.S. projects.

Attorney General Meese has consistently claimed that he did not tell Casey about the diversion memorandum, or ask him about the diversion, even though Meese recognized it as a bombshell as soon as his staff reported it to him. The reason Attorney General Meese gave for not asking Casey about the diversion memorandum was that he thought it inappropriate to do so until North was questioned. Attorney General Meese also testified that, despite the fact that Casey mentioned a claim that proceeds had been diverted to U.S. projects, Attorney General Meese did not feel the conversation could logically have led to questions regarding a diversion of those proceeds to the Contras without revealing to Casey what Meese knew. Attorney General Meese testified that, "I felt it was not appropriate to discuss this with anyone, even as good a friend as Mr. Casey, until I found out what it was all about." So, in a meeting that lasted between 30 minutes and an hour, Meese, according to his testimony, avoided the subject.

## NOVEMBER 23: INVESTIGATION AND OBSTRUCTION CONTINUE

The Attorney General's investigation continued to build on Sunday, November 23 toward the afternoon interview with North. From 9:00 A.M. to noon, Cooper and McGinnis completed more interviews at the CIA. Reynolds and Richardson returned to the NSC to continue their document review, although they apparently never did complete it.

At the CIA, Cooper and McGinnis interviewed Charles Allen, Duane Clarridge, George Jameson, and David Doherty. McGinnis interviewed Clarridge, who told him that the CIA's involvement in November 1985 was limited to providing to North the name of a proprietary airline to fly oil drilling equipment to Iran. Clarridge also explained that he made arrangements for flight clearances.

Meanwhile, North, who had told the Attorney General he was not available for an interview until the afternoon because he wanted to go to church, called McFarlane Sunday morning and asked to meet with him. McFarlane was getting ready to leave for church himself and told North to meet him at his office at noon. North said he would bring his attorney. North arrived alone at McFarlane's office at 12:30 P.M. North told McFarlane everything was on track except for one thing that could be a problem: the diversion. According to McFarlane, he asked North if the diversion had been approved and North replied that he would not do anything that was not approved. North said that the diversion was a matter of record in a memorandum he had written for Poindexter.

At that point, attorney Thomas Green arrived at McFarlane's office. Green told McFarlane he had been an Assistant U.S. Attorney and had dealt with problems of this kind before. Green advised McFarlane and North to state the story truthfully and let the chips fall where they may. Not long thereafter, Richard Secord arrived as well, but by that time, McFarlane had to leave for an appointment.

From approximately 12:45 P.M. to 2:00 P.M., Attorney General Meese, Reynolds, Cooper, and Richardson met to discuss the upcoming interview of North. North arrived, alone, at approximately 2:15 P.M. Meese did most of the questioning. Richardson and Reynolds took notes.

The Attorney General began by telling North he wanted all the facts, and did not want North to coverup to protect himself or the President. He then asked North to explain the arms sales from the beginning. North replied with a combination of fact and fiction. All the while he knew that the Attorney General was acting under orders from the President and that the Attorney General's findings would be reported back to the President.

North said he was unaware of the first shipment of 504 TOWs until after it occurred. Regarding the November 1985 HAWK shipment, North said he received a call from McFarlane in Geneva who told him to contact Israeli Defense Minister Rabin to help Israel move something to Iran. North then claimed that Defense Minister Rabin told him it was oil-related equipment. North sent Secord to help with the shipment. North also called Duane Clarridge at the CIA to get a CIA proprietary to fly the equipment. When Secord saw the shipment in Israel, he told North the cargo was 18 or 19 HAWK missiles. The implication in North's statements—that he was unaware until informed by Secord that the flight was to contain HAWK missiles—was false. As North subsequently admitted in his public hearing testimony, he knew the nature of the cargo from his first involvement in the November shipment.

While lying to the Attorney General about other aspects of the November 1985 HAWK shipment, North admitted that his statements about that shipment in the NSC chronology and at the November 20, 1986, meeting to review Casey's draft testimony were false. As discussed above, North had claimed in the chronology and at the meeting that the United States had to force the Iranians to return the HAWK missiles. In his interview with the Attorney General, North admitted that it was the Iranians who were dissatisfied and demanded their money back.

Attorney General Meese then asked North to describe the money flow. Again, North lied. North said the money passed from the Iranians to the Israelis who in turn paid into a CIA account which reimbursed the Army for the weapons. North made no mention of Secord or the Lake Resources account through which the money had actually passed.

The Attorney General turned to the di-version. He directed North's attention to the section of the memorandum describing how the "residuals" would go to the Nicaraguan Resistance. North appeared to be "visibly surprised." He asked if they had found a "cover memo." Reynolds said that none had been found—without first questioning North as to whether he recalled a cover memo, or to whom it had been directed, or what it said. After Reynolds informed North that no cover memo had been found, the Attorney General asked North if they should have found a cover memo, and North said "no."

The Attorney General asked North if he had discussed the diversion with the President. North replied that Poindexter was the point of contact with the President.

Attorney General Meese pointed out that if the President had approved the diversion, North probably would have a record of it. North agreed and said he did not think it was approved by the President. The Attorney General asked whether other files might contain a document indicating Presidential approval, and North said he would check.

The Attorney General asked North if there was anything more. North said that only the February 1986 shipment and the second shipment had produced residuals to the Contras. North also said that only three people in the Government knew of the diversion—Poindexter, McFarlane, and himself. North said the CIA did not handle the "residuals" and, though some in the CIA may have suspected a diversion, he did not think anyone at the CIA knew. If North's testimony at the public hearings was truthful, then these statements, too, were lies. At the hearings, North testified that Casey knew, approved, and was enthusiastic about the diversion as early as February 1986.

And of course, North was aware when he spoke to the Attorney General that Earl knew of the diversion.

Attorney General Meese then confirmed to North that he had to share this information with the President and determine if he was aware of it. Meese again asked North about other problem areas, including complaints from people who financed the deals and lost money. North responded only that Ghorbanifar had lost money in a "sting."

The North interview concluded at 5:55 P.M. as the Attorney General was returning. North was not told what would happen next. Although the Justice Department officials noticed North's surprise that they had a copy of the diversion memorandum North had written, no one asked North if he had shredded or otherwise disposed of documents, nor did the Justice Department officials take any steps to secure North's remaining documents.

That evening, North called McFarlane and Poindexter. Afterwards, North shredded additional documents at his office until at least 4:30 A.M., when a security guard noticed that North's office had not been secured for the day. North responded to the officer's security report by claiming that when the officer checked the office, North was in the bathroom.

## NOVEMBER 24: INFORMING THE PRESIDENT

Early Monday morning, November 24, McGinnis called George Jameson of the CIA to ask certain limited questions, and Cooper researched possible criminal violations. Attorney General Meese planned to meet with the President, the Vice President, McFarlane, Poindexter, and Regan.

McGinnis continued to speak that morning with CIA personnel about the money flow. During one of his conversations, he was told of a rumor at CIA that the surplus funds had been diverted to the Contras. McGinnis told Cooper of this rumor. Cooper then told McGinnis about the diversion memorandum and the North interview.

Cooper went to the State Department Monday morning to obtain Hill's notes relating to the November 1985 HAWK shipment. At first Hill was reluctant to surrender them. he agreed, however, only when Sofaer told him they were needed for a criminal investigation.

The Attorney General called the head of the Justice Department's Criminal Division, William Weld, at 9:55 A.M. On the previous Friday in an early morning staff meeting attended by Reynolds and Cooper among others, Weld had urged that the Criminal Division should be involved in the weekend inquiry. He had argued, for example, that the Criminal Division had already made representations to a court denying any U.S. Government involvement in arms sales to Iran, and that the Criminal Division should know the facts. Attorney General Meese told Weld during their Monday morning call that the Criminal Division was being left out of the Iran investigation on purpose and not as a result of negligence. Weld inferred that the Attorney General had been informed that Weld had argued for Criminal Division involvement. Weld told Meese that he had registered a concern at the Friday meeting about Meese's personal involvement in the investigation, warning: "If you tried to carry too much water here some might spill on you."

Early Monday morning, Attorney General Meese called McFarlane to arrange a second interview. They met alone at the Justice Department and no one took notes. Meese asked if McFarlane knew about the diversion. McFarlane responded that he learned of it from North during the Tehran mission in May 1986. McFarlane told Attorney General Meese that North claimed to have approval for the diversion.

McFarlane testified that the only other question Attorney General Meese asked was whether he had told anyone else about the diversion. Meese, however, could not recall asking that. Meese never asked McFarlane if the President had approved the diversion, nor did he show McFarlane the diversion memorandum. Meese did not ask McFarlane why he had not told him about the diversion during their Friday interview. McFarlane did not mention that he had spoken to Poindexter and North after North's interview with the Attorney General.

Attorney General Meese went to the White House at 11:00 A.M. to meet with the President and Regan pursuant to an appointment he had made earlier that morning. Meese testified that he told the President that his team had found a memorandum at the NSC which included plans to divert excess funds from the Iran arms sales to the Contras. Attorney General Meese also said that North and McFarlane had confirmed this diversion. The President, Meese said, was very surprised. Meese told the President there was more factfinding to do before he could give him a full report at the National Security Planning Group (NSPG) meeting.

Regan had a different recollection of the morning events. Regan testified that Attorney General Meese told him about the diversion prior to meeting with the President.

Regan described his own reaction to news of the diversion as "horror, horror, sheer horror." According to Regan, Attorney General Meese told him that North had done the diversion, and Regan said the President needed to be immediately informed. Attorney General Meese said he did not want to tell the President until he could nail down some other things. They went to see the President, but told him only that the factfinding inquiry had uncovered some serious problems and that they would need to meet later that afternoon. They set a meeting for 4:15 P.M.

No one took notes of the Attorney General's morning meeting with the President. Regan recalled that Meese had papers with him from which he seemed to be reading. However, according to Regan, Attorney General Meese never told him there actually was a memorandum spelling out the diversion. Regan testified that Meese "kept using the phrase, 'I have got a few last-minute things to button up before I can give you the details.'"

Attorney General Meese returned to the White House for the 2:00 P.M. NSPG meeting. Richardson's notes indicate that prior to that, the Attorney General met briefly with the Vice President at 1:40 P.M. Attorney General Meese, however, testified that this meeting occurred after 4:00 P.M. Continuing the pattern, Meese met with the Vice President alone and no notes were taken. Meese reported that the Vice President was unaware of the diversion.

Back at the Department of Justice, Reynolds and Cooper had arranged to meet at 2:00 P.M. with attorney Tom Green. Green and Reynolds had a long-standing professional relationship, so Green approached Reynolds for a meeting.

Reynolds and Cooper both understood that Green had spoken to North after North's Sunday interview with the Attorney General. Yet Green's version of the events differed sharply from what North had told them. First, Green said the idea to divert funds to the Contras originated with Albert Hakim, while North had tagged Amiram Nir with originating the plan. Green claimed there were no illegalities because the diverted money did not belong to the United States. Green urged that the facts not be made public because it would risk the lives of contacts in Iran as well as the hostages.

Green also recounted other facts which differed from what North had said the day before. In contrast to North's version of the money flow, Green explained that the diversion was accomplished by routing the money through Hakim's financial network. Green said that Hakim told the Iranians that in order to foster good relations, the Iranians should make a contribution for the use of the Contras or of the United States. Green also claimed North felt he was doing the "Lord's work."

Sometime on Monday, Reynolds told Meese what Green had said about the diversion. Attorney General Meese, however, testified that he recalled no mention of the fact that money went through Hakim's financial network and concluded from what Reynolds told him that Green "added nothing particularly new. . . ."

At the White House, the NSPG met from 2:00 P.M. to 3:45 P.M. Present were the President, the Vice President, Poindexter, Casey, Attorney General Meese, Secretary Weinberger, Secretary Shultz, Regan and George Cave. Although the sole topic at the meeting was the Iran initiative, neither Attorney General Meese nor Regan mentioned the di-version, nor did either ask any one present about it.

After the NSPG meeting, Attorney General Meese met with Poindexter from 4:15 P.M. to 4:20 P.M. to find out what he knew of the diversion. Although North had told the Attorney General that Poindexter was the point of contact with the President, the Attorney General chose to meet alone with him and to take no notes.

Poindexter told Attorney General Meese that North had given him only enough hints about the diversion to know what was going on, but that he had not inquired further. Poindexter testified that the Attorney General never asked him if the President knew of the diversion. Although Meese testified at his deposition that he thought he had asked that question, he stated at the public hearings that he had not asked so direct a question, but only whether anyone else in the White House knew. Poindexter testified that he did not tell the Attorney General he actually approved the diversion, because he wanted the President and his staff to retain deniability.

Poindexter told the Attorney General that he knew that when the diversion became public he would have to resign, and would defer to the Attorney General's judgment on the timing of his resignation. Attorney General Meese asked no further questions because he needed to meet with the President at 4:30 P.M. as scheduled. The Attorney General, however, never went back to Poindexter to obtain additional details after meeting with the President.

Attorney General Meese met alone with the President and Regan. According to Meese, he told the President that Poindexter had confirmed the fact of the diversion. According to Regan, Meese was informing the President for the first time of the diversion of funds from the arms sales into Swiss bank accounts controlled by the Contras. Regan said the President appeared crestfallen. The Attorney General told the President that the person primarily responsible was North, but that Poindexter had some inkling of the diversion and let it happen.

According to Regan, the conversation then turned to making the information public. Regan suggested they establish a commission to investigate the facts as soon as possible. Regan also suggested that the President announce the situation at the press conference and turn questions over to Meese. The President said they should think about the matter overnight and decide how it should be handled.

## NOVEMBER 25: THE PUBLIC LEARNS OF THE DIVERSION

By Tuesday morning, November 25, the Attorney General's investigation was largely over. What had started as an effort to resolve differing testimony over the November 1985 HAWK shipment had led to the discovery of an illicit connection between the Iran initiative and the secret Contra support activities. Evidence had been destroyed; false statements had been made; important questions had been skirted or avoided. Nevertheless, the secret of the diversion had been uncovered. On this day, the American people would find out.

Attorney General Meese's day began with a 6:30 A.M. call from Casey, whom the Attorney General had not yet interviewed about the diversion. Casey told the Attorney General that Regan had advised him of the diver-

sion, and asked Meese to drive by his house on the way to work. The Attorney General arrived at 6:45 A.M., with Richardson in the car. Richardson did not go into Casey's house. Richardson testified that he never sat in on meetings between Casey and the Attorney General. Meese once again held a crucial meeting without witnesses or notes.

Attorney General Meese testified that, at this meeting, Casey was adamant that the diversion needed to be publicly announced as quickly as possible. This description of Casey's position is substantially different from Casey's position the day before when he met with Regan.

While the Attorney General was at Casey's house, Regan called to speak to him. Regan told the Attorney General he wanted to meet with Poindexter at 8:00 A.M. to accept Poindexter's resignation.

Meese returned to his car and called Poindexter, who was just arriving at the White House. He asked Poindexter to meet him at the Department of Justice, where they spoke privately for 15 minutes before Poindexter met with Regan. The Attorney General told Poindexter the time had come to submit his resignation. Poindexter agreed to resign. They then discussed North's transfer back to the Marine Corps. Attorney General Meese told Poindexter he did not think North had done anything illegal.

Poindexter returned to the White House and was eating breakfast in his office when Regan came in and told him to have his resignation ready for the regular 9:30 A.M. meeting with the President. Regan then asked Poindexter how the diversion could have happened. Poindexter replied he had thought something was going on with North. Regan asked why he never looked into it; Poindexter replied, according to Regan:

I knew it would hurt the Contras, and the way those guys on the Hill are jerking around, . . . I was afraid it would hurt them too much, so I didn't look into it.

In Poindexter's testimony, however, he did not recall Regan asking him about the diversion. Both Regan and Poindexter agree that Regan never asked Poindexter whether the President knew.

At 9:30 A.M., the Vice President, Regan, Meese, and Poindexter met with the President. Poindexter told the President that he was aware of the plan to divert funds to the Contras, and he tendered his resignation in order to give the President "the necessary latitude to do whatever you need to do." The President told Poindexter that it was in the tradition of a Naval officer to take responsibility. Poindexter then shook hands with those present and left. Poindexter testified that he did not tell the President that he had actually approved the diversion, because matters were in flux and he wanted more time to think about it.

After Poindexter left the meeting, those remaining discussed North's fate. It was agreed that North should be immediately reassigned to the Marine Corps. A resignation was not necessary because North was not a Presidential appointee. No one informed North that he would be reassigned. He learned of it for the first time while watching the President's statement and Meese's press conference on television at noon that day.

Sometime that morning Poindexter called North and, according to North's notes, dis-cussed the disclosure of the Contra connection. North's notes contain a reference to "put it off on Ghorbanifar."

At 10:15 A.M. the President met with the National Security Council to brief them on developments. From 11:00 A.M. to noon, the President, Regan, Secretary Shultz, Attorney General Meese, and Casey briefed Congressional leaders. Attorney General Meese began by telling them about the diversion. Meese said North was involved with possibly one or two other NSC staff or consultants. The President said that this was the only incident of this kind and that Poindexter, although not a participant, had known of it and had therefore resigned.

House Majority Leader Jim Wright then asked if the diversion was done with knowledge or approval of anyone in the U.S. Government. Attorney General Meese answered that North had approved it. Representative Wright asked about Poindexter, and Meese responded that Poindexter knew the money was going to the Contras but did not know the details. Senate Minority Leader Robert Byrd then asked if Poindexter's resignation was requested. The President responded that Poindexter volunteered to resign, in the Navy tradition.

Senator Nunn expressed concern about NSC staff involvement in covert operations. The President replied that the NSC staff had served the country well, citing the opening to China as an example. Senator Nunn replied that he drew a distinction between a diplomatic initiative and a covert operation.

Representative Wright then asked if the CIA knew of the diversion. Casey responded, "No, I didn't." Casey then volunteered that McFarlane learned of the diversion in April or May 1986.

## November 25, 1986: The Attorney General's Press Conference

The Presidential statement and subsequent press conference by the Attorney General began at noon and lasted approximately 45 minutes. Attorney General Meese began the press conference with a disclaimer of sorts, stating that the inquiry was not yet complete because "all information was not yet in." Nonetheless, his responses contained several purported conclusions.

Meese was asked how the diversion came to his attention. He responded that, through a review of reports and other materials, there was a hint that some money was available to be used for another purpose. He elaborated that the diversion had accounted for some $12 million to $30 million. Meese was asked if the CIA knew of the diversion. He responded that none of the statutory members of the National Security Council knew, including Casey.

Later, in describing the money flow, Meese said the money went directly from the Israelis into bank accounts held by the Contras. This version of events, although consistent with North's statements, was contradicted by the diversion memorandum, which described how the money would be transferred by the Israelis into an account maintained by "a private United States corporation" and then transferred to the Contras.

Meese was asked about arms shipments prior to the January 1986 Finding. He responded that there was one transaction in which Israel shipped weapons without authorization from the United States, and that the weapons so shipped were returned to Israel. Attorney General Meese added that the August, September and November 1985 shipments were between Israel and Iran and "did not involve, at that time, the United States."

Attorney General Meese specifically stated that the President had not known about the November 1985 HAWK shipment until February 1986. Thus the Attorney General said: The President was informed generally that there had been an Israeli shipment of weapons to Iran sometime during the late summer, early fall of 1985, and then he later learned in February of 1986 details about another shipment that had taken place in November of 1985, which had actually been returned to Israel in February of 1986.

These statements were contrary to what he and Cooper had learned regarding CIA participation in the November 1985 HAWK shipment and regarding McFarlane's conversation with Shultz on November 18, 1985. Attorney General Meese's statements were also contrary to the information Meese had received from Secretary Shultz on November 22 that the President had told Shultz 3 days earlier that he (the President) had known of the November 1985 HAWK shipment at the time. Attorney General Meese did not tell these facts to the press.

When asked whether the diverted funds were owed to the United States, Meese responded that all money owed to the United States had been paid to the United States. Meese said, "We have no control over that money. It was never United States funds, it was never property of the United States officials, so we have no control over that whatsoever." Meese later testified that a good case could be made that such funds were held in "constructive trust" for the United States, that is, that all profits reaped belong in the U.S. Treasury.

Attorney General Meese also stated at the

press conference that, to the best of his knowledge, no American was present for, or participated in, negotiating the price of the arms to Iran. Meese's source for this statement is also unclear.

FBI Director William Webster watched the Attorney General's press conference on television, and thereby learned of the diversion. After the press conference, Webster walked across the street to the Department of Justice and told Meese that a criminal investigation was warranted. The Attorney General stated that he had turned the inquiry over to the Criminal Division to determine which, if any, statutes were violated. Webster then raised the problem of securing NSC records. Attorney General Meese assured Webster that the Justice Department would take the appropriate steps to secure the records. Webster went back to the FBI and told his Assistant Director to gear up for the anticipated investigation.

Sometime that afternoon, Secord, after being besieged by the press at his office, went to a hotel to consult with Tom Green. North joined them. North received two phone calls at the hotel. One was from the Vice President calling to express his regrets about North's dismissal. The other was from the President. North stood at attention while the President spoke to him. There is some dispute about the substance of this conversation. North testified that the President told him, "I just didn't know," which North understood to be a reference to the diversion. Earl testified that, when North returned to the office, North had told him that the President had called and said, "It is important that I not know." North testified that perhaps he told Earl that the President felt it was important that North know that he, the President, did not know of the diversion. Craig Coy, who was present when North related the Presidential conversation to Earl, testified that he did not recall North saying anything about the President's statements concerning his knowledge. Hall testified that North told her that President had said, "I just didn't know."

There is no dispute, however, that during the phone call the President told North that he was "a national hero." Indeed, the President has publicly acknowledged making this statement.

At 4:40 P.M., Meese was called by Israeli Prime Minister Peres. The Prime Minister told Meese that the Government of Israel was concerned about Meese's claims in his press conference and was about to issue a statement. Prime Minister Peres said the Israelis had transferred "defensive arms" at the request of the United States. He also told Meese that the Israelis had not paid anything to any Contra account. The Prime Minister explained that the Iranians paid directly into an account in Switzerland maintained by an American company. He indicated that Israel—which had been asked by U.S. officials early on to take the rap if the arms sales became public—was not going to take the blame for the diversion.

Amiram Nir made the same point in a call to North. North's notes of that call show that Nir complained about Meese's statements and asked what basis Meese had for making them. Nir pointed out that, far from ever telling him that any funds were diverted, North had always told him there was a shortage of funds. Indeed, Nir questioned why the Israelis had been made to pay for replacement weapons if there was an excess of funds. Nir told North he could not back his story. He said that statements made by the Attorney General regarding Israeli deposits

283

to Contra accounts and other matters were simply false.

During the afternoon of November 25, the NSC staff secured North's office. In reviewing her files at the time, Fawn Hall discovered that she had not substituted the copies of the documents she had altered on November 21 for the copies of unaltered versions of the documents in North's files. She also found PROF notes that were similar to those shredded Friday night, along with minutes of the Tehran meeting in May 1986 that she had saved to read. Hall knew that the NSC security staff soon would be closing the office, so she called North and told him to come back to the office, indicating to him the urgency of her request and signalling that it involved a problem with documents. North said that he and his attorney would come back to the office.

Before they arrived, Hall took the documents upstairs and placed copies of the altered documents inside her boots, inexplicably leaving the originals of the altered versions on her desk. She then went to Earl's office and solicited his help in pulling the PROF notes from he pile of remaining documents. Earl was going to put the PROF notes in his jacket, but Hall told him she would do it. She then told him to watch the open entrance to his office while she hid the PROF notes under her clothes. Earl assured her that the documents were not visible.

North and his attorney [Tom Green] then arrived at North's office, where North took a phone call in his private office with only Hall present. Hall asked North if he could detect anything against her back, and he said he could not. Hall left the office with North and the attorney. Their briefcases were inspected by the NSC security staff, and they were allowed to pass. In the hallway, Hall indicated to North that she wanted to give him the documents. He told her to wait until they were outside.

Hall, North, and the attorney walked outside. Hall made a motion to North (she was planning to pass the documents), but the attorney said, according to Hall, "No, wait until we get inside the car." Once in the car, Hall pulled out the documents, gave them to North, and told North that she had not finished substituting the altered documents for the originals. The attorney drove them to their cars and, according to Hall, asked her what she would say if asked about the shredding. Hall replied that she would say "We shred every day," to which the attorney said, "Good."

There is no evidence as to whether the attorney knew in advance that Hall had documents on her person. That evening, the attorney withdrew from North's representation. Subsequently, North's new attorney returned documents to the NSC.

## NOVEMBER 26: CRIMINAL INVESTIGATION UNDERWAY

By Wednesday morning, November 26, Meese was prepared for the investigation to enter a new phase. At 9:15 A.M., he met with Justice Department attorneys Burns, Trott, Reynolds, Cooper, Bolton, Cribb, Korten, Weld, and Richardson. The Attorney General began the meeting by announcing to Weld that this was the day for the handoff of the investigation to the Criminal Division. Weld said he wanted to assign the investigation to two experienced attorneys in the Public Integrity Section, which typically handles prosecutions of public officials and Independent Counsel inquiries. Attorney General Meese stated he also wanted Deputies Mark Richard and John Keeny to participate.

## NOVEMBER 27: A THANKSGIVING PHONE CALL

November 27 was Thanksgiving. Fawn Hall received a telephone call at home from Jay Stephens, an attorney on the White House Counsel's staff. Press reports had appeared claiming that documents pertinent to the Iran-Contra Affair had been shredded at the NSC. Stephens asked Hall whether those reports were true. Hall told Stephens exactly what she had earlier told North's attorney her response would be to such a question: "we shred everyday." Hall admitted during the public hearings that she misled Stephens to believe that nothing unusual had occurred.

## FINAL STEPS

The NSC security officer had secured North's office on November 25. The FBI took over joint custody of the documents at the NSC on Friday, November 28.

Also on November 28, Hall went to the office of North's new attorney to deliver messages that North had received. When Hall returned to the NSC, Craig Coy introduced her to FBI agents, who asked to interview her over the weekend. Hall left her new office

that evening with NSC aide Robert Earl, and they agreed not to tell the FBI about the removal of documents from the NSC offices. The next day, after learning that Earl had retained an attorney, Hall arranged for one as well.

On December 1, Reynolds planned to meet with Tom Green, who had become Secord's attorney. Criminal Division officials were opposed because Reynolds was a potential witness. Eventually, it was agreed that William Hendricks (Deputy Chief of the Justice Department's Public Integrity Section) would sit in. Green wanted immunity for his client and made several new assertions. He said McFarlane lied about the November 1985 shipment and that CIA "subordinates" knew the cargo was weapons. Hendricks suggest that Secord come forward without immunity. Green rejected that idea and predicted the principals would "clam up" if an independent counsel were named.

At 2:20 P.M., Meese met with Burns, Cooper, Bolton, Cribb, Weld, Hendricks, and Richard to discuss the investigation. This meeting focused on whether to apply for an Independent Counsel. There was concern that North and Poindexter might not be persons covered by the Independent Counsel statute. The consensus, however, was that sufficient evidence of a conflict of interest existed that the Justice Department should apply for an Independent Counsel. Weld took it upon himself to draft the application that night. Weld mentioned only North in the application as a possible target because he felt there were insufficient facts to name others.

On December 19, an Independent Counsel was appointed.

PART

# THE ENTERPRISE

# CHAPTER 21

# Introduction to the Enterprise

By the summer of 1986, the organization that Richard Secord ran at Lt. Col. Oliver L. North's direction controlled five aircraft, including C-123 and C-7 transports. It had an airfield in one country, warehouse facilities at an airbase in another, a stockpile of guns and military equipment to drop by air to the Contras, and secure communications equipment obtained by North from the National Security Agency (NSA).

Flying the planes were veteran pilots and crew, many experienced in covert operations. At any given time, about 20 airmen were paid consultants to a Panamanian corporation formed by Secord and Albert Hakim at North's direction; their salaries were paid from secret Swiss accounts controlled by Secord and Hakim.

In Robert Dutton, a recently retired U.S. Air Force lieutenant colonel, the organization had an expert in special operations. Dutton was reporting to an NSC official, Oliver North, and a retired Air Force general, Richard Secord, both of whom indicated that the operation was authorized by the President of the United States. This private air force was but a part of the organization that Secord and Hakim called the "Enterprise."

This part of the Report explores the activities of the Enterprise and addresses questions such as: Where did the Enterprise get the money? How did it spend it? Who profited? What amount of the Iranian arms sales proceeds was spent on the Contras (the so-called "diversion")? What happened to the $10 million that Brunei contributed? What other covert operations did the Enterprise conduct or plan?

Witnesses testifying before the Committees could not easily define the Enterprise. To Hakim, Secord's partner, the Enterprise was a covert organization with a chain of command headed by North; it was also a business with a chain of Swiss accounts that he set up and partially owned. Secord first described the Enterprise as the group of offshore companies that carried out the Iran and Contra operations, but later testified that it was fair to describe the Enterprise as his own covert operations organization formed at the request of North and Poindexter to carry out all of the operations described in his testimony. Secord declared that he "exercised overall control" over the Enterprise, but acknowledged that he depended upon North's support.

North described Secord's network of off-shore companies as a private commercial organization, but he also stated that it was the starting point for the creation of an organization that would conduct activities similar to those of the Central Intelligence Agency (CIA), including counterterrorism. Poindexter never defined the Enterprise, but stated that he found attractive the idea of a "private organization properly approved, using nonappropriated funds in an approved sort of way."

Secord consistently turned to the same group of individuals in order to accomplish the tasks that North assigned to him. Albert Hakim, an Iranian-born American citizen, was his partner and, by agreement, Secord and Hakim were to share equally in any Enterprise profits. Hakim controlled the Enterprise's bank accounts. Rafael Quintero, a Cuban exile formerly associated with the CIA, handled the logistics of arms deliveries from various locations in Central America. Glenn Robinette, a former CIA officer-turned-consultant, investigated those who made accusations about operations of the Enterprise and performed other tasks, among them, installation of a security system at North's residence. Thomas Clines, a former CIA official-turned-investor and consultant, served as the primary broker for the Enterprise's arms transactions.

The relationships were not new. Secord had been in contact with the group throughout his career; apparently he trusted these individuals and they trusted him. Secord, as an Air Force officer, and Clines, as a CIA officer, worked together in the late 1960s when both were assigned to the CIA station in Laos, and developed a close relationship. When Secord returned from Laos he was stationed at the Pentagon. Clines took the opportunity to introduce him to a number of Clines' CIA associates, including Quintero. Clines also introduced Secord to Edwin Wilson, a former CIA officer who had become enormously successful in international business dealings. In the mid 1970s, Secord was stationed in Iran where he exercised substantial influence over purchasing decisions of the Iranian Air Force. At about this time, according to Hakim, Wilson bought, or was given, an interest in one of Hakim's companies and Wilson became "acquainted" with Hakim's "Iranian operations." Hakim's Iranian operations included, among other things, an effort to sell electronic intelligence systems to the Iranian Government. The operations also involved payoffs to Iranian Air Force and Army Generals through "bearer letters" and numbered Swiss accounts. Hakim and Secord claimed that they first met on unfriendly terms in 1976 or 1977 when Secord recommended against a contract that Hakim proposed to the Iranian Government.

After Secord returned from Iran, his relationship with Wilson became more involved. In 1981, Secord and Clines became subjects of a Department of Justice conflict-of-interest and bribery investigation stemming from their relationship with Wilson. In addition, in 1982, Clines became a target of a Department of Justice investigation concerning fraudulent overbillings of the U.S. Government by the Egyptian American Transport Company (EATSCO), 49 percent of which was owned by Clines.

Secord retired from the Air Force in May 1983 because the Wilson story and the ongoing Justice Department investigation had placed a cloud over his military career. Two months later, EATSCO pleaded guilty to criminal and civil overbilling charges. Clines, on behalf of the corporate entity that held his 49 percent interest, paid a $10,000 criminal fine and a $100,000 civil fine as part of the settlement. In July 1984 the Justice Department closed the EATSCO case and in January 1986, it closed the conflict-of-interest and bribery investigation of Secord and Clines. No indictments or other prosecutorial action followed.

Hakim kept in communication with Secord after Secord left Iran. When Hakim learned that Secord was considering retirement, he tried to recruit Secord as a partner to revive his security sales company, Expantrade. By offering security systems to foreign governments, Hakim believed that "you have a deep penetration in that government and therefore you can do a lot of business."

Secord agreed with the concept and in May 1983, immediately upon his retirement, joined Hakim. Secord became Hakim's equal partner in a new company, Stanford Technology Trading Group International (STTGI), headquartered in Vienna, Virginia, outside of Washington, D.C. STTGI, relying on Secord's contacts, tried to develop contracts in the security field in Saudi Arabia and elsewhere. In 1984, when North recruited Secord to help with arms supply to the Contras, Hakim and Secord found a major project that would steadily grow more complex—as the ensuing chapter shows.

# CHAPTER 22

# The Enterprise

Almost $48 million flowed into the Enterprise. It came from contributions directed to the Enterprise by North from Carl "Spitz" Channell and Richard Miller, third countries, and others. It came from the sales of arms to the Contras and missiles to Iran. It came from the sale of weapons to the CIA. The total would have been at least $10 million greater had the Brunei contribution not been misdirected.

All of the Enterprise's money went into Swiss bank accounts managed by an expert in handling money, Willard Zucker, and was protected by the world's most stringent secrecy laws. But the Enterprise did not rely solely on Swiss law to preserve the confidentiality of its operation. Zucker created a maze of companies through which money could be passed without trace. The corporate operations of the Enterprise were befitting of its covert charter.

One of the main objectives of the Committees was to penetrate this secrecy—to find out where the money came from, and where it went; and thus, to learn about the operations and organization of the Enterprise.

In the financial records of the Enterprise, the Committees found that:

— The plan—which North attributed to Casey—to create a worldwide private covert operation organization, with significant financial resources, was being implemented through a network of offshore companies administered in Switzerland.

— The Enterprise took in nearly $48 million during its first 2 years. Its income-generating capacity came almost entirely from its access to U.S. Government resources and connections: the contributions directed to it by North, the missiles sold to Iran, and the brokering of arms to the Contras as arranged by North.

— The Enterprise generated a substantial amount of its income from the sale of arms to Iran. Before its operations came to a halt, the Enterprise managed to divert at least $3.8 million from the Iran arms sale profits to the Contras.

— The Enterprise spent almost $35.8 million. It used its resources to finance covert operations not reported to Congress as required by law and, in some instances, not disclosed to the President.

— The income of the Enterprise exceeded its expenditures by $12.2 million.

— Secord, Hakim, and Clines took self-determined "commissions" from the $12.2 million surplus to reward themselves for their work on arms deliveries to the Contras and the CIA. The commissions totaled approximately $4.4 million, with an average markup of about 38 percent over the cost of the arms—not 20 percent as asserted by Secord.

— Contrary to their testimony that they only took "commissions" out of the Enterprise accounts, Hakim and Secord also took approximately $2.2 million from the $12.2 million surplus for personal business ventures and personal use. One of these business ventures involved plans to sell weapons to the Contras at substantial profits; another called for the sale of weapons to Iran.

— $5.6 million of the $12.2 million surplus was left in Enterprise accounts managed in Switzerland when the Enterprise ceased its operations in November, 1986. An additional $2.2 million from earlier commission payments and profit distributions remained in separate accounts managed in Switzerland for the benefit of the individual members of the Enterprise.

In the following seven sections, the Committees describe these findings in detail. The first section describes the Enterprise's records and explains the network of companies and bank accounts through which the Enterprise operated. The second traces the sources of the Enterprise's funds and North's role in generating them. The third describes the Enterprise's expenditures. The fourth examines the diversion. The fifth shows what happened to the "surplus," the excess ($12.2 million) of revenues over expenditures, and

discusses Hakim's efforts to pass money to North. The sixth section describes where the Enterprise funds are now, and the seventh tells the story of what happened to the misdirected Brunei contribution.

## SECTION 1: THE SWISS CONNECTION, THE SECRET ACCOUNTS AND COMPANIES, AND THE COVERT CHARTER

### The Swiss Connection

The Enterprise's records were maintained by Compagnie de Services Fiduciaries (CSF). CSF is a Swiss fiduciary company, owned and administered on a daily basis by Willard I. Zucker, a U.S. citizen and former Internal Revenue Service (IRS) lawyer who has resided in Switzerland for 20 years. CSF establishes tax haven offshore companies to hold the funds of its clients, satisfying the necessary formalities and keeping the books. It also accepts its clients' funds, keeping them in its name with a bank or investment house.

A Swiss fiduciary company has no exact counterpart in the United States. The client employing a Swiss fiduciary such as CSF—which uses Panamanian or Liberian companies, Swiss bank accounts, and offshore trust accounts—buys a triple layer of secrecy, a formidable barrier against identification of the location of money.

Starting in 1971, Zucker provided banking-type services to Hakim. The Zucker-Hakim relationship continued into the 1980s; thus, Zucker's services were available when Secord became Hakim's partner in 1983. As early as June 1984, Zucker visited the United States and met with Secord about a Hakim-Secord business project that involved supplying military equipment to an unnamed resistance group.

Zucker was a discreet, efficient, and rapid channel for moving money. By merely telephoning Zucker in Switzerland, Hakim, and later Secord, could order the movement of funds from Swiss bank accounts to the destination of their choice without a paper trace to either of them. With bank accounts in international tax havens and financial centers, CSF would simply issue a check from the most appropriate location. When necessary, Hakim could direct Zucker to set up a new Swiss bank account and an offshore shell company to act as the nominal owner of the account. If Secord or Hakim wanted $50,000 in cash that could not be traced to a Swiss account, Zucker could arrange for that, too; Zucker would call upon business associates and other U.S. contacts to provide the cash and Zucker, in turn, would reimburse his sources.

Thus, Zucker—who had a license to practice law in the United States, all the powers of a Swiss fiduciary, an inside knowledge of the IRS, and experience in meeting the needs of clients such as Hakim—was a covert operator's model banker, accountant, lawyer, and money manager.

## The Covert Charter

North testified that as early as 1984 Casey wanted to establish an offshore entity capable of conducting operations in furtherance of U.S. foreign policy that was "stand-alone"—financially independent of appropriated funds and, in turn, Congressional oversight. During the first half of 1985, the Enterprise simply purchased arms and resold them to the Contras at a profit, which was distributed to its partners. It had no continuing assets of its own and conducted no operations apart from selling arms to the Contras. During this period, North steered contributions from Country 2 to accounts controlled by Contra leader Adolfo Calero in Miami. Calero transferred over $11 million to an Enterprise company named Energy Resources, Inc. Energy Resources paid approximately $9 million for arms which were delivered to the Contras, and the profit of over $2 million was distributed to Secord, Hakim and Clines.

Starting in July of 1985, however, the donations raised by North were no longer sent to Calero's account, but were sent directly to accounts of the Enterprise. Using these funds, the Enterprise then begun to take shape as the "stand-alone" self-financed entity capable of conducting covert actions for the U.S. Government which Casey, according to North, had envisioned. In April and mid-May 1985, three new companies were established: Lake Resources, Gulf Marketing, and Udall Research Corp; and in September 1985, Albon Values and Dolmy Inc. were added to the roster. Most of the funds from Energy were eventually moved to Lake. Lake became the funnel for contributions to the expanded Enterprise organization.

As the network of companies and accounts grew, North asked Secord to produce a chart setting forth the organization of the Enterprise as envisioned by Casey. As North put it:

A: Director Casey had in mind, as I understood it, an overseas entity that was capable of conducting operations or activities of assistance to U.S. foreign policy goals that was a stand-alone—

Q: Self-financed?

A: That was self-financing, independent of appropriated monies and capable of conducting activities similar to the ones that we had conducted here. . . .

Q: Did I understand you to say . . . that the chart that you had drawn by Hakim, which is Exhibit [OLN] 328, was a chart to reflect that concept?

A: . . . that chart was something that I had asked General Secord for.

Q: Was it intended to reflect the concept as described by Director Casey?

A: Yes.

Hakim testified that in February 1986, with the assistance of CSF, he had the chart drawn on a computer and then gave it to Secord. (See figure 22-1)

The chart was the blueprint for the off-the-shelf covert organization that Casey envisioned. It depicts three types of companies: collecting companies, treasury companies, and operating companies (collectively the "Enterprise Companies"). Hakim stated that the idea was that each collecting company would serve as the sole receiver of funds for the Enterprise for a period of time. When the first collecting company became too visible it could be cast aside and the next company would be taken off the "shelf" and brought into use. Thus, secrecy would be preserved.

The treasury companies show the global scope of the plan. Each treasury company was responsible for holding funds for operations in a distinct region of the world: South America, the Middle East, and Africa. Africa was included because, according to Hakim, Secord said—allegedly in jest—

"who knows, if we do a good job, the President may send us to Angola."

Each of the regional treasury companies, Hakim explained, would supply funds to "operating companies" within their respective regions. Each operating company would perform specific operations, and thus, the exposure of any single company would not bring down the entire network. For example, Toyco was to be used for the purchase and sale of weapons—euphemistically called "toys"—for the Contras, while Udall was to be used to run the air resupply operations.

The final element of the chart, the section for reserves marked with an "R," reflects the plan for continuing operations—the essential ingredient for an "off-the-shelf," "self-sustaining" organization. Hakim stated that the "R" stood for the "Reserves" that were to hold the capital necessary for the Enterprise to become self-sufficient. Appropriately, the chart provides that the reserves would be held by CSF Investments Ltd., the Bermuda branch of CSF that invests and manages funds of CSF clients.

In Central America, where activity was the most intense, the Enterprise fully developed the network of companies set forth on the blueprint. Albon Values, the Central American treasury company, directed $4.3 million of its funds to two Central American operating companies: Toyco S.A. and Udall Research Corporation. Performing their operational roles, Toyco purchased arms for the Contras and made payments to Contra leaders, while Udall, among other things, bought and operated the aircraft for the resupply operation. Udall also leased land in Costa Rica, where it built an emergency airstrip for the aircraft dropping supplies in Nicaragua.

# Figure 22-1. Exhibit AH-1: Diagram of the Enterprise

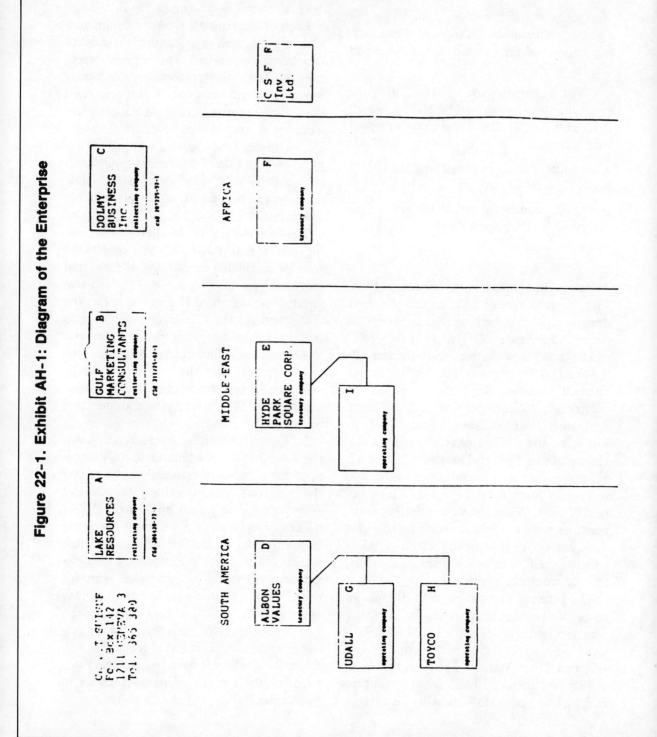

In short order, Zucker could create or dissolve a corporation as circumstances required.

## SECTION 2: INCOME GENERATION

Table 22-1 and Figure 22-2 summarize the sources of the Enterprise income, from December 1984 to December 1986.

The details of each of these income-raising efforts are set forth in other chapters of this Report. The summary here demonstrates that every single source of Enterprise income involved North and the use of U.S. Government resources. Indeed, Secord flatly acknowledged this connection.

Table 22–1.–Enterprise Income[1] *1985 and 1986*

| Source | Amount |
|--------|-------:|
| Arms Sales to the Contras (Calero) | $11,348,926 |
| Total | $11,348,926 |
| Donations for the Contras: | |
|     Institute for North-South Issues (Miller) | 60,000 |
|     IBC (Miller) | 429,839 |
|     IC, Inc. (Miller) | 1,307,691 |
|     Country 3 | 2,000,000 |
|     Joseph Coors | 65,000 |
|     Total | 3,862,530 |
| Arms Sales to Iran: | |
|     Second Channel | 3,600,000 |
|     Israel | 2,685,000 |
|     Khashoggi | 25,000,000 |
|     Total | 31,285,000 |
| Other: | |
|     Arms Sales to the CIA | 1,200,000 |
|     Interest Income and Miscellaneous | 262,637 |
|     Total | 1,462,637 |
| Grand Total Income | 47,959,093 |

[1] Based upon analysis of the CSF ledgers and supporting bank records, H6378-79.

North helped generate the Enterprise's revenues, and, in turn, Secord and Hakim accommodated North's requests for funds and services. At North's request, the Enterprise bought a ship, sent radios to a foreign political party, and provided money to Drug Enforcement Administration (DEA) agents for a covert operation. Hakim testified that, as a result of these kinds of demands, he was not sure who was making the decisions about the use of the Enterprise's funds—North acting as an official of the U.S. Government, or he and Secord. As Hakim put it: "whoever designed this structure, had a situation that they could have their cake and eat it too. Whichever they wanted to have, a private organization, it was private; when they didn't want it to be a private organization it wasn't."

## The Cash Balances

The Enterprise companies built up substantial cash balances, which totaled almost $5.5 million by the time the operations came to a halt in December 1986. Table 22-2 summarizes the ending monthly cash balances for the Enterprise companies and the Reserves. Hakim testified that he understood that North wanted a pool of funds available in Switzerland for the Contras and any other purpose he might designate. Secord testified that he was "generating money to keep the Enterprise going." Later, in an interview, he elaborated:

The majority of the money was in [the Enterprise accounts] to provide operating capital for a very, very large enterprise which owned a ship, and which was preparing to buy a two million dollar 707, and which was preparing to

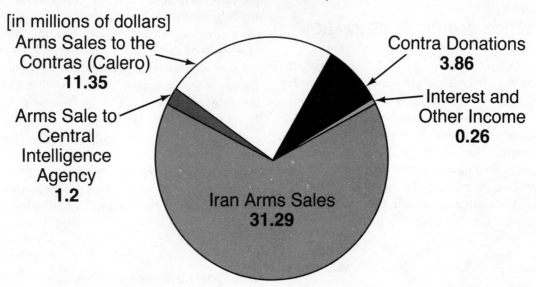

Figure 22-2.
# Enterprise Income
($47.96 Million).

[in millions of dollars]
Arms Sales to the
Contras (Calero)
**11.35**

Contra Donations
**3.86**

Interest and
Other Income
**0.26**

Arms Sale to
Central
Intelligence
Agency
**1.2**

Iran Arms Sales
**31.29**

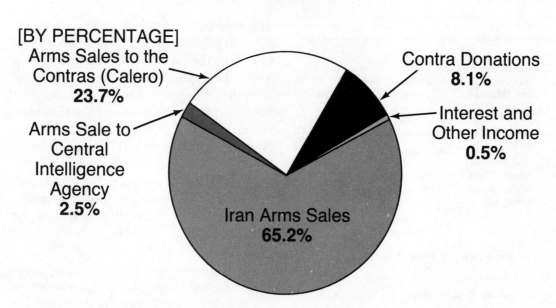

[BY PERCENTAGE]
Arms Sales to the
Contras (Calero)
**23.7%**

Contra Donations
**8.1%**

Interest and
Other Income
**0.5%**

Arms Sale to
Central
Intelligence
Agency
**2.5%**

Iran Arms Sales
**65.2%**

Source: Compagnie de Services Fiduciaires ledgers.

set up permanent headquarters in Europe for a joint Iranian-American commercial venture.

### Table 22-2.—Estimated Ending Monthly Cash Balances [1]

| Month Ending | Enterprise [2] Companies | Reserves | Total |
|---|---|---|---|
| Dec. 84...... | $10,957 | .............................. | $10,957 |
| Jan. 85....... | 418,939 | .............................. | 418,939 |
| Feb ........... | 344,591 | .............................. | 344,591 |
| Mar........... | 3,543,489 | .............................. | 3,543,489 |
| Apr........... | 4,128,476 | .............................. | 4,128,476 |
| May ......... | 1,573,472 | .............................. | 1,573,472 |
| June......... | 1,515,879 | .............................. | 1,515,879 |
| July......... | 1,316,089 | .............................. | 1,316,089 |
| Aug ......... | 725,123 | .............................. | 725,123 |
| Sept ......... | 1,561,631 | .............................. | 1,561,631 |
| Oct............ | 1,123,709 | .............................. | 1,123,709 |
| Nov ......... | 918,867 | .............................. | 918,867 |
| Dec........... | 513,595 | .............................. | 513,595 |
| Jan. 86...... | 394,166 | .............................. | 394,166 |
| Feb .......... | 6,755,693 | .............................. | 6,755,693 |
| Mar........... | 4,106,152 | $2,000,000 | 6,106,152 |
| Apr........... | 2,462,197 | 2,000,000 | 4,462,197 |
| May ......... | 8,799,871 | 2,000,000 | 10,799,871 |
| June......... | 5,269,057 | 4,200,000 | 9,469,057 |
| July.......... | 2,019,829 | 4,200,000 | 6,219,829 |
| Aug ......... | 612,383 | 4,200,000 | 4,812,383 |
| Sept ......... | 1,144,218 | 4,200,000 | 5,344,218 |
| Oct............ | 1,944,486 | 4,200,000 | 6,144,486 |
| Nov ......... | 1,441,331 | 4,200,000 | 5,641,331 |
| Dec........... | 1,299,127 | 4,200,000 | 5,499,127 |

[1] Based upon an analysis of the CSF Ledgers and supporting bank account records. During the month of May the bank account balances went as high as $23 million; the money was rapidly spent, however, pursuant to the Iran arms transactions. Ending monthly balances, shown here, present a more accurate picture of cash freely available to the Enterprise.

[2] Includes funds controlled by Energy, Lake, Gulf, Udall, Albon, Dolmy, ACE, Hyde Park, ToyCo, Stanford Tech Services, S.A., and Defex SA. ACE was created for the Contra air resupply operation. Stanford Tech Services paid American Express bills for Hakim and Secord.

## SECTION 3: EXPENDITURES

All told, the Enterprise spent almost $35.8 million—out of the nearly $48 million it took in—on covert operations. Table 22-3 and Figure 22-3 summarize the expenditures.

When asked about the cash balances, North testified that Casey wanted the Enterprise to become a self-sustaining operation so that "there [would] always be something there which you could reach out and grab . . . at a moment's notice." But North also said that he was surprised by the size of the balance, adding, "I am not willing at this point to accuse anybody." He also acknowledged that he had been told in September 1986—even though the cash balances were then approximately $5.3 million—about a shortage of money available for the Second Channel Iranian initiative.

Throughout 1985 and the first half of 1986, Enterprise cash surpluses, including the Reserves, were increasing. They reached their height in May 1986. As of May 1, 1986, the funds in the accounts of the collecting companies, treasury companies, operating companies (collectively the "Enterprise companies") and the Reserves, contained approximately $10.8 million.

In October 1986, at the same time New York businessman Roy Furmark was threatening to expose the initiative if the Iran arms financiers were not paid, the Enterprise companies and the Reserves still had a total cash balance in the vicinity of $6.1 million.

## Central American Expenditures

In the beginning, the Enterprise simply sold arms to the Contras. Its Contra arms-brokering operation—complete with an offshore company and an offshore account—was only the first stage for the full-service covert organization that, according to North, Casey envisioned.

From December 1984 through July 1985, Calero transferred $11.3 million to Secord.

Secord used the money to provide five arms shipments, described by Secord as Phases I through IV (one of the five shipments was a supplement to a previous one). Secord spent a total of $9.4 million for the arms he sold to Calero, including transportation costs; however, the total cost—including commissions for Secord, Hakim, and Clines—exceeded $11.3 million; the shortfall was made up with other Enterprise funds, including donations from the private fund-raising network.

### Table 22-3.—Enterprise Expenditures [1]

**1. CENTRAL AMERICA:**

Arms Purchased for Sale to Calero:

| | |
|---|---|
| Defex [2] | $7,487,606 |
| Transworld Arms | 1,390,532 |
| Total | 8,878,138 |

Arms Purchased and Donated to Southern front Defex ....... 864,407

Air Resupply:

| | |
|---|---|
| C–123 (Doan Helicopter) | 475,000 |
| C–123 (Hanson Sale) | 250,000 |
| Maule Aircraft (Maule Air) | 183,238 |
| Caribous (Propair Inc.) | 1,096,966 |
| Airfield | 125,000 |
| Southern Air Transport [3] | 1,991,512 |
| Corporate Air Services | 437,688 |
| Aero Contractors | 70,756 |
| East | 657,804 |
| Central American Contractor | 192,233 |
| Quintero | 198,376 |
| David Walker | 110,000 |
| Other [4] | 73,367 |
| Total | 5,861,940 |

Contra Leaders and Others:

| | |
|---|---|
| Calero | 200,000 |
| Contra Leader | 59,500 |
| Contra Leader | 155,000 |
| Calero's Broker | 200,000 |
| Contra Leader | 50,000 |
| Total Contra | 664,500 |

Legal Support:

| | |
|---|---|
| Shea and Gardner | 20,000 |
| Tom Green | 90,000 |
| Sharp, Green, and Lankford | 1,671 |
| Total | 111,671 |
| Other | 130,217 |
| Total | 16,510,873 |

**2. MID-EAST (IRAN ARMS):**

| | |
|---|---|
| Payments to CIA for Arms | 12,237,000 |
| Israel [5] | 732,250 |
| Southern Air Transport | 1,151,000 |
| Aeroleasing | 226,998 |
| CIA Proprietary Airline | 127,700 |
| Related Costs | 457,700 |
| Advance to Richard Second | 260,000 |
| Total | 15,192,648 |

**3. WORLD WIDE:**

| | |
|---|---|
| Erria (North Africa) | 743,409 |
| DEA Agents | 30,150 |
| Radios for foreign government | 100,000 |
| Defex [2] (Arms sold to CIA) | 2,226,987 |
| Total Contra | 3,100,546 |

**4. OTHER** ....... 967,953

Total Expenditures ....... 35,772,020

[1] Based upon an analysis of CSF ledgers and supporting bank account records, H6344–62.
[2] These expenditures include payments to Alkasser totalling $1.5 million. According to Richard Secord, Alkasser is an agent for Defex and the $1.5 million covered arms purchases from Defex. The expenditures also include prepaid transportation costs.
[3] According to Southern Air's records, this includes $598,390 for delivery of arms to Calero and the Southern Front.
[4] Includes $48,165 which, as of 10-22-86, remained in ACE's bank account.
[5] Payment for leasing of aircraft.

From February until May 1986, the Enterprise purchased approximately $3.1 million of military equipment from Defex, a Portuguese arms supplier. It delivered some of the arms, paid for largely by the Iranian weapon sales and third-country contributions, in three airlifts which took place in March, April, and May 1986 (described by Secord as phases V through VII). Additional arms purchased during the same period (the "stranded shipment") never reached the Contras.

In addition, the Enterprise spent approximately $5.9 million for air resupply operations, which had been planned by North, Secord, Clines, and Quintero in July 1985. It acquired an air force, purchasing two C-123 cargo aircraft, two Caribou aircraft, and three Maule aircraft.

Operating the airplanes was expensive: the Enterprise paid Corporate Air Services a

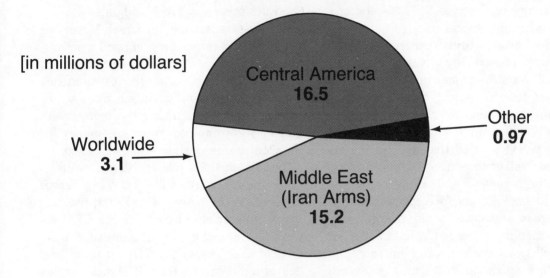

Figure 22-3.
**Enterprise Expenditures, December 1984
thorugh December 1986**
($47.96 Million).

[in millions of dollars]

Central America
**16.5**

Other
**0.97**

Worldwide
**3.1**

Middle East
(Iran Arms)
**15.2**

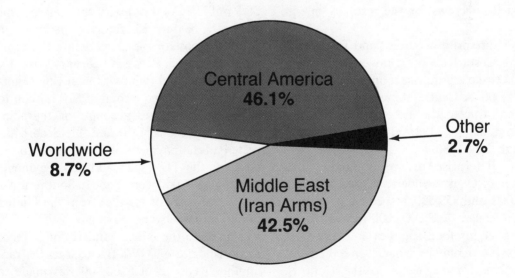

Central America
**46.1%**

Other
**2.7%**

Worldwide
**8.7%**

Middle East
(Iran Arms)
**42.5%**

Source: Compagnie de Services Fiduciaires ledgers.

total of $437,688, directly and indirectly, for the crews used in the resupply operation. Southern Air Transport received approximately $2 million for aircraft spare parts, fuel, and other services in connection with the resupply operation. Eagle Aviation Services and Technology, Inc. (EAST), another Gadd company, received $657,804 for providing other air services.

David Walker, a British expert in guerrilla warfare recruited by North, received $110,000 for his services on May 5, 1986. Secord noted that during the July meeting in Miami it was decided that the resistance needed "to get into some of the urban areas." North testified that in 1985, he authorized Walker to perform military operations "in Managua and elsewhere in an effort to improve the perception that the Nicaraguan resistance could operate anywhere that it so desired." Later, Walker provided two technicians to help carry out a military operation in Nicaragua. Secord and Hakim testified that in 1986 Walker provided air crews for the resupply operation.

The Enterprise acquired land for an airstrip in Costa Rica for a down payment of $125,000 and a purchase money mortgage of $4,875,000. A Central American contractor who constructed the airfield, received payments totaling $192,233 from February through July 1986.

The Enterprise disbursed funds to a number of Contra leaders. It paid $50,000, $155,000, and $59,500, respectively, to three Contra leaders, and $400,000 to Calero and his broker for food supplies and other expenses. North may have had even more complex plans for payments to the Contras. Figure 22-4 summarizes expenditures related to the Contras.

## The Mideast: Expenditures for the Iran Operations

The Enterprise was involved in every NSC-connected shipment of weapons to Iran from November 1985 on. The net surplus generated by these transactions for the benefit of the Enterprise was $16.1 million.

The first transaction, the Israeli November 1985 HAWK shipment, generated a net surplus of $850,317. According to Secord, the Israelis told North that the extra money could be used for "whatever purpose we wanted." After discussing the matter with North, Secord agreed to use the money for the Contras and testified that he did so.

The Enterprise's role in the next transaction—the sale of the 1,000 TOWs in February—was more active. The Enterprise was the "commercial cut-out" for the CIA, receiving the money for the missiles from Ghorbanifar, paying the CIA for them, and delivering them to Iran. The net surplus from this transaction was approximately $5.5 million. As it did with the Calero arms sales, the Enterprise received payment to cover the cost of the arms before the arms were purchased. Between February 7 and 18, 1986, Khashoggi (who was financing Ghorbanifar) transferred a total of $10 million to the Lake Resources account for the shipment. On February 10 and 11, Secord directed a total payment of $3.7 million to the CIA for the TOWs. In addition, payments totaling $484,000 were made to Southern Air for the delivery of missiles from the United States to Israel; one payment of $185,000 was made to the Israeli Ministry of Defense to transport the TOWs from Israel to Iran; another payment of $100,000 was made to the Israeli Ministry of Defense for other related activities; and $31,500 was paid to

Figure 22-4.

# Expenditures Relating to the Contras

($16.5 Million)

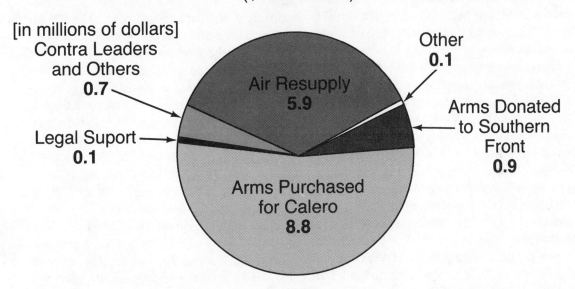

[in millions of dollars]
Contra Leaders and Others
**0.7**

Legal Suport
**0.1**

Air Resupply
**5.9**

Other
**0.1**

Arms Donated to Southern Front
**0.9**

Arms Purchased for Calero
**8.8**

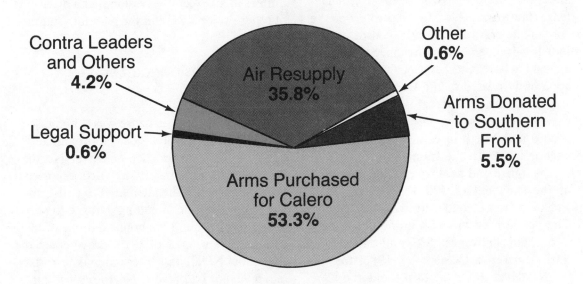

Contra Leaders and Others
**4.2%**

Legal Support
**0.6%**

Air Resupply
**35.8%**

Other
**0.6%**

Arms Donated to Southern Front
**5.5%**

Arms Purchased for Calero
**53.3%**

Source: Compagnie de Services Fiduciaires ledgers.

an Israeli bank for miscellaneous expenses.

The Enterprise's role was the same in the third transaction—the deliveries of the HAWK replacement parts to Iran in May and August 1986, and the shipment of TOWs to Israel to replenish the TOWs sold to Iran in September 1985. The net surplus from this transaction was approximately $8.3 million.

Khashoggi financed the May transaction for Ghorbanifar, transferring $15 million to the Lake Resources account on May 14 and 16, 1986, for the HAWK parts. On May 15 and 16, the Israeli Ministry of Defense transferred a total of $1,685,000 to the Lake Resources account for the TOWs. After Khashoggi's first payment was received, Secord directed the Enterprise to pay $6.5 million to the CIA to cover the cost of the HAWK spare parts and the TOWs. In order to pay for the delivery of the HAWK parts, the TOWs, and McFarlane's trip to Iran, the Enterprise paid $667,000 to Southern Air and $447,250 to the Israeli Ministry of Defense. Dutton received $40,000 to cover the cost of the crew and other expenses on the Israel-to-Iran leg of the mission. Secord also appears to have received $260,000 which was apparently related to the Iran transactions.

Finally, the Enterprise paid $205,015 for expenses of chartering corporate aircraft for Secord and North in connection with their negotiations with the Iranians.

The fourth and final transaction consisted of the shipment of 500 TOWs from U.S. stocks to Iran through the Second Channel. The net surplus was $1.4 million. The Second Channel advanced $3.6 million to Hyde Park Square on October 29, 1986, for the TOWs. Hyde Park, in turn, paid the CIA $2,037,000 for the missiles and incurred other expenses aggregating $161,240.

## Worldwide Projects

The Enterprise's expenditures were not limited to Central America and the Middle East. In May 1986, North directed Secord to purchase a ship for other covert operations. Accordingly, the Enterprise spent $743,409 on the purchase and operation of a Danish vessel named the *Erria*.

North directed a project with DEA agents to try to free certain hostages which contemplated paying bribes and, indirectly, a $2 million ransom to their captors. North turned to businessman and philanthropist H. Ross Perot, who agreed to provide $2 million for the project. In addition, North called upon the Enterprise which paid $30,150 to the DEA agents for their expenses.

At North's request, the Enterprise paid $100,000 for radios supplied to a political party of a foreign nation. Another project involved an attempted propaganda effort in a foreign country. North disclosed to the Committees in an executive session that a number of other projects were in the planning stages.

## The North Residence Security System

Another Enterprise expense was a home security system, which cost approximately $16,000, for the residence of Oliver North. As early as September 1985, North reported harassment which he attributed to anti-Contra demonstrators, including damage to part of the fence around his home and one of his cars. In the spring of 1986, the press reported that Abu Nidal, the international terrorist and assassin, had placed North on his "hit" list. When the FBI advised North that it was not authorized to provide protection, North made a request to Poindexter for assistance. Poindexter did not follow up on the matter. According to the Marine Corps, North did not request protection for his home from the Corps, an option that was available to him. North told Secord about the problem and Secord offered to help.

Secord asked Glenn Robinette, an ex-CIA officer with experience in electronic surveillance and security, for assistance. Secord had hired Robinette in late March to do investigative work related to the Avirgan and Honey lawsuit, at a fee of $4,000 a month plus expenses. Robinette examined the North residence and met first with Mrs. North, then with North and Secord. Robinette proposed a security system designed primarily to provide protection from trespassers, not terrorists, at a cost of $8,500. According to Robinette, North responded to the effect, "Please try to keep it along those lines. Remember, I am a poor lieutenant colonel."

Robinette paid the installers of the system, which included a remote control electronic gate, approximately $13,900—$6,000 in May and roughly $7,900 on July 10th when the installation of the system was complete. At the time of each payment, Robinette reported to Secord, rather than North, for reimbursement because he was "working for Secord." Secord reimbursed Robinette for his time and expenses with $7,000 in cash and a $9,000 check drawn by Zucker from Enterprise funds and mailed to Robinette at Secord's request.

On August 6, 1986, at a meeting in the White House, North told Members of the House Permanent Select Committee on Intelligence, who were inquiring about his involvement with the Contras, that he had installed, at his own expense, a security system to protect his family from anti-Contra demonstrators.

North testified that a bill never came for the security system and that he assumed that "an accommodation was worked between Mr. Robinette and General Secord to make a gift out of [the] security system." Secord, in an interview, denied that he made the gift or approved it. From Secord's viewpoint, there was a misunderstanding: Robinette asked for his expenses and Secord never realized that those expenses were for the security system rather than for investigative work. Robinette testified as follows:

Q: When you went to General Secord to seek reimbursement [for the final payment to the security company], you told him what you were seeking reimbursement for, didn't you?

A: Yes, sir.

Q: He knew he was paying you for the security system, didn't he?

A: That would be my understanding, sir. I usually told him what I was asking to be paid for.

Q: There is no question about it, is there?

A: No, sir, there is no question about it.

In December 1986, North realized that the gift of the security system "just didn't look right." By that time, North had been named in the Justice Department application for the appointment of an Independent Counsel. North called Robinette and asked him to send a bill. Since the system had already been paid for, Robinette assumed that North wanted to make it appear that he (North) had actually paid the bill. Robinette, who told Secord that he was going to send North a bill, sent North two back-dated bills of payment due, dated months earlier but actually written and delivered at the same time in December 1986.

North, in turn, wrote two back-dated letters, designed to fit with Robinette's bills, which told a false story about financial arrangements relating to the security system. In the first, dated May 18, 1986, but written in December 1986, North stated that it was his understanding that he could pay for the system either through 24 monthly installments or by making his house a demonstration unit. North concluded the letter by informing Robinette that he was selecting the second option. In the second letter, dated october 1, 1986, but also written in December, North apologized for the delay in responding to the first and second notices and reminded Robinette that he wished to pay for the system by making his home available as a demonstration unit. In his testimony, North stated that he typed at least one of the letters on a demonstration typewriter in a typewriter store, rather than using a home typewriter.

On the morning of March 16, 1987, as Robinette went out to get his morning paper, he was interviewed by a reporter about the driveway gate which was part of the North security system. Robinette stated that he installed the gate for North at no charge, hoping that North "might steer business his way" and that he would be able to put in gates for North's neighbors. Later in the day, North called Robinette, asking to meet with him on the following day at his lawyer's office, and requesting that Robinette bring copies of the back-dated letters.

Robinette gave the letters to North's attorneys, but did not say they were spurious. Robinette then went to see Secord who, upon learning that Robinette had sent North a bill for the security system, stated, "You did the right thing." That same afternoon Robinette received a call from North's attorney, who told him not to protect North, and to "tell the truth, tell the truth, tell the truth." He also advised Robinette to get an attorney. Robinette did so. Later, after receiving immunity, he related the above-described events to the Independent Counsel and the Committees.

North testified that in fabricating the letters in December 1986, "I did probably the grossest misjudgment that I have made in my life." North offered no explanation as to why he also created the false record, other than that the gift "just didn't look right."

## Unexplained Cash Expenditures

The CSF ledgers record expenditures of approximately $902,110 during the period from March 1985 to October 1986 without identifying their specific purpose. Two transactions accounted for the bulk of these funds. The first involved a $260,000 cash disbursement on May 21, 1986. In the second transaction, $310,000 was withdrawn from the Hyde Park account on July 18, 1986. The ledgers state that in both cases, the funds were "in transit," but where they went is unknown. In addition, the Enterprise transferred $152,200 to an account called Codelis. Finally, Hakim, Secord, and Clines received cash totaling $179,610 from various Enterprise accounts; these transactions were listed as "business expenses," and were in amounts of up to $50,000 each.

## SECTION 4: THE DIVERSION—HOW MUCH?

The Iran arms sales generated a $16.1 million surplus for the Enterprise. The Enterprise managed to spend part of that money, $3.8 million, for the Contras before its operations were stopped.

As of November 19, 1985, the day before the first money from the Iran arms transactions was deposited into the Enterprise, the Enterprise had a cash balance of approximately $1 million. From November 20, 1985 through December 1986, the Enterprise received an additional $2.4 million in donations for the Contras. During the same period, the Enterprise spent approximately $7.2 million on behalf of the Contras. The shortfall—$3.8 million—was diverted from the Iran arms sale surplus.

The diversion did not take place by accident. In fact, North helped set the price of the arms so that a surplus would be created which could be used for the Contras. According to Secord, North consistently instructed him to use the surpluses generated from the Iranian arms sales for the Contra project. North apparently thought that at least $6 million of the Iran surplus from the May transaction alone would be used for the Contras. He sent Poindexter a PROF note on May 16, saying that the Enterprise had "more than $6 million available for immediate disbursement." Poindexter testified that he believed that the Enterprise was giving the Contras all of the surplus from the Iran arms sales.

## SECTION 5: PROFITS—WHO MADE WHAT

### Breaking the Code Names

Hakim was both a promoter and a salesman: The Enterprise was a great opportunity to make a great deal of money and, he said, at the same time, to serve both his new country, the United States, and his native country, Iran. Hakim added:

> I never pretended to undertake the tasks I was asked to perform for philanthropic purposes and I made that clear to all of those with whom I [w]as involved—including General Secord, Lieutenant Colonel North, the CIA, and the Iranians.

The Enterprise fulfilled Hakim's objective: without risking any of its own or Hakim's money, the Enterprise made extraordinary profits through weapons sales. Its revenues of $48 million exceeded its expenses by $12.2 million. Secord preferred to speak of this money as "residuals" or "surplus" rather than profit because he did not want to be called a "profiteer."

Not only was the structure and operation of the Enterprise cloaked in secrecy, so was the distribution of its profits. The CSF records indicate that $6.8 million of the $12.2 million "surplus" was distributed as profits directly or indirectly to five entities: "Albert Hakim, Korel Assets, C. Tea, Scitech, and Button." In addition, $4.2 million was transferred to CSF to be held in a fiduciary capacity for the Enterprise as "Reserves." The balance, $1.2 million, remained at the end of 1986 as undistributed cash in the Enterprise's operating companies.

## Korel Assets

Hakim testified that Korel Assets was a corporation that held Secord's profit share. The records of the Enterprise support Hakim's testimony. Profit distributions to Korel match, often to the last dollar, distributions to Secord's equal partner, Hakim.

According to the CSF Ledgers, $1.62 million was transferred out of the Enterprise accounts for the benefit of "Korel Assets." Most of this money was distributed to the Korel Assets Fiduciary Fund where it remained unspent. However, $269,000 was transferred either directly from the Enterprise accounts or indirectly through the Korel Fiduciary Fund to the U.S. or elsewhere. The Committees have traced most of this money to: Secord's personal bank account (including payments for a personal airplane) ($74,600); payments for Secord's Porsche ($31,825); payments for a stay by Secord at a health farm ($3,075); and cash withdrawals where Secord signed the withdrawal slips ($33,000). An additional $126,492 went for other purposes.

Secord testified that he was unaware that Korel Assets stood for him and that it held his profit share. He claimed that the money he personally received from Switzerland came through Hakim as personal loans or as payments for work unrelated to the Enterprise. Hakim never mentioned Korel to Secord. As far as Secord was concerned, the money for the Porsche was a loan from Hakim (even though Secord signed no note and paid no interest), and the money for the airplane was Secord's share of a consulting fee. Hakim denied that the money for a Porsche was a loan and indicated that in both cases he took the money from Secord's profit share.

## "Button"

On May 20, 1986, the Enterprise transferred $200,000 to "B. Button." The money was wired out of an Enterprise account to CSF, which agreed to hold the funds for "B. Button" under a CSF fiduciary agreement. The transfer was recorded in the Button Capital Ledger as a distribution for the benefit of Button.

Hakim's explanation of the Button money changed during his deposition. He initially testified that the Button fund was set up to pay death benefits for the pilots in the Contra air operation and that Button meant "Button up or something." When told of a handwritten note by Zucker referring to "Mrs. Belly Button," Hakim said that Button meant "bellybutton" and gave an almost incomprehensible explanation. Hakim, who denied that Button stood for anyone's name, failed to explain why "Button" had a Capital Ledger, as if it were sharing profits.

Two days later, Hakim stated that the $200,000 was a death benefit for Mrs. North and her family in the event of North's death. The Capital Ledger "Button" referred to distributions for the benefit of North. Shortly thereafter, Hakim produced the "B. Button" fiduciary agreement which showed that $200,000 was being held by Zucker for B. Button. And after being shown the reference to "Mrs. Bellybutton," Hakim admitted that it was the code name for Mrs. North. (Button was short for North's codename—Bellybutton.)

Hakim testified that he had proposed to Secord that a $500,000 death benefit be set up in connection with North's trip to Tehran in May 1986, but that Secord had rejected the proposal telling Hakim that he did not "understand a soldier's life." Hakim then proposed $200,000, and Secord acquiesced. Hakim said that his motive was humanitarian: he had become extremely fond of North (whom he had met only once) and wanted to relieve North's anxieties about his family. He asserted he never told North about the Button Fund, but did say if North did not return from Tehran "as long as one of us is alive you need not worry about your family."

The death benefit for North had not emerged in Secord's prior interviews and public testimony. When asked about Hakim's testimony, Secord acknowledged that Hakim told him of the need for "insurance coverage" for North. Secord claimed that he told Hakim that they "couldn't set up an insurance coverage for Ollie North," but that North could be covered by the $200,000 death benefit fund which had been set up in November 1985 for the pilots involved in the resupply operation. He recalled opposing the notion of a $500,000 fund.

North offered a third version. He testified that in early March, just after he met Hakim, Hakim told him, "If you don't come back, I will do something for your family."

The matter did not end with the creation of the Button Fund. Hakim also testified that he sought a way to give money to Mrs. North for the education of the North children, after he learned from Secord that North was worried about college costs. Hakim testified that he decided to offer Mrs. North $15,000, representing the annual interest on the $200,000 Button account, and that he asked Zucker to try to pass money to Mrs. North in a "legal, proper way." According to Hakim, Zucker telephoned Mrs. North directly, and told her that he was representing an anonymous admirer of her husband who wanted to help her family financially and

that he wished to meet with her in Philadelphia.

Secord gave a different version. He testified that Hakim never said anything to him about giving money to Mrs. North, but had mentioned only that Zucker was a "wizard" at making money for other people, and that he might be able to advise Mrs. North on investments. Secord stated that he told Hakim that the Norths did not have any money to invest, and that you could not make "chicken soup out of chicken feathers." Although Secord considered it a "bad idea," Hakim insisted that he ask North. Secord called North at least twice about the matter. In particular, Hakim spoke to Secord about the "requirement" to put a North child in college. As a result, Secord testified, Mrs. North met with Zucker when he came to Philadelphia in the spring. North testified that he sent his wife to Philadelphia for the meeting with Zucker, but that

[t]he purpose, as I understood it, of that meeting was that my wife would be in touch with the person who would, if I didn't return, do something for my family.

Hakim testified that Zucker came up with the idea of having a client of his, a real estate developer, employ Mrs. North. Hakim stated that he told Zucker, "if the guy doesn't have an opening, cannot pay for it, we will pay for it. In other words we [would have] paid the guy to pay her so she would work." In September, Zucker called a Washington lawyer, David Lewis. Lewis testified that he visited Zucker in Geneva on October 10, 1986. Zucker asked Lewis if he had a client who could pass money to the wife of a White House official disguised as compensation for her services in a real estate transaction. The money, Zucker explained, was due her husband. The husband's name, to the best of Lewis' recollection, was Lt. Col. North. Zucker said that Lewis' client would be reimbursed through a Swiss account, or any other account in the world. Lewis demurred. He reported this attempt to the Committees and the Independent Counsel in February 1987 after he realized the significance of the conversation. Secord testified that he knew nothing about this effort.

No money, so far as the Committees can determine, was ever passed to the Norths by Zucker or Hakim. $15,000 was transferred, however, to STTGI on May 5, 1986. The transmittal instructions contained the notation, in Zucker's writing, "Mrs. Bellybutton."

There is no evidence that North knew of the effort to pass money to his family through Lewis. Hakim stated, "I put a wheel into motion and then if North's family wanted to open the door . . . they could. If they wanted to close the door . . . they also could do that."

## The Surplus

The $12.2 million in Enterprise surplus was distributed in a number of ways. (See Figure 22-5, Breakdown of $12.2 million surplus). The CSF ledgers indicate that Secord, Hakim, and Clines took part of the surplus as commissions on arms sales to the Contras. But Secord and Hakim did not stop with the self-determined commissions. The ledgers also indicate that they took part of the $12.2 million as seed money for risky personal business ventures, for personal expenditures, and for the Button fund. Finally, Secord and Hakim transferred part of the surplus to CSF

to be held as Reserves for future projects by Hakim, Secord, and North.

## The Commissions

Approximately $4.4 million of the Enterprise profits went to Secord, Hakim, and Clines as commissions on arms sales to the Contras and the CIA—even though North testified that he did not intend to make anyone a rich man from the sales. Apparently, Secord and Hakim never negotiated with Calero or anyone else for these commissions; they simply took what they wanted out of the general pool of money in the Enterprise accounts. Hakim described the basic arrangement in his testimony as follows:

Q: Your gross income comes from third parties, contributions from third countries, private contributions, profits on the sale of arms to Iran.

So really as far as the profit that you take or the leftover in the enterprise you really negotiate with yourself as to the amount of profits, do you not?

A: That is correct.

Q: And that makes it very flexible for you as to whether or not you want to claim 75 percent or 50 percent or 30 percent, isn't that basically the situation?

A: You are correct, sir. . . .

Q: You simply negotiate with yourself?

A: Yes.

As noted, Secord described each arms shipment as a separate phase, Phases I–VII. The final shipment for the Contras, purchased in August of 1986, never made it to

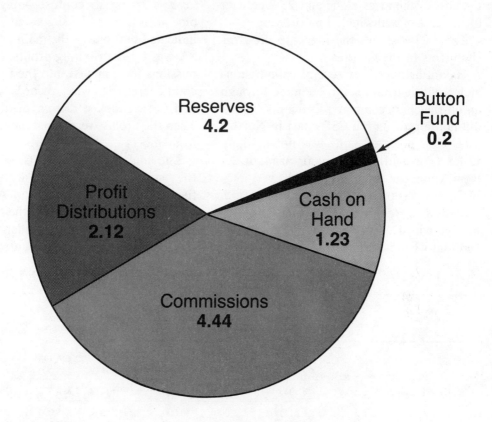

Figure 22-5.
**Breakdown of $12.19 Million Surplus**
(in millions)

Reserves
**4.2**

Button
Fund
**0.2**

Profit
Distributions
**2.12**

Cash on
Hand
**1.23**

Commissions
**4.44**

Source: Compagnie de Services Fiduciaires ledgers.

the Contras and thus Secord did not describe it as a "Phase"; here, it is referred to as the Stranded Shipment.

The CSF ledgers indicate that on Phases I through IV, Secord and Hakim allocated themselves and Clines a total of approximately $2.7 million, equal to 31.6 percent of the cost of the arms alone and 28.7 percent of the cost of arms including delivery.

Table 22-4 shows the mark-up on arms shipments to the Contras.

Hakim arranged for several commissions and profit distributions to be made through an off-the-chart company, Defex SA, which did not appear on the CSF chart in North's safe. The choice of name was not random. Defex (Portugal) was a major arms dealer from whom the Enterprise bought weapons. Defex SA was owned by the Enterprise and, according to Hakim and Secord, had no connection with Defex (Portugal). Hakim testified that when he transferred funds to Defex

SA, "people" would think that the funds were being used to purchase arms from Defex (Portugal). Secord testified that Defex SA was a "cover mechanism" set up by Hakim to disguise the source of money paid to arms dealers.

Hakim could not remember exactly whom he was trying to confuse—maybe Eastern bloc arms dealers, he suggested. The ledgers indicated that one of the main uses of Defex SA was for distributing profits. Often, commissions were moved into the Defex SA account, creating wire records and ledger entries that looked like payments to Defex. Then the profits were wired out of Defex SA to members of the Enterprise.

The final commission distribution was for the "stranded shipment." In August 1986, the restrictions of the Boland Amendment were about to be lifted and the CIA was to resume its role as arms supplier to the Contras. Hakim and Clines decided that they

Table 22–4.—Mark-up on Arms Purchased for Contras According to CSF Ledgers

| Phase | Cost of arms | Cost of transportation | Related delivery costs[1] | Total costs | Total commissions per ledger | Commissions as a percent of total cost | Commissions as a percent of arms cost |
|---|---|---|---|---|---|---|---|
| I–III[2] | $6,491,159 | $566,385 | $98,100 | $7,155,644 | $2,446,493 | 34.19 | 37.69 |
| IV | 2,044,258 | 118,500 | 73,220 | 2,235,978 | 252,000 | 11.27 | 12.31 |
| Total Phases I–IV | 8,535,417 | 684,885 | 171,320 | 9,391,622 | 2,698,493 | 28.73 | 31.62 |
| V | 222,003 | 121,000 | 10,000 | 353,003 | 345,000 | 97.73 | 155.40 |
| VI | 229,279 | 120,000 | 66,780 | 416,059 | 229,303 | 55.11 | 100.01 |
| VII | 413,158 | 0 | 142,127 | 555,285 | 301,168 | 54.24 | 72.89 |
| Stranded shipment | 2,227,001 | 0 | 0 | 2,227,001 | 861,327 | 38.68 | 38.68 |
| Post phase IV | 3,091,441 | 241,000 | 218,907 | 3,551,348 | 1,736,798 | 48.91 | 56.18 |
| Grand total | 11,626,858 | 925,885 | 390,227 | 12,942,970 | 4,435,291 | 34.27 | 38.15 |

[1] Related Transportation Costs includes 'bonuses' paid to Quintero, for assistance on arms deliveries and other miscellaneous expenses. SC4103. Secord Test. 5/5/87 at 54.

[2] The commissions paid on phases I–III were in lump sums for all three phases and cannot be accurately allocated to the individual phases.

Source: CSF Ledgers, bank documents, and information provided by Secord and Hakim.

should have one last distribution. They made it a large one. The purchase price of the weapons was about $2.2 million. The weapons were purchased, but delivery to the Contras was never completed. Hence, the weapons were known as the "stranded shipment" and were ultimately sold for a $1 million loss to an intermediary who later sold the weapons to the CIA.

But the loss was not limited to $1 million. Hakim testified that he and Clines proposed that the group reward itself for their work with a fee of $861,327, which is equal to 39 percent of the cost of the weapons. According to Hakim, Secord approved the commission and the division of profits among the group. The profits were split on a 30/30/30/10 basis: $258,398 each to Hakim, Korel Assets, and Clines, and $86,133 to Scitech.

## Other Profit Distributions

In addition to commissions, the partners took more than $2.1 million in profit distributions from the Enterprise accounts. Apparently, $420,000 of this money was used by Secord, Hakim, and Clines for personal and other purposes. The balance, approximately $1.7 million, was invested in a variety of business ventures.

While most of these business ventures had no connection to the Enterprise, one venture involved proposed sales of military equipment to the Contras and another contemplated sales of military equipment to the Iranians. Zucker played an active role in the ventures as an adviser. In at least one case, he was also a potential partner.

## The Reserves

The Enterprise transferred $4.2 million to CSF to be held in three fiduciary accounts referred to as the "Reserves." A large part of the Reserve monies appear to have come from the proceeds of the Iranian arms sales.

According to the CSF fiduciary agreements, Hakim was the owner of the Reserves; Secord testified, however, that the Enterprise was the beneficial owner of the Reserves and Hakim acknowledged that the Reserves were treated as the Enterprise's money. Table 22-6, Distributions to Reserves, shows the amount of each Reserve, the operational company from which the monies were taken, and the date each Reserve was established.

Hakim testified that Reserve 2, containing $2,000,000, was to be used to pay money to persons associated with the Second Channel. According to Hakim, if the Second Channel initiative was successful, the money was to be invested for those persons in the joint Iranian-U.S. venture which was being planned; if the Second Channel was unsuccessful, it would be used as baksheesh. Reserve 1, containing an additional $2,000,000, was to be used for any purpose, including "operational purposes."

The CSF fiduciary agreement governing Reserve 1—the one for covert operations—provided that should Hakim die, Secord would have direct control over it and should

Table 22–6.—Distributions to Reserves[214]

| Reserve | Date | Amount | Source |
|---------|------|--------|--------|
| Reserve 1 | 3/05/86 | $2,000,000 | Gulf Marketing |
| Reserve 2 | 6/18/86 | 2,000,000 | Hyde Park |
| Reserve 3 | 6/18/86 | 200,000 | Hyde Park |

[214] Based upon CSF Ledgers.

Secord die, North would have direct control. Should North die, the remaining portion of the Reserve would be divided equally among the estates of all three men. The instructions to CSF were irrevocable without the consent of all the beneficiaries. Hakim said that in setting up Reserve 1, he simply followed the structure of the Enterprise from top to bottom as he understood it—with North on the top.

North testified that he specifically requested that some Reserve funds be put aside for a number of special activities. Those activities included recovering military equipment, setting up a propaganda operation in foreign countries, and influencing domestic politics in foreign countries.

Secord and North testified briefly about the origin of the Hakim "wills"—the provisions for continuing control over the Reserves in the event of Hakim's death. Secord told the Committees that he knew Hakim had made arrangements to cover a catastrophe but professed ignorance of the details. North claimed to have been totally in the dark as to the arrangements. He noted, however, that at one point he asked Secord what would happen to the money if "both you guys go down on some airplane flight." According to North, Secord responded, "Don't worry, arrangements will be made so that these operations can continue." Hakim claimed that he told North that if he, Hakim, died, North would be in total control.

Neither Secord nor Hakim had a clear recollection of the purpose of Reserve 3 containing $200,000. Hakim suggested that it might have been set up to cover "death benefits" for those working on the resupply operation, or as a set aside for a Secord-Hakim business venture. Secord remembered setting aside $200,000 for death benefits. He insisted, however, that there was only one such fund and it was converted into the Button fund. The purpose of Reserve 3 remains a mystery.

## SECTION 6: WHERE IS THE MONEY NOW

The Enterprise generated a surplus of $12.2 million. Some of this surplus went directly to Secord, Clines, and Hakim. Substantial funds, $7.8 million, however, remained under management in Switzerland when the Enterprise ceased its operations. This money was apparently frozen by Swiss authorities at the request of the Justice Department.

Of the $7.8 million, approximately $2 million is held in CSF fiduciary accounts for the benefit of Hakim, Korel Assets and Scitech. Approximately $200,000 remains in the Button account and another $4.2 million is held as reserves for the Enterprise by CSF. The balance, $1.2 million, is in the Enterprise's Swiss bank accounts, unallocated for any purpose. Table 22-7 shows the location of the $7.8 million.

The participants have different ideas of what should happen to the money. Secord testified that the money belongs to the Enterprise and that is up to Hakim, as the owner of the Enterprise, to decide what to do with it. He would recommend to Hakim that the money, after expenses, be donated to the William Casey Fund for the support of the Contras.

Likewise, North testified that he would send "that money, every nickel of it, to the Nicaraguan Resistance, which was indeed the original purpose of setting up all those non-U.S. government entities."

Hakim said that he was entitled to, and

Table 22-7.—Individuals and Entities that Control Unspent Enterprise Funds

| Description | Transferred from Enterprise | Investment Income | Withdrawals | Balance 12-31-86 | Total |
|---|---|---|---|---|---|
| Cash in Enterprise Companies | | | | $1,227,173 | $1,227,173 |
| **Reserves Held by CSF:** | | | | | |
| Reserve 1 | $2,000,000 | 144,398 | 15,246 [1] | 2,129,152 | |
| Reserve 2 | 2,000,000 | 75,583 | 23,673 [1] | 2,051,909 | |
| Reserve 3 | 200,000 | 7,915 | 50,769 [2] | 157,146 | 4,338,207 |
| **CSF Fiduciary Funds:** | | | | | |
| Hakim | 1,613,649 | 301,743 [3] | 1,655,799 [4] | 259,593 | |
| Button | 200,000 | 14,330 | 2,339 [1] | 211,991 | |
| Korel | 1,434,121 | 218,192 | 105,278 [5] | 1,547,035 | |
| Sci Tech | 458,424 | 34,535 | 302,822 [6] | 190,137 | 2,208,756 |
| Total [7] | | | | | 7,774,136 |

[1] CSF management fees.
[2] CSF management fees and a transfer to Sharp, Green, and Lankford.
[3] Generally, all funds transferred to CSF came from Enterprise accounts. One notable exception was $258,300 transferred by Hakim from his California bank account on May 29, 1986, to his CSF fiduciary account to repay a CSF loan. These funds are included in Hakim's income amount.
[4] Traced, for the most part, to Hakim's U.S. bank accounts and Hakim projects.
[5] Traced to Secord's bank account and payments made for Secord's bills.
[6] Traced, for the most part, to Secord/Hakim business ventures.
[7] CSF records indicate that, as of 12-31-86, all of the money was held for CSF by Merrill, Lynch, Pierce, Fenner, and Smith, Inc. (Geneva office).
Source: CSF Ledgers, H6363A.

promised a substantial interest in, the Enterprise funds. Hakim recognized that North's view of who owned the funds differed from his but realized he would benefit either way—either he would profit from opening the trade door to Iran, or he would fight North for a share of the money. Hakim declared that if the United States had tried to end the Iran initiative, "I guarantee you that I would have put up a big fight to get as much as I could from that money before letting it go." Hakim also testified that "obligations" were still outstanding to the Iranians who helped open the Second Channel.

## SECTION 7: BRUNEI CONTRIBUTION

If not for a typographical error, the Enterprise would have received an additional $10 million generated by U.S. Government ef-

forts: the misdirected contribution from the Sultan of Brunei.

In December 1985, Congress amended Boland to provide explicitly that solicitation by the State Department of humanitarian aid for the Contras from third countries was not precluded. Solicitation of lethal assistance was not addressed. The National Security Planning Group decided to pursue such third-country funding at a meeting with the President on May 16, 1986. These funds would bridge the gap until the anticipated resumption of U.S. aid in the fall.

The Administration estimated that the earliest that aid could be made available to the Contras through the normal appropriations channels was August or September 1986. In the face of continued House opposition and the likelihood of a filibuster in the Senate, Secretary Shultz advocated seeking aid from third countries as the course of least resistance. He believed that it was highly improbable that Congress would support a re-programming of some money from the Department of Defense for non-military aid to the Contras and he argued that it would be desirable to approach other countries. Secretary Shultz was asked to draw up a list of possible donors.

In discussions at the State Department following the National Security Planning Group meeting, Secretary Shultz ruled out any countries receiving U.S. aid or whose political relationship with the United States was otherwise delicate. The Secretary's criteria eliminated all the obvious candidates, including nations in the Middle East. In early June, Assistant Secretary Elliott Abrams recommended the Sultanate of Brunei—a tiny, oil-rich nation on the northwest coast of Borneo—and the Department agreed. Abrams described how the selection was made:

Take a list of countries in the world and exclude those with insufficient resources to make a humanitarian contribution. Exclude further those which are right-wing dictatorships, or which are, if you will, on the other side, allied with the Soviet Union. Then exclude those . . . over which we can be said to have some leverage. You are left essentially with oil producers. Then look for non-Arab—since I had been to Ambassador Murphy already, non-Middle East non-Arab oil producers. Venezuela, I thought, would not do this. You are down to Brunei.

Since Secretary Shultz planned to travel to Asia in June 1986, Abrams was tasked with getting an appropriate account number in the event of a successful solicitation of Brunei for a contribution to the Contras. Abrams approached North, who, with Poin-dexter's concurrence, gave Abrams the number of the Enterprise's Lake Resources account in Switzerland. Abrams was not told that this was an account controlled by North, Hakim, and Secord for disbursing lethal (not humanitarian) aid to the Contras.

But either North or his secretary made a mistake. In writing down the account number or in typing it, North or his secretary apparently inverted the first two digits, so that the correct account number at Credit Suisse, *386*-430-22-1, became *368*-430-22-1. North gave Abrams a typed card containing the erroneous number and Abrams gave it to the Secretary of State. The Secretary of State was informed by Abrams that the account belonged to the Contras; Abrams said he had received that information from North.

Abrams, carrying North's account number and using the cover name "Mr. Kenilworth," met with an official of Brunei in London on August 9, 1986, and successfully solicited a $10 million contribution for humanitarian aid. Abrams gave the Bruneian official the Swiss account number from North.

On September 15, Brunei confirmed to the State Department that "arrangements have been consummated." But North advised Abrams three days later that no funds had been received. The State Department went back to Brunei and was told that transferring the funds would require the U.S. to "wait for a short while before the transaction is completed."

By November, the funds still had not arrived in the Lake Resources account. This remained true as of November 25, when the Attorney General announced discovery of the diversion. On December 1, Secretary Shultz instructed Charles Hill to brief the State Department's Legal Adviser, Abraham

Sofaer, on the circumstances surrounding the solicitation. According to Sofaer, this was the first time he learned about the Brunei contribution.

When he was informed of the Brunei contribution, Sofaer directed the U.S. Ambassador to advise the Brunei Government that if the funds were still under its control, they should be frozen. But on December 4, 1986, Brunei informed the State Department that it had sent the funds to the designated account in August and could not withdraw the transfer. Sofaer testified that on December 4, he received the approval of officials at the Justice Department and the White House to approach the Swiss Ambassador in Washington with a request that all accounts related to Lake Resources and Oliver North be frozen. Simultaneously, he ordered a cable sent to the U.S. Ambassador in Switzerland instructing that the same request be made. The request became effective the following morning. The problem, however, was that nobody in Washington—not even Oliver North— knew where the Brunei funds had gone. A diplomatic coup had become a diplomatic fiasco. The fiasco continued into 1987.

With the assistance of Swiss authorities aided by the State Department, the Committees determined that the Brunei funds had ended up in the Credit Suisse account of a person described by the Swiss as a wealthy Swiss businessman involved in the shipping business who alleged that the $10 million flowed into his account in connection with a shipping transaction. The account-holder had withdrawn the $10 million transfer shortly after it arrived at Credit Suisse and placed it in a certificate of deposit at another Swiss bank in Geneva, where it had been collecting interest.

In May 1987, the matter was placed in the hands of a Swiss Magistrate, who, with the Committees' encouragement, froze the certificate of deposit. The Government of Brunei was notified by the State Department and asserted its claim. The Committees understand that, as of this writing, the $10 million has been returned to Brunei, but the interest remains frozen.

Swiss authorities have declined to reveal the identity of the individual who received the funds. The Committees were assured by the Swiss Magistrate, however, that the individual is neither a principal in the investigation, nor related to any of the principals.

# CHAPTER 23

# Other Privately Funded Covert Operations

Under the plan that Lt. Col. Oliver L. North attributed to Director of Central Intelligence William Casey, profits from the Iran arms sales were to fund not just the Contras, but other covert operations of the Enterprise as well. Before the Iran arms sales became public, Lt. Col. Oliver L. North had begun implementing certain projects he and Casey believed the Enterprise could perform.

"We always assumed," North said later "that there would come a time again, as indeed it did, where the Congress would make available the moneys necessary to support the Nicaraguan freedom fighters." When that happened, the Enterprise, functioning free of government scrutiny and with ample funds, could carry out other covert projects; many were intended "to be conducted jointly [with] . . . other friendly intelligence services" while others would be limited to activities conducted by North, Secord and Hakim.

Even before the Enterprise was formed, however, North was operating with non-appropriated funds on another project that the Government could not do because it was contrary to United States policy—the ransom of the hostages.

## THE DEA RANSOM OPERATION

Before the Iran initiative was conceived, the NSC staff was working on a plan to ransom the hostages. Confronted with the policy of the U.S. Government of not paying for the hostages release, North found a loophole by using private funds.

Edward V. Hickey, Jr., an Assistant to the President, attended a meeting of the Terrorist Incident Working Group (TIWG) in January 1985. Hickey noted that the area in Lebanon, where the hostages were held, was a known area of narcotics trafficking. Hickey had a personal interest in the hostages. He had known William Buckley, the CIA Chief of Station in Beirut who had been kidnapped on March 16, 1984.

Hickey asked his long-time friend, a DEA Special Agent (Agent 1), if DEA could help to locate Buckley and the other hostages. Agent 1 reported that another DEA Special

Agent (Agent 2) had contacts in the Middle East who might be able to help. Shortly thereafter, Agents 1 and 2 met with Hickey and Hickey's military aid General Matthew Caulfield. Agent 2 told Hickey that he had an excellent source with impressive contacts in Lebanon.

Following this meeting, Hickey met with Deputy National Security Adviser John Poindexter and encouraged him to include the DEA in the Hostage Locating Task Force (HLTF). On February 13, 1985, National Security Adviser McFarlane notified the Departments of State, Defense, and Justice and the CIA that the Task Force would report to the TIWG and it would include the DEA. The DEA was to be represented on the Task Force by Abraham Azzam, an Arabic speaking agent of Lebanese heritage. Funding for the Task Force would come from the CIA.

With the approval of DEA Administrator Mullen, the DEA provided Agents 1 and 2 with $20,000 for travel, expenses and for payments to their sources for information on the hostages. If the DEA's sources were productive, they were to be turned over to the CIA for further operational handling. Agents 1 and 2 were instructed to report to Azzam, who in turn was to report to DEA Deputy John Lawn.

Agents 1 and 2 were not to be involved operationally in securing the release of the hostages; their function was to assist in obtaining intelligence information regarding the location of the hostages. According to Lawn, he gave these instructions because Federal law provides that DEA's responsibility is for operations that concern drug-related law enforcement. (See Figure 23-1.)

In February 1985, Azzam, Agent 1, and Agent 2 met with Agent 2's source in Geneva and in New York. The source claimed that he had contacts who could arrange to pay off individuals in Lebanon who had enough influence over the captors to arrange for the release or escape of the hostages. He added that $50,000 was needed to begin operations, and that the hostages could be released if the United States sold weapons, tanks, airplanes, and other military equipment to those controlling the holders of the hostages. Oliver North, the NSC staff member responsible for terrorism issues, later told the agents the United States could not sell weapons.

Under the Task Force authorization, the CIA was to pay for hostage information. But the CIA was reluctant to do so without proof that Agent 2's source was legitimate and would produce valuable information. Agent 1, Agent 2, Hickey, and Caulfield then met with Poindexter to explain their need for funds. Poindexter told them he would look into the matter.

In early March 1985, Hickey arranged a meeting among North, Agent 1, Agent 2, Azzam, and Caulfield. At the meeting, the agents explained their efforts to North and informed him that the CIA was reluctant to provide the money. In a follow-up phone call to North on March 12, 1985, Caulfield said the DEA's efforts were "not very sophisticated." He explained that the plan now called for four hostages to be released in exchange for $1 million per hostage, once the $50,000 was paid to the source. North's notes of the conversation reflected his own reaction: "fundamental decision: Do we pay ransom?" North answered his own question with his actions: he became the operational leader of the project.

Soon thereafter, the DEA agents arranged

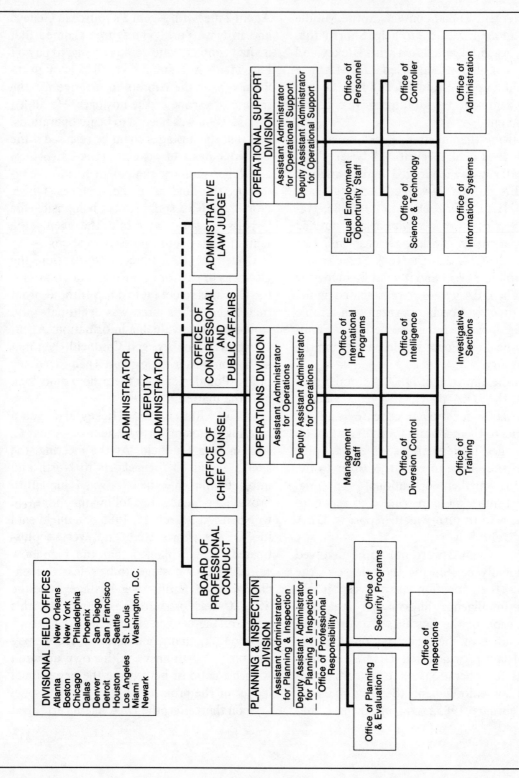

**Figure 23-1.   Organization Chart of the Drug Enforcement Administration.**

DIVISIONAL FIELD OFFICES
Atlanta          New Orleans
Boston           New York
Chicago          Philadelphia
Dallas           Phoenix
Denver           San Diego
Detroit          San Francisco
Houston          Seattle
Los Angeles      St. Louis
Miami            Washington, D.C.
Newark

ADMINISTRATOR
DEPUTY ADMINISTRATOR

BOARD OF PROFESSIONAL CONDUCT

OFFICE OF CHIEF COUNSEL

OFFICE OF CONGRESSIONAL AND PUBLIC AFFAIRS

ADMINISTRATIVE LAW JUDGE

PLANNING & INSPECTION DIVISION
Assistant Administrator for Planning & Inspection
Deputy Assistant Administrator for Planning & Inspection
Office of Professional Responsibility

Office of Planning & Evaluation

Office of Security Programs

Office of Inspections

OPERATIONS DIVISION
Assistant Administrator for Operations
Deputy Assistant Administrator for Operations

Management Staff

Office of International Programs

Office of Diversion Control

Office of Intelligence

Office of Training

Investigative Sections

OPERATIONAL SUPPORT DIVISION
Assistant Administrator for Operational Support
Deputy Assistant Administrator for Operational Support

Equal Employment Opportunity Staff

Office of Personnel

Office of Science & Technology

Office of Controller

Office of Information Systems

Office of Administration

October 1987
Source: U.S. Department of Justice.

320

for two CIA officers to meet Agent 2's source in New York. The two officers were sufficiently convinced of the value of the source to authorize the $50,000 expenditure from the CIA. Agent 1 received the money on March 18 from a CIA officer and signed a form acknowledging that he was responsible to account for it. Agent 1 paid the money to the source in two installments: $20,000 on March 19, and $30,000 on April 20, after the source had returned from a trip to Lebanon.

On May 2, 1985, upon the source's return from another trip to Lebanon, he told the agents that he now needed to give $200,000 to his contact, who would locate Buckley and obtain proof that he was still alive. After that payment, the source said, it would take an additional $1 million per hostage to secure their release.

Azzam became concerned when he learned that the source's contact was known to the DEA as a narcotics trafficker and a thief.

Azzam voiced his concerns to CIA officials who agreed that the $200,000 should not be paid until the source produced proof that his contacts had access to Buckley. The proof was to consist of photographs of the hostage with current newspapers, or similar items, showing the date of the proof.

North told Azzam he could get the ransom money of $1 million per hostage. When Azzam asked North where he would get it, North asked him not to inquire. Azzam surmised correctly that North was planning to get the money from H. Ross Perot, a Texas industrialist. Azzam told this to the CIA officers. The next day, North called Azzam to express his anger that Azzam had told the CIA. Azzam could not understand North's anger. He believed that the CIA was to be a full partner given that DEA could not legally

have any operational capabilities. Reportedly, Perot was upset that his role had been compromised and complained to Poindexter and McFarlane.

In early May 1985, the source went to Lebanon to obtain the required proof while Agents 1 and 2 waited in Cyprus. The source produced a document that allegedly was proof of access to Buckley. Azzam directed Agent 1 to bring the document to him for verification by expert analysts from the CIA and FBI laboratories. Despite these instructions, Agent 1 presented the "proof" first to North, a signal in Azzam's eyes that Agents 1 and 2 regarded North as their principal supervisor.

On May 14, 1985, Azzam and Agent 1 took the document to the CIA. The Agency found the evidence unacceptable. The CIA and FBI technical reports which were produced two weeks later were inconclusive.

Because the first evidence the source produced was at best inconclusive and at worst fabricated, the CIA developed a series of questions to the hostages only they could answer. When the source refused to return to Lebanon and submit the questions, the CIA and Azzam declined to authorize the $200,000. According to the CIA's Deputy Director for Operations, Clair George, the plan was a "scam, a fake" nothing more than "hocus pocus."

## North Continues the Initiative

Notwithstanding this account of their source, Agents 1 and 2 urged North to continue working with them. On May 22, 1985, according to North's notes, the two Agents assured North that their source could produce the hostages if given $200,000 for payments to officials in Lebanon and $2 million for two hostages. The agents explained that they needed to change their operating procedures: they wanted to report directly to the NSC staff to get the DEA "off their backs." They advised North to contact DEA Administrator Lawn or Attorney General Meese directly to ensure that they could proceed without interference.

On June 7, 1985, in a memo to McFarlane, North detailed the DEA operation. He wrote that, "at the request of the two DEA officers who originated the contact in Lebanon, I met with their asset [source] in Washington . . ." North informed McFarlane that the $2,200,000 would be provided by a "donor," but that "travel arrangements and operational costs are currently being financed from funds normally available to the Nicaraguan resistance." He added that "our normal point-of-contact of these matters is not yet aware."

Finally, North recommended in the memorandum that McFarlane approve the plan and ask the Attorney General to detail Agents 1 and 2 to the NSC for 30 days. McFarlane initialed the "approve" line at the bottom of the memo. McFarlane handwrote just under the approve line, "North to follow up 6/10 with AG."

McFarlane testified that he did not realize the full meaning of North's memorandum regarding his use of funds "normally available" to the Contras. "To tell you the truth," McFarlane testified, "it is my own oversight. . . . If I had been careful about reading [North's memorandum] I would have [understood its true significance]."

Around June 10, North prepared a memorandum for Attorney General Meese describing how the DEA agents would deposit the $200,000 and open an account for the remaining $2 million, which was to be provided by the "donor to bribe those in control of the hostages." North asked the Attorney General to assign the DEA agents to "this organization [NSC staff] for a period not to exceed 30 days." Attorney General Meese complied with North's request. That assignment would last for over one year.

Once the DEA agents were assigned to North, they reported directly to him, except for occasional, cursory briefings to Lawn. They wrote no reports of their activities and made no entries in the DEA informant files regarding contacts with their sources. Further, they immediately destroyed their notes after orally reporting to North.

The agents embarked on the operation as planned. In late May, Jay Coburn, an employee of H. Ross Perot, had delivered $200,000 in cash to North and Agent 1 without obtaining a receipt. North placed the money in his office safe and told Agent 1 that a nongovernmental employee would have to handle the money. Agent 1 suggested his brother, who had experience in security matters. The plan called for Agent 1 and his brother to meet with their source on Cyprus and for the brother to give him the money. If everything went well, they would arrange for the $2 million to be deposited and available for "contacts," who would arrange the release and transportation of two hostages.

True to the plan, North gave the brother the $200,000 in cash and $11,000 in Calero traveler's checks for expenses. Agent 1 and his brother travelled to Cyprus in late June of 1985, where the brother gave the source the $200,000 to take to Lebanon.

Two unrelated events then intervened: the hijacking on June 14, 1985, of TWA flight 847 by Lebanese terrorists, and in early June the death of one of the source's contacts in

Lebanon. As a result, the DEA source claimed to be leery about approaching anyone associated with the hostage holders. The source, after a trip to Lebanon, reported that the hostages possibly could be freed in exchange for arms. The agents concluded that this was not feasible. Ironically, this same course was about to be pursued by the United States in the Iran initiative.

## Late 1985 and Early 1986: North Presses On

In December 1985, Charles Allen of the CIA became Chairman of the Hostage Location Task Force. Allen already was involved in the Iranian initiative. North also recruited an Army Major of the Defense Intelligence Agency, who had an intelligence background in the Middle East. North or Allen then picked the Major to serve as "team leader or chief of staff, organizer, et cetera."

The Major described Agents 1 and 2 as "street toughs in camel hair coats," who were "street-smart but not very knowledgeable of other federal agencies . . . outside their own, nor knowledgeable certainly in any way, shape or form, about Middle East or international relations or politics or the military." At their first meeting, the DEA agents told the Major and Allen that they did not want to deal with the Operations Directorate at the CIA; Allen told them that the Major would be their CIA contact.

On January 14, 1986, Agent 1 and the Major went to New York to meet with and evaluate a new DEA "source," who, if acceptable, would be paid from CIA funds. On January 28, 1986, the Major reported to North his reservations about the source and the whole operation. North said that he liked the DEA agents because they were "action oriented." From that point on, the Major sensed that North was deliberately keeping him uninformed. Allen testified that he believed the DEA agents were working only to obtain intelligence information and were not involved operationally in hostage-release activities.

In January 1986, the Major expressed to Allen his concern regarding the propriety of using money to gain the hostages' release. Allen replied that North had told him that the President had said he would "go to Leavenworth if necessary" to free the hostages. The Major also recalled that in March 1986, while Allen and the Major were generally discussing how to finance efforts to free the hostages, Allen commented that, "Ollie was already into his Contra money for the hostages. . . ." The Major did not pursue this remark.

In late April 1986, the Major submitted a paper to North analyzing a range of options to gain the release of the hostages. When the Major met with North to present his paper, he urged North to abandon any effort to gain the release of the hostages by providing arms to Iran. Indeed, his paper warned that a faction in Iran might leak such a sale "simply to embarrass the present Administration." North was noncommittal and "made no comment on [the Major's] noting that it was against official U.S. policy . . . [and] encouraged terrorism." In late May 1986, the Major left the Task Force.

## The DEA Agents Become Operational Again

In May 1986, at the very time that North was preparing to accompany McFarlane to Tehran, he continued to work with the DEA agents to ransom the hostages for $1 million each. When the plan finally was executed, it occurred simultaneously with the McFarlane mission to Tehran.

According to the new plan, certain Lebanese elements would be paid $1 million to rescue each hostage. Once the hostages were freed, it was decided they would be taken by the Enterprise ship *Erria* to Cyprus. While the Enterprise provided the expense money, North turned once again to H. Ross Perot for funding of the ransom. In June 1986, Jay Coburn, Perot's aide, flew to Cyprus in a private plane. Coburn was to provide $2 million upon the release of the hostages. After Coburn arrived, Clines appeared in Cyprus with the *Erria*, but the plan collapsed: the contacts demanded the money before releasing the hostages, but the DEA agents refused to pay until the hostages were freed.

Soon after the June 1986, DEA mission failed, North told McFarlane that Perot had complained that he lost his money on the operation, and that North had failed to keep him informed. North asked McFarlane to mollify Perot. McFarlane eventually saw Perot and asked him "not to be too hard on Ollie."

In August and September 1986, Agent 1 called North about two possible sources on the hostages. North told Agent 1 he could not "touch them" and referred him to Dewey Clarridge at the CIA. On October 14, 1986, North met with Lawn. North expressed his appreciation for the DEA agents' efforts, but acknowledged that their efforts had failed. With that, U.S. efforts to ransom the hostages ended.

## The Attorney General's Role

Throughout the DEA operation, private funds were used to pay the expenses of the agents and to provide the ransom money. Yet, as discussed in Chapter 27, the use of nonappropriated funds to finance Government operations is inconsistent with the provisions of the Constitution requiring that all monies spent by the Government be appropriated by Congress.

The evidence points toward the conclusion that the Attorney General approved the use of private funds for the ransom/resource operations. McFarlane testified that Attorney General Meese had advised that while Government funds could not be used, private monies could be used to bribe foreign officials to free the hostages. Agent 2 testified that Lawn told him that the Attorney General had personally approved Agent 2's participation in the NSC hostage effort. Agent 2 told the Committees that Lawn had given him instructions that the DEA agents not handle the private money personally. Agent 1 stated that North gave him the money-handling instructions and attributed them to the Attorney General.

The Attorney General denied knowing of the specifics of Perot's involvement in the plan, although his telephone logs reflect some contact with Perot during 1985. Then, on November 26, 1986, after the diversion became public, the Attorney General telephoned Perot. A note taken by Meese's aide on December 3, 1986, reflects an instruction by the Attorney General to call Perot to check on whether he would respond that the Attorney General knew of or authorized the payments.

Administrator Lawn's testimony regarding his knowledge of using private money to ransom the hostages also contradicted documentary evidence. Lawn at first testified that he was never told that the money would be paid by a private donor. Lawn was then shown a copy of his handwritten notes of a briefing of the plan by Agent 2 which reads, in part: "donor money, not CIA;" "facilitators will not handle funds;" and "contact with donor." Lawn then admitted that "obviously I was told that there was donor money and I was obviously told that it was not CIA money. I don't recall hearing that. I don't recall recording that. But this obviously is my handwriting." As to the notations that the agents would not themselves handle the private funds but only facilitate the delivery of the funds, Lawn admitted: "I assume that I was told. I am sorry, I just don't recollect having been told."

## Policy Considerations Were Ignored

President Reagan repeatedly has stated since 1981 that the United States would not pay ransom to terrorists who kidnapped Americans, a policy adhered to by Administrations of both parties over the years. There are practical reasons for such a policy. Clair George, the Deputy Director for Operations, stated: "You don't trade for hostages . . . because now everybody is going to sell them for something." Former Deputy Director of the CIA, John McMahon stated that ransom payments could become a source of funds for terrorists. When they "run out of funds, they would kidnap the nearest U.S. businessman, get a ransom and then they'd fill their coffers for a year. When they needed more, they would ransom another one."

The DEA operation had all these short-comings plus an additional one: it was inconsistent with the simultaneous effort to gain the release of the hostages through the Iran initiative. It is reasonable to believe that the Lebanese hostage holders would be less likely to release the hostages at the request of Iran, at the same time as they were being offered $1 million per hostage in the DEA initiative.

There was little consideration of these factors. The DEA initiative was not discussed at a meeting of the NSC; there were no policy papers; and no consultation with the Secretaries of Defense and State. Secord summed up the process when he testified that "it did not occur to me at the time that these two [efforts] clashed," but he acknowledged that "they could have collided." Some on the NSC staff characterized the payments to the hostages holders as "bribes" not ransom, and the operation as a rescue, not a payoff.

## THE OTHER OPERATIONS

### Israel

During 1985 and 1986, North planned several projects involving the Israelis, taking advantage of the close working relationship he had developed with Nir, an adviser to Prime Minister Peres. Later, though, North testified that none of the projects ever moved past the planning stages. The projects were not described.

### The Lebanese Operation

Another initiative undertaken by North involved the use of DEA and Israeli contacts to fund and equip a force in Lebanon. North described the proposed force as part of a "long term operation" to give the United States some future military leverage on the ground in Lebanon.

North sent Poindexter a PROF note in June 1986 about Secord's progress in working with a Lebanese group on a hostage rescue operation: "After the CIA took so long to organize and then botched the Kilburn effort, Copp [Secord] undertook to see what could be done through one of the earlier DEA developed [Lebanese] contacts. Dick [Secord] has been working with Nir on this, and now has three people in Beirut and a 40-man . . . force working for us. Dick rates the possibility of success on this operation as 30% but that's better than nothing." In closed testimony before the Committees, North indicated that the project was never carried out even though "we spent a fairly significant amount of money on . . . [this additional] DEA operation."

Peter Kilburn, a 60-year-old librarian at the American University in Beirut, was kidnapped on November 30, 1984. U.S. sources believed that, unlike the other hostages, Kilburn was being held by a criminal faction in Lebanon. At one point in the fall of 1985, North had contemplated allocating Enterprise funds to support an operation intended to free him. The plan was terminated when Kilburn was murdered allegedly by agents of Mu'ammar Qaddafi shortly after the American air raid on Libya in April 1986.

## Other Countries

Other projects contemplated by North involved aiding anticommunist resistance groups around the world. North told the Committees that he and Director Casey "had several discussions about making what he called off-the-shelf, self-generating activities that would be able to do a number of these things. He had mentioned specifically an ongoing operation." In addition, North testified, "I concluded within my own mind the fact that it might require [other ongoing] operations [as well]." In testimony before the Committees, North explained his motivation for assisting resistance groups. "We cannot be seen . . . in the world today as walking away and leaving failure in our wake. We must be able to demonstrate, not only in Nicaragua, but . . . elsewhere where freedom fighters have been told, we will support you, we must be able to continue to do so."

In April 1986, North asked Secord and his partner Albert Hakim to use $100,000 from the Lake Resources Swiss accounts to purchase conventional radio phone equipment for donation to a political party in a foreign country. On April 29, two representatives of a U.S. manufacturer met in Miami with Secord and one of Secord's associates, and the purchasing agent for the political party. At the meeting, the purchasing agent agreed to buy $100,000 of the radio equipment, and Secord—upon North's request—arranged for the Enterprise to wire this amount to the manufacturer.

## The *Erria*

Another of North's projects involved the purchase by the Enterprise of the M/V *Erria,* a small coastal freighter of Danish registry used to transport goods between Europe and the Middle East. The *Erria,* built in 1973, was small, only 163 feet long, and weighed 710 tons. Before its purchase, the *Erria* was owned by its captain, Arne Herup.

In 1984 and 1985, the *Erria* was used to run weapons to the Persian Gulf and then to Nigeria and Central America. Because of its Danish registry, the *Erria,* was able to escape the scrutiny of customs officials. "When we ended up needing a ship to perform a certain task," recalled North, "there was nowhere to get one on short notice, and so this organization [the Enterprise] produced it practically overnight." Poindexter testified that Secord offered the ship because the Department of Defense could not provide a ship suitable for the covert operation. According to North, Casey said "we can't find one anywhere else, get a ship. It didn't cost the taxpayers of the United States a cent." The money came from the Iran arms sales and other Enterprise funds.

The *Erria* first came to the attention of the Enterprise in April 1985, when it carried arms purchased through Secord to the Contras. En route to Central America, the *Erria* came under surveillance by an unidentified "fishing boat" which Captain Herup assumed was Cuban. Herup took evasive action and brought the cargo successfully to a Central American country. Herup's actions impressed Secord's associate, Thomas Clines, and when North needed a ship in April 1986, for covert operations, Clines suggested to Hakim that the Enterprise purchase the *Erria* from Herup, and keep him as Captain.

Hakim bought the ship for $312,000 through Dolmy Business, Inc., one of the Panamanian companies owned by the Enterprise, on April 28, 1986. Herup was asked to remain as captain for at least six months, with Danish agent Tom Parlow of SA Chartering continuing as the ship's agent. Hakim and Clines told Herup that they were working for the CIA and that at some future date they might ask him to transport technical equipment for covert operations. They promised that when the project was finished, the ship would be returned to Herup at no cost.

## The Proposed Charter to the CIA for a Covert Operation

The first mission North contemplated for the *Erria* was for an extended covert operation. On April 28, 1986, Secord sent a KL-43 message to North proposing that the CIA charter the vessel for that purpose: ". . . Abe [Hakim] still in Copenhagen with our lawyer finalizing purchase of ship. Deal has been made after three days of negotiation. The Danish captain is up and eager for the mission—he now works for us. We are asking . . . [of the CIA] for firm fixed price contract of $1.2 million for six months. He will probably balk at this price . . ."

As Secord predicted, the Agency felt the rate was excessive (several times the prevailing rate for similar assets) and it balked at chartering the ship. In addition, the CIA informed North that it was not interested on technical grounds and that it did not feel that security could be maintained because of the ship's previous use by North's associates to ferry arms to Central America. The Agency indicated that Tom Clines' involvement was a negative factor of major proportions.

North persisted in his efforts to have the CIA lease the ship. He then enlisted Poindexter's help. In a May 14 memorandum, Vincent M. Cannistraro of the SC staff urged Poindexter to take the matter up with Casey:

Status of Ollie's Ship. Ollie has offered the use of a Danish vessel for [a covert operation]. He first offered CIA a six month lease. CIA told me that they thought it was too expensive, and the cost and time involved in refitting the vessel for [the] mission made the alternative option . . . more attractive. Ollie then offered to [perform the mission] using his own resources. [C/NE] has told me that because of the alleged involvement of one Tom Clines (who was involved with Wilson and Terpil), CIA will have nothing to do with the ship.

In the end, Casey supported Clair George's decision that the ship was not suitable for Agency use.

## The Odyssey of the *Erria*

On May 9, 1986, the *Erria* commenced its operations under its new owners, the Enterprise. The ship was to travel to pick up technical equipment for a covert operation.

On May 16 Herup was ordered to abort the mission and return to Larnaca, Cyprus. The new plan for the ship was to pick up any American hostages released as a result of the DEA initiative. En route to Larnaca, Herup received instructions to take up a position off the coast of Lebanon and to await further directions.

As described earlier in this Chapter, the DEA hostage ransom plan failed. Accordingly, after a 48-hour wait, Hakim ordered the ship to sail on to Larnaca. On June 5, Herup received instructions to head for Gibraltar, but at the last moment the ship was diverted to Cagliari, Sardinia. From there, he was told to take the ship to Setubal, Portugal, to await an arms cargo from Defex. The cargo at Setubal was not ready for loading, and Herup was instructed to return to Copenhagen, where he arrived on July 4.

The *Erria* then was ordered to Szczecin,

Poland, where it arrived on July 10. The cargo it picked up was marked "machine parts," but actually consisted of 158 tons of Communist-bloc weapons, including AK-47 assault rifles, hand grenades, mortars, and a variety of ammunition. The shipment was consigned to Energy Resources International, an Enterprise company.

The *Erria*'s next stop was Setubal, Portugal, where on July 19, it loaded an additional 222 tons of arms from Defex Portugal in the presence of Parlow and Clines. Herup was told to set his course for a Central American port. According to Hakim, the total cargo, which he called the "stranded shipment," cost $1.7 million; Secord placed the cost at about $2.4 million. En route to Central America, Parlow called Herup and told him to stop the ship: Congress was in the process of repealing the Boland Amendment. The vessel sat in the water for 4 days. Captain Herup then was ordered to return to Portugal, where he was met by Clines.

The Enterprise decided to find a buyer for the 380-ton cargo of arms now on board the *Erria*. Defex sold the arms to an intermediary for $1.2 million. The intermediary, in turn, sold the cargo for $2,156,000 (including transportation), to the CIA, which did not want to deal with the Enterprise because of Clines' involvement. The arms were transferred from the *Erria* to another ship on September 20 for delivery to the CIA.

Hakim and Secord continued their efforts. Herup was ordered to take the now-empty *Erria* to Haifa, Israel, where it was to receive a new shipment of arms. So as not to run afoul of the Arab boycott, the name of the ship was altered to read, "*Ria,*" and false entries were placed in the Captain's log. On October 13, at Haifa, Herup loaded a crate containing eight tons of Eastern Bloc arms that Nir had promised for the Contras. The captain also had been told he was to pick up pharmaceuticals for Iran. No pharmaceuticals were loaded.

Herup was then ordered to go to Fujairah in the Gulf of Oman. The Iranians had promised North two Soviet T-72 tanks, but after the *Erria* waited 6 weeks in the Gulf, the plan failed to materialize. On December 9, Herup was ordered to open the Israeli crate. He found only 600 well-used AK-47 assault rifles and 15 cases of ammunition—valued at approximately $100,000—a cargo not worth transporting to Central America.

After the revelations of the Iran-Contra covert operations in November 1986, Clines or Hakim ordered the *Erria* on December 14 to return to Eilat, Israel, where the crate of weapons that had been received in Haifa were unloaded.

The *Erria* returned to Denmark later in December. Its missions on behalf of the Enterprise were at an end.

## CONCLUSION

The *Erria* was in a sense a metaphor for the other operations of the Enterprise—ventures that began with ambitious expectations but accomplished nothing. But the fate of these ventures cannot obscure the danger of privatization of covert operations or the fact that the participants in the Enterprise had audacious plans for covert operations. Had the architects of the other operations been emboldened by success, and not frustrated by failure, the Committees can only conjecture, with apprehension, what other uncontrolled covert activities on behalf of the United States lay in store.

# PART VI

# CONCLUSIONS AND RECOMMENDATIONS

# CHAPTER 24

# Covert Action in a Democratic Society

The Iran-Contra Affair raises fundamental and troublesome questions about the secret intelligence operations of the U.S. Government. Can such operations, and particularly covert action, be authorized and conducted in a manner compatible with the American system of democratic government and the rule of law? Is it possible for an open society such as the United States to conduct such secret activities effectively? And if so, by what means can these operations be controlled so as to meet the requirements of accountability in a democratic society?

These questions became the center of public debate in the mid-1970s, after revelations of controversial Central Intelligence Agency (CIA) activities and extensive investigations by a Presidential Commission and Select Committees of the House and the Senate.

The result of those inquiries was a concerted effort by the executive and legislative branches to adopt laws and procedures to control secret intelligence activities, including covert actions, and to ensure that they would be conducted only with the prior authorization of the President and timely notice to Congressional committees specially constituted to protect the secrecy necessary for effective operations.

Experience has shown that these laws and procedures, if respected, are adequate to the task. In the Iran-Contra Affair, however, they often were disregarded. The flexibility built into the legislation and rules to allow the executive branch to deal with extraordinary situations was distorted beyond reasonable bounds. Laws intended to reflect a spirit of comity between the branches were abused when that commitment to cooperation was abandoned.

The Director of the Central Intelligence Agency, William J. Casey, and other Government officials showed contempt for the democratic process by withholding information that Congress was seeking and by misrepresenting intelligence to support policies advocated by Casey.

## WHAT IS COVERT ACTION?

The term "covert action" refers to a specific type of clandestine activity that goes beyond the collection of secret intelligence. It is an attempt by a government to influence political behavior and events in other countries in ways that are concealed.

Covert action is not defined in statute. Executive Order 12333, however, issued by President Reagan in 1981, refers to covert action as special activities which are defined as:

> Special activities mean activities conducted in support of national foreign policy objectives abroad which are planned and executed so that the role of the United States government is not apparent or acknowledged publicly, and functions in support of such activities. . . .

## COVERT ACTION AND THE LAW

Covert action operations pose challenges for the political processes of the United States. As with other secret intelligence programs and more sensitive defense projects, appropriations and expenditures of these operations must necessarily be kept from the public domain. Thus, covert assistance to foreign governments and groups does not receive the open debate other assistance programs do.

Paramilitary covert actions are in the "twilight area" between war, which only Congress can declare, and diplomacy, which the President must manage. This type of activity is especially troublesome as a constitutional separation of powers issue.

The National Security Act of 1947 created both the National Security Council (NSC) and the Central Intelligence Agency. The law authorized the CIA to advise the NSC on intelligence matters, to correlate and evaluate intelligence, and "to perform such other functions and duties related to intelligence

affecting national security as the National Security Council may from time to time direct." While Congress has never provided specific authority for the CIA or any other elements of the Government to conduct covert actions, it has continued to appropriate funds for these activities.

When Secretary of Defense James Forrestal asked the Director of Central Intelligence (DCI) in 1947 whether the CIA was empowered to conduct covert activities, the Director replied that the CIA could do so if the NSC approved the activities and Congress appropriated funds to carry them out.

A CIA's legal counsel put it in similar terms:

> If the President gave us a proper directive and Congress gave us the money, we had the administrative authority to carry out [covert actions].

After public allegations of CIA efforts to "destabilize" the Allende regime in Chile, Congress sought to insure Presidential accountability for covert actions and notification of all appropriate Congressional committees, including those on foreign affairs. The Hughes-Ryan Amendment of 1974 provided:

> No funds appropriated under the authority of this chapter or any other Act may be expended by or on behalf of the Central Intelligence Agency for operations in foreign countries, other than activities intended solely for obtaining necessary intelligence, unless and until the President finds that each such operation is important to the national security of the United States.

The Hughes-Ryan Amendment also required the President "to report, in a timely fashion, a description and scope of such operations to the appropriate committees of Congress." There were six such committees at that time.

The investigations by the Church Committee in 1975 and 1976 failed to turn up proof that Presidents had ordered assassinations of foreign officials, but some senior officials indicated it was their belief that some Presidents had secretly approved such activities. Many in Congress felt that the problem was not so much that the CIA was undertaking covert action without the proper authority, but that Executive approval had been given in a deliberately ambiguous manner.

Congress responded with the Hughes-Ryan Amendment which altered the approval process of CIA covert action operations. By requiring that the President personally approve all covert actions as important to the national security, Congress sought to make the President responsible for all covert operations. The U.S. Government might still be able to deny publicly the responsibility for specific actions, but within the Government there would be an accountable source of authority—the President.

By 1977, both Houses of Congress established permanent select committees for intelligence oversight. This increased from six to eight the number of "appropriate committees" to be notified under the terms of the Hughes-Ryan Amendment. The resolution establishing the Senate Select Committee on Intelligence expressed the sense of the Senate that the Committee should be notified of "significant anticipated intelligence activities." The term was intended to ensure that notice of Presidential Findings under the Hughes-Ryan Amendment would occur prior to the implementation of the operation. In 1980, Congress replaced the notifica-

tion provisions of the Hughes-Ryan Amendment by amending the National Security Act of 1947 to add a new section 501 on Congressional oversight of intelligence activities. For the first time, the language on notice of "significant anticipated intelligence activities" was written into law.

Under the new law, notification had to be given only to the Intelligence Committee of each house, rather than to eight committees. Moreover, in extraordinary circumstances affecting the national interests of the United States, the President may choose to limit prior notice to the chairmen and ranking minority members of the Intelligence Committees and the majority and minority leaders of the two Houses, a total of eight Members.

Although the law gave the President some flexibility on notification, there was no exception from the requirement for a Presidential Finding as a precondition to all covert action operations. Presidential accountability remained the cornerstone of the system of control over covert actions.

When President Reagan took office, he pledged to revitalize U.S. intelligence and to dispel the "suspicion and mistrust . . . [that] can undermine this nation's ability to confront the increasing challenge of espionage and terrorism."

As part of the effort to restore confidence, the President issued Executive Order 12333 in which he eased some of the restrictions on CIA activities. The new order pledged continued obedience to the law and retained the provision that only the CIA could conduct covert actions in peacetime unless the President designated another agency to do so. The Executive Order also applied the Hughes-Ryan Amendment's Finding requirement to all covert actions, not just to those of the CIA.

In keeping with standard American political processes, a basic structure of covert action procedures evolved within the law. A system of interlocking statutes, executive orders, and national security directives had been established by three successive Administrations.

For the goals of this system of accountability and oversight to be fulfilled, several steps had to be taken. First, the President had to approve specifically, and accept responsibility for, each covert action by signing a Finding before the operation proceeded. Second, the Congressional Intelligence Committees had to be notified either before the operation began or in a "timely fashion" thereafter. Third, for oversight of intelligence activities to be meaningful, intelligence officials had to respond candidly to Congressional inquiries and provide Congress and officials in the executive branch with objective intelligence analyses so that proposed actions could be evaluated objectively.

In the Iran-Contra Affair, the principles of this process of accountability and oversight would get their severest test.

## MISUSE OF FINDINGS

The Findings process was circumvented. Covert actions were undertaken outside the specific authorizations of Presidential Findings. At other times, covert actions were undertaken without a Presidential Finding altogether. Actions were undertaken through entities other than the CIA, including foreign governments and private parties. There were claims that the Findings could be used to override provisions of the law. The statutory option for prior notice to eight key congressional leaders was disregarded throughout, along with the legal requirement to notify the Intelligence Committees in a "timely fashion."

## Dispensing with Presidential Findings

In reaction to the adoption of the second Boland Amendment in October 1984, the NSC staff took an increasingly active role in support of the Contras. The NSC staff raised money for the Contras and, with Richard Secord's assistance, created an organization outside the Government to procure arms and resupply the Contras. While the President has said that supporting the Contras was his own idea, he told the Tower Board that he was unaware that the NSC staff was directly assisting the Contras. In any event, there was no Presidential Finding authorizing these activities. National Security Adviser Robert C. McFarlane testified that he was unaware of the magnitude of Oliver North's operation although both North and Admiral John M. Poindexter disputed McFarlane's denials.

Efforts coordinated by North to ransom hostages constituted another instance in which the legal requirements for a Finding were dispensed with. This was in contravention of the President's own directive, Executive Order 12333, which provided specifically that all covert actions be contained in Presidential Findings. Not only was a Finding dispensed with, but funds to support the operation were raised from private sources. The operation was pursued despite the objection of CIA and some DEA officials, and Congress was not notified.

There was also no written Finding when the CIA became involved in the covert shipment of arms to Iran in 1985. As McFarlane subsequently expressed, "[t]he President was all for letting the Israelis do whatever they wanted to do." In November 1986, McFarlane asserted that the Attorney General had opined that U.S. participation in the initial Israeli shipments could be justified on the grounds that the President had made a "mental Finding." The Attorney General testified to his view that the President's concurrence was tantamount to an oral Finding and thus sufficient legal authorization for the program.

The use of Findings to ensure Presidential responsibility for covert action operations also was disregarded in the diversion of money from the Iran program to the Contras, which itself was never authorized by a Finding. Neither the January 17, 1986, Finding relating to the Iran arms sales, nor any Finding relating to assistance to the Contras authorized the diversion of funds. Poindexter testified that he believed the diversion would become politically controversial if exposed, so he decided not to tell the President in order to give him "deniability."

## Using Findings to Avoid Laws

At times, certain members of the Administration used Findings to avoid legal requirements. A project to stockpile weapons for the Contras is a case in point.

In the summer of 1983, the CIA feared that Congress might refuse to appropriate funds for the Contras in the next fiscal year 1984. The Agency thus devised a way of bypassing the appropriations process: the Department of Defense (DOD) would secretly transfer military equipment to the CIA without charge. The Agency would

then dispense the equipment to the Contras in the following fiscal year even if Congress cut off aid. To justify its request, the CIA pointed to the broad Presidential Finding authorizing assistance to the Contras even though nothing was said in that Finding about a donation of DOD materiel to the Contras through the CIA.

The Finding that was supposed to enhance control over covert action operations was invoked to justify an evasion of one of the Constitution's most fundamental safeguards, the dependence of the executive branch upon Congress for specific appropriations. In the end, the proposal was not implemented because DOD would not transfer the equipment to the CIA free of charge.

## NOT PLAYING IT STRAIGHT WITH CONGRESS

The concept of Presidential responsibility was not the only principle undercut during the Iran-Contra initiative. Accountability to Congress for intelligence operations also was ignored. For Congress to exercise its constitutional and statutory responsibility for oversight, it must first be notified of significant intelligence activities and then be given truthful and comprehensive information about them.

## Misleading Testimony

Congress was not notified of either the Iran initiative or the NSC staff's covert operation in support of the Contras. Senior intelligence officials, including the Director of

Central Intelligence, misled Congress, withheld information, or failed to speak up when they knew others were giving incorrect testimony.

For example, Clair George (CIA Director for Operations), the CIA's Chief of Central America Task Force (C/CATF), and Elliott Abrams (Assistant Secretary of State), testified in October 1986, before the House Permanent Select Committee on Intelligence (HPSCI) on the shooting down of the Hasenfus flight. Abrams testified that the U.S. Government was not involved in the Hasenfus operation. George and the C/CATF knew that the testimony was incorrect, but neither corrected Abrams. George later apologized to the Select Committees.

## Misuse of Intelligence

The democratic processes also are subverted when intelligence is manipulated to affect decisions by elected officials and the public. This danger is magnified when a Director of Central Intelligence, like Casey, becomes a single-minded advocate of policy. Although Deputy Director of Central Intelligence, John McMahon testified that no such intelligence manipulation took place, there is evidence that Director Casey misrepresented or selectively used available intelligence to support the policy he was promoting, particularly in Central America.

Intelligence misrepresentations for policy purposes occurred in the spring of 1986, when the Sandinistas pursued Contra fighters into Honduras. Such raids had periodically occurred since mid-1985. Neither Honduras nor the United States made an issue of these incursions because they were limited in scope and aimed at the Contras. At that time, the Sandinista raid was considered routine by the CIA Intelligence Directorate which noted, "[t]he Sandinistas probably believed that there would, as usual, be no Honduran reaction to the incursions and that their forces could quickly move out and return to Nicaragua."

The White House response ignored this assessment, blamed Congress for encouraging the raid, and used the incident to authorize emergency military aid to Honduras. Press spokesman Larry Speakes stated at the daily White House briefing on March 25, 1986:

> Within 48 hours of the House rejection of aid to the Nicaraguan resistance, Sandinista military units crossed into Honduras in a large scale effort to attack UNO and FDN camps.

Actually, the first Sandinistas crossed the border on March 20, the same day as the House action, and began to retreat across the border by March 24, before Speakes gave his briefing. They were back in Nicaragua before President Reagan signed the authorization for emergency military assistance to Honduras.

Casey, however, wanted CIA analysts to highlight, rather than minimize, the raid's significance in Agency reports. In an April 3 memorandum, Casey instructed the Deputy Director of Intelligence to use the available material on the Sandinista incursion:

> to alert the world that the Sandinistas were preparing and trying to knock the Contras out while we debated in the U.S. and can have another bigger try if we debate another two weeks.

# CONCLUSIONS

Out of necessity, covert activities are conducted, and nearly all are approved and monitored, in secret. Because they are not subject to public debate and scrutiny, they must be examined carefully within the practical constraints imposed by the need for operational security. It has been the United States' historic achievement to develop a system of law, using statutes, executive orders, regulations, notification procedures, that provides this scrutiny and protection. The Committees conclude:

(a) Covert operations are a necessary component of our Nation's foreign policy. They can supplement, not replace, diplomacy and normal instruments of foreign policy. As National Security Adviser Robert McFarlane testified, "it is clearly unwise to rely on covert action as the core of our policy." The government must be able to gain and sustain popular support for its foreign policy through open, public debate.

(b) Covert operations are compatible with democratic government if they are conducted in an accountable manner and in accordance with law. Laws mandate reporting and prior notice to Congress. Covert action Findings are not a license to violate the statutes of the United States.

(c) As the Church Committee wrote more than a dozen years ago. "covert actions should be consistent with publicly defined United States foreign policy goals." But the policies themselves cannot be secret.

(d) All Government operations, including covert action operations, must be funded from appropriated monies or from funds known to the appropriate committees of the Congress and subject to Congressional control. This principle is at the heart of our constitutional system of checks and balances.

(e) The intelligence agencies must deal in a spirit of good faith with the Congress. Both new and ongoing covert action operations must be fully reported, not cloaked by broad Findings. Answers that are technically true, but misleading, are unacceptable.

(f) Congress must have the will to exercise oversight over covert operations. The intelligence committees are the surrogates for the public on covert action operations. They must monitor the intelligence agencies with that responsibility in mind.

(g) The Congress also has a responsibility to ensure that sensitive information from the executive branch remains secure when it is shared with the Congress. A need exists for greater consensus between the Legislative and executive branches on the sharing and protection of information.

(h) The gathering, analysis, and reporting of intelligence should be done in such a way that there can be no question that the conclusions are driven by the actual facts, rather than by what a policy advocate hopes these facts will be.

It has been observed that a country without enemies has no need of an army or an intelligence agency.

The United States of America, as a great power with worldwide interests, will continue to have to deal with nations that have different hopes, values, and ambitions. These differences will inevitably lead to conflicts. History reflects that the prospects for peaceful settlement are greater if this country has adequate means for its own defense, including effective intelligence and the means to influence developments abroad.

Organized and structured secret intelligence activities are one of the realities of the world we live in, and this is not likely to change. Like the military, intelligence services are fully compatible with democratic government when their actions are conducted in an accountable manner and in accordance with law.

This country has been fortunate to have a military that is sensitive to the constraints built into the Constitution and to the necessity of respecting the Congress' responsibilities. This attitude of the military has won the trust of the American people, as George C. Marshall, the Chief of Staff of the Army during World War II, explained to one of his officers:

But we have a great asset and that is that our people, our countrymen, do not distrust us and do not fear us. Our countrymen, our fellow citizens, are not afraid of us. They don't harbor any ideas that we intend to alter the government of the country or the nature of this government in any way. This is a sacred trust. . . .

Like the military, the intelligence services can function only with the trust and support of their countrymen. If they are to earn that trust, they must heed Marshall's words.

# CHAPTER 25

# Powers of Congress and the President in the Field of Foreign Policy

Under our Constitution, both the Congress and the Executive are given specific foreign policy powers. The Constitution does not name one or the other branch as the exclusive actor in foreign policy. Each plays a role in our system of checks and balances to ensure that our foreign policy is effective, sustainable and in accord with our national interests.

Key participants in the Iran-Contra Affair had serious misconceptions about the roles of Congress and the President in the making of foreign policy. Poindexter testified, referring to his efforts to keep information about the covert action in support of the Contras from the Congress, "I simply did not want any outside interference." North testified, "I didn't want to show Congress a single word on this" same covert action. In Poindexter's and North's view, Congress trespassed on the prerogatives and policies of the President and was to be ignored or circumvented when necessary. If Congress denied the President funds to implement his foreign policy, they believed that the President could and should seek funds from private parties and foreign governments. If Congress sought to investigate activities which were secretly taking place, they believed executive branch officials could withhold information to conceal operations. These practices were required, in their judgment, to promote the President's policies.

## FOREIGN POLICY AS A SHARED POWER

The sharing of power over foreign policy requires consultation, trust, and coordination. As President Reagan told a joint session of Congress on April 27, 1983: "The Congress shares both the power and the responsibility for our foreign policy."

In the aftermath of the Vietnam war, Secretary of State Henry Kissinger observed:

> The decade-long struggle in this country over executive dominance in foreign affairs is over. The recognition that the Congress is a coequal branch of government is the dominant fact of national politics today. The executive accepts that the Congress must have both the sense and the reality of participation; foreign policy must be a shared enterprise.

The need for such a cooperative relationship was stressed in the testimony received by these Committees from Secretary of State George Shultz and Secretary of Defense Caspar Weinberger. Each recognized that both Congress and the Executive had fundamental duties in the area of foreign policy.

Secretary Shultz rejected the notion that there is a need "to lie and cheat in order to be a public servant or to work in foreign policy." He emphasized that Congress and the President must work cooperatively on foreign affairs:

> [W]e have to respect the fundamental duties of our colleagues on the Hill, but we have to expect them to respect ours and what that means is . . . while we have a system of separation of powers in the way it is constituted, it inevitably means we also have a system of sharing powers. . . .

> You have to have a sense of tolerance and respect and a capacity to work together and a desire to do it, for us to share information, for you to put forward your ideas, not to keep telling us all the time how to run things. But keep tabs. To have a way of interacting. . . .

Secretary Weinberger was asked at the hearings whether frequent consultation with Congress on foreign policy issues was a valuable opportunity for the President. He replied:

> Indeed, yes, sir. Not only because it is very useful to have the advice . . . but I also think

that it is important for the longer-range success of any kind of activity, because I have frequently made the point in private meetings that we can't fight a war on two fronts.

> We can't fight with the enemy, whoever it may be, and we can't fight with the Congress at the same time.

## CONCLUSION

The questions before these Committees concerning the foreign policy roles of Congress and the President are not abstract issues for legal scholars. They are practical considerations essential to the making of good foreign policy and the effective functioning of government. The theory of the Constitution is that policies formed through consultation and the democratic process are better, and wiser, than those formed without it.

The Constitution divided foreign policy powers between the legislative and executive branches of government. That division of power is fundamental to this system, and acts as a check on the actions of each branch of government. Those who would take shortcuts in the constitutional process—mislead the Congress or withhold information—show their contempt for what the Framers created. Shortcuts that bypass the checks and balances of the system, and excessive secrecy by those who serve the President, do not strengthen the President. They weaken the President and the constitutional system of government.

# CHAPTER 26

# The Boland Amendments and the NSC Staff

Beginning in 1983, Congress responded to the President's policy toward the Contras principally through its power over appropriations—one of the crucial checks on Executive power in the Nation's system of checks and balances. Because the President's program depended upon providing financial assistance to the Contras, appropriations bills became the forum for debating what the Nation's policy should be.

Aid to the Contras was controversial from the beginning. The Kissinger Commission, unanimous on virtually all other recommendations about Central America, could not agree on the Contras. The Administration's justifications for aid to the Contras were sometimes contradictory. The President publicly denied that his goal was to overthrow the Sandinista Government. Yet the Contras pursued only one goal—to topple the Sandinistas.

In Congress, the two Chambers found themselves at odds, with the House generally denying or restricting and the Senate generally supporting aid for the Contras. Votes in each Chamber were often decided by razor-thin margins.

Ultimately, restrictions on assistance to the Contras were embodied in the Boland Amendments, named after their chief sponsor, Representative Edward P. Boland. While Congress applied various requirements to support for the Contras in each of the six fiscal years from October 1, 1982, to September 30, 1987, the legislation for fiscal years 1983, 1985, and 1986 embodied the most important restrictions and will be designated Boland, I, II, and III, respectively.

The Boland Amendments were compromises between supporters of the Administration's programs and opponents of Contra aid. As compromises, they were written not with the precision of a tax code, but in the language of trust and with the expectation that they would be carried out in good faith. None expected the Administration to secretly seek loopholes, or to lead Congress to believe that support was not being given to the Contras when, in fact, it was.

**Boland I was in effect from September 27, 1982, to December 7, 1983, and said: "None of the funds provided in this Act may be used by the Central Intelligence Agency or the Department of Defense to furnish military equipment, mili-**

tary training or advice, or other support for military activities, to any group or individual, not a part of a country's armed forces, for the purpose of overthrowing the government of Nicaragua or provoking a military exchange between Nicaragua and Honduras." This law remained in effect the following year, but from December 8, 1983, to October 3, 1984, Contra funding was also limited to $24 million. Boland II was in effect from October 3, 1984, to December 3, 1985, and was intended, according to its authors, to end all United States funding for the Contras. But others say the amendment's wording did not make that clear. It said: "During fiscal year 1985, no funds available to the Central Intelligence Agency, the Department of Defense, or any other agency or entity of the United States involved in intelligence activities may be obligated or expended for the purpose or which would have the effect of supporting, directly or indirectly, military or paramilitary operations in Nicaragua by any nation, group, organization, movement, or individual." From August 8, 1985, to March 31, 1986, Congress approved $27 million to be spent for so-called "humanitarian," or non-lethal, aid to the Contras. Later Congress said the U.S. could also share intelligence with the Contras. Boland III, from December 4, 1985, to October 17, 1986, continued the restriction on spending by the intelligence agencies, except that now they could provide communications equipment and related training as well as intelligence "information and advice." A secret amount of money was appropriated for that. On October 18, 1986, full military aid to the Contras was restored.

## THE BOLAND AMENDMENTS WERE VIOLATED IN LETTER AND SPIRIT

Boland II forced the CIA to withdraw from its role of financing, arming, training, clothing, feeding, and supervising the Contras. But the vacuum was quickly filled. Acting to carry out the President's direction to keep the Contras together "body and soul," North, with the express approval of Poindexter and at least the acquiescence of McFarlane, took over where the CIA left off. With North as the action officer, the NSC staff raised funds from third countries, directed whether those funds should be sent to Secord or Calero, recruited the Enterprise to handle the logistics, helped the Enterprise run the resupply operation for the men in the field, and gave the ultimate directions to Secord and his aides on how to conduct the operation. Even an ambassador, Lewis Tambs, took orders from North on opening a front against the Sandinistas.

An isolated act of assisting the Contras may have presented a close question of law under Boland II and III. But the NSC staff's activities were not so limited. Its support for the Contras was systematic and pervasive. As the CIA had done before Boland II, the NSC staff now ran the Contra insurgency. According to Poindexter, North "was the switching point that made the whole system work. . . . I viewed Ollie as the kingpin to the Central American opposition once the CIA was restricted."

Moreover, while the NSC staff started its support of the Contras at least in part with private funds, the diversion gave it control over funds that belonged to the United States. The profits that were skimmed were generated by the sale of weapons belonging to the United States. The profits that were skimmed were generated by the sale of weapons belonging to the United States. North, sometimes with the assistance of Earl, fixed the mark-up to ensure that there would be money to divert. The Secord-Hakim Enterprise was not only brought into the sales as the "agent of the CIA," but, according to

Hakim's and Secord's testimony, functioned at North's direction.

Because Boland II and III both prohibited direct or indirect use of the United States funds, the diversion was a flagrant violation of those proscriptions.

Even the amendment to Boland III, authorizing the State Department to solicit humanitarian funds for the Contras, was abused by the NSC. When Brunei agreed to transfer $10 million, North gave Abrams the account number of Lake Resources. According to Abrams, North represented that this account was one of Calero's and that the money would be used for non-lethal expenditures. But, in fact, it was controlled by the Enterprise and was used to pay for arms for the Contras, to pay their leaders, and to finance the military airlift. Giving Abrams the Lake Resources account was a deliberate effort to divert funds solicited for humanitarian purposes to lethal ends, and was foiled only because of an error in the account number.

The Administration only recently has asserted that Congress lacked the authority to restrict the President's options in Nicaragua in the manner it did. As in the case of the Sciaroni opinion, at no time prior to public disclosure of alleged violations of the Boland Amendments did the Administration come forward to challenge their constitutionality. On the contrary, Congress and the American people were routinely being assured that the statutes were being observed, "in letter and in spirit." As President Reagan himself stated during a press conference on April 14, 1983, "But what I might wish or our government might wish still would not justify us violating the law of the land."

Surely an Administration should identify in a timely fashion those laws it claims a constitutional prerogative to ignore or subvert. But even beyond the aura of disingenuousness, the attack on the constitutionality of the Boland Amendment falls, in the Committees' collective opinion, far short of the mark.

The analysis must begin, of course, with an appropriate statement of what is, and is not, in issue. Some have attempted, for example, to cast the Boland Amendments as violative of the Supreme Court's famous dictum in *United States* v. *Curtiss-Wright Export Corp.,* referring to:

> the very delicate, plenary and exclusive power of the President as the sole organ of the federal government in the field of international relations—a power which does not require as a basis for its exercise an act of Congress . . ."

But one does not have to be a proponent of an imperial Congress to see that this language has little application to the situation presented here. We are not confronted with a situation where the President is claiming inherent constitutional authority in the absence of an Act of Congress. Instead, to succeed on this argument the Administration must claim it retains authority to proceed in derogation of an Act of Congress—and not just any act, at that. Here, Congress relied on its traditional authority over appropriations, the "power of the purse," to specify that no funds were to be expended by certain entities in a certain fashion.

Bearing this in mind, the Committees believe a more instructive decision than *Curtiss-Wright* is *Dames & Moore* v. *Reagan.* There, the Supreme Court upheld Executive Orders issued by President Carter to govern the treatment of claims against Iran after resolution of the hostage crisis 1979 and

1980. Chief Justice Rehnquist, then an associate justice, wrote for the Court and quoted portions of a concurring opinion filed by Justice Jackson in the *Steel Seizure Case.* According to Chief Justice Rehnquist:

> When the President acts pursuant to an express or implied authorization from Congress, he exercises not only his powers but also those delegated by Congress. In such a case the executive action "would be supported by the strongest presumptions and widest latitude of judicial interpretation, and the burden of persuasion would rest heavily upon any who might attack it." When the President acts in the absence of congressional authorization he may enter a "zone of twilight in which he and Congress may have concurrent authority, or in which its distribution is uncertain." In such a case, the analysis becomes more complicated, and the validity of the President's action, at least so far as separation-of-powers principles are concerned, hinges on a consideration of all the circumstances which might shed light on the views of the Legislative Branch toward such action, including "congressional inertia, indifference or quiescence." Finally, *when the President acts in contravention of the will of Congress, "his power is at its lowest ebb"* and the Court can sustain his actions "only by disabling the Congress from action on the subject."

As the Committees have already noted, the Administration's activities in support of the Contras were conducted in direct contravention of the will of Congress. It follows, then, that the President's constitutional authority to conduct those activities was "at its lowest ebb."

It strains credulity to suggest that the President has the constitutional prerogative to staff and fund a military operation without the knowledge of Congress and in direct disregard of contrary legislation. To endorse such a prerogative would, in the language of *Dames & Moore,* "[disable] the Congress from action on the subject" and leave the Administration entirely unaccountable for such clandestine initiatives.

In Federalist 75, Alexander Hamilton cautioned against granting the President too much authority over foreign affairs:

> The history of human conduct does not warrant that exalted opinion of human virtue which would make it wise in a nation to commit interests so delicate and momentous a kind as those which concern its intercourse with the rest of the world to the sole disposal of a magistrate, created and circumstanced, as would be a president of the United States.

While each branch of our Government undoubtedly has primacy in certain spheres, none can function in secret disregard of the others in any sphere. That, in essence, was the Administration's attempt here.

Congress must be able to depend upon the President for the execution of laws. It cannot be thrust into an adversarial role in which it must treat representations from the President's staff with skepticism and incredulity. If the President believes that a law has provisions that are unconstitutional, he must either veto it or put Congress on notice of his position—as he did with portions of Gramm-Rudman. The one option the executive branch does not have is to pretend that it is executing the law when it is, in fact, evading it.

The American system works well only when its branches of government trust one another. The Iran-Contra Affair is a perfect example of how to destroy that trust.

# CHAPTER 27

# Rule of Law

SIR THOMAS MORE: The law, Roper, the law. I know what's legal not what's right. And I'll stick to what's legal. . . .

WILLIAM ROPER: So now you'd give the Devil benefit of law!

MORE: Yes. What would you do? Cut a great road through the law to get after the Devil?

ROPER: I'd cut down every law in England to do that!

MORE: Oh? And when the last law was down, and the Devil turned round on you—where would you hide, Roper, the laws all being flat? This country's planted thick with laws from coast to coast—Man's law, not God's—and if you cut them down—and you're just the man to do it—d'you really think you could stand upright in the winds that would blow them?

—*A Man for All Seasons* by Robert Bolt

Too many laws were "cut down" in the Iran-Contra Affair by officials who, like Roper, decided that the laws inhibited pursuit of their goals.

This process began when members of the National Security Council staff decided "to take some risks" with the law, in John Poindexter's words, in order to continue support for the Contras. At the end, as Oliver North acknowledged, they were engaging in conduct such as lying to Congress that they knew was plainly "wrong."

The Committees were charged by their Houses with reporting violations of law and "illegal" or "unethical" conduct, and if the Committees are to be true to their mandates, they cannot hesitate to draw the inevitable conclusions from the conduct these officials displayed during this affair.

The judgments of these Committees are not the same as those required of the Independent Counsel. He must decide whether there was criminal intent behind any violation, whether there are any extenuating circumstances, and whether prosecution is in the public interest. The Committees express no opinions on these subjects and our comments in this section are purposely general so as not to prejudice any individual's rights. Our focus is not on whether the technical and demanding requirements of criminal statutes have been met, but on whether the policy underlying such statutes has been frustrated. Moreover, the list of statutes implicated by the Iran-Contra Affair is not exhaustive.

Because of the importance of the Boland Amendment to this investigation, this Report considers the applicability of that Amendment to the NSC in a separate chapter. The only issue under the Boland Amendment that is addressed in this chapter is the legality of the diversion. The Boland Amendment aside, however, the Committees find that activities in the Iran-Contra Affair, including the diversion, were conducted and later covered up by members of the NSC staff in violation of the Constitution and of applicable laws and regulations.

## USE OF DONATED FUNDS TO EVADE CONGRESS' POWER OF THE PURSE

### Overview

The Committees find that the scheme, taken as a whole, to raise money to conduct a secret Contra-support operation through an "off-the-shelf" covert capacity (the Enterprise) operating as an appendage of the NSC staff violated cardinal principles of the Constitution.

Several witnesses at the public hearings contended that the covert action to support the Contras did not violate the Boland Amendment because it was financed by contributions, not appropriated funds. The Boland Amendment by its terms, they maintained, only prevented the President from spending appropriated funds to support the Contras. But that ignores a greater principle. The Constitution contemplates that the Government will conduct its affairs only with funds appropriated by Congress. By resorting to funds not appropriated by Congress—indeed funds denied the executive branch by Congress—Administration officials committed a transgression far more basic than a violation of the Boland Amendment.

The power of the purse, which the Framers vested in Congress, has long been recognized as "the most important single curb in the Constitution on Presidential Power." The Framers were determined not to combine the power of the purse and the power of the sword in the same branch of government. They were concerned that if the executive branch had both the power to raise and spend money, and control over the armed forces, it could unilaterally embroil the country in war without consent of Congress, notwithstanding Congress' exclusive power to declare war.

When members of the executive branch raised money from third countries and private citizens, took control over that money through the Enterprise, and used it to support the Contras' war in Nicaragua, they bypassed this crucial safeguard in the Constitution. As Secretary of State George Shultz testified at the public hearings: "You cannot spend funds that the Congress doesn't either authorize you to obtain or appropriate. That is what the Constitution says, and we have to stick to it."

### The Power of the Purse and the Constitution

Article I, Section 9, Clause 7 of the Constitution, the appropriations clause, provides:

> No money shall be drawn from the Treasury, but in consequence of appropriations made by law.

The appropriations clause was intended to give Congress exclusive control of funds spent by the Government, and to give the democratically elected representatives of the people an absolute check on Executive action requiring expenditure of funds.

The Framers viewed Congress' exclusive power of the purse as intrinsic to the system of checks and balances that is the genius of the United States Constitution.

James Madison, the principal architect of the Constitution, explained:

> The House of Representatives alone can propose the supplies requisite for the support of government. They, in a word, hold the purse. . . . This power of the purse may, in fact, be regarded as the most complete and effectual weapon with which any constitution can arm the immediate representatives of the people for obtaining a redress of every grievance, and for carrying into effect every just and salutary measure.

Col. George Mason, another Constitutional Convention delegate, stated, ". . . the purse and the sword ought never to get into the same hands, whether legislative or executive. . . ."

This concept has been a guiding constitutional principle for 200 years. As President Reagan stated at an October 22, 1987, press conference: "The President of the United States cannot spend a nickel. Only Congress can authorize the spending of money."

Congress' exclusive control over the expenditure of funds cannot legally be evaded through use of gifts or donations made to the executive branch. Were it otherwise, a President whose appropriation requests were rejected by Congress could raise money from private sources or third countries for armies,

military actions, arms systems, and even domestic programs.

The Government may, of course, receive gifts. However, consistent with Congress' constitutionally exclusive power of the purse, gifts like all other "miscellaneous receipts" must, by statute (31 U.S.C. Section 484) be placed directly into the Treasury of the United States, and may be spent only pursuant to a Congressional appropriation.

The Constitutional process that lodges control of Government expenditures exclusively in Congress is further enforced by the Anti-Deficiency Act (31 U.S.C. Section 1341) which prohibits an officer of the United States from authorizing an expenditure that has not been the subject of a Congressional appropriation, or that exceeds the amount of any applicable appropriation. Thus it provides:

> An officer or employee of the United States Government may not make or authorize an expenditure or obligation exceeding an amount available in an appropriation or fund for the expenditure or obligation; or involve [the] government in a contract or obligation for the payment of money before an appropriation is made unless authorized by law.

Violations of the Anti-Deficiency Act are made crimes by 31 U.S.C. Section 1350.

## Use of the Enterprise to Mask the Fact that the U.S. Government Had Taken Control of the Donations

The constitutional scheme, which these laws amplify, is thus a simple one. Congress is dependent upon the executive branch to execute the law it passes; and the executive branch is dependent upon Congress to appropriate the funds to carry on its activities. This mutual dependence is at the heart of the system of checks and balances.

The Constitutional plan did not prohibit the President from urging other countries to give money directly to the Contras. But the Constitution does prohibit receipt and expenditure of such funds by this Government absent an appropriation. This prohibition may not lawfully be evaded by use of a nominally private entity, if the private entity is in reality an arm of the Government and the Government is able to direct how the money is spent.

The law with respect to when a nominally private company is an arm of the Government such that expenditure of its funds is governed by rules applicable to expenditure of Government funds is summarized in *Motor Coach Industries, Inc. v. Dole*, 725 F.2d 958, 964–65 (4th Cir. 1984). There, the Court articulated a multifactor approach for resolving when an ostensibly private entity like a trust is a Federal entity:

> We must consider, at a minimum, the purposes for which the trust was established; the public or private character of the entity spearheading the trust's creation; the identity of the trust's beneficiary and administrators; the degree of control exercised by the public agency over disbursements and other details of administration; and the method by which the trust is funded.

Lake Resources, the flagship of the Enterprise, was created by Richard Secord and Albert Hakim at North's request in July 1985. North did not like the way Contra leader Adolpho Calero was spending the donations received earlier, and he wanted more

control over expenditures. By North's own admission, Lake Resources was to be an "off-the-shelf" company to conduct a "full service covert action" in support of the Contras and other governmental projects. North referred to it in his PROF messages to Poindexter as "our Lake Resources company."

North was responsible, directly or indirectly, for virtually all the income of Lake Resources and the other companies in the Enterprise, and he had the power to direct its expenditures. North instructed Secord to spend money for airplanes, an airstrip, and munitions for the Contras and Secord did. He instructed Secord to spend money on radios for a political party in a foreign country and Secord did. He instructed Secord to spend its money for a ship to conduct an intelligence operation and Secord did. He instructed Secord to spend cash in support of a Drug Enforcement Agency operation to free U.S. hostages and Secord did.

North had secure communication devices in his office and those of all principal operatives in the covert action. Using these devices, North was able to maintain control of the most minute details of the operation. On one occasion, he even instructed pilots on the coordinates to be used in a weapons drop to the Contras inside Nicaragua.

Lake Resources was created for the very purpose of conducting Government operations while evading the Congressional appropriations power. In describing Director of Central Intelligence William Casey's plan for an off-the-shelf covert capacity, North testified:

Q: Do you remember giving testimony about the fact that Director Casey wanted something that he could pull off the shelf and that is why he was excited about the fact that you were now able to generate some surpluses that could be used?

A: That is correct.

Q: Why don't you give us a description of what he said, or as you understood it, what he meant by pulling something off the shelf?

A: Director Casey had in mind, as I understood it, an overseas entity that was capable of conducting operations or activities of *assistance to U.S. foreign policy goals* that was a stand-alone.

Q: Self-financed?

A: That was self-financing, independent of appropriated monies and capable of conducting activities similar to the ones that we had conducted here. (Emphasis added.)

The concept of an off-the-shelf covert company to conduct operations with funds not appropriated by Congress is contradictory to the Constitution. The decision to use the Enterprise to fight a war with unappropriated funds was a decision to combine the power of the purse and the power of the sword in one branch of government.

Referring to the concept of having independently financed entities conduct covert actions to avoid Congressional review, Secretary Shultz said: "This is not sharing power, this is not in line with what was agreed to in Philadelphia. This is a piece of junk and it ought to be treated that way."

As former Secretary of State Henry Kissinger recently wrote with particular reference to the use of the proceeds of the Iranian arms sales:

On the formal level the case is obvious. The Executive branch cannot be allowed—on any claim of national security—to circumvent the Congressional prerogative over appropriations by raising its own funds through the sale of government property.

## Legal Advice

The President may have received support for use of third country funds from a decision at the June 1985 National Security Policy Group meeting, which he attended, to seek the advice of Attorney General William French Smith before any funds were obtained from third countries.

At that meeting, Secretary Shultz warned that solicitation of third-country funds that the Government could control might be an "impeachable offense," attributing this opinion to Chief of Staff James Baker. Casey disagreed and offered to obtain an opinion from Attorney General Smith.

When Casey approached the Attorney General the following day, however, he drew the question narrowly, asking only whether Nicaragua's neighbors could be urged to help the Contras. The Committees have received evidence that Attorney General Smith gave an oral opinion that this would not be unlawful. As noted above, the Constitution does not prohibit a President from urging foreign countries and private citizens to give money to causes which the President supports, so long as this Government does not take control of the money.

But no representatives of the Justice Department were ever asked to express an opinion that it was constitutional for members of the executive branch to do what they did here—raise money from third countries and private parties, put the money in an entity controlled by the Executive, and direct its expenditure for projects of the executive branch. Nor did any legal officer of the Government ever suggest that it was lawful or constitutional to divert proceeds from the sale of U.S. property for purposes forbidden by the Congress.

The oral, on-the-spot advice of Attorney General Smith to Casey that Central American countries could be approached may in the transmission have been given a broader interpretation. The Committees simply do not know. But the Iran-Contra Affair cannot stand as a precedent for bypassing the constitutional requirement for appropriations. Securing funds, without Congressional authorization, to fund Government programs run by Government officials, is a direct violation of the Constitution that cannot be condoned.

## SECTION 501 OF THE NATIONAL SECURITY ACT AND RELATED REGULATION

The Committees find that the failure to notify the House Permanent Select Committee on Intelligence and the Senate Select Committee on Intelligence of the covert action to support the Contras violated the Congressional notice provisions of Section 501 of the National Security Act; and that the delay in notifying Congress of the Iran arms sales abused whatever flexibility Congress built into the statute.

Section 501 of the National Security Act requires that Congress be notified of all covert actions conducted by any agency of Government. The statute provides:

The Director of Central Intelligence *and the heads of all departments, agencies and other entities of the United States involved in intelligence activities* shall:

(1) keep the Select Committee on Intelligence of the Senate and Permanent Select Committee on Intelligence of the House of Representatives (hereinafter in this section referred to as the "Intelligence Committee") fully and currently informed of all intelligence activities *which are the responsibility of, are engaged in by or are carried out for or on behalf of any department, agency, or entity of the United States,* including any significant anticipated intelligence activity. (Emphasis added.)

There are only two exceptions or qualifications to the requirement of prior notice. First, the relevant head of a department, in lieu of notifying both Intelligence Committees, may notify the two ranking Members of each Intelligence Committee, and the two ranking Members of each House of Congress. This requires a personal decision by the President of the United States.

Second, the Act recognizes that there are circumstances under which the President may not have provided any prior notice to Congress. In such a case, he must "fully inform the Intelligence Committees in a timely fashion" with a "statement of the reasons for not giving prior notice." This also requires a personal decision by the President.

The notification provision of Section 501 serves vital purposes for both Congress and the executive branch. First, the required notification allows for beneficial congressional input in decisions that may affect important national interests. As former Director of Central Intelligence William E. Colby said during consideration of the Act, discussion with Congressional officials of planned covert actions "enables the Executive to get a sense of Congressional reaction and avoid the rather clamorous repudiation which has occurred in certain cases. . . . I think that is a helpful device."

Second, notification enables Congress to fulfill its constitutionally mandated role of monitoring Executive actions in the area of national defense and foreign policy lest covert actions entangle the country in overt hostilities. As a mechanism for consultation between the executive and legislative branches, notification helps to address the anomaly of formulating plans for secret action within a democracy.

The language of Section 501, as well as its legislative history, was the product of a delicate compromise between Congress and the executive branch. The purpose of the compromise was to avoid a confrontation with President Carter, who maintained there might be situations in which he should not be required to give prior notice, and that a statute requiring such disclosure in every case would interfere with his constitutional responsibilities. After lengthy consultation with the Administration, the statute was crafted so as to permit the Congress and the President to continue to disagree. This was done by the inclusion of a preamble that states that the notice requirements apply "to the extent consistent with all applicable authorities and duties, including those conferred upon the executive and legislative branches of the Government," and by recognizing that there might be circumstances where prior notice is not given.

Deferral of notice was intended to be the exception, not the rule. For example, Senator Dee Huddleston, the lead sponsor of the bill, stated:

I myself believe that the only constitutional basis for the President to withhold prior notice of a significant intelligence activity would be exigent circumstances when time does not permit prior notice; in such a case

the committee could be notified as soon as possible.

Similarly, Senator Daniel Inouye said during consideration of the Conference Report on the Intelligence Oversight Act:

I am of the firm belief that the only time the President has the constitutional authority to withhold prior notice to the intelligence committees would be in matters of extreme exigency. In my experience as chairman of the Intelligence Committee and as a continuing member of that committee, and after 4 years of reviewing the covert operations of our intelligence system, I cannot conceive of any circumstance which would require the withholding of prior notice except where the nation is under attack and the President has no time to consult with Congress before responding to save the country.

The Administration's conduct in the Iran-Contra Affair was inconsistent with these standards.

## The Contra Covert Operation

Under Section 501, the President alone can make a determination to delay notice of a covert operation. The President did not make a personal determination that notice of the NSC staff's Contra support activity should either be delayed or limited. Indeed, he has publicly disclaimed knowledge of the covert action. Thus, prior notice to Congress of the covert action by the NSC staff was required.

No notice of any kind was ever sent to Congress concerning the Contra covert action conducted by the NSC staff. On the contrary, the NSC staff took every step to keep

Congress from discovering its activities. The covert action was carried out in violation of the Congressional notice provisions of the National Security Act.

## The Iranian Arms Sales

The President did know of the Iran arms sales, and he made a deliberate decision not to notify Congress. Thus, Congress did not learn of direct arms sales to Iran, approved by the Finding of January 17, 1986, until the press reported it in November 1986. Congress did not learn of the December 5, 1985, Finding approving U.S. participation in the Israeli shipments until Poindexter's testimony was compelled under a grant of immunity. As a consequence of the President's decisions not to notify Congress, the operation continued for over a year through failure after failure, and when Congress finally did learn, it was not through notification by the Administration, but from a story published in a Beirut weekly.

The flexibility afforded the President for providing notice to Congress was abused by this delay. The reason cited for not notifying Congress was not that there was insufficient time to notify Congress—the only reason recognized in the legislative history justifying absence of prior notice—but that leaks might result and could endanger the hostages. There was no evidence to support such a rationale. The hostages had value to their holders only while they were alive. The Intelligence Committees frequently are entrusted with information about covert operations in which disclosure would put American lives at risk. Moreover, the information the Administration withheld from Congress was given at various times to an Iranian interme-

diary who failed several CIA lie detector tests, officials of the Government of Iran, officials of the Government of Israel, officials of the Government of a European country, private Israeli businessmen, and private U.S. citizens who did not have security clearances, such as Hakim.

It is a fair conclusion, therefore, that the Administration chose not to notify Congress of the arms-for-hostages initiative precisely because it anticipated Congress' objections and knew that the Secretaries of State and Defense would not defend the initiative. Indeed, the Iran initiative was contrary to longstanding national policies and to common sense, and the Administration might have abandoned the plan rather than disclose it to Congress.

All covert actions can be supported by strong arguments for secrecy. If the Administration can use these arguments as reasons to withhold notice where its plans are most suspect, Section 501 of the National Security Act is all but nullified. It is precisely when a covert action is suspect and potentially embarrassing that Congressional notice is most important. It is also then that the Administration is most in need of independent evaluations and criticism of proposed policies. And it is then when Congress, the representative of the people, must be given at least the opportunity to be heard in secret before action that could be calamitous for the Nation is carried out.

## The DEA Hostage Rescue Operation

In 1985 and 1986, the NSC used DEA agents to conduct a covert operation designed to free the hostages. The details of this operation are described in Chapter 23 of this Report. Congress must be notified of such operations under Section 501 of the National Security Act.

No notice of any kind was provided to Congress about this operation, and no decision was ever made by the President that prior notice should be withheld or delayed. Thus, failure to notify Congress of the DEA covert operation violated the law.

## EXECUTIVE ORDER 12333, AND NSDD 159

The procedures applicable to covert actions are governed not only by statutes, but by executive orders and National Security Decision Directives (NSDDs). These are written regulations signed by the President of the United States, and are binding on the entire executive branch until they are rescinded or changed by the President. They, too, were violated.

Executive Order 12333 issued by the President provides that "no agency except the CIA . . . may conduct any special activity (elsewhere defined to include covert actions overseas) unless the President determines that another agency is more likely to achieve a particular objective."

There was no Presidential determination that the NSC staff should conduct the Contra covert operation, and thus the NSC staff's covert action in support of the Contras violated the President's executive order.

Similarly, National Security Decision Directive 159, promulgated by the President, provides that no covert action overseas may be conducted by any agency of Government unless it is authorized by a written Finding signed by the President.

There was no written Finding signed by the President approving the covert action by the NSC staff in support of the Contras. Thus the NSC staff's activity violated this directive.

## VIOLATIONS OF 18 U.S.C. SECTION 1001

We have described elsewhere (Part IV) the elaborate efforts by Government officials to conceal their Contra-support activities from Congress.

It is enough to say here that, among other things, Congress was told by an Administration official orally and in writing in 1985 that the NSC staff was not engaged in fundraising or arranging military support for the Contras. Congress was personally told by North in 1986 that he was not engaged in fundraising or giving military advice to the Contras. Congress was told in testimony by Administration officials in October 1986 that the Government had no connection to the plane carrying Eugene Hasenfus. And Congress was told in testimony by Administration officials in October, November, and December 1986 that the Administration was not involved in raising funds for the Contras from foreign countries, including specifically funds from Country 2.

These statements were all untrue. They were made by officials who had varying degrees of knowledge about the facts they discussed. Some of the statements may have been unintentionally misleading and made by officials who were themselves deceived; others were outright falsehoods.

Most of these statements were not under oath. But for the branches to operate in a cooperative relationship, Congress must be able to rely on statements even if unsworn. Congress and the executive branch are partners, not adversaries.

The law recognizes this, and the false statement statute, 18 U.S.C. 1001, provides felony criminal penalties for knowingly false, fictitious, and fraudulent statements to Congress, even if not made under oath.

Some officials claimed they were forced to choose between making false statements and revealing information they believed should remain secret. Government officials may claim any valid privilege including executive privilege, as a basis for refusing to answer questions or provide documents, and thus set in motion procedures for lawfully resolving the claim. But under the U.S. legal system, public officials do not have the option of making false statements to Congress.

## THE DIVERSION—BOLAND AMENDMENT

The Committees find that the diversion of arms sales proceeds to the Contras' war effort was an evasion of the Boland Amendment no matter how narrowly that noncriminal statute is construed.

The Boland Amendment provides that "no funds *available to* the Central Intelligence Agency, the Department of Defense, or any other agency or entity involved in intelligence activities" may be spent for military support of the Contras. (Emphasis added.)

The missiles that were sold to Iran in 1986 came from Department of Defense stocks. The missiles had been purchased with money appropriated for the Department of Defense by Congress, and the missiles belonged to the Department of Defense. The Department of Defense sold the missiles to the Central Intelligence Agency, and the Central Intelligence Agency sold the missiles to Iran.

The memorandum to the President dated January 17, 1986, outlining the arms sales the President approved that day spells this out very clearly. It states that the CIA would purchase the missiles from DOD and would sell the missiles "directly" to Iran, using an "agent"—i.e., the various Enterprise companies—to handle the actual transactions.

Iran paid $28.5 million for those weapons. In the ordinary course, the purchase price is paid to the seller, i.e., the CIA. In this case, however, National Security Adviser Poindexter decided, on North's recommendation, that only a portion of the money should go to the CIA, with the rest remaining in the custody of Secord's companies before being used to support the Contras. Thus, Poindexter testified:

Q: Who decided how that money would be used?

A: The—my guidance to Colonel North what he requested and I approved, was that those funds should be used for support of the contras in Central America so they could keep pressure on the Sandinistas.

Q: So the decision—and I think you said earlier in your testimony, "the buck stops here"—the decision as to how that money was to be used was made by you?

A: Was my decision; that is correct.

Poindexter could also have decided that all of the purchase price be remitted to the CIA. North testified as follows:

Q: The question was, if those higher-ups in the U.S. Government from whom you sought approval decided that the $10 million [residue] should not, any part of it, be sent to the contras but should all come back to the U.S. Treasury, that is what would have happened isn't it?

A: Yes.

Given the Enterprise's status as an agent, and the NSC staff's control over the pricing and the proceeds of the arms sales, the full purchase price was available to the CIA. These funds, generated from the sale of U.S. weapons, could no more be diverted to the Contras than the weapons themselves.

## PROCEEDS OF ARMS SALES—FUNDS OF THE UNITED STATES

The Committees find that the full proceeds of the arms sales to Iran belong to the U.S. Government. Consequently, these funds are governed by statutes applicable to Government funds, including statutes prohibiting conversion of U.S. Government funds to unauthorized purposes.

As already noted in the previous section, Secord's Enterprise received the purchase price for the missiles in its capacity as agent for the United States. This conclusion is strongly supported by the documentary and testimonial evidence. The President approved the arms sales based on the January 17, 1986, memorandum, which states that the purchase price "would be transferred to an agent of the CIA," and that the CIA would "deliver the weapons to Iran through the agent." That memorandum is consistent on this point with other documents in the Committees' possession.* Moreover, as noted above, the Enterprise conducted itself in a manner consistent with its status as an agent of the United States, spending money for Government purposes—for the Contras, for a foreign country, for a ship, and for a DEA operation—all at the direction of Government officials. The Enterprise's profits from the Iran arms sales were not the result of entrepeneurial risks or skills. The Government determined the price which the Enterprise paid for the missiles and approved and negotiated the price at which the missiles were sold to Iran.

Government funds include not only funds in the physical possession of the Government, but funds that, although in the possession of another, are under the Government's control. When an agent of the Government collects money owed to the Government by a customer of the Government, the money belongs to the Government and cannot be converted to some other use. *Arbuckle* v. *United States,* 146 F.2d 657 (D.C. Cir. 1944).

---

*Other memorandums confirm the Enterprise's role as agent in the Iran arms sales. The proposal to sell missiles directly to Iran first appeared in a December 9, 1985, memorandum from North to Poindexter, suggesting "using Secord as our conduit." A memorandum by CIA General Counsel Stanley Sporkin dated January 15, 1986, makes three separate references to an "agent" who would supply the weapons to Iran and "act as a middleman with our authority." And the January 17, 1986, Memorandum to the President makes the final proposal to have the CIA transfer the weapons "directly" to Iran "using an authorized agent as necessary."

The chief legal officer of the United States appears to be in agreement with the Committees on this point. The Attorney General of the United States took the position in an official request for assistance to the Central Authority of Switzerland, dated December 12, 1986, that the full proceeds of the arms sales were funds of the United States; and gave similar testimony to these Committees. Thus, referring to these funds he said: "I would say that as a general matter, it is highly probable that those funds should be on a constructive trust theory or agency theory the property of the United States."

Government funds coming into the hands of an officer or agent of the United States must be paid immediately into the Treasury (31 U.S.C. Sections 484, 3302) and may not be applied to some other use (18 U.S.C. Section 641). Consequently, it is the Committees' judgment that all funds derived from the proceeds of the sale of arms to Iran currently in the custody of the Enterprise or its representatives belong to the United States and by law should be returned to the United States Treasury forthwith.

## IRAN ARMS SALES: ARMS EXPORT CONTROL ACT

The Committees find that the Administration's approval of the transfer of weapons to Iran by Israel violated the Arms Export Control Act (AECA).

All the HAWKs and TOWs that Israel transferred to Iran in 1985 had earlier been obtained from the United States under the AECA. Agreements between this country and Israel prohibited Israel from transferring the arms to any third country without first obtaining written consent of the United States.

Under the AECA, the President may not provide that consent unless: (1) the United States itself would transfer those arms to that country; (2) the transferee country (here Iran) agrees in writing that it will not further transfer the items without obtaining the consent of the President; and (3) the President notifies Congress of the transfer (22 U.S.C. Section 2753(a)).

The President's authorization of the 1985 Israeli transfers to Iran were made without even a pretense of compliance with the AECA or Israel's written agreements with the United States. No written consent was sought or given; and even if Israel had sought a written consent, this Government could not have given it without changing its own regulations. This is so because Iran, which was considered a terrorist nation by the United States and which was the subject of a U.S. arms embargo, was not eligible for direct sales. No written Iranian retransfer assurances were obtained nor could they have been. Finally, no notice was given to Congress.

In 1985, the Secretary of Defense stated vigorously to the President that he believed the sales were illegal. He restated his belief before these Committees in 1987:

A: But my feeling about that was, as I've mentioned to you earlier, that the Export Control Act doesn't permit a blanket approval in advance or anything of that kind and does not permit exports, did not permit exports to Iran, neither that Act nor some others, and did not permit the Israelis to export anything we hadn't specifically authorized.

Q: So if Israel had earlier purchased arms from the United States under the Arms Export Control Act and not pursuant to an intelligence activity, your position was that the law forbade them to transfer them to any third country without going through varius kinds of waivers and reporting requirements?

A: Yes. Right.

Later he testified:

Q: So it would have been—you're saying it would have been a violation of law for Israel to have—?

A: I don't know of anything that would have taken it out of the normal course. I haven't researched the problem and had a legal opinion on it. My view is that our Arms Export Control Act would make that kind of transaction illegal, yes. That is just my own conclusion.

The Administration takes the position that the CIA may transfer weapons as part of an intelligence operation, outside the context of the AECA, by using the President's powers under the National Security Act. That is the approach the President used in 1986 regarding his January 17, 1986, Finding. However, no such Finding existed for the sale of 504 TOWs; only a retroactive Finding existed for the November 1985 HAWKs sale; and the weapons transferred by Israel to Iran were governed by the AECA having been earlier transferred to Israel pursuant to that Act.

The Department of Justice, in a legal opinion on December 17, 1986, concluded that the 1985 Israeli shipments did not violate the AECA. In reaching this conclusion, the opinion assumed that Israel was acting solely as a "conduit" in a direct sale by the United States to Iran; that the United States promptly replenished all Israeli weapons with identical weapons; that the Israelis had no financial interest in the transaction; and that the United States asked Israel to engage in these transfers as an accommodation to the United States. The opinion also recognized that its conclusion depended on the correctness of these assumptions.

The assumptions are, in fact, incorrect. It was the Israelis who first suggested and engaged in the arms sales. Israel was more than a conduit. The initiative was considered a joint venture by the United States and Israel; Israel ended with newer TOWs than it started with; and the prolonged negotiations over replenishment reveal the financial interest Israel had in the transaction. Since its assumptions were incorrect, the legal conclusion of the Department of Justice opinion must be discounted. Moreover, even if the assumptions were correct, it is not clear that the Department of Justice legal opinion is correct.

## VIOLATION OF 18 U.S.C. SECTION 1505 AND THE PRESIDENTIAL RECORDS ACT

The destruction or alteration of documents or the giving of false testimony to frustrate a Congressional inquiry is a felony if done with "corrupt" intent—i.e., the purpose of impeding an inquiry (18 U.S.C. Section 1505).

Even if a subpoena has not been issued, an individual on notice of a planned Congressional inquiry cannot lawfully alter or destroy documents for the purpose of preventing Congress from developing the facts if he knows such documents may be subpoenaed or requested. E.g., see *United States* v. *Vesich,* 724 F.2d 471 (5th Cir. 1984); *United States* v. *Tallant,* 407 F.Supp. 878, 888 (N.D. Ga. 1975).

Starting at least as early as November 10, 1986, the Administration was put on notice that various Congressional committees planned inquiries into the sale of arms to Iran. Both the House and Senate Intelligence Committees told the White House of the inquiries and arranged for Poindexter and Casey to appear before them on Friday, November 21, 1986. Thereafter, several Administration officials took actions which had the effect of concealing this Government's participation in the Israeli shipments that violated the Arms Export Control Act.

On November 18, 1986, 3 days before the scheduled appearance of Casey and Poindexter, Presidential aides began to focus on the legal problems attending U.S. involvement in the Israeli shipments made prior to the January 17, 1986, Finding. Then during the next 3 days, several Administration officials involved in the pre-Finding shipments told conforming stories denying U.S. involvement in these shipments, at times using a false cover story that the United States had been told the Israelis were shipping oil-drilling equipment, not arms. These officials wrote this false cover story into NSC chronologies; they told the false cover story in one version or another to Congress and to the Attorney General; and they destroyed documents that would have revealed the truth.

The full facts concerning this effort, in the face of imminent Congressional probes, to alter the historical record, are described in Part IV. Whether or not any of the individuals had the requisite criminal intent to violate

18 U.S.C. Section 1505, their conduct violated the very thrust of that law—to ensure that Congress' access to the truth would not be obstructed.

## IRAN: THE PRESIDENTIAL RECORDS ACT

Government employees do not have the discretion to destroy or alter embarrassing or incriminating documents. The Presidential Records Act was enacted after Watergate for the very purpose of ensuring that official records would be preserved. The Act has no criminal penalties but it was willfully violated by Poindexter in destroying the December 1985 Finding.

## CONCLUSION

Article II, Section 3 of the Constitution directs that the President "shall take care that the laws be faithfully executed." The "take care" clause was derived from the English Bill of Rights, which forbade the King from suspending laws that he did not like. As Justice Jackson stated, the "take care" clause signifies "that ours is a government of laws, not of men."

The "take care" clause embodies the principle of accountability. As Gouverneur Morris, one of the Constitutional Convention delegates, stated, the Framers were quite cognizant that "without . . . ministers the Executive can do nothing of consequence." At the same time, however, they understood that a government of the people could not function unless the elected chief executive was responsible for the actions of his appointed subordinates. In 1789, Madison wrote that "[N]o principle is more clearly laid down in the Constitution, than that of responsibility." The "take care" clause so unpretentious in its wording, made accountability compatible with delegation. Although they recognized that executive power must be exercised by subordinate departments, the Framers nevertheless required the President to superintend the actions of those departments, thus correcting the tendency of "plurality in the executive . . . to conceal faults and destroy responsibility."

The President's responsibility to supervise his appointees was vigorously debated in the first session of Congress when the President's power to remove Cabinet officers was questioned. Many of the members had been delegates to the Constitutional convention or the ratifying conventions, and they had firsthand knowledge of the Framers' intent. One Member of Congress, Fisher Ames, stated, "The executive powers are delegated to the President with a view to have a responsible officer to superintend, control, inspect, and check the officers necessarily employed in administering the laws." "If anything in its nature"

is executive, James Madison explained, "it must be that power which is employed in superintending and seeing that the laws are faithfully executed." Representative Lee answered his own rhetorical question, "Is not the President responsible for the Administration? He certainly is."

In modern government, with its hundreds of thousands of employees, a President obviously cannot personally supervise the acts of all who act in his name. But if the "take care" clause has any vitality, it invests in a President the responsibility for cultivating a respect for the Constitution and the law by his staff and closest associates. When the President's National Security Adviser, who had daily contact with the President, can assume that he is carrying out the President's wishes and policy in authorizing the diversion; when NSC staff members believe that the destruction of official documents is appropriate and the deception of Congress is proper; and when laws like the Boland Amendment can be treated as if they do not exist, then clearly there has been a failure in the leadership and supervision that the "take care" clause contemplated.

# CHAPTER 28

# Recommendations

It is the conclusion of these Committees that the Iran-Contra Affair resulted from the failure of individuals to observe the law, not from deficiencies in existing law or in our system of governance. This is an important lesson to be learned from these investigations because it points to the fundamental soundness of our constitutional processes.

Thus, the principal recommendations emerging from the investigation are not for new laws but for a renewal of the commitment to constitutional government and sound processes of decisionmaking.

The President must "take care" that the laws be faithfully executed. This is both a moral and legal responsibility.

Government officials must observe the law, even when they disagree with it.

Decisionmaking processes in foreign policy matters, including covert action, must provide for careful consideration of all options and their consequences. Opposing views must be weighed, not ignored. Unsound processes, in which participants cannot even agree on what was decided (as in the case of the initial Iranian arms sale) produce unsound decisions.

Congress' role in foreign policy must be recognized, not dismissed, if the benefit of its counsel is to be realized and if public support is to be secured and maintained.

The Administration must not lie to Congress about what it is doing. Congress is the partner, not the adversary of the executive branch, in the formulation of policy.

Excessive secrecy in the making of important policy decisions is profoundly antidemocratic and rarely promotes sound policy decisions.

These recommendations are not remarkable. They embody the principles on which this country's success has been based for 200 years. What is remarkable is that they were violated so freely and so repeatedly in the Iran-Contra Affair.

Congress cannot legislate good judgment, honesty, or fidelity to law. But there are some changes in law, particularly relating to oversight of covert operations, that would make our processes function better in the future. They are set forth below:

## 1. Findings: Timely Notice

The Committees recommend that Section 501 of the National Security Act be amended to require that Congress be notified prior to the commencement of a covert action except in certain rare instances and in no event later than 48 hours after a Finding is approved. This recommendation is designed to assure timely notification to Congress of covert operations.

Congress was never notified of the Iranian arms sales, in spite of the existence of a statute requiring prior notice to Congress of all covert actions, or, in rare situations, notice "in a timely fashion." The Administration has reasoned that the risks of leaks justified delaying notice to Congress until after the covert action was over, and claims that notice after the action is over constitutes notice "in a timely fashion." This reasoning defeats the purpose of the law.

## 2. Written Findings

The Committees recommend legislation requiring that all covert action Findings be in writing and personally signed by the President. Similarly, the Committees recommend legislation that requires that the Finding be signed prior to the commencement of the covert action, unless the press of time prevents it, in which case it must be signed within 48 hours of approval by the President.

The legislation should prohibit retroactive Findings. The legal concept of ratification, which commonly arises in commercial law, is inconsistent with the rationale of Findings, which is to require Presidential approval before any covert action is initiated.

The existing law does not require explicitly that a Presidential Finding approving a covert operation be in writing, although executive orders signed by both Presidents Carter and Reagan required that they be in writing. Despite this requirement, a PROF note by McFarlane suggested that the initial arms sales to Iran were approved by a "mental finding," and there is conflicting testimony about whether certain actions were orally approved by the President. The requirement of a written Finding will remove such uncertainties in the future.

## 3. Disclosure of Written Findings to Congress

The Committees recommend legislation requiring that copies of all signed written Findings be sent to the Congressional Intelligence Committees.

Since existing law does not require that covert action Findings be in writing, there currently is no requirement that written Findings be disclosed to Congress. The existing practice has been not to provide the Intelligence Committees with a signed written Finding.

## 4. Findings: Agencies Covered

The Committees recommend that a Finding by the President should be required before a covert action is commenced by any department, agency, or entity of the United States Government regardless of what source of funds is used.

The existing statutes require a Presidential Finding before a covert action is conducted only if the covert action uses appropriated funds and is conducted by the Central Intelligence Agency (CIA). By executive order and National Security Decision Directive (NSDD), Presidential Findings are required before covert actions may be conducted by any agency. Nonetheless, both the National Security Council (NSC) and the Drug Enforcement Administration (DEA) became

363

engaged in covert actions without Presidential Findings fully authorizing their involvement.

The executive order requirement is sound. In the Committees' judgment, Presidential Findings for covert actions conducted by any agency should be required by law. Experience suggests that Presidential accountability, as mandated by the Finding requirement, is equally as important in the case of covert actions conducted by agencies other than the CIA.

The Committees also believe the Finding requirement should apply regardless of the source of funding for the covert action.

### 5. Findings: Identifying Participants

The Committees recommend legislation requiring that each Finding should specify each and every department, agency, or entity of the United States Government authorized to fund or otherwise participate in any way in any covert action and whether any third party, including any foreign country, will be used in carrying out or providing funds for the covert action. The Congress should be informed of the identities of such third parties in an appropriate fashion.

Current law does not require a Finding to state what agencies, third parties, or countries will be utilized in conducting a covert action. The Iran-Contra investigation demonstrates that disclosure of what U.S. agencies (such as the NSC), private parties, or foreign countries will be engaged in covert actions are matters of considerable importance if Congress is to fulfill its oversight responsibilities adequately.

The record of the Iran-Contra investigation reflects repeated efforts by the executive branch to obtain funds from third countries for covert operations and for other causes the Administration supports.

These actions raise concerns of two kinds. First, there is a risk that foreign countries will expect something in return. Second, in an extreme case such as that presented by the record of these hearings, the use of third country or private funds threatens to circumvent Congress' exclusive power of the purse.

### 6. Findings: The Attorney General

The Committees recommend that the Attorney General be provided with a copy of all proposed Findings for purposes of legal review.

The first Iranian arms Finding of December 5, 1985, was not reviewed by the Attorney General. The Attorney General did give oral advice on the January 17 Finding but did not do the analysis or research that a written opinion would have entailed. The President, the intelligence community, and Congress are entitled to a review by the country's chief legal officer to ensure that planned covert operations are lawful.

### 7. Findings: Presidential Reporting

The Committees recommend that consistent with the concepts of accountability inherent in the Finding process, the obligation to report covert action Findings should be placed on the President.

Under current law, it is the head of the intelligence entity involved which has the obligation to report to Congress on covert action. Yet policy choices are inherently part of the Findings process and it is the President who must authorize covert operations through the signing of Findings.

## 8. Recertification of Findings

The Committees recommend that each Finding shall cease to be operative after one year unless the President certifies that the Finding is still in the national interest. The executive branch and the Intelligence Committees should conduct frequent periodic reviews of all covert operations.

## 9. Covert Actions Carried Out by Other Countries

The Committees believe that the definition of covert action should be changed so that it includes a request by an agency of the United States to a foreign country or a private citizen to conduct a covert action on behalf of the United States.

## 10. Reporting Covert Arms Transfers

The Committees recommend that the law regulating the reporting of covert arms transfers be changed to require notice to Congress on any covert shipment of arms where the transfer is valued at more than $1 million.

Under current law, the Administration must report covert arms transfers involving any single item valued at more than $1 million. Since a TOW or a HAWK missile is individually worth less than $1 million, this reporting requirement did not apply to the Iranian arms sales even though two shipments involved $10 million in arms or more. It is the value of a transfer, not the value of each component of a transfer, that matters.

## 11. NSC Operational Activities

The Committees recommend that the members and staff of the NSC not engage in covert actions.

By statute the NSC was created to provide advice to the President on national security matters. But there is no express statutory prohibition on the NSC engaging in operational intelligence activities.

## 12. NSC Reporting to Congress

The Committees recommend legislation requiring that the President report to Congress periodically on the organization, size, function, and procedures of the NSC staff.

Such a report should include a list of duties for each NSC staff position from the National Security Adviser on down, and whether incumbents have been detailed from a particular department or agency. It should include a description of the President's guidelines and other instructions to the NSC, the National Security Adviser, and NSC staff for their activities. Particular attention should be paid to the number and tenure of uniformed military personnel assigned to the NSC.

## 13. Privatization

The Committees recommend a strict accounting of all U.S. Government funds managed by private citizens during the course of a covert action.

The record of the Iran-Contra hearings reflects use of private parties to conduct diplomatic missions and covert actions. Private parties can be of considerable use to the Government in both types of ventures and their use should be permitted. However, the record reflects that funds generated during a covert action are subject to abuse in the hands of a private citizen involved in conducting a covert action.

## 14. Preservation of Presidential Documents

The Committees recommend that the Presidential Records Act be reviewed to determine how it can be made more effective. Possible improvements include the establishment of a system of consultation with the Archivist of the United States to ensure complete compliance with the Act, the creation of a program of education of affected staff as to the Act's provisions, and the attachment of criminal penalties for violations of the Act.

During the Iran-Contra hearings, Oliver North, John Poindexter, Fawn Hall, and others admitted to having altered and destroyed key documents relating to their activities. Such actions constitute violations of the Presidential Records Act, which was intended to ensure the preservation of documents of historical value that were generated by the Chief Executive and his immediate staff.

## 15. CIA Inspector General and General Counsel

The Committees recommend that a system be developed so that the CIA has an independent statutory Inspector General confirmed by the Senate, like the Inspectors General of other agencies, and that the General Counsel of the CIA be confirmed by the Senate.

The CIA's internal investigation of the Iran-Contra Affair—conducted by the Office of the Inspector General—paralleled those of the Intelligence Committees and then the Iran Committees. It contributed to, and cooperated with, the Tower Board. Yet, the Office of the Inspector General appears not to have had the manpower, resources or tenacity to acquire key facts uncovered by the other investigations.

The Committees also believe the General Counsel plays an important role in these matters and accordingly should be confirmed by the Senate.

## 16. Foreign Bank Records Treaties

The Committees recommend that treaties be negotiated with foreign countries whose banks are used to conceal financial transactions by U.S. citizens, and that these treaties covering foreign bank records specify that Congress, not just the Department of Justice, has the right to request, to receive, and to utilize such records.

Many of the important records relating to the Iran-Contra Affair were generated by foreign banks that were used by the Enterprise for the covert arms sales to Iran and the Contra supply operation. The Independent Counsel has sought access to these Swiss bank records pursuant to a treaty with Switzerland. But the Independent Counsel and the Justice Department do not believe the Congressional Committees are entitled under the terms of the treaty to receive these records. New treaties should assure Congress of access to such records and should streamline the process for obtaining them. The Independent Counsel had not received all of the Swiss bank records after 9 months of waiting. Given the use of foreign banks by drug dealers, terrorists, and others involved in unlawful activity, it is more essential than ever that binding secrecy not be a shield for serious criminal conduct.

## 17. National Security Council

The Committees recommend that all statutory members of the National Security Council should be informed of Findings.

## 18. Findings Cannot Supercede Law

The Committees recommend legislation affirming what the Committees believe to be the existing law: that a Finding cannot be used by the President or any member of the executive branch to authorize an action inconsistent with, or contrary to, any statute of the United States.

## 19. Improving Consistency in Dealing with Security Breaches

The Committees recommend that consistent methods of dealing with leaks of classified information by government officials be developed.

The record of these hearings is replete with expressions of concern by executive branch officials over the problem of unauthorized handling and disclosure of classified information. The record is also replete with evidence that high NSC officials breached security regulations and disclosed classified documents to unauthorized persons when it suited their purposes. Yet no steps have been taken to withdraw or even review clearances of such people.

## 20. Review of Congressional Contempt Statutes

The Committees recommend that the Congressional contempt statutes be reviewed by the appropriate Committees.

There is a need, in Congressional investigations, for a swift and sure method of compelling compliance with Congressional orders for production of documents and the obtaining of testimony. These investigations raised questions about the adequacy of existing statutes.

In addition, new legislation should make clear that a Congressional deposition, including one conducted by staff, is a "proceeding" at which testimony may be compelled under the immunity statute, 18 U.S.C. Section 6001 *et. seq.*

## 21. Review of Special Compartmented Operations Within the Department of Defense

The Committees recommend that oversight by Intelligence and Armed Services Committees of Congress of special compartmented operations within the Department of Defense be strengthened to include systematic and comprehensive review of all such programs.

## 22. Review of Weapons Transfers by Chairman of Joint Chiefs of Staff

The Committees recommend that the President issue an order requiring that the Chairman of the Joint Chiefs of Staff should be consulted prior to any transfer of arms by the United States for purposes of presenting his views as to the potential impact on the military balance and on the readiness of United States forces.

## 23. National Security Adviser

The Committees recommend that Presidents adopt as a matter of policy the principle that the National Security Adviser to the President of the United States should not be an active military officer and that there should be a limit placed on the tour of military of-

367

cers assigned to the staff of the National Security Council.

## 24. Intelligence Oversight Board

The Committees recommend that the Intelligence Oversight Board be revitalized and strengthened.

## 25. Review of Other Laws

The Committees suggest that appropriate standing Committees review certain laws for possible changes:

a. Should restrictions on sales of arms to certain countries under the Arms Export Control Act ("AECA") and other statutes governing overt sales be made applicable to covert sales?
b. Should the Hostage Act be repealed or amended?
c. Should enforcement or monitoring provisions be added to the AECA so that we better control retransfers of U.S.-manufactured arms by countries to whom we sell them?

## 26. Recommendations for Congress

a. The Committees recommend that the oversight capabilities of the Intelligence Committees be strengthened by acquisition of an audit staff.
b. The Committees recommend that the appropriate oversight committees conduct review of sole-source contracts for potential abuse.
c. The Committees recommend that uniform procedures be developed to ensure that classified information is handled in a secure manner and that such procedures should include clear and strengthened sanctions for unauthorized disclosure of national security secrets or classified information which shall be strictly enforced.

## 27. Joint Intelligence Committee

The Committees recommend against consolidating the separate House and Senate Intelligence Committees into a single joint committee. We believe that such consolidation would inevitably erode Congress' ability to perform its oversight function in connection with intelligence activities and covert operations. Congress has structured its system for effective oversight in this area to meet the need for secrecy that necessarily accompanies intelligence activities and the creation of a single oversight committee would simply add nothing to this effort.

# SECTION II

# THE MINORITY REPORT

# Minority Report

## of

Representative Dick Cheney
  of Wyoming

Representative William S. Broomfield
  of Michigan

Representative Henry J. Hyde
  of Illinois

Representative Jim Courter
  of New Jersey

Representative Bill McCollum
  of Florida

Representative Michael DeWine
  of Ohio

Senator James McClure
  of Idaho

Senator Orrin Hatch
  of Utah

*Members, House Select Committee to
  Investigate Covert Arms Transactions
  with Iran*

*Members, Senate Select Committee on
  Secret Military Assistance to Iran and the
  Nicaraguan Opposition*

# Minority Staff

Thomas R. Smeeton
*Minority Staff Director*

George W. Van Cleve
*Chief Minority Counsel*

Richard J. Leon
*Deputy Chief Minority Counsel*

| | | | |
|---|---|---|---|
| *Associate Minority Counsel* | Robert W. Genzman | *Minority Editor/Writer* | Michael J. Malbin |
| *Assistant Minority Counsel* | Kenneth R. Buck | *Minority Executive Assistant* | Molly W. Tully |
| *Minority Research Director* | Bruce Fein | *Minority Staff Assistant* | Margaret W. Dillenburg |

## Associate Staff

*Representative Broomfield*

*Representative Hyde*
*Representative Courter*
*Representative McCollum*
*Representative DeWine*

## House of Representatives

Steven K. Berry
David S. Addington
Diane S. Dornan
Dennis E. Teti
Tina L. Westby
Nicholas P. Wise

## Associate Staff

*Senator McClure*
*Senator Hatch*

## Senate

Jack Gerard
Dee Benson

PART I

# INTRODUCTION

# CHAPTER 1

# Introduction

President Reagan and his staff made mistakes in the Iran-Contra Affair. It is important at the outset, however, to note that the President himself has already taken the hard step of acknowledging his mistakes and reacting precisely to correct what went wrong. He has directed the National Security Council staff not to engage in covert operations. He has changed the procedures for notifying Congress when an intelligence activity does take place. Finally, he has installed people with seasoned judgment to be White House Chief of Staff, National Security Adviser, and Director of Central Intelligence.

The bottom line, however, is that the mistakes of the Iran-Contra Affair were just that—mistakes in judgment, and nothing more. There was no constitutional crisis, no systematic disrespect for "the rule of law," no grand conspiracy, and no Administration-wide dishonesty or coverup. In fact, the evidence will not support any of the more hysterical conclusions the Committees' Report tries to reach.

No one in the government was acting out of corrupt motives. To understand what they did, it is important to understand the context within which they acted. The decisions we have been investigating grew out of:

— Efforts to pursue important U.S. interests both in Central America and in the Middle East;
— A compassionate, but disproportionate, concern for the fate of American citizens held hostage in Lebanon by terrorists, including one CIA station chief who was killed as a result of torture;
— A legitimate frustration with abuses of power and irresolution by the legislative branch; and
— An equally legitimate frustration with leaks of sensitive national security secrets coming out of both Congress and the executive branch.

Understanding this context can help explain and mitigate the resulting mistakes. It does not explain them away, or excuse their having happened.

## The Committees' Report and the Ongoing Battle

The excesses of the Committees' Report are reflections of something far more profound. Deeper than the specifics of the Iran-Contra Affair lies an underlying and festering institutional wound these Committees have been unwilling to face. In order to support rhetorical overstatements about democracy and the rule of law, the Committees have rested their case upon an aggrandizing theory of Congress' foreign policy powers that is itself part of the problem. Rather than seeking to heal, the Committees' hearings and Report betray an attitude that we fear will make matters worse. The attitude is particularly regrettable in light of the unprecedented steps the President took to cooperate with the Committees, and in light of the actions he already has taken to correct past errors.

A substantial number of the mistakes of the Iran-Contra Affair resulted directly from an ongoing state of political guerrilla warfare over foreign policy between the legislative and executive branches. We would include in this category the excessive secrecy of the Iran initiative that resulted from a history and legitimate fear of leaks. We also would include the approach both branches took toward the so-called Boland Amendments. Congressional Democrats tried to use vaguely worded and constantly changing laws to impose policies in Central America that went well beyond the law itself. For its own part, the Administration decided to work within the letter of the law covertly, instead of forcing a public and principled confrontation that would have been healthier in the long run.

Given these kinds of problems, a sober examination of legislative-executive branch relations in foreign policy was sorely needed. It still is. Judgments about the Iran-Contra Affair ultimately must rest upon one's views about the proper roles of Congress and the President in foreign policy. There were many statements during the public hearings, for example, about the rule of law. But the fundamental law of the land is the Constitution. Unconstitutional statutes violate the rule of law every bit as much as do willful violations of constitutional statutes. It is essential, therefore, to frame any discussion of what happened with a proper analysis of the Constitutional allocation of legislative and executive power in foreign affairs.

The country's future security depends upon a modus vivendi in which each branch recognizes the other's legitimate and constitutionally sanctioned sphere of activity. Congress must recognize that an effective foreign policy requires, and the Constitution mandates, the President to be the country's foreign policy leader. At the same time, the President must recognize that his preeminence rests upon personal leadership, public education, political support, and interbranch comity. Interbranch comity does not require Presidential obsequiousness, of course. Presidents are elected to lead and to persuade. But Presidents must also have Congressional support for the tools to make foreign policy effective. No President can ignore Congress and be successful over the long term. Congress must realize, however, that the power of the purse does not make it supreme. Limits must be recognized by both branches, to protect the balance that was intended by the Framers, and that is still needed today for effective policy. This mutual recognition has been sorely lacking in recent years.

## WHY WE REJECT THE COMMITTEES' REPORT

Sadly, the Committees' Report reads as if it were a weapon in the ongoing guerrilla warfare, instead of an objective analysis. Evidence is used selectively, and unsupported inferences are drawn to support politically biased interpretations. As a result, we feel compelled to reject not only the Committees' conclusions, but the supposedly "factual" narrative as well.

We always knew, of course, that there would be differences of interpretation. We had hoped at the start of this process, however, to arrive at a mutually agreeable statement of facts. Unfortunately, that was not to be. The narrative is not a fair description of events, but an advocate's legal brief that arrays and selects so-called "facts" to fit preconceived theories. Some of the resulting narrative is accurate and supported by the evidence. A great deal is overdrawn, speculative, and built on a selective use of the Committees' documentary materials.

The tone of the Report flows naturally from the tone of the Committees' televised hearings. We feel strongly that the decision to air the hearings compromised some intelligence sources and methods by broadcasting inadvertent slips of the tongue. But one thing television did do successfully was lay bare the passions that animated too much of the Committees' work. Who can forget the massive displays of travelers' checks being shown to the country to discredit Col. North's character, weeks before he would be given a chance to reply? Or the "j'accuse" atmosphere with which witnesses were confronted, beginning with the first week's prosecutorial confrontation with General Se-

cord, as Members used the witnesses as objects for lecturing the cameras? These tactics had little to do with factfinding, or with a careful review of policies and institutional processes.

Our reasons for rejecting the Committees' Report can best be understood by sampling a few of its major conclusions. By presenting these examples, we hope to alert conscientious readers—whether they agree with our interpretations or not—to take the narrative with a very large grain of salt. Regrettably, readers seeking the truth will be forced to wade through a mass of material to arrive at an independent judgment.

## The President's Knowledge of the Diversion

The most politically charged example of the Committees' misuse of evidence is in the way it presents the President's lack of knowledge about the "diversion"—that is, the decision by the former National Security Adviser, Admiral John Poindexter, to authorize the use of some proceeds from Iran arms sales to support the Nicaraguan democratic Resistance, or Contras. This is the one case out of thousands in which the Committees—instead of going beyond the evidence as the Report usually does—refused instead to accept the overwhelming evidence with which it was presented. The Report does grudgingly acknowledge that it cannot refute the President's repeated assertion that he knew nothing about the diversion before Attorney General Edwin Meese discovered it in November 1986. Instead of moving forward from this to more meaningful policy questions, however, the Report seeks, without any support, to plant doubts. We will never know what was in the documents shredded by Lt. Col. Oliver L. North in his last days on the NSC staff, the Report says. Of course we will not. That same point could have been made, however, to cast unsupported doubt upon every one of the Report's own conclusions. This one seems to be singled out because it was where the President put his own credibility squarely on the line.

The evidence shows that the President did not know about the diversion. As we discuss at length in our chapter on the subject, this evidence includes a great deal more than just Poindexter's testimony. Poindexter was corroborated in different ways by the President's own diaries and by testimony from North, Meese, Commander Paul Thompson (formerly the NSC's General Counsel), and former White House Chief of Staff Donald Regan. The conclusion that the President did not know about the diversion, in other words, is one of the strongest of all the inferences one can make from the evidence before these Committees. Any attempt to suggest otherwise can only be seen as an effort to sow meritless doubts in the hope of reaping a partisan political advantage.

## The Idea for the Diversion and the Use of Israeli Evidence

In the normal course of the narrative's hundreds of pages, the lack of objectivity stems more from the way it selects, and makes questionable inferences, from a scarcity of evidence, rather than a deliberate decision to ignore what is available. This becomes most obvious when we see a witness dismissed as being not credible for one set of events, and then see the same witnesses' uncorroborated

testimony become the basis for a major set of assertions about other events. If these flip-flops could be explained by neutral rules of evidence, or if they were random, we could treat them more lightly. But something quite different seems to be at work here. The narrative seems to make every judgment about the evidence in favor of the interpretation that puts the Administration in the worst possible light. Two examples involving North will make the point clearly. The first has to do with when he first got the idea for a diversion.

North testified that he first got the idea for diverting some of the Iran arms sale proceeds to the Contras from Manucher Ghorbanifar at a London hotel meeting in late January 1986. He acknowledged that the subject of using the residuals to replenish Israeli weapon supplies, and for related operations, came up in a discussion with Amiram Nir, an Israeli official, in late December or early January. North specifically said, however, that the Nir conversation had nothing to do with the Contras.

The Committees also received a chronology from the Israeli Government, however, that claimed North told Israeli supply officials in New York on December 6 that the Contras needed money, and that he intended to use proceeds from the Iran arms sales to get them some. When North was asked about the December 6 meeting, he reiterated that he did not recall discussing the Contras with anyone involved in the Iran initiative before the late January meeting with Ghorbanifar.

The Committees' Report has used the Israeli chronology, and the timing of North's alleged December 6 conversation, to suggest that the idea of gaining funds for the Nicaraguan Resistance was an important consideration that kept the Iran arms initiative alive, more than a month before the President signed the Finding of January 17. The problem with making this important inference is that we have no way of knowing whether the Israeli chronology is accurate. It may be, but then again it may not. The Government of Israel made its chronology available to the Committees fairly late in our investigations, and consistently refused to let key Israeli participants give depositions to the Committees' counsel.

We have no quarrel with the fact that Israel, or any other sovereign nation, may refuse to let its officials and private citizens be subject to interrogation by a foreign legislature. The United States, no doubt, would do the same. But we do object vehemently to the idea that the Committees should use unsworn and possibly self-serving information from a foreign government to reject sworn testimony given by a U.S. official—particularly when the U.S. official's testimony was given under a grant of immunity that protected him from prosecution arising out of the testimony for any charge *except perjury.*

Even if North did mention the Contras to the Israeli supply officials in early December, however, the inference made from the timing would be unfair. The Committees have no evidence that would give them any reason to believe that anyone other than North even considered the Contras in connection with the Iran arms sales before the January Finding. Poindexter specifically testified that he first heard of the idea when North asked him to authorize it in February. North testified that he first mentioned the idea to the Director of Central Intelligence, William J. Casey, at about the same time, in late January or early February, after the post-finding London meeting. More importantly, North and Poindexter both testified that no one else in the U.S. Government was told about a diversion before this time. What that means is that the diversion cannot possibly have been a consideration for people at the policymaking level when the President decided to proceed with the Iran initiative in January.

## Off-the-Shelf, Privately Funded Covert Operations

Paradoxically, the Committees seem to have had no difficulty swallowing North's testimony that Director Casey intended to create a privately funded, off-the-shelf covert operations capability for use in a variety of unforeseen circumstances. This is despite the fact that two people close to Casey at the CIA, Deputy Director of Central Intelligence John M. McMahon and Deputy Director for Operations Clair George, both denied Casey would ever have countenanced such an idea. "My experience with Bill Casey was absolute," said George. "He would never have approved it."

We have to concede the possibility, of course, that Casey might have discussed such an idea speculatively with North without mentioning it to others at the CIA. As with so many other questions, we will never know the answers with certainty. Casey's terminal illness prevented him from testifying between December 1986 and his death in May 1987. Nevertheless, it is interesting to note how much the majority is willing to make of one uncorroborated, disputed North statement that happens to suit its political purpose, in light of the way it treats others by North that are less convenient for the narrative's thesis.

379

## The Allegation of Systematic Cover-up

The Report also tries to present the events of November 1986 as if they represent a systematic attempt by the Administration to cover up the facts of the Iran initiative. The reason for the alleged coverup, it is suggested, was to keep the American people from learning that the 1985 arms sales were "illegal."

There can be no question that the Administration was reluctant to make all of the facts public in early November, when news of the arms sales first came out in a Lebanese weekly. It is clear from the evidence that this was a time when covert diplomatic discussions were still being conducted with Iran, and there was some basis for thinking more hostages might be released. We consider the Administration's reticence in the early part of the month to have been completely justifiable.

However, as November 1986 wore on, Poindexter and North did falsify the documentary record in a way that we find deplorable. The outstanding fact about the late November events, however, is that Attorney General Meese understood the importance of getting at the truth. Working on a very tight schedule, Meese and three others from the Department of Justice managed to uncover the so-called "diversion memorandum" and reported it to the President. The President immediately removed Poindexter and North from the NSC staff. Shortly afterwards, he asked for an Independent Counsel to be appointed, appointed the Tower Board, and supported the establishment of select Congressional investigative committees, to which he has given unprecedented cooperation.

The Committees' Report criticizes Meese for not turning his fact-finding operation into a formal criminal investigation a day or two earlier than he did. In fact, the Report strongly tries to suggest that Meese either must have been incompetent or must have been trying to give Poindexter and North more time to cover their tracks. We consider the first of these charges to be untrue and the second to be outrageous. We shall show in a later chapter that Meese worked with the right people, and the right number of them, for a national security fact-finding investigation. Whatever after-the-fact criticism people may want to make, it is irresponsible to portray the Administration, in light of Meese's behavior, as if it were interested in anything but learning the truth and getting it out as quickly as possible.

## The "Rule of Law"

Finally, the Committees' Report tries—almost as an overarching thesis—to portray the Administration as if it were behaving with wanton disregard for the law. In our view, *every single one* of the Committees' legal interpretations is open to serious question. On some issues—particularly the ones involving the statutes governing covert operations—we believe the law to be clearly on the Administration's side. In every other case, the issue is at least debatable. In some, such as the Boland Amendment, we are convinced we have by far the better argument. In a few others—such as who owns the funds the Iranians paid Gen. Richard Secord and Albert Hakim—we see the legal issue as being close. During the course of our full statement, we shall indicate which is which.

What the Committees' Report has done with the legal questions, however, is to issue a one-sided legal brief that pretends the Administration did not even have worthwhile arguments to make. As if that were not enough, the Report tries to build upon these one-sided assertions to present a politicized picture of an Administration that behaved with contempt for the law. If nothing else would lead readers to view the Report with extreme skepticism, the adversarial tone of the legal discussion should settle the matter.

## OUR VIEW OF THE IRAN-CONTRA AFFAIR

The main issues raised by the Iran-Contra Affair are not legal ones, in our opinion. This opinion obviously does have to rest on some legal conclusions, however. We have summarized our legal conclusions at the end of this introductory chapter. The full arguments appear in subsequent chapters. In our view, the Administration did proceed legally in pursuing both its Contra policy and the Iran arms initiative. We grant that the diversion does raise some legal questions, as do some technical and relatively insubstantial matters relating to the Arms Export Control Act. It is important to stress, however, that the Administration could have avoided every one of the legal problems it inadvertently encountered, while continuing to pursue the exact same policies as it did.

The fundamental issues, therefore, have to do with the policy decisions themselves, and with the political judgments underlying the way policies were implemented. When these matters are debated as if they were legal—and even criminal—concerns, it is a sign that interbranch intimidation is replacing and debasing deliberation. That is why we part

company not only with the Committees Report's answers, but with the very questions it identifies as being the most significant.

There are common threads to what we think went wrong with the Administration's policies toward Central America and Iran. Before we can identify those threads, however, we will give a very brief overview of the two halves of the Committees' investigations. For both halves, we begin with the context within which decisions were made, describe the decisions, and then offer some judgments. After taking the parts separately, we will then be in a position to talk about commonalities.

## NICARAGUA

The Nicaraguan aspect of the Iran-Contra Affair had its origins in several years of bitter political warfare over U.S. policy toward Central America between the Reagan Administration and the Democratic House of Representatives. The United States had supported the Sandinistas in the last phase of the dictatorial regime of Anastasio Somoza and then gave foreign aid to Nicaragua in 1979 and 1980, the first years of Sandinista rule. By 1980, however, the Sandinistas had shed their earlier "democratic reformer" disguise and begun to suppress civil liberties at home and export revolution abroad. As a result, the United States suspended all aid to Nicaragua in the closing days of the Carter Administration.

During the early years of the Reagan Administration, the Soviet Union and its allies dramatically increased their direct military support for Nicaragua, and their indirect support, through Nicaragua, of Communist guerrillas in El Salvador. The Reagan Administration decided to provide covert support for the Nicaraguan democratic Resistance in late 1981, and Congress agreed. By late 1982, however, Congress adopted the first of a series of so-called "Boland Amendments," prohibiting the CIA and Defense Department from spending money "for the purpose of overthrowing the Government of Nicaragua or provoking a military exchange between Nicaragua and Honduras." The House voted for this "limitation" by a margin of 411-0, in large part because everyone understood that the Administration could continue to support the Resistance as long as the purpose of the support was to prevent the revolution from being exported to El Salvador.

This approach left many unsatisfied. Some within the Administration wanted a broader attack on the Sandinista regime. Some within Congress wanted to end all support for the Contras and begin moving back toward the 1979–80 policy of providing economic assistance to the Sandinistas. Neither side of the policy debate was politically strong enough to prevail. Instead, during the course of the next several years, Congress and the Administration "compromised" on a series of ambiguous formulas.

Meanwhile, the Soviet buildup accelerated, and Sandinista support for the insurgents in El Salvador continued. In May 1983, the House Intelligence Committee, chaired by Representative Edward P. Boland, reported:

It is not popular support that sustains the insurgents [in El Salvador]. As will be discussed later, this insurgency depends for its lifeblood—arms, ammunition, financing, logistics and command-and-control facilities—upon outside assistance from Nicaragua and Cuba. This Nicaraguan-Cuban contribution to the Salvadoran insurgency is long standing. It began shortly after the overthrow of Somoza in July 1979. It has provided—by land, sea and air—the great bulk of the military equipment and support received by the insurgents.

Despite this finding, House Democrats succeeded in late 1983 in limiting appropriated support for the Resistance to an amount intentionally calculated to be insufficient for the full fiscal year. The funds ran out by late spring or summer 1984. By October, the most stringent of the Boland Amendments had taken effect. Paradoxically, Congress' 1983–85 decisions came in a context in which it was continuing to pass laws that accused the Sandinistas of violating the non-aggression provisions of the charter of the Organization of American States—a violation that the OAS charter says calls for a response by other member nations, including the United States.

## Actions

By the late spring of 1984, it became clear that the Resistance would need some source of money if it were to continue to survive while the Administration tried to change public and Congressional opinion. To help bridge the gap, some Administration officials began encouraging foreign governments and U.S. private citizens to support the Contras. NSC staff members played a major role in these efforts, but were specifically ordered to avoid direct solicitations. The President clearly approved of private benefactor and third-country funding, and neither he *nor his designated agents* could constitutionally be prohibited from encouraging it. To avoid political retribution, however, the Administration did not inform Congress of its actions.

In addition to encouraging contributions, the NSC's North, with varying degrees of authorization and knowledge by National Security Advisers Robert C. McFarlane and Admiral John Poindexter:

— Helped coordinate or facilitate actions taken by private citizens and by certain U.S. Government officials to direct money, arms, or supplies from private U.S. citizens or foreign governments to the Nicaraguan Resistance;
— Provided the Resistance with expert military judgment or advice to assist in the resupply effort; and
— Together with others in Government, provided the Resistance with intelligence information that was useful in the resupply effort.

Poindexter and North testified that they both believed these activities were legally permissible and authorized. They also said that the President was kept generally informed of their coordinating role. The President has said, however, that he was not aware of the NSC staff's military advice and coordination.

Because the Boland Amendment is an appropriations rider, it is worth noting that there is no evidence that any substantial amounts of appropriated taxpayer funds were used in support of these efforts. In addition, the NSC staff believed—as we do—that the prohibition did not cover the NSC. At no time, in other words, did members of the President's staff think their activities were illegal. Nevertheless, the NSC staff did make a concerted effort to conceal its actions from Congress. There is no evidence, however, to suggest that the President or other senior Administration officials knew about this concealment.

## Judgments

The effort to raise foreign government and private funds for the Resistance raised about $35 million between mid-1984 and mid-1986—virtually all of it from foreign countries. In addition, the much discussed and unauthorized diversion orchestrated by North and Poindexter contributed about $3.8 million more. Without this support, according to uncontroverted testimony the Committees received, there can be no question that the Resistance would have been annihilated. In other words, the support clearly did make an important strategic difference in the 2 years it took the Administration to persuade Congress to reverse its position. The short-term benefits of the effort are therefore undeniable. The long-term costs, however, seem not to have been adequately considered.

We do believe, for reasons explained in the appendix to this introductory chapter and in our subsequent chapters on Nicaragua, that virtually all of the NSC staff's activities were legal, with the possible exception of the diversion of Iran arms sale proceeds to the Resistance. We concede that reasonable people may take a contrary view of what Congress intended the Boland Amendments to mean.

Notwithstanding our legal opinions, we think it was a fundamental mistake for the NSC staff to have been secretive and deceptive about what it was doing. The requirement for building long-term political support means that the Administration would have been better off if it had conducted its activities in the open. Thus, the President should simply have vetoed the strict Boland Amendment in mid-October 1984, even though the Amendment was only a few paragraphs in an approximately 1,200 page-long continuing appropriations resolution, and a veto therefore would have brought the Government to a standstill within 3 weeks of a national election. Once the President decided against a veto, it was self-defeating to think a program this important could be sustained by deceiving Congress. Whether technically illegal or not, it was politically foolish and counterproductive to mislead Congress, even if misleading took the form of artful evasion or silence instead of overt misstatement.

We do believe firmly that the NSC staff's deceits were not meant to hide illegalities. Every witness we have heard told us his concern was not over legality, but with the fear that Congress would respond to complete disclosure with political reprisals, principally by tightening the Boland Amendments. That risk should have been taken.

We are convinced that the Constitution protects much of what the NSC was doing— particularly those aspects that had to do with encouraging contributions and sharing information. The President's inherent constitutional powers are only as strong, however, as the President's willingness to defend them. As for the NSC actions Congress could constitutionally have prohibited, it would have been better for the White House to have tackled that danger head on. Some day, Congress' decision to withhold resources may tragically require U.S. citizens to make an even heavier commitment to Central America, perhaps one measured in blood and not dollars. The commitment that might eliminate such an awful future will not be forthcoming unless the public is exposed to and persuaded by a clear, sustained and principled debate on the merits.

## IRAN

The Iran arms sales had their roots in an intelligence failure. The potential geopolitical importance of Iran for the United States would be obvious to anyone who looks at a map. Despite Iran's importance, the United States was taken by surprise when the Shah fell in 1979, because it had not developed an adequate human intelligence capability there. Our hearings have established that essentially nothing had been done to cure this failure by the mid-1980's. Then, the United States was approached by Israel in 1985 with a proposal that the United States acquiesce in some minor Israeli arms sales to Iran. This proposal came at a time when the United States was already considering the advisability of such sales. For long term, strategic reasons, the United States had to improve relationships with at least some of the currently important factions in Iran. The lack of adequate intelligence about these factions made it important to pursue any potentially fruitful opportunity; it also made those pursuits inherently risky. U.S. decisions had to be based on the thinnest of independently verifiable information. Lacking such independent intelligence, the United States was forced to rely on sources known to be biased and unreliable.

Well aware of the risk, the Administration nonetheless decided the opportunity was worth pursuing. The major participants in the Iran arms affair obviously had some common and some conflicting interests. The key question the United States had to explore was whether the U.S. and Iranian leadership actually felt enough of a common interest to establish a strategic dialogue.

## Actions

To explore the chance for an opening, the President agreed first to approve Israeli sales to Iran in 1985, and then in 1986 to sell U.S. arms directly. The amounts involved were meager. The total amount, including all of the 1985 and 1986 sales combined, consisted of 2004 TOW antitank missiles, 18 HAWK antiaircraft missiles, and about 200 types of HAWK spare parts.

There was a strong division of opinion in the Administration about the advisability of these arms sales, a division that never abated. Unfortunately, this served as a pretext for Poindexter's decision not to keep the Secretaries of State or Defense informed about the detailed progress of the negotiations between the United States and Iran. One reason for the failure to inform appears to have been a past history in which some Administration officials may have leaked sensitive information as a way to halt actions with which they disagreed. Poindexter's secretive inclinations were abetted by Secretary Shultz, who all but invited Poindexter not to keep him informed because he did not want to be accused of leaking. They also were abetted by Secretary Weinberger, who—like Shultz—was less than vigorous about keeping himself informed about a policy he had good reason to believe was still going forward.

The first deals with the Iranian Government were flawed by the unreliability of our intermediary, Manucher Ghorbanifar. For all of his unreliability, however, Ghorbanifar

helped obtain the release of two U.S. hostages and did produce high Iranian officials for the first face-to-face meetings between our governments in 5 years. At those meetings, one of which was held in Tehran in May 1986, U.S. officials sought consistently to make clear that we were interested in a long-term strategic relationship with Iran to oppose the Soviet Union's territorial interests. As concerned as the President had become personally for the fate of the hostages—including the CIA's Beirut station chief, William Buckley, who was repeatedly tortured until he died—the hostages were always presented in these negotiations as obstacles to be overcome, not as the reason for the initiative. But Ghorbanifar appeared to have misled both sides, and the Iranian officials seemed to be interested only in weapons, and in using the hostages for bargaining leverage.

After the Tehran meeting, the United States was able to approach a very high Iranian official using a Second Channel arranged by Albert Hakim and and his associates. There is little doubt about Hakim's business motives in arranging these meetings; there is equally little doubt that this channel represented the highest levels of the Iranian Government. Discussions with this channel began in the middle of 1986 and continued until December. They resulted in the release of one further hostage and U.S. officials expected them to result in some more. Perhaps more importantly, these discussions appear to have been qualitatively different from the ones conducted through the First Channel arranged by Ghorbanifar, and included some talks about broad areas of strategic cooperation.

As a result of factional infighting inside the Iranian Government, the initiative was exposed and substantive discussions were suspended. Not surprisingly, given the nature of Iranian politics, the Iranian Government has publicly denied that significant negotiations were underway. Congress was not informed of the Administration's dealings with Iran until after the public disclosure. The failure to disclose resembled the Carter Administration's similar decisions not to disclose in the parallel Iranian hostage crisis of 1979–81. President Reagan withheld disclosure longer than Carter, however—by about 11 months to 6.

## Judgments

The Iran initiative involved two governments that had sharp differences between them. There were also very sharp internal divisions in both Iran and the United States about how to begin narrowing the differences between the two countries. In such a situation, the margin between narrow failure and success can seem much wider after the fact than it does during the discussions. While the initial contacts developed by Israel and used by the United States do not appear likely to have led to a long-term relationship, we cannot rule out the possibility that negotiations with the Second Channel might have turned out differently. At this stage, we never will know what might have been.

In retrospect, it seems clear that this initiative degenerated into a series of "arms for hostage" deals. It did not look that way to many of the U.S. participants at the time. Nevertheless, the fact that the negotiations never were able clearly to separate the long-term from the short-term issues, confirms our instinctive judgment that the United States should not have allowed arms to become the currency by which our country's

bona fides were determined. There is no evidence that these relatively minor sales materially altered the military balance in the Iran-Iraq war. However, the sales damaged U.S. credibility with our allies, making it more difficult, among other things, for the Administration to enforce its preexisting efforts to embargo arms sales to Iran.

The decision to keep Congress in the dark for 11 months disturbs all Members of these Committees. It is clear that the Reagan Administration simply did not trust the Congress to keep secrets. Based on the history of leaks we shall outline in a later chapter, it unfortunately had good reason to be concerned. This observation is not offered as a justification, but as an important part of the context that must be understood. To help remove this concern as an excuse for future Administrations, we are proposing a series of legislative and administrative recommendations to improve both Congress' and the executive branch's ability to maintain national security secrets and deter leaks.

## DIVERSION

The lack of detailed information-sharing within the Administration was what made it possible for Poindexter to authorize the diversion and successfully keep his decision to do so from the President. We have already indicated our reasons for being convinced the President knew nothing about the diversion. The majority Report says that if the President did not know about it, he should have. We agree, and so does the President. But unlike some of the other decisions we have been discussing, the President cannot himself be faulted for this one. The decision was Admiral Poindexter's, and Poindexter's alone.

As supporters of a strong Presidential role in foreign policy, we cannot take Poindexter's decision lightly. The Constitution strikes an implicit bargain with the President: in return for getting significant discretionary power to act, the President was supposed to be held accountable for his decisions. By keeping an important decision away from the President, Poindexter was acting to undercut one foundation for the discretionary Presidential power he was exercising.

The diversion also differs from the basic Nicaragua and Iran policies in another important respect: we can find nothing to justify or mitigate its having occurred. We do understand the enthusiasm North displayed when he told the Committees it was a "neat idea" to use money from the Ayatollah, who was helping the Sandinistas, to support the Contras. But enthusiasm is not a sufficient basis for important policy decisions. Even if there were nothing else wrong with the diversion, the decision to mix two intelligence operations increased the risk of pursuing either one, with predictably disastrous repercussions.

Unlike the Committees' majority, we believe there are good legal arguments on both sides of the question of whether the proceeds of the arms sales belong to the U.S. Government or to Secord and Hakim. For that reason, we think it unlikely, under the circumstances, that the funds were acquired or used with any criminal intent. Nevertheless, the fact that the ownership seems unclear under current law does not please us. We do believe that Secord and Hakim were acting as the moral equivalents of U.S. agents, even if they were not U.S. agents in law.

The diversion has led some of the Committees' Members to express a great deal of concern in the public hearings about the use of private citizens in covert operations in settings that mix private profits with public benefits. We remain convinced that covert operations will continue to have to use private agents or contractors in the future, and that those private parties will continue to operate at least partly from profit motives. If the United States tries to limit itself to dealing only with people who act out of purely patriotic motives, it effectively will rule out any worthwhile dealing with most arms dealers and foreign agents. In the real world of international politics, it would be foolish to avoid working with people whose motives do not match our own. Nevertheless, we do feel troubled by the fact that there was not enough legal clarity, or accounting controls, placed on the Enterprise by the NSC.

## THE UNCOVERING

It is clear that officials of the National Security Council misled the Congress and other members of the Administration about their activities in support of the Nicaraguan Resistance. This occurred without authorization from outside the NSC staff. It is also clear that the NSC staff actively misled other Administration officials and Congress about the Iran initiative both before and after the first public disclosure. The shredding of documents and other efforts at covering up what had happened were also undertaken by NSC staff members acting on their own, without the knowledge, consent, or acquiescence of the President or other major Administration officials, with the possible exception of Casey.

In the week or two immediately after the Iran initiative was disclosed in a Lebanese weekly, the President did not tell the public all that he knew, because negotiations with the Second Channel were still going on, and there remained a good reason for hoping some more hostages might soon be released. Once the President learned that not all of the relevant facts were being brought to his attention, however, he authorized the Attorney General immediately to begin making inquiries. Attorney General Meese acted properly in his investigation, pursuing the matter as a fact-finding effort because he had no reason at the time to believe a crime had been committed. Arguments to the contrary are based strictly on hindsight. In our opinion, the Attorney General and other Justice Department officials did an impressive job with a complicated subject in a short time. After all, it was their investigation that uncovered and disclosed the diversion of funds to the Contras.

## COMMON THREADS

The different strands of the Iran-Contra Affair begin coming together, in the most obvious way, on the level of personnel. Both halves of the event were run by the NSC, specifically by McFarlane, Poindexter, and North. With respect to Nicaragua, the Boland Amendment just about ruled all other agencies out of the picture. With respect to Iran, the other parts of the executive branch—from the State and Defense Departments to the CIA—seemed more than happy to let the NSC be in charge.

It is ironic that many have looked upon these events as signs of an excessively powerful NSC staff. In fact, the NSC's roles in the Iran and Nicaragua policies were exceptions rather than the rule. The Reagan Administration has been beleaguered from the beginning by serious policy disagreements between the Secretaries of State and Defense, among others, and the President has too often not been willing to settle those disputes definitively. The press accounts written at the time Poindexter was promoted to fill McFarlane's shoes saw his selection as a decision to have the National Security Adviser play the role of honest broker, with little independent power. This image of the NSC lasted almost until the Iran arms initiative became public. Poindexter was seen as a technician, chosen to perform a technical job, not to exercise political judgment.

Once the NSC had to manage two operations that were bound to raise politically sensitive questions, it should have been no surprise to anyone that Poindexter made some mistakes. It is not satisfactory, however, for people in the Administration simply to point the finger at him and walk away from all responsibility. For one thing, the President himself does have to bear personal responsibility for the people he picks for top office. But just as it would not be appropriate for the fingers to point only at Poindexter, neither is it right for them only to point to the top.

Everyone who had a stake in promoting a technician to be National Security Adviser should have realized that meant they had a responsibility to follow and highlight the political consequences of operational decisions for the President. Even if the Cabinet officials did not support the basic policy, they had an obligation to remain engaged, if they could manage to do so without constantly arguing the President's basic policy choice. Similarly, Chief of Staff Donald Regan may not have known, or had reason to know, the details of the Iran initiative or Contra resupply effort. But he should have known that North's responses to Congressional inquiries generated by press reports were too important politically to be left to the people who ran the NSC staff.

The discussion of personnel ultimately gets around to the importance of political judgment. We can be more precise about what that means, however, if we consider the common threads in the decisions we have already labelled as mistakes. These have included:

— The President's decision to sign the Boland Amendment of 1984, instead of vetoing it;

— The President's less-than-robust defense of his office's constitutional powers, a mistake he repeated when he acceded too readily and too completely to waive executive privilege for our Committees' investigation;

— The NSC staff's decision to deceive Congress about what it was doing in Central America;

— The decision, in Iran, to pursue a covert policy that was at odds with the Administration's public expressions, without any warning signals to Congress or our allies;

— The decision to use a necessary and constitutionally protected power of withholding information from Congress for unusually sensitive covert operations, for a length of time that stretches credulity;

— Poindexter's decision to authorize the diversion on his own; and, finally,

— Poindexter and North's apparent belief that covering up was in the President's political interest.

We emphatically reject the idea that through these mistakes, the executive branch subverted the law, undermined the Constitution, or threatened democracy. The President is every bit as much of an elected representative of the people as is a Member of Congress. In fact, he and the Vice President are the only officials elected by the whole Nation. Nevertheless, we do believe the mistakes relate in a different way to the issue of democratic accountability. They provide a good starting point for seeing what both sides of the great legislative-executive branch divide must do to improve the way the Government makes foreign policy.

## Congress

Congress has a hard time even conceiving of itself as contributing to the problem of democratic accountability. But the record of ever-changing policies toward Central America that contributed to the NSC staff's behavior is symptomatic of a frequently recurring problem. When Congress is narrowly divided over highly emotional issues, it frequently ends up passing intentionally ambiguous laws or amendments that postpone the day of decision. In foreign policy, those decisions often take the form of restrictive amendments on money bills that are open to being amended again *every year,* with new, and equally ambiguous, language replacing the old. This matter is exacerbated by the way Congress, year after year, avoids passing appropriations bills before the fiscal year starts and then wraps them together in a governmentwide continuing resolution loaded with amendments that cannot be vetoed without threatening the whole Government's operation.

One properly democratic way to ameliorate the problem of foreign policy inconsistency would be to give the President an opportunity to address the major differences between himself and the Congress cleanly, instead of combining them with unrelated subjects. To restore the Presidency to the position it held just a few administrations ago, Congress should exercise the self-discipline to split continuing resolutions into separate appropriation bills and present each of them individually to the President for his signature or veto. Even better would be a line-item veto that would permit the President to force Congress to an override vote without jeopardizing funding for the whole Government. Matters of war and peace are too important to be held hostage to governmental decisions about funding Medicare or highways. To describe this legislative hostage taking as democracy in action is to turn language on its head.

## The Presidency

The Constitution created the Presidency to be a separate branch of government whose occupant would have substantial discretionary power to act. He was not given the power of an 18th century monarch, but neither was he meant to be a creature of Congress. The country needs a President who can exercise the powers the Framers intended. As long as any President has those powers, there will be mistakes. It would be disastrous to respond to the possibility of error by further restraining and limiting the powers of the office.

Then, instead of seeing occasional actions turn out to be wrong, we would be increasing the probability that future Presidents would be unable to act decisively, thus guaranteeing ourselves a perpetually paralyzed, reactive, and unclear foreign policy in which mistake by inaction would be the order of the day.

If Congress can learn something about democratic responsibility from the Iran-Contra Affair, future Presidents can learn something too. The Administration would have been better served over the long run by insisting on a principled confrontation over those strategic issues that can be debated publicly. Where secrecy is necessary, as it often must be, the Administration should have paid more careful attention to consultation and the need for consistency between what is public and what is covert. Inconsistency carries a risk to a President's future ability to persuade, and persuasion is at the heart of a vigorous, successful presidency.

A President's most important priorities, the ones that give him a chance to leave an historic legacy, can be attained only through persistent leadership that leads to a lasting change in the public's understanding and opinions. President Reagan has been praised by his supporters as a "communicator" and criticized by his opponents as an ideologue. The mistakes of the Iran-Contra Affair, ironically, came from a lack of communication and an inadequate appreciation of the importance of ideas. During President Reagan's terms of office, he has persistently taken two major foreign policy themes to the American people: a strong national defense for the United States, and support for the institutions of freedom abroad. The 1984 election showed his success in persuading the people to adopt his fundamental perspective. The events since then have threatened to undermine that achievement by shifting the agenda and refocusing the debate. If the President's substantial successes are to be sustained, it is up to him, and those of us who support his objectives, to begin once again with the task of democratic persuasion.

## AFTERWORD: SUMMARY OF LEGAL CONCLUSIONS

### Nicaragua

The main period under review during these investigations was October 1984 through October 1986. During this period, various versions of the Boland Amendment restricted the expenditure of appropriated funds available to agencies or entities involved in intelligence activities from being spent directly or indirectly to support military or paramilitary operations in Nicaragua. In August 1985, the State Department was authorized to spend $27 million to provide humanitarian assistance to the Nicaraguan democratic Resistance. In December 1985, the CIA was authorized to spend funds specifically appropriated to provide communications equipment and training and to provide intelligence and counterintelligence advice and information to assist military operations by the Resistance. On October 18, 1986, $100 million in direct military support for the Contras was made available for fiscal year 1987. Our understanding of the effect of these prohibitions rests on both statutory and constitutional interpretations.

(1) The Constitution protects the power of the President, either acting himself or through agents of his choice, to engage in whatever diplomatic communications with other countries he may wish. It also protects the ability of the President and his agents to persuade U.S. citizens to engage voluntarily in otherwise legal activity to serve what they consider to be the national interest. That includes trying to persuade other countries to contribute their own funds for causes both countries support. To whatever extent the Boland Amendments tried to prohibit such activity, they were clearly unconstitutional.

(2) If the Constitution prohibits Congress from restricting a particular Presidential action directly, it cannot use the appropriation power to achieve the same unconstitutional effect. Congress does have the power under the Constitution, however, to use appropriations riders to prohibit the entire U.S. Government from spending any money, including salaries, to provide covert or overt military support to the Contras. Thus, the Clark Amendment prohibiting all U.S. support for the Angolan Resistance in 1976 was constitutional. Some members of Congress who supported the Boland Amendment may have thought they were enacting a prohibition as broad as the Clark Amendment. The specific language of the Boland Amendment was considerably more restricted, however, in two respects.

(a) By limiting the coverage to agencies or entities involved in intelligence activities, Congress chose to use language borrowed directly from the Intelligence Oversight Act of 1980. In the course of settling on that language in 1980, Congress deliberately decided to exclude the National Security Council (NSC) from its coverage. At no time afterward did Congress indicate an intention to change the language's coverage. The NSC therefore was excluded from the Boland Amendment and its activities were therefore legal under this statute.

391

(b) The Boland prohibitions also were limited to spending that directly or indirectly supported military or paramilitary operations in Nicaragua. Under this language, a wide range of intelligence-gathering and political support activities were still permitted, and were carried out with the full knowledge of the House and Senate Intelligence Committees.

(c) Virtually all, if not all, of the CIA's activities examined by these Committees occurred after the December 1985 law authorized intelligence sharing and communications support and were fully legal under the terms of that law.

(d) If the NSC had been covered by the Boland Amendments, most of Oliver North's activity still would have fallen outside the prohibitions for reasons stated in (b) and (c) above.

## Iran

The Administration was also in substantial compliance with the laws governing covert actions throughout the Iran arms initiative.

(1) It is possible to make a respectable legal argument to the effect that the 1985 Israeli arms transfers to Iran technically violated the terms of the Arms Export Control Act (AECA) or Foreign Assistance Act (FAA), assuming the arms Israel transferred were received from the United States under one or the other of these statutes. However:

(a) Covert transfers under the National Security Act and Economy Act were understood to be alternatives to transfers under the AECA and FAA that met both of these latter acts' essential purposes by including provisions for Presidential approval and Congressional notification.

(b) The requirement for U.S. agreement before a country can retransfer arms obtained from the United States is meant to insure that retransfers conform to U.S. national interests. In this case, the Israeli retransfers occurred with Presidential approval indicating that they did so conform.

(c) The Israeli retransfer and subsequent replenishment made the deal essentially equivalent to a direct U.S. sale, with Israel playing a role fundamentally equivalent to that of a middleman. Since the United States could obviously have engaged in a direct transfer, and did so in 1986, whatever violation may have occurred was, at most, a minor and inadvertent technicality.

(2) A verbal approval for covert transactions meets the requirements of the Hughes-Ryan Amendment and National Security Act. Verbal approvals ought to be reduced to writing as a matter of sound policy, but they are not illegal.

(3) Similarly, the President has the constitutional and statutory authority to withhold notifying Congress of covert activities under very rare conditions. President Reagan's decision to withhold notification was essentially equivalent to President Carter's decisions in 1979–1980 to withhold notice for between 3 and 6 months in parallel Iran hostage operations. We do not agree with President Reagan's decision to withhold notification for as long as he did. The decision was legal, however, and we think the Constitution mandates that it should remain so. If a President withholds notification for too long and then cannot adequately justify the decision to Congress, that President can expect to pay a stiff political price, as President Reagan has certainly found out.

## Diversion

We consider the ownership of the funds the Iranians paid to the Secord-Hakim "Enterprise" to be in legal doubt. There are respectable legal arguments to be made both for the point of view that the funds belong to the U.S. Treasury and for the contention that they do not. If the funds do not belong to the United States, then the diversion amounted to third-country or private funds being shipped to the Contras. If they did belong to the United States, there would be legal questions (although not, technically, Boland Amendment questions) about using U.S.-owned funds for purposes not specifically approved by law. The answer does not seem to us to be so obvious, however, as to warrant treating the matter as if it were criminal.

# PART II

# THE FOREIGN AFFAIRS POWERS OF THE CONSTITUTION AND THE IRAN-CONTRA AFFAIR

# CHAPTER 2

# The Foreign Affairs Powers and the Framers' Intentions

Judgments about the Iran-Contra Affair ultimately must rest upon one's views about the proper roles of Congress and the President in foreign policy. There were many statements during the public hearings, for example, about the rule of law. But the fundamental law of the land is the Constitution. Unconstitutional statutes violate the rule of law every bit as much as do willful violations of constitutional statutes. It is essential, therefore, to frame any discussion of what happened with a proper analysis of the Constitutional allocation of legislative and executive power in foreign affairs.

One point stands out from the historical record: the Constitution's Framers expected the President to be much more than a minister or clerk. The President was supposed to execute the laws, but that was only the beginning. He also was given important powers, independent of the legislature's, and these substantively were focused on foreign policy.

Our analysis will cover three chapters. The first will be about the debates in and around the Constitutional Convention of 1787 and will show the Constitutional Convention of 1787 and will show the particular importance of what Alexander Hamilton called "energy in the executive" in this policy area. The second reviews historical examples. It shows that, throughout the Nation's history, Congress has accepted substantial exercise of Presidential power—in the conduct of diplomacy, the use of force and covert action—which had no basis in statute and only a general basis in the Constitution itself. The third considers the applicable court cases and legal principles.

Taken together, the three chapters will show that much of what President Reagan did in his actions toward Nicaragua and Iran were constitutionally protected exercises of inherent Presidential powers. However unwise some of those actions may have been, the rule of law cannot permit Congress to usurp judgments that constitutionally are not its to make. It is true that the Constitution also gives substantial foreign policy powers to Congress, including the power of the purse. But the power of the purse—which forms the core of the majority argument—is not and was never intended to be a license for Congress to usurp Presidential powers and functions. Some of the statutes most central to the Iran-Contra Affair contain a mixture of constitutionally legitimate and illegitimate prohibitions. By the end of the three chapters, we will be in a position to start sorting them out.

## "Necessary and Proper" and the "Invitation to Struggle"

The 1972 Senate Foreign Relations Committee's report recommending the War Powers Act, and the 1974 report of the Select Committee on Intelligence Activities (chaired by Senator Frank Church and known as the Church Committee), both tried to support an all but unlimited Congressional power by invoking the "Necessary and Proper" clause. That clause says Congress may "make all Laws which shall be necessary and proper for carrying into Execution the foregoing [legislative] Powers, and all other Powers vested by this Constitution in the Government of the United States, *or in any Department or Officer thereof.*" The argument of these two prominent committees was that by granting Congress the power to make rules for the other departments, the Constitution meant to enshrine legislative supremacy except for those few activities explicitly reserved for the other branches.

One must ignore 200 years of constitutional history to suggest that Congress has a vast reservoir of implied power whose only limits are the powers *explicitly* reserved to the other branches. It seems clear, for example, that Congress could not legislate away the Supreme Court's power of judicial re-view, even though judicial review is not mentioned explicitly in Article III. The same applies to the Presidency. The Necessary and Proper clause does not permit Congress to pass a law usurping Presidential power. A law negating Presidential power cannot be treated as if it were "necessary and proper for carrying" Presidential powers "into Execution." To suggest otherwise would smack of Orwellian Doublespeak.

The issue for this investigation, therefore, is not whether Congress and the President both have a legitimate role in foreign policy. Clearly, both do. Rather, the question is how to interpret the powers the two branches were given. All three of the Government's branches were given both express and implied powers. Congress does not have the authority to arrogate all of the implied power to itself. What we need to determine is whether these implied powers all fall into an undefined war zone, or whether there are theoretical and historical principles that allow one to decide when powers are more properly exercised by one branch or another.

Countering a view held by some Constitutional analysts, the minority argues that the Framers meant the Constitution to compensate for the overly weak government set up by the Articles of Confederation. During the Constitutional Convention, the Presidency's power over foreign policy increased. The President was given discretion to use force without declaration of war and the power to be make treaties. Advocates of a strong national government also pressed their case in the *Federalist* papers.

# CHAPTER 3

# The President's Foreign Policy Powers in Early Constitutional History

Our review of the Constitutional Convention concluded that the original document left a great deal to be worked out in practice. The *Federalist* does not change this conclusion. It does give us a theoretical basis, however, for seeing that the subsequent historical development of the President's foreign policy powers was no aberration. This is evident in the early development of diplomatic power, in presidential deployments of force, and in the use of secret agents for intelligence and covert activities.

## DIPLOMACY

**The disputes over Presidential power were implicit from the the moment the new Constitution took effect. President Washington, for example, angered many when he kept the United States neutral in the war between France and England of 1793. He decided against honoring the 1778 Treaty of Alliance between France and the United States and refused for 8 months to call a special session of Congress on the subject.**

Some Members of these Committees seem to have taken the positions (1) that Congress can require the President to notify it whenever the President prepares or begins to conduct secret negotiations or covert operations, whatever the circumstances, and/or (2) that Congress may constitutionally use its appropriations power to prohibit certain forms of communication between the President (or the President's employees in the White House and State Department) and other governments or private individual. We consider negotiations and communications with foreign governments or individuals to be Presidential powers protected by the Constitution, without reservation. They fall comfortably within precedents established during the Washington Administration which have never been successfully challenged since. The constitutional validity of withholding information about sensitive, covert operations involves additional considerations that will be discussed separately later.

## USE OF FORCE

We do not intend to turn this report into an argument about war powers. We have no doubt that we disagree with some of our esteemed colleagues on this issue, but there is no point in getting sidetracked. Nevertheless, we consider it important to say something about the power Presidents traditionally have exercised under the Constitution, to use force with and without prior congressional authorization. This history clearly supports our basic contention that the Constitution expected the President to be much more than a clerk. It will also provide a context for discussing the less drastic projections of U.S. power that fit under the rubric of covert action.

**Quoting from a 1973 hearing on the War Powers Resolution, the minority provides samples of the 118 instances in which force was used by a President without Congressional authorization. These include President Johnson's 1965 decision to send troops to the Dominican Republic and President Kennedy's naval quarantine of Cuba in 1962.**

## INTELLIGENCE AND COVERT ACTIONS

We end this review of historical precedent with a brief overview of intelligence and covert actions authorized by past Presidents. That history begins in the earliest days of the Nation. As Representative Hyde mentioned during Admiral Poindexter's testimony on July 17, the Continental Congress—which did not have a separate executive branch—set up a Committee of Secret Correspon-

dence made up of Benjamin Franklin, Robert Morris, Benjamin Harrison, John Dickinson and John Jay. On October 1, 1776, Franklin and Morris were told that France would be willing to extend credit to the revolutionaries to help them buy arms. They wrote:

> Considering the nature and importance of [the above intelligence,] we agree in opinion that it is our indispensable duty to keep it a secret from Congress. . . . As the court of France has taken measures to negotiate this loan in the most cautious and secret manner, should we divulge it immediately we may not only lose the present benefit but also render the court cautious of any further connection with such unguarded people and prevent their granting other loans of assistance that we stand in need of.

Beginning with George Washington, almost every President has used "special agents"—people, often private individuals, appointed for missions by the President without Senate confirmation—to help gain the intelligence about which Jay wrote, and to engage in a broad range of other activities with or against foreign countries. The first such agent was Gouverneur Morris, who was sent to Great Britain in 1789 to explore the chances for opening normal diplomatic communications. At the same time, Britain sent a "private agent" to the United States who communicated outside normal channels through Secretary of Treasury Alexander Hamilton instead of through the Francophile Secretary of State, Thomas Jefferson. Washington's agents were paid from a "secret service" fund he was allowed to use at his discretion, without detailed accounting.

During the country's first century, Presi-

400

dents used literally hundreds of secret agents at their own discretion. Congress did give the President a contingency fund for these agents, but never specifically approved, or was asked to approve any particular agent or activity. In fact, Congress never approved or was asked to approve covert activity in general. The Presidents were simply using their inherent executive powers under Article II of the Constitution. For the Congresses that had accepted the overt presidential uses of military force summarized in the previous section, the use of Executive power for these kinds of covert activities raised no constitutional questions.

## CONCLUSION

Presidents asserted their constitutional independence from Congress early. They engaged in secret diplomacy and intelligence activities, and refused to share the results with Congress if they saw fit. They unilaterally established U.S. military and diplomatic policy with respect to foreign belligerent states, in quarrels involving only third parties. They enforced this policy abroad, using force if necessary. They engaged U.S. troops abroad to serve American interests without congressional approval, and in a number of cases apparently against explicit directions from Congress. They also had agents engage in what would commonly be referred to as covert actions, again without Congressional approval. In short, Presidents exercised a broad range of foreign policy powers for which they neither sought nor received Congressional sanction through statute.

This history speaks volumes about the Constitution's allocation of powers between the branches. It leaves little, if any, doubt that the President was expected to have the primary role of conducting the foreign policy of the United States. Congressional actions to limit the President in this area therefore should be reviewed with a considerable degree of skepticism. If they interfere with core presidential foreign policy functions, they should be struck down. Moreover, the lesson of our constitutional history is that doubtful cases should be decided in favor of the President.

# CHAPTER 4

# Constitutional Principles in Court

The historical examples given in the preceding section point the way toward a proper understanding of the Executive's foreign policy powers as those powers have evolved under the Constitution. The assertion by Presidents, and the acceptance by Congress, of inherent presidential powers in foreign policy were the normal practice in American history before the 1970s, not an aberration. The history therefore creates a strong presumption against any new constitutional interpretation that would run counter to the operative understanding in the legislative and executive branches that has endured from the beginning.

The Supreme Court has used history in just such a presumptive way. In the Opinion of the Court in the "flexible tariff" delegation case of *Field* v. *Clark,* Justice Harlan wrote:

> The practical construction of the Constitution, as given by so many acts of Congress [involving similar delegations], and embracing almost the entire period of our national existence, should not be overruled unless upon a conviction that such legislation was clearly incompatible with the law of the land.

The point of this quotation is not that historical usage must slavishly be followed. Rather, it is that historical precedents—especially ones that began almost immediately, with the support of many who participated in the 1787 Convention—carry a great deal of weight in any discussion about what the Constitution was supposed to mean in the real world of government.

The historical examples clearly undermine the position of the staunchest proponents of Congressional power: that Presidents were intended to be ministerial clerks, whose only authority (except for subjects explicitly mentioned in Article II) must come from Congress. But that still leaves two other possibilities that must be considered when judging the constitutional validity of executive action. One is that a particular exercise of presidential power may have been acceptable in the past only because Congress had not yet spoken on the subject. The other is that at least some exercises of implied power (i.e., power not explicitly stated in Article II) are so central to the office that they remain beyond the constitutional reach of legislative prohibition. The Supreme Court precedents discussed below show that many of the major

Iran-Contra actions undertaken by President Reagan, his staff, and other executive branch officials, fall into the constitutionally protected category.

## THE STEEL SEIZURE CASE AND INHERENT PRESIDENTIAL POWER

Justice Robert Jackson's concurring opinion in the *Steel Seizure Case (Youngstown Sheet and Tube Co.* v. *Sawyer)* is often used as a basis for outlining the logically possible constitutional relationships between legislative and executive power. In the case's most famous dictum, Jackson wrote:

> We may well begin by a somewhat over-simplified grouping of practical situations in which a President may doubt, or others may challenge, his powers, and by distinguishing roughly the legal consequences of this factor of relativity.
>
> 1. When the President acts pursuant to an express or implied authorization of Congress, his authority is at its maximum, for it includes all that he possesses in his own right plus all Congress can delegate. . . .
>
> 2. When the President acts in absence of either a congressional grant or denial of authority, he can only rely upon his own independent powers, but there is a twilight in which he and Congress may have concurrent authority, or in which its distribution is uncertain. . . .
>
> 3. When the President takes measures incompatible with the express or implied will of Congress, his power is at its lowest ebb, for then he can rely only upon his own constitutional powers minus any constitutional powers of Congress over the matter. Courts can sustain exclusive presidential control in such a case

only by disabling the Congress from acting upon the subject.

The major issues in the Iran-Contra investigation have to do with incidents about which Congress ostensibly has spoken. In other words, putting aside issues of statutory construction to be argued in later chapters, they all fall into Jackson's third category, the one where presidential power is supposedly at its weakest. Even in this category, however, Jackson conceded that Congress is "disabled" from interfering with some matters.

The President does not have plenary power to do whatever he wants in foreign policy; Congress does have some legislative powers in the field. However, there are some foreign policy matters over which the President is the "sole organ" of government and Congress may not impinge upon them.

## THE PRESIDENT AS THE "SOLE ORGAN" FOR DIPLOMACY

We have shown that the Constitution gives the President some power to act on his own in foreign affairs. What kinds of activities are set aside for him? The most obvious—other than the Commander-in-Chief power and others explicitly listed in Article II—is the one named in *Curtiss-Wright:* the President is the "sole organ" of the government in foreign affairs. That is, the President and his agents are the country's eyes and ears in negotiation, intelligence sharing and other forms of communication with the rest of the world.

This view has long and until recently unchallenged history. As was mentioned in the earlier historical section, the phrase originated in Alexander Hamilton's *Pacificus* papers of 1793 and was used by John Marshall in a House floor debate in 1800. The 1860 lower court decision of *Durand* v. *Hollins* described the President as "the only legitimate organ of the government, to open and carry on correspondence or negotiations with foreign nations, in matters concerning the interests of the country or of its citizens."

Justice Jackson also referred to the concept in an opinion written just four years before the *Steel Seizure Case*. In *C. & S. Air Lines* v. *Waterman Corp.*, a case involving a Civilian Aeronautics Board decision to deny an airline a license to serve foreign countries, Jackson said:

> Congress may of course delegate very large grants of its power over foreign commerce to the President. [Citation omitted.] The President also possesses *in his own right* certain powers conferred by the Constitution on him as Commander-in-Chief and as the Nation's organ in foreign affairs. For present purposes, the order draws vitality from either or both sources.

Finally, to complete this brief history, the passage from *Curtiss-Wright* with the "sole organ" reference was quoted and reaffirmed in *Dame & Moore* v. *Regan* in 1981.

## The "Sole Organ" and the Boland Amendments

What are the implications for the Iran-Contra investigation of characterizing the President as the "sole organ" of foreign policy? For one thing, it is beyond question that Congress did not have the constitutional power to prohibit the President from sharing information, asking other governments to contribute to the Nicaraguan resistance, or entering into secret negotiations with factions inside Iran. Such conversations are paradigms of what Chief Justice John Marshall said in *Marbury* v. *Madison:* "The President is invested [by the Constitution] with important political powers in the exercise of which he is to use his own discretion." In addition, as Marbury made clear, these powers do not stop with the President. To make them effective, the President may exercise his own discretion through agents of his own choice.

> To aid him in the performance of these duties, he is authorized to appoint certain officers who act by his authority and in conformity with his orders. In such cases, their acts are his acts; and *whatever opinion may be entertained of the manner in which executive discretion may be used, still there exists, and can exist, no power to control that discretion. . . .*

> The conclusion from this reasoning is, that where the heads of departments are the political or confidential agents of the executive, merely to execute the will of the president, or rather to act in cases in which the executive possesses a constitutional or legal discretion, nothing can be more perfectly clear than that their acts are only politically examinable.

What follows from Chief Justice Marshall's opinion in *Marbury* is that if Congress cannot prevent the President from exercising discretion over a particular matter, neither may it prevent the President's personal staff on the National Security Council, the Departments of State and Defense, the Intelligence Community, or the President's *ad hoc* personal representatives, from performing

404

the same tasks on the President's orders and in his own name.

Many, if not all, of the actions by representatives of the U.S. government that have been alleged to run counter to the Boland amendments were essentially forms of information sharing and diplomatic communication. To the extent that such activities by the NSC staff, CIA, State Department or Defense Department were covered by the amendments—and we shall argue that many were not—we believe the activities were constitutionally protected against limitation by Congress. The executive was not bound to follow an unconstitutional effort to limit the President's powers.

## PROTECTING AMERICAN CITIZENS ABROAD

One inherent presidential power particularly relevant to the Iranian side of this investigation is the power to protect the lives and interests of American citizens abroad.

In July 1854, U.S. Navy Commander George S. Hollins demanded reparations from Nicaragua after a U.S. official was injured during a riot. When he failed to receive satisfaction, Hollins ordered his ships to bombard San Juan del Norte, otherwise known as Greytown. Calvin Durand then sued Hollins in the Circuit Court for the Southern District of New York for damages the bombardment had caused to his property. In its opinion denying Durand's claim, the court said:

> As the executive head of the nation, the president is made the only legitimate organ of the general government, to open and carry on cor-

respondence or negotiations with foreign nations, in matters concerning the interest of the country or of its citizens. It is to him, also, the citizens abroad must look for protection of person and of property, and for the faithful execution of the laws existing and intended for their protection. For this purpose, the whole executive power of the country is placed in his hands, under the constitution, and the laws passed in pursuance thereof. . . .

## THE CONSTITUTIONAL LIMITS TO CONGRESSIONAL RESTRICTIONS

All of these court decisions demonstrate that the President was meant to have a substantial degree of discretionary power to do many of the kinds of things President Reagan did in Iran and Central America. They do not suggest that a President can do anything he wants. Congress and President were given different resources and different modes of influencing the same policy arenas. Both President and Congress can sway the U.S. posture toward Nicaragua or Iran, for example, but each have their own characteristic tools to bring to bear on the subject. What the Constitutional separation of powers protects is not the President's or Congress's precise sway over particular events. That is for the individual occupants of each branch to earn. But the Constitution does prevent either branch from using its own powers, or modes of activity, to deprive the other branch of its central functions.

Congress may not use its control over appropriations, including salaries, to prevent the executive or judiciary from fulfilling Constitutionally mandated obligations. The implication for the Boland amendments is obvious. If any part of the amendments would have used Congress's control over salaries to prevent executive actions that Congress may not prohibit directly, the amendments would be just as unconstitutional as if they had dealt with the subject directly.

## CONCLUSION

The Constitution gives important foreign policy powers both to Congress and to the President. Neither can accomplish very much over the long term by trying to go it alone. The President cannot use the country's resources to carry out policy without congressional appropriations. At the same time, Congress can prohibit some actions, and it can influence others, but it cannot act by itself, and it is not institutionally designed to accept political responsibility for specific actions. Action or implementation is a peculiarly executive branch function.

The Constitution's requirement for cooperation does not negate the separation of powers. Neither branch can be permitted to usurp functions that belong to the other. As we have argued throughout, and as the Supreme Court reaffirmed in 1983, "the powers delegated to the three branches are functionally identifiable." The executive branch's functions are the ones most closely related to the need for secrecy, efficiency, dispatch, and the acceptance by one person, the President, of political responsibility for the result. This basic framework must be preserved if the country is to have an effective foreign policy in the future.

PART

# NICARAGUA

# CHAPTER 5

# Nicaragua:
# The Context

It is impossible to understand the motivations for the Administration's actions without first understanding the strategic and political context within which it was operating. In describing these circumstances, it is necessary to begin with the fact that the Sandinista Government in Nicaragua is a Communist regime that openly espouses the expansionist, Leninist doctrine of "revolution without borders." Because of this, and because the Sandinistas have behaved in a manner consistent with the doctrine by supporting Communist insurgencies elsewhere in Central America, Nicaragua has become a direct threat to the stability of the governments of its neighbors and to U.S. security interests.

**The minority recounts a 1980 speech by a member of the House Intelligence Committee, Rep. C.W. "Bill" Young of Florida, who objected to the Carter Administration's assessment that the Sandinistas were following democratic procedures. He complained that Presidential orders barred Congressional staff members from talking to CIA analysts about Nicaragua, a circumstance he said suggested the intelligence was being manipulated—the same charge the majority report makes against the Reagan Administration.**

During the period between January 1982 and January 1985, while Congress was vacillating and pinching pennies, the Soviet Union and its allies provided about $500 million in military aid alone to Nicaragua. By early 1985, at the time of the cutoff of U.S. taxpayer military assistance to the Resistance, the Sandinista armed forces included 62,000 troops. Their arsenal also included nearly 150 tanks (of which more than 110 were T-55 Soviet battle tanks that were clearly superior to any other tank in the region), 200 other armored vehicles (mostly machine-gun-armed BTR-60 and BTR-152 personnel carriers that can carry an infantry squad), 300 missile launchers, 45 airplanes, and 20 helicopters, including the deadly Soviet MI-24 HIND-D "flying tanks" that General Singlaub described as "the most effective people killing machine[s] in the world."

During 1985, the already high level of aid accelerated. According to publicly available material provided by the State Department, the Soviet Union, Cuba, and Eastern Bloc

**Figure 5-1.**

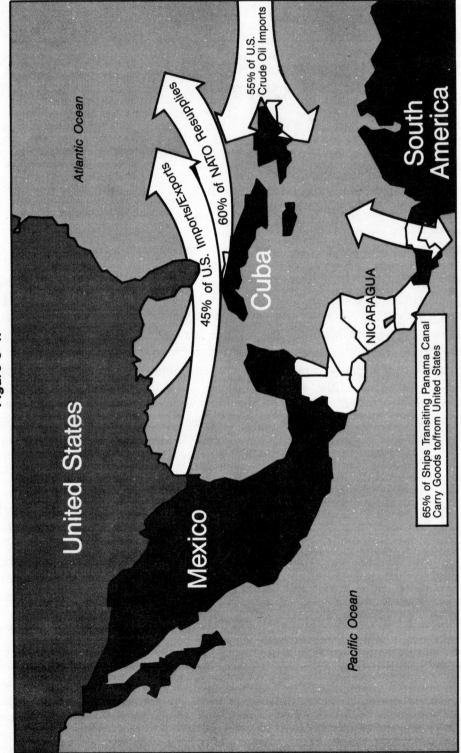

countries gave Nicaragua another $150 million in military aid in 1985. (In addition to the Soviet Union and Cuba, Nicaragua is receiving aid from Czechoslovakia, North Korea, Libya, and the Palestine Liberation Organization, among others.) That figure for military aid jumped to $580 million for 1986 alone. Between December 1982 and October 1986, according to Defense Intelligence Agency estimates discussed in these Committees' public hearings, the same countries gave $1.34 *billion* in military aid and *another* $1.8 *billion* in economic aid to the Nicaraguan Government. The net result is that Nicaragua has far and away the largest armed force in all of Central America, and that does not even take into account approximately 2,500 to 3,000 advisers from the Soviet Union, Cuba, and other Soviet bloc countries. In contrast, all U.S. humanitarian and military aid to the Resistance during the entire 1980s amounted to approximately $200 million, $100 million of which came in the fiscal year from October 1, 1986 to September 30, 1987.

These numbers only begin to give a picture, however, of the reasons for viewing Nicaragua as a threat to the region. According to former National Security Advisor Robert C. McFarlane:

The danger is not Nicaraguan soldiers taking on the United States, it is that country serving as a platform from which the Soviet Union or other surrogates like Cuba can subvert neighboring regimes and ultimately require the United States to defend itself against a Soviet threat, whether by spending more dollars on defense that we didn't need to, to worry about our southern border, whether we need to worry more about the Panama Canal now that Russians are here, whether we need to be concerned about the half of our oil imports that come from refineries in the Caribbean within MIG range of Nicaragua, and we have not had to think about these things for a long time.

The danger, it should be obvious from what McFarlane said, is not simply that posed to other Central American countries by Nicaragua's own armed forces.

According to information presented during General Singlaub's testimony, the Nicaraguans are building a 10,000-foot-long airstrip at Punta Huete. As Representative Hyde observed, the runway is "capable of accommodating any Soviet aircraft in their inventory. That includes the Backfire bomber, the Bear-D reconnaissance aircraft, and it's strictly a military facility with antiaircraft guns deployed around the airfield." Singlaub agreed, and said that what made the airfield significant was that it would accommodate intercontinental as well as short-range aircraft.

Nor is this all. The Soviet Union has an intelligence collection facility at Lourdes near Havana, Cuba, that is able to monitor maritime, military and space communications as well as telephone conversations in the Eastern portion of the United States. A similar base in Nicaragua would mean a similar capability for the Pacific and West Coast. Finally, the Nicaraguans are building the Corinto port facility that is being made into a deep water port able to accommodate submarines. The Soviet presence in Nicaragua, in other words, when combined with its presence in Cuba, could mean a Soviet base on both ends of the Caribbean as well as the only Soviet port in the Pacific outside the Soviet Union itself. The latter, Singlaub said, "would give them for the first time a base from which they could threaten the West

Coast of the United States." So there is plenty of reason for a President of the United States to think the Nicaraguan Government is not merely unfortunate for its own people, but a distinct threat to the security of the region and, ultimately, to the United States.

When President Reagan sought to bring pressure on the Nicaraguan Government by aiding the Resistance, he was doing something more than merely furthering his own policy goals. According to the findings of the Congress of the United States and the terms of the OAS charter, the President was obliged to do what he could to act against Nicaragua's aggression against its neighbors. The finding would not have permitted the President to violate laws that explicitly prohibited the use of appropriated funds for a particular purpose. Beyond these explicit prohibitions, however, the President was not only permitted by his inherent foreign policy powers under the Constitution, but was positively obliged to do whatever he could, within the law, to respond to Nicaragua's behavior.

Because of this obligation, it is not proper to assert that the President should have gone out of his way to avoid any actions that some of the Boland Amendment's sponsors might arguably have wished to prohibit. Although no President is required to so interpret a law on any subject within his constitutional authority, such a response might have made sense as an act of prudence and comity if Congress had only passed a prohibition. The fact, however, is that Congress put two sets of obligations on the President, one mandating action and the other restricting it. Under the circumstances, the President had a duty to try to satisfy both of the mandates, to whatever extent he could possibly do so.

# CHAPTER 6

# The Boland Amendments

People listening to the public hearings on the Iran-Contra Affair heard many statements about the "spirit of the Boland Amendments." Everyone knows, the argument goes, that Congress wanted to cut off all U.S. aid to the Nicaraguan resistance. Congress did not anticipate that anyone on the National Security Council staff would support private and third-country fundraising or give advice to and help coordinate the private resupply effort. Col. North's activities were a clear attempt, the argument concludes, to circumvent the law.

There are three basic problems with this line of reasoning. First, as previously discussed, the Constitution does not permit Congress to prevent the President or his designated agents from communicating with the Nicaraguan resistance or from encouraging other countries and private citizens to support the resistance. Second, as Justice Frankfurter said in *Addison* v. *Holly Hill Co.,* "Congress expresses its meaning by words. . . . It is no warrant for extending a statute that experience may disclose that it should have been made more comprehensive." One of the reasons there was so much discussion of the "spirit of the law" at the

hearings is, as we shall show, that it is difficult to argue the letter of the law had been violated. Finally, even this last statement concedes too much. The fact is that Congress was not animated by a single "spirit" when it passed the Boland Amendments. It is necessary, therefore, to take account of the political history in the first part of this chapter as well as the statutory history in the rest.

## THE "SPIRIT" OF OCTOBER 1984

We have already noted that at the same time Congress was denying appropriations for the anti-Sandinista resistance, it was also declaring the Sandinista Government to be in violation of a provision of the OAS Charter that calls for a response by the President. In addition, Congress has changed its collective mind virtually every year over policy toward Nicaragua. The United States gave aid to the Sandinistas in fiscal 1980, took aid away from the Sandinistas at the end of 1980 for fiscal year 1981, and then gave covert support to the democratic resistance in 1981 for

413

fiscal year 1982. For fiscal 1983, Congress denied aid "for the purpose of overthrowing the government," a restriction that was all but meaningless and therefore adopted by the House unanimously. For fiscal year 1984, Congress removed the language about purpose but limited the amount of assistance to a level that it knew would not last for the full year. Then, the strictest version of the Boland Amendment was adopted for fiscal 1985—partly, it is often said, because Congress was upset at allegedly not having been informed about the CIA's role in connection with the mining of Nicaraguan harbors.

## THE WORDS OF THE BOLAND AMENDMENT

The real legal issue turns, therefore, on the exact words of the Boland Amendment. Before turning to those words, however, it is important to bear in mind that they were a rider, or a limitation amendment, to an appropriations bill. The Boland Amendment was not, for example, like the Hatch Act, which prohibits specific (political) activities by civil servants whether they are on the job or off. Nor is it like the Neutrality Act, which also prohibits defined activities and makes them criminal. An appropriations rider, even if it reaches salaries, is nothing more than a limitation on the way Federal funds may be used. It does not reach a person's whole life and does not make activities criminal.

What were the precise "funds available," to use Mr. Boland's words, whose use was prohibited? The relevant language read as follows:

During fiscal year 1985, no funds available to the Central Intelligence Agency, the Department of Defense, or any other agency or entity of the United States involved in intelligence activities may be obligated or expended for the purpose or which would have the effect of supporting, directly or indirectly, military or paramilitary operations in Nicaragua by any nation, group, organization, movement or individual.

The terms of this prohibition apply to funds made available to specific arms of the executive branch. The fiscal 1983 prohibition of aid "for the purpose of overthrowing the government" applied only to funds available to the Department of Defense and Central Intelligence Agency. The fiscal 1985 law broadens the prohibition to include "any other agency or entity of the United States involved in intelligence activities." The obvious question, given Col. North's activities in behalf of the democratic resistance, is whether the staff of the National Security Council (NSC) is an "agency or entity" covered by the act.

**The minority disputes suggestions that the National Security Council was an agency or entity involved in intelligence activities. It says legislative history of various intelligence measures supports the argument that it was not. A 1980 Senate bill that drafted a charter for the intelligence agencies, for example, omitted the NSC from its long list of covered agencies. The Intelligence Oversight Act of 1980, which was drawn from the proposed charter, contained only a general statement that it applied to the Director of Central Intelligence and all departments, agencies, and other entities involved in intelligence activities. The Boland Amendment used similar terms to describe which agencies were restricted from aiding the Contras.**

## SHARING INFORMATION AND INTELLIGENCE UNDER THE BOLAND AMENDMENT

A review of the legislative history of the Boland Amendment and related subsequent amendments makes clear that it was lawful for Col. North and others to provide intelligence to the resistance leadership. The legislative history also makes clear that it is reasonable to view the Boland Amendment as allowing the type of information transfer, advice, and coordination that Col. North and others provided to the Contra resupply effort.

## Advice for and Coordination of the Resupply Operation

The language and legislative history of the Boland Amendment, as modified by the "communications" and "advice" provisions, also make clear that Col. North and other U.S. Government officials could legally provide general advice, coordination, and information with respect to the Contra resupply operation that began in late 1985.

The Boland Amendment provides that:

> No funds . . . may be obligated or expended for the purpose or which would have the effect of *supporting,* directly or indirectly, *military or paramilitary operations* in Nicaragua. [Emphasis added.]

This language does not prohibit all support, but only support of a specific kind. The question that always arose, however, was what kind of support would constitute indirect support of a military operation inside Nicaragua? After the "communications" and "advice" provisions were enacted in 1985, the Chairmen of the House and Senate Intelligence Committees disagreed about their meaning—particularly as they might apply to a resupply operation, as opposed to specific military or paramilitary operations in Nicaragua.

Rep. Hamilton, in a December 4, 1985, letter, took the position that the law prohibited advice about "logistical operations upon which military or paramilitary operations depend." Senator Durenberger, in a letter dated the next day, however, said that he believed the law meant to allow just such advice. Faced with these conflicting interpretations, the CIA, after a careful analysis of the legislative history, chose to accept the position that most clearly represented a harmonization of the points of difference between the two Chambers:

> The legislative history, therefore, seems to draw distinctions between, on the one hand, participation, planning, and providing advice (which would not be permitted in support of paramilitary operations) and, on the other hand, information sharing, including advice on the delivery of supplies. . . . There is no clear indication that Congress intended to prohibit the CIA from giving advice on supply operations, and some indication that it did intend to distinguish between mere information-sharing and actual participation in such operations. Furthermore, there would appear to be a valid distinction between permissible, general military resupply operations and operations in the context of specific military operations, which were not authorized. . . .

> Merely passing intelligence on Sandinista gun or radar placements, weather conditions, flight vectors, and other information to assist in the delivery of supplies for general maintenance of the forces in the field would not

seem to be prohibited, both because this would not constitute "participation," and because this would not be "integral" to a "paramilitary operation" as contemplated by Congress."

We agree with the legal conclusions reached in this memorandum. Based on these conclusions, we would argue that virtually all, if not all, of Col. North's activities in support of the democratic resistance would have been legal even if the Boland Amendment had applied to the NSC. By extension, we believe that virtually all, if not all, of the activities of employees of other executive branch agencies and entities that were covered were also legal. The worst that can be said of all of these people is that they adopted one side of a reasonable dispute over interpretation. In that dispute, the opinions of the Senate are every bit as much of a valid indicator of Congress's intention as the House's. There is no way, therefore, that behavior undertaken in reliance on the Senate's legislative record can fairly be interpreted as an intentional flouting of the law.

# CHAPTER 7

# Who Did What to Help the Democratic Resistance?

The public hearings of these Committees presented a confusing picture of U.S. assistance to the Nicaraguan democratic Resistance during the period of the Boland Amendments. The overall impression the Committees' majority tried to create was that the government was engaged in a massive effort to subvert the law. A careful review shows, however, that this simply was not the case. The NSC staff's activities fell into two basic categories. Some were the kinds of diplomatic communication and information sharing that Congress may not constitutionally prohibit, even if Congress had intended the Boland Amendment to apply to the NSC. Others, with the possible exception of the diversion, were in accordance with the law, as we have analyzed it in the preceding section.

Given the nature of the strategic threat in Central America, we also believe President Reagan had more than a legal right to pursue this course of assistance to the Contras. We believe he was correct to have done so. The mixed signals Congress was giving indicates that many members agreed. Our *only* regret is that the Administration was not open enough with Congress about what it was doing.

We have no intention here of trying to present all of the evidence the Committees received about what each person did. If we did, our dissent would have to be as long as the Committees' narrative. Frankly, we believe the mind-numbing detail in that narrative obscures as much as it reveals, leaving readers with some fundamentally mistaken impressions.

## THE PRESIDENT

President Reagan gave his subordinates strong, clear and consistent guidance about the basic thrust of the policies he wanted them to pursue toward Nicaragua. There is some question and dispute about *precisely* the level at which he chose to follow the operational details. There is no doubt, however, about the overall management strategy he followed. The President set the U.S. policy toward Nicaragua, with few if any ambiguities, and then left subordinates more or less free to implement it.

417

## THE VICE PRESIDENT

There is *no* evidence that Vice President George Bush knew about either the Contra resupply effort or the diversion of funds to the democratic Resistance. The Vice President's staff does acknowledge having learned about General Secord's resupply operation from Felix Rodriguez in August 1986. The staff members informed the relevant agencies, but said they did not think the issue warranted informing Bush at the time. The testimony all says the subject was not discussed with the Vice President. Two April scheduling memoranda did use the word "resupply" in connection with one Rodriguez visit to the Vice President's office, but there is no reason to infer from a single phrase that the Vice President's staff had full knowledge of a subject the NSC staff was deliberately keeping from them.

## NATIONAL SECURITY COUNCIL STAFF

Robert McFarlane and John Poindexter appear to have had different views of what the President wanted, and what the law would allow, the NSC staff to do. It is important to be clear, however, that with the possible exception of some small fraction of NSC staff salaries, overhead, and small amounts of travel expenses—all of which could legitimately have been used in any event to maintain contact by the NSC staff with the Resistance leadership and others—no appropriated funds were devoted to the efforts discussed below.

Robert McFarlane testified that he believed (1) that the NSC staff was covered by the Boland Amendment, and (2) that one of the principal purposes of the amendment was to prevent the government from raising funds in support of the Resistance. He testified that he took this position for political reasons, not on the basis of an analysis of the law. It should be noted, however, that although McFarlane says he was quite vocal on the point of NSC coverage, Commander Paul Thompson, formerly the NSC's legal counsel, has a different recollection. Thompson said that he remembers a discussion in which he and McFarlane considered whether the NSC might conceivably be covered and then decided that the issue was moot because nothing the NSC staff was doing would be a violation even if it were covered.

## Conclusion

In sum, the NSC's activities, aside from its normal duties, generally fell into two categories. One involved information sharing with the democratic Resistance and encouraging contributions that—with the possible exception of the diversion—were perfectly legal. Activities such as these could not constitutionally have been prohibited by statute. The second category involved North's military advice to the Resistance and detailed coordination of the resupply effort. Since the NSC was not covered by the Boland Amendment, these activities were clearly legal. But even if one assumes the NSC were covered, we showed earlier that the amendment did not prohibit general military advice and resupply coordination. Some of these latter activities, however, perhaps could have been reached by Congress without violating the Constitution. It was to protect these unpopular, but legal activities from possibly being made illegal that we believe the NSC staff misled Congress. There is no evidence that the President knew more than general information about this side of North's activities, or anything at all about the deceptions of Congress.

# STATE DEPARTMENT

Little or no evidence surfaced during these hearings to suggest that the State Department was used wittingly or unwittingly to circumvent the Boland Amendment. Individuals such as Louis Tambs (Ambassador to Costa Rica) and Robert Owen (who had a contract relationship with UNO under a grant agreement with the Nicaraguan Humanitarian Assistance Office, or NHAO) did assist North with the resupply effort, but this was done without the knowledge and blessing of their superiors at the Department. Owen's assistance arguably took place during his "off" hours, but Tambs' assistance with the establishment of the Point West airfield was clearly done in the course of his long, ambassadorial day. Even Tambs' activities, however, fell within the normal, *legal and constitutionally protected* scope of activity for an ambassador. His error was to bypass his superiors in the State Department by reporting outside channels to North.* That is, the error—like that of a CIA station chief, "Tomas Castillo"—was a matter of violating his own department's policy rather than violating the law.

---

*Ambassador Tambs had been a friend of Col. North's going back to 1982 when Tambs was a consultant to the NSC. Later when Tambs was the Ambassador to Colombia, North personally saw to it that troops were sent to the embassy in Colombia to protect Tambs when his life was threatened by drug dealers.

# Elliott Abrams

The main State Department focus of the Nicaragua side of the Committees' investigation, however, was Elliott Abrams, Assistant Secretary of State for Inter-American Affairs. Abrams was the main spokesman for the Contra program. As chairman of the Restricted Interagency Group (RIG), Abrams therefore was a natural object of suspicion for those opposed to Contra aid.

The theory that seemed to structure the investigation of Abrams' role was that he either knowingly assisted and advised North, or that he realized what North was doing but ignored it to let North keep the Resistance alive while the Administration fought for renewed Congressional aid. There was a third possibility testified to by Abrams, however: that North effectively kept Abrams in the dark. The evidence more clearly substantiates what Abrams said than either of the other, more conspiratorial theories. In this respect, Abrams was more of a victim than a co-conspirator. He was deliberately kept uninformed by North and Poindexter, just as were the President, Secretaries Shultz and Weinberger, the Intelligence Oversight Board's Bretton Sciaroni, and the United States Congress.

Abrams was not engaged in any conduct that even remotely qualified as a violation of the Boland prohibitions or of any other law.

**Abrams' other major area of testimony was his statements to the Senate Intelligence Committee on November 25, 1986. He said there had been no solicitation of third countries, even though he had been directly involved in soliciting money from the Sultan of Brunei.**

There is no question that Abrams exercised very poor judgment in his SSCI [Senate

Select Committee on Intelligence] testimony by attempting to answer questions regarding third country fundraising in a technically correct, but misleading, manner to protect the confidence of Brunei. Abrams himself described it as an indefensible and foolish act that he greatly regretted. He surely could have asked the Senators to let him refrain from answering the question until he had a chance to discuss the matter with the Secretary. Ultimately, Abrams apologized to the Senate Intelligence Committee for his error, six months before these hearings began.

## THE CIA'S ROLE

The Central Intelligence Agency was not a major player in the Administration's efforts to help the Nicaraguan Resistance during the period of the prohibitory Boland Amendments. That was partly because the amendments explicitly limited the CIA and other intelligence agencies. In addition, the CIA, as an agency, wanted to avoid even coming close to the edge of the law. As Admiral Poindexter said in our public hearings, "They wanted to be careful and Director Casey was very sensitive to this, they wanted to keep hands-off as much as they could."

Of course, the agency could not simply keep hands off. For one thing, it was expected throughout this period to continue intelligence gathering and political support for the Resistance. At the same time, the CIA felt it had to be responsive both to Congress's mandate and to the Administration's strong support for the Contras. The result was an extremely difficult situation for career professionals who had to implement policy at the operational level. The Chief of the Central American Task Force described his feelings this way:

> I knew almost from the beginning that I was caught between the dynamics of a giant nutcracker of the Legislative on the one hand and the Executive on the other, and I was in the center of a very exposed position.

**The minority recounts the CIA's involvement with the airstrip in Costa Rica and the Contra air resupply operation and criticizes Agency officials for incomplete testimony to Congress in October of 1986. But it concludes that the statements to legislators were "not a byproduct of an orchestrated conspiracy to keep Congress in the dark."**

## Conclusion

The CIA had to work under difficult, politically charged circumstances. To protect the agency, its personnel steered a wide berth around the prohibitions of the law. This was particularly difficult to do in an environment in which people were dying for a cause the Administration and the agency supported. There were misunderstandings in management, and errors in judgment, particularly in Congressional testimony. But the blame for this situation must rest upon unclear laws, and a vacillating Congressional policy, at least as much as it does upon the career professionals who were faced with the Herculean task of implementing the law.

## PRIVATE FUNDRAISING

The private fundraising activities in support of the Contras conducted by Carl R. (Spitz) Channell and Richard Miller received considerable attention in the news reports surrounding the Iran-Contra affair. The fundraising efforts were also the focus of early criminal prosecutions by the Independent Counsel, and were explored somewhat during our public hearings. They have also received significant attention in the Majority's Report, where it is portrayed in a lengthy chapter as a project devoid of proper purposes.

We cannot agree with the analysis and conclusions of the Majority Report. We agree that a private fundraising effort organized and conducted by Mr. Channell raised funds for the Nicaraguan democratic Resistance; and we agree that the manner in which the fundraising activities were carried out can be criticized. We are in particular concerned that a rather sizable portion of the donated funds appears not to have actually gone to the Contras. But we disagree with the majority's theme that the fundraising activities represented an illegal conspiracy imbued throughout with criminal intent and improper motivations. Based on the evidence, we see the private contributors as being worthy of praise rather than scorn. For the most part, their actions represented good faith activities of well-intentioned American citizens motivated by a genuine—and completely legal—desire to do what they could to help the Contras in a time of need. The private actions, especially those of the donors, were patriotic responses in harmony with the policies of the President that were designed to rebut the growing spread of Soviet communism in North America. Our basic conclusions are as follows:

— Channell developed the private fundraising organizations and controlled their solicitations. Colonel North did not solicit money. He did not conspire with Channell to commit tax fraud. Any suggestion that North deliberately created or nurtured the fundraising network to provide tax write-offs, tax expenditures, or backdoor Federal financing for the Contras, is wholly without support from the evidence.

— President Reagan had no specific knowledge of the private fundraising efforts. He generally believed the persons he met with had donated to a media campaign designed to generate support for further Contra funding by Congress.

— President Reagan met with individuals in the White House to thank them for their long term support for his policies, not for a particular contribution to Channell's organization.

— This investigation unfairly chastised conservative fundraising efforts that supported foreign policy goals inconsistent with those of the majority of Congressional Democrats. However, the Committees failed to investigate parallel fundraising efforts by organizations that support the Communist forces in Central America, and use Members of Congress in their fundraising.

— Finally, the private fundraising investigation of our Committees needlessly harassed private citizens whose political views happen to be contrary to the views held by the majority, by asking them questions that intruded on their privacy and were irrelevant to the Committees' investigation.

## Conclusions

It is fully legal for private individuals to raise money for weapons, and then send that money to bank accounts controlled by the Nicaraguan democratic Resistance. The information to which Channell pled guilty was not about raising money for lethal aid for the Contras *per se,* but about using a tax exempt corporation, NEPL, to do so. Channell formed several entities in his fundraising network to respond to the complicated tax laws covering charitable and political activities. There is no evidence that indicates North knew about the tax problem, much less conspired with Channell and Miller. This conclusion is supported by the fact that Channell did not know of any contributors who donated money because NEPL was tax exempt who would not have donated if NEPL were not tax exempt. As for Colonel North's other activities, there is no evidence that North instructed Channell to use NEPL to raise money for the Contras. In addition, he did not solicit money from contributors. There can be no question that North knowingly conveyed the impression that he favored what Channell was trying to do, but there is nothing wrong with the White House openly endorsing private activities in support of Administration policy.

## Left Wing Private Fundraising

Conservative fundraising organizations have been criticized during this investigation because they have raised money to support policy goals that a majority of the Democratic Members of Congress did not support. Clearly, it is permissible under current law to raise money for foreign political movements, including military activities. If there were any question about this, the Committees should—for the sake of a balanced, fair record—have devoted similar resources investigating organizations that support left-wing forces in Central America opposed to United States foreign policy that use Members of Congress in their fundraising.

Several organizations have opposed United States policy in Central America by sending money and supplies to El Salvador. The most notable is the Committee in Solidarity with the People of El Salvador (CISPES) which Assistant Secretary Abrams described as an organization that "essentially serves as a front for the FMLN guerrillas in El Salvador". According to a 31 page set of State Department cables about these groups that was introduced by Rep. Bill McCollum as a Committee exhibit, CISPES was founded in 1980 by the leader of the Salvadoran Communist Party, Shafik Handal. This Washington, D.C. based organization coordinates efforts of a major U.S. support network. CISPES activities are said to include, among other things, a program to send material aid to Central American struggles and "creative harassment" at public appearances and speaking engagements of individuals who support U.S. policy.

New El Salvador Today (NEST) is an organization that has worked closely with CISPES on fundraising, volunteer training, and other activities. NEST has raised funds for projects in areas of El Salvador controlled by the Communist insurgents.

There have been allegations, included in the State Department cables, to the effect that much of the money received by organizations such as these ends up in the coffers of guerrilla groups, or being used to provide welfare services that help the FMLN's political program in areas the FMLN controls. According to a State Department interview with former Salvadoran leftist guerrilla leader, Miguel Castellanos, the Western Democracies became the largest source of cash for the guerrillas during the 1980s. Castellanos served on the finance committee of the Popular Forces of Liberation (PFL) in 1978 and defected in 1985. He stated that the guerrilla groups set up institutions to collect donations from leftist humanitarian organizations and use that money without concern for its original purpose. Approximately 70% of the money which purported to go for humanitarian assistance actually went for the purchase of arms.

## Overstepping the Bounds

With the time it saved not investigating groups on the left, the private fundraising investigation has needlessly harassed private citizens who happen to hold conservative foreign policy views. Witnesses were forced to travel long distances and testify concerning money which they legitimately gave to political organizations. Committee attorneys questioned witnesses about their political activity, religious affiliations, educational backgrounds, employment history, political lineage, roommate's political contributions, social associations, and more. The subpoenas issued to many of Channell's contributors required tax returns, correspondence related to Nicaragua, documents concerning political contributions and other broad categories of personal papers, without any apparent effort being made to limit the material to items that fell within the Committees' legitimate mandate to investigate governmental activities.

If Congress wants to be worthy of trust as an institution, it has to restrain itself. Just as the President ultimately has to accept responsibility for the actions of any one subordinate who zealously steps over the line, so too must these Committees bear the responsibility for the actions of one of its own staff, even if—or especially because—they were not typical of the Committees' work as a whole.

## CONCLUSION

Our analysis of the past two chapters has largely been about legal questions. It has shown the Administration did stay within the law. By giving the Administration a clean bill of legal health, however, we do not intend to be endorsing the wisdom of everything it was doing. Notwithstanding our legal opinions, we think it was a fundamental mistake for the NSC staff to have been secretive and deceptive about its actions. The requirement for building long term political support means that the Administration would have been better off if it had conducted its activities in the open. Thus, the President should simply have vetoed the strict Boland Amendment in mid-October 1984, even though the amendment was only a few paragraphs in an approximately 1,200 page long continuing appropriations resolution, and a veto therefore would have brought the Government to a standstill within three weeks of a national election. Once the President decided against a veto, it was self-defeating for anyone to think a program this important could be sustained by deceiving Congress. Whether technically illegal or not, it was politically foolish and counterproductive to mislead Congress, even if misleading took the form of artful evasion or silence instead of overt misstatement.

We do believe firmly that the NSC staff's

deceits were not meant to hide illegalities. Every witness we have heard told us his concern was not over legality, but with the fear that Congress would respond to complete disclosure with political reprisals, principally by tightening the Boland Amendments. That risk should have been taken.

We are convinced that the Constitution protects much of what the NSC staff was doing—particularly those aspects that had to do with encouraging contributions and sharing information. The President's inherent constitutional powers are only as strong, however, as the President's willingness to defend them. As for the NSC actions Congress could constitutionally have prohibited, it would have been better for the White House to have tackled that danger head on. Some day, Congress's decision to withhold resources may tragically require U.S. citizens to make an even heavier commitment to Central America, perhaps one measured in blood and not dollars. The commitment that might eliminate such an awful future will not be forthcoming unless the public is exposed to and persuaded by a clear, sustained, and principled debate on the merits.

PART IV

# IRAN

# CHAPTER 8

# The Iran Initiative

Simple plots make for stirring fiction. Sometimes, amateur historians fall into the temptation of presenting events as if all lines inevitably and always pointed toward the already known conclusion. That is not the way events happen in the real world. The Iran chapters of the majority report create the impression that its authors have fallen into the amateur historian's trap. The narrative tries to simplify events and motivations for the sake of a story line. That does a disservice to history. The record ought to reflect the complex motives of the participants in these operations. The motives may be difficult to determine, but papering the difficulties over will not help future generations learn from what happened.

The majority report seems alternately to be torn between two theses about the Iran Initiative: that it was strictly an arms-for-hostages deal or that, starting in December 1985 or January 1986, it was driven by a desire to provide funds for the Contras. Additionally, the Iran sections of the report continue the majority's portrayal of the Administration as a gang of law-breakers who would do virtually anything to achieve their objectives, while invoking an exaggerated fear of leaks to keep the truth about activities from Congress.

This portrayal is patently absurd. The hostages were important to President Reagan. He probably did fall victim to his own compassion, and let their personal safety weigh too heavily on him. But it is clear from all the evidence we have that the initiative was pursued primarily for strategic reasons. We may disagree with the underlying assumptions, or with the decision to sell arms, but any honest review of the evidence must acknowledge these intentions, and with the fact that strategic considerations played an important part in the discussions conducted through the so-called Second Channel.

Similarly, the use of residuals to benefit the Contras was certainly seen as a plus—a "neat idea"—by North and Poindexter. But Contras funding never *drove* the Iran initiative. A sober look at the amount of money involved would make that clear to anyone. At most, the residuals were seen as a peripheral benefit from a policy whose justification lay elsewhere.

We shall show in this section of our report that the Administration did, in fact, substantially comply with the legal requirements.

Moreover, the decision not to notify Congress was not based on an anti-democratic obsession with secrecy, but was based on the same sound reasoning that led the Carter Administration to the identical decision not to report operations during the Iranian hostage crisis of 1979 and 1980.

## STRATEGIC OPENING, OR ONLY AN ARMS-FOR-HOSTAGES DEAL?

The majority report systematically downplays the importance of strategic objectives in the Iran initiative. We believe, to the contrary, that the record is unambiguous on the following facts: (1) that strategic objectives were important to the participants at all times; (2) that the objectives were credible, (3) that they were the driving force for the initiative at the outset, and (4) that without such a strategic concern, the initiative would never have been undertaken.

One of the most disappointing forms of evidence-slanting throughout the majority's narrative is that it refuses adequately to present the key witnesses' accounts of their own motives, in their own words, from the hearing record. That failure is most glaring in connection with the witnesses' statements about the strategic motives behind the Iran policy. We have no intention of trying to recite all of the evidence here. We are convinced, however, that anyone who reads the material we cite will recognize the bias involved in presenting what purports to be any analysis of the arms sales without including the participants' own explanations of their motivations. The majority may not agree with the Administration's strategic reasoning, but it is simply unfair to ignore it.

The President's words are probably the most important here. Dale Van Atta, a reporter, knew the essential facts of the initiative in February 1986. The President was willing to talk to him on February 24, on the condition that the information not be used until the hostages came home. Van Atta asked the President about the hostages. Instead of answering in kind, the President spoke about strategic matters.

> All right. The Iranian situation. We have to remember that we had a pretty solid relationship with Iran during the time of the Shah. We have to realize also that that was a very key ally in that particular area in preventing the Soviets from reaching their age old goal of the warm water ports, and so forth. And now with the take-over by the present ruler, we have to believe that there must be elements present in Iran that—when nature takes its inevitable course—they want to return to different relationships . . . We have to oppose what they are doing. We at the same time must recognize we do not want to make enemies of those who today could be our friends.

## U.S. INTELLIGENCE WEAKNESSES IN IRAN

Although the motives were clearly present for trying to develop a new relationship with Iran, the means were not. In an important respect, the Iran initiative had at least one of its roots in an intelligence failure. There are two different intelligence issues raised by the Iran initiative. One is that intelligence gaps or weaknesses influenced U.S. decisions. We agree with this point. The other is that intelligence was "cooked"

# Figure 8-1. Map of Middle East

Source: Central Intelligence Agency,
Office of Congressional Affairs

Boundary representation is
not necessarily authoritative.

**Middle East**

— International boundary

★ National capital

Mercator Projection

0    250    500 Kilometers

0    250    500 Nautical miles

429

to match the preconceived conclusions of policy makers. We strongly disagree with this charge, to the extent that it relates to the information generated by the executive branch. We do believe, however, that some officials—most notably, Admiral Poindexter and Director Casey—failed adequately to present the U.S. intelligence community's assessment to the President at a crucial moment of decision.

There was near unanimity inside the government on the weakness of U.S. intelligence in Iran. Director Casey reportedly conceded the point, and his former deputy, John McMahon, agreed. Casey believed that the need for intelligence was one of the main reasons for going ahead with the initiative. Robert McFarlane and John Poindexter both lamented the dearth of intelligence on internal Iranian politics and Iranian support for terrorism, which left them vulnerable and "flying blind". In particular, U.S. policy makers lacked the information necessary to assess the influence and *bona fides* of the Iranian officials with whom they were dealing.

The core problem was a lack of well-placed human agents within Iran. The CIA's Deputy Director for Operations, Clair George, is responsible for clandestine human intelligence collection. He freely acknowledged that the Directorate was not collecting the information necessary to influence or deal with Iran. In the opinion of some intelligence professionals the CIA's weakness of human intelligence collection reflects a long-term shift toward a greater reliance on more exotic, technical collection methods, which are considered "clean" and safe compared to the messy business of running human spies.

430

## The Issue of "Cooked" Intelligence

One of the many dramatic charges Secretary Shultz made about his own Administration involved this assessment of the Iran-Iraq war. Responding to Senator Inouye, Shultz said that the failure to separate "the functions of gathering and analyzing intelligence from the function of developing and carrying out policy" resulted in the Administration getting faulty information on which to base its judgments and decisions.

I hate to say it, but I believe that one of the reasons the President was given what I regard as wrong information, for example about Iran and terrorism was that the agency or the people in the CIA were too involved in this. So that is one point. And I feel very clear in my mind about this point. And I know that long before this all emerged, I had come to have great doubts about the objectivity and reliability of some of the intelligence I was getting.

Despite Secretary Shultz's statement, these committees have found absolutely no evidence to support allegations of intelligence bias within the CIA. As Deputy CIA Director Gates has observed, one of the best guarantees against an intelligence bias is the widespread circulation of CIA analyses on Capitol Hill, particularly the intelligence committees' scrutiny of virtually everything the CIA and intelligence community produces. With the exception of one controversial 1982 report, neither committee has exhibited any concern over the objectivity of analysis within Casey's CIA, despite the committees' often stormy relationship with the Director. Shultz is also refuted by former Deputy CIA Director McMahon who, in response to a deposition question regarding the Secretary's assertions, said: "It wouldn't happen. This is just so [expletive deleted] outrageous, I can't stand it. That is just so damn false, and I think George Shultz got away with murder on that one." McMahon also said he asked Director Webster "why the hell he didn't challenge Shultz on that." Webster, according to McMahon, said he did ask Shultz, but "I guess he hasn't heard from Shultz yet."

## THE ISRAELI CONNECTION

The Administration's reliance on Israeli intelligence has raised questions about Israel's role in the Iran initiative. That role probably will never be fully understood. The Tower Commission Report, supplemented by some new material in the majority narrative, lays out the basic outline. We have too little confirmed evidence, however, and too many conflicting theories, to sort it all into neat packages.

Israel was more than a passive message bearer at the outset of the initiative. In addition, it weighed in to help keep the initiative on track at several points later. These included, among other things, an August 2, 1985 visit Kimche paid to McFarlane to seek authorization for the first Israeli TOW transfer; Nir's January 1986 proposal to keep the initiative moving forward at a time when U.S. interest appeared to be flagging, and Peres' February 1986 letter to and September 1986 communication with President Reagan.

## Shultz v. Shultz—Suckers or Big Boys?

The question that arises out of all this is whether Israel was playing on U.S. ignorance to draw the United States into the Iran arms transactions. At a November 10, 1986 meeting between the President and his top advisors, Secretary Shultz said, according to Donald Regan's notes, that he "Thinks Israeli [sic] suckered us into this so we can't complain of their sales." Shultz apparently expanded on this point in a private meeting he held with the President ten days later. A briefing paper Shultz brought with him to that meeting stated:

> Much if not all of the incentive on the Israeli side of the project may well have been an Israeli "sting" operation. The Israelis used a number of justifications to draw us into this operation—intelligence gains, release of hostages, high strategic goals, . . . Israel obviously sees it in its national interest to cultivate ties with Iran, including arms shipments. Any American identification with that effort serves Israeli ends, even if American objectives and policies are compromised.

We are inclined to agree with Shultz that Israel was actively promoting the initiative because the initiative suited Israel's own national interest. We disagree, however, with the idea that the United States was being played for a sucker. We believe the U.S. Government responsibly made its own judgments, and its own mistakes.

431

## HOSTAGES AND THE IRAN INITIATIVE

We are convinced, as we have argued, that the Iran initiative started as a desire to pursue a strategic opportunity, and that these considerations always remained important. At the same time, there can be no question—as the President himself acknowledged—that the President's personal concern for the hostages added a sense of urgency that skewed our negotiating tactics, and helps explain the imprudently wishful thinking that led Poindexter and Casey to proceed despite repeated disappointments.

It is important to note that the President has an affirmative duty under U.S. law to do everything in his power to secure the release of Americans illegally imprisoned or held hostage abroad.

## DEA ACTIVITIES

We shall digress briefly from the Iran initiative at this point to discuss another effort the Administration undertook to gain the release of the hostages in Lebanon. This one involved Drug Enforcement Administration (DEA) agents and began in early 1985. The majority is highly critical of this effort in its report. This is puzzling to us, because if the DEA operation had succeeded, there would have been no temptation to mix concern for the hostages with the strategically more important talks with Iran.

The majority repeatedly describes the DEA activities, which were under North's direction, as an overt attempt to pay ransom for the hostages. Indeed, a number of the points made by the majority depend on the ransom theme. The importance of this claim,

to the overall thesis of the majority report is that, if true, it would show a predisposition toward paying ransom that would tend to confirm an interpretation of the Iran initiative as an arms-for-hostages deal. We too would be troubled if ransom were being contemplated. But, according to the evidence received in the Committees' investigation, the DEA rescue plans contemplated bribes as the means to gain the hostages' release. There was no attempt to pay ransom to the captors.

The majority discounts the testimony of one of the two DEA agents involved, whom we shall call Agent 1. The agent clearly stated that the plan was to offer bribes to certain individuals, and not to pay ransom to those who had directed the capture of the hostages. The agent emphasized that none of the captors had solicited ransom. Rather, money was to be delivered as bribes to those who could effect the release of the hostages, not to the people who actually controlled the terrorist organization. The idea was to find individuals who could be paid off without the knowledge of those in control. The money was intended to go directly to these individuals.

In the final analysis, the DEA efforts to free the hostages must be viewed in perspective. The President was personally committed to do all that he could to bring the hostages home, and there was intense national pressure to do so. Accordingly, the Administration initiated several alternative programs, including the plan to use DEA assets in Lebanon. DEA efforts ultimately failed, and in hindsight these efforts could have been better implemented. Nonetheless, the facts show that many involved in these activities acted at great personal risk and with the best of intentions. Moreover, the

Administration deserves recognition for its efforts to explore every promising avenue for the release of the hostages.

## THE SECOND CHANNEL

It is tempting, knowing Buckley's fate and the depth of the President's feeling, to portray U.S. policy as having become "hostage to the hostages." The hostages did become too prominent. Negotiations conducted through the First Channel, arranged by Ghorbanifar, never got off the arms-for-hostages track, despite repeated U.S. efforts. Once discussions began through the Second Channel, however, they began to take in broader geopolitical issues. Some aspects might potentially have been promising. Others, such as the Da'wa prisoners, should have been turned off from the beginning.

The actual results of the Second Channel negotiations—a small shipment of arms, the release of one hostage—were similar to the earlier agreements conducted through the First Channel. Two elements of the Second Channel meetings were different, however. First, although some of the same people participated in meetings held through both of the channels, the Second Channel meetings involved a different, more powerful leadership. Second, the Iranians this time clearly seemed to recognize that if the hostage problem could be finally resolved, the United States and Iran had important, mutually compatible interests that might well sustain a substantially increased level of cooperation.

The precise elements of the strategic relationship being discussed were decidedly mixed, however. Some were beneficial to the United States, such as the exchanges of infor-

mation over mutual geopolitical interests in the region. Others, such as proposed Da'wa release, were not. North may have been correct in saying that the position he endorsed on the Da'wa did not exactly contradict publicly stated U.S. policy. This technical accuracy does not begin to account, though, for the way such a position would have undermined U.S. credibility. It is another example of the NSC staff thinking about literal compliance, without adequately considering the long term political consequences.

## CONCLUSION: THE ROLE OF THE NSC STAFF, AND OTHERS

The Tower Commission concluded that the Iran initiative was pursued with a flawed decision process managed by the NSC staff, and suggested that the procedural flaws were responsible for some of the initiative's substantive errors. The Tower board, we believe, underestimated the extent to which major issues were aired and argued before the President from November 1985 through January 1986. But the board was right to say that the lack of regular procedures, fostered by an excessive concern for secrecy, short-circuited the process of periodic review and evaluation—both of the substantive desirability of continuing the initiative, and of the decision not to notify Congress.

To describe what happened simply in terms of the process, however, leaves some important questions unanswered. It is true that good organization can help make sound decisions more likely. But organization, at best, is a tool. The real flaw in the NSC's Iran negotiations, as well as in the NSC's deceptions of Congress over Nicaragua, came from

433

errors in judgment. The question, therefore, is: what can an administration do to ensure that people with the appropriate breadth and depth of judgment are fully involved in the process at the appropriate stages? The majority report seems to want to get at this issue by legislating organization for the executive branch down to the finest detail. We are convinced, however that no one formula will work best for all Presidents.

**The minority assesses the role NSC principals and staff played. It says Poindexter was not the sort of man who initiated policy and says he had little feel for domestic political strategy. According to the minority, White House Chief of Staff Donald T. Regan should have seen "red warning flags" when North became the subject of Congressional inquiries and should have had the same reaction when the Iran arms deal was never reviewed by the full NSC after the January finding. While Secretaries Weinberger and Shultz were denied information, the minority asserts that both knew enough to raise objections. The minority says Weinberger's inaction is excusable because he had been told repeatedly by Poindexter that the President's mind was made up on pursuing the arms sales. It says, however, that Shultz was better informed and had more reason and opportunity to take action. The minority says Shultz should have found out more about the Iran initiative or resigned in protest.**

It is at least theoretically possible that the idea of a strong cabinet government, with a weak NSC staff, will not meet any President's needs in today's international climate. That is, with the constant pressure of events and the inevitability of interdepartmental disagreement, it is possible that future Presidents will decide that some important issues over the course of a full term inevitably will require them to have something more than an honest broker as National Security Adviser. If the need is inevitable, Presidents would be well advised to choose people who are known for their independent skills at understanding the strategic politics of international relations, both domestically and abroad. President Reagan certainly reached this conclusion when he picked Frank Carlucci to replace Poindexter, and we expect that General Powell will also turn out to be a person with the requisite sense of judgment. But Presidents should not simply assume that the Iran-Contra affair automatically proves the inevitable need for an independently powerful NSC staff. President Reagan's approach toward governing automatically requires something from the cabinet that was not supplied in this case. The model, in other words, was never given much of a chance.

# CHAPTER 9

# Iran: The Legal Issues

These Committees' hearings and the majority report have trivialized important disagreements over international policy, and the political relationships between the legislative and executive branches. In an attempt to gain partisan advantage, the majority has focused upon legal disputes, trying to portray the Committees' role as that of prosecutor. We have indicated several times that we have some policy disagreements with the Administration's actions of 1984–86. We disagree, for example, with the decision to sell arms to Iran and to withhold notification to Congress for as long as the President did in this case. We also think it was a political mistake for the President not to have confronted Congress over the Boland Amendment in 1984. In neither case, however, do we think the Administration made serious legal missteps. Our reasoning with respect to the Boland Amendment was laid out in an earlier chapter.

The minority argues that the 1985 arms shipments by Israel for the most part were not violations of the Arms Export Control Act, which requires the President to notify Congress of covered arms sales and get a special waiver if the proposed sale is to a country certified by the State Department as supporting terrorism. Transfers of arms by American allies must have Presidential permission and follow the same rules. The minority notes that Israel received oral authorization for its shipments. The report does not address the issue of waivers and concludes that "substantive provisions" of the act were met. It says Presidents have an inherent power, under exceptional circumstances, to delay the notification of Congress required by law.

## CONCLUSION

We conclude that the Administration was in substantial compliance with the law during each of the Iran arms transactions. The arms sales of 1985 from Israel to Iran did not violate the terms of the AECA or FAA. It is reasonable to assume that the weapons Israel shipped to Iran in 1985 were originally supplied under AECA or FAA. These two statutes permit the President or the Secretary of State to consent to retransfers. In these instances, oral authorization was given for the transfers. Moreover, the formal reporting re-

435

quirements do not apply because each of these transactions involved munitions valued at less than $14 million. The AECA and FAA seek to ensure that such retransfers foster the national security interests of the United States. The Israeli shipments were made with the agreement of American authorities and were premised on U.S. views about America's own national security interests. The substantive purposes of the AECA and FAA were met.

Moreover, the 1985 Israeli sales to Iran did not violate the requirements for Presidential authorizations or Findings under the National Security Act and the Hughes-Ryan Amendment. The National Security Act provides an alternative route apart from the AECA and FAA under which the Administration was in compliance with the law during the 1985 transactions. The terms under which the President may use the National Security Act meet all of the underlying purposes of the AECA and FAA. Therefore, Congress has been satisfied to let the one approach be a substitute or alternative route to the other.

The Hughes-Ryan Amendment contains no requirement that Presidential Findings be reduced to writing. The November-December 1985 Finding reflected in written form that the President had been briefed before the shipments on the efforts made to obtain the release of the hostages, and that the President himself had found these efforts were important to the national security of the United States. Therefore, in both the oral Findings of 1985, and the written November-December 1985 Finding, the President accordingly ratified all prior actions and directed further actions to be taken. With regard to the 1986 transactions, the President's January 17, 1986, Finding clearly satisfied the Hughes-Ryan Amendment.

Finally, the 1986 arms sales did not violate the National Security Act's requirements for notifying Congress. Certainly, the National Security Act requires agencies involved in intelligence activities to keep the intelligence committees of Congress "fully and currently informed of all intelligence activities." However, the law specifically contemplates situations in which notifying the appropriate Congressional members might be too risky. The act requires that in instances in which the President has not given prior notice of intelligence operations, he must inform the intelligence committees in a "timely" fashion.

The decision not to notify must rest on Presidential discretion. The reporting requirements of the National Security Act cannot limit the constitutional authority of the President to withhold prior notification of covert activities in exceptional circumstances. In this case, the lives of hostages were at stake such that premature notification was extraordinarily dangerous to the lives of American citizens. We conclude that, in circumstances such as these, the President must have the discretion to determine when notification is "timely." If Congress, after the fact, disagrees with the way in which the President has exercised his discretion, the appropriate remedy is a political and not a legal one.

# CHAPTER 10

# The Use or "Diversion" of the Iran Arms Sales Proceeds

"What did the President know, and when did he know it?" That was Senator Howard Baker's famous crystallizing question about President Nixon from the Senate Watergate hearings of 1973. Political tensions were heightened in the Iran-Contra Affair when the same question was asked about the so-called "diversion" of funds from the Iran arms sales to the Nicaraguan democratic resistance. The very term "diversion," given currency by Attorney General Edwin Meese's press conference of November 25, 1986, had the sound of illegality.

Beginning with the first public revelations about the Iranian arms sales in early November 1986, reaction in the United States was a mixture of curiosity, puzzlement, and controversy. The Attorney General's press conference added a new dimension to the furor. The prospect that money had been sent to the Contras during the period of the Boland Amendments greatly intensified the scrutiny the Iran initiative received in the media. Speculation ran unchecked. The Attorney General put the amount that might have been diverted at $10 million to $30 million. Members of the Congressional investigating committees suggested that the amount might

have been as high as $50 million. Ultimately, the diversion received more scrutiny than any other aspect of the Iran-Contra Congressional investigations.

The evidence is overwhelmingly clear, however, that the President did not in fact know about the diversion, despite Democratic wishes to soft-peddle the point by attacking Adm. Poindexter's credibility. In addition, the use of the word "diversion" itself assumes that the funds belong to the United States. We shall show later in this chapter that the legal questions surrounding the ownership of the proceeds from the Iran arms sales are by no means settled. Before we can reach these points, however, it is first necessary to explain what the diversion was, how it came about, and how much was transferred.

## HOW DID THE DIVERSION HAPPEN?

The concept of transferring a portion of the excess proceeds from an arms sale to another project was not a new one. Gen. Singlaub explained that he and North had discussed this concept in connection with arms sales to an entirely different country in early 1985. When the Israeli arms sales to Iran begin in 1985, the U.S. was aware that the Iranians were paying relatively high prices for the arms compared to what Israel had paid for them. This meant that the United States could reasonably conclude that some funds were being put to other uses by Israel.

Secord and North were both aware that the Contras needed money. By late 1985, they had both been involved in obtaining funds and arms for the Resistance. The specific decision to transfer a portion of Iranian arms sales proceeds to the air resupply operation was the result of a number of factors, one of which was General Secord's involvement in both operations.

## HOW MUCH WAS DIVERTED?

The most reasonable calculations show that approximately $3.8 million of proceeds from the Iran arms transactions was spent for the support of the Nicaraguan Resistance. During the period that the "Enterprise" received income from the Iranian transaction (November 1985 through November 1986), it also had other funds available for support of the Resistance that totaled $3.4 million. Much of this money came from foreign and private domestic donations specifically earmarked for the Contras. During that same period of time, the "Enterprise" spent approximately $7.2 million in support of the Contras. If one subtracts the $3.4 million in non-Iran funds designated for the Resistance, then the remainder of the $7.2 million, or $3.8 million, was the total amount of the diversion.

## WHO AUTHORIZED THE DIVERSION?

The diversion was authorized by Poindexter. The Committees were careful when taking testimony on this point to make sure that the principal witnesses would testify in private session before they had a chance to hear the crucial public testimony of this particular point. Thus, Poindexter testified in private session, before North's closed session or public testimony, that he had authorized the diversion at North's request. North corroborated this point in his own executive session testimony before he could have known anything about what Poindexter had said.

Poindexter also testified that he believed he had the authority to make the decision on his own to approve the use of the Iranian arms sales surplus for the Nicaraguan Resistance. He said that because he had worked for the President for a number of years, he felt he knew what the President would want to have done in this situation. Poindexter stated that to him, the diversion appeared to involve the use of what could be considered either third-country funds, or private funds, to support the Contras, and that he believed the President favored the use of such private or third-country funds to support them. Therefore, in his view, the President would have agreed to the use of surplus funds in such a manner. However, Poindexter said, because he thought it would be politically (as opposed to legally) controversial to use the funds to support the Contras, he decided not to inform the President of it so the President could truthfully deny knowledge if the diversion were revealed.

The President has stated, however, that he would not have consented to the diversion had he known about it. He has also stated that in his opinion, Admiral Poindexter did not have the authority to make the decision without the President's approval.

The Committees have received no documentary evidence or testimony which shows that any other U.S. Government official approved or in any other way was involved in agreeing to the diversion. Col. North testified that Director Casey knew about, and was supportive of, the diversion, but North did not suggest that Casey's approval was either sought or required.

## THE PRESIDENT KNEW NOTHING ABOUT THE DIVERSION

The evidence available to these Committees shows that the President did not know about the diversion. The President has made this point repeatedly. The Committees have received sworn testimony supporting the President on this point from four individuals with first-hand knowledge, and from another individual who directly corroborates some of this key testimony. The plain fact of the matter is that the Committees have no testimony or documentary evidence to the contrary.

### Diversion Memorandums

Although their accounts of how the diversion was authorized were consistent, North and Poindexter had different recollections about the extent to which the diversion had been documented. North said he believed he had written five memorandums seeking approval of diversions, but that he had later destroyed them. Poindexter said he did not recall seeing most of these memorandums, although he thought it was possible that he

had seen the original of the surviving April diversion memorandum and then had destroyed the section that dealt with the diversion. However, the references to the diversion apparently usually occupied one or two paragraphs in a multipage document. Given the amount of paper normally flowing through the National Security Adviser's office, it would not be surprising if Poindexter had simply forgotten or overlooked these references.

In any event, the Committees have no evidence to suggest that *any* of these North memorandums, which were addressed to Poindexter, ended up going to the President. The Committees actually have some documentary evidence supporting the testimony that they did not go to the President. Poindexter's practice on some occasions was to brief the President orally with respect to what he considered to be the key points of lengthy memorandums, such as the one supporting the January 17 Finding. That is probably what he did with the April diversion memo, using the "Terms of Reference" portion that did not contain a reference to the diversion.

## CONCLUSION

The diversion has led some of the Committees Members to express a great deal of concern in the public hearings about the use of private citizens in covert operations in settings that mix private profits with public benefits. We remain convinced that covert operations will continue to have to use private agents or contractors in the future, and that those private parties will continue to operate at least partly from profit motives. If the United States tries to limit itself to dealing only with people who act out of purely patriotic motives, it effectively will rule out any worthwhile dealing with most arms dealers and foreign agents. In the real world of international politics, it would be foolish to avoid dealing with people whose motives do not match those of the United States. Nevertheless, we do feel troubled by the fact that there was not enough legal clarity, or accounting controls, placed on the Enterprise by the NSC.

Whether viewed with foresight or hindsight, and regardless of its legal status, the decision to use part of the proceeds of the Iran arms sales for the benefit of the Contras was extremely unwise. Even if the diversion is determined by the courts to have been legally permissible, it was the result of poor judgment on the part of U.S. Government officials. The decision to proceed with the Iran arms sales was itself fraught with great potential for controversy and disagreement. There was no sound basis whatsoever for adding to the political risks of the operation by bringing into it another hotly debated aspect of American foreign policy.

It was equal folly not to tell the President of the planned use of the proceeds of the arms sales. The question of legality aside, the President should have been given the opportunity to exercise his own good judgment to instruct the participants not to allow the diversion.

The diversion decision was not the first time an unwise operation has been undertaken in the conduct of American foreign affairs, and, unfortunately, it undoubtedly will not be the last. At a minimum, the decision should generate a fuller awareness in the executive branch of the serious negative ramifications of risky and short-range decisions that have not had a full airing in the Presidential office, let alone in the halls of Congress.

The decision also serves to underscore the tremendous pressures placed on the Chief Executive and his staff in carrying out an effective and coherent foreign policy in Central America or elsewhere when Congress unnecessarily and unwisely abuses its power of the purse to manage foreign affairs with an inconsistent on-again, off-again policy. Congress needs to learn that to be an effective participant in the field of foreign affairs, it must afford Presidents from either party the latitude to plan and implement an effective foreign policy based on clear decisions that are free from annual change. When Congress learns this, the world will be more stable for us and our allies.

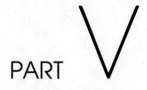

PART V

# DISCLOSURES
# AND INVESTIGATIONS

# CHAPTER 11

# From the Disclosure
# to the Uncovering

On Tuesday, November 4, 1986 the *New York Times* carried a front page story disclosing a portion of the Iran initiative. Only three weeks later, on November 25, 1986, the Attorney General of the United States announced that officials of his department had discovered a diversion of funds from that initiative to the use of the Nicaraguan resistance. This chapter describes our view of the events of November 1986.

We reach three principal conclusions. *First,* the President's decisions about how much to disclose were motivated by his effort to balance the need for protection of hostages and secret diplomatic discussions with the public's need for information. *Second,* once the President decided that the Administration did not have a complete picture of the Iran initiative, the Attorney General undertook an aggressive effort to obtain the facts. He then made the information available promptly to the President and to the public. *Third,* the President and the Attorney General discovered and disclosed the essential facts, despite efforts on the part of certain members of the NSC staff and others to cover up certain events, including the diversion. There is no evidence that the President directed, encouraged, or in any way condoned this coverup, a point the majority spares no effort to gloss over. In our opinion, the Attorney General and his associates did an impressive job with a complicated subject in a very short time. Far from being inept, or parties to a cover up, the Department of Justice was responsible for uncovering the diversion of Iran arms sale proceeds to the Contras.

## EARLY NOVEMBER

The Iranian initiative was disclosed for political reasons by high level dissident Iranian religious officials. The *New York Times* report was based on a report from a Lebanese weekly, *Al-Shiraa.* Its report was in turn based on a politically inspired leak from Iranian dissidents bent on retaliation for efforts by the Iranian Government to curb their support for wide scale terrorism and possibly to reach an accommodation with the United States. At least one of the key dissidents has recently been executed by that Government.

American officials had learned of the pending disclosure of McFarlane's May trip to Tehran at a secret meeting in Europe a week before the disclosure appeared in the press. Their immediate concern was for the lives of remaining American hostages. They also wanted to continue the secret discussions, as did officials of the Government of Iran. In addition, there were serious questions about the impact of the disclosures on a significant American ally, Israel.

During the week after the *New York Times* story, there were vigorous disagreements within the Administration about what, if anything, the Administration should disclose about the Iran initiative. As the situation was later described by former Chief of Staff Donald Regan:

I recall discussing with other members of the staff, "The cover is blown here. We have got to go public with it. We have got to tell the Congress, we have got to tell the American public exactly what went on so they were aware of it."

Mr. Smilijanich. What did Admiral Poindexter recommend?

Mr. Regan. [His recommendation was] Absolutely not. It was later reported in local papers here that we had a shouting match . . . [W]e did have a difference of opinion—a strong one. . . . His reasoning was a good one, that Jacobsen had just come out as a hostage, North was preparing to go to London and actually did go to London that first weekend in November— what was it, the 8th or 9th, in through there [to meet with Iranian officials]—and there's a possibility of two more prisoners coming out, two of the original ones, and maybe even the additional three, the later ones. And why blow that chance? We got to keep the lid on this, we got to deny it, we're endangering their lives.

And then I might add here, a very dramatic thing happened. I recall it vividly. Jacobsen had a Rose Garden ceremony welcoming him back. He had said in his remarks he had cautioned the media about discussing this. On the way back, as the President and he were mounting the steps to the colonnade to go back into the Oval Office, there were shouted questions from the media about, "What are you going to do about the hostages, what about the others that are there?" And Jacobsen turned and very emotionally said, "For God's sake, don't talk about that, that is exactly what I have been saying, you are endangering lives of the people I love, these are my friends." That made quite an impression on the President. And even though that same day I urged him again to get this story out, he said, "No, we can't Don,' he said, "We can't endanger those lives." And he didn't.

Regan's testimony shows the Administration's concern for the hostages. North's notes of a meeting with Iranian representatives on November 7, three days after the New York Times story, show both the desire to continue the negotiations and a concern for the hostages:
—"Holding to no comment—
—We recog.(nize) that public statement, RR admitting mtgs. w/ [2d Channel] wd be dangerous for you and Speaker
—Need to know WTF going on
· Press release
· [Second Channel] told in Frankfurt 2 host (two hostages)."

## NOVEMBER 10–20

Public pressure for an account of the Administration's dealings with Iran led during

444

November to meetings, a speech and press conference by the President, and testimony by various Administration officials before Congressional committees. Questions were raised both inside and outside the Administration about the Administration's compliance with civil statutes governing Executive-Legislative branch relations in the conduct of covert activities and arms transfers. The President and his advisers continued to grapple with the question of how to balance the diplomatic concerns just described with the need for public disclosure.

According to Regan's notes of a November 10 meeting, the President opened the discussion with a statement to the effect that "as a result of media, etc. must have a statement coming out of here. . . . Some things we can't discuss because of long term considerations of people with whom we have been talking about the future of Iran."

## TESTIMONY AND CHRONOLOGIES

The need for additional, detailed information on the Iran initiative was intensified by the need to testify before the Intelligence Committees on November 21. It became clear that the Administration had only an incomplete "institutional memory" on the origin and conduct of that highly compartmented initiative and that different participants had conflicting memories of certain key 1985 events.

The events surrounding the creation of false and misleading chronologies have been discussed in detail during the hearings and there is no need to review the matter here. These chronologies misstated the fact of the President's authorization for the 1985 arms

shipments, the Israeli participation in those shipments, and contemporaneous knowledge by United States Government officials of the nature of those shipments. It is sufficient to note that the preparation of these materials was almost exclusively the work of then present and former members of the NSC staff, particularly North and McFarlane. Their false presentation of these events appears to have been acquiesced in, either knowingly or unknowingly, by Casey and Poindexter.

## JUSTICE DEPARTMENT INVESTIGATION

We think that the suggestion that the Attorney General's investigative procedures changed in some irregular manner after the discovery of a possible diversion is particularly unfair. We encourage any reader who is interested in this issue to review the colloquy on this subject between the Attorney General and Senator Mitchell in which Senator Mitchell raised this issue and then dropped it after the Attorney General directly challenged him for doubting Meese's testimony about it.

The Attorney General's November 25 press conference report was based principally on admissions made to him on November 23 by North. At the press conference, the Attorney General repeatedly made clear that there were a large number of matters on which his information was uncertain and subject to additional review and correction. At that time, Justice Department officials were not aware of any document shredding or altering by North and others. As McFarlane testified, although he did not participate in the shredding he did not inform Meese that North had told him it might occur. Similarly, Justice Department officials had no immediate way to determine that several of these officials gave them misleading or inaccurate answers to their questions. The majority's pointless cavilling about this press conference is very much indicative of the quality of their work in this area. As noted, despite this attempt at a coverup by certain NSC officials, the Attorney General's investigation turned up the facts that are still the essential ones today.

There is no evidence that the President directed, encouraged, or otherwise in any way condoned a coverup. We reject as completely unsupported by the record any suggestion that the Attorney General or his staff ignored signs of potential criminal behavior or consciously sought not to obtain information in an effort to assist or protect the President. After intense scrutiny, by two Congressional committees with a very staff, it is clear that the Attorney General and his staff conducted themselves honorably and disclosed to the President and the public their findings without regard to any political damage which would ensue.

# CHAPTER 12

# The NSC's Role
# in Investigations

The majority chapter entitled "NSC Involvement in Criminal Investigations and Prosecutions" raises questions about the connection between the work of the National Security Council and traditional law enforcement activities. Unfortunately, the majority combines carelessly assembled information about matters which any fair-minded person would conclude raise no important issues, with scattered and conclusory judgments about matters where real questions of judgment exist.

Because of the necessity for accurate and timely information about threats to persons or property posed by those who may wish to cause harm for reasons connected to the foreign policy of the United States, the national security community must sometimes be involved in pending criminal investigations undertaken by domestic law enforcement agencies. The real question is not whether but when and how much involvement is appropriate. To answer this question requires a close examination of the reasons for such involvement and the manner in which such involvement is responded to by law enforcement officials.

The record of the various investigations discussed by the majority shows that law enforcement agencies outside the NSC, from the Department of Justice, to the FBI and Customs Service, responded in an appropriate manner to requests for investigations prompted by such reasons. In addition, the record of several of the investigations in which NSC personnel became involved reveals that NSC involvement in these activities, at least at their preliminary stages, was appropriate. However, their involvement in others was questionable at best.

The circumstances of each case will determine whether such involvement was appropriate. We encourage each reader to examine the facts of each investigation carefully to make this determination.

Basically, the majority alleges that certain Administration officials, particularly Colonel North, became improperly involved in a number of investigations relating to Contra activities. However, the majority's highly critical analysis is based on a flawed methodology. In view of the majority's intent to show that Col. North acted improperly, it is noteworthy that the majority in most cases declined to ask Col. North himself, during six days of public testimony, about these allegations against him. During the Committees' investigation, the majority obtained information on these matters from witnesses who were in contact with North, but North was never asked to give his side of these events. The majority uses selected entries from North's written notes of conversations and meetings, but even though these entries are often abbreviated and cryptic, the majority declined to ask North to explain them. Instead, the majority attempted to interpret what these notes "suggest." In light of this flawed methodology, the majority's conclusions regarding purported interference with various investigations cannot be considered objective.

PART VI

# PUTTING CONGRESS' HOUSE IN ORDER

# CHAPTER 13

# The Need to Patch Leaks

Throughout the majority report, much is made of the Administration's concern for secrecy. That concern is protrayed almost exclusively, if not exclusively, as the desire of some lawbreakers to cover the tracks of their misdeeds. We agree that the National Security Council staff, under Admiral Poindexter, let its concern over secrecy go too far. We should not be so deceived by self-righteousness, however, that we dismiss the Admiral's concern as if it had no serious basis. Our national security, like it or not, does depend on many occasions on our ability to protect secrets. It is easy to dismiss the specific Iran arms sales decisions about executive branch compartmentalization, and about withholding information from Congress for almost a year, as having been excessive. Everyone on these Committees would agree with that conclusion. But unless we can understand the real problems that led the NSC staff to its decision, future Administrations will once again be faced with an unpalatable choice between excessive secrecy, risking disclosure or foregoing what might be a worthwhile operation.

Time after time over the past several years, extremely sensitive classified information has been revealed in the media. Predictably, both Congress and the Administration have blamed each other. In fact, both are culpable. It is important for these Committees to recognize this truth forthrightly. As Secretary Shultz said, quoting Bryce Harlow, "trust is the coin of the realm." But trust has to be mutual. Some people on these Committees seem to want to bring criminal prosecutions against former Administration officials for not speaking candidly to Congress. It is true that the business of government requires the Administration to be considered trustworthy by Congress. But so too must Congress prove itself trustworthy to the Administration.

We do not mean, by our focus on congressional leaks, to suggest that we turn our eyes from the same problem in the executive branch. Executive branch leaks are every bit as serious as legislative branch ones. But as long as there is a consensus on this point, we do not feel a need to dwell on it here. At the end of this chapter, we will recommend legislation to help address the issue of executive branch leaks along with our suggestions for the legislative branch.

There is much less consensus in Congress, however, about leaks from the legislative branch. Those problems are real.

PART 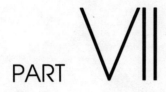 VII

# RECOMMENDATIONS

# CHAPTER 14

# Recommendations

The majority report reaches the conclusion, accurately in our opinion, that the underlying cause of the Iran-Contra Affair had to do with people rather than with laws. Despite this laudable premise, the majority goes on to offer no fewer than 27 recommendations, most involving legislation and several of them multifaceted. Some of the recommendations unfortunately betray Congress' role in the legislative-executive branch struggle by proposing needlessly detailed rules for the organization of the executive branch. At the same time, the majority recommendations barely touch the problem of leaks, and say nothing at all, to no one's surprise, about Congress' misuse of massive continuing appropriations resolutions to conduct foreign policy.

We do not intend here to give a detailed critique of the majority recommendations. We do believe that requiring the President to notify Congress of all covert operations within 48 hours, without any exceptions, would be both unconstitutional and unwise. Many of the remaining recommendations seem to us to be unconscionably meddlesome. No good reasons are offered for prohibiting military officers, such as General Powell, from being National Security Adviser. No good reasons are offered for having the National Security Council produce regular staff rosters for Congress. And so forth, and so on. It all strikes as more of the same: an attempt to achieve grand policy results by picking away at the details.

In the spirit of offering recommendations, however, we are pleased to present some of our own.

## Recommendation 1: Joint Intelligence Committee

*Congress should replace its Senate and House Select Committees on Intelligence with a joint committee.*

Congress has realized that limiting the number of people with access to sensitive information can help protect the information's security. The House and Senate took worthwhile first steps to limit the number of Members and staff engaged in intelligence oversight by establishing Select Committees on Intelligence. Unfortunately, as we have seen, security still is not tight enough. The time has now come, therefore, for taking the next logical steps.

Given the national security stakes involved, Congress and the Administration must find a remedy for restoring mutual trust. One major step in that direction can be taken by merging the existing House and Senate intelligence committees into a joint committee, along the lines of legislation (H.J. Res. 48) sponsored by Representative Henry Hyde and a bipartisan group of 135 cosponsors. Such a committee need not have the 32 Members (plus four exofficio) and 55 staff now needed for two separate committees. Fewer Members, supported by a small staff of apolitical professionals, could make up the single committee. In recognition of political reality, the majority-party membership from each House would have a one vote edge.

A joint intelligence panel would drastically diminish the opportunities for partisan posturing and substantially reduce the number of individuals with access to classified and sensitive information. This would not only minimize the risk of damaging unauthorized disclosures but would also significantly increase the likelihood of identifying leak sources—something that rarely occurs now because so many people are in the "intelligence information loop." Furthermore, with the possibility of discovery so much greater, potential leakers would be strongly deterred from unauthorized disclosures.

To achieve both efficiency and secrecy in congressional consideration of intelligence matters, a Joint Intelligence Committee must have legislative as well as oversight jurisdiction. Otherwise, the two Houses would not give the Joint Committee the deference the two existing intelligence committees enjoy. Neither would the intelligence agencies have the budget-based incentives to cooperate with the Joint Committee as they have now with the two select committees. Inadequate

jurisdiction might also prompt the various committees in each House with historical interests in intelligence to reassert themselves. That could trigger increased fractionalization of the congressional oversight process, with the concomitant proliferation within the Congress of access to sensitive intelligence information.

## Recommendation 2: Oath and Strict Penalties for Congress.

*To improve security, the Joint Intelligence Committee (or the present House and Senate committees) should adopt a secrecy oath with stiff penalties for its violation.*

Creating a joint committee will not by itself guarantee the security of intelligence information. Also essential is committee self-discipline. Earlier, we pointed out how the reputations of the Senate and House Intelligence Committees have been sullied by leaks from Members or staff. As the importance of congressional oversight, and the reputation for leaking, both grow, foreign intelligence agencies are discouraged from unguarded cooperation with the United States. Change is therefore urgent both to stanch the flow of leaks and to symbolize to foreign countries that Congress is serious about preserving the confidentiality of secrets.

One significant change that would help further both goals would be to require an oath of secrecy for all Members and staff of the intelligence committees. Such an oath would not be an American novelty. As we have already noted, the Continental Congress' Committee on Secret Correspondence required all of its members and employees to pledge not to divulge, directly or indirectly, any information that required secrecy.

The proposed oath should read: "I do

solemnly swear (or affirm) that I will not directly or indirectly disclose to any unauthorized person any information received in the course of my duties on the [Senate, House or Joint] Intelligence Committee except with the formal approval of the Committee or Congress."

The Committee Rules should be amended to compel permanent expulsion from the committee of any member or staff person who violates his or her oath. While proceedings remain pending, the accused would be denied access to classified information. The rules of the House and Senate should also be amended to provide that the Intelligence Committee would be authorized to refer cases involving the unauthorized disclosure of classified information to the Ethics Committees. The rules should make it clear that the Ethics Committees may recommend appropriate sanctions, up to and including expulsion from Congress.

This approach is well within the Constitution's expulsion power and the power of each House to set rules for its own proceedings. The power of each House of Congress to expel Members for misbehavior by two-thirds vote is virtually uncircumscribed. Historically, fifteen Senators and four Representatives have been expelled. Fourteen of the Senators were expelled for supporting the Confederate secession. The fifteenth, Senator Blount, was for conspiring with Indian tribes to attack Spanish Florida and Louisiana. The House and Senate also have considered and refused expulsion on twenty-four occasions for charges as varied as corruption, disloyalty, Mormonism, treasonable utterances, dueling, and attacking other Members of Congress. Expulsion decisions of Congress are probably beyond judicial review.

Any set of recommendations that limits itself to Congress would not be adequate to respond to the problem of leaks. Therefore, we recommend a more balanced approach that would stiffen the penalties for others who participate in this activity.

## Recommendation 3: Strengthening Sanctions

*Sanctions against disclosing national security secrets or classified information should be strengthened.*

Current federal law contains many provisions prohibiting the disclosure of classified information, but each of the existing provisions has loopholes or other difficulties that make them hard to apply. The section that covers the broadest spectrum of information, "classified information," only prohibits knowing, unauthorized communication to a foreign agent or member of a specified Communist organization.

Another set of provisions contains no such limit on the recipient of the information, but applies only to information related to the national defense. For some specified information, unauthorized disclosure or transmission is criminal under any circumstances. The transmission of other "information relating to the national defense" to an unauthorized person is also illegal if a person has reason to believe the information would be used to injure the United States or to benefit a foreign nation. The problem with these provisions is that they cover only "information relating to the national defense" rather than the full range of national security information whose secrecy the government has a legitimate reason to protect.

A third set of provisions in current law is limited to nuclear weapons production. A fourth is limited to information about ciphers or communications intelligence. This is the law that the National Security Agency Director, General William E. Odom, believes should be applied more vigorously against both federal employees and the press.*

Finally, a fifth provision—also limited in the information it protects—makes illegal the disclosure of agents' identities. This law is also restricted to disclosures by someone who (a) has authorized access to the identity from classified information or (b) is engaged

in a "pattern of activities intended to identify and expose covert agents" with reason to believe the publicity would impair the foreign intelligence activities of the United States. The latter limitation means that the agent disclosure law does not cover most normal press disclosures, such as the ones we mentioned earlier about reports based on these committees' work, because they are not normally part of a pattern or practice of identifying covert agents.

In order to close these loopholes, Rep. Bill McCollum has introduced a bill (H.R. 3066) co-sponsored by all the other Republican members of the House Iran Committee. The bill is limited to current and past federal employees in any branch of government. For these people, the bill would make it a felony knowingly to disclose classified information or material (not just specific national defense information) to any unauthorized person, whatever the intent.

Another approach that would supplement the McCollum bill would be to introduce substantial civil penalties for the knowing disclosure of classified information to any unauthorized person. The penalties might range from administrative censure to a permanent ban on federal employment and a fine of $10,-000. The advantage of giving the Justice Department the option of using a civil statute would be (a) that the standard for proof would be the preponderance of evidence rather than proof beyond a reasonable doubt and (b) the law could stipulate that contested violations should be heard in secret, without a jury. These procedures should not encounter constitutional difficulties in light of the Supreme Court's broad endorsement of controls on the disclosure of classified information in *Snepp* v. *U.S.*

---

*The following is quoted from Molly Moore, "Prosecution of Media for Leaks Urged," The Washington Post, Sept. 3, 1987, p. A4:

"I don't want to blame any particular area for leaking," said Odom, who added, "There's leaking from Congress . . . there's more leaking in the administration because it's bigger. I'm just stuck with the consequences of it.

Leaks have damaged the [communications intelligence] system more in the past three to four years than in a long, long time." . . .

Odom said he has encouraged the administration to use an obscure law that prohibits disclosures of "communications intelligence." Odom said he has referred several cases involving news leaks to the Justice Department since 1985 but said the department has declined to prosecute any of them. The department said it has not prosecuted any so far. . . .

"Generally, when I'm with a group of journalists, I can usually see two or three people who fall in the category of those who probably could be successfully prosecuted," Odom told the reporters.

The following material, from the same press briefing, is from Norman Black, "Gen. Odom blames leaks for 'deadly' intelligence loss," Associated Press dispatch published in The Washington Times, Sept. 3, 1987, pp. 1, 12:

Asked to provide examples, Gen. Odom said he didn't want "to get specific right now and compound the things, but a number of sources have dried up in some areas which you are all familiar with, in the past year or two.

A number of years ago there was a case that had to do with a Damascus communication. . . . It was a leak. It attributed this thing to an intercept. And the source dried up immediately," Gen. Odom said.

Asked then about Libya, he replied, "Libya, sure. Just deadly losses."

## Recommendation 4: Gang of Four

*Permit the President to notify the "Gang of Four" instead of the "Gang of Eight" in special circumstances.*

Representative Broomfield has introduced a bill that, among other things, would permit the President on extremely sensitive matters to notify only the Speaker of the House, House Minority Leader, Senate Majority Leader and Senate Minority Leader. Under current law, limited notification means notification of these four plus the chairmen and ranking minority members of the two intelligence committees. On the principal that notifying fewer people is better in extremely sensitive situations, we would be inclined to support legislation along these lines that would ratify what has already come to be an informal occasional practice.

## Recommendation 5: Restore Presidential Power to Withstand Foreign Policy by Continuing Resolution

*Require Congress to divide continuing resolutions into separate appropriations bills and give the President an item veto for foreign policy limitation amendments on appropriations bills.*

The way Congress made foreign policy through the Boland Amendment is all too normal a way of doing business. Congress uses end of the year continuing resolutions to force its way on large matters and small, presenting the President with a package that forces him to choose between closing down the Government or capitulating. Congress should give the President an opportunity to address the major differences between himself and the Congress cleanly, instead of combining them with unrelated subjects. To restore the Presidency to the position it held just a few Administrations ago, Congress should exercise the self-discipline to split continuing resolutions into separate appropriation bills and present each of them individually to the President for his signature or veto. Even better would be a line-item veto that would permit the President to force Congress to an override vote without jeopardizing funding for the whole government.

SECTION III

# SUPPLEMENTAL AND ADDITIONAL VIEWS

# Additional Views of Chairman Daniel K. Inouye and Vice Chairman Warren B. Rudman

We wish to acknowledge the bipartisan spirit that characterized our Committee's work and resulted in a Report signed by all of the Democrats and a majority of the Republican Members of the Senate Select Committee. We wish also to recognize the outstanding leadership of our distinguished colleague, Representative Lee Hamilton, Chairman of the House Select Committee.

Tragedies like the Iran-Contra Affair unite our Government and our people in their resolve to find answers, draw lessons and avoid a repetition. In investigations of this magnitude—which involve serious questions relating to the proper functioning of our Government—it is just as important to lay aside partisan differences and avoid unjustified criticisms as it is to make the justified criticisms set forth in the Report. In that spirit, we wish to recognize the cooperation that we received from the White House throughout this inquiry.

**The Senators express their appreciation to the President for allowing the Committees to review excerpts from his personal diaries. They also urge the White House to consent to the Committees' only outstanding request, for access to additional information from the main White House computer. But they note that even in this last matter the White House has been cooperative so far.**

# Additional Views of Honorable Peter W. Rodino, Jr., Honorable Dante B. Fascell, Vice Chairman, Honorable Thomas S. Foley, Honorable Jack Brooks, Honorable Louis Stokes, Honorable Les Aspin, and Honorable Edward P. Boland

We have all joined in voting for the joint Report of the Select Committees, and wish to commend the Chairmen and the staff for their extraordinary efforts in assembling the voluminous factual information gathered during our investigation and crafting it into a fair and credible report. Obviously, it would have been impossible to draft a report with which all the Members of the Committees would have agreed in every particular; the subject is far too complex, the information subject to too many different shadings, and the unresolved questions too numerous to expect unanimity. Nonetheless, we wish to emphasize our strong support for the Report in general and for the work of the leadership of the Committees in producing a document that a majority of Members could endorse.

We would emphasize, however, that the Report is based solely on the documents, testimony, and other information available to the Committees. Unfortunately, not all information requested by the Committees was in fact made available, and this has deprived us of material that quite possibly could resolve a number of key issues.

**In contrast to Senators Inouye and Rudman, the Representatives say that "the White House did not provide the Select Committees with all documents and information requested in the past months." Not provided, they say, was certain information from the White House computers, including PROF notes that may still be retrievable from computer tapes, and other documents that may be on word-processor floppy disks, including possible memos on the diversion of funds to the Contras.**

# Additional Views of Honorable Peter W. Rodino, Jr., Honorable Dante B. Fascell, Vice Chairman, Honorable Jack Brooks, and Honorable Louis Stokes

We support the joint report of the Select Committees and are pleased that a bipartisan majority of Members of the House and Senate voted to adopt it. In particular, we wish to commend the Chairmen of the two panels for their fair and impartial leadership during the investigation and for their efforts to produce an objective report based on the facts we discovered. We also believe it is important to take note of the painstaking, professional work of the staffs of the Committees over the past several months. They have done an extraordinary job in preparing for and guiding us through the public hearings, and in assembling the massive amount of information the Committees gathered into a comprehensive and readable report.

While we support the Committees' report, we are including in these views some additional comments on the difficulties caused by delayed document production by the executive branch, on the Attorney General's role in the Iran-Contra matter, and on NSC involvement in criminal investigations and prosecutions.

**In the longest of the Additional Views, the Representatives say the Committees were not able to answer every question about the Iran-Contra Affair. Part of the reason, in their view, was that the Administration, particularly the Justice Department, took too long delivering some requested materials. The Representatives also question Attorney General Meese's conduct, notably his preliminary inquiry of the matter in November 1986. They also argue that the majority report is wrong to absolve Federal law enforcement agencies of blame when they acceded, in whole or in part, to NSC requests that slowed or stopped several criminal investigations.**

# Additional Views of Senator David L. Boren and Senator William S. Cohen

As the work of the Iran-Contra Committees comes to a close, it is important to focus on the future and, in particular, on how to strengthen Congressional oversight of intelligence activities. This issue has been a matter of great concern to us since becoming the Chairman and Vice Chairman of the Senate Select Committee on Intelligence in January.

In order to go forward constructively from this point, we believe it is essential that all the information developed with respect to CIA's involvement in this affair should be included in the final Report. This is important both to the Intelligence Committees in Congress and to the Director of Central Intelligence in order to be clear as to what happened, to evaluate effectively what should be done as a result, and to determine ways to avoid similar problems in the future.

Moreover, it should be noted that the Iran-Contra Committees also developed information concerning the CIA which did not pertain directly to the Iran-Contra affair, but which raises concerns for the Intelligence Committee. It is our intention to pursue these matters consistent with our oversight responsibility.

**Senators Boren and Cohen criticize certain CIA employees for assisting the Contras "in a manner contrary to both Agency policy and restrictions imposed by law." The Senators also point out that the CIA involved itself in the covert sale of arms to Iran without a Presidential Finding and suggest that CIA officers may have allowed that to happen because, as they saw it, they were just helping carry out an NSC program. Senators Boren and Cohen also fault the Agency for offering distorted intelligence to support Administration policies.**

# Additional and Separate Views of Senator Howell T. Heflin

This Report should be viewed clearly for what it is—a consensus report. I do not agree with all of the language in the Report, nor do I agree with all of its conclusions and recommendations.

At the beginning of the hearings, I stated that we were beginning a process of investigation, of affirmation, and of restoration. The investigation and affirmation have been completed, we should now finish the process of restoration.

The Congressional investigation into the Iran-Contra Affair is concluded with the publication of this Report. The investigation has been long, controversial, though, at times uplifting. While the two Congressional Committees have finished their tasks, the Independent Counsel is still investigating this matter. It is the responsibility of the Independent Counsel and, ultimately, the courts, to determine whether any criminal laws were violated. This was not the Committees' task.

I believe that the very essence of a democracy is an informed electorate. Clearly, the hearings have fulfilled this role. They have served to educate the American people about the strategic importance of the Middle East and the dangers we are facing in Central America. Additionally, the investigation and the hearings have confirmed my support for a democratic outcome in Nicaragua and have strengthened my resolve to see an end to the Soviet and Cuban presence and the Marxist expansion in Central America.

**Senator Heflin gives support to a long-standing proposal that the Senate and House Intelligence Committees be merged into one. That, he says, would "enhance secrecy" and "promote a better relationship between the Executive and Legislative branches." He also suggests that the Chairman of the Joint Chiefs of Staff be made a statutory member of the National Security Council.**

# Additional Views of
# Senator David L. Boren

A project of this kind involves hundreds of people and literally thousands of hours of work. This report represents a good faith attempt to accommodate the views of the many individuals involved and to reflect a consensus as to the facts and conclusions of the elected officials responsible for this process. Not surprisingly, with eleven Members of the United States Senate and fifteen Members of the House of Representatives the final product cannot completely satisfy everyone involved on each particular point. Nevertheless, I support this Report and accept generally its concepts.

While accepting generally this Report, I cannot say that I accept every statement contained in the Report, nor can I say that I would represent each fact or conclusion in precisely the same way.

**Senator Boren gives three examples. First, he says the Committees did not give enough attention to "alleged improper propaganda activities engaged in by the Department of State." Second, he believes the Committees were not proper forums "in which to determine, even by implication, whether and which criminal laws have been broken and by whom." And third, he says, "I am concerned that the report may imply that secrecy in all circumstances is wrong," even though "the taxpayers have invested significant amounts of money" in developing intelligence agencies and capabilities. The Senator also discusses the shortcomings of the Committees' investigation, saying, for example, that the merged Senate-House Committees were too large.**

# Supplemental Views of Senator James A. McClure

In his opening statement before the Committee, Col. North testified, "It is sort of like a baseball game in which you [Congress] are both the player and the umpire. It's a game in which you call the balls, and the strikes, and where you determine who is out, or who is safe. And, in the end you determine the score and declare yourself the winner."

Today, it appears that what Col. North predicted is exactly what happened. For many reasons, I have decided that I cannot agree with the Majority, which has indeed declared itself the winner. Therefore, I have joined seven of my colleagues in filing dissenting views which I believe are more objective than the committees' report. However, there are some additional points which I would like to make briefly.

Most important, what do we know today that we didn't know a year ago, when the Iranian arms sale and the funds diversion were first made public by the Administration? What do we have to show for the months of effort and millions of dollars of taxpayers' money that we have spent? We

have identified more of the individuals involved and spent countless hours going over their respective role. We have plotted the intricate financial arrangements and reviewed thousands of written documents, recorded conversations and witnesses' testimony.

Certainly, we know many more of the details, but we have really only shown that President Reagan was forthcoming and honest when he told the American public that he was unaware of certain of his staff's activities. As Secretary of State Shultz told the Committees, the essential facts unearthed by Attorney General Meese and his investigators remain the essential facts today.

**Senator McClure argues that the Committees' investigation was largely unnecessary. In the end, he says, all it showed was that President Reagan told the truth. He also says lying is appropriate in certain circumstances, and so North's critics are being hypocritical when they piously complain that he lied. McClure concludes by saying it should be remembered that North and Poindexter were fighting communism.**

# Additional Views
# of Congressman
# William S. Broomfield

In my view, the Congressional Iran/Contra investigation went on too long and yielded few results. Since Attorney General Meese publicly announced the Iran/Contra connection nearly a year ago, there have been hearings by several Congressional committees, a full-scale investigation by the Senate Intelligence Committee, and partial investigations by other committees. The President's Special Review Board (Tower Commission) was formed last December and reported in February. The Select Committees were formed in January and conducted public hearings and other proceedings through September.

Prior to formation of the Select Committees, I emphasized that the Committees' true role was to garner the facts, get those facts out to the American people, and recommend corrective action if necessary. I also stated my reservations about the length of time for which the Committee were formed, the absence of a specific budget figure, and the absence of adequate security procedures. My fear was that the Committees would embark on an open-ended and unfocused investigation that would wander beyond its legitimate objectives yet fail to perform its proper mission. This fear has been realized.

What do we have to show for all the activity in Congress? The consensus appears to be that—aside from unearthing considerable detail—the Committees made little progress in resolving even the factual issues. The basic outlines of the story have not changed much since the Attorney General's announcement, no less the Tower Commission's extensive report.

**Representative Broomfield says the Committee hearings seemed too much like a trial, dwelling on sensational factual revelations; instead, they should have been a vehicle for public education. Broomfield says the President did make policy errors, but largely because he got flawed advice. He says the Iran arms sales policy was incorrectly implemented. Although he says the President cannot be blamed, North, Poindexter, and perhaps others may be guilty of improprieties and illegalities. Broomfield believes the Administration should have consulted with Congress but also says Congress shares blame for politicizing oversight of the Nicaragua policy.**

# Supplemental Views of Senator Orrin G. Hatch

Much has been said in the foregoing reports about the Constitutional roles of Congress and the President in foreign affairs. I concur with the views of my fellow Republicans in our minority report on that subject, and offer the following supplementary remarks.

The framers of the Constitution anticipated a Congress with significant powers and with a checking function on the President. But the framers also created a chief executive with real power. It is, I believe, a common misperception that the framers, in creating the Presidency at the Constitutional Convention, were driven only by a desire to avoid the tyrannical power of the English kings. Such was not the case in the American colonies by the year 1787. It is true that the abuses of power of the English monarchs had been the principal impetus for the colonists to flee England, and to later fight the Revolution; and the dictatorial excesses of King George III were well understood and sought to be avoided by the framers. But when the Constitutional Convention convened in Philadelphia, the delegates were more concerned about the ineffectiveness of the Continental Congress, and about the lack of any coherent foreign policy for their fragile new nation, than they were about the abusive power of kings. John Jay's Federalist Paper No. 64 is an especially informative summary of the manner in which the framers viewed the power of the President in foreign affairs.

As finally written, the Constitution provided for a Congress, a chief executive, and a judiciary, each with considerable authority.

**Senator Hatch says the Constitution empowered the President to take the lead in the nation's foreign affairs, and the Iran-Contra Affair ought to teach the nation that the President needs the power the Constitution grants him without excessive second-guessing and micromanaging by Congress. Unnecessary Congressional interference, he says, helped lead to the Iran-Contra Affair.**

# Supplemental Views of Congressman Henry Hyde

One unanticipated benefit of the Iran Contra hearings was the surprising emergence of so many strict constructionists among members of the Joint Investigating Committee. It is heartening to see the ranks of those devoted to law and order increasing, notwithstanding the selectivity of their devotion.

In earlier days, we were conditioned to favor appeals to "the higher law" over mere statutory expressions, depending on who made the appeal and the degree of left-ward tilt to their cause.

We have seen high minded demonstrators trespass on military installations, splash animal blood on draft records, illegally picket within 500 feet of the South African Embassy, conduct sit-ins to obstruct C.I.A. university recruitment, and deliberately violate our immigration laws to provide sanctuary to a chosen few.

These acts of civil and criminal disobedience are routinely applauded by many who turn a cold shoulder, a blind eye and a deaf ear towards such appeals when made by, for example, Fawn Hall on behalf of her former boss, Lt. Col. Oliver North.

Ms. Hall's testimony that "sometimes you have to go above the written law . . ." has been much remarked in the press, but we are less often reminded that she was echoing Thomas Jefferson, who on September 20, 1810 wrote to John Colvin:

> A strict observance of the written law is doubtless *one* of the high duties of a good citizen, but it is not *the highest.*

**Representative Hyde argues that it is too simplistic to say the Administration should not have violated the Boland Amendments under any circumstances. Vacillating U.S. policy toward the Contras may have made it necessary not to interpret them in the strictest terms. The Founding Fathers, he says, intended to give the President general control of the nation's foreign policy, and given the threat of communism in Central America the President is justified in using that power. The hearings, he says, were overly self-righteous and moralistic. Under President Reagan, the United States has, he says, rightly reasserted itself as the "party of liberty in the world."**

# Additional Views of
# Senator William S. Cohen

The Iran-Contra Affair was a significant departure from the constitutional processes which normally control the operations of the Government. While the affair was an aberration in this sense, it also demonstrated a recurring problem which has afflicted Administrations of both parties—albeit without such bizarre, unseemly, and far-reaching results.

When an Administration adopts objectives whose goals, however defensible, are at odds with actions taken by the Congress, or with its own publicly acknowledged positions, it embarks on a perilous course. Subordinates of any President are motivated primarily by a desire to carry out his wishes, whatever the obstacles. Without an appreciation of the balance between the branches, such subordinates may be ignoring the law, even if it means taking actions which violate publicly stated U.S. policy.

Normally, there are enough checks and balances within the governmental framework that such anomalies are detected and corrected early on. In the national security area, however, where secrecy is necessarily a tool of the trade, there is a greater potential that secrecy will neutralize the normal checks and balances of government. This was clearly demonstrated in the Iran-Contra Affair.

Part of the responsibility to ensure this does not happen rests with the President.

**The need for secrecy, Senator Cohen says, does not justify deceiving Congress. The press, he says, first exposed the Iran-Contra Affair, and the Government then intervened to make corrections. This report, Cohen says, overstates its case on occasion. It was particularly inappropriate, he says, for the Committees to make even tentative judgments about legality. The Senator questions whether the majority report's section on NSC involvement in criminal investigation should have been included since no malfeasance was proved. And, he says, the report dwells too long on the activities of the State Department's Office of Public Diplomacy.**

473

# Supplemental Views of
# the Honorable Bill McCollum

In good conscience I could not sign the majority report of this Committee because there are just too many things with which I disagree. While I have signed the dissenting views prepared by House Minority Staff, there are areas where my interpretation of evidence and testimony presented to us differs and I have some additional views which I feel compelled to set forth here.

The Iran/Contra hearings gave Americans a unique look inside a Presidential Administration. They also gave a sobering look at the results of the unwillingness of a President to have a Constitutional showdown with Congress over his powers, a lack of trust among people in our government, and a lack of a clearly defined and effective policy for combatting terrorism and rescuing hostages.

Partisan bickering was the most distressing thing about the hearings. It got in the way of our purpose, which was to bring out the facts, to determine the President's credibility, and, finally, to recommend law and policy changes that reach far beyond these hearings.

The cloud hanging over the President on the issue of his credibility was removed. The President told the truth when he said he did not know of the diversion and that his knowledge of various aspects of the affair was limited. Of course, the buck stops with the President, and he must accept responsibility for the errors and omissions of his appointees.

**During the hearings, Representative McCollum says, Administration critics were highly partisan and overzealous. The President, he says, should have openly confronted Congress over the Boland Amendments, obviating the need for the secret activities that led to the hearings. He says part of the blame thrown at Tomas Castillo, the pseudonym for the CIA station chief in Costa Rica, should have been directed at his superiors. The Iran-Contra Affair occurred, he also says, partly because of excessive Government leaks and the nation's failure to form an effective counterterrorism policy. And, he says, the majority is wrong to say the scandal might not have occurred if the Government were not so heavily directed by political appointees rather than career officers.**

# Additional Views of Senator Paul Trible

I have joined the majority of my colleagues in this Report because its interpretation of the facts, the law, and policy considerations in most instances squares with my own. I am not, however, in accord with the majority in every particular, nor do I assess the roles of our institutions in precisely the same way.

The essence of the Iran-Contra Affair lay in the decision by a few within the National Security Council Staff to embark on a self-destructive journey into the privatization of foreign policy. The pitfalls associated with this departure from long established principles of government are well chronicled in the Report. The main lessons are: that a Presi-dent's staff, no matter how well intentioned, must always be accountable; that a President who is deceived and from whom information is intentionally withheld is a President be-trayed; and that truth, trust and respect for the rule of law and the Constitution are in-dispensable to the success of our free society.

**One large failing that led to the scandal, Senator Trible says, was vesting so much authority in the hands of private citizens—Secord and Hakim—who were partly motivated by profit. Another problem is the Government's failure to reach con-sensus on the nation's foreign policy. Congress shares blame for that. And he is not happy with the "sweeping character of the [report's] indict-ment" of the President.**

# About the Editors

**Joel Brinkley,** White House correspondent for *The New York Times,* was the Washington editor of the *Times'* Iran-Contra coverage through most of 1987. His previous assignments have included covering the CIA, the Contras, and other Central America issues. In the summer of 1985, he was the first to write that Lieutenant Colonel Oliver L. North was directing the Contra war from the White House.

Mr. Brinkley is a 1975 graduate of the University of North Carolina at Chapel Hill and has worked for the Associated Press, the *Richmond* (Va.) *News Leader* and the *Louisville Courier-Journal.* He joined the *Times'* Washington bureau in 1983.

He won the Pulitzer Prize for International Reporting in 1980 and has also received more than a dozen other national journalism awards.


**Stephen Engelberg** writes about the CIA and the other intelligence agencies for the Washington bureau of *The New York Times.* He covered the Iran-Contra Affair even before it was known by that name and remained on it full-time through the fall of 1987.

After graduating from Princeton in 1979 he worked for the *Norfolk Virginian-Pilot* and in the Washington bureau of the *Dallas Morning News.* He joined the *Times'* Washington bureau in 1984 as an editor. He has covered a wide range of intelligence stories, including the Walker family espionage ring and the other spy cases that made 1986 "the year of the spy." He has been the *Times'* chief reporter on intelligence coverage since 1986.